SITUATIONAL METHOD ENGINEERING: FUNDAMENTALS AND EXPERIENCES

IFIP – The International Federation for Information Processing

IFIP was founded in 1960 under the auspices of UNESCO, following the First World Computer Congress held in Paris the previous year. An umbrella organization for societies working in information processing, IFIP's aim is two-fold: to support information processing within its member countries and to encourage technology transfer to developing nations. As its mission statement clearly states,

> *IFIP's mission is to be the leading, truly international, apolitical organization which encourages and assists in the development, exploitation and application of information technology for the benefit of all people.*

IFIP is a non-profitmaking organization, run almost solely by 2500 volunteers. It operates through a number of technical committees, which organize events and publications. IFIP's events range from an international congress to local seminars, but the most important are:

- The IFIP World Computer Congress, held every second year;
- Open conferences;
- Working conferences.

The flagship event is the IFIP World Computer Congress, at which both invited and contributed papers are presented. Contributed papers are rigorously refereed and the rejection rate is high.

As with the Congress, participation in the open conferences is open to all and papers may be invited or submitted. Again, submitted papers are stringently refereed.

The working conferences are structured differently. They are usually run by a working group and attendance is small and by invitation only. Their purpose is to create an atmosphere conducive to innovation and development. Refereeing is less rigorous and papers are subjected to extensive group discussion.

Publications arising from IFIP events vary. The papers presented at the IFIP World Computer Congress and at open conferences are published as conference proceedings, while the results of the working conferences are often published as collections of selected and edited papers.

Any national society whose primary activity is in information may apply to become a full member of IFIP, although full membership is restricted to one society per country. Full members are entitled to vote at the annual General Assembly, National societies preferring a less committed involvement may apply for associate or corresponding membership. Associate members enjoy the same benefits as full members, but without voting rights. Corresponding members are not represented in IFIP bodies. Affiliated membership is open to non-national societies, and individual and honorary membership schemes are also offered.

SITUATIONAL METHOD ENGINEERING: FUNDAMENTALS AND EXPERIENCES

Proceedings of the IFIP WG 8.1 Working Conference, 12-14 September 2007, Geneva, Switzerland

Edited by

Jolita Ralyté
University of Geneva, Switzerland

Sjaak Brinkkemper
Utrecht University, The Netherlands

University of Technology, Sydney, Australia

Springer

Situational Method Engineering: Fundamentals and Experiences

Edited by J. Ralyté, S. Brinkkemper, and B. Henderson-Sellers

p. cm. (IFIP International Federation for Information Processing, a Springer Series in Computer Science)

ISSN: 1571-5736 / 1861-2288 (Internet)

ISBN 978-1-4419-4483-2
Printed on acid-free paper

eISBN: 13: 978-0-387-73947-2

9 8 7 6 5 4 3 2 1
springer.com

Preface

This proceedings volume contains the papers of the scientific program of the IFIP Working Group 8.1 working conference on Situational Method Engineering: Fundamentals and Experiences. The conference has been held from 12 to 14 September 2007 at the University of Geneva in Switzerland.

Since the early 1980s, the IFIP WG8.1 working conferences have provided a forum for the presentation and exchange of research results and practical experiences within the field of information systems development methods. After two successful Method Engineering conferences in Atlanta in 1996 and in Kanazawa in 2002, it is now time again to provide a forum for the exchange of ideas in and give a state of the art overview in Method Engineering. The conference programme features three invited keynote presentations, paper presentations and one interactive panel session. Besides, tutorials have been arranged to learn about the basics of Method Engineering. The format of a working conference allows for extensive paper discussions featured by discussant reviews in plenary sessions.

Over the last decade Method Engineering, defined as the engineering discipline to design, construct and adapt methods, including supportive tools, has emerged as the research and application area for using methods for systems development. Hundreds of methods have been published ranging from generic methods to methods for specific projects or domains. We mention: Unified Process, RUP, DSDM, SSADM, Merise, UML, OPEN Process Framework for general systems development; ARIS and DEM for ERP implementations; Scrum, XP (Xtreme Programming), Crystal in the agile movement; T-map for Testing; Attribute Driven Design method and TOGAF for software architecture; Archimate and Dynamic Architecture (DYA) for enterprise architecture.

Several theories have emerged as basic instruments in Method Engineering. Meta-modelling proves useful to identify the concepts and internal structure of a method, and provides means for building method support tools. Methods are understood to be built from so-called method fragments or method chunks, which are stored in a method base and can be assembled in a newly configured method. Perspectives and viewpoints aid in distinguishing processes, deliverables and events in systems development. Situational method engineering was coined to deal with the adaptation of a generic method to the actual situation of a project. Tool support for method engineering turns out to be not yet as successful as process management tools and metaCASE tools seem not to make it beyond the arena of specialists.

Many issues are still open for research. Studies in particular domains reveal that specific project needs are not covered, thus asking for method extensions or for specialized domain methods. Another issue is the classification and granularity of method fragments, or method chunks, that are to be configured into new methods. The notion of situationality of a method and of the suitability of method fragments has been investigated but still requires more theory and experimentation. The same applies for assembly and configuration of methods and tools, where formal construction techniques and assembly guidelines are to be explored. Most method engineering activities are nowadays performed from open methods or from corporate knowledge infrastructures and require further investigation. Experience reports and empirical validation of all these issues in industrial contexts will contribute to the theory building in the area of Method Engineering.

The conference organizers have send out a call for papers through the usual channels of international mailing lists of researchers active in Method Engineering. A total of 47 papers were received and each paper has been reviewed by four members of the program committee, recruited from IFIP 8.1 members and other researchers active in method engineering domain. The overall quality of the papers was very high, and very well fitting to the scope of Method Engineering. During the conference preparation meeting in Geneva the program committee decided to accept 23 papers for presentation in the main program and publication in this volume. For the poster session 5 papers were selected.

We wish to thank the members of the international program committee and the additional reviewers, who assisted in making a good selection for a high quality program. A special word of thanks goes to the chairman of IFIP Working Group 8.1, Barbara Pernici of the Politecnico di Milano, and the leader of the Matis team of the University of Geneva, Michel Léonard for their support and advice. We furthermore thank the keynote speakers and tutorial organizers for their willingness to present the latest views in our conference. We finally want to thank Mehdi Snene for his work on the conference management system, and Inge van de Weerd for the design and maintenance of the conference website.

We wish you a pleasant reading and a fruitful use of our research results in your applications or research in methods for information systems development.

Jolita Ralyté
Sjaak Brinkkemper
Brian Henderson-Sellers

Conference Committee

General Chair

Brian Henderson-Sellers, University of Technology, Sydney, Australia

Program Chairs

Jolita Ralyté, University of Geneva, Switzerland
Sjaak Brinkkemper, Utrecht University, The Netherlands

Organising Chair

Mehdi Snene, University of Geneva, Switzerlands

Web Master

Inge van de Weerd, Utrecht University, The Netherlands

Program Committee

Pär J. ÅGERFALK, Ireland
Jacky AKOKA, France
David AVISON, France
Per BACKLUND, Sweden
Albertas ČAPLINSKAS, Lithuania
Massimo COSSENTINO, Italy
Rébecca DENECKERE, France
Xavier FRANCH, Spain
Cesar GONZALEZ-PEREZ, Spain
John GRUNDY, New Zealand
Peter HAUMER, USA
Frank HARMSEN, The Netherlands
Remko HELMS, The Netherlands
Manfred JEUSFELD, The Netherlands
Paul JOHANNESSON, Sweden
Frederik KARLSSON, Sweden
John KROGSTIE, Norway
Susanne LEIST, Germany

Michel LÉONARD, Switzerland
Mauri LEPPANEN, Finland
Kalle LYYTINEN, USA
Isabelle MIRBEL, France
Haralambos MOURATIDIS, UK
Mohan NARASIPURAM, Hong Kong
Selmin NURCAN, France
Antoni OLIVE, Spain
Leon J. OSTERWEIL, USA
Oscar PASTOR, Spain
Juan PAVÓN, Spain
Barbara PERNICI, Italy
Anne PERSSON, Sweden
Yves PIGNEUR, Switzerland
Klaus POHL, Germany
Naveen PRAKASH, India
Erik PROPER, The Netherlands
Colette ROLLAND, France
Matti ROSSI, Finland
Motoshi SAEKI, Japan
Guttorm SINDRE, Norway
Monique SNOECK, Belgium
Il-Yeol SONG, USA
Juha-Pekka TOLVANEN, Finland
Richard WELKE, USA
Robert WINTER, Switzerland

Additional Referees

Lena AGGESTAM, Sweden
Tobias BUCHER, Switzerland
Stephan KURPJUWEIT, Switzerland
Valeria SEIDITA, Italy
Maurice VERHELST, Belgium
Jonas SJÖSTRÖM, Sweden

Table of Contents

Keynote Talks

Fundamentals

Situational Method Engineering

Meta-modelling Approaches

Perspectives on Method Engineering

Method Quality

Domain Specific Methods

Process Improvement

Organisation Modelling

Panel

Domain-Specific Modeling: The Killer App for Method Engineering?

Steven Kelly
MetaCase
stevek@metacase.com
http://www.metacase.com

Abstract. The method creation heyday of the 1980s was characterized by convivial chaos, leading to the idea of a discipline of method engineering. Before it could grow, the unification and marketing machine of UML crushed method development into "one size fits all" design by committee in the 1990s. A scattering of brave souls went against the current, creating modeling languages specific to their own problem domain, and were rewarded with significantly higher productivity. As they seek to scale their solutions, they need help from the research world to analyze their results, and to bring to bear the learning from the early days of method engineering.

1 Introduction

The 1980s were in many ways the heyday for the creation of new modeling languages and associated processes, together known then as methods. It seemed everybody with software development experience and a theoretical bent was creating their own method. Many of the methods shared common features, whether by shared ancestry, loaning, or convergent evolution. These factors gave rise to the idea of a discipline of method engineering, to improve the process of creating a new method.

The 1990s poured cold water on the fledgling discipline, as UML progressively out-marketed or subsumed most common methods. Rather than a chaotic yet convivial mass of method creators, method development largely became something only a single committee were doing. Some brave souls carried on under the radar, but always with the stigma of working on a "non-standard" modeling language. Their reward was often significantly higher productivity, as their modeling language was made to fit tightly with just their problem domain, and production quality code could often be generated directly from the models.

Please use the following format when citing this chapter:

Kelly, S., 2007, in IFIP International Federation for Information Processing, Volume 244, Situational Method Engineering: Fundamentals and Experiences, eds. Ralyté, J., Brinkkemper, S., Henderson-Sellers B., (Boston Springer), pp. 1-5.

With the turn of the millennium, there were already some published success stories of Domain-Specific Modeling [1]. Metamodeling tools offered method engineers automatic tool support of any modeling language they chose to specify, significantly reducing the cost of building and supporting a new method. The method engineering research community began to emerge from hibernation, gaining new members and a new direction. Rather than assembling methods from smaller common building blocks, the focus was now on creating entirely new modeling languages, and the skills and tools necessary for that task.

Now, the giants of Microsoft and Eclipse have joined the fray, bringing the ideas of Domain-Specific Modeling to the masses. More mature tools go beyond the giants' entry-level offerings, providing support for true method engineering: new parts are created whenever necessary, but existing fragments can be reused, and several modeling languages are integrated into an effective whole. To push the field further requires four things:

1. understanding the state of the art from mature tools and previous research,
2. empirical research on the use of DSM in the field,
3. condensing that information and experience into advice for method engineers,
4. hypothesizing from it a set of new requirements for the next generation of tools.

As guardians of point 1 and one of the few trustworthy parties to carry out point 2, the method engineering community is thus in a unique position of responsibility. Those unaware of past results or current practice will leap to points 3 and 4 to form unfounded conclusions, sending research and practice back to the dark ages. Many commercial attempts to jump on the bandwagon are doing just that, with productivity of "UML-based MDA" only increasing by 35% [2], and of "Software Factories" by 20% [3]. Even allowing for the vagaries of these particular cases, one by a major MDA tool vendor and one by the most referenced users of Software Factories, these meager productivity increases compare poorly with the 500%–1000% commonly encountered with better-founded DSM approaches [1].

2 Meta- and meta-meta-development, but no development?

In order to achieve our goals, we must first know and agree what those goals are. In our Working Group, the focus is on the planning, analysis, design and evaluation of information systems. Conspicuously absent from the list is the construction of information systems: their implementation in a programming language. This omission is all the odder when one looks at other working groups in TC8, and sees that none of them include a focus on construction in general; only for specific kinds of systems such as smart cards. How can this be? Construction is clearly central, the one phase without which there is no hope whatsoever for a project, and without which there would be no information systems, good or bad, for us to study. Construction is also more clear-cut than many phases, amenable to hard scientific analysis: an IF statement is unequivocal, whereas a UML Association can mean different things to different people.

Perhaps the answer lies in that very clarity. In other phases we can believe that we have a generic solution: there is enough fuzziness that a concept of "Requirement" or "Entity" can be seen as applicable to almost any project. In the unforgiving glare of compilers, let alone users, a particular part of a program can clearly be found lacking. Bubble sort may be fine for a PC home address book, but too sluggish in other domains such as mobile phones or enterprise databases. Academic research strives to come up with results that are universally true, but IS construction is clearly dependent on the domain.

Whilst only implicit by omission for construction, this situational contingency has always been recognized by WG 8.1 for IS development methods: different modeling languages are suited for different problem domains. Historically, such domains have been considered broadly, e.g. vertical domains such as banking, or horizontal domains such as database systems. Modeling languages have taken a similarly broad outlook, e.g. ER diagrams for database design. This breadth was taken to its extreme in UML, which claims to be a universal method for any discrete software system. Unsurprisingly, in reaching out for this goal UML has grown to include a great number of modeling concepts, each of whose semantics are deliberately vague.

3 Broad or Narrow?

While UML claims to be able to model everything from space shuttles through database applications to mobile phones, no one development group needs this breadth. Rather, each group works in a far narrower domain: not just mobile phones, say, but user-visible applications for the Nokia Series 60 range of phones. As this is one of many thousands of other such domains in IS, a modeling language developed specifically for this situation can thus be a much better fit than UML. Such a Domain-Specific Modeling language could have fewer modeling techniques, and their concepts would be much more precise. Above all, the concepts can be at a significantly higher level of abstraction: rather than having a general "Event" causing transitions in a State Diagram, their can be different concepts for events like "Button Press", "Soft key press", or "Incoming call".

When comparing other related domains, e.g. Ericsson mobile phones, it quickly becomes apparent that while there may be a number of similarities between the DSM languages, there is no way to produce an integrated modeling language without losing precision or introducing significant bloat. However, the differences between the modeling languages pale into insignificance when compared to the difference between the code written in the two related domains. Partly because of different underlying components, frameworks and platforms, but above all because of separate evolution of in-house standards and traditions, the code in the two domains is virtually unrecognizable. What remains common, however, is that for either domain it is a relatively simple task for an expert developer to specify the mapping from their DSM language to their code.

Generating full production quality code directly from high-level models has long been a goal of the software industry. Earlier attempts have largely failed, except in a few narrow domains. Unfortunately, while narrowness has been a virtue for good code generation, it is normally bad news for business. Another major factor in the failure of earlier code generation attempts has been the difference between the code different groups expect or want, as seen above. Since an expert from the group is now creating a domain-specific code generator, that problem is largely overcome, as are issues of vendor lock-in and long change cycles. Narrowing down the problem domain space that the modeling language and generator need cover also addresses another problem: earlier generated code tended to be bloated and inefficient, having to cope with so many possible situations.

4 Back to the Future?

Any right-thinking UMLer will of course respond with the standard argument: standards (pun unavoidable). But will the sky really fall if we use more than one modeling language? DSM has consistently shown productivity increases greater than any since the move from assembly language to 3rd Generation Languages. These figures stand up to empirical experiment [e.g. 4] and industrial experience of several hundred developers working on hundreds of products over a dozen years [5].

Looking back at assembly languages, we can note an interesting fact: there was a different language for each family of chips. Indeed, there could be more than one language for a family: assembler vendors added their own higher-level constructs, which did not map one-to-one with a single machine code instruction on that chip. Was the move from assembly language to 3GLs therefore a welcome escape from a confusing plethora of languages to a single universal language, e.g. C? Emphatically not, although many students and practitioners today seem to have assumed this. Rather, there was a surprisingly broad range of languages available, and many focused on a specific domain, e.g. scientific programming, business systems or graphics.

The move was also a gradual one, with the majority of systems at the start of the 1980s still being built in assembler. Some groups made the move earlier than others, but all made it for the same reason: the productivity in the 3GL was higher than in assembler. The main reasons for this were that one statement in a 3GL corresponds to several in assembly language, and that 3GL statements are closer to the way we look at the world, rather than the way a chip interacts with binary data. Both these reasons are also factors in why DSM is more productive than programming in a 3GL.

The rate of evolution of hardware has always been higher than that of software, possibly constituting another factor: users of a 3GL did not have to rewrite their programs each time a new chip was released. Instead, one compiler writer rewrote the mapping for the new chip, and all users of that 3GL simply upgraded to the new compiler version. Again, with DSM the situation is similar: to cope with a change in platform version, or even platform or programming language, there is no need to build all models from scratch, or even to edit them at all. Instead, the expert developer updates the generator, and all models by all developers now produce code for the new platform.

5 Conclusion

In the 1980s, the focus of method engineering was on helping method users to select from among the many available modeling languages. With the advent of UML, the choice has been so restricted that the focus has shifted to other areas such as requirements or processes. With Domain-Specific Modeling, there is a call for a new category of developer, creating a modeling language for their group. Whether that group is a single project, a company, or even similar projects across many companies, the task of building a new modeling language is a challenge.

Method engineering research of the 1990s led to some of the meta-metamodels and metamodeling tools that are easing the adoption of DSM, enabling today's method engineers to concentrate on building a good language, rather than getting stuck down in reinventing the wheel of modeling tool construction. The basic task of identifying suitable constructs has been analyzed from dozens of industrial cases, giving useful initial guidance to the method engineer [6].

To move forward, method engineers will need advice on modularization and continuous integration of models by separate developers, research results on the changes needed in version control systems for models, new algorithms for identifying and displaying differences between similar models, and above all empirical studies on which modeling approaches work, which do not, and where these results hold. Those building tools for method engineers will need theory and in-depth analysis: are the existing meta-metamodels really different, or are people twisting UML and MOF semantics to get closer to some actual set of useful constructs.

To be relevant, researchers in method engineering must be at least as smart as the method engineers. Having had the pleasure of working with many of today's method engineers, I can promise you this is a tough challenge. In my quarter century in this field, I have only met one group that could make that claim: the method engineering researchers of the early 1990s, now 15 years older. It is high time for this conference, and for a new group of leading lights. I have every hope for the class of 2007!

References

1. DSM Case Studies and Examples, 26.5.2007; http://www.dsmforum.org/cases.html
2. M. Burber and D. Herst, Productivity Analysis — Model-Driven, Pattern-based development with OptimalJ, 26.5.2007 http://www.theserverside.com/tt/articles/article.tss?l=SymposiumCoverage
3. J. Warmer, Case Study: Building a Flexible Software Factory using Small DSLs and Small Models, (unpublished discussion from talk), Code Generation 2007
4. R.B. Kieburtz, L. McKinney, J.M. Bell, J. Hook, A. Kotov, J. Lewis, D.P. Oliva, T. Sheard, I. Smith and L. Walton, A software engineering experiment in software component generation, *18th International Conference on Software Engineering (ICSE'96)*, 1996
5. Nokia case study, MetaCase, 1999; www.metacase.com/papers/MetaEdit_in_Nokia.pdf
6. J. Luoma, S. Kelly and J-P. Tolvanen, Defining Domain-Specific Modeling Languages: Collected Experiences, 4th OOPSLA Workshop on DSM, TR-33, University of Jyväskylä, 2004

Method Engineering: Trends and Challenges

Colette Rolland
CRI, Université Paris 1 Panthéon – Sorbonne, 90, rue de Tolbiac, 75013
Paris, France
rolland@univ-paris1.fr

Method Engineering (ME) is the discipline to study engineering techniques for constructing, assessing, evaluating and managing methods for developing Information Systems Development Methods (ISDM). Method engineering can therefore, be seen as concerned with meta-methods. The prevalent research view point has been the one of a meta-method supporting the selection and integration of ISDM parts that together form a new *situational method* i.e. a method adapted to the situation of a specific ISD project. Research in Situational Method Engineering (SME) has not exclusively, but undoubtedly produced a large portfolio of assembly-based approaches.

The talk will build upon the results achieved in SME to suggest cross fertilization with other disciplines and to raise research challenges for our community.

The position of the author is on one hand, that some of the results achieved can be 'exported' to other fields to the benefit of the SME research whereas on the other hand, our discipline can expand its scope by 'importing' views and approaches that other communities are developing on similar issues.

Please use the following format when citing this chapter:

Rolland, C., 2007, in IFIP International Federation for Information Processing, Volume 244, Situational Method Engineering: Fundamentals and Experiences, eds. Ralyté, J., Brinkkemper, S., Henderson-Sellers B., (Boston Springer), pp. 6.

Supporting Situational Method Engineering with ISO/IEC 24744 and the Work Product Pool Approach

Cesar Gonzalez-Perez
European Software Institute
cesargon@verdewek.com
http://www.verdewek.com/work

Abstract. The advantages of situational method engineering (SME) as an approach to the development, specification and application of methods are significant. However, taking this approach into practice in real-world settings is often a daunting task, because the necessary infrastructure and superstructure are not currently available. By infrastructure, we mean the underpinning theoretical and technological foundations on which SME is based; in this regard, this paper explains how the ISO/IEC 24744 metamodel solves many long-standing problems in methodology specification and enactment that other approaches, such as OMG's SPEM, cannot. By superstructure, we mean the exploitation mechanisms, often in the form of tools and decision procedures, that allow individuals and organisations to obtain value out of SME during their daily activities. Without these, SME is often seen as a purely theoretical exercise with little practical purpose. In this regard, we this paper also introduces the work product pool approach, which departs from the conventional view that methodologies must be described in a process-centric fashion to focus on a product-centric worldview, thus providing teams the capability to adopt an opportunistic and people-oriented setting in which to conduct their work.

1 Introduction

The method engineering approach [3, 13] builds upon the assumption that no specific methodology can solve enough problems and, therefore, methodologies must be specifically created for a particular set of requirements. In order to make this feasible and cost-effective, the old principles of modularity and reuse are utilised, and methodologies are said to be assembled from pre-existing method components, rather than created from scratch. Method components, consequently, take a very

---

Please use the following format when citing this chapter:

Gonzalez-Perez, C., 2007, in IFIP International Federation for Information Processing, Volume 244, Situational Method Engineering: Fundamentals and Experiences, eds. Ralyté, J., Brinkkemper, S., Henderson-Sellers B., (Boston Springer), pp. 7-18.

preeminent role in method engineering, since they comprise the raw material from which methodologies are obtained. Method components are often said to be stored into a repository, and the kinds of method components, as well as the relationships that are possible between these kinds, are given by an underpinning metamodel. Several metamodels have been proposed, such as OMG's SPEM 1.1 [16], SPEM 2.0 [18] (still under development) and ISO/IEC 24744 [12]. Of these, the latter is especially oriented towards method engineering, providing specific support for extant issues that other proposals, such as the ongoing versions of OMG's SPEM, have not been able to solve. This support occurs at two levels: on the one hand, the appropriate theory is established, so that a viable method engineering-based solution can be developed on top of it. This involves issues such as the interactions between the product and process sides of a methodology, or the specification of the endeavour domain from the metamodel domain. On the other hand, the necessary exploitation mechanisms are developed, so that an ISO/IEC 24744-based methodological solution can be used in practice to solve real problems, going beyond a mere academic exercise.

The next section briefly introduces the ISO/IEC 24744 standard metamodel. Section 3 focuses on infrastructural issues, describing the major theoretical aspects that are solved by the ISO/IEC 24744 standard metamodel, and explaining how they are relevant for the method engineering approach. Section 4, on the other hand, focuses on superstructural issues, describing how the work product pool approach works on top of repositories and methodologies in order to let software developers achieve their goal, i.e. deliver working software.

2 The ISO/IEC 24744 Standard Metamodel

ISO/IEC 24744 is an International Standard that defines a metamodel for development methodologies. Although it is geared towards *software* development methodologies, there is nothing in it that can prevent it from being applied to systems development methodologies or even other areas.

In this context, a *metamodel* means a semi-formal language capable of describing methodologies, and that these methodologies are models themselves. This is similar to what other metamodels (such as OMG's SPEM) claim to do, but with a larger scope. The ISO/IEC 24744 metamodel covers the following domain areas:

- Work units, also known as the process aspect of methodologies. This describes the work that has to be done in order to obtain the system to be delivered. SPEM and other metamodels also cover this area.
- Work products, also known as the product aspect of methodologies. This describes the artefacts that must be used and/or created in order to obtain the system to be delivered. SPEM and other metamodels also cover this area, although at a very high level of abstraction.
- Producers, also known as the people aspect of methodologies. This describes the roles, teams and tools that actually perform the work units and create or use the work products mentioned above. SPEM and other metamodels barely cover this area.

- Stages, also known as the temporal aspect of methodologies. This describes how work units, work products and producers relate to each other over time, providing a macro-structure for the methodology (and, consequently, to endeavours). SPEM and other metamodels often mix this area together with work units, using the same class in the metamodel to specify the "what" and the "when". This poses heavy limitations on the modularisation of methodologies, which, arguably should be avoided in a method engineering context.
- Model units, also known as the modelling aspect of methodologies. This describes the modelling building blocks that developers can use in order to construct the work products mentioned above. SPEM and other metamodels do not cover this area, assuming that UML or other modelling language will be adopted and magically made to work with the methodology.

The following sections describe the details of some of the particularities of ISO/IEC 24744 and how they make it especially appropriate for method engineering.

3 Theoretical Aspects

The theory underpinning ISO/IEC 24744 departs from the classic views implemented by other metamodels in some aspects, but still conforms to a very conventional object-oriented worldview. The following sections describe the details of this theory, focussing on how it can provide the infrastructure for the implementation of a method engineering solution.

3.1 The Strict Metamodelling Paradigm

According to the OMG's worldview, models represent their subjects strictly by means of "instance-of" relationships. In other words, a subject is an "instance-of" the entity that models it. No "instance-of" relationships may occur other than these. Because of this, elements organise themselves into layers, sometimes called "metalevels" in the literature, connected only by "instance-of" relationships. This is often depicted as the widely know stack of metalevels, usually labelled M0, M1, etc. This worldview is called the strict metamodelling paradigm, and, although prevalent within the OMG's technology suite, it has been widely criticised from academia [2, 7]. To the best of our knowledge, no convincing reasons have been shown to exist as of why the strict metamodelling paradigm should be accepted. On the contrary, it is usually presented as an *a priori* statement that is to be obeyed without further explanation.

ISO/IEC 24744 departs from this stance, and organises elements according to the communities of people that are involved in their production and usage (Figure 1). On the one hand, method engineers maintain repositories of method components and may use them to create methodologies, which, in turn, are used by software developers to create software products. Method engineers and software developers are two different communities that establish the boundaries between three different domains: the metamodelling domain, the methodology domain, and the endeavour domain. Each domain is a representation of the domain "below" it, in the sense that methodologies represent endeavours and metamodels represent methodologies [5]. The concept of *representation* has been explored in the software engineering literature (e.g. [9, 20]), and goes beyond that of "instance-of". A full discussion of the concept of representation is out of scope of this paper; please see [7] for an extended treatment.

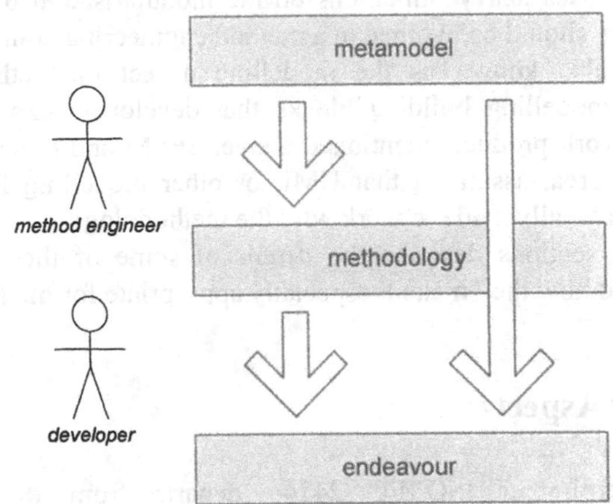

Figure 1. Overall structure of ISO/IEC 24744. Boxes depict domains, and arrows depict the representation relationships between domains. Stick figures depict the communities that are directly related to each domain or relationship between domains, as described in the main text.

The absence of the artificial restrictions imposed by the strict metamodelling paradigm, together with the flexible yet grounded concept of representation, gives ISO/IEC 24744 some capabilities that are discusses in the following sections.

3.2 Dual-Layer Modelling

The most important consequence of using the concept of representation as a means to relate domains, rather than that of "instance-of", is that the metamodel domain can exert control over multiple domains at the same time. With a traditional, strict metamodelling-based approach, a methodology is seen as an instance of a metamodel, and an endeavour as an instance of a methodology; therefore, there is no way in which a metamodel and an endeavour can be directly related. In other words, the designers of a metamodel cannot put in the metamodel anything that regulates how the endeavours that will be generated from the methodologies that will be obtained from the metamodel being designed will look like. For example, let us consider that the designers of a metamodel want to capture the fact that all the work products created during the application of any methodology must have a version number. Using a strict metamodelling approach, this is impossible, because work products exist in the endeavour domain, which is an instance of the methodology domain; therefore, the WorkProduct class, with its VersionNumber attribute, belongs to the methodology domain. The metamodel designers are free to design the metamodel as they wish, but cannot dictate anything about the methodology domain.

Methodologies are supposed to be put together by method engineers, not metamodel designers. Therefore, the metamodel designer cannot guarantee that all the work products created during the application of any methodology derived from the metamodel being designed will have a version number.

Using a representation-based approach, the chain of reasoning that led us to conclude that the WorkProduct class belongs to the methodology domain does not need to happen. On the contrary, a community-oriented perspective is taken. ISO/IEC 24744 assumes that any conceivable methodology will use work products, and therefore the concept of a work product is universal enough as to be "frozen" as part of the metamodel. In other words, the WorkProduct concept is provided to the method engineering community as raw material from which they can construct method components and populate repositories. The WorkProduct class, with its VersionNumber attribute, belongs to the metamodel domain. Its instances (i.e. specific work products, such as the requirements specification document that I can see on my desk as I type this) still belong to the endeavour domain. We must realise that this means that the representation relationship that links the WorkProduct class and its instances travels across the methodology domain; a class in the metamodel is being instantiated in the endeavour. This would be illegal in a strict metamodelling environment, but is perfectly reasonable in ISO/IEC 24744. The result is that the ISO/IEC 24744 metamodel is perfectly capable to exert control on the endeavour domain (e.g. determine that every work product will have a version number) as well as the methodology domain (see Figure 1).

Common sense dictates that the final purpose of any software development methodology is to produce working software. Therefore, any approach for the specification of methodologies should take into account the enactment (or application) of methodologies onto specific endeavours. Using a programming simile, we can say that an approach to methodology specification that does not take into account their enactment is akin to a programming language that can express programs but does not take into account the possibility of running them. The ability for a metamodel to provide classes that get instantiated at the endeavour level is not a plus, but something that should be essential. Furthermore, tracing between endeavour-level elements and methodology-level elements (method components) should be directly addressed by the structure of the metamodel. ISO/IEC 24744 achieves this by pairing classes that represent endeavour-level elements and methodology-level elements into *powertype patterns* [6], in which the methodology-level class (the powertype) partitions the endeavour-level class (the partitioned type). For example, ISO/IEC 24744 includes the classes Task and TaskKind. Task represents an actual task as performed at the endeavour level. TaskKind, on the other hand, represents a kind of task as documented in a methodology. Task has attributes such as StartTime or Duration. TaskKind has attributes such as Name or Purpose. Evidently, every task "is-of" a particular task kind. This is shown in the metamodel by pairing Task and TaskKind into the powertype pattern Task/*Kind, meaning that the TaskKind class (the powertype) partitions the Task class (the partitioned type) (
Figure 2).

Figure 2. Powertype pattern formed by the Task and TaskKind classes in ISO/IEC 24744.

Since most metamodel classes are paired into powertype patterns, they are used together as well: a powertype pattern is "instantiated" as a whole. In fact, method components are created in ISO/IEC 24744 as clabjects [1], i.e. dual-faceted entities that exhibit a class facet plus an object facet. The object facet is obtained as a conventional instance of the methodology-level (powertype) class in the powertype pattern, whereas the class facet is obtained as a conventional subtype of the endeavour-domain class in the powertype pattern. Within a method component clabject, both facets, class and object, represent exactly the same concept, but using different representational mechanisms.

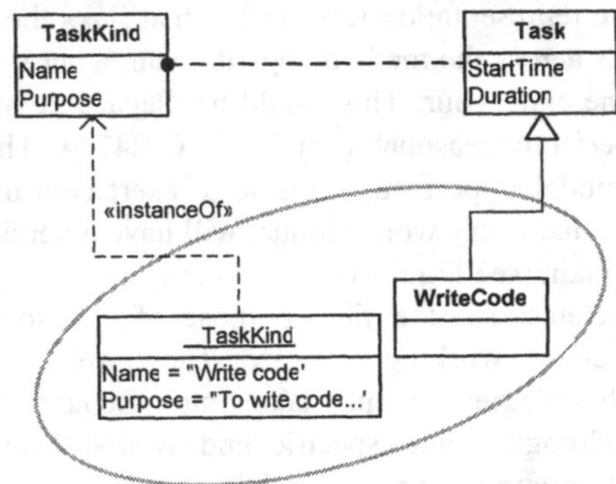

Figure 3. The "instantiation" of a powertype pattern. A regular object is instantiated from the TaskKind class, and a regular class is obtained by subtyping the Task class. Both together form a clabject (depicted by the ellipse), which is the implementation of a method component.

For example, if we were to "instantiate" the Task/*Kind powertype pattern to define a "Write code" task method component, this would involve creating an object as instance of TaskKind and giving values to its attributes (Name="Write code" and Purpose="To write code..."); and then creating a class (named WriteCode, for example) as subtype of Task, which would inherit its attributes (StartTime and Duration). The object with Name="Write code" and the WriteCode class (components of the clabject) represent the same concept, i.e. the task specification of writing code (Figure 3). The class facet will be useful as a template from which instantiation is possible during enactment, while the object facet is useful as "data" at the methodology level.

3.3 Product/Process Interaction

Another aspect that is often neglected by metamodelling approaches is that of the integration between the product and process aspects of methodologies. If we still agree that the final purpose of any software development methodology is to produce working software, it should be clear that, at least from a motivational standpoint, methodologies should be product- rather than process-driven. To put it unceremoniously, process is a necessary evil. Process is necessary to transform ambiguous, incomplete and conflicting expectations given by stakeholders into hopefully working software. The ultimate purpose of a methodology, however, is obtaining the software, not performing the process. Interestingly, most metamodels for development methodologies are strongly process-focussed, sometimes even being called simply "processes" (hence the "P" in "SPEM"). The product aspect is usually assumed to be solved externally by the adoption of an all-encompassing modelling language such as UML [17, 19]. Such inattention to product results in a poor integration between process and product, because, given that the product aspect of the methodology to be used is unknown to the metamodel, very few assumptions about it can be made and, therefore, the interfaces between process and product elements in the metamodel must be kept to a minimum.

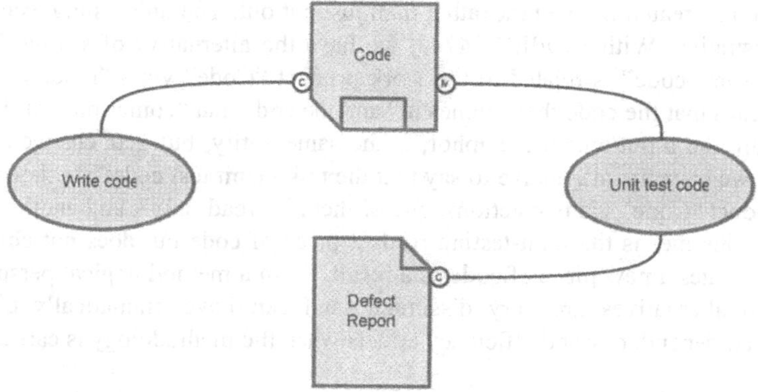

Figure 4. Action diagram showing that the "Write code" task kind creates work products of the "Code" and "Defect Report" kinds, and that the "Unit test code" task kind modifies work products of the "Code" kind and creates work products of the "Defect Report" kind.

ISO/IEC 24744 takes a different route, namely, that of modelling not only the process aspect but also the product aspect of methodologies. The former involves everything related to the tasks, processes, techniques and stages that describe the work- and time-oriented nature of the methodology, whereas the latter is concerned with everything related to the models, documents, languages, notations and model units from which models can be built. In other words, the product aspect of a methodology describes, with very fine details, the modelling languages (plus their potential forms of depiction) that may be used within an endeavour that follows the methodology. The whole of UML, for example, would be subsumed as part of a methodology defined as an instance of ISO/IEC 24744 (Figure 4).The major advantage of this approach is that, since the metamodel includes classes that represent both process and product aspects of the methodology, it can also specify rich interfaces between them. Conventional, process-focussed metamodels such as SPEM use an input/output approach to relate work products to the tasks that interact with them. For example, using SPEM, we can say that the work product "Code" is an output of task "Write code", and an input to task "Unit test code". The input/output approach, however, is not rich enough to describe the variety of ways in which tasks can act upon work products. Consider the above mentioned task "Unit test code". When a developer performs that task, she starts with some code, unit-tests it, and then ends up with some code. Is the code at the end the same work product as the code at the beginning? With SPEM, we can only say, at the methodology level, that the work product "Code" is an input to "Unit test code" and also an output; it is not possible to reflect whether the outgoing product is a new instance of the Code work product kind, or the same instance that came in. ISO/IEC 24744 uses a richer approach, based on the concept of actions. An action is a usage event that a task performs upon a work product. An action is of a specific type: create, read-only, modify or delete. We can express a similar meaning to what in SPEM is conveyed by saying that the work product "Code" is an output of task "Write code" by saying in ISO/IEC 24744 that the task "Write code" is related to the work product "Code" via a "create" action. Notice that this meaning is richer, since we are specifying that the code is being created by the task rather than just put out. The unit testing example is more illustrative. With ISO/IEC 24744, we have the alternative of saying that the task "Unit test code" is related to the work product "Code" via a "modify" action, which means that the code that "comes in" and the code that "comes out" of the task, to maintain the input/output metaphor, is the same entity, but gets changed by the task. But we have the alternative to say that the task "Unit test code" is related to the work product "Code" via two actions: one of them is "read-only", and another one is "create". This means that unit-testing reads a piece of code but does not change it, and then creates a new piece of code as a result. From a methodological perspective, these two alternatives are very dissimilar, and can have dramatically different traceability, dependency and efficiency effects when the methodology is carried out.

4 Methodology Exploitation

Method engineering assumes that methodologies are assembled from method components and made available to their users, i.e. software developers. In order for software developers to reap the benefits of using these methodologies, the appropriate tools and techniques have to be provided as well. The following sections explore how software developers can exploit a methodology by using an alternative enactment approach and the work product pool approach.

4.1 Enactment Approaches

As we have said, most metamodels for development methodologies are strongly process-focussed. This is often reflected in the adoption of the metaphor that the organisation is a machine that executes the methodology as if it were a computer programme. Consequently, metamodels such as OMG's SPEM describe processes in terms of work breakdown structures and task precedence, borrowing from the most classical management styles.

This clashes frontally with the current trend towards agility [4, 22]. It is our personal experience that organisations often take advantage of nudging their systems, acting opportunistically when possible, and leveraging unexpected circumstances, even when an agile style of work is not explicitly encouraged, and more so when it is. Conventional management practices, on the contrary, try to impose up-front plans, which, from a methodological perspective, are sometimes seen as the one-off enactment of method components at the beginning of the endeavour. In other words, if a project plan is supposed to specify what is going to happen in terms of actual tasks and work products, why can't we instantiate the appropriate method components at the beginning of the project in a large big-bang enactment event and leave them sitting there for later use? Changes to the plan are supposed to be minor (as compared to the overall magnitude to the plan) and can surely be addressed by destroying or creating a few extra objects.

Let us consider, for a moment, that an up-front project plan is not possible or not wanted. The "plan a little, design a little, code a little" approach has been proposed a number of times in the context of evolutionary lifecycles [15], and most agile approaches also share that an up-front plan is not a good idea. In a context like this, a big-bag enactment event at the beginning of the endeavour is not feasible. Quite to the contrary, the enactment of the methodology must proceed little by little as time goes by and new method components in the methodology are "ready" to be instantiated. Recall from Section 3.2 that most method components are clabjects, and that it is their class facet which gets instantiated at the endeavour level.

The fact that enactment is done just-in-time means that the exact situation of the endeavour can be known and analysed prior to the instantiation of a method component. For example, imagine a "Write code" task kind specified in a methodology. Using a traditional approach, this task kind would have to be instantiated at the beginning of the endeavour and assigned a start time and duration well ahead of the actual time of performance. Since exact dates and durations cannot be known beforehand with precision, rough estimates would be probably used. This is, incidentally, the same problem that conventional project plans usually find. Using a just-in-time enactment approach, the "Write code" task kind would not be instantiated until a developer actually needs to write some code; at that precise moment, an instance of the task kind is created, the situation of the whole endeavour is evaluated, and the most favourable start time and duration values are assigned to the task. Of course, anything is possible between these two extremes. Our point here is that just-in-time enactment presents an interesting alternative to the more traditional, one-off variant.

4.2 The Work Product Pool Approach

The *work product pool* can be conceived as a central repository where all the intermediary work products managed by the endeavour are stored. We must take into account that the work product pool is an abstract construct and very rarely it is actually implemented as a real database or information store. In any case, more often than not it would contain pointers to the actual work products rather than the work products themselves. Initially, when the endeavour starts, the work product pool contains very few products, such as those that are internally available (e.g. a reusable asset database) or those that are externally provided (e.g. a needs statement). As tasks being to be carried out, and actions to be performed, existing work products are read, modified and deleted, and new work products are created, changing the population of the pool. Eventually, the final system (i.e. the ultimate goal of the endeavour) appears in the pool and the endeavour can be considered complete.

This approach sees work products as the drivers of the endeavour, and tasks as secondary elements that operate on them and transform them as necessary. This fits nicely with our discussion of process- vs. product-centric methodologies in Section 3.3. It is also highly compatible with the notion of microprocesses described by [8], and with the fountain model of [10].

A question still remains, namely, determining which method components are "ready" to be enacted at any point in time. In our previous example, we assumed that a developer needed to write some code, and that the situation of the endeavour was such that writing code was feasible. This means that the developer had the appropriate role and that all the work products that are necessary in order to write code are available in the work product pool. It is possible to build a tool that implements an algorithm that automatically finds which task kinds of a given methodology are *candidate* task kinds, i.e. are ready to be enacted if a particular user wishes. A candidate task kind is one that can be enacted at a given point in time because:

- The user requesting the enactment has a role that is mapped, as per the methodology specification, to that kind of task.
- The organisation carrying out the methodology is performing at a capability level equal or higher to that of the task kind.
- All the work products that are necessary to perform a task of the given kind are present in the pool.

An algorithm capable of verifying these three conditions is easily implementable on top of ISO/IEC 24744 because of the following characteristics of the metamodel:

- ISO/IEC 24744 contains classes that represent both the endeavour as well as the methodology domains. This allows ISO/IEC 24744-based tools to manipulate information belonging to both domains in an integrated fashion, and trace back and forth as necessary. A metamodel that only models the methodology domain will find it very difficult (if not impossible) to implement this algorithm.
- ISO/IEC 24744 directly supports the concept of capability or maturity levels as defined by standards such as CMMI [21] or ISO/IEC 15504 [11]. This provides an additional dimension to methodologies, which can be adjusted according to the desired capability of the performing organisation.
- ISO/IEC 24744 implements rich semantics for the interface between process and product aspects of the methodology, allowing the algorithm to "reason" about the dependencies between work products and therefore determine whether the required products for any particular task are present in the pool or not. A metamodel based on a more conventional input/output approach would be unable to attain this.

A tool that implements an algorithm like this would allow a software developer to display a list of candidate task kinds at any point in time and choose, from that list, any one that she wishes to enact. As we have said, which task kinds are candidate to be enacted is determined just in time depending on the role of the developer, the organisation's performing capability level, and the contents of the work product pool at that precise point in time. The major advantages of this approach as opposed to a conventional, plan-driven one, are two. First of all, it takes advantage of as much information as possible, since it defers enactment to the last possible moment, resulting in optimal decisions and a decreased need for corrections. Secondly, it is highly opportunistic, meaning that the state of the endeavour (primarily given by the contents of the work product pool) is what determines, at any point in time, the next steps that must be taken. This, in turn, supports the appearance of complex emergent behaviours, which have been described as a key component of modern business environments [14].

5 Conclusions

In this paper we have introduced the ISO/IEC 24744 standard metamodel, focussing on how it can help the implementation of a method engineering solution from both infrastructural and superstructural perspectives. On the one hand, ISO/IEC 24744 can provide the theoretical background for method engineering to model the methodology and endeavour domains together and maintain the relationships between them, which is fundamental to keep the necessary traceability during enactment. Also, this metamodel provides rich semantics to model the interface between the process and product sides of methodologies, allowing a better connection between these two often separated worlds. On the other hand, we have shown how these properties make it possible that an algorithm can be implemented on top of ISO/IEC 24744 that can determine what method components of a methodology can be enacted at any point in time. Such just-in-time enactment has the advantages over conventional, up-front enactment that it uses as much information as possibly available (requiring less rework) and that it is highly opportunistic, supporting the emergent behaviours that usually occur in modern business environments.

We acknowledge that the advantages provided by ISO/IEC 24744 come to a price: the theoretical underpinnings of the metamodel, based on powertype patterns and clabjects, depart from the conventional strict metamodelling paradigm often found in the literature. As with any other new technology, a moderately steep learning curve is to be expected. We hope that the gains will be worth it.

References

1. Atkinson, C. and T. Kühne, 2000. Meta-Level Independent Modelling. In *International Workshop on Model Engineering at 14th European Conference on Object-Oriented Programming*. 12-16 June 2000.

2. Atkinson, C. and T. Kühne, 2001. Processes and Products in a Multi-level Metamodeling Architecture. *Int. J. Software Eng. and Knowledge Eng.* **11**(6): 761-783.
3. Brinkkemper, S., 1996. Method Engineering: Engineering of Information Systems Development Methods and Tools. *Information and Software Technology*. **38**(4): 275-280.
4. Chau, T., F. Maurer, and G. Melnik, 2003. Knowledge Sharing: Agile Methods vs. Tayloristic Methods. In *12th IEEE International Workshop on Enabling Technologies: Infrastructure for Collaborative Enterprises (WETICE 2003)*. IEEE Computer Society. 302-307.
5. Gonzalez-Perez, C. and B. Henderson-Sellers, 2005. A Representation-Theoretical Analysis of the OMG Modelling Suite. In *The 4th International Conference on Software Methodologies, Tools and Techniques*. 28-30 September 2005. Frontiers in Artificial Intelligence and Applications 129. IOS Press: Amsterdam. 252-262.
6. Gonzalez-Perez, C. and B. Henderson-Sellers, 2006. A Powertype-Based Metamodelling Framework. *Software and Systems Modelling*. **5**(1): 72-90.
7. Gonzalez-Perez, C. and B. Henderson-Sellers, 2007. Modelling Software Development Methodologies: A Conceptual Foundation. *Journal of Systems and Software*. **(in press)**.
8. Greenfield, J. and K. Short, 2004. *Software Factories*: John Wiley & Sons.
9. Guizzardi, G., 2007. On Some Modal Properties of Ontologically Well-Founded Structural Conceptual Models. In *CAiSE 2007*. LNCS (in press). Springer-Verlag
10. Henderson-Sellers, B., 1992. *A Book of Object-Oriented Knowledge*. New York: Prentice-Hall.
11. International Organization for Standardization / International Electrotechnical Commission, 2004. ISO/IEC 15504-1: 2004. *Software Process Assessment - Part 1: Concepts and Vocabulary*.
12. International Organization for Standardization / International Electrotechnical Commission, 2007. ISO/IEC 24744. *Software Engineering - Metamodel for Development Methodologies*.
13. Kumar, K. and R.J. Welke, 1992. Methodology Engineering: a Proposal for Situation-Specific Methodology Construction, in *Challenges and Strategies for Research in Systems Development*, W.W. Cotterman and J.A. Senn (eds.). John Wiley & Sons: Chichester (UK). 257-269.
14. Lycett, M., R.D. Macredie, C. Patel, and R.J. Paul, 2003. Migrating Agile Methods to Standardized Development Practice. *IEEE Computer*. **36**(6): 79-85.
15. McConnell, S., 1996. *Rapid Development*. Redmond: Microsoft Press.
16. Object Management Group, 2005. formal/05-01-06. *Software Process Engineering Metamodel Specification*, version 1.1.
17. Object Management Group, 2005. formal/05-07-04. *Unified Modelling Language Specification: Superstructure*, version 2.
18. Object Management Group, 2006. ad/2006-08-01. *Software & Systems Process Engineering Meta-Model*, version 2.0.
19. Object Management Group, 2006. formal/05-07-05. *Unified Modelling Language Specification: Infrastructure*, version 2.
20. Seidewitz, E., 2003. What Models Mean. *IEEE Software*. **20**(5): 26-31.
21. Carnegie Mellon Software Engineering Institute, 2002. CMMI-SE/SW/IPPD/SS, V1.1, Continuous. *CMMI for Systems Engineering/Software Engineering/Integrated Product and Process Development/Supplier Sourcing, Continuous Representation*, version 1.1.
22. Thomsett, R., 2002. *Radical Project Management*. Upper Saddle River, NJ: Prentice-Hall.

Multi-Grounded Action Research in Method Engineering: The MMC Case

Fredrik Karlsson[1] and Pär J. Ågerfalk[2,3,4]
1 Methodology Exploration Lab, Dept. of Informatics (ESI),
Örebro University, SE-701 82 Örebro, Sweden
Email: fredrik.karlsson@esi.oru.se,
2 Dept. of Information Science, Uppsala University, Sweden
3 Jönköping International Business School,
P.O. Box 1026, SE-551 11 Jönköping, Sweden
4 Lero – The Irish Software Engineering Research Centre
University of Limerick, Limerick, Ireland
Email: agpa@jibs.hj.se

Abstract. There appears to be two schools of information systems development methods research that largely pursue their own agendas without many cross-references. On the one hand there is the method engineering research and on the other hand there is the method-in-action research. There seems to be much to be gained from integrating these two schools, developing knowledge that both has the formality (rigor) and reflects its enactment in practice. To achieve this, the research approach adopted has to embrace this duality. In this paper we explore how Multi-Grounded Action Research (MGAR) can contribute to achieving this aim. MGAR has been used in the development of a Method for Method Configuration, a research product that integrates the strengths of both schools.

1 Introduction

As noted by Ågerfalk and Fitzgerald [1], there appears to be two schools of information systems development method (ISDM) research that largely pursue their own agendas without many cross-references. On the one hand there is the method engineering (ME) research which has to a large extent concentrated on deriving situational methods from atomic method fragments or larger method chunks [2-7]. This school of ISDM research has paid limited attention to what actually happens in software development projects where the situational method is used. On the other hand, there is the method-in-action research that focuses specifically on how espoused ISDMs are enacted in practice [e.g. 8, 9, 10]. This school of ISDM research, while having contributed extensively to our understanding of method use,

Please use the following format when citing this chapter:

Karlsson, F., Ågerfalk, P.J., 2007, in IFIP International Federation for Information Processing, Volume 244, Situational Method Engineering: Fundamentals and Experiences, eds. Ralyté, J., Brinkkemper, S., Henderson-Sellers B., (Boston Springer), pp. 19-32.

seems to neglect the intricate task of defining and validating consistent method constructs.

Another way to put it is that there has been a lot of research on (a) the construction of situational methods out of existing method parts, and (b) the relationship between espoused methods and methods-in-action. According to Ågerfalk and Fitzgerald [1], a basic flaw in the research of type (a) is that it often does not pay sufficient attention to actual method use. Perhaps focusing too much on what people should do, rather than on what they actually do. A basic flaw in research of type (b), on the other hand, is that it often does not pay sufficient attention to the formality (rigour) required to ensure method consistency. That is, too little focus on how to codify successful development practices into useful ISDMs. Another flaw is that (b) usually does not acknowledge the difference between what is termed base method [11] and situational methods, perhaps even confusing the latter with method-in-action (i.e. an ISDM as enacted in practice).

As pointed out by Ågerfalk and Fitzgerald [1], there seems to be much to be gained from integrating these two schools, and they even suggest method rationale could be an important link between the two. They argue that since ISDMs fundamentally are linguistic expressions as result of and basis for social action, we need to understand the complex social reality that shapes methods-in-action. On the other hand, it is imperative to use that understanding as a basis for formal construction, verification and validation of ISDMs. Subsequently, it becomes critical for the adopted research process to reflect this duality. The aim of this paper is to explore how Multi-Grounded Action Research (MGAR) can contribute to method engineering research. This is explored through reflecting on its use in the development of Method for Method Configuration (MMC), a research product where the rigor of ME research is combined with the social sensitivity of the method-in-action school.

The paper proceeds as follows. Section 2 contains an in-depth discussion of the MGAR approach. While the focus of this paper is on the MGAR approach as such, to facilitate understanding, Section 3 then provides a brief overview of the main research product, MMC. Following this, Section 4 provides empirical experiences from applying MGAR and provides an in-context perspective of the research approach. Finally, the paper ends with a concluding discussion in Section 5.

2 Multi-Grounded Action Research

MMC is the result of a collaborative project involving the Swedish research network VITS (with participants from Örebro University and University College Borås), University of Limerick, Ireland, and three Swedish software developing organizations: Volvo IT (a multi-national software and technology consultancy organization), Posten IT (the information technology division of Posten AB), and Precio (a mid-sized software consultancy company).

The research method used was that of Multi-Grounded [12] Action Research. Similar to grounded action research [13] it draws on the well-established qualitative research method Grounded Theory, particularly as it has evolved in the tradition of

Strauss and Corbin [14]. In a multi-grounded approach evolving as well as existing theory play an important part in data collection and analysis [cf. 15]. The idea is to ground theory not only in empirical data, but also internally and in other existing knowledge of theoretical character. This gives rise to three grounding processes, which were applied in this research: internal grounding, external grounding and empirical grounding.

Internal grounding means reconstructing and articulating 'background knowledge', that is, knowledge that might otherwise be taken for granted. For example, it is important to identify and explicate the basic assumptions behind MMC to understand how and when it is applicable. Internal grounding also includes defining concepts used and their interrelationships. The important contribution of this process in this particular research is a consistent conceptual model of MMC, free from ambiguities and with concepts that are anchored in explicit values and goals. That is, it ensures that the developed knowledge (MMC in our case) is logically consistent [16]. External grounding is concerned with relationships between the developed knowledge (its concepts and internal relationships) and other knowledge of a theoretical character. This is relevant for putting forward similarities and differences between the evolving knowledge and other existing knowledge. In our case, this meant ensuring that MMC builds on existing ME wisdom in a constructive way and that it does not contradict relevant previous studies. Empirical grounding emphasizes the importance of applying developed knowledge in practice to validate the concepts and their relationships in an empirical environment. In this context we use 'applying' in a broad sense, involving analysis, design and implementation, as well as test and evaluation. In our case, this involved designing parts of MMC together with qualified practitioners as well as gaining experience from using MMC in real projects when specifying situational ISDMs. Furthermore, as we learn more about the domain we research, knowledge can also be generated through classification of empirical phenomena, which results in refinement of the theoretical knowledge and thus triggers further internal and external grounding.

Our MGAR approach can be understood in terms of the traditional 'canonical' action research method with cycles of diagnosing, action planning, action taking, evaluating, and specifying learning [17]. The research project consisted of two such MGAR cycles, which are elaborated further in the sections below. Within these two cycles seven smaller 'action cases' [18] were performed, as shown in Table 1. An action case means involving competent practitioners in collaborative design and evaluation efforts. Problems and design decisions are discussed and taken together by researchers and practitioners, which means continuous feedback and interaction between the two [19]. The selection of action cases was based on finding a mixture of different organization-wide ISDMs and organizations. The choice of organizations was based on two premises: they had to use different, preferably well-known, organization-wide ISDMs, and they had to agree to put aside resources to enable the kind of collaboration envisaged. The organizations in this study ranged from quite small to very large and the ISDMs used in these organizations were the Rational Unified Process (RUP) and the Microsoft Solution Framework (MSF) – see Table 1. Furthermore, each action case served a specific purpose towards the final research product and was related to the action cycle discussed below.

Table 1. Action cases in chronological order

Action case	Business	ISDM	Case role
1. Volvo IT – pre case	Large	RUP	Method configuration diagnosis
2. Volvo IT	Large	RUP	MMC design, configuration application
3. ESI	Small	RUP	MMC validation, configuration application
4. Posten IT	Large	RUP	MMC redesign & validation, configuration application
5. Posten IT	Large	RUP	MMC redesign & validation, reconstruction of configuration
6. Precio	Medium	MSF	MMC validation, creating configuration
7. Precio	Medium	MSF	MMC validation, reconstruction of configuration

2.1 The First Multi-Grounded Action Research Cycle

The first MGAR cycle was carried out between spring 2000 and spring 2002. During this cycle the first three action cases in Table 1 were carried out, together with the research collaborators Volvo IT and ESI.

Phase 1 – Diagnosing (Action case 1): Difficulties related to tailoring an organization-wide method for a specific project was explored at Volvo IT through a series of workshops with a systems development project requiring a situational ISDM. Problems with the current way of tailoring the organization-wide ISDM were documented. Based on principles from the situational ME literature, a vision of how to improve method configuration was formulated. The data sources from this phase were: log books from three workshop sessions, organization-wide ISDM (the RUP), situational method, project deliverables. Data analysis was done using problem analysis [20] and conceptual models. Problem analysis was used to separate real problems from symptoms. Conceptual models of the organization-wide ISDM were created to facilitate understanding of experienced phenomena, using UML and other standard techniques.

Phase 2 – Action planning (Action case 2): A set of design principles for improved method configuration was developed in a series of workshops. These were anchored in the formulated vision, prioritized problems, and principles from the situational ME literature. The proposed design principles were: the principle of modularization, the principle of method rationale for selecting method parts and the principle of a multi-layered reuse model. The data sources from this phase were: log books from two planning sessions and the vision document.

Phase 3 – Action taking (Action case 2 & 3): Based on the design principles, a prototype of MMC was developed. In a series of workshops, a conceptual structure and a classification schema were chiseled, along with a number of instructions for the method engineer role. The four main concepts were: the method fragment (based on established situational ME principles [4]), the base method (the organization-wide ISDM), the configuration package, and the configuration template. The latter two concepts were introduced to facilitate modular reuse of method configurations.

Volvo IT provided a set of existing projects as input for the design sessions and emerging concepts were tried against those projects' requirements. A summary of the work so far was presented at an international workshop [21]. When MMC had stabilized sufficiently, it was used in a small scale project at ESI, which enabled active participation throughout the project. The chosen base method was the RUP. Identified data sources were: log books from twelve design sessions and a preliminary version of MMC.

Phase 4 – Evaluation (Action case 3): The first full-scale evaluation of MMC was based on the active participation in the ESI project. The business objectives of the systems development project were to offer the situational information about personnel to internal users and external users outside the organization. The first author was project manager and method engineer during this project. Five different data sources were of interest from this phase: the situational ISDM that was used during the project, defined reusable assets, project artifacts, project results, and the project log book.

The data sources were analyzed with a focus on encountered problems and achieved design goals. Documented problems were traced to possible causes. For example, some of these causes could be traced back to the situational method and MMC, the systems developer's knowledge of the base method, or a combination. The developed software was evaluated through interviews with end users and change requests tracking. [22].

Phase 5 – Specifying learning: On the basis of the data analysis in Phase 4, lessons learnt, including practical advices on how to use the proposed meta-method, and change requests were outlined. A summary of the work so far was published in an international journal [11].

2.2 The Second Multi-Grounded Action Research Cycle

The second MGAR cycle included four action cases as shown in Table 1. These were carried out together with Posten IT and Precio between autumn 2002 and autumn 2004.

Phase 6 – Diagnosing: The diagnosing phase was based on the specified lessons learnt from the first MGAR cycle. These lessons were analysed from two different perspectives: design flaws in the MMC prototype were identified, and the need for a CAME-tool based on MMC was identified (note that the tool aspect is beyond the scope of this paper and is only mentioned here for completeness). Data sources during this phase were the lessons learnt and change requests from the first action research cycle. The data analysis, like in Diagnosing during the first MGAR cycle, was done using problem analysis [20], to separate real problems from symptoms.

Phase 7 – Action planning (Action case 4 & 5): Based on lessons and change requests from the first MGAR cycle, the set of design principles was refined. It resulted in a set of sub-principles:

- The principle of modularization: self-contained modules, internally consistent and coherent modules, support for information-hiding and implementable in a CAME-tool;

- The principle of method rationale for selecting method parts: support analysis of potential to achieve rationality resonance, and support 'method-in-action' [23] decisions;
- The principle of a multi-layered reuse model.

Phase 8 – Action taking (Action cases 4–7): MMC was redesigned based on the refined principles. A new modularization concept was introduced, based on a modification of an existing ME concept: the method component. This concept was integrated with the two concepts configuration package and configuration template. As a consequence of this redesign, the classification schema was changed as well. The method rationale and method component concepts were presented at international conferences [24, 25] and in an international journal [26]. During this phase the following data sources were produced: log books from four design sessions and MMC.

The redesigned MMC was used in live projects at Posten IT and Precio. In these projects, RUP and MSF were used as base methods. In total MMC was used in four different project settings as shown in Table 1. Two of the projects included reconstruction of existing situational methods into reusable assets and the remaining two projects focused actual tailoring of ISDMs.

Phase 9 – Evaluation (Action cases 4–7): Evaluation of MMC (Phase 8) was performed during its use at Posten IT and Precio. Through-out these projects, group interviews were performed with project members. The following data source was used during the evaluation: log books from six configuration workshops, situational methods, defined reusable assets, project artifacts, and four group interviews. Theses data sources were analyzed with a focus on encountered problems and achieved design goals.

Phase 10 – Specifying learning: On the basis of the data analysis in Phase 9, lessons learnt and change requests were outlined. As during the first MGAR cycle the first category contains practical advice and the second category contains identified design flaws that have had subsequent design implications.

3 The Method for Method Configuration – MMC

The aim of the research product MMC is to support method configuration, as a specific kind of ME, which we define as: the planned and systematic adaptation of a specific method through the use of reusable assets. The foundation of MMC is its conceptual framework, shown in Fig. 1. MMC provides the possibility to work with reusable assets of ISDMs through the three core concepts: the method component [24, 26], the configuration package [27], and the configuration template [27]. Together they constitute types of reusable assets of different magnitude.

A method component is the smallest meaningful and coherent part of an ISDM, and the organization-wide ISDM (base method) has to be represented as a set of such components in order to use MMC. Method components are used as modularization blocks that are excluded, added and exchanged from the base method. For example, an ISDM might include a method component concerned with software packaging;

involving copying the software on distributable medium, printing handbooks, and designing a cardboard box with a selling cover. In projects where the final product is delivered using the Internet such a component is often considered superfluous and can be excluded.

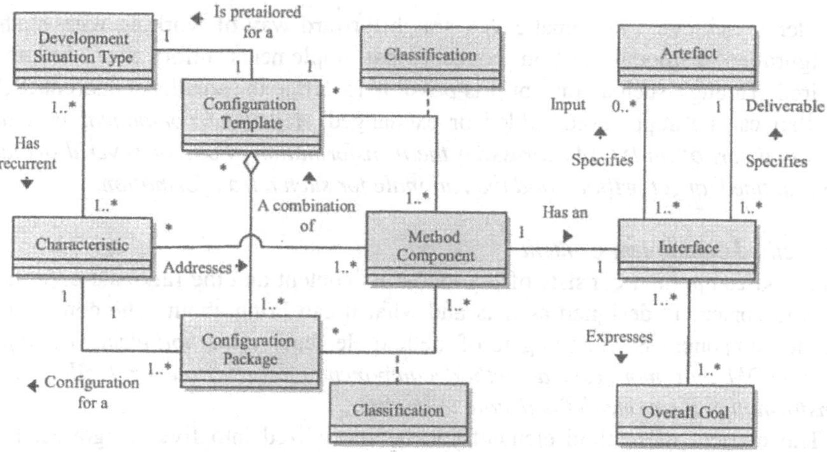

Fig. 1. A conceptual meta-model of Method for Method Configuration

Configuration packages and configuration templates are used to represent situational versions of an ISDM. The main difference between these two concepts is how much of a situational method they represent. Briefly, a configuration package can be described as a pre-made method configuration designed to fit one single specific development characteristic. If we continue on the short example in the previous paragraph it is likely that we are working with a characteristic of Internet delivery. In such a case the characteristic should affect method components aiming for product distribution. The result of how such method components are selected with respect to this characteristic is represented in the configuration package. This selection of components can, if required, include components from complementing ISDMs.

Real-life development situations obviously comprise a combination of several characteristics. For example, a single project may involve a number of diverse characteristics, such as unstable requirements, low degree of management support, a new technical platform and Internet delivery. The configuration template then represents this more complex configuration, and is a pre-configuration of the complete organization-wide ISDM for a typical project situation in the organization. A configuration template is constructed from a selection of configuration packages (each one representing a characteristic) and can be viewed as an aggregate of configuration packages. Hence, a configuration template reflects a recurring development pattern in an organization.

The remainder of this section is structured based on the three core concepts introduced above. For an extensive presentation of these concepts and content examples see Karlsson and Wistrand [26], Wistrand and Karlsson [24] and Karlsson [27].

3.1 The Method Component Concept

In order to achieve a systematic yet straightforward way of working with method configuration a modularization concept that implements information hiding is required. Through such a concept it is possible to define the smallest coherent ISDM part that can be suppressed, added or exchanged: *A method component is a self-contained part of an ISDM expressing the transformation of one or several artifacts into a defined target artifact, and the rationale for such a transformation.*

The Method Component Content

A method component consists of two parts: its content and the rationale expressing why the content is designed as it is and what it can bring about. The content of a method component is an aggregate of method elements: *A method element is a part of an ISDM that manifests a method component's target state or facilitates the transformation from one defined state to another.*

The concept of method element can be specialized into five categories. First, there are three interrelated parts frequently mentioned in the literature: *prescribed action*, *concept*, and *notation*. Prescribed actions together with sequence restrictions guide the performance of activities and tell project members what actions to take in specific situations. In performing these actions, the concepts direct developers' attention towards specific phenomena in the problem domain. Hence, concepts are used to express an understanding of the problem domain, and also of the ISDM itself. The results of the prescribed actions are documented using a specific notation, which gives the concepts a concrete representation.

Second, based on empirical observations from MGAR Cycle 1, these categories are complemented with *artifact* and *actor role* as two further sub-types of method element. Project members tended to discuss ISDMs from an artifact perspective during method configuration and software development projects. This is also in line with previous research emphasizing the importance of 'keeping the focus on what is being produced' [28]. Artifacts act as deliverables from the transformation process as well as input to this process. Our use of the term input should not be interpreted in terms of a precondition. ISDMs are here viewed as heuristic procedures and consequently specified inputs are considered to be recommended inputs. However, a method component needs to have at least one input. Otherwise the method component will not have any meaningful support in the method. One exception is method components that initiate new activities that are later integrated with the result from other method components. The selection of actor roles are determined by the prescribed actions that need to be part of the transformation process. Actor roles are played either as drivers or as participants of the prescribed actions in the method component. Observations from MGAR Cycle 1 show that actor roles are important when mapping the situational ISDM to the actual work organization.

The rationale part of the method component concept consists of two parts: *goals* and *values*. Method elements exist for reasons, which are made explicit by means of associating method elements to the goals. These goals are anchored in values of the method creator [1]. Taken together, goals and values are often considered important constituents of an ISDM's underlying perspective or 'philosophy' [23]. When working with method configuration according to MMC, method rationale is more important than the deliverable as such. Through the method rationale it is possible to address the goals that are essential in order to fulfill the overall goal of a specific project. Prescribed actions and artifacts are only means to achieve something and method rationale can thus help developers not to loose sight of that ultimate result, and also help them find alternative ways forward.

The Method Component Interface

The second purpose of the method component concept is to hide unnecessary details during method configuration, providing a sort of encapsulation. Thus, we draw on how the component concept is traditionally used in software engineering [29]. How a task is executed is not interesting from an external view of a component. A user of a component is primarily interested in the results offered by the component and the required inputs needed to achieve those results. The reduction of complexity is achieved through the method component interface: *A method component interface is a selection of method fragments and rationale that are relevant for the task at hand.*

The interface creates an external view of method components. The interface's content depends on the task at hand [26]. Empirical observations from MGAR Cycle 1 show that the method component's overall goals and the artifacts are central during method configuration. Therefore, they are part of the interface during method configuration as shown in Fig. 1. Artifacts are, as discussed above, designated as input and/or deliverable (output). This is necessary in order to deal with the three fundamental actions that can be performed on an artifact: create, update and delete. In cases when an artifact is only created by a method component, it is classified as a deliverable. If the artifact can be updated by the same method component it is classified as input as well. Furthermore we stipulate that a component can take one or several input artifacts, but has only one deliverable. Finally, the interface also expresses the overall goals of the method component representing the method rationale. These goals are used during method configuration and when discussing the rationality resonance possible to achieve during a project with certain characteristics.

3.2 The Configuration Package

Method configuration is about deciding whether or not method components in a base method are to be performed, and to what extent. This is done through the focus a characteristic has on the rationale of a method; rationale that is expressed through the method components' interfaces. A characteristic is viewed as a question about one aspect of the development situation type [11]. This question can have one or more possible answers that constitute the characteristic's dimension; one possible answer is termed configuration package in MMC. Each characteristic addresses one or several method components and their purpose of existence. Hence, each configuration package has a scope: the method components that are of interest for classification based on the characteristic. The scope is defined in order to reduce the number of classification operations that have to be performed when creating a configuration package.

Thus, a configuration package is a classification of method components (see Fig. 1) with regard to how relevant their overall goals are for a specific answer in a characteristic's dimension. An example of a characteristic is 'Business processes already well understood?' which could address method components about business modeling. Two possible answers are 'We have good knowledge about existing business processes' and 'We have no knowledge about existing business processes.' In this case the dimension consists of two answers, or configuration packages. Thus component-based method configuration links to the idea of larger reusable blocks of method modules, blocks termed configuration packages: *A configuration package is a configuration of the base method suitable for a characteristic's value.*

The classification of method components is based on a two-dimensional classification schema. The vertical dimension focuses how much attention should be devoted to a particular method component: 'None,' 'Insignificant,' 'Normal' or 'Significant'. If at this stage a method component is found to be unimportant, it can be classified as 'Omit' outright. The three aspects of the horizontal dimension: 'Satisfactory,' 'Unsatisfactory' and 'Missing' cut across the vertical dimension. This dimension is referred to as the potential for achieving rationality resonance, based on the content of the base method. Together this schema provides different variants of the fundamental method configuration scenarios [24] that need to be supported: selection, exchange and addition.

3.3 The Configuration Template

The configuration package concept is used together with characteristics to simplify analysis of the base method. Still, we can conclude that software projects are not simple, nor are situational methods. Consequently, we need configurations that reflect this more complicated picture where characteristics exist in combinations. The configuration template concept is used for this purpose: *A configuration template is a combined method configuration, based on one or more configuration packages, for a set of recurrent project characteristics* (see Fig. 1). Hence, configuration templates make it possible to tailor the base method more efficiently. The concept as such allows reuse of combined configuration packages that target development situation types common within the organization. Configuration packages on the other hand are used to narrow the analysis and to reduce the complexity.

The situational method is based on a selected configuration template and is the ISDM delivered to the project team for use. This method is then turned into method-in-action when enacted by the project team members. Thus there is a difference between the tailored version of the base method and the method-in-action [1]. Experiences from the latter should be fed back to the configuration process, in order to improve configuration templates and/or configuration packages. This feedback is typically done continuously throughout the project, for example, at the end of each iteration, or during project close-out.

4 Multi-Grounded Action Research in Action

4.1 Volvo IT – Emphasis on External Theoretical Grounding

From a retrospective point of view theoretical grounding has played an important part during the research process. One clear example is the introduction of modularization concepts, a joint decision by the researchers and the practitioners.

The method fragment concept was used during the initial development of the first version of MMC, with a starting point in the process model [11]. Each process fragment has a purpose, based on the assumption that prescribed actions are prescribed for reasons. The effect on product fragments was then traced through the relationship between the process and product model. Since it was found difficult to balance precision and cost when using method fragments [11], a modified version of the method component concept was later introduced [24]. The major changes to the method component concept were the introduction of two distinctive views, the operationalization of the interface concept and viewing method components as non-hierarchic. These changes were introduced in order to reduce the number of details to present to the method engineer.

4.2 Posten IT – Emphasis on Internal Grounding

The empirical work at Posten IT included two action cases during the second MGAR cycle. The systems development aim of the first action case was to adapt an existing IS to new regulations, and in the second case to implement and host an IS in the electronic government area. The first case was a reconstruction project from a research point of view. Hence, the research aim was to test possibilities for reconstructing reusable patterns, based on how a project had been working. In the second case a configuration team was to deliver reusable patterns for an upcoming project. Both projects shared some features and parts of situational ISDMs.

During one of the joint introduction sessions for the work at Posten IT the impact of internal grounding became obvious. The tool mentor working with these project teams found an inconsistency in the activity diagram that presented MMC's overall process structure [11]. One of the decision points in the diagram was placed illogically. This error had the following consequence when searching for a configuration template as the base for a situational method: if a configuration template could not be found when trying to define a situational method it triggered an input to manage a change request for a template. But since no appropriate configuration template could be found, the result would always be defining a new configuration template. Subsequently, an improvement was to directly trigger the prescribed action for defining a configuration template.

4.3 Precio – Emphasis on Empirical Grounding

The empirical work at Precio shared similarities with the studies conducted at Posten IT, although Precio used MSF as their base method rather than RUP. Two action cases were carried out with Precio during the second MGAR cycle: one reconstruction case and one case where method configuration was conducted in preparation for an upcoming project. The reconstruction case concerned a booking system involving two companies sharing the new IS. The second project concerned extending an existing IS with a report module. The idea was to find reusable parts during reconstruction and configuration work and hopefully share the configuration packages between the two projects.

The empirical grounding during these two action cases showed that the artifact focus of a method component together with method rationale is a natural starting point for method engineers and project team members when discussing methods. For example, the project manager of the booking system project expressed that 'it is easy to translate to the use of deliverables' and a team member of the Report module project expressed method components as 'easy to grasp.'

However, the team members of the Report module project suggested design improvements for the method component interface concerning the use of method rationale. They expressed in unison a need for more 'precise goals' to capture what a component's deliverable could be used for subsequently. At that time, the conceptual framework only allowed the interface to contain one goal. This limitation meant that it was impossible to express multiple purposes of a method component. The participating developers stressed that the resulting artifact of a method component sometimes 'is used for different purposes.' Hence, the current design thus limited their potential to discuss method components. This design restriction had forced rewriting goals, found in the base method, into one comprehensive goal for each component, which then became ambiguous. As a result the conceptual design of the method component was changed to include the possibility to express multiple purposes in the method component's interface.

5 Concluding Discussion and Lessons Learned

In this paper we have shown how Multi-Grounded Action Research (MGAR) can be used in method engineering research, in our case to devise a Method for Method Configuration (MMC). This research approach combines the need to capture knowledge of how systems development methods are used and tailored in organizations with how to formalize such knowledge, and evaluate it in use. MGAR has proved to be a relevant and valuable approach in the development of MMC. The approach provides a balanced research method that has been instrumental in combining ME rigor with the social sensitivity of the method-in-action school.

In terms of MGAR, four major lessons can be learned from this research project. First, the three grounding processes (internal, theoretical and empirical) are not to be seen as a division of work between researchers and practitioners, where the researchers do the theoretical and internal grounding and the practitioners do the empirical grounding. Neither are they a classification schema for where the work is carried out. Instead, they constitute processes carried out together; processes with a specific focus. An example is the inconsistency discussion at Posten IT, which shows how internal grounding was carried out at the research site and involved joint efforts by practitioners and researchers.

Second, these three grounding processes are intertwined. This means that attention between the different processes can shift continuously. During a project meeting it is, for example, possible to cover each process several times. This, however, can raise difficulties when it comes to tracing the origin of data. For example: Was the inconsistency discussion generated from internal or empirical grounding? In this case it was clearly internal grounding since the discussion had a conceptual focus. It was, however, induced by empirical grounding, witheout which the problem would not have been identified.

Third, as is the case with Grounded Theory, MGAR opens a box with a vast amount of empirical data. This is certainly another reason for why it is difficult to trace data as the project moves on, sometimes in a rather fast pace. Since data is of no use if it is not documented and analysed properly, it is important to have a well functioning way of working with documentation. For this purpose, it is possible to use existing theories as filters. In our case, design decisions about evolving concepts were important together with method configuration results and judgments about the concepts in use.

Finally, working with industry may imply a trade-off between relevance and external theoretical anchoring. When solving day-to-day problems, external theoretical grounding easily falls into the background. Effectively, this means that developed knowledge may not always build on and develop existing research, which a conscious focus on external theoretical grounding then becomes a way to avoid.

References

1. P.J. Ågerfalk and B. Fitzgerald, in: In Advanced Topics in Database Research, edited by K. Siau (PA: Idea Group, Hershey, 2006), pp. 63-78.
2. S. Brinkkemper, Method engineering: engineering of information systems development methods and tools, *Information and Software Technology*. **38**(4), 275–280, (1996).
3. S. Brinkkemper, M. Saeki, and F. Harmsen, Meta-modelling based assembly techniques for situational method engineering, *Information Systems*. **24**(3), 209–228, (1999).
4. A.F. Harmsen, *Situational Method Engineering* (Moret Ernst & Young Management Consultants, Utrecht, The Netherlands, 1997).
5. J. Ralyté, R. Deneckère, and C. Rolland, Towards a Generic Model for Situational Method Engineering in: Advanced Information Systems Engineering, 15th International Conference, CAiSE 2003, LNCS 3084, Springer-Verlag, pp.202-218.
6. C. Rolland and N. Prakash, A Proposal For Context-Specific Method Engineering in: Method Engineering: Principles of method construction and tool support, edited by S. Brinkkemper, K. Lyytinen, and R. Welke (Chapman & Hall, 26–28 August 1996).
7. A.H.M. ter Hofstede and T.F. Verhoef, On the Feasibility of Situational Method Engineering, *Information Systems*. **22**(6/7), 401–422, (1997).
8. D.E. Avison and G. Fitzgerald, Where now for development methodologies? *Association for Computing Machinery. Communications of the ACM*. **46**(1), 78, (2003).
9. L.D. Introna and E.A. Whitley, Against Method-*ism*: Exploring the limits of method, *Information Technology & People*. **10**(1), 31–45, (1997).

10. N.L. Russo and E. Stolterman, Exploring the assumptions underlying information systems methodologies: their impact on past, present and future ISM research, *Information Technology & People*. **13**(4), 313–327, (2000).
11. F. Karlsson and P.J. Ågerfalk, Method Configuration: Adapting to Situational Characteristics while Creating Reusable Assets, *Information and Software Technology*. **46**(9), 619-633, (2004).
12. M. Lind and G. Goldkuhl, How to develop a Multi-Grounded Theory: The Evolution of a Business Process Theory, *Australian Journal of Information Systems*. **13**(2), 69-85, (2006).
13. R. Baskerville and J. Pries-Heje, Grounded action research: a method for understanding IT in practice, *Accounting, Management and Information Technologies*. **9** 1-23, (1999).
14. A.L. Strauss and J.M. Corbin, *Basics of qualitative research: techniques and procedures for developing grounded theory* (SAGE, Thousand Oaks, CA, 1998).
15. H.K. Klein and M.D. Myers, A Set of Principles for Conducting and Evaluating Interpretive Field Studies in Information Systems, *MIS Quarterly*. **1** 67-94, (1999).
16. A.S. Lee, A Scientific Methodology for MIS Case Studies, *MIS Quarterly*. **13**(1), 33-51, (1989).
17. R. Baskerville and A.T. Wood-Harper, Diversity in information systems action research methods, *European Journal of Information Systems*. **7** 90-107, (1998).
18. K. Braa and R. Vidgen, Interpretation, intervention, and reduction in the organizational laboratory: a framework for in-context information system research, *Accounting, Management and Information Technologies*. **9**(1), 25–47, (1999).
19. L. Mathiassen, Collaborative Practice Research, *Information Technology & People*. **15**(4), 321-345, (2002).
20. G. Goldkuhl and A. Röstlinger, *Joint elicitation of problems: An important aspect of change analysis*, in *Human, Organizational, and Social Dimensions of Information Systems Development*, D.E. Avison, J.E. Kendall, and J.I. DeGross, Editors. 1993: North-Holland. p. 107–125.
21. F. Karlsson, P.J. Ågerfalk, and A. Hjalmarsson, Process Configuration with Development Tracks and Generic Project Types in: Proceedings of the 6th CAiSE/IFIP8.1 International Workshop on Evaluation of Modelling Methods in Systems Analysis and Design (EMMSAD'01)(4–5 June 2001).
22. F. Karlsson, Method Configuration - A Systems Development Project Revisited in: The Fourteenth International Conference on Information Systems Development (ISD 2005), edited by A.G. Nilsson, et al. (Springer, Karlstad, Sweden, 14-17 August, 2005).
23. B. Fitzgerald, N.L. Russo, and E. Stolterman, *Information Systems Development - Methods in Action* (McGraw-Hill, London, 2002).
24. K. Wistrand and F. Karlsson, Method Components - Rationale Revealed in: The 16th International Conference on Advanced Information Systems Engineering (CAiSE 2004), edited by A. Persson and J. Stirna (Riga, Latvia, June 7 - 11, 2004).
25. P.J. Ågerfalk and K. Wistrand, Systems Development Method Rationale: A Conceptual Framework for Analysis in: Proceedings of the 5th International Conference on Enterprise Information Systems (ICEIS 2003)(Angers, France, 23–26 April 2003).
26. F. Karlsson and K. Wistrand, Combining method engineering with activity theory: theoretical grounding of the method component concept, *European Journal of Information Systems*. **15** 82-90, (2006).
27. F. Karlsson, *Method Configuration - Method and Computerized Tool Support* (Linköping University, Linköping, 2005).
28. J. Cameron, Configurable Development Processes, *Communications of the ACM*. **45**(3), 72-77, (2002).
29. P. Stevens and R. Pooley, *Using UML - Software Engineering with Objects and Components* (Addison Wesley, Essex, England, 2006).

Situational Method Engineering

On the Differentiation of "Context" and "Project Type"

Tobias Bucher, Mario Klesse, Stephan Kurpjuweit, Robert Winter
Institute of Information Management, University of St. Gallen
Mueller-Friedberg-Strasse 8, 9000 St. Gallen, Switzerland
{tobias.bucher, mario.klesse, stephan.kurpjuweit, robert.winter}@unisg.ch
http://www.iwi.unisg.ch

Abstract. Based on the experience that there cannot be a "one-size-fits-all" method, different situational method engineering approaches are examined in this paper. The result of the analysis shows that "situations" are conceptualized very imprecisely. Therefore, we propose to differentiate between "context" and "project type" in situational method engineering. Especially context is neglected in existing method engineering approaches. To close this gap, we enhance existing method engineering processes by adding three steps to facilitate the identification of context factors and project type factors, enabling the engineering of both contextual and project type-specific methods. Furthermore, we propose a set of extensions to the method engineering meta model that allow the method engineer to differentiate between "context" and "project type" in describing situational methods.

1 Introduction

Since its first theoretical foundation almost four decades ago, the "sciences of the artificial" [1] have evolved into a key research paradigm in the study of information systems development that is commonly referred to as "design research" [2, 3, 4]. Unlike research in behavioral or natural sciences, design research is not aimed at explaining the behavior of a system that is observable to the researcher but rather at creating solutions to specific problems of practical relevance. Typical outputs produced by design research are representational constructs (e.g. ontologies), models (e.g. architecture models, process models), methods, and instantiations (e.g. prototypes, reference models) [2, 3].

This paper aims at contributing to the state-of-the-art in a particular subset of design research, namely method engineering. Traditionally, method engineering (ME) is concerned with the processes of designing, constructing, and adapting methods

---

Please use the following format when citing this chapter:

Bucher, T., Klesse, M., Kurpjuweit, S., Winter, R., 2007, in IFIP International Federation for Information Processing, Volume 244, Situational Method Engineering: Fundamentals and Experiences, eds. Ralyté, J., Brinkkemper, S., Henderson-Sellers B., (Boston Springer), pp. 33-48.

directed at the development of information systems [5]. According to the definition of Alter, an information system (IS) can be understood as a specific subtype of a work system [6, 7]. Therefore, we refer to the objects that are to be engineered or transformed by means of a method as work systems (WS) in the following.

According to Brinkkemper, a method is "[...] an approach to perform a systems development project, based on a specific way of thinking, consisting of directions and rules, structured in a systematic way in development activities with corresponding development products" [5].

In order to be applicable for WS development, methods need to be adapted to the specific characteristics of the so-called development situation or project situation. This approach is commonly referred to as "situational method engineering" [8, 9, 10] and may be ascribed to the so-called "contingency model" proposed by Fiedler [11]. According to this scientific theory, there is no "best way" of organizing or leading an organization. On the contrary, there are various internal and external factors that influence organizational effectiveness, and therefore the organizational style must be contingent upon those factors. This theory was often transferred to WS development in the past [12, 13, 14] and apparently also to the ME field.

The paper at hand is aimed at contributing to the ME discipline by proposing a new approach to situational ME that explicitly addresses the difference between "context" and "project type". The remainder of this paper is therefore structured as follows: In section 2, related work on situational ME is discussed. Based on the conclusion that there is no generally accepted understanding of what is meant by the term "situation", a model of context and project type within WS development ME (cf. [15]) is proposed in section 3. Section 4 is dedicated to the discussion of extensions to the ME meta model that has been proposed by Heym [16] and Gutzwiller [17]. The extensions recommended in this paper allow for the differentiation between "context" and "project type" when describing situational methods. In section 5, a procedure model for the engineering of contextual and project-specific methods (cf. [15]) is sketched. Implications and further research opportunities are discussed in the concluding section 6.

2 Discussion of Related Work

Change constructions of generic artifacts such as models or methods always bear reference to an initial artifact (model, method, partial model, method fragment, method chunk) in contrast to which they are configured and/or composed with regard to the characteristics of a specific scenario or project type.

Correspondingly, vom Brocke differentiates between the two modification techniques "configuration" and "aggregation" [18]. The configuration technique follows the so-called adaptive principle, i.e. subsequent changes are explicitly allowed for and planned already at the moment of the initial construction of the artifact. On the other hand, the aggregation technique follows the compositional principle, permitting subsequent changeability that is, at least to a certain degree, almost unrestricted.

Following this systematization, we propose to divide adaptation mechanisms of the ME discipline into "situational method configuration" on the one hand and "situational method composition" on the other hand (cf. [18]).

2.1 Situational Method Configuration

The distinguishing mark of situational method configuration is the adaptation of a so-called base method against the background of a specific development situation or project situation of WS development [19, 20]. According to Karlsson and Ågerfalk, the adaptation process of a generic method is organized in three distinct phases:

- *Defining Configuration Packages.* A Configuration Package (CP) represents the configuration of a base method with respect to the characteristics of one single, well-defined part of a development situation.
- *Combining CPs in Configuration Templates.* A Configuration Template (CT) represents the comprehensive configuration of a base method with respect to a vector of recurrent project characteristics mapped onto a development situation that comprehends several delimited characteristics. Thus, a CT is based on a specific combination of CPs.
- *Selecting a CT that is adequate for the project situation.* By identifying the characteristics of a project situation and matching them with the characteristics of a CT, an adequate configuration of the base method with respect to the project situation can be obtained.

The configuration process proposed by Karlsson and Ågerfalk [19] is characterized by its systematic structure and its intuitive comprehensibility [19, 20]. However, the authors do not provide a proper definition of what is actually meant by the terms "development situation" and "project situation" respectively (cf. table 1). They merely point out that a development situation "is an abstraction of one or more existing or future software development projects with common characteristics" [19] but fail to offer any guidance in identifying and/or defining those characteristics.

2.2 Situational Method Composition

The fundamental idea of situational method composition is the selection and orchestration of artifact fragments with respect to the specifics of a WS development situation. Unlike situational method configuration, the composition process is not aimed at configuring one single base method but at combining and aggregating several method chunks in order to establish new constructional results. This approach to situational ME is widely-used and discussed in-depth in the scientific literature [5, 8, 10, 21, 22, 23, 24, 25].

Based on the seminal contributions of Brinkkemper [5] and Harmsen [8], the composition process can as well be subdivided into three phases:

- *Identifying situational characteristics.* Those characteristics can be used for characterizing specific development project types as well as artifacts and artifact fragments.

- *Decomposing generic artifacts into artifact fragments.* In order to fill the method base, generic artifacts need to be decomposed into artifact fragments. Furthermore, the artifact fragments and their interrelationships need to be described by use of the situational characteristics identified afore.
- *Composing artifact fragments into a situational method.* The actual composition of a situational method takes place by choosing and orchestrating artifact fragments according to well-defined construction or composition principles in order to fit the situational characteristics of the development project.

Although even early contributions to situational method composition put significant emphasize on the necessity to identify situational characteristics [5, 8, 9, 22], merely three articles offer some guidance regarding this requirement:

Punter and Lemmen [23] propose to apply the MADIS modeling framework [26, 27] for the characterization of the problem situation at the one side and the artifact fragments on the other side. The underlying idea of MADIS is that the WS development process can be viewed at different levels of abstraction (object system modeling, conceptual IS modeling, data system modeling, implementation modeling). At each level, identical aspect domains (goal structure, environmental interaction, functional structure, entity structure, process structure, system dynamics, allocation aspect, realization aspect) have to be considered as part of the development process [23].

According to Rolland and Prakash [25], a development situation is characterized both by the problem domain and the subject area. Within the problem domain, the situational factors complexity (simple, moderate, complex) and risk (low, moderate, high) are evaluated for both the target domain and the project domain [25]. With respect to the specification of the problem domain, the authors refer to Franckson [28] but fail to explicitly derive or state reasons for the choice of the situational factors.

Van Slootes and Hodes [10] propose a list of 17 contingency factors whose values (ranging between low and high) influence the project approach, i.e. the specific method that has been adapted to fit the project context. The list of contingency factors comprises characteristics that are primarily external to the method application, i.e. they describe the environment to which the method is adapted and in which it is deployed.

2.3 Concepts Used for Specifying Situational Characteristics

Irrespective of the preferred way of configuring (cf. section 2.1) or composing (cf. section 2.2) generic methods with regard to the characteristics of a specific scenario or project type, there is general agreement among all authors dealing with issues of situational ME that one needs to explain the characteristics of the relevant development situation and to adapt generic methods with respect to these situational characteristics. However, there is also obvious dissent among the authors about what exactly is meant by the term "situational". Table 1 gives an overview of some related concepts.

Aside from the contributions of Punter and Lemmen [23], Rolland and Prakash [25], and van Slooten and Hodes [10], current research in the field of situational ME offers no support at all in how to actually specify WS development situations. Therefore, this paper is aimed at bridging the gap by proposing a terminological differentiation between the concepts "context" and "project type" as well as by sketching a procedure model that incorporates the idea of differentiating between context and project type into the situational method construction processes (cf. [15]).

Table 1. Concepts Used for Specifying Situational Characteristics

Author	Concept	Concept Description
Baumoel [21]	Reference Context	Reference contexts are abstractions of project types that share common characteristics.
Brinkkemper [5], Brinkkemper et al. [22], Harmsen [8]	Project Environment	Since every project is different, the project environment must be characterized according to a list of contingency factors.
Karlssoon and Ågerfalk [19], Karlsson et al. [20]	Project Situation	The project situation describes the characteristics of a specific software development project.
	Development Situation	A development situation is an abstraction of one or more existing or future software development projects with common characteristics.
Punter and Lemmen [23]	Project Environment	The project environment is characterized by the problem situation and its contingency. Both the problem situation and the method fragments are described using the MADIS framework.
Rolland and Prakash [25]	Situation	The development situation is characterized by the problem domain and the subject area. Within the problem domain, the situational factors complexity and risk are evaluated for both the target domain and the project domain.
van Slooten and Hodes [10]	Project Context	The project context is made up of contingency factors that affect the project approach. Project context is external to method application.
	Project Approach	The project approach is the result of the configuration process of methods/method components.

3 "Situation" as Combination of "Context" and "Project Type"

All existing method concepts in the ME discipline comprise a procedure/activity model to accomplish the creation or transformation of a certain artifact [29], also referred to as "product" by some authors [30]. While for IS development methods this artifact is usually an information system [31], the concept of a method is also applicable for engineering and transformation of work systems [21]. As stated in the introduction, we stick to the term "work system" [6, 7] to subsume all systems which can be constructed by using methods. These systems comprise one or more system elements that are to be engineered or changed by the method. In the following, we use the term "transformation" for any engineering or change of a WS.

Consequently, a method can be viewed as a systematic aid that helps transforming a WS from an initial state to a target state (cf. figure 1). In the following, we designate the WS that is transformed by the method's activities WS_S, its initial state S_A, and its target state S_Z. WS_S comprises a set of system elements [32] that are transformed by the method.

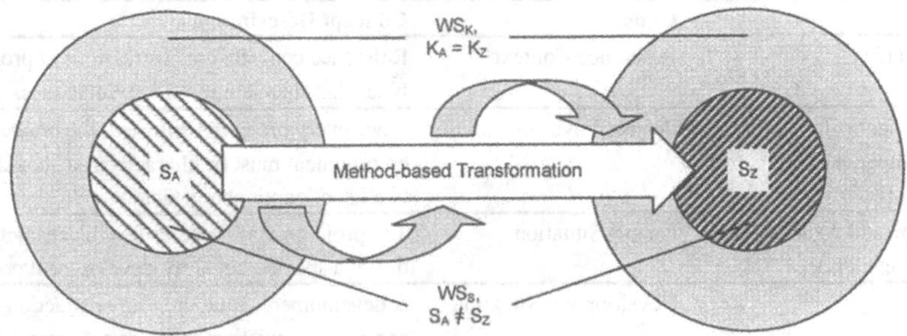

Fig. 1. Context and Project Type of Work Systems within ME [15]

The tuple (S_A, S_Z) is qualified as "situation" by some authors [19, 20, 25]. A more suitable designation for "situation" might be "project type" or "task type". A project type can be characterized by an initial WS state and a designated WS target state:

$$S_A := \text{initialStateOf}[WS_S] \quad (1)$$

$$S_Z := \text{targetStateOf}[WS_S] \quad (2)$$

$$\text{Project Type} := (S_A; S_Z) \quad (3)$$

Table 2 exhibits two exemplary project types that occur in data warehouse (DWH) development.

Table 2. Exemplary ME Project Types

Method Artifact WS_S	Project Type	Initial State S_A	Target State S_Z
Informational/analytical IS landscape and its supporting IT processes (for elements see e.g. [33, 34, 35])	"Green field" approach to DWH development (initial development)	Elements are non-existent	Data warehouse is implemented and filled with initial data; Development, operation, and support processes are established
	"Consolidation" approach to DWH development (by integrating extisting, independent data marts)	Independent data marts are existent, maintained, and are regularly refreshed with data; Data between data marts is inconsistent; DWH is non-existent	Data warehouse is implemented and filled with initial data; Development, operation, and support processes are established; Former data marts are abolished; Platforms are reused as far as possible

The project type has significant impact on the effectiveness and efficiency of method application [21]. This fact leads to the concept of situational ME where methods or method chunks are treated as situation-specific (cf. section 2). For each project type, a suitable method has to be constructed either by recombining existing method chunks or by adapting an existent method to the respective project type. A way to systematically identify project types is presented by Baumoel [21].

Besides the project type, there are other – environmental – contingency factors (e.g. [36]) that also have significant impact on the effectiveness and efficiency of method application. It is a matter of fact that each WS_S is part of a larger WS; e.g. an information system is part of an IS landscape, an IS landscape is part of a company, and a company is part of a business network. We refer to this larger work system as WS_G, with WS_S as a subset of WS_G. All elements that are not part of WS_S but part of WS_G can be referred to as environmental work system of WS_S. This environment WS_K is outside of the transformation scope of a method. It may comprise non-transformable system elements. Although it is out of the method's transformation scope, the state of these environmental WS elements may influence the applicability of transformation procedures or techniques (e.g. in form of restrictions).

In the following, we refer to the state of this environment as "context". The context is invariant during method application:

$$K_A := \text{initialStateOf}[WS_K] \tag{4}$$

$$K_Z := \text{targetStateOf}[WS_K] \tag{5}$$

$$\text{Context} := K_A = K_Z = K = \text{stateOf}(WS_K) = \text{stateOf}\,(WS_G \setminus WS_S) \tag{6}$$

Table 3 lists some exemplary context element states of a method and their potential impact on method applicability.

Table 3. Exemplary ME Contexts

Method Artifact WS_S	Context Description	Possible Impact
Informational/analytical IS landscape and its supporting IT processes (for elements see e.g. [33, 34, 35])	Large company (more than 10'000 employees) and large DWH	Building a permanent organizational unit for data warehousing is strongly indicated to maintain the data warehouse [37]
	Medium company (number of employees between 1'000 and 10'000) and small DWH	Building a permanent organizational unit for data warehousing is not cost-effective to maintain the data warehouse. Instead roles should be integrated into the existing business organization [38]

In summary, both context and project type are relevant factors to be considered during method construction and application.

For our understanding of project type, a development methodology to identify and structure project types has been proposed by Baumoel [21]. Most existing ME approaches are designed to consider the project type (cf. section 2). For the concept of context, however, such a methodology is missing, and context is neglected in existing ME approaches. Therefore, we describe a three-step procedure for the engineering of both contextual and project type-specific methods in the section 5. This procedure can be integrated into any existing situational ME methodology (cf. step 4 of the process outlined in section 5). Since the context and project type may become very complex due to the theoretically unlimited size of the work system WS_S itself as well as of the environment of WS_S, relevant factors have to be identified that describe context(s) and project type(s) at the best possible rate. Afterwards, these factors can be used as configuration parameters or as method metadata as it is proposed for situation descriptors in situational ME approaches [25]. Before turning to the process, however, necessary extensions to the ME meta model are introduced that allow for the differentiation between context and project type in the description of situational methods.

4 Extensions to the Method Engineering Meta Model

Based on a review of different approaches to method construction and method implementation, Heym [16] and Gutzwiller [17] identified five constituent elements of a method: design activities, documents specifying design results, roles, techniques, and the information model of the method. By analyzing a total of twelve scientific contributions to the ME body of literature, Braun et al. [29] validated this set of elements that can be used for the description of generic methods. Therefore, it is reasonable to conclude that these five elements of work system design methods represent a "core" meta model.

As we have outlined in the paper at hand, this core is incomplete and insufficient for the adequate characterization of situational methods. We therefore propose to extend the ME core meta model by adding the three concepts "adaptation mechanism", "context", and "project type". In accordance with situational ME literature and with the ideas presented in the paper at hand, we regard "situation" as combination of context and project type. Any tuple of context characteristics and project type characteristics is referred to as situation. Furthermore, we introduce the "method fragment" as connecting factor for the adaptation mechanism element. According to Brinkkemper's definition that has been stated in section 1, a method provides goal-oriented instructions and recommendations [5]. Design activities describe the tasks that have to be executed (what?), and techniques specify possible ways in which the results can be achieved (how?). Therefore, we denote the combination of these two core elements as method fragment.

Our interpretation of the method fragment concept is largely in accordance with the so-called general method fragment meta model that has been derived by Cossentino et al. [39]. According to their research, a method fragment consists of the elements design activity, technique (referred to as "guidance"), role (referred to as "actor"), and design result (referred to as "artifact"). In our understanding, design activities and techniques are intrinsically tied to design results. Therefore, we dissent from Cossentino et al. solely with respect to the inclusion of the role element. In contrast to their perception, we do not explicitly call for the inclusion of roles. However, a role description may be attached to a design activity where required. The extended ME meta model is depicted in figure 2. Our extensions are highlighted by use of shaded element boxes and bold connectors.

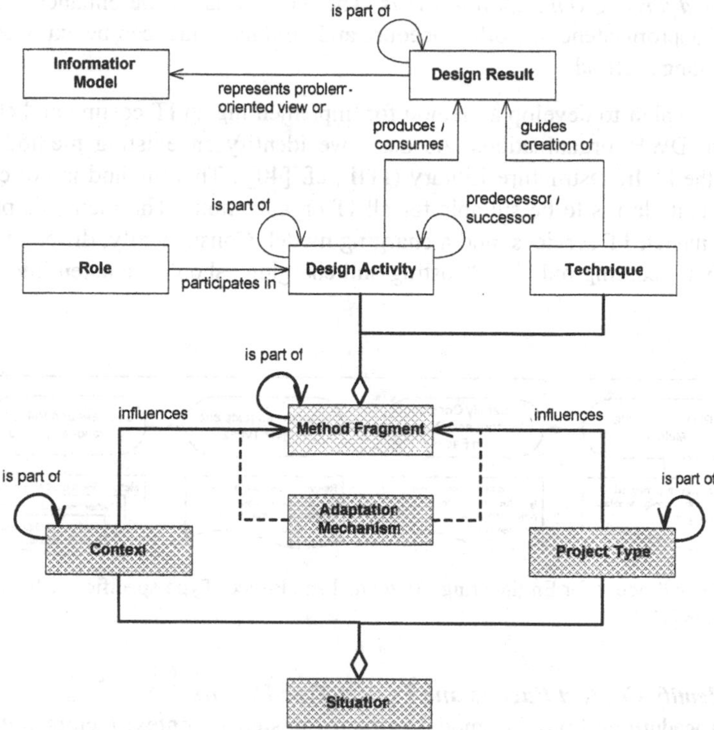

Fig. 2. Extended Method Engineering Meta Model

5 A Process for Engineering Contextual and Project Type-specific Methods

The purpose of the process proposed in this section is to identify the situations, i.e. tuples of context and project type, in which a method (or a method fragment) has to be valid, and to engineer a method that is suitable for these situations. The procedure can be combined with any ME methodology (cf. e.g. section 2). It consists of four steps, incorporating the selected method construction methodology as fourth step (cf. figure 3). In the following, we describe each step and illustrate it with an example of designing a method in the field of data warehousing.

Step 1: Plan or Evaluate Method

As we have shown in section 3, both context and project type influence the appropriateness of method application as well as the design of the method's product/artifact. Therefore, as a prerequisite for identifying factors that describe the context(s) and the project type(s), at least a rough idea about the method itself and the method's product has to exist. We distinguish between two initial situations of our process:

- *No method for a given situation exists yet.* Thus, a method has to be built from scratch. To this end, a procedure model and a product model of the method have to be outlined first.

- *A method for a given situation exists.* The method has to be enhanced for situational appropriateness. Both procedure and product model can be extracted from the existing method.

Example. We plan to develop a method for implementing an IT costing and charging process for DWH organizations. As basis we identify an existing method that is based on the IT Infrastructure Library (ITIL, cf. [40]). This method is not context-specific, i.e. it claims to be suitable for all IT organizations. The method's products are a cost model, IT services, and a charging model. Consequently, different project types such as "costing only" or "costing and charging" should be taken into consideration.

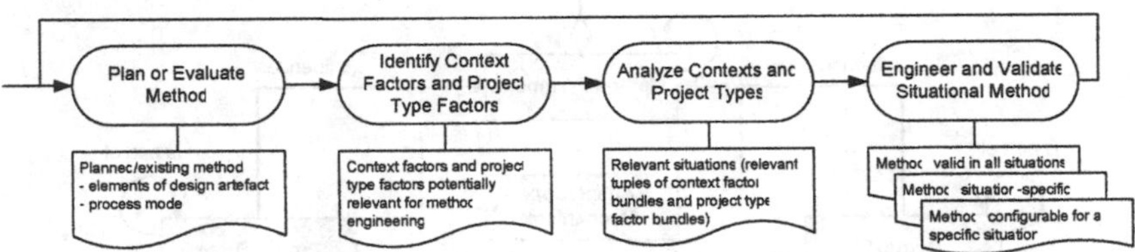

Fig. 3. Generic Process for Engineering Contextual and Project Type-specific Methods (adapted from [15])

Step 2: Identify Context Factors and Project Type Factors

For the procedure and product model extracted in step 1, context factors and project type factors are identified. This step includes a systematic screening of the existing body of knowledge about the product and of existing procedures to design the products and includes:

- Existing models, methods, procedure models, and theories about the method's artifact,
- existing generic knowledge about procedure models, and
- experience from practice projects or gained by observation.

The list of factors describing context and project type may become very long. To reduce it to potentially relevant factors, the following criteria should be applied:

- There is empirical or theoretical evidence that the factors have an impact on the method artifact and/or on the procedure to design the artifact.
- Context factors are invariant during method application.
- Project type factors change their values/characteristics during method application, i.e. they are part of the method's product.

To compact the list, both context factors and project type factors should be classified and aggregated/systematized into a hierarchy. For each factor, possible values and/or the values' range have to be specified.

At this juncture, techniques that are commonly used in behavioral and natural sciences are applied to the design research process in order to support the construction of design science artifacts. As pointed out by March and Smith [3] as well as by Cao et al. [41], interaction between different research paradigms, their methods, techniques, and activities are important since they complement each other in creating solutions to specific problems that are observable in the entrepreneurial world. The combination or "triangulation" (cf. [42]) of different methods and techniques will eventually lead to more enlightening and relevant research results and construction outcomes.

However, it is of particular importance to note that not all relevant context factors and/or project type factors are necessarily quantifiable in a trivial way. This is especially true if it comes to factors assessing organizational structures, complex social environments [43], workplace culture, or power. In this case, measurement constructs must be elaborated that can be used as auxiliary means for attributing numerical values to variables that would otherwise be non-quantifiable. This can be accomplished with the help of structural equation modeling (cf. e.g. [44]). A structural equation model (SEM) consists of a set of hypothetical constructs (so-called latent variables), a set of exogenous variables, and a set of endogenous variables. The model components are linked with each other by "directed" (i.e. causal) relationships. Ultimate goal of SEM is the prediction of interrelationships between endogenous, non-quantifiable variables through observation of exogenous, quantifiable variables.

Example. By screening the body of literature, two potentially relevant context factors and one project type factor restricting the applicability of the ITIL-based method can be found: the maturity stage of the IT organization and systems [45] and the organizational positioning of the DWH service provider [37] influence the context, and the coordination form between IT and business organization [46] influences the project type. Maturity can be assessed by CMMI stages of the IT processes [47]. Organizational positioning can be measured by the activities that are within responsibility of the DWH organization and of the business organization [48]. The coordination form can be expressed with the responsibility center concept (cost center, profit center, investment center) [49].

Step 3: Analyze Contexts and Project Types

In reality, not all context factor values and not all project type factor values do exist in any combination. Consequently, a method does not have to address all possible permutations of context factor values and project type factor values but only those combinations occurring with a certain frequency in practice. To extract these combinations, an exploratory empirical investigation can be conducted. This investigation should survey all potentially relevant factors and their values in the population for which the method should be applicable. Relevant context factor value combinations and project type factor value combinations can be extracted by factor analysis and cluster analysis techniques (cf. e.g. [50]) – yet another use case of integrating techniques from behavioral and natural sciences into the design research process. The results of these analyses are contexts bundling context factor values that are common in reality and project types that bundle project type factor values that occur in a multiplicity of settings.

The identified context(s) and project type(s) can be summarized in matrix format (cf. figure 4). As already stated before, a tuple of context(s) and project type(s) is referred to as situation. A situation can relate to one or multiple contexts as well as to one or multiple project types. Moreover, it is important to note that certain combinations of context and project type might not exist in reality. Therefore, the complete enumeration of all situations might not lead to success at any rate.

	Project Type A	Project Type B	Project Type C	Project Type ...
Context a	Situation 1	Situation 2		Situation 3
Context b		Situation 4		Situation 5
Context c			Situation 6	
Context ...		Situation 7		Situation 8

Fig. 4. The Context vs. Project Type Matrix (exemplary illustration)

Example. The analysis of the context factors and project type factors led to the following results: DWH organizations have reached a medium to high level of maturity today [51]. Most DWH organizations are responsible for costs only [52] and positioned as "DWH competence centers" or "business service providers" according to their activity profile [48]. Thus, the matrix shows two contexts ("medium to high maturity, DWH competence centers" and "medium to high maturity, business service provider") and one project type ("costing only").

Step 4: Engineer and Validate Situational Method

For these situations, either a monolithic method or multiple method fragments that can be composed into a situational method have to be constructed. Depending on the ME approach (cf. section 2), the resulting methods can be of the following types:

- *Method, configurable for a specific situation.* This type of method can be applied to a real world setting by analyzing the context factors and project type factors and by configuring it with respect to the situation at hand. Consequently, step 4 of our process can correspond either to a method configuration process as proposed by Karlsson and Ågerfalk [19, 20] (cf. section 2.1) or to a method composition process as proposed by Brinkkemper [5] and Harmsen [8] (cf. section 2.2). In particular the first two phases of the configuration process ("defining configuration packages" and "combining configuration packages in configuration templates") and the first phase of the composition process ("identifying situational characteristics") are supported by our process. By identifying and analyzing relevant contexts and project types, the situational appropriateness of configuration packages, configuration templates, characterizations of specific development situations, and descriptions of artifacts and artifact fragments can be improved significantly. Furthermore, our process adds value to the both the configuration and the composition approach since it particularizes the individual concepts used for specifying situational characteristics (cf. table 1).
- *Method, situation-specific.* This type of method is applicable only in one or more situations for which it was specifically developed. As one can see in the context vs. project type matrix (cf. figure 4), the characteristic trait of situation-specificity can either consist in context-specificity (method is specific to one particular context but applicable for multiple project types, cf. e.g. situations 2 and 6

in the illustration), project type-specificity (method is specific to one particular project type but applicable for multiple contexts, cf. e.g. situation 1 in the illustration), or simultaneous context-specificity and project type-specificity (method is specific to one situation consisting of one context and one project type, cf. e.g. situations 3, 4, 5, 7, and 8 in the illustration). Situation-specific methods represent the output of any approach to situational ME, be it situational method configuration or situational method composition. The differentiation between context and project type can help not only in the process of engineering methods but also in describing the scope of method (or method fragment) applicability [5, 8].

- *Method, valid in all situations.* This type of method is applicable in all situations (i.e. in all combinations of context and project type) that have been identified in step 3. Consequently, this type of method represents a generalization of situation-specific methods as outlined before.

Regardless of the method type, the method has to be validated by applying it in a real world situation for which it is claimed to be valid.

Example. Since the most probable situation for method application is a (more or less) mature DWH competence center that is responsible for costs only, a method for implementing an IT costing process has to be developed and validated for this situation only.

6 Conclusion and Further Research

Our discussion of existing ME approaches showed that nearly all approaches claim to incorporate situational factors. Nevertheless, the existing engineering methodologies do not detail what these situational factors comprise of and how they can be identified. In our paper, we have presented a novel approach to situational ME. Based on the conclusion that context and project type are different determinants of method applicability, we have proposed a procedure model that incorporates both context and project type into situational method construction processes. Our procedure model guides the identification of relevant context and project type factors, examines their occurrences in practice, and classifies them into situations defined as tuple of context and project type. For these situations, suitable methods can be constructed that might be more appropriate than generic methods focusing solely on single situational aspects that are a subset of our definition at the most. With evidence about the frequency of occurrence of contexts and project types in practice, the method engineering discipline can concentrate on developing methods for the most common (i.e. most relevant) situations.

Based on the initial work presented in this paper as well as in our previous work (cf. [15]), three broad categories of research opportunities exist:

- First, our process needs to be validated at large. In the paper at hand, we have proposed a procedure and provided substantial reasons for its meaningfulness based on an extensive literature review as well as on our own experience. In order to prove the practicability and feasibility of the process, we have evaluated single steps (in particular steps 2 and 3) for different domains (cf. e.g. [48, 53]). The validation of the process as a whole is subject to further research.

- Secondly, our process could be extended to cover epistemologically valid method construction processes by evaluating and combing existing ME approaches described in section 2. This opportunity for further research has been sketched in the description of step 4 of our process. However, we believe that further work is necessary. The development of a reference process or even of a method for method construction itself (a so-called "meta method") would help method engineers to design new methods more systematically.
- Thirdly, a reference information model of method fragments and their context(s)/project type(s) could be designed. As stated in section 5, the differentiation between context and project type can be of value for describing the scope of method (or method fragment) applicability. The existence of a reference information model would enable storing and managing situational method elements in an electronic method base, and therefore enhance the potential for reusability of method fragments.

7 References

1. H.A. Simon, *The Sciences of the Artificial* (MIT Press, Cambridge, 1969).
2. A.R. Hevner, S.T. March, J. Park, and S. Ram, Design Science in Information Systems Research, *MIS Quarterly*, **28**(1), pp. 75-105 (2004).
3. S.T. March and G.F. Smith, Design and Natural Science Research on Information Technology, *Decision Support Systems*, **15**(4), pp. 251-266 (1995).
4. J.G. Walls, G.R. Widmeyer, and O.A. El Sawy, Building an Information System Design Theory for Vigilant EIS, *Information Systems Research*, **3**(1), pp. 36-59 (1992).
5. S. Brinkkemper, Method Engineering - Engineering of Information Systems Development Methods and Tools, *Information and Software Technology*, **38**, pp. 275-280 (1996).
6. S. Alter, Work Systems and IT Artifacts - Does the Definition Matter?, *Communications of the Association for Information Systems*, **17**(14), pp. 299-313 (2006).
7. S. Alter, 18 Reasons Why IT-reliant Work Systems Should Replace "The IT Artifact" as the Core Subject Matter of the IS Field, *Communications of the Association for Information Systems*, **12**(23), pp. 366-395 (2003).
8. F. Harmsen, *Situational Method Engineering* (Moret Ernst & Young Management Consultants, Utrecht, 1997).
9. K. Kumar and R.J. Welke, Methodology Engineering - A Proposal for Situation-specific Methodology Construction, in: Challenges and Strategies for Research in Systems Development, edited by W. Cotterman and J.A. Senn (John Wiley & Sons, 1992), pp. 257-269.
10. K. van Slooten and B. Hodes, Characterizing IS Development Projects, in: Method Engineering - Principles of Method Construction and Tool Support, edited by S. Brinkkemper, K. Lytinnen, and R.J. Welke (Chapman & Hall, 1996), pp. 29-44.
11. F.E. Fiedler, A Contingency Model of Leadership Effectiveness, *Advances in Experimental Social Psychology*, **1**, pp. 149-190 (1964).
12. B. Arinze, A Contingency Model of DSS Development Methodology, *Journal of Management Information Systems*, **8**(1), pp. 149-166 (1991).
13. R.J. Schonberger, MIS Design - A Contingency Approach, *MIS Quarterly*, **4**(1), pp. 13-20 (1980).

14. P. Weill and M.H. Olson, An Assessment of the Contingency Theory of Management Information Systems, *Journal of Management Information Systems*, **6**(1), pp. 59-85 (1989).
15. T. Bucher and M. Klesse, Contextual Method Engineering, University of St. Gallen, Institute of Information Management, Working Paper, 2006.
16. M. Heym, Methoden-Engineering - Spezifikation und Integration von Entwicklungsmethoden für Informationssysteme, University of St. Gallen, Ph.D. Thesis, 1993.
17. T. Gutzwiller, *Das CC RIM-Referenzmodell für den Entwurf von betrieblichen, transaktionsorientierten Informationssystemen* (Physica, Heidelberg, 1994).
18. T. Bucher, S. Kurpjuweit, and B. Dinter, Risikomanagement im Data Warehousing - Situative Komposition einer methodischen Vorgehensweise, in: DW2006 - Integration, Informationslogistik und Architektur, edited by J. Schelp, R. Winter, U. Frank, B. Rieger, and K. Turowski (Gesellschaft für Informatik, Bonn, 2006), pp. 35-59.
19. F. Karlsson and P.J. Ågerfalk, Method Configuration - Adapting to Situational Characteristics while Creating Reusable Assets, *Information and Software Technology*, **46**(9), pp. 619-633 (2004).
20. F. Karlsson, P.J. Ågerfalk, and A. Hjalmarsson, Method Configuration with Development Tracks and Generic Project Types, Paper Accepted for the 6th CAiSE/IFIP8.1 International Workshop on Evaluation of Modeling Methods in System Analysis and Design (EMMSAD'01), http://citeseer.ist.psu.edu/503218.html, 2001.
21. U. Baumoel, Strategic Agility through Situational Method Construction, in: Proceedings of the European Academy of Management Annual Conference (EURAM2005), edited by R. Reichwald and A.S. Huff (http://www.euram2005.de, 2005).
22. S. Brinkkemper, M. Saeki, and F. Harmsen, Assembly Techniques for Method Engineering, in: Proceedings of the 10th International Conference on Advanced Information Systems Engineering (CAiSE'98), Springer, LNCS 1413, 1998, pp. 381-400.
23. T. Punter and K. Lemmen, The MEMA-Model - Towards a New Approach for Method Engineering, *Information and Software Technology*, **38**(4), pp. 295-305 (1996).
24. J. Ralyté, Ingénierie des Méthodes a base de Composants, Université Paris 1 - Sorbonne, Ph.D. Thesis, 2001.
25. C. Rolland and N. Prakash, A Proposal for Context-Specific Method Engineering, in: Method Engineering - Principles of Method Construction and Tool Support, edited by S. Brinkkemper, K. Lytinnen, and R.J. Welke (Chapman & Hall, 1996), pp. 191-207.
26. L.J.B. Essink, A Modelling Approach to Information System Development, in: Information Systems Design Methodologies - Improving the Practice, edited by T.W. Olle, H.G. Sol, and A.A.V. Stuart (North-Holland, 1986).
27. L.J.B. Essink, A Conceptual Framework for Information Systems Development Methodologies, in: First European Conference on Information Technology for Organizational Systems (EurInfo 1988), edited by H.J. Bullinger (North-Holland, 1988).
28. M. Franckson, The Euromethod Deliverable Model and Its Contribution to the Objectves of Euromethod, in: IFIP-TC8 International Conference on Methods and Tools for the Information Systems Life Cycle, edited by A.A.V. Stuart and T.W. Olle (North-Holland, 1994), pp. 131-149.
29. C. Braun, F. Wortmann, M. Hafner, and R. Winter, Method Construction - A Core Approach to Organizational Engineering, in: Proceedings of the 20th Annual ACM Symposium on Applied Computing (SAC 2005), edited by H.L. Haddad, Lorie M.; Omicini, Andrea; Wainwright, Roger L. (ACM, Santa Fe, 2005), pp. 1295-1299.
30. N. Prakash, On Method Statics and Dynamics, *Information Systems Journal*, **24**(8), pp. 613-637 (1999).
31. D. Truex and D. Avison, Method Engineering - Reflections on the Past and Ways Forward, Proceedings of the Ninth Americas Conference on Information Systems (AMCIS 2003), 2003.

32. J. Ruegg-Stuerm, *Das neue St. Galler Management-Modell - Grundkategorien einer integrierten Managementlehre* (Paul Haupt, Bern, 2002).
33. W.H. Inmon, *Building the Data Warehouse* (Wiley, New York, 2002).
34. W.H. Inmon, J.D. Welch, and K.L. Glassey, *Managing the Data Warehouse* (Wiley, New York, 1997).
35. R. Kachur, *Data Warehouse Management Handbook* (Prentice Hall, 2000).
36. B. Ives, S. Hamilton, and G.B. Davis, A Framework for Research in Computer-Based Management Information Systems, *Management Science*, **26**(9), pp. 910-934 (1980).
37. R. Winter and M. Meyer, Organization of Data Warehousing in Large Service Companies - A Matrix Approach Based on Data Ownership and Competence Centers, Proceedings of the Seventh Americas Conference on Information Systems (AMCIS 2001), 2001.
38. C. Limacher, Organisationskonzept und Erfolgsfaktoren fuer den Betrieb und die Weiterentwicklung einer Data Warehouse Loesung am Beispiel des Universitaetsspitals Zuerich, University of St. Gallen, Bachelor Thesis, 2005.
39. M. Cossentino, S. Gaglio, B. Henderson-Sellers, and V. Seidita, A Metamodelling-based Approach for Method Fragment Comparison, in: The 18th International Conference on Advanced Information Systems Engineering, edited by T. Latour and M. Petit (Presses Universitaire de Namur, Luxembourg, 2006), pp. 419-432.
40. Office of the Government of Commerce, *Introdction to ITIL* (Stationary Office, London, 2005).
41. J. Cao, J.M. Crews, M. Lin, A. Deokar, J.K. Burgoon, and J.F. Nunamaker Jr, Interactions between System Evaluation and Theory Testing - A Demonstration of the Power of a Multifaceted Approach to Information Systems Research, *Journal of Management Information Systems*, **22**(4), pp. 207-235 (2006).
42. E.J. Webb, D.T. Campbell, R.D. Schwartz, L. Sechrest, and J.B. Grove, *Unobtrusive Measures - Nonreactive Research in the Social Sciences* (Rand McNally, Chicago, 1966).
43. R. Lamb and R. Kling, Reconceptualizing Users as Social Actors in Information Systems Research, *MIS Quarterly*, **27**(2), pp. 197-235 (2003).
44. R.B. Kline, *Principles and Practice of Structural Equation Modeling* (Guilford Press, New York, 2005).
45. C.A. van Lengen and J.N. Morgan, Chargeback and Maturity of IS Use, *Information & Management*, **25**(3), pp. 155-163 (1993).
46. W.P. McKinnon and E.A. Kallman, Mapping Chargeback Systems to Organizational Environments, *MIS Quarterly*, **11**(1), pp. 5-20 (1987).
47. D.M. Ahern, A. Clouse, and R. Turner, *CMMI Distilled - A Practical Introduction to Integrated Process Improvement* (Addison Wesley, 2003).
48. M. Klesse and R. Winter, Organizational Forms of Data Warehousing - An Explorative Analysis, in: Proceedings of the 40th Hawaii International Conference on System Sciences (HICSS-40), edited by IEEE Computer Society (IEEE Computer Society, Los Alamitos, 2007).
49. M.J. Earl, *Management Strategies for Information Technologies* (Prentice Hall, 1989).
50. B.G. Tabachnick and L.S. Fidell, *Using Multivariate Statistics* (Allyn & Bacon, 2006).
51. P. Chamoni and P. Gluchowski, Integrationstrends bei Business-Intelligence-Systemen - Empirische Untersuchung auf Basis des Business Intelligence Maturity Model, *Wirtschaftsinformatik*, **46**(2), pp. 119-128 (2004).
52. M. Klesse, Leistungsverrechnung im Data Warehousing - Ergebnisse einer empirischen Studie, University of St. Gallen, Institute of Information Management, Working Paper, 2005.
53. T. Bucher and R. Winter, Classification of Business Process Management Approaches - An Exploratory Analysis, *BIT - Banking and Information Technology*, **7**(3), pp. 9-20 (2006).

Examining Key Notions for Method Adaptation

Mehmet N. Aydin
University of Twente, Department of Information Systems and Change Management. P. O. Box 217, 7500 AE, Enschede, The Netherlands,
m.n.aydin@utwente.nl

Abstract. It is a well-known fact that IS development methods are not used as prescribed in actual development projects. That is, every ISD method in a development project is subject to its modifications because its peculiarities and emerging situations cannot be understood adequately in a prescribed manner. Though the idea of method modifications has been studied exclusively under the subject matter called situational method development, the underlying notions (situation, context, agency, and method fragment) for its theoretical basis are not grounded explicitly in the literature. In this paper, we articulate appropriate accounts for these key notions and induce a conjecture so-called method adaptation referring to a process or capability in which agents holding intentions through responsive changes in, and dynamic interplays between, contexts, and method fragments develop a situated fragment for a specific project situation. As concluding remarks, theoretical implications of method adaptation are discussed.

1 Introduction

This research is concerned with situated method development, which is a particular subject in the research domains of information systems development [1] and method engineering [2], aiming to contribute to the understanding of how to achieve a method that fits a project situation. It has been acknowledged as a promising research endeavor to overcome a long-standing problem with information systems development (ISD) methods [2]. That is, as methods are not used as prescribed in practice, they fall short in supporting practitioners in the development of information systems for, for instance, a globally networked organisation using new development approaches such as agile systems development.

Please use the following format when citing this chapter:

Aydin, M. N., 2007, in IFIP International Federation for Information Processing, Volume 244, Situational Method Engineering: Fundamentals and Experiences, eds. Ralyté, J., Brinkkemper, S., Henderson-Sellers B., (Boston Springer), pp. 49-63.

While new methods are promoted as a panacea for well-publicized ISD failures, old ones have been criticized that they are rigid, comprehensive and are built upon the idea that a method can be used for all projects which brings on a "one-size-fits all" issue [3]. In fact a fundamental problem still remains that methods, irrespective to their preferred features (agility, state-of-the art knowledge foundations), by nature involve certain thinking and often prescribe certain actions for ISD [4]. The subject matter at hand addresses this "one-size-fits all" issue and aims to deal with how an ISD method is developed and can be supported so that the resulting method, so-called situated method, fits a project situation. The idea behind a situated method is that any prospective method to be used for a development project is subject to certain adjustments because of the fact that the method is limited to its preferred thinking and prescribed actions for ISD which cannot fully accommodate the uniqueness of a project situation. In this regard, such adjustments are needed for the method along with a premise that the resulting method can provide a well-suited means for ISD and in turn reduce the risk of its failures. As shown in the succeeding sections, the existing studies appear to lack an appropriate theoretical ground that illuminates the underpinnings of these adjustments, which are referred as method adaptation. It is this missing ground that urges us to investigate what accounts the idea of situated method development. So, the goal of this paper is to articulate its underlying key notions at a foundation level.

The research can be considered as explorative research which employs a broader view on the subject matter by applying a stratification research model and use logical arguments to induce a conjecture so-called method adaptation. Basically, the stratification model adopted in this research has four modes of the analysis of relevant research [5]: (i) a classification system which includes generic categories of those studies having affinities with method development and situated method development in particular; (ii) a taxonomy which reflects basic dimensions for studying situated method development; (iii) a conceptual system in which we critically examine the conceptual elements of a few selected studies; and finally (iv) a theoretical system which includes a generic model along with a number key constructs and their relations. Notice that conceptual system and theoretical system analysis is within the scope of this paper.

The paper is outlined as follows. Having presented the motivation of the research in this introduction section, we sketch the overall research scope as well as relevant research in the second section. It is the third section where we start presenting the articulation of key notions, and providing basic understandings of the key notions. This eventually leads us to the next step whereby we incorporate their basic understandings into a conjecture that we call method adaptation. In light of this conjecture we furthermore briefly discuss three basics models proposed in the literature and conclude with its theoretical implications and future research.

2 Research Background

In a practical sense, the subject of this work is about supporting (human and non-human) an agent to make a method work for a project situation. This is often performed by a project manager or other actor responsible for the project. But usually there is more than one actor involved in this task and surely more actors have stakes in the outcome of this task –a situated method. This task is usually performed at the early stages of a project and can result in, for instance, a project plan, project proposal, or system development plan.

Among all the cited problems and issues hindering a better use of methods, it is argued by many scholars that methods by nature have their own limited views on the reality of IS development Truex et al. [6] assert that: "By adopting a single engineering concept of method all of our thinking about information systems development becomes imprisoned by this one concept. The method is not only our way of thinking about systems development; it is our way of thinking about "thinking about systems development".

Scholars in both the ISD research literature (see, for example, [7, 8]) and method engineering (ME) (see, for example, [4, 9]) address this issue from their own perspectives. In fact, the reactions of scholars in method engineering to problems concerning methods are set forth along with the call for 'methodology engineering' in [10, 11], 'method engineering' by Brinkkemper and his colleagues [9, 11, 12, 13]. Kumar and Welke [9] propose that "...we need a formal (as opposed to ad-hoc) and efficient (as opposed to time and money wasting) methodology for developing ISD methods which are situation appropriate (as opposed to universal) and complete (an opposite to partial), and at the same time rely on the accumulated experience and wisdom of the past (as opposed to built from scratch)" (p. 322).

At a high level, [14] distinguishes three research domains (the ISD research, Method Engineering, and Implementation research) that contribute to an understanding of situated method development. The ISD and ME research domains provide insights into the way or process (situated) method development takes places. The ISD and Implementation research domains help us employ the content of such a way (including characteristics and/or elements used in this process). [14] indicates that situated method development related studies adopt a number of key notions (situation, context, agency, method fragment) as basic elements for their models, but their articulation along with theoretical ground needs to be done explicitly. Because of this lack of explicitness, for instance, these basic notions have been incorporated with different interpretations in research domains. What is interesting to see in this review is that most of the studies mentioning and adopting these notions fall short in incorporating the essential attributes, as we shall discuss them later on, and often do not provide explicit definitions of the terms. In particular, the notion of *agency* as part of situated method development is undervalued in the prevailing models. Only Baskerville and Stage [15] emphasise the matter, but as a conceptual system their proposed model requires factual validity in an empirical setting and lacks unambiguous descriptions of certain elements (situation, context). With regard to the conceptual system review mode, the common terms in the aforementioned studies are conceptualized as sensitizing notions in their model building. We claim that the treatments of these notions are partial as they provide alternative or complementary viewpoints.

We contend that the prevailing models show alternative approaches to situated method development along with their pros and cons. For the examination of alternative approaches we propose to investigate situated method development as a phenomenon. The examination should be done at a fundamental level where its key underlying notions are naturally revealed and articulated. This examination will provide a beginning for the foundation of the phenomenon for which we induce a conjecture in section four.

3 Articulations of Key Notions

A detail literature review indicates that there are four essential notions (situation, context, agency, and method fragment) underlying situated method development. We shall now examine each notion in turn. By examining we mean to understand how the notion is treated in its corresponding research domain and thereafter incorporate its meaning into our research context. For instance, to understand how the notion of situation is treated in literature, we have identified and discussed three relevant studies in the research domain of linguistics, cognitive psychology, and sociology. For the notion of context, we have discussed relevant studies in the research domain of pragmatics and decision-making. For the notion of agency, we have examined the theory of intention in the philosophy of mind. The treatments of these notions are provided in their own discourses and at different levels of detail. It should be noted that to avoid any misunderstanding on the adopted notions we stick to their original meanings and remain clear about how relevant their meanings are to our subject. Let us start with situation.

The Notion of Situation. The term situation refers to, "the way in which something is placed in relation to its surroundings" [16] or "a set of circumstances in which one finds oneself, or location and surroundings of a place" [17]. The key words are here circumstances, surroundings, and placing them in a certain way. This placement has to do with cognitive activities (i.e., making sense of surrounding, circumstances, and relating with a cognitive scheme) and/or physical activities (performing an activity to do so). In Latin the term in situ as an adverb or adjective indicates a similar meaning stating that "in the natural or original position or appropriate place" [16]. The term has been used extensively in IS research in different ways, but its meaning is often reduced to a number of factors without articulating its essential features or their interplay in relation to human knowledge and action tied to its philosophical treatment. In this sense, we briefly discuss its use in sociology, linguistics, and cognitive science, and aim to come to its essential features (Table 1).

Perhaps the most comprehensive exposition of the term to appear so far in linguistics is in [18] titled "Situation and Attitudes" and associative studies that deal with situation semantics and propose a mathematical theory of situation. In sociology, it is the work of Suchman [19], entitled "Plans and Situated Action" which introduces "situated action". In cognitive science, especially in connection with artificial intelligence, Endsley [20] and her colleagues introduce "situational awareness" to emphasize "the knowing of what is going on". Three studies in this work are representative studies which help us find three complementary views on the notion of situation. In doing so, we have been able to reason about the underlying features of situation in connection with the idea of situated method.

Regarding the theory of situation [18], which has been applied in various areas including design theory, linguistics, and artificial intelligence [21], it aims to incorporate intentions and circumstances of the agents in the communication process. [22] recognises the need to rethink the foundations of situation semantics and provide the following definitions: "Situations are contrasted with worlds; a world determines the answer to every issue, the truth-value of every proposition. A situation corresponds to the limited parts of reality we perceive, reason about, and live in. What goes on in these situations will determine answers to some issues, but not all. (p. 1)"

Table 1. The very notion of situation in three complementary studies

Representative study	Associated Disciplines	Essential features of the very notion of situation
Theory of Situation	Linguistics	Partial reality, Realism, Relations
Situational Awareness	Cognitive Psychology	Employment of cognitive mechanisms and relevant factors for human knowing
Situated Actions	Sociology	Interactions, Partial plans and other resources subsumed and produced

Regarding 'situated action', Lucy Suchman [19] introduces this term to underscore that actions take place in the context of particular, concrete, and possibly material and social, circumstances. She contrasts her account with the traditional view of human actions, specifically goal-directed behaviour as studied in cognitive science, asserting that plans are taken to be either formal structures that control a purposeful action or abstractions over its instances. Alternatively, her account as drawn from ethno-methodology contends that: plans are representations of actions and in the course of situated action, representation occurs when otherwise transparent activity becomes problematic in some way. Further she asserts that a central resource for achieving the objectivity of situations is language, which stands in a generally indexical relationship to circumstances that it presupposes, produces and describes. As a consequence of the indexicality of language, mutual intelligibility is achieved on each occasion of interaction with reference to situation particulars, rather than being discharged once and for all by a stable body of sharing.

The third representative study which introduces 'situational awareness' (SA), employs the models of human thinking proposed in cognitive science [20]. By 'situational awareness' Endsly [20] means, "...perception of the elements in the environment within a volume of time and space, the comprehension of their meaning and projection of their status in the near future". She argues that although the elements of SA vary widely in several disciplines, the nature of SA and the mechanisms used for achieving it are common (for instance, perception, comprehension and projection are proposed as three 'levels' underlying SA and blended with, but different from, the decision-making perspective that SA is aimed to facilitate decision-making). By drawing on associated empirical studies, they argue that certain elements (goals, expectations, mental models, schema, and automaticity) influence SA and are vital for the agency's internal representation of state. It should be noted that SA is concerned about the state of knowledge that has to do with the references to confirmed schemas and the 'yet-to-be-tested' hypothesis, rather than the process of achieving this. Many factors (e.g., task under or overload, fatigue, psychological stress) may also degrade SA, but they are, as claimed, independent constructs. It is suggested that other terms like shared situational awareness, shared understanding and distributed /shared cognition should be used for a collective version of the SA as it has an originally individual focus. It is also suggested that factors like culture, experience, personality, sex, and age as 'structural factors' are different from 'situational factors' such us mood, time pressure, stress, ambiguity, etc.

Our understanding of the term situation has some commonalities with the three representative studies. That is, situation is about:

- A limited portion of the world - partial reality - as emerging over location and time
- Characterization (confined and yet-to-be-tested hypothesis)
- Subsumed and produced partial reality for planning (concerning future- and present-directed act)

An important corollary of partial reality is that a situation as constructed by the agency is about knowing of the agency and it is in the head of an agency. This view is in line with what [23] called "radical constructivism" which is developed following Kant (1724-1804), Vico (1668-1744), and Piaget (1896-1980). This view employs the basic principles of radical constructivism, such as that knowledge is not passively received either through the senses or by way of communication; the function of cognition is adaptive, tending towards fit or viability; cognition serves the subject's organisation of the experiential world, not the discovery of an objective ontological reality.

By drawing on the principles of radical constructivism, a constituent of a situation is not a thing-in-itself, but something that the cognizing subject has constructed by making distinctions and coordination in his or her perceptual field [24]. For the purpose of an analytical examination however, we see the three constituents – context, agency and method fragment- as distinct elements ('things-in-themselves') though each of them construes and includes the other two.

The Notion of Context. In a broader sense the term context refers to a collection of relevant conditions and surrounding influences that make a project situation unique and comprehensible [25]. The complexity of context as a subject has been acknowledged by many scholars, including [21]. [26] argues that relevant discussions on this subject in philosophy evolve from its narrowest meaning about the consideration of texts in linguistics, to its broadest meaning, something to do with 'situated cognition'- that is invariably situated, as elaborated in the field of pragmatism. In particular, a traditional view of the notion of context suggests that contexts are pre-existing and stable environments that perhaps include unobservable factors that cause agencies to behave in partly unpredictable ways [26]. This view appears to be akin to what [26] calls the optimistic claims stating that for all classes of cognitive tasks and processes, there is a uniform context matrix - whatever the features or factors are granted, such that for all situations in the class, the outcome of any process in the class is determined by the values taken by the matrix in the situation.

This is often contrasted with the contemporary view which asserts that all contextual regularities, conditions and any other relevant features, are assumed to be dynamically activated and accomplished in the situation [27]. Context has also been studied as a central notion in human decision-making. [28] illuminates the dynamics of context and the employment of reasoning for 'practical' decision-making. Practical decision-making, as discussed by [28], is reminiscent of naturalistic decision-making, an adopted orientation in this work.

Different kinds of context are introduced with a duality character [29] such as 'immediate' or 'proximate' contexts. These include features pertaining to actual surroundings in situ versus 'distal' or 'mediate' contexts which cover background knowledge, cognitive frames, or assumptions about on-going, up-coming, or even priori activities relevant in situ. Another distinction is made between so-called primary and secondary context, the extent to which influencing characteristics are stable [28]. In relation to this duality character, [26] defends a 'mixed model of inquiry', which combines rationalist reliance either on fact or principles with a consideration for appropriateness to the situation at hand. This is indeed where the pragmatics view of context stands and of which several accounts are proposed. [30], for instance, advocates this view and argues that ambiguity is inherent in contextualization, decontextualization, and recontextualization (hereafter called 'contextualizing') through which one may effectively marginalize certain agencies and their legitimate interpretations by virtue of an institutionally embedded context.

Human agency is central to contextualization. In connection with this work, of course, method fragments are also considered during this contextualization. But exclusion of the agency and method fragments is in effect when the context is framed and reframed along with the cognitive structure and processes [24]. After successive approximation, this eventually leads to an appropriate context under consideration with respect to, upon, and in which the decision is made. Accordingly, cognitive structures change through the process of adaptation by assimilation and accommodation. This is boldly marked in the radical constructivism along with the principle stating that the function of cognition is adaptive and serves the agency's framing or organizing of the experiential world, not the discovery of an objective ontological reality [23]. We employ the ideas of 'contextualizing', 'framing', 'appropriation' in relation to the very notion of context.

The Notion of Agency. Cognitive elements come into place at the outset of situated cognition when contextualizing takes place in situ where the agency is supposed to make a decision and to perform actions. But what cognitive elements are manifest in human thinking and actions? It has been argued for a long time that desire and belief are the elements that have certain direct impacts on human thinking and actions. There is no doubt that beliefs and desires are always present in the cognitive structures and process with some effects, but contemporary studies in the field of the philosophy of mind, including [31] and his associates, have questioned their direct effects in the course of actions and corresponding decision- making.

Granting that human knowing, more broadly thinking, and actions are inherent in determining situation, we turn our discussion to what cognitive elements are necessary for situated method development. In principle, human thinking is subject to the complexity of interplay between many cognitive elements such as beliefs, norms, motives, goals, and intentions. The accounts on each term or their combinations along with counter arguments are readily available in philosophy as a reference discipline as well as in certain applied sciences (management science, IS research, organisational science) where the prospective accounts are adopted. By drawing upon the works of [32] in the philosophy of mind and Husserl (1859-1938) and proponent scholars in the philosophy science, our aim in this section is to show that as a cognitive element, the notion of intention serves best to explain the interplay between the method fragments, the agency, and the context.

In the dictionary [16] and every day language, the term intention is synonymous for volition, purpose, and significance, and indicates "a determination to act in a certain way". Other derivations and uses of the term appear as intent, intentionality, doing with an intention, or doing something intentionally. To ground explanations concerning their differences would require a long philosophical treatise which belongs to the philosophy of mind, but the treatment of intention and intentionality in [32] and [32] is relevant to our subject. The treatment of the terms intention and intentionality should be separated as the former has been articulated in relation to action, planning and practical rationality [31], and the latter is proposed in phenomenology, a particular school of thought in the philosophy. Intention is considered a state of mind (what it is to *intend to something*) and a characteristic of action (*having an intention* to do something or doing something *intentionally*).

'Intentionality' derives from the Latin verb 'intendere', which means "to point" or "to aim at", and Brentano (1838-1917) accordingly characterized the intentionality of mental states and experiences as their feature of each being 'directed toward something'. Intentionality in this technical sense then subsumes the everyday notion of doing something "intentionally": an action is intentional when done with a certain "intention", i.e., a mental state of "aiming" toward a certain state of affairs.

One of the most comprehensive expositions of the term intention is in the work of Michael Bratman [31]. His treatment reveals complexity and the essence of its characteristics and functions along with two forms (future- and present-directed). [31] extensively discusses his account in relation to planning theory and agent rationality, for which we cannot condense the body of literature he employs in a few pages. The forms and kinds of intention he proposed however, are especially useful for characterizing the agency action in method adaptation.

Upon the deeper examination of the idea of intending to act, which channels a future-directed form of intention, or having an intention to act, which is present-directed action, he contends that intentions are neither desires nor beliefs but plans, and that plans have an independent place in practical thinking. One of the central facts about intentions essential for this work is that they are conduct-controlling pro-attitudes and serve as inputs for further practical reasoning. According to [31], distinct from normal beliefs, both desires and intentions are pro-attitudes, which have a motivational function for an act. As distinct from desires or other weak proposition attitudes such as beliefs and goals, (considered *potential influencers of action*) intentions are *conduct-controlling* pro-attitudes. As such, intentions are parts of partial plans for action, required by an agency that must make complex plans but cannot make the plans complete. The partial plans play a central role in practical reasoning, aimed at adjusting and completing prior but partial plans, and help extend the influence of deliberation beyond the present moment and facilitate coordination within the agent's life and, socially, between agents.

The Notion of Method Fragment. Philosophical treatment of the term method is often done implicitly while discussing the matters about, for instance, rationality of agency, reasoning in the formation of thinking and action. In fact the definition of method holds a very strong affinity with these matters, but its elaboration is beyond the scope of this work. We therefore turn to the IS research literature to articulate the notion of method and method fragment. Recall the definition of (ISD) method: an explicit way to structure one's thinking and actions. It is the *one,* as we term agency that has some affinity and involvement in a project [33]. The method does not do anything itself though there are certain parts of method that perform some activities together with an agent (modelling, testing, coding, etc.). What is interesting to see is that a method structures or helps someone to structure other agencies' thinking and actions. This is done together or without the others agencies at the time (t1) which occurs before the actual execution (t2) of the structured thinking and actions. That is where an intriguing relation with t1 and t2 begins because,

- It is very optimistic to think that the context at t2 is truly taken into account in this structuring at t1;
- It is too idealistic to consider that the agent who makes use of the method to achieve this structure has the same intention embedded in the methods (i.e. incongruence of the agent's perceived situation with the situation held by the method);
- It is too strong, and possibly incorrect, to surmise that the agents who hopefully hold and practice in the context at t2 will have the same intentions as presumed.

We argue that structuring at t1 and under the context c1, one's thinking and actions to be executed at t2 under the context c2 is a yet-to-be-tested hypothesis. Namely, neither the method to be situated nor the agent who wishes to achieve a situated method can justify or even claim the structured thinking and actions will be realized as intended and contextualized. But, if this is so, what is the rationale behind a situated method?

First and foremost, a meaning of situated method is revised in that it is not with a fine-grained description of the method that we are concerned, but instead the intentions attached to a number of key deliberative actions to be appropriate to the contexts under consideration. We also note that method as inanimate agency holds 'frozen-rational' of its producer. It is necessary to explicate how this frozen-rational with its collectives are proposed to be situated, when present. If it does not include this aspect (i.e. how it is to be situated), it fails to hold the very idea of situated method. [33] criticizes methods on this matter, and proposes a framework containing four essential elements: the 'problem situation' (similar to the term context we use), the intended problem solver (methodology user), the problem-solving process (the method), and the evaluation of the above three. The proposed framework has certain interesting features pertaining to the goal, as opposed to forcing the method user to use the method, that *facilitate* the designer to come to her own method. For this purpose, the designer and user are encouraged to ask a number of questions and critically examine the intention of every action needed. Some examples: What are the methodology users' value sets? What believes do they hold as being "good"? For example, which of the economic, political, cultural, or technical values do the methodology users consider as uppermost? In this context what values do the methodologies advocate? How congruent are these with methodology users' values?

4 Incorporating the Four Essential Notions for Method Adaptation

As discussed above that the four essential notions are often conceived from what we call a basic or simplistic view, they need to be extended to comprehensive and possibly richer meanings. We consider the notion of 'situation' a phenomenon with which the agency perceives, reasons about, and lives in at certain time. Three complementary views on situation -Theory of Situation, Situational Awareness, and Situated Actions, summarized in Table 1, indicate underlying features of this construct, which is essentially a composite one. By employing the theory of situation [18] we contend that situation is partial reality at best which has to do with the relations among the collectives under consideration. By employing the idea of situational awareness [20], we argue that the agency needs to use all kinds of cognitive elements and mechanisms to be aware of the position held on and reason about what we intend to do. By employing the idea of situated action [19], situated method is enacted by interactions among its collectives along partial plans.

By drawing on the conception of situation we conjecture that agency, context, and fragment are essential for situated method development. Situated method is regarded as a phenomenon because it is:

- Based on partial reality construed by the agency that forms the intention in the context at a certain time and in place,
- Enacted and re-constructed for the context in which the agencies' thinking and actions are structured and referred thereof

Table 2. An extension of four essential notions for situated method development

Four essential notions	Basic View (Simplistic)	Extension
Situation	characterized by a number of factors that influence or are being influenced by a method fragment	the limited parts of reality that the agency perceive, reason about, and live in
Context	Described in terms of aspects or collectives in the process	dynamic interplays among collectives of work practice as situated and characterized by the agency
Agency	adheres to enactment of proposed fragment in the work practice	interplays among fragments with a certain intention in and for the context
Method fragment	description of a methodical artefact or any coherent part thereof	comes into play with the agency in the context when structuring one's thinking and actions

The following summarises our conceptions of three notions (see Table 2).

Regarding *context*, Andler's [34] account gives a hint about two aspects of a context: On the one hand it is perceived, and perhaps influenced by means of the agency's own fragments (fragments already used a priori by the agent) and proposed fragments (the fragments not used a priori by the agent). On the other hand it influences the agency's fragments and proposed fragments. It has then a duality character on 'to influence' and 'being influenced', which is manifest in the process of contextualizing, de-contextualizing, and re-contextualizing. In other words, this process is about 'characterization of context for situation awareness'. This characterization includes, as referred to in [20], perception, comprehension, and projection. It is this characterization that uses a number of factors considered salient to the situation at hand. Most of these characteristics are nothing more than subjective views of the situation. By drawing on the literature of social cognition, we contend that characterization remains effective when the relations among the characteristics of the situation can be present to achieve a 'yet-to-be-tested hypothesis', sometimes represented as heuristics. As time progresses in situated method development and more insights are gained along emergent attributes of the context, relations among the characteristics are subverted and (re)formed as the meanings and their importance is characterized again.

Agency, is at the heart of situated method development where it interacts with the fragments (owned and proposed) in and for the context. The agency conducts characterization of the context in which all collectives (other agencies having one of the roles as identified, methodical artefacts as shall be elaborated below), and other constituents of the situation are considered. At any moment during this characterization the agency may need to determine what to do with the fragments owned and proposed (i.e., how to structure the agents' thinking and actions in the situation foreseen). This determination is an intentional action of the situation at hand and involves a human decision-making process. We argue that the concept of intention, along with its main functions and forms (future- and present-directed), paves the way for an account of the agency theorizing the way an agent structures his own and/or the user's thinking and action for constructing a situated method. Accepting that the situation at hand and that which is foreseen (where the actions are performed intentionally whether or not the associated intentions agree with the proposed one) are partially construed and relative to the agency, uncertainty is always inherent in situated method development and in determination of the fragments. Therefore, a body of knowledge concerning 'decision-making under uncertainty' is used to understand how decision-making is achieved in situated method development. In particular, naturalistic decision-making accounts are found to be appropriate as their particular view on decision matters fits our orientation on the subject matter.

Regarding *(method) fragment*, which is of course, present in situated method development and is a cognitive element that presupposes agents' future-directed intentions and is materialized in different forms (template, procedure, technique, etc.). Due to this cognitive aspect, a method fragment influences the way a designer structures her thinking and actions that affect the way the user structures and realises her thinking and actions. Various intriguing interplays occur between the agency and method fragments that will be elaborated later on, but to give an example, consider a simple case where the designer adopts the fragment without any change (i.e., the designer role is not effective). In this case, the fragment becomes more dominant in situated method development (i.e., it directly structures its user's thinking and actions). But that is only one direction of the influence; the other manifested as the method fragment is subject to change in the execution of the proposed fragment (i.e., the proposed fragment is enacted and modified in a context). These two aspects of fragment, similar to context, show a duality of method fragment (simply, 'to influence' and 'being influenced') which manifests the process of contextualizing, de-contextualizing, and re-contextualizing of the fragment. In other words, this process is about 'characterization of method fragment for situation awareness'.

As we have incorporated basic understandings of the key notions for situated method development, we are ready to induce the proposition about the meaning of adaptation for situated method development as well as the conjecture asserting how the underlying notions can be understood better.

Proposition: Adaptation Underpinning Situated Method Development. Adaptation is essential to situated method development because the agents in a 'perfect' sense cannot arrive at matching, adjusting, and/or transferring elements of a situated method where the context is unique and relative for each agency.

Conjecture: Method Adaptation Process (MAP). Given that three concepts (context, fragment, and the agency) emphasise the idea of modifications, changes on, and interplays among them, we conjecture that the 'Method Adaptation Process', in short 'method adaptation' or 'MAP', is a process or capability in which agents holding intentions through responsive changes in, and dynamic interplays between, contexts, and method fragments develop a situated fragment for a specific project situation.

Notice that with this conjecture, we consider a situation as a collection of three essential concepts: Agent, Context, and Fragment. The conjecture does not claim how these interplays may occur, but asserts that this interplays come into an end in the form of a situated method. In the following, we refer to three studies [35, 36, 14] to discuss briefly how these interplays can manifest in terms of models. We shall briefly mention the corresponding interplays as incorporated in their proposed models.

The interplays between context and fragment are incorporated explicitly in the Configuration Process [35]; on the other hand, the interplays between agent and context are implicit in the model. The S3 Model of Situational Method Engineering in [36] puts a special emphasis on the explicit interplay between context and fragment and on the implicit interplays between agent and fragment. This implicit mentioning of the other interplays in [35] and [36] is not surprising because the notion of agency is not central to their articulation of the idea of situated method development.

Baskerville and Stage [15] propose a social process for situated method development along with the premise that a method should be situated at the ISD level where ISD activities are carried out. Similar to the previous two basic models, characterization of a context in terms, a number of elements are suggested though their mutual relations are not addressed in such a characterization. In relation to the Social Process for Method Fragment Adaptation in [15], the process as proposed is a good example of a special emphasis on the explicit interplay between agent and context and on the implicit interplays between agent and fragment.

To conclude with the examination of the conjecture in relation to the basic models, we contend that as they correspond to specific interplays, they put special emphasis on the interplays between agent, context, and fragment with different degrees and explicitness. These models can be seen as specific patterns reflecting specific orientation on the subject matter.

5 Conclusion

This paper is concerned with theoretical underpinnings of situational method development, which concerns about how to make a method work for a project situation. In literature, various approaches, models or alike are proposed to describe or prescribe how to achieve a situated method, which is a method that fits a project situation. Based on the review of relevant studies in ISD and method engineering research domains, we point out that there is a lack of explicit articulation of key notions underlying situated method development. Eventually, upon the deeper examination of key notions in various disciplines, including cognitive psychology, philosophy of mind, and linguistics, we induce a proposition about the meaning of adaptation for situated method development and a conjecture called method adaptation. This conjecture states that situation, as a combining construct, embraces the other notions context, fragment and agency. As such, method adaptation asserts that there are intriguing interplays among these key notions. We briefly discuss the specific interplays that are found in basic models proposed for situated method development in literature. One implication of method adaptation is that method, context and the agent are not passive elements in these interplays but purposively intervene in the agent's knowledge about how to handle construction of situated method. This implies that we should advance in our thinking about the effect of method in these interplays rather than reducing its meaning to certain aspects and attributes. To show how to advance in thinking, we suggest looking beyond its 'frozen' rationale captured and often implicit in the presence of the method, and possibly capture its creator's way of structuring the intended user's thinking and actions.

This conjecture may suggest two basic directions for future research. First, it seems that this conjecture gives a hint about a need for a generic model that explains possible interplays among the key notions [37]. If this is possible, the existing basic models can be considered as specific patterns that can be induced from a generic model [38]. Description of a generic model should be made in an ambiguous way so that the comparison of the generic model with other models can be made explicitly. Second, empirical justifications of the specific interplays may be needed to show the feasibility of studying certain models in practice. In fact, this is one of the immediate needs for conducting relevant research to better understand how situated method development occurs in practice. The deeper articulation of its underlying key notions may accommodate the one intending to carry out follow-up research.

References

1. D. Avison, D and G. Fitzgerald, Reflections on Information Systems Development 1988-2002, in: Information Systems Development - Advances in Methodologies, Components, and Management, edited by M. Kirikova, J. Grundspenkis, W. Wojtkowskiet (Kluwer Academic/ Plenium Publishers, 2002), pp. 1-11.
2. K. Kumar and R. J. Welke, Methodology Engineering: A Proposal for Situation-Specific Methodology Construction, in: Challanges and Strategies for Research in Systems Development Method, edited by W. W. Cotterman, J. A. Senn (John Wiley & Sons, 1992).
3. G. J. Hidding, Reinventing Methodology: *Communications of the ACM*, **40**(11) (1997)
4. B. Fitzgerald, The Use of Systems Development Methodologies in Practice: A Field Study. *Information Systems Journal*, **7**, 201-212 (1997).
5. J. Webster and R. T. Watson, Analyzing the Past to Prepare for the Future: writing a Literature Review, *MIS Quarterly* **26**(2), xiii-xxiii (2002).
6. D. Truex, R. Baskerville, and J. Travis, Amethodical system development: the deffered meaning of systems development method. *Accounting, Management & Technology*, 10,53-79 (2000).
7. J. Iivari and H. Linger, Knowledge Work as Collaborative Work: A Situated Activity Theory View. HICCS99, Hawaii, USA (1999).
8. T. W. Olle, H. G., Sol, and A. A. Verrijn-Stuart, Information Systems Design Methdologies: A Comparative Review. Amsterdam, North-Holland (1982).
9. S. Brinkkemper, Method Engineering: Engineering of Information Systems Development Methods and Tools, *Journal of Systems and Software*, **38**, 275-280 (1996).
10. R. J. Welke, K. Kumar and H. van Dissel, Methodology Engineering: Een voorstel om te komen tot situationeel specifieke methode-ontwikkeling, *Informatie*, **33**(5), 11-20 (1981).
11. K. Kumar and R. J. Welke, Methodology Engineering: A Proposal for Situation-Specific Methodology Construction. in: Challanges and Strategies for Research in Systems Development Method , edited by W. W. Cotterman, J. A. Senn (John Wiley & Sons, 1992).
12. C. van Slooten, S. Brinkkemper, A Method Engineering Approach to Information Systems Development, in: Information System Development Process, by N. Prakash, C. Rolland and B. Pernici (Elsevier Science Publishers, North-Holland, 1993).
13. F. Harmsen, S. Brinkkemper, and H. Oei, Situational Method Engineering for Information Systems Projects. in: Methods and Associated Tools for Information Systems Life Cycle, edited by T. W. Olle and A. V. Stuart (North-Holland, Amsterdam, 1994), pp. 169-194.
14. M. N. Aydin, F. Harmsen, and J. van Hillegersberg, Taxonomic Dimensions for Studying Situational Information Systems Development, In: Situational Method Engineering: Fundamentals and Experiences, edited by J. Ralyté, S. Brinkkemper and B. Henderson-Sellers, IFIP Series in print (2007).
15. R. Baskerville and J. Stage, Accommodating emergent work practices: Ethnographic choice of method fragments. In: Realigning research and practice: The social and organisational perspectives (Kluwer Academic Publishers, Boston, 2001), pp. 11-27.
16. Merriam-Webster, (February 13, 2005); http://www.m-w.com.
17. OED - Oxford English Dictionary, (Feb 13, 2005; http://www.oed.com
18. J. Barwise and J. Perry, *Situations and Attitudes* (Cambridge, MIT-Bradford, 1983).
19. L. A. Suchman, *Plans and situated actions: The problem of human-machine communications* (Cambridge University Press, Cambridge, 1987).
20. M. R. Endsley, Design and Evaluation for Situation Awareness Enhancement. the Proceedings of the Human Factors Society 32nd Annual Meeting, Human Factors Society, Santa Monica, CA, 97-101 (1988).
21. P. R. Cohen and H. J. Levesque, Persistence, Intention and Commitment. In: Proceedings of Timberline workshop on Reasoning about Plans and Actions, 297-338 (1987).

22. J. Perry, Semantics and Situation, Routledge Encyclopedia of Philosophy, retrieved from http://www-csli.stanford.edu/~john/PHILPAPERS/sitsem.pdf on March 13, 2002, (1987)
23. E. von Glasersfeld, Piaget's Legacy: Cognition as Adaptive Activity In: A. Riegler, M. Peschl and A. von Stein (Eds.). Understanding representation in the cognitive sciences - Does representation need reality? New York/Dordrecht: (Kluwer Academic/Plenum Publishers, 1997) 283-287.
24. J. Piaget, Piaget's Theory. In P. Mussen (Ed.) Handbook of child psychology. (Wiley, 1983).
25. L. Hasher and R. T. Zacks, Automatic Processing of Fundamental Information: the Case of Frequency of Occurrence. *American Psychologist*, **39**(12), 1372-1388, (1984).
26. B. Rogoff and J. Lave, *Everyday Cognition: Its Development in Social Context* (Harvard University Press, 1984).
27. P. Linell and D. P. Thunqvist, Moving in and Out of Framings: Activity Contexts in Talks with Young Unemployed People Within a Training project. *Journal of Pragmatics*, **35**(3), 409-434 (2003).
28. J. –Ch. Pomerol and P. Brézillon, About some relationships between knowledge and context. Modeling and Using Context (CONTEXT-01). Lecture Notes in Computer Science, Springer Verlag, 461-464 (2001).
20. E. Schegloff, In another context, Duranti, in: Rethinking Context: Language as an Interactive Phenomenon, edited by A. Goodwin, (Cambridge: Cambridge University Press, 1992), pp. 193-227
30. J. L. Mey, Context and (dis)ambiguity: a pragmatic view, *Journal of Pragmatics*, **35**, 331-347.
31. M. Bratman, Intention, Plans and Practical Reason. Harvard University Press (1987).
32. Morrison, James C. (1970) Husserl and Brentano on Intentionality. Philosophy and Phenomenological Research, 31, 27-46 (2003).
33. N. Jayaratna, *Understanding and Evaluating Methodologies* (McGraw-Hill, Berkshire 1994).
34. D. Andler. Context: the case for a principles epistemic particularism, *Journal of Pragmatics*, **35**(3), 349-371 (2003)
35. C. van Slooten, Situated Methods For Systems Development, Doctoral Dissertation, University of Twente (1995).
36. F. Harmsen, *Situational Method Engineering*. (Moret Ernst & Young Management Consultants, Utrecht ,1997).
37. Aydin, M. N. Decision-Making and Support for Method Adaptation, PhD Dissertation, University of Twente, ISBN: 90-365-2375-3 (2006)
38. Mirbel and J. Ralyté, Situational Method Engineering: Combining assembly-based and roadmap driven approaches, *Requirements Engineering*, **11**(1):58-78 (2006).

Method Chunks Selection by Multicriteria Techniques: an Extension of the Assembly-based Approach

Elena Kornyshova[1,2], Rébecca Deneckère[1], and Camille Salinesi[1]
1 CRI, University Paris 1 – Panthéon Sorbonne
90, rue de Tolbiac, 75013 Paris, France,
2 ECD, Saint-Petersburg State University of Economics and Finance
21, Sadovaia Str, 191023 Saint-Petersburg, Russia
{elena.kornyshova,rebecca.deneckere,camille}@univ-paris1.fr,
WWW home page: http://crinfo.univ-paris1.fr/

Abstract. The work presented in this paper is related to the area of situational method engineering (SME). In this domain, approaches are developed accordingly to specific project specifications. We propose to adapt an existing method construction process, namely the assembly-based one. One of the particular features of assembly-based SME approach is the selection of method chunks. Our proposal is to offer a better guidance in the retrieval of chunks by the introduction of multicriteria techniques. To use them efficiently, we defined a typology of projects characteristics, in order to identify all their critical aspects, which will offer a priorisation to help the method engineer in the choice between similar chunks.

1 Introduction

It is now clearly assumed that one development process cannot fit all the existing problems and development contexts. This assumption has lead to the development of the Method Engineering domain, and more particularly of Situational Method Engineering (SME) [0] [0]. In this domain, approaches have been developed to adapt existing methods to deal with the specifications of the project at hand. It allows the construction of a specific process to meet the requirements of each particular situation by reusing and assembling parts of existing methodologies called either fragments [0], chunks [0], patterns [0], etc, that, similarly to a software component, can be treated as separated unit. The knowledge encapsulated in these small method parts is generally stored in a classic library repository called Method Base [0] [0] [0].

Please use the following format when citing this chapter:

Kornyshova, E., Deneckère, R., Salinesi, C., 2007, in IFIP International Federation for Information Processing, Volume 244, Situational Method Engineering: Fundamentals and Experiences, eds. Ralyté, J., Brinkkemper, S., Henderson-Sellers B., (Boston Springer), pp. 64-78.

Following a complete assembly SME approach consists of executing the following phases: (a) identification and formalisation of the method chunks, (b) storage in a method chunks base, (c) chunks selection following the project needs, and (d) assembling of the selected method chunks. In this paper, we will consider the SME aspect regarding the selection of chunks in the repository. In our proposal, we refer to the notion of "chunk" to describe every type of small method parts (considered also as fragment or as pattern). The problem of chunk retrieval is an important part of this process and has to be easy and effective.

The assembly based approach [0] uses a process (assembly process model – APM) that guides the engineer in the elaboration of a requirement map and uses this map in order to select a set of related chunks. The final selection is then realised with the help of similarity measures inspired from those proposed by [0] and [0]. They distinguish two types of measures: those which allow to measure the similarity of the elements of *product models* and those which allow to measure the closeness of *process models* elements.

The similarity measures are provided in order to compare the method requirements with the solutions proposed by the selected chunks but their application is difficult. First, the difference between the formulation of requirements to achieve and of requirements that can be achieved is more or less inexistent, which made the requirements map creation difficult. Second, the results obtained by an application of the similarity measures are not simple to handle. Furthermore, the cost of a project can increase as, in order to offer a good comparison, method engineers have to manage an increasing number of artefacts, which induce a combinatory explosion of all the values to calculate. Finally, even if all these issues are solved, the final selected chunks may be quite similar; this means that the method engineer has to choose one over the other and to discriminate between them.

To solve these difficulties, we propose an extension of the APM by the introduction of multicriteria (MC) techniques (or MC methods). Our objectives are to (a) guide chunk retrieval and (b) to propose a priorisation of the selected chunks in order to guide the method engineer into the final selection process. In order to use the full potentiality of the MC techniques, we also propose a project characteristics typology, in order to identify all its critical aspects. This typology is an adaptation of two similar works. The first one is the typology created by Kees Van Slooten and Bert Hodes in [0] to prove that the project approach is affected by the project context. The second was made by Isabelle Mirbel and Jolita Ralyté in [0]. In this work, they define the concept of Reuse frame and they apply it to the assembly approach. Their reasons are threefold: (a) to help the chunk selection by better qualifying them, (b) to enable the use of more powerful matching techniques to retrieve them when looking at similar methodological problems and (c) to express better methodological needs for a specific project, improving this way the chance to get adequate and useful method chunks. The merging of these two existing typologies and their adaptation to be used by MC techniques will multiply the process efficiency.

Our approach is presented in this paper as follows: In the section 2, we give a brief introduction in MC techniques. The section 3 describes the assembly-based approach extended by MC techniques with an example. The section 4 presents conclusion and future works.

2 Multicriteria Techniques

Multicriteria techniques currently dominate in the field of decision-making [0], [0]. They appeared at the beginning of the Sixties, and their number and application contexts increase continually. For example, these techniques are employed for requirements priorisation [0], to choose evolution scenario [0], or to make operational decisions [0].

Generally, a decision-making problem is defined by the presence of alternatives. The traditional approach consists in using only one criterion to carry out the selection between alternatives. The traditional example is the selection of the projects according to the net present value (NPV). However, using a single criterion is not sufficient when the consequences of the alternatives to be analyzed are important [0].

The goal of the multicriteria decision-making (MCDM) techniques consists in defining priorities between alternatives (actions, scenarios, projects) according to multiple criteria. In contrast to monocriterion approach, MC techniques allow a more in-depth analysis of problem because of taking into consideration various aspects. Nevertheless, their application has proved more difficult.

In spite of their complexity, MC techniques are often chosen and used by companies. In general, the MC formulation of a problem is based on the definition of [0]:

- alternatives set represented by "concurrent" actions,
- criteria (attributes) set defined by parameters to be considered for priorisation,
- alternatives evaluations according to criteria (partial evaluations, which are obtained by assignment of values to each alternative according to all criteria),
- aggregation rules (to select an alternative, it is necessary to incorporate the partial evaluations in a general evaluation). The aggregation rules differ in different techniques.

According to this, the decision-making steps are defined as follows:

1. diagnostics of problem (necessity to define priorities),
2. identification of problem's parameters: alternatives, criteria,
3. alternatives partial estimations,
4. priorities definition.

Five families of MCDM techniques can be considered: MAUT [0], AHP [0], outranking techniques [0], weighting techniques [0], and fuzzy techniques [0]. These are not detailed here for the sake of space.

3 Extended Assembly-based Approach

Using MC techniques allow to integrate new parameters into method chunk selection. We propose to adapt namely the assembly based SME approach by integrating of MC techniques expression.

The basic and extended APM are illustrated in Fig. 1 using the MAP formalism [0].

The intentional modelling of MAP provides a generic model based on intentions (goals) and the possible strategies to achieve each intention. The map is presented as a graph where nodes are *intentions* and edges are *strategies*. The directed nature of the graph shows which intentions can follow which one. An edge enters a node if its manner can be used to achieve its intention. Since there can be multiple edges entering a node, the map is able to represent the many manners that can be used for achieving an intention. The map includes two predefined intentions: "Start" and "Stop", which mean accordingly the beginning and the end of the process. An important notion in process maps are the *sections* witch represent the knowledge encapsulated in a triplet <source intention, strategy, target intention>, in other terms, the knowledge corresponding to a particular process step to achieve an intention (the target intention) from a specific situation (the source intention) following a particular technique (the strategy).

In the following figure, the basic components of APM are presented by solid lines, and the components proposed to extend the basic approach are exposed by dashed lines.

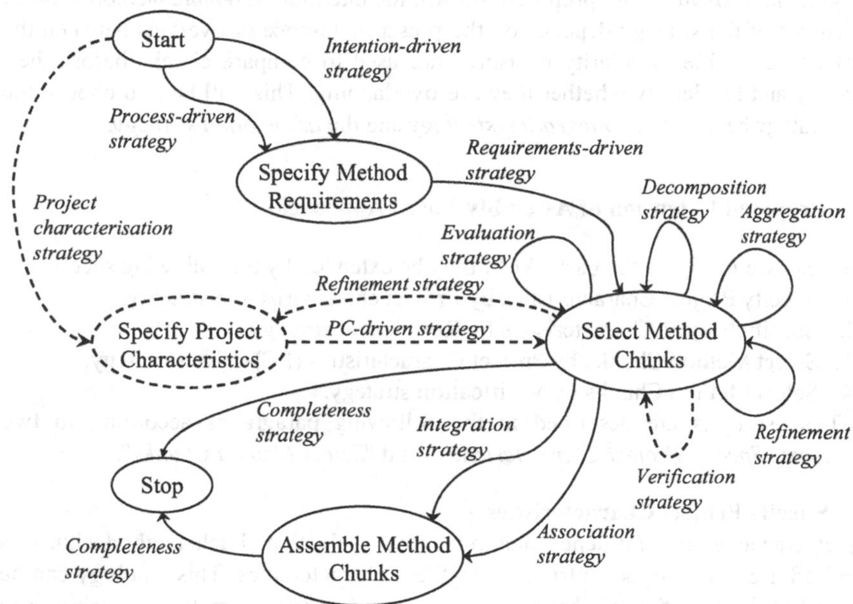

Fig. 1. Basic and extended APM

This map is described in the following sections. Firstly, we present the basic APM, secondly, the extended one, and, finally, an illustrative example.

3.1 Basic Assembly-based Approach

The APM [0] is based on the notion of "chunk" as a representation of a method small unit. It proposes different ways to select them that match requirements as well as different strategies to assemble them. It is based on the achievement of two key intentions: *Select method chunks* and *Assemble method chunks*. Achieving the first intention leads to the selection of chunks from the method base that matches the requirements. The second intention is satisfied when the selected chunks have been assembled in a consistent manner.

The process starts by selecting candidate chunks that are expected to match the requirements expressed in a requirements map. Guidelines suggest formulating queries to the method base in order to identify the chunks that are expected to match part or the totality of the requirements. A set of strategies (*decomposition, aggregation, refinement, decomposition, aggregation)* help to refine the candidate chunk selection, but, any time a chunk has been retrieved, it can be validated by applying an *evaluation strategy*. This helps in evaluating the degree of matching of the candidate chunk to the requirements. This is based on similarity measures between the requirements map and the map of the selected chunk.

When at least two chunks have been selected, the method engineer can progress to the assembly of these chunks. Two strategies, namely the *integration strategy* and the *association strategy*, are proposed to fulfil the intention *Assemble method chunks*. The choice of the strategy depends on the presence/absence of overlaps between the chunks to assemble. Similarity measures are used to compare chunks before their assembly and to identify whether they are overlapping. This will help to choose the right strategy between the *integration strategy* and the *association strategy*.

3.2 Proposed Extension of Assembly-based Approach

As we can see in Fig. 1, the basic APM may be extended by the following sections:

1. Specify Project Characteristics by Project characterisation strategy,
2. Specify Project Characteristics by Refinement strategy,
3. Select Method Chunks by Project Characteristics (PC)-driven strategy,
4. Select Method Chunks by Verification strategy.

These sections are described in the following paragraphs according to two intentions: *"Specify Project Characteristics"* and *"Select Method Chunks"*.

3.2.1 Specify Project Characteristics

Project characteristics influence method chunks selection. Each method chunk is described according to its contribution to these characteristics. This typology can be enriched by introduction of characteristics proper to concrete methods (such a used approach, tool presence, notation, difficulty etc).

Project characteristics typology

Project characteristics describe the main properties of IS development project. Their difference with method requirements of basic APM lies in the way of definition and presentation. The method requirements are analysed and expressed in the form of requirements map, whereas the project characteristics form a predefined typology that method engineer investigates in order to choose those, which are needed for a project.

Based on studies [0] [0], we propose a typology of project characteristics, which includes four dimensions: organisational, human, application domain, and development strategy.

The typology of project characteristics is illustrated on Tables 1, 2, 3, and 4. The characteristics proposed in this table are either inspired from the works presented in [11] and [12] or suggested in this paper. In order to differentiate them in the table, we identify the source (1) as the work of Van Slooten [11], the source (2) as Mirbel's [12] and ours will be noted as the source (3).

The organisational dimension highlights organisational aspects of IS development project and includes the following characteristics: management commitment, importance, impact, time pressure, shortage of resources, size, and level of innovation (Table 1).

Table 1. Organisational dimension.

Characteristic	Values	Source
Management commitment	{low, normal, high}	(1), (2), (3)
Importance	{low, normal, high}	(1), (3)
Impact	{low, normal, high}	(1), (2), (3)
Time pressure	{low, normal, high}	(1), (2), (3)
Shortage of resources	{low, normal, high}	(1), (2), (3)
	{human, means}	(1), (2)
	{financial resources, human resources, temporal resources, informational resources}	(3)
Size	{low, normal, high}	(1), (2), (3)
Level of innovation	{low, normal, high}	(1), (2), (3)
	{business innovation, technology innovation}	(2), (3)

The human dimension describes the qualities of persons involved into IS development project. It includes the following characteristics: resistance and conflict, expertise, requirements clarity and stability, user involvement, stakeholder number (Table 2).

Table 2. Human dimension

Characteristic	Values	Source
Resistance and conflict	{low, normal, high}	(1), (3)
Expertise (knowledge, experience, and skills)	{low, normal, high}	(1), (2), (3)
	{tester, developer, designer, analyst}	(2), (3)
Clarity and stability	{low, normal, high}	(1), (2), (3)
User involvement	{real, virtual}	(2), (3)
Stakeholder number	num	(3)

The application domain dimension includes formality, relationships, dependency, complexity, application type, application technology, dividing project, repetitiveness, variability, and variable artefacts (Table 3).

Table 3. Application domain dimension.

Characteristic	**Values**	**Source**
Formality	{low, normal, high}	(1), (2), (3)
Relationships	{low, normal, high}	(1), (3)
Dependency	{low, normal, high}	(1), (2), (3)
Complexity	{low, normal, high}	(1), (3)
Application type	{intra-organization application, inter-organization application, organization-customer application}	(2), (3)
Application technology	{application to develop includes a database, application to develop is distributed, application to develop includes a GUI}	(2), (3)
Dividing project	{one single system, establishing system-oriented subprojects, establishing process-oriented subprojects, establishing hybrid subprojects}	(1), (2), (3)
Repetitiveness	{low, normal, high}	(3)
Variability	{low, normal, high}	(3)
Variable artefacts	{organisational, human, application domain, and development strategy}	(3)

The development strategy dimension gathers source system, project organization, development strategy, realization strategy, delivery strategy, tracing project, and goal number (Table 4).

Table 4. Development strategy dimension.

Characteristic	Values	Source
Source system	{code reuse, functional domain reuse, interface reuse}	(2), (3)
	{weak, medium, strong}	(2), (3)
Project organization	{standard, adapted}	(1), (2), (3)
Development strategy	{outsourcing, iterative, prototyping, phase-wise, tile-wise}	(1), (2), (3)
Realization strategy	{at once, incremental, concurrent, overlapping}	(1), (2), (3)
Delivery strategy	{at once, incremental, evolutionary}	(1), (2), (3)
Tracing project	{weak, strong}	(1), (2), (3)
Goal number	{one goal, multi-goals}	(3)

Specify Project Characteristics by Project characterisation strategy

This section consists in the identification of characteristics for a given project. The method engineer explores the project characteristics typology and brings out the project critical aspects, which are crucial for the current project.

Specify Project Characteristics by Refinement strategy

The refinement strategy is similar to this one of the basic APM. The distinction is concluded in a refinement objective. The selection result may be presented by a set of method chunks, which are homogeneous, i.e. have the same description with regard to previously identified project characteristics. Then, additional information is required to define more precisely the differences between homogeneous method chunks. In this case, the refinement aims to specify more closely the project characteristics.

3.2.2 Select Method Chunks

Select Method Chunks by PC-driven strategy

The PC-driven strategy consists in application of MC techniques for selecting alternatives method chunks.

This section can be itself refined by a process map (illustrated on Fig. 2), which contains two main intentions: *"Define weights"* and *"Define priorities"*.

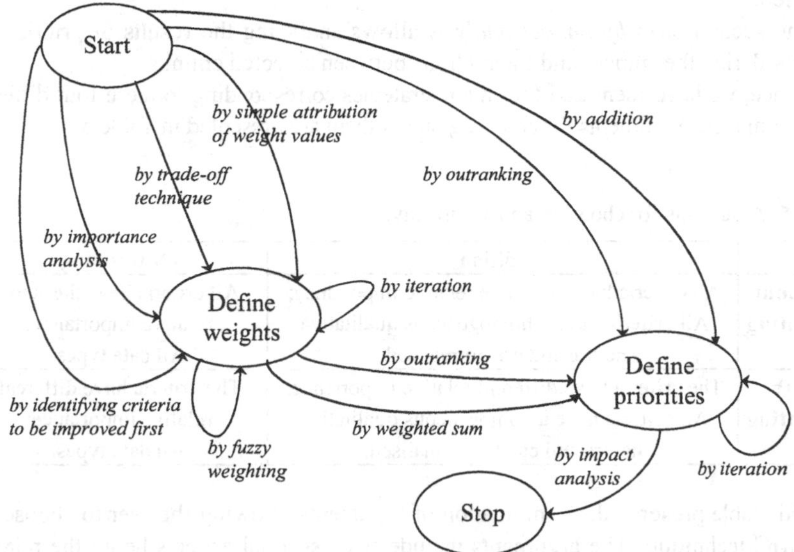

Fig. 2. Select Method Chunks by PC-driven strategy's process map

The choice between these two intentions is made according to needs for criteria weighting. Criteria weighting enables to analyse their relative importance. When they are not weighted, it means that their relative importance is equal.

These two strategies are developed in the following paragraphs (for more details on outranking and weighting techniques, see Appendix 1).

1. *Define weights.* This intention can be achieved *"by simple attribution of weight values"*, *"by identifying criteria tot be improved first"* (SWING), *"by trade-off technique"* (trade-off weighting), and *"by importance analysis"* (SMART). The choice between these possibilities can be carried out in function of decision-maker preferences. This intention can be achieved *"by iteration"* (when the result must be specified) and *"by fuzzy weighting"* (when fuzzy values are needed).

2. *Define priorities* (Priorisation). There are two ways to achieve this intention that are: priorisation strategy with or without weighting and priorisation strategy with

weighting. The objective of this stage is to aggregate the alternatives evaluations into a unique (aggregated) evaluation and to priory alternatives.

Priorisation strategy without weighting. To carry out this strategy, we suggest application of the following strategies: *"by outranking"* (outranking) without weighting or *"by addition"*. The addition of values requires that all of them must have a homogeneous qualitative nature and be normalised. The outranking can be applied to all data types (quantitative and qualitative) and does not require the normalisation. However, it is most complicated.

Priorisation strategy with weighting. The possible strategies are *"by outranking"* (outranking) with weighting or *"by weighted sum"* (weighting techniques). .The difference between the given strategies is similar to the previous selection.

This intention too can be completed *"by iteration"* if the result has to be specified.

The section *Stop by impact analysis* allows analysing the results of priorisation by considering the impact and interactions between selected chunks.

Hence, we have identified four main strategies corresponding to these four different MC techniques. Arguments for choosing one of them are presented in Table 5.

Table 5. Arguments for choosing a main strategy.

	Addition	**Outranking**
Without weighting	All criteria have the same relative importance; All criteria have a homogeneous qualitative nature and are normalised.	All criteria have the same relative importance; All data types.
With weighting	The criteria have different relative importance; All criteria have a homogeneous qualitative nature and can be normalised.	The criteria have different relative importance; All data types.

This table presents the combination of arguments allowing the user to choose the right MC technique. The arguments include two essential aspects being the relative importance of the criteria ("same" or "different") and their nature ("all" or "homogeneous qualitative and normalised").

Select Method Chunks by Verification strategy

This strategy aims at verifying adequacy of chunks selected by MC techniques: if the result is not sufficient, other project characteristics are needed for final decision-making. Then the section *"specify project characteristics by refinement"* is available.

3.3 Example

To illustrate our proposal, we have selected method chunks that deal with information system (IS) security within requirements engineering (RE).

Five chunks of RE methods designed for analysing IS security were identified: NFR Framework [0], KAOS [0], Secure Tropos [0], GBRAM [0], and Misuse Cases [0]. The comparison of these methods is presented in [0]. Within this example, we illustrate only one part of extended APM that concerns the application of MC techniques in SME.

The given project is described by:

- the great influence on the whole organisation;
- the need for ensuring the greater progress;
- the organisation does not have the experts in this field and does not plan to employ them;
- the need for a better explanation of method chunks and their application.

The method engineer has chosen three project characteristics (since the weights of the others are equal to zero) and has described the method chunks according to methods properties. Thus, these methods chunks are compared according to six criteria, which concern two groups: project characteristics and proper method characteristics. The first group includes impact, level of innovation, and expertise. The second group comprises guidance, approach, and formalism.

Depending on project description, the method engineer has defined the following preferences rules for these criteria:

- *Impact on organisation:* maximum;
- *Level of innovation:* maximum;
- *Required expertise:* minimum;
- *Guidance:* a predefined taxonomy is better than heuristics, which is better than a simple guidelines;
- *Approach:* a systemic approach is better than exploratory, which is better than explanatory.
- *Formalism:* a formal approach is better than semi-formal one, which is better than informal one.

The summary of chunks evaluation is presented in Table 6.

Table 6. IS security chunks evaluation.

Criteria	NFR Framework	KAOS	Secure Tropos	GBRAM	Misuse Cases
Project Characteristics					
Impact	high	low	high	low	normal
Level of innovation	high	high	low	high	high
Expertise	normal	high	high	normal	low
Method Chunk Characteristics					
Guidance	predefined taxonomy	reuse of generic refinement patterns, heuristics	*No guidance*	documents analysis, heuristics	guidelines
Approach	explanatory	exploratory	systemic	*Not applicable*	explanatory
Formalism	semi-formal	formal	formal	informal	informal

In order to compare these chunks and to select one of them, which is more adapted to the given project, we have applied three different calculations: simple addition, weighted sum, and outranking with weighting.

1) The *simple addition* was applied to the first three criteria, which are "*quantifiable*". Two method chunks, which are the best ones, present the result: NFR Framework and Misuse Cases (See Table 7).

Table 7. Method selection with simple addition.

Criteria	NFR Framework	KAOS	Secure Tropos	GBRAM	Misuse Cases
Impact	3	1	3	1	2
Level of innovation	3	3	1	3	3
Expertise	2	1	1	2	3
	8,00	5,00	5,00	6,00	**8,00**

2) In the case of *weighted sum*, we add the weights assigned to criteria. These weights are defined by importance analysis (Appendix 1). The chunk "Misuse Cases" is the best one (see Table 8).

Table 8. Method selection with weighted sum.

Criteria	Weights	NFR Framework	KAOS	Secure Tropos	GBRAM	Misuse Cases
Impact	0,30	3	1	3	1	2
Level of innovation	0,20	3	3	1	3	3
Expertise	0,50	2	1	1	2	3
		2,50	1,40	1,60	1,90	**2,70**

3) To apply the outranking technique, we selected ELECTRE [0] (Appendix 1). All calculations are not presented here for the sake of space. The concordance and discordance matrices developed in our case study are shown in Table 9 (Table 9.a – concordance matrix; Table 9.b – discordance matrix). Application of outranking techniques allows considering the last three criteria, which are not quantifiable.

Table 9. Method selection with outranking.

a)

	Fr1	Fr2	Fr3	Fr4	Fr5
Fr1	X	0,45	0,45	0,85	0,85
Fr2	0,60	X	0,50	0,85	0,75
Fr3	0,65	0,80	X	0,65	0,65
Fr4	0,35	0,60	0,50	X	0,35
Fr5	0,60	0,30	0,35	0,70	X

b)

	Fr1	Fr2	Fr3	Fr4	Fr5
Fr1	X	0,33	0,67	0,50	0,50
Fr2	1,00	X	1,00	0,50	1,00
Fr3	1,00	0,67	X	0,67	1,00
Fr4	1,00	0,67	1,00	X	0,33
Fr5	0,67	1,00	0,67	1,00	X

As we can see, only one alternative (NFR Framework) dominates the others without any particular shortcoming in terms of discordance. As a result, this first chunk is selected.

Application of different MC techniques for selecting method chunks gives different results. The simple addition is the simplest technique, but it implies the following disadvantages: a) it does not take into account the relative importance of criteria and b) it is applicable only for numeric or easy quantifiable criteria. The weighted sum supports the criteria relative importance, but saves the restrictions on data type (quantitative). The outranking technique is more complex, its application requires additional skills. Nevertheless, the result is defined more precisely with consideration of all data types. In this case, the chunk "NFR Framework" was selected in order to analyse the requirements of IS security.

Hence, the approaches using diverse MC techniques imply a selection of different method chunks. For this reason, we recommend to use one of strategies described above to specify and to select the method chunks (by addition, by weighting, or by outranking) according to available criteria.

4 Conclusion

We have proposed an adaptation of the existing assembly process with the introduction of MC techniques. The two approaches (basic and extended) may be combined within the same method engineering process as it will offer a more complete guidance to select chunks.

Our objective is twofold. Firstly, we offer the possibility to the method engineer to qualify the method chunks by their correspondence with projects and to choose between similar chunks by an application of MC techniques. Secondly, we propose to characterise the project and the chunks to improve their selection. This typology allows to identify all their critical aspects and to weight them. Within our example, we showed the utility of application of MC techniques and revealed that different MC techniques give different selection result.

In near future, our research perspectives include:

- improve the guidance;
- adapt other situational methods by integrating MC techniques;
- improve the typology presented in this paper in order to take into account other critical characteristics;
- extend the MC techniques application to the field of System Engineering based on MC techniques chunks.

References

1. S. Brinkkemper, Method Engineering: engineering of information systems development method and tools, Information and Software Technology, 38(7), (1996), pp 275-280
2. A.F. Harmsen, Situational Method Engineering, (Moret Ernst Young, 1997)
3. A.F. Harmsen, J.N. Brinkkemper, and J.L.H. Oei , Situational Method Engineering for information Systems Project Approaches, Int. IFIP WG8. 1 Conference in CRIS series: "Methods and associated Tools for the Information Systems Life Cycle", (North Holland, 1994)

4. C. Rolland, V. Plihon, and J. Ralyté, Specifying the reuse context of scenario method chunks, Proceedings of the 10th CAiSE'98 (Pisa, Italy, 1998)
5. R. Deneckere and C. Souveyet, Patterns for Extending an OO Model with Temporal Features, Object Oriented Information Systems (OOIS), (Paris, France, 1998)
6. J. Ralyté, Reusing Scenario Based Approaches in Requirement Engineering Methods: CREWS method base, Proc. 10th DEXA'99, (Los Alamitos, CA, USA, 1999), pp 305-309
7. M. Saeki, CAME: the first step to automated software engineering, Process Engineering for OOPSAL 2003 Workshop, (COTAR, Sydney, 2003)
8. J. Ralyté and C. Rolland, An Assembly Process Model for Method Engineering, Proceedings of the 13th CAISE'01, (Interlaken , Switzerland , 2001) pp. 267-283
9. S. Castano and V. De Antonellis, A Constructive Approach to Reuse of Conceptual Components, Proceedings of Advances in Software Reuse: Selected Papers from the Second International Workshop on Software Reusability, (Lucca, Italy, 1993)
10. G. Bianco, V. De Antonellis, S. Castano, and M. Melchiori, A Markov Random Field Approach for Querying and Reconciling Heterogeneous Databases. Proceedings of the 10th DEXA'99,(Florence, Italy, 1999)
11. K. Van Slooten, B. Hodes, Characterising IS development project, IFIP WG 8.1 Conference on Method Engineering, (Chapman and Hall, 1996), pp. 29-44
12. Mirbel and J. Ralyté, Situational Method Engineering: Combining Assembly-Based and Roadmap-Driven Approaches, Requirements Engineering, 11(1), (2006), pp. 58–78
13. M. Baudry and N. Vincent, Multicriteria decision making, First annual meeting on health science and technology, (Tours, France, 2002)
14. J.A. Gómez-Limón, L. Riesgo, and M. Arriaza, Multi-Criteria Analysis of Factors Use Level: The Case of Water for Irrigation, Proceedings of the 25th International Conference of Agricultural Economists, (2003)
15. K. Wiegers, First Things First: Prioritizing Requirements, Software Development, vol. 7, no. 9, (1999)
16. E. Papadacci, C. Salinesi, and L. Sidler, Panorama des approches d'arbitrage dans le contexte de l'urbanisation du SI, Revue des sciences et techniques de l'information (RSTI), (Hermes, France, 2006)
17. D. Bouyssou, Outranking methods, In Encyclopedia of Optimization, (Kluwer, 2001)
18. B. Roy, Multicriteria Methodology for Decision Aiding, (Dordrecht, Kluwer Academic Publishers, 1996)
19. C. Zopounidis, Décisions financières et analyse multicritère, Encyclopédie de Gestion, (Ed. Economica, Paris, 1997), pp. 915-925
20. R.L. Keeney and H. Raiffa, Decisions with Multiple Objectives: Preferences and Value Trade-Offs, (Cambridge University Press, 1993)
21. T.L. Saaty, The Analytic Hierarchy Process, (NY, McGraw Hill, 1980)
22. R.L. Keeney, Foundations for Making Smart Decisions, IIE Solutions, 31, No. 5, (1999), pp. 24-30
23. R. Fuller and C. Carlsson, Fuzzy multiple criteria decision making: Recent developments, Fuzzy Sets and Systems, 78, (1996), pp. 139-153
24. C. Rolland, N. Prakash, and A. Benjamen, A Multi-Model View of Process Modelling, Requirements Engineering Journal, (1999)
25. L. Chung, B. A. Nixon, E. Yu and J. Mylopoulos, Non-functional requirements in software engineering, (Kluwer Academic Publishers, 1999)
26. Dardenne, A. Lamsweerde, and S. Fickas, Goal-directed Requirements Acquisition, Science of Computer Programming, 20, (Elsevier, 1993), pp. 3-50
27. P. Bresciani, P. Giorgini, F. Giunchiglia, J. Mylopoulos, and A. Perini, TROPOS: An Agent Oriented Software Development Methodology, Journal of Autonomous Agents and MultiAgent Systems, 8(3), (2004), pp. 203-236

28. A.I. Anton, Goal Identification and Refinement in the Specification of Software-Based Information Systems", Ph.D. Dissertation, Georgia Institute of Technology, (Atlanta, USA, 1997)
29. Alexander, Misuse cases help to elicit non-functional requirements, Computing & Control Engineering Journal, 14 (1), (2003), pp. 40-45
30. M. Lassoued and C. Salinesi, Shall IS Security be Treated Differently in the light of the Open World Assumption? A Literature Review, Centre de Recherche en Informatique, University Paris 1, Internal Report, (2006)
31. Kangas, J. Kangas, and J. Pykäläinen, Outranking Methods As Tools in Strategic Natural Resources Planning, 35(2), (Silva Fennica, 2001) pp. 215–227
32. J. Mustajoki, R.P. Hamalainen, and A. Salo, Decision Support by Interval SMART/SWING – Incorporating Imprecision in the SMART and SWING Methods, 36(2), (Decision Sciences, 2005), pp. 317-339
33. M. Poyhonen, R.P. Hamalainen, On the convergence of multiattribute weighting methods, European Journal of Operational Research, 129(3), (2001), pp. 569-585

Appendix 1

This appendix presents a brief description of two groups of MC techniques: outranking and weighting techniques.

Outranking techniques

Outranking techniques [0], [0], [0] are inspired from the theory of social choice [0]. There are two kinds of approaches in the family of outranking techniques: ELECTRE (created by Roy, since 1968) and PROMETHEE (created by Brans J.P., Mareschal B., and Vincke Ph, since 1984) [0], [0]. The most known technique is ELECTRE (ELimination Et Choix Traduisant la REalité, B. Roy / Elimination And Choice Corresponding to Reality). Outranking techniques serve for approaching complex choice problems with multiple criteria and multiple participants. Outranking indicates the degree of dominance of one alternative over another. Outranking techniques enable the utilization of incomplete value information and, for example, judgments on ordinal measurement scale.

It includes the following steps:

1. Calculation of the indices of concordance and discordance on the basis of estimation of two given alternatives. These indices define the concordance and discordance following the assumption that alternative A is preferred to alternative B. The principle is that the decision maker estimates that alternative A is at least as good as B if the majority of the attributes confirm it (concordance principle) and the other attributes (minority) are not strong enough (discordance principle).

2. Definition of levels for the concordance and discordance indices. If the concordance index is higher then defined level and the discordance one is lower, then an alternative is preferred to the other. If it is note the case, alternatives are incompatible (what means that A is preferred to B according to criterion X, and B is preferred to A according to the criterion Y).

3. Elimination of dominated alternatives. Then a first alternatives subset is obtained, which can be either equivalent, or incompatible.

4. Iterative application of stages 2 and 3 with "lower" levels of concordance and discordance indices. A more restricted subset of alternatives is then carried out.

The procedure is applied until a suitable subset is obtained. A last subset includes the best alternatives. The order of the obtained subsets determines the alternatives scale according to their criteria given suitability.

The ELECTRE family has several members: ELECTRE I (for choice problems), ELECTRE II, ELECTRE III, ELECTRE IV (for ranking problems), ELECTRE TRI (for alternatives sorting). An advantage of outranking techniques is that they are based on step-by-step identification of decision makers' preferences. A detailed analysis makes it possible to the decision makers to formulate his preferences and to define compromises between the criteria. The incompatibility relation can be employed to find the contradictory pairs of alternatives, to stop on a subset whose choice is justified (with available information). Difficulties can appear during the weight definition by the decision maker. Moreover, the appearance of the cycles (when alternative A is preferred to B, B is preferred to C and C is preferred to A) is rare but is not excluded.

Weighting techniques

Weighting techniques include SMART (Simple Multiattribute Technical Rating), SWING, and Trade-off weighting [0], [0], and [0]. They are characterised by a weight assignment to the decision criteria. Aggregation of the evaluations is based on weighted sum.

The SMART technique (proposed by W. Edwards), which appeared the first, includes the following stages: criteria scaling according to their importance, criteria attribution of a value from 1 to 100, calculation of the relative importance of each criterion. We call it definition of criteria weights by importance analysis.

In SWING weighting (D. Winterfeldt и W. Edwards), all criteria are supposed bad. The expert chooses the one, which must be improved firstly and a value of 100 is attributed to this criterion. The same operation is carried out with the other criteria to determine their values (by identifying criteria to be improved first).

In Trade-off weighting (H. Raiffa and R.L. Keeney) the decision maker compares two hypothetical alternatives according to two criteria; other criteria are invariable. The weights of these two criteria are refined so that the values of two given weighted alternatives have the same importance for the decision maker. This operation is repeated until all the weights are defined.

Reuse Mechanisms in Situational Method Engineering

Jörg Becker, Christian Janiesch, Daniel Pfeiffer
European Research Center for Information Systems (ERCIS)
University of Münster, Leonardo-Campus 3, 48149 Münster, Germany
{becker,janiesch,pfeiffer}@ercis.de,
WWW home page: http://www.ercis.de

Abstract. Methods describe systematic procedures to overcome problems. It has been widely acknowledged that methods have to be adapted to the context of their application in order to maximize their impact. Since the original proposal of situational method engineering, numerous approaches have been introduced to tackle this problem. In order to efficiently design situation specific methods it is necessary to reuse existing knowledge. Reuse mechanisms have emerged in different research areas that can be transferred to method engineering. The objective of this paper is to identify relevant reuse mechanisms for method engineering and to review the literature for their usage. Thereof, we derive suggestions for the improvement of existing method engineering approaches and the design of new ones.

1 Introduction

Methods describe systematic procedures to overcome problems. Problems can be characterized as the discrepancy between an as-is and a to-be situation. It is widely accepted that a universal method which can be used without modification in all situations is not feasible [1-6]. Rather, appropriate methods for problem solving must be chosen, adapted, or designed depending on the specific characteristics of a situation, such as qualification, number of employees, or available time. In the method engineering community, terms like domain specific method engineering [7, 8] or situational method engineering [9-11] have been used to voice this special circumstance.

To design a method that meets the specific needs of a situation is very time-consuming and costly. Hence, it is not efficient to build situation specific methods from scratch. Rather, it makes sense to reuse existing knowledge to reduce the cost of construction and evaluation. For this purpose reuse approaches such as components, reference models, or patterns have evolved. These approaches have been successfully applied in diverse contexts. The underlying principles of these

Please use the following format when citing this chapter:

Becker, J., Janiesch, C., Pfeiffer, D., 2007, in IFIP International Federation for Information Processing, Volume 244, Situational Method Engineering: Fundamentals and Experiences, eds. Ralyté, J., Brinkkemper, S., Henderson-Sellers B., (Boston Springer), pp. 79-93.

approaches are so called reuse mechanisms. The aim of this paper is to explicate these mechanisms from a method engineering perspective and to propose directions for the improvement of existing and the design of new adaptable methods.

Accordingly, the paper is structured as follows: Following this motivation, a classification of reuse and adaptation approaches and their mechanisms is introduced to provide the basis for the analysis. In Section 3, approaches of situational method engineering are reviewed concerning their exploitation of reuse mechanisms. Section 4 includes a discussion of the literature review as well as a classification of the mechanisms. It concludes the analysis with an outlook and proposal for possible future directions of research on situational method adaptation. The paper closes with a short summary of the main results.

2 Reuse Approaches and Mechanisms

2.1 Reuse approaches

Reuse means to apply the experiences of a former projects to solve an actual problem [12]. This implies that an existing knowledge base is utilized to avoid starting from scratch. For the reuse of knowledge different approaches have been developed that can be found in a similar form in software engineering, conceptual modeling, or method engineering:

Patterns (P): A pattern defines a template to solve a commonly occurring problem [13]. It contains a problem description and the abstract structure of a possible solution. It is necessary to specialize the pattern and to fill the abstract solution with additional information in order to meet the specific conditions of the actual case. A pattern can be applied, when the issue at hand maps with the general problem specification in the pattern. Examples are analysis patterns which contain the knowledge on how to appropriately represent a certain fact in systems analysis or requirements engineering [14]. Patterns are also used to guide model-based design of software [15].

Components (CO): Components are independent items that can be aggregated to form a new artifact [16, 17]. They have been derived from recurrently occurring elements or they are formulated to reach compliance with a certain standard. Components provide a partial solution to a defined problem. Compared with patterns they are more concrete as they can be used without modification. They act as building blocks that can be assembled based on certain rules to achieve an intended solution. Process building blocks are an example for model components [18]. It can be argued that components may also be configured or specialized before or after aggregation. For the sake of selectiveness of mechanisms we have not included this in the overview.

Modules (M): Modules or generic packages are abstract objects which have to be instantiated to be of concrete use. The idea originates from the need in software engineering to know data types before run-time [19]. By implementing a non-type specific package, it can be reused, i.e. instantiated, for various data types. The concept of generic packages [20] carries the idea on to offer unique data structures that can be reused for various data types. Lately, the idea to instantiate reference models emerged [26].

Reference model (RM): A reference model is a robust yet flexible model which comprises universal information that suits more than one situation [22]. Reference models contain information which is relevant for a class of modeling scenarios. The information within these models is applicable to several organizations in different domains. Reference models can be used as-is, but commonly, they are adapted to the specific conditions of a situation. They represent common or best practices and often offer a normative suggestion to solve a certain problem. Compared with components, reference models do not just provide a small part of a solution but they are more comprehensive. Similar to patterns reference models normally also have to be adapted to meet the specific conditions of an organization. Examples for reference models are the Y-CIM model [23] or the Retail-H [24]. Reference models are used by enterprise systems vendors to specify the functionality of their systems [21].

These reuse approaches are rather complementary then competing. For example a reference model can be split up into components and later be aggregated. A reference model can also be part of a pattern. Reference models imply a top down approach. Components help to construct a solution bottom up. Patterns can, depending on their granularity, address both ways. In the next section we want to analyze what basic mechanisms are employed by the reuse approaches.

2.3 Reuse Mechanisms

All reuse approaches are based on a common set of reuse mechanisms [25, 26], which enable their definition and application.

Analogy Construction (AC): An analogy implies the transfer of information from one subject to another. This mechanism is very flexible as it can be drawn from any aspect of an artifact. It is for example used by patterns (P/AC). Patterns employ this mechanism in order to be applicable in domains they were not specifically constructed for. The application of a pattern requires a conclusion by analogy to establish a fit between the problem description in the pattern and the actual situation. Also, reference models or their parts can be the basis of an analogy construction (RM/AC), e.g. as proposed by the ebXML initiative [27]. By the annotation of relevant parts of the reference model, its elements can be reused in different situations.

Aggregation (A): Aggregation assembles independent parts to form a composite. This mechanism is applied by components (CO/A) (cf. e.g. [16, 28]). Interface descriptions of model components offer information on the possibility to combine or integrate the different components and their general compatibility [29]. One might also argue that there are also reference models which support aggregation. These models are not available as monolithic blocks but rather as independent elements that can be assembled [25]. This is rather a special case which does not conform well with our definition of a reference model as one universal model. Hence, we do not consider aggregation a relevant mechanism for reference models.

Configuration (C): Configuration means to modify certain elements of an artifact based on predefined rules that refer to specific project situations. Reference models can be designed as configurable artifacts (RM/C). They are provided with explicit configuration points, which specify model variants regarding purpose-specific characteristics [21, 26]. Based on the specific values assigned to configuration parameters a reference model is projected into a company-specific model. Model elements are removed or modified depending on the parameters. The actual procedure of model projection can be automated based on the prior annotation of configuration parameters to the model.

Specialization (S): Through specialization a particular artifact is derived from a more general artifact by adopting, extending and/or partially modifying the more general one [30]. Reference models can support specialization (RM/S). These reference models have a higher level of abstraction than their organization-specific counterparts. They offer only a relatively low number of model elements. Patterns also use the specialization mechanism in order to transform the solution structure into a concrete solution (P/S).

Instantiation (I): Instantiation selects a specific value or object from a predefined domain with multiple possible occurrences. Instantiation can be applied on modules (M/I). In order to prepare them for this mechanism they must be annotated with placeholders [19, 20]. The placeholders are added during the construction of the module. When a specific module is created, the placeholders are filled with valid occurrences with respect to the particular circumstances. Depending on the properties of the domain, numeric or alphanumeric attributes, distinct elements, or even composed clusters can be defined as placeholders.

Table 1 maps the different reuse mechanisms to their corresponding reuse approaches.

Table 1. Mapping of Identified Mechanisms to Approaches

Mechanism / Approach	Pattern	Component	Module	Reference Model
Analogy Construction	P/AC			RM/AC
Aggregation		CO/A		
Configuration				RM/C
Specialization	P/S			RM/S
Instantiation			M/I	

3 Utilization of Reuse Mechanisms in (Situational) Method Engineering

Since the establishment of the method engineering as an own research field within the IS discipline in the 1990's many suggestions for the design of methods and the combination of their components have been published. In this section the current state-of-the-art of (situational) method engineering research is examined and compared.

In IS literature a method is not considered as a single monolithic block but rather consisting of a set of fragments [e.g. 11, 31, 32, 33], also called chunks [e.g. 34] or components [e.g. 35, 36]. These fragments can have a very different granularity and they can describe the product (what is created) as well as the process aspect (how is it created) of a method. The fragments can comprise a single activity or construct but they can also contain a complete method. Hence, a method engineering project can start with a set of atomic method fragments which must be assembled as well as an existing method which has to be modified [37]. Method engineering research has mainly focused on the first strategy so far [38]. Contrary to that, reuse mechanisms primarily focus on an existing artifact and only additionally consider its design by the aggregation of predefined components. Both strategies are viable approaches to (situational) method engineering as the corresponding mechanisms can be widely found in the method engineering literature as the following review shows (cf. Table 2).

Table 2. Overview of Reuse Mechanisms in Method Engineering Approaches

No.	Reference	Reuse Mechanism	Denotation of the Reuse Mechanism	Objects of the Reuse Mechanism
1	Baskerville and Stage [39]	Aggregation	Accommodation	Method Fragments
		Specialization	Accommodation	Method Fragments
2	Bajec et al. [38]	Configuration	Process Configuration	Base Method, Configuration Rules, Project Characteristics
3	Becker et al. [40]	Configuration	Method Configuration	Configurable Method
4	Brinkkemper et al. [10, 11, 31]	Aggregation	Method Assembly	Method Fragments
5	Cameron [41]	Aggregation	Tailoring	Work Product Descriptions, Work Breakdown Structures
6	Fitzgerald [4]	Aggregation	Method Tailoring	Original Formalized Methodologies
7	Greiffenberg [42]	Aggregation	Creation of Meta Model	Concepts
		Specialization	Choice of Reference Meta Model Scope	Reference Meta Models
		Analogy Construction	Creation of Meta Model	Typing Patterns
8	Gupta and Prakash [16]	Aggregation	Method Assembly	Method Components
9	Henninger [43]	Specialization	Refinement and Tailoring	Software Development Resources
10	Karlsson et al. [36, 44, 45]	Configuration	Configuration Framework	Base Method, Configuration Package, Configuration Template
11	Kumar and Welke [9]	Aggregation	Methodology Engineering	Methodology Components
12	Leppänen [46]	Aggregation	Method Engineering Methodical Skeleton	Contextual Method Components
13	Nuseibeh [47]	Aggregation	Template Reuse	Viewpoint Templates
		Instantiation	Instantiation	Viewpoint Templates

No.	Reference	Reuse Mechanism	Denotation of the Reuse Mechanism	Objects of the Reuse Mechanism
		Specialization	Inheritance	Super Templates
14	Odell [48]	Specialization	Single Framework Modeling	Kernel Meta Model
15	Patel et al. [49]	Aggregation	Selection and Assembly	Method Fragments
		Specialization	Method Tailoring	Method Fragments
16	Punter and Lemmen [32]	Aggregation	Assembly	Method Fragments
17	Ralyté et al. [30, 34, 37, 50]	Aggregation	Assembly-based strategy	Method Chunks
		Specialization	Extension-based strategy, Paradigm-based strategy	Method Chunks, Meta Models
		Analogy Construction	Paradigm-based strategy	Meta Models
18	Rossi et al. [51, 52]	Aggregation	Method Construction	Method Components
		Specialization	Method Refinement	Meta Models
19	Saeki and Wenyin [33]	Aggregation	Method Integration	Meta Models
20	van Offenbeek and Koopman [53]	Specialization/ Analogy Construction	Fit	Scenarios

Harmsen [11], Brinkemper [10] and Brinkkemper et al. [31] focus in their situational method engineering approach in particular on the recombination of method fragments and, thus, are using the mechanism of aggregation. They describe rules in the context of the aggregation to guide the assembly of method fragments. Comparable approaches were for example published by Fitzgerald et al. [4], Gupta and Prakash [16], Punter and Lemmen [32], and Saeki and Wenyin [33]. Kumar and Welke [9] handle methodology components similarly but also stress the disassembly of old methods prior to the assembly of new methods. Cameron [41] puts so called work products together and chooses their temporal order to define a specific development process. Baskerville and Stage [39] as well as Patel et al. [49] emphasize the need to adapt a method after the aggregation by means of deletion, addition and/or modification. This so called method accommodation is considered an application of the specialization mechanism.

Greiffenberg [42] has published a comprehensive approach for the development of modeling languages. Greiffenberg specifies a meta modeling language, a reference meta model, a set of meta modeling patterns as well as a process model for method engineering. Following Greiffenberg, the construction of a meta models is based on concepts. For this purpose the mechanism of aggregation is used. Furthermore, Greiffenberg includes the mechanism of specialization for selecting from the reference model. Analogy construction is taken into consideration by the application of meta modeling patterns.

Henninger et al. [43] and van Offenbeek and Koopman [53] base their methodology on existing scenarios or available resources. They gather contextual factors such as risk to guide the adaptation process of a method. The procedure results ultimately in a refined method that is a specialized version of the original or that is analog to the original. The refinement process is strongly depending on the fit of original model to the specific problem. A configuration in terms of specific adaptation points or parameters is not in focus.

Karlsson and Ågerfalk [45], Karlsson [44], and Karlsson and Wistrand [36] are one of the few authors in method engineering who directly address the mechanism of configuration. Adaptations of methods are performed by the use of configuration packages which rest upon a base method. To manage complex situations with a number of characteristics, configuration packages are combined to configuration templates. Based on the characteristics of a project, an acceptable configuration template is chosen and applied on the base method. Thus, the base method is configured according to the project needs. The configuration of the method focuses only the procedure model. Due to this fact, the modeling language and the resulting products are only indirectly taken into consideration. A comparable approach that also focuses the process part of the method is suggested by Bajec et al. [38]. Becker et al. [40] transfer the mechanisms of configurative reference modeling to the domain of method engineering.

Leppänen [46] also makes use of method components that can be aggregated to form situation-specific methods. He, however, focuses on forming an ontology that assists the selection and combination, i.e. integration, of these components. He provides comprehensive interfaces that explicate the compatibility of method components. However, his ontology is not intended to be the basis for any further configuration and, thus, only provides a means to perform method aggregation.

The approach of Nuseibeh [47] focuses on the multi-perspectivity of software development with the ViewPoint Framework. Due to the abstraction of viewpoints to viewpoint templates, this can be understood as a method engineering approach. New methods can be designed by the combination of viewpoint templates. On the basis of an abstract super template, specialization (inheritance) results in a more specific sub template. By applying the instantiation mechanisms on a viewpoint template, a viewpoint is created.

Odell [48] suggests a basic vocabulary for describing modeling languages, which is called kernel meta model. With the aid of the kernel meta model, which is based on the mechanism of specialization, it is possible to derive specific concepts of meta models. For example, the concept *relation* from the kernel meta model can be specialized as *is super type of*.

Ralyté and Rolland [37] provide a generic process model for situational method engineering. With a map notation they describe different strategies to construct a method that meets the contingencies of a project situation. The *assembly-based strategy* reuses method chunks from a repository and compiles them by applying the aggregation mechanism [30]. The *extension-based approach* uses the specialization mechanism on an existing method and employs patterns to provide novel additions to it [34]. The *paradigm-based approach* takes a meta-model that belongs to a certain theoretical framework as starting point. By analogy construction and specialization the meta model is adapted to the specific needs. Mirbel and Ralyté [50] include the a detailed refinement of a project specific method by each project member. They describe the aggregation of method chunks for the development of project specific methods. For adapting the method with respect to the necessity of every project member, they suggest the adaptation of the procedure (roadmap) of the project specific method by the mechanism of specialization; e.g. the user is able to choose between a prosaic way and use case diagrams to document a requirements analysis depending on his expertise.

Tolvanen [51] and Rossi et al. [52] are highlighting the iterative, incremental aspects of method engineering. They assume that due to the inadequate acknowledgement of the application domain at the beginning of the method engineering project, only a part of the language specification is possible. Thus, an iterative process for evaluation and refinement of the method is necessary to reach an adequate description level for the method. This includes adaptation (specialization) and addition of missed constructs (aggregation). Becker et al. [54] also argue that the feedback of situational adaptations has to be considered in the evolutionary development of a method.

In the next section the results of this literature review are analyzed and implications for method engineering research are derived.

4 Discussion of the Literature Review

Reuse mechanisms can be classified according to different dimensions. One possibility of segmentation is to take the costs of preparation, i.e. the engineering of the situational method, as the first dimension and the cost of utilization, i.e. the reciprocal value of the degree of guidance in adaptation, as second dimension [25, 55].

The costs of preparation depend on how much effort is necessary before a certain mechanism can be used. To be able to apply the mechanisms of *configuration*, rules must be defined and the model elements must be annotated according to the rules. This process is very time-consuming. It is necessary to define the domains of valid values to be able to apply an *instantiation* of the corresponding placeholders. *Aggregation* can specify constraints which restrain the possible combinations of components but such rules are not obligatory. *Specialization* can exclude certain sorts of modification and allows the general adaptation of models. An *analogy construction* can always be applied and does not require any preparation.

The costs of utilization vary on how much the modeler is instructed when a certain mechanism is employed. The guidance in the case of *configuration* is high and consequently, the costs of utilization are low. When the parameters are filled with values the model can be automatically configured. Interactions with the user are only necessary to resolve possible conflicts. *Instantiation* specifies the domain of possible values but gives no hints what values to choose in a certain situation. This leads to higher efforts and thus, higher costs of utilization. The guidance of *aggregations* and *specialization* depends on whether any restrictions have been specified. Aggregation can be directed by interface definitions and specialization can be supported by detailed descriptions of the required actions. *Analogy construction* offers no instructions at all on how to proceed and, hence, it results in the highest cost of utilization. In Fig. 1 the different mechanisms are arranged in a portfolio.

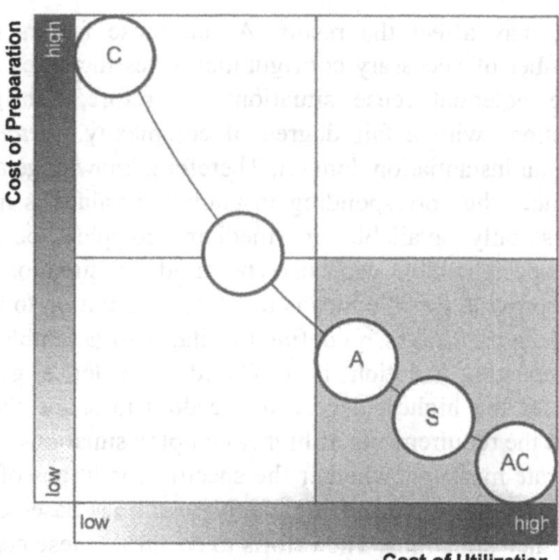

Fig. 1. Cost of Preparation and Cost of Utilization of Reuse Mechanisms [25, 56]

A different possibility to assess reuse mechanisms is by the complexity of the reuse situation and the rate of repetition of the corresponding conditions. In Fig. 2 the different mechanisms are juxtaposed.

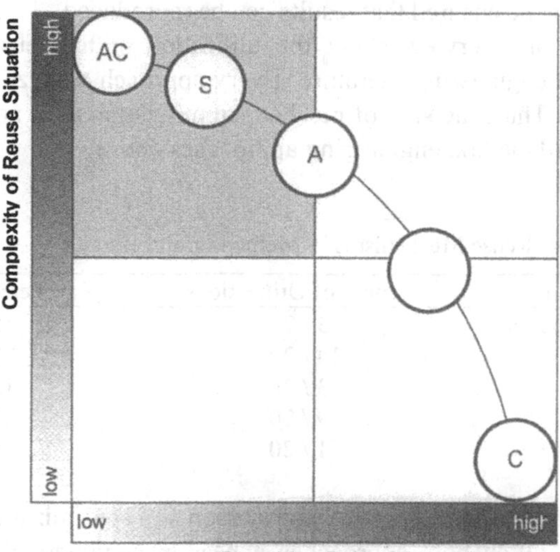

Fig. 2. Applicability of Mechanisms Concerning the Complexity of the Situation and the Repetition Rate of Reuse

The complexity of the reuse situation describes how many contingency factors influence the suitability of a solution. *Configuration* requires anticipating all circumstances that may affect the result. As all these factors can be mutually dependent, the number of necessary configuration rules increases strongly with the complexity of the potential reuse situations. Therefore, configuration is only applicable in situations with a fair degree of complexity. *Instantiation* makes it necessary to define an instantiation domain. Therefore, knowledge about the relevant aspects that influences the corresponding instantiation values is needed. However, this knowledge is only available in medium complex potential situations. Aggregation and specialization can also be used in situations with a higher complexity as they provide flexible means to adapt the solution to the specific needs of a situation. *Aggregation* takes predefined artifacts to assemble a solution; with *specialization* an existing solution is modified with loose guidance. *Analogy construction* provides the highest degree of freedom to shape the result and can, therefore, also meet the requirements of highly complex situations.

The repetition rate measures whether the specific conditions of a reuse situation are unique or rather regularly reoccurring. *Configuration* is based on rules that fit to a number of predefined situations. The efforts to construct these configurations rules only pay off when the repetition rate of the situation is high and, thus, the rules can be applied in more than one situation. *Instantiation* also leads to relatively high cost of preparation but is less strongly coupled with a set of specific situations. *Aggregation* and *specialization* can be used in a much wider variety of situations. Hence, both of them do not depend on a high repetition rate of each single reuse situation. As *analogy construction* does not induce high costs of preparation but can help to construct a solution that meets the specific needs of a project, it can also be applied when the reuse situation is unique. On the downside, its repeatability is very low so that it cannot be ensured that results can be reproduced.

Table 3 gives an overview about the utilization of the reuse mechanisms in situational method engineering literature. Every approach analyzed employs one or more mechanisms. Thus, the sum of mechanism utilization does not add up with the sum of the reviewed method engineering approaches above.

Table 3. Utilization of Reuse Mechanisms in Method Engineering

Reuse Mechanism	Number of Utilizations	Percentage
Analogy Construction	3 / 20	15 %
Aggregation	14 / 20	70 %
Configuration	3 / 20	15 %
Specialization	9 / 20	45 %
Instantiation	1 / 20	5 %

The analysis shows that especially aggregation and specialization are included in many approaches. Often both approaches appear in conjunction (6 out of 20, i.e. 30 %). Analogy construction is related to specialization as a specialization with a very high degree of freedom can lead to similar results as an analogy construction [26]. Furthermore, analogy construction is rarely employed; often it is only used in combination with specialization [37, 42, 53].

It can also be deducted that the configuration and instantiation of methods has not been sufficiently addressed yet. While instantiation was used in only one approach in conjunction with two others, configuration only appeared thrice. Furthermore, when configuration was used, it was always the only mechanism employed in the approach.

Hence, so far method engineers have focused mainly on mechanisms with low costs of preparation but rather high costs of utilization (cf. gray box in Fig. 1). This means that the costs of designing method engineering approaches are comparably low, but only little guidance is given on how to construct a situation specific method. Consequently, method engineering research has mainly focused on complex and singular situations where extensive preparations are not feasible (cf. gray box in Fig. 2). Hence, future method engineering research should also look at less complex but repetitive situations. With domain specific methods [52, 57] the first results from this research stream can be observed.

Ultimately, however, the goal has to be to engineer well-balanced methods, which utilize the most applicable reuse mechanisms for their intended reuse scenario. Since there are as many scenarios, i.e. situations, as there are possible ways to adapt a method no universal answer can be derived from this analysis. However, it is to assume that certain general assumptions hold true:

- If a (part of the) method is used and adapted more often than others and this adaptation can be explicated beforehand, it should be a configurable method.
- If a (part of the) method's general path of adaptation can be foreseen but is not as clearly laid out as with configuration, it should be a method that can be adapted by instantiation.
- If a (part of the) method is very extensive and used in heterogeneous environments so that only a small amount of the originally intended method is used, but this part is used as is, it should be a component-based method.
- If a (part of the) method is used and adapted in a diverse way and only limited adaptations have to take place to create variants, specialization should be used.
- If a (part of the) method is used only seldom and adapted in a very diverse way, the method should be adapted by analogy construction.

Naturally, a method engineering approach can combine multiple of these mechanisms to form an adaptable situational method. For example, a situational method can be aggregated from adaptable components. Some of the components can be configurable, some might only be instantiable or specializable. Some might not even exist and have to be engineered by analogy construction on demand.

Preliminary quantitative analysis hints at the fact that making only a limited but integral part of a method configurable or instantiable, eases the adaptation of the overall method considerably. Cf. for evidence concerning model component configuration of business documents [58]. In this case it was observed that certain central components of a method have been used more often than others. Making only them configurable already allows the method engineering to reduce the adaptation effort of the overall method considerably without reengineering the whole method. This observation goes along with the Pareto principle observed in other areas.

5 Conclusion

It has been widely acknowledged that methods have to be adapted to the context of their application in order to maximize their impact. Situational method engineering is considered to be a reasonable approach to support this adaptation process to reuse existing knowledge.

As preliminary analysis has shown that there are at least three commonly accepted approaches to knowledge reuse that are relevant to method engineering: patterns, components, and reference models. Each of these approaches uses one or more of five distinct reuse mechanisms which facilitate employing existing knowledge to a new situation. A subsequent literature review revealed that only two of these mechanisms are used frequently within situational method engineering: aggregation and specialization. The other three, configuration, analogy construction, and instantiation, all have a specific purpose in method engineering. Their application, however, involves different costs in preparation and utilization compared with the other two mechanisms.

The results at hand, therefore, suggest that a *mechanism mix* should be used when engineering methods that are to be situationally adapted. Central method parts, e.g. aggregateable components, which are used often, should be configurable or at least instantiable, parts of lesser detail and specificity should be specializable or available to analogy construction. It should be avoided to solve all adaptation problems with lesser structured mechanisms as reproducibility and lack of guidance cannot be qualitatively compensated by the cost savings in the preparation of a method.

This entails for method engineers to rethink their method proposals and to consider the herein described mechanisms to enrich and refine their methods with configuration, instantiation, aggregation, specialization, and if necessary analogy construction. It is by no means prescriptive to use more than one of the mechanisms. However, situations may be very diverse – why should not method adaptation be diverse as well?

Future research on this topic will have to deal with an analysis of the actual utilization of the mechanisms of situational methods in case studies. This analysis may point out which mechanisms are considered to be more efficacious than others by method users and can give hints on fruitful future research directions. Furthermore, it will allow validating the five general assumptions we explicated in the previous section.

References

1. F.P. Brooks, Essence and Accidents of Software Engineering, *IEEE Computer* **20**(4), 10-19 (1987).
2. M. Lindvall and I. Rus, Process Diversity in Software Development, *IEEE Software* **17**(4), 14-18 (2000).
3. K. Kautz, The Enactment of Methodology: The Case of Developing a Multimedia Information System, in: Proc. 25th International Conference on Information Systems (ICIS 2004) (Washington, D.C., 2004), pp. 671-683.

4. B. Fitzgerald, N.L. Russo, and T. O'Kane, Software Development: Method Tailoring at Motorola, *Communications of the ACM* **46**(4), 65-70 (2003).
5. K. Wistrand and F. Karlsson, Method Components – Rationale Revealed, in: Proc. 16th International Conference on Advanced Information Systems Engineering (CAiSE 2004) (Riga, 2004), pp. 189-201.
6. A.H.M. ter Hofstede and T.F. Verhoef, On the Feasibility of Situational Method Engineering, *Information Systems* **22**(6/7), 401-422 (1997).
7. S. Kelly, M. Rossi, and J.-P. Tolvanen, What is Needed in a MetaCASE Environment?, *Enterprise Modelling and Information Systems Architectures* **1**(1), 25-35 (2005).
8. J. Luoma, S. Kelly, and J.-P. Tolvanen, Defining Domain-Specific Modeling Languages - Collected Experiences, in: Proc. 4th Object-Oriented Programming Systems, Languages, and Applications Workshop on Domain-Specific Modeling (OOPSLA 2004) (Vancouver, 2004).
9. K. Kumar and R.J. Welke, Methodology Engineering: A Proposal for Situation-specific Methodology Construction, in: Challenges and Strategies for Research in Systems Development, edited by W. W. Cottermann and J. A. Senn (John Wiley & Sons Ltd., Chichester, 1992), pp. 257-269.
10. S. Brinkkemper, Method Engineering - Engineering of Information Systems Development Methods and Tools, *Information and Software Technology* **38**(4), 275-280 (1996).
11. A.F. Harmsen, *Situational Method Engineering* (Twente, Utrecht, 1997).
12. K. Wimmer and N. Wimmer, Conceptual modeling based on ontological principles, *Knowledge Acquisition* **4**(4), 387-406 (1992).
13. C. Alexander, *A Pattern Language: Towns, Buildings, Constructions* (Oxford Univ. Press, New York, 1977).
14. M. Fowler, *Analysis Patterns: Reusable Object Models* (Addison-Wesley, Menlo Park, 1996).
15. E. Gamma, R. Helm, R. Johnson, and J. Vlissides, *Design Patterns: Elements of Reusable Object-Oriented Software* (Addison-Wesley, Reading, 2005).
16. D. Gupta and N. Prakash, Engineering Methods from Method Requirements Specifications, *Requirements Engineering* **6**(3), 135-160 (2001).
17. C. Szyperski, D. Gruntz, and S. Murer, *Component Software: Beyond Object-Oriented Programming* (Addison-Wesley, London, 2003).
18. J. Becker, L. Algermissen, T. Falk, D. Pfeiffer, and P. Fuchs, Model Based Identification and Measurement of Reorganization Potential in Public Administrations – the PICTURE-Approach, in: Proc. 10th Pacific Asia Conference on Information Systems (PACIS) (Kuala Lumpur, 2006), pp. 860-875.
19. P. Slater, Output from generic packages, *ACM SIGAda Ada Letters* **XV**(3), 76-79 (1995).
20. T.C. Jones, Reusability in Programming: A Survey of the State of the Art, *IEEE Transactions on Software Engineering* **10**(5), 488-493 (1984).
21. M. Rosemann and W.M.P. van der Aalst, A Configurable Reference Modelling Language, *Information Systems* **32**(1), 1-23 (2007).
22. J. Becker, M. Kugeler, and M. Rosemann, *Process Management: A Guide for the Design of Business Processes* (Springer, Berlin, 2007).
23. A.-W. Scheer, *Business Process Engineering: Reference Models for Industrial Enterprises* (Springer, Berlin et al., 2002).
24. J. Becker and R. Schütte, *Handelsinformationssysteme* (Redline Wirtschaft, Frankfurt am Main, 2004).
25. J. vom Brocke, Design Principles for Reference Modelling – Reusing Information Models by Means of Aggregation, Specialisation, Instantiation, and Analogy, in: Reference Modeling for Business Systems Analysis, edited by P. Fettke and P. Loos (Idea Group Publishing, Hershey, 2007), pp. 47-75.

26. J. Becker, P. Delfmann, and R. Knackstedt, Adaptive Reference Modeling: Integrating Configurative and Generic Adaptation Techniques for Information Models, in: Proc. Reference Modeling Conference (RefMod) (Passau, 2006).
27. C. Crawford: Core Components Technical Specification - Part 8 of the ebXML Framework. Version 2.01. UN/CEFACT (2003)
28. S. Brinkkemper, M. Saeki, and F. Harmsen, Meta-modelling Based Assembly Techniques for Situational Method Engineering, *Information Systems* **24**(3), 209-228 (1999).
29. M. Leppänen, Contextual Method Integration, in: Advances in Information System Development, edited by G. Knapp, G. Wojtkowski, J. Zupancic, and S. Wrycza (Springer, 2007).
30. J. Ralyté and C. Rolland, An Assembly Process Model for Method Engineering, in: Proc. 13th International Conference on Advanced Information Systems Engineering (CAiSE 2001). Lecture Notes in Computer Science. Vol 2068 (Interlaken, 2001), pp. 267-283.
31. S. Brinkkemper, M. Saeki, and F. Harmsen, Assembly Techniques for Method Engineering, in: Proc. 10th International Conference on Advanced Information Systems Engineering (CAiSE 1998). Lecture Notes in Computer Science (Pisa, 1998), pp. 381-400.
32. T. Punter and K. Lemmen, The MEMA-model: towards a new approach for Method Engineering, *Information and Software Technology* **38**(4), 295-300 (1996).
33. M. Saeki and K. Wenyin, Specifying Software Specification & Design Methods, in: Proc. 6th International Conference on Advanced Information Systems Engineering (CAiSE 1994) (Utrecht, 1994).
34. J. Ralyté and C. Rolland, An Approach for Method Reengineering, in: Proc. 20th International Conference on Conceptual Modeling (ER 2001) (Yokohama, 2001), pp. 471-484.
35. X. Song, Systematic Integration of Design Methods, *IEEE Software* **14**(2), 107-117 (1997).
36. F. Karlsson and K. Wistrand, Combining Method Engineering with Activity Theory: Theoretical Grounding of the Method Component Concept, *European Journal of Information Systems* **15**(1), 82-90 (2006).
37. J. Ralyté, R. Deneckère, and C. Rolland, Towards a Generic Model for Situational Method Engineering, in: Proc. 15th International Conference on Advanced Information Systems Engineering (CAiSE 2003) (Klagenfurt, 2003), pp. 95-110.
38. M. Bajec, D. Vavpotič, and M. Krisper, Practice-driven Approach for Creating Project-specific Software Development Methods, *Information and Software Technology* **49**(4), 345-365 (2007).
39. R. Baskerville and J. Stage, Accommodating Emergent Work Practices: Ethnographic Choice of Method Fragements, in: Proc. IFIP TC8/WG8.2 Working Conference on Realigning Research and Practice in IS Development: The Social and Organisational Perspective (Boise, ID, 2001), pp. 12-28.
40. J. Becker, R. Knackstedt, D. Pfeiffer, and C. Janiesch, Configurative Method Engineering: On the Applicability of Reference Modeling Mechanisms in Method Engineering, in: Proc. 13th Americas Conference on Information Systems (AMCIS 2007) (Keystone, CO, 2007).
41. J. Cameron, Configurable Development Processes, *Communications of the ACM* **45**(3), 72-77 (2002).
42. S. Greiffenberg, *Methodenentwicklung in Wirtschaft und Verwaltung* (Verlag Dr. Kovac, Hamburg, 2003).
43. S. Henninger, A. Ivaturi, K. Nuli, and A. Thirunavukkaras, Supporting Adaptable Methodologies to Meet Evolving Project Needs, in: Proc. Joint Conference on XP Universe and Agile Universe (Chicago, IL, 2002), pp. 33-44.
44. F. Karlsson: Method Configuration: Method and Computerized Tool Support. Linköping (2005)

45. F. Karlsson and P.J. Ågerfalk, Method Configuration: Adapting to Situational Characteristics While Creating Reusable Assets, *Information and Software Technology* **46**(9), 619-633 (2004).
46. M. Leppänen: An Ontological Framework and a Methodical Skeleton for Method Engineering: A Contextual Approach. Jyväskylä (2005)
47. B.A. Nuseibeh: A Multi-Perspective Framework for Method Integration. London (1994)
48. J. Odell, Meta-modelling, in: Proc. OOPSLA'95 Workshop on Metamodelling in OO (Austin, TX, 1995).
49. C. Patel, S. de Cesare, N. Iacovelli, and A. Merico, A Framework for Method Tailoring: A Case Study, in: Proc. 2nd OOPSLA Workshop on Method Engineering for Object-Oriented and Component-Based Development (Vancouver, 2004).
50. I. Mirbel and J. Ralyté, Situational Method Engineering: Combining Assembly-based and Roadmap-driven Approaches, *Requirements Engineering* **11**(1), 58-78 (2006).
51. J.-P. Tolvanen: Incremental Method Engineering with Modeling Tools: Theoretical Principles and Empirical Evidence. Jyväskylä (1998)
52. M. Rossi, B. Ramesh, K. Lyytinen, and J.-P. Tolvanen, Managing Evolutionary Method Engineering by Method Rationale, *Journal of the Association for Information Systems* **5**(9), 356-391 (2004).
53. M.A.G. van Offenbeek and P.L. Koopman, Scenarios for System Development: Matching Context and Strategy, *Behaviour & Information Technology* **15**(4), 250-265 (1996).
54. J. Becker, C. Janiesch, S. Seidel, and C. Brelage, A Framework for Situational and Evolutionary Language Adaptation in Information Systems Development, in: Advances in Information System Development, edited by G. Knapp, G. Wojtkowski, J. Zupancic, and S. Wrycza (Springer, 2007).
55. A. Mili, S.F. Chmiel, R. Gottumukkala, and L. Zhang, An Integrated Cost Model for Software Reuse, in: Proc. 22nd International Conference on Software Engineering (Limerick, Ireland, 2000), pp. 157-166.
56. J. Becker, C. Janiesch, and D. Pfeiffer, Towards more Reuse in Conceptual Modeling: A Combined Approach using Contexts, in: Proc. 19th International Conference on Advanced Information Systems Engineering (CAiSE 2007) Forum (Trondheim 2007).
57. G. Guizzardi, L.F. Pires, and M.J.v. Sinderen, On the Role of Domain Ontologies in the Design of Domain-Specific Visual Modeling Languages, in: Proc. 17th ACM Conference on Object-Oriented Programming, Systems, Languages and Applications (OOPSLA 2002) (Seattle, WA, 2002).
58. C. Janiesch, Implementing Views on Business Semantics: Model-based Configuration of Business Documents, in: Proc. 15th European Conference on Information Systems (ECIS 2007) (St. Gallen, 2007).

Developer Driven Approach to Situational Method Engineering

Antero Järvi[1], Harri Hakonen[2], and Tuomas Mäkilä[1]

[1] Department of Information Technology, University of Turku, Finland
[2] Aginit Oy, Turku, Finland
antero.jarvi@utu.fi

This position paper reflects SME into software development. We argue that to apply SME in software development projects, construction of method fragments should also take place during the project by the method users. The topic is current due to two key technologies, EPF and SPEM, that enable illustrative and prompt method construction. The paper looks at the relevant background in both SME and software development processes, identifies four levels of method management work, discusses the method reuse strategy, and presents an example of on-the-fly method construction.

1 Introduction

Our background is on software engineering and on pragmatic research with the companies. Currently, we focus on process modeling technologies and their utilization in, for example, reducing the process/project gap. To retain the applicability of the results we work with the processes and process frameworks that are in real use. It has turned out that our work is closely related to Situational Method Engineering (SME) in the Information Systems field, and we see direct applicability of the SME concepts in the software development projects. In what follows, we use 'process' and 'method' as synonyms.

The topic of this paper has become significant due to recent technological advances that have improved our ability to create, organize, reuse, and manage methods. Two key technologies are The Software Process Engineering Metamodel (SPEM) and The Eclipse Process Framework (EPF). SPEM is a standard for defining processes and process components and it is fostered by Object Management Group (OMG). Currently, version 2.0 is at the final stage of standarization [1]. EPF is an open source project that provides tools and content for software process engineering [2]. The EPF Composer supports for all essential SPEM modeling mechanisms although it is not fully SPEM compliant.

Situational Method Engineering (SME) focuses on providing techniques and tools for creating and using project specific methods, instead of having a single generic method. The fundamental goal is to achieve flexibility, as opposed to rigid methods, without sacrificing control over the development project. There are several approaches for pursuing this goal that are reviewed and summarized

Please use the following format when citing this chapter:

Järvi, A., Hakonen, H., Mäkilä, T., 2007, in IFIP International Federation for Information Processing, Volume 244, Situational Method Engineering: Fundamentals and Experiences, eds. Ralyté, J., Brinkkemper, S., Henderson-Sellers B., (Boston Springer), pp. 94-99.

in [3]. The majority of SME methods approach the goal by creating situational method fragments that are selected according to project's situation and then assembled into a project specific method. Another strategy is to start with a full method framework comprising of myriad of method contents capable of supporting a wide range of project situations. A workable method is obtained by configuring the framework with the characteristics of a particular project, or common characteristics of several projects. This approach is widely used in software development industry; a well known example of such commercial method frameworks is Rational Unified Process (RUP) [4].

Distinctive work in flexible processes in the software engineering field includes Boehm's risk-based approach for making methodology decisions that integrate agile and plan-driven practices [5]. In Cockburn's approach, a method is selected according to staffing size and system criticality [6]. Even though this aims at pre-selecting the method, changing the selected method during the project is not uncommon. This indicates the difficulty of seeing the situational forces in advance and the volatility of the project situation.

While these approaches have many differences, they all share a common attribute: separation of method design from its use in terms of time and participation roles. Methods are designed almost solely in advance by method engineers. Also, project specific methods are typically created at the beginning of the project by a method engineer that is external to project's staffing. Recent approaches shift part of the method design into method users' responsibility. Mirbel and Ralyté describe a two step method approach: The first step builds a new method adapted for project situation, while the second step allows the method users to configure further the obtained method for their particular needs [7]. However, the method users do not create new solutions for the situation, but they select what existing method guidance is used in the project. This is very different from a practice-driven approach by Ivar Jacobson et al. [8]. The approach puts a reusable practice in the center of process design; teams will mix and match practices to create efficient ways of working. Practices are used in a framework that allow, for example, to track how value is created and captured in work products.

The hallmarks of recognized SME approaches – separating software process design from its use, externalizing process knowledge and structuring the process modules to form a coherent system – form only one possible strategy for coping with the complexity and uncertainty of current software projects [9]. We argue that this strategy should be complemented with developer driven method design also during the project execution in the real project context.

2 Method management strategy

We identify four levels of method engineering. Firstly, *method library management* takes a facilitating viewpoint to process use. A practical goal is to maintain method content modularized so that method use and reuse in the other three levels is expedient. This level is the responsibility of method engineers and higher management. Secondly, *project specific method design* describes a method for a particular project situation. The method imposes control onto the development, but leaves choices open where need for adaptation is anticipated. This level implements planned process flexibility. Thirdly, *method fitting* is the responsibility of the process users. Based on the project's real situation, the users select method content that best fits their needs. The fitting is constrained by the project specific method. Fourthly, *on-the-fly method construction* responses to unanticipated situations. A new method fragment is created in the project's process context. The constructed fragment communicates the plan for coping with the situation to all participants, and documents it for further use in process improvement activities.

The balance between these four levels of method engineering should be treated as a strategic choice depending on the company's business and individual project's method needs. One of the main issues is the balance between repeatability and helping the project staff to manage the unanticipated situations. It is evident that one scheme does not fit all needs; some companies operate in a highly dynamic business environment, whereas others operate in a stable business context [10]. The former will not benefit from rigid method repositories. Instead, the strategy should emphasize facilitation of the on-the-fly method construction with method fragments that reflect the teams true capabilities and can be combined flexibly and promptly. The project situation, involving both the business and engineering contexts, resolves on what levels we should put the emphasis.

Business context involves any goals that the project has in addition to producing the deliverables. Requirement of high predictability of cost and time of delivery, need to demonstrate quality or progress during the project, and creating reusable software components highlight the need for the project specific method design. High emphasis on time-to-market and innovative or technically challenging products require maneuverability of the teams. In this kind of surroundings the method is used as a facilitator of team capabilities in unexpected situations. This calls for on-the-fly method construction.

Engineering context involves the predictability and the stability of the method needs in a project. For example, a project affected by many forces not controlled by itself has unpredictable method needs. An unstable project has characteristics that change over time, for example, growing project staff or decision to outsource parts of development. The less predictable and stable the project is, the more we have to rely on on-the-fly method construction.

3 Method reuse strategy

The reusability of a method fragment is determined by its project situation coverage and the engineering scope it impacts, illustrated in Fig. 1. Wide project situation coverage implies high reuse value, whereas a fragment with narrow coverage describes a solution to an unfrequent situation. The upper levels of method management strategy should concern fragments of high reuse value. Wide engineering scope means that the fragment affects several development disciplines, and thus, should not be tampered with from a local point of view without proper authorization. Fragments with narrow engineering scope are localized and have well-defined and explicit interdependencies in the process.

Every company has a unique mixture of method needs from each of the quadrants, and the challenge is to make the method quadrants work together. Method fragments in the on-the-fly quadrant are solutions to local and possibly unique situations. The challenge is how to construct methods on the fly without impeding software development. The practice quadrant together with the disciplined quadrant is the home ground of SME allowing specific method design for wide range of process types. The challenge is the compatibility and composability of the method fragments so that they can form a seamless method. The disciplined quadrant captures the backbone and dominant assumptions of methods. The challenge is how to retain the process user's ability to modify the method using fragments from practice quadrant [10]. The specialized methods do not involve the reuse aspect, but are highly efficient end-to-end methods for a specific development purpose.

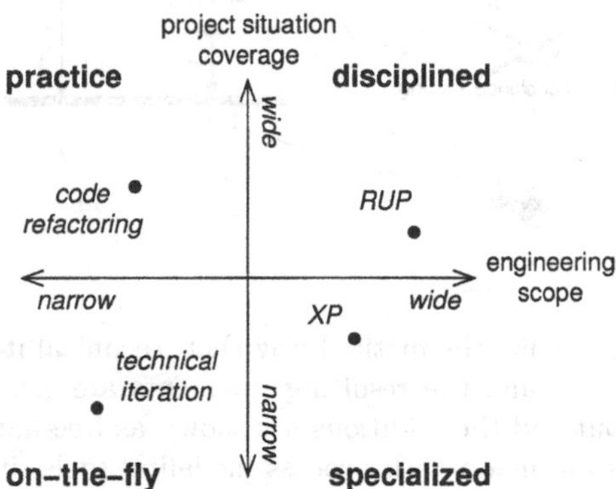

Fig. 1. Project situation coverage and engineering scope characterize the reuse strategy of a method fragment. 'Technical iteration' is an example of the result of on-the-fly construction, 'code refactoring' is a highly reusable fragment having only a local impact, 'RUP' is an example where project dependent practices are intertwined into a process backbone. 'XP' is specialized method for situations including on-site customer, single development team and no architectural risks.

4 Example of the on-the-fly method construction

The following example serves two purposes: Firstly, it shows a typical on-the-fly constructed fragment, and secondly, it illustrates how effortless on-the-fly construction can be made. The example in Fig. 2 is taken from a real project using an agile development process in *Gaudí Software Factory* [11]. The method modification concerns using a customer requirement driven development iteration as a stating point for creating an iteration where the focus is on solving the technical challenges of the product and new customer requirements are not added. The customer driven acceptance testing is replaced with exploratory testing that is run by the technical expert. 'Write user manual' is removed as unnecessary and 'Refactor' is added to improve the code quality.

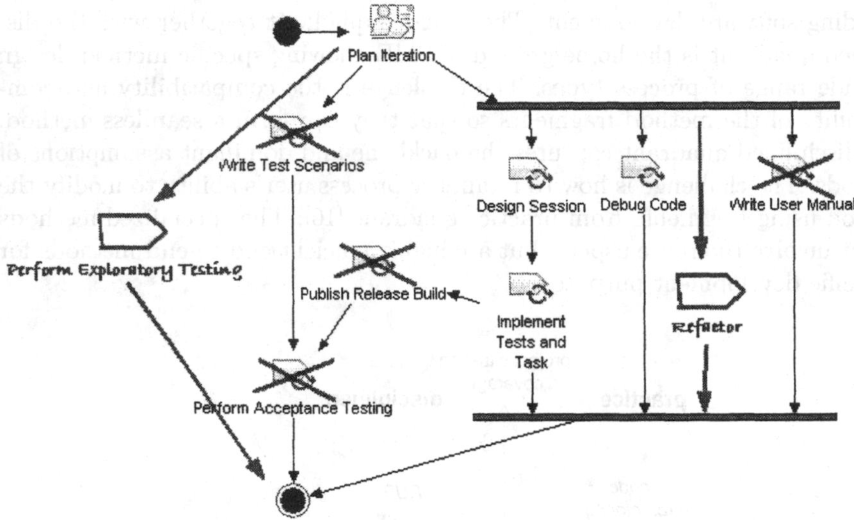

Fig. 2. Example of developing the method fragment 'technical iteration' in on-the-fly construction. The starting and the resulting fragments are combined. The removed activities are crossed out and the additions are shown as free-hand symbols. In practice, the modifications are made with process modeling tools, in this case EPF 1.0. Free-hand graphics is used here for illustrative purposes.

The example demonstrates that on-the-fly construction does not go into details, instead it should focus on devising a plan rather than writing guidance. When this is combined with reusing existing process fragments (e.g. 'refactor' in the example) the construction becomes rapid. The fragment representation is understandable, it communicates the created solution, and shows explicitly the dependencies of the fragment so that they can be taken into account. Finally, the created fragment would probably be useful in other projects and can be analyzed and refined into a reusable practice.

5 Conclusion

The recent development in process standards and tools makes on-the-fly method and method fragment construction feasible in practice. This enables us to allocate part of process management work to development teams: (i) The methods can reach down to operational level development work as it is carried out in the project, narrowing the process/project gap, and (ii) the actual process needs in projects can be captured by on-the-fly construction and they can be communicated to process management to keep processes up to date.

Integrating on-the-fly method construction into existing process management practices is not straightforward. We have presented four levels of process management strategy, and outlined a framework for understanding the reuse strategy and realization of the fragments. However, there are open questions on, for example, structuring of method libraries, composability of method fragments and backbones, roles and responsibilities in process management, and process improvement practices. On-the-fly method construction itself needs further research, in particular the required tool support, the modeling conventions, and sufficient content and level of details in the constructed models.

References

1. Object Management Group. *Software Process Engineering Metamodel Specification, v2.0 Final Adopted Specification ptc/07-03-03*, 2007. http://www.omg.org/cgi-bin/doc?ptc/07-03-03.
2. Eclipse process framework project homepage. http://www.eclipse.org/epf/. Accessed on May 31 2007.
3. Mauri Leppänen. Conceptual evaluation of methods for engineering situational ISD methods. *Softw. Process Improve. Pract.*, 11:539–555, 2006.
4. Philippe Kruchten. *The Rational Unified Process: An Introduction (Second Edition)*. Addison-Wesley Professional, March 14 2000.
5. Barry Boehm and Richard Turner. *Balancing Agility and Discipline, A Guide for the Perplexed*. Addison-Wesley, 2003.
6. Alistair Cockburn. Selecting a projects methodology. *IEEE Software*, pages 64–71, July/August 2000.
7. Isabelle Mirbel and Jolita Ralyté. Situational method engineering: combining assembly-based and roadmap-driven approaches. *Requirements Engineering*, 11:58–78, 2006.
8. Ivar Jacobson, Pan-Wei Ng, and Ian Spence. Enough of processes: Let's do practices part I. *Dr.Dobb's Journal*, April 2007.
9. Ivan Aaen. Software process improvement: Blueprints versus receipes. *IEEE Software*, pages 86–93, October 2003.
10. Antero Järvi, Tuomas Mäkilä, and Harri Hakonen. Changing role of SPI — opportunities and challenges of process modeling. In *The Proceedings of the 13th European Conference, EuroSPI 2006*, LNCS 4257, 2006.
11. Ralph-Johan Back, Luka Milovanov, and Ivan Porres. Software development and experimentation in an academic environment: The Gaudí factory. In *Product Focused Software Process Improvement*, LNCS 3547, 2005.

Characterizing Knowledge Intensive Tasks indicating Cognitive Requirements;
Scenarios in Methods for Specific Tasks

S.J. Overbeek[1], P. van Bommel[2], H.A. (Erik) Proper[2], and D.B.B. Rijsenbrij[2]

[1] e-office B.V., Duwboot 20, 3991 CD Houten, The Netherlands, EU
Sietse.Overbeek@e-office.com

[2] Institute for Computing and Information Sciences, Radboud University Nijmegen, Toernooiveld 1, 6525 ED Nijmegen, The Netherlands, EU
{P.vanBommel, E.Proper, D.Rijsenbrij}@cs.ru.nl

Abstract. Methods for specific tasks can among others be identified in conceptual modeling of information systems and requirements engineering in software development. Such methods dictate a specific way of working by describing necessary knowledge intensive tasks to fulfill while applying the method. An actor may experience difficulties when trying to fulfill tasks as part of a method application, related to the cognitive abilities required to fulfill a certain task versus the specific cognitive abilities possessed by the actor. This paper specifically focusses on the cognitive abilities required to fulfill a knowledge intensive task while applying a method for specific tasks. This is based on a categorization and characterization of knowledge intensive tasks and on scenarios in conceptual modeling of information systems and requirements engineering.

1 Introduction

Methods for specific tasks contain a *way of working*, which is the strategy determining the manner how the method should be applied. This includes the necessary knowledge intensive tasks to fulfill when using a method in a certain context. When fulfilling a certain task, an actor that is applying a method may experience difficulties during a task's fulfillment. Independent of other reasons that may contribute to the existence of those difficulties, the research reported in this paper is concerned with the *cognitive* abilities necessary to execute a certain task while applying a method, as is shown in figure 1. As is described by Meiran [6] and Schraagen et al. [8], research in task analysis has a cognitive basis in psychological research. Analyzing task fulfillment from a cognitive viewpoint may yield knowledge underlying an actor's task performance. The research reported in this paper is part of an ongoing research effort to better understand cognitive settings of actors that are applying a method for specific tasks versus the cognitive abilities required to fulfill a typical task. As part of this ongoing research, it is also our wish to provide automated support to assist

Please use the following format when citing this chapter:

Overbeek, S. J., van Bommel, P., Proper, H. A. (Erik), Rijsenbrij, D. B. B., 2007, in IFIP International Federation for Information Processing, Volume 244, Situational Method Engineering: Fundamentals and Experiences, eds. Ralyté, J., Brinkkemper, S., Henderson-Sellers B., (Boston Springer), pp. 100-114.

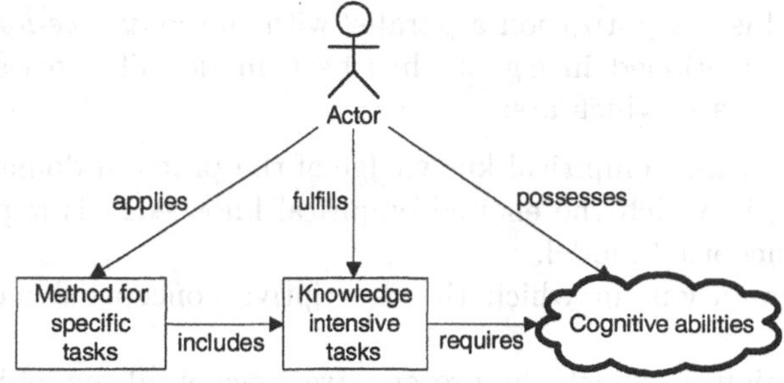

Fig. 1. Cognitive abilities during task fulfillment in a method.

an actor (characterized by a certain cognitive setting) in fulfilling a certain task (characterized by the cognitive abilities required to fulfill it). This automated support should be able to guide an actor that is applying a method through task fulfillment if his cognitive setting may cause difficulties in fulfilling a task.

To better understand knowledge intensive tasks and the nature of it, basic definitions are discussed in section 2.1. Then, the distinguished tasks are classified by their properties indicating an actor's requirements from a cognitive point of view. These properties are further elaborated in sections 2.2 and 2.3 and materialized in methods for specific tasks within conceptual modeling of information systems and requirements engineering (see sections 3 and 4). This leads up to two scenarios in which required cognitive abilities are denoted while fulfilling tasks in conceptual modeling and requirements engineering. Section 5 briefly compares our model with other approaches in the field and outlines benefits of our approach compared to others. Section 6 concludes this paper.

2 Categorizing and Characterizing Knowledge Intensive Tasks

Exploring the fundamentals of knowledge intensive tasks is necessary to gain a better understanding of that what we would like to categorize and characterize. The following subsections provide definitions and a cognition-based characterization of knowledge intensive tasks.

2.1 Basic Definitions

As the notion *knowledge intensive task* suggests, knowledge is very important and also emphatically present during an actor's fulfillment of a knowledge intensive task. It is relevant to mention that, according to Liang [4], knowledge can be regarded as 'wrapped' in information, whilst information is 'carried' by data (expressions in a symbol language). To be able to reason about those tasks on a conceptual level, a general categorization of knowledge intensive tasks is suggested. For this categorization a parallel with the *inductive-hypothetical research strategy* mentioned in e.g. [9] has been made. This research strategy consists of five phases, which are:

1. Initiation, in which empirical knowledge of the problem domain is elicited.
2a. Abstraction, in which the elicited empirical knowledge is applied in a descriptive conceptual model.
2b. Theory formulation, in which the descriptive conceptual model is made prescriptive.
3a. Implementation, in which the prescriptive conceptual model is empirically tested.
3b. Evaluation, a comparison of the elicited empirical knowledge (1) with the prescriptive empirical model (3a).

Following the research approach, possible knowledge intensive tasks that can be fulfilled can be abstracted to a pattern of three types:

1. `Acquisition` tasks, which are related with the *acquisition* of knowledge. This can be illustrated by a student reading a book in order to prepare himself for an exam.
2. `Synthesis` tasks, which are related with the actual utilization of the acquired knowledge. An example is a student who utilizes knowledge (acquired by reading a book) while performing an exam.
3. `Testing` tasks, which are related with the identification and application of knowledge in practice inducing an improvement of the specific knowledge applied. E.g. a student who failed an exam studies a teacher's feedback on his exam. Then a re-examination attempt follows to improve his previously acquired and utilized knowledge.

The execution of an acquisition task can be compared to going through an *initiation* phase of the inductive-hypothetical research strategy to acquire knowledge and to understand the problem domain well enough so that the acquired knowledge can be abstracted to conceptual models as a next step. The *abstraction* and *theory formulation* phases of the aforementioned research strategy can be compared to the nature of a synthesis task, viz. applying elicited knowledge into a descriptive and a prescriptive conceptual model. The nature of an *implementation* phase and an *evaluation* phase is comparable to what is conducted in a testing task, namely to gain feedback by testing earlier elicited and applied knowledge. In the research strategy this can be translated to testing the prescriptive conceptual model and further the comparison of the elicited knowledge from the initiation phase with the prescriptive empirical model from the implementation phase. Now the set of tasks can be represented as:

$$\mathcal{TA} \triangleq \{\texttt{acquisition}, \texttt{synthesis}, \texttt{testing}\} \quad (1)$$

A specific instantiation of such a task is expressed by $\mathsf{Task} : \mathcal{TI} \to \mathcal{TA}$, where $\mathcal{TI}$ is a set of *task instances* which are fulfilled by an actor. Given a task instance i of a task $\mathsf{Task}(i)$, we can view the actor that is specifically fulfilling a task instance as a function $\mathsf{Fulfillment} : \mathcal{AC} \to \mathcal{TI}$. Here, $\mathcal{TI}$ is a set of task instances which are fulfilled by an actor (which is part of a set of actors $\mathcal{AC}$).

2.2 Characterization of Knowledge Intensive Tasks

The following properties are going to be discussed to characterize knowledge intensive tasks:

- The property of *satisfaction* is related with a need for knowledge during a task's fulfillment and the eventual disappearance of that need.
- *Relevance* is concerned with whether or not knowledge acquired is deemed appropriate during the fulfillment of a task.
- The *applicability* property expresses to what extent knowledge is applicable in a task.
- When knowledge is applied it should meet its requirements. This is indicated by the *correctness* property.
- The *faultiness* property is necessary to be able to determine whether or not applied knowledge contains flaws.
- To correct already applied knowledge containing flaws, the *rectification* property can be determined.

Formally, the set of task properties can be represented as:

$$\mathcal{CP} \triangleq \{\texttt{satisfaction}, \texttt{relevance}, \texttt{applicability}, \texttt{correctness}, \texttt{faultiness}, \texttt{rectification}\} \quad (2)$$

The properties shown in table 1 are globally discussed independent from each other in the following sections. We understand that there may be other properties requiring specific cognitive abilities when fulfilling knowledge intensive tasks, but in this paper we will limit ourselves to the mutually independent properties mentioned above. The function $\mathsf{Characterization} : \mathcal{TA} \rightarrow \wp(\mathcal{CP})$ specifies which properties belong to a certain task. So following from table 1 an actor fulfilling e.g. an acquisition task should have the cognitive abilities to adhere to the *satisfaction* as well as the *relevance* property.

Table 1. Characterization of knowledge intensive tasks by their properties

	$\mathcal{CP}$					
$\mathcal{TA}$	Satisfaction	Relevance	Applicability	Correctness	Faultiness	Rectification
Acquisition	×	×	–	–	–	–
Synthesis	–	–	×	×	–	–
Testing	×	–	×	–	×	×

2.3 Definitions of Knowledge Intensive Task Properties

Before materializing the six task properties of table 1 in methods for specific tasks, the properties themselves are elaborated in this section.

Satisfaction The first property that is discussed is the property of *satisfaction*. A task has a *satisfaction* property, if a need for certain knowledge is present during task fulfillment and that need is indulged if the required knowledge is acquired. The need for knowledge is influenced by what an actor already has received in the past. This can be modeled as a function:

$$\mathsf{Need} : \mathcal{AS} \rightarrow (\wp(\mathcal{KA}) \rightarrow \mathcal{KA} \mapsto [0,1]) \tag{3}$$

The set $\mathcal{AS}$ contains *actor states*. The introduction of an actor state is necessary to understand how an actor's need for knowledge changes over time. The set $\mathcal{KA}$ represents the *knowledge assets* an actor may receive. These *assets* are tradeable forms of knowledge, i.e. knowledge which actors can exchange with each other. This may include knowledge obtained by viewing a Web site or a document or by conversing with a colleague. When an instructor explains a learner how to drive a car for instance, the explanation may contain valuable knowledge assets for the learner. $\mathsf{Need}_t(\mathcal{S}, k)$ is interpreted as the residual need for a knowledge asset k of an actor in state t after the set $\mathcal{S}$ has been presented to an actor, where $t \in \mathcal{AS}$, $k \in \mathcal{KA}$ and $\mathcal{S} \subseteq \mathcal{KA}$. The set $\mathcal{S}$ can be interpreted as the personal knowledge of an actor (also called a knowledge profile). When an actor a in state t experiences a knowledge asset k, then this actor will end up in a new state denoted as $t \ltimes k$:

$$\ltimes : \mathcal{AS} \times \mathcal{KA} \rightarrow \mathcal{AS} \tag{4}$$

No more knowledge is required by an actor if his need for knowledge deteriorates after experiencing the required knowledge, which is denoted by $\mathsf{Need}_{t \ltimes k}(\mathcal{S}, k) = 0$. Note that $\mathsf{Need}_{t \ltimes k}(\mathcal{S}, k) \equiv \mathsf{Need}(t \ltimes k, \mathcal{S}, k)$. However, it is not always necessary to include an actor's state for some of the task properties discussed and can, therefore, be omitted if desired.

An actor's *input* and *output* of knowledge are also considered as important concepts as part of the task properties. Input and output of knowledge assets can be represented as:

$$\mathsf{In}, \mathsf{Out} : \mathcal{AS} \rightarrow (\mathcal{AC} \rightarrow \wp(\mathcal{KA})) \tag{5}$$

Now that an indicator of the need for knowledge and the notation for input and output of knowledge have been explained, the satisfaction property can be assembled:

$$\mathsf{Satisfaction} : \mathsf{Need}_t(\mathcal{S}, k) > 0 \wedge k \in \mathsf{In}_t(a) \Rightarrow \mathsf{Need}_{t \ltimes k}(\mathcal{S}, k) = 0 \tag{6}$$

The satisfaction property includes an actor having a need for knowledge asset k while experiencing state t. To be able to adhere to the satisfaction property, such an actor receives knowledge asset k while in state t. When the actor is in a succeeding state $t \ltimes k$ the need for that specific knowledge asset k deteriorates indicating his specific needs have been satisfied. So if an actor still requires, say, knowledge assets k_1 and k_2 to complete a task, that actor should continue to gather knowledge until $\mathsf{Need}(\mathcal{S}, k_1) = 0$ and $\mathsf{Need}(\mathcal{S}, k_2) = 0$. An acquisition task as well as a testing task have this property. Both tasks require knowledge input, meaning that an actor is satisfied if the required knowledge has been obtained.

Relevance A task has a *relevance* property if, during fulfillment of a task, the knowledge acquired is indeed needed by an actor. To acquire relevant knowledge, an actor should experience a need for the knowledge to be acquired and an actor's knowledge profile should not already contain the knowledge to be acquired:

$$\mathsf{Relevance}: k \in \mathsf{In}(a) \Leftrightarrow \mathsf{Need}(\mathcal{S}, k) > 0 \wedge k \notin \mathcal{S} \tag{7}$$

To make sure that an actor solely acquires relevant knowledge, the relevance property should be adhered to when executing an acquisition task.

Applicability A task has an *applicability* property if knowledge is applied during task fulfillment and that applied knowledge has a useful effect on successfully completing the task. To understand to what extent knowledge is applicable for a task, i.e. has a useful effect for completing the task, the following function is necessary:

$$\mathsf{Applicable}: \mathcal{TI} \times \mathcal{KA} \mapsto [0,1] \tag{8}$$

If a knowledge asset k is not applicable at all for a task instance i the function equals 0: $\mathsf{Applicable}(i,k) = 0$. If a knowledge asset k is most applicable for a task, the function equals 1. An actor adheres to the *applicability* property only if a certain knowledge asset k is applicable during a task instance:

$$\mathsf{Applicability}: k \in \mathsf{Out}(a) \Leftrightarrow \mathsf{Applicable}(i,k) > 0 \wedge k \in \mathcal{S} \tag{9}$$

The applicability property is not relevant for an acquisition task, because knowledge is not applied in such a task.

Correctness A task has a *correctness* property when the knowledge that is applied is useful for the specific task and the applied knowledge meets its requirements. To be able to determine whether or not applied knowledge is correct it should thus meet its *requirements.* The following function is therefore introduced:

$$\mathsf{Requirement} \subseteq \mathcal{KA} \times \wp(\mathcal{RQ}) \tag{10}$$

Suppose that a knowledge asset k should meet two requirements r_1 and r_2 which are part of a set of requirements $\mathcal{R}$. Then if knowledge k is applied and indeed meets its requirements this is indicated by $(k, \{r_1, r_2\}) \in \mathsf{Requirement}$. The correctness property can now be conceived as follows:

$$\mathsf{Correctness}: \mathsf{Applicable}(i,k) > 0 \wedge k \in \mathsf{Out}(a) \Leftrightarrow (k, \mathcal{R}) \in \mathsf{Requirement} \wedge k \in \mathcal{S} \tag{11}$$

Faultiness A *faultiness* property is part of a task if it is necessary to indicate if certain knowledge that has been obtained by an actor is not meeting its requirements:

$$\mathsf{Faultiness}: \mathsf{In}(a) = \mathcal{K} \wedge (k, \mathcal{R}) \notin \mathsf{Requirement} \wedge k \in \mathcal{K} \Rightarrow \mathsf{Out}(a) = \{k\} \tag{12}$$

Suppose that an actor a obtains a knowledge set $\mathcal{K}$. If an actor a observes that a knowledge asset $k \in \mathcal{K}$ does not meets its requirements this specific asset is returned as output to indicate that it is faulty.

Rectification A task has a *rectification* property if it is part of the task to locate erroneously applied knowledge and then to rectify and return that knowledge so that it does meet its requirements. If an actor receives a knowledge asset k_1 and that knowledge does not meet its requirements $\mathcal{R}$ i.e. the knowledge is wrongly applied, then the actor broadcasts knowledge asset k_2 which does meet the requirements instead. This improvement process by an actor is denoted as *rectification*:

$$\mathsf{Rectification}: \mathsf{In}(a) = \{k_1\} \wedge (k_1, \mathcal{R}) \notin \mathsf{Requirement} \Rightarrow \mathsf{Out}(a) = \{k_2\} \wedge (k_2, \mathcal{R}) \in \mathsf{Requirement} \wedge k_1 \preceq k_2 \quad (13)$$

The notation $k_1 \preceq k_2$ is verbalized as *the knowledge in* k_1 *is contained within* k_2 and is modeled by the function:

$$\preceq : \mathcal{KA} \rightarrow \mathcal{KA} \quad (14)$$

In terms of an actor's need for knowledge, the knowledge containment relation is defined as:

$$k_1 \preceq k_2 \equiv k_1 \preceq_{\mathsf{Need}} k_2 \equiv \mathsf{Need}(\{k_2\}, k_1) = 0 \quad (15)$$

Here, $k_1 \preceq_{\mathsf{Need}} k_2$ represents the knowledge containment relation in the context of the knowledge need represented by 'Need'. In the notation of the rectification property we have omitted Need and denoted knowledge containment as $\preceq$. It is also possible that a certain knowledge asset is contained within more than one knowledge asset. Therefore the + operator concatenates knowledge assets:

$$+ : \mathcal{KA} \times \mathcal{KA} \rightarrow \mathcal{KA} \quad (16)$$

The concatenation of e.g. knowledge assets k_2 and k_3 is therefore shown as $k_2 + k_3$. The function $k_1 \preceq (k_2 + k_3)$ expresses that the knowledge in k_1 is contained within k_2 and k_3.

In order to have a graphical representation of the discussed definitions, an object-role model (ORM) is presented in figure 2. For details on object-role models, see e.g. [2]. Thus far we have focussed on a theory about knowledge intensive tasks and their properties. In the next section a scenario in conceptual modeling of information systems is introduced to illustrate the theory in the context of a method for specific tasks.

3 Cognitive Requirements in Conceptual Modeling Tasks

The discussed theoretical model comes to life when it is illustrated by a practical situation in the process of conceptual modeling. An example of a method for conceptual modeling of information systems is object-role modeling (ORM). ORM is a fact oriented method and makes use of natural language statements by examining them in terms of elementary facts. ORM has a specific *way of working* which makes it a suitable method to study the cognitive requirements needed to fulfill possible knowledge intensive tasks while applying the method. Halpin [2] shows that the way of working in ORM is called the *Conceptual Schema Design Procedure* (CSDP), consisting of seven steps:

1. Transform familiar information examples into elementary facts, and apply quality checks.

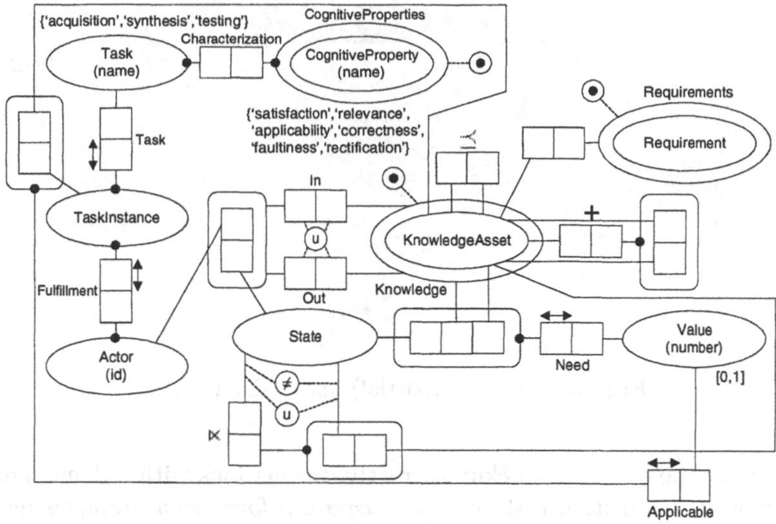

Fig. 2. Object-role model of knowledge intensive task properties.

2. Draw the fact types, and apply a population check.
3. Check for entity types that should be combined, and note any arithmetic derivations.
4. Add uniqueness constraints, and check clarity of fact types.
5. Add mandatory role constraints, and check for logical derivations.
6. Add value, set comparison and sub-typing constraints.
7. Add other constraints and perform final checks.

To let the theoretical model as discussed in section 2 materialize in a practical ORM modeling situation, suppose that a certain actor *a* who is acting as an *ORM modeler* wishes to create a conceptual model of an information system. Therefore, the ORM modeler walks through the seven steps as mentioned above. In this section we will focus on *step one* only, because the first step is already complex enough to illustrate our theory in the ORM method.

When initiating step one, an ORM modeler fulfills several knowledge intensive tasks. To understand how our theory materializes in an ORM method, a fragment of an information system's intended functionality is considered. One function of the information system to be modeled is to provide insight in a user's own knowledge profile. A partial screen mockup of an information system which should eventually include such functionality is shown in figure 3. The partial mockup shown is part of an application called DEXAR (Discovery and eXchange of Revealed knowledge) which is also currently under development as part of our research [7]. DEXAR is an application that assists the user in discovering and retrieving knowledge by implementing a question and answer mechanism with the user. The knowledge assets retrieved by the user are then stored in a (searchable) profile as can be seen in figure 3.

Part of the modeling task is to clarify the meaning of the functionality intended. Conversations between a domain expert and the ORM modeler are therefore needed to clarify the required functionality and to let the ORM mod-

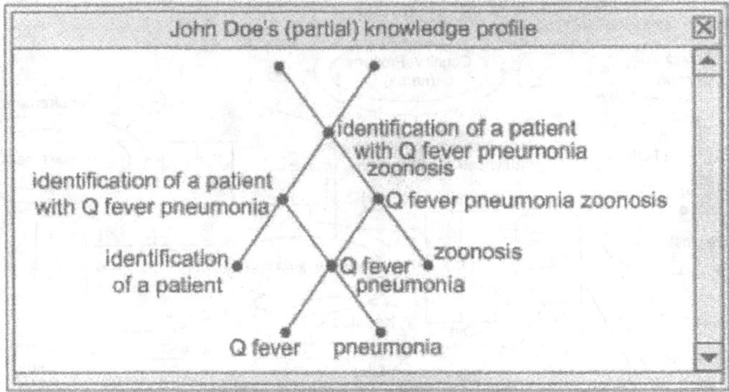

Fig. 3. Showing a (partial) knowledge profile.

eler interpret the example mockup correctly. Discussions with a domain expert are part of an acquisition task instance *acquire information examples* denoted by i_1, thus $\mathsf{Task}(i_1) = \mathtt{acquisition}$. Furthermore we can say that, with respect to the partial DEXAR functionality, the ORM modeler responsible for acquiring the information examples has a *need* for those information examples. An information example can be interpreted as information that is presented to the modeler, i.e. graphical information, information on forms, tabularly information, etc. The need for knowledge k concerning an information example is formally expressed as $\mathsf{Need}(\mathcal{S}, k) > 0$, where $\mathcal{S}$ is the personal knowledge profile of the ORM modeler in this case. During fulfillment of task instance i_1 several knowledge assets can be discerned which can be of importance:

k_1 **The knowledge profile of a user should be displayed as a lattice.**
k_2 **The user may browse through the lattice to learn about previously acquired knowledge and to gain insight in his own profile as a whole.**
k_3 **A lattice should consist of index expressions.**

When executing the acquisition task instance i_1, the modeler needs to satisfy the *satisfaction* property, denoted as: $\forall_{n \in \{1,2,3\}}[\mathsf{Need}_t(\mathcal{S}, k_n) > 0 \wedge k \in \mathsf{In}_t(a) \Rightarrow \mathsf{Need}_{t \ltimes k_n}(\mathcal{S}, k_n) = 0]$. In order to acquire knowledge that is not irrelevant, the modeler should satisfy the *relevance* property as follows: $\forall_{n \in \{1,2,3\}}[k_n \in \mathsf{In}(a) \Leftrightarrow \mathsf{Need}(\mathcal{S}, k_n) > 0 \wedge k_n \notin \mathcal{S}]$.

The knowledge gathered thus far is to be stated in terms of *elementary facts* as step one of the ORM method dictates. Basically, an elementary fact asserts that a particular object has a property, or that one or more objects participate in a relationship, where that relationship cannot be expressed as a conjunction of simpler (or shorter) facts. For example, to say that ORM is a modeling language and C++ is a programming language is to assert two elementary facts. Task instance i_1 is now followed by a second task instance i_2. Task instance i_2 is concerned with the creation of elementary facts based on the acquired knowledge k_1, k_2 and k_3 thus far. So this task instance can be referred to as *create elementary facts* and can be classified as a synthesis task.

The ORM modeler applies the knowledge acquired to generate four different elementary facts:

k_4 User has KnowledgeProfile displayed as Lattice
k_5 User browses through Lattice
k_6 Lattice contains Knowledge
k_7 Lattice consists of IndexExpressions

The *applicability* property now determines if the elementary facts are applicable for task instance i_2: $\forall_{n\in\{4,5,6,7\}}[\mathsf{Out}(a) = \{k_n\} \Leftrightarrow \mathsf{Applicable}(i_2, k_n) > 0 \wedge k_n \in \mathcal{S}]$. Once applied, the *correctness* property determines if the knowledge applied meets the requirements: $\forall_{n\in\{4,5,6,7\}}[\mathsf{Applicable}(i_2, k_n) > 0 \wedge k_n \in \mathsf{Out}(a) \Leftrightarrow (k_n, \mathcal{R}) \in \mathsf{Requirement} \wedge k_n \in \mathcal{S}]$. The set R contains the requirements for correctly conceiving elementary facts in ORM. Two possible requirements $r_1, r_2 \in \mathcal{R}$ can be:

r_1 The first letter of object types should be capitalized.
r_2 Each elementary fact should assert a binary relationship between two object types.

Knowledge asset k_4 does not meet requirement r_2, however, because three instead of two objects are part of k_4. In this case the correctness property fails: $(k_4, \{r_2\}) \notin \mathsf{Requirement}$ and the modeler should first alter elementary fact k_4.

When altering k_4, the modeler fulfills a testing task instance i_3 denoted as *correct errors in elementary facts.* A testing task has four properties as can be viewed in table 1. The improvement process or 'quality checks' that are part of task instance i_3 should satisfy the four properties. The *faultiness* property of task instance i_3 stipulates that asset k_4 does not meet requirement r_2: $\mathsf{In}(a) = \mathcal{K} \wedge (k_4, \{r_2\}) \notin \mathsf{Requirement} \wedge k_4 \in \mathcal{K} \Rightarrow \mathsf{Out}(a) = \{k_4\}$. Now when fulfilling task instance i_3, the modeler desires at least one or perhaps more knowledge assets that do meet requirement r_2. To be able to meet the requirement, the modeler, currently in a state t, has a desire to split up knowledge asset k_4 into two new knowledge assets: $k_{4'}$ and $k_{4''}$. These assets should be part of the modeler's profile $\mathcal{S}$ at state $t \ltimes k_{4'} \ltimes k_{4''}$. Therefore the *satisfaction* property is part of the task: $\forall_{n\in\{4',4''\}}[\mathsf{Need}_t(\mathcal{S}, k_n) > 0 \wedge k_n \in \mathsf{In}_t(a) \Rightarrow \mathsf{Need}_{t\ltimes k_n}(\mathcal{S}, k_n) = 0]$. When the newly produced knowledge assets are applied during the task, they should be relevant enough to reach the task's goal. The *applicability* property is thus also part of the task: $\forall_{n\in\{4',4''\}}[k_n \in \mathsf{Out}(a) \Leftrightarrow \mathsf{Applicable}(i_3, k_n) > 0 \wedge k_n \in \mathcal{S}]$. Finally, the *rectification* property determines if requirement r_2 has been met by replacing k_4 with assets $k_{4'}$ and $k_{4''}$: $\mathsf{In}(a) = \{k_4\} \wedge (k_4, \{r_2\}) \notin \mathsf{Requirement} \Rightarrow \mathsf{Out}(a) = \{k_{4'}, k_{4''}\} \wedge (k_{4'}, \{r_2\}) \in \mathsf{Requirement} \wedge (k_{4''}, \{r_2\}) \in \mathsf{Requirement} \wedge k_4 \preceq (k_{4'} + k_{4''})$. Remember from section 2.3 that the knowledge containment relation can be determined by the $\preceq$ symbol and that concatenated knowledge assets are represented by the $+$ symbol. In the property above, the following knowledge containment relation is depicted: $k_4 \preceq (k_{4'} + k_{4''})$. This can be verbalized as: *the knowledge in k_4 is contained within the concatenation of $k_{4'}$ and $k_{4''}$*. The resulting facts are then displayed as follows after the completion of testing task instance i_3:

$k_{4'}$ User has KnowledgeProfile
$k_{4''}$ KnowledgeProfile is displayed as Lattice
k_5 User browses through Lattice

k_6 Lattice contains Knowledge
k_7 Lattice consists of IndexExpressions

The following section shows how the defined task properties can be situated in a requirements engineering scenario by focussing on the way of working of COLOR-X, which is an example of a requirements engineering method.

4 Cognitive Requirements in Requirements Engineering Tasks

In the previous section a scenario in conceptual modeling of information systems has been presented in which our theory came alive. We will now elaborate a scenario in the area of requirements engineering. Requirements engineering is an indication for the first phase of a software development process, in which the main objective is to correctly understand the needs of the system's customers or users: *What* is the system supposed to do. The process of understanding these needs or requirements, i.e. requirements engineering, can be defined as the systematic process of developing requirements through an iterative cooperative process of analyzing the problem, documenting the resulting observations in a variety of representation formats, and checking the accuracy of the understanding gained [5]. The Ph.D. thesis of Burg [1] illustrates the COLOR-X method for requirements engineering. The COLOR-X way of working covers requirements specification, verification and validation phases. In this section we will limit ourselves to how the knowledge intensive tasks of section 2.1 can be fulfilled in a *requirements specification* phase indicating the cognitive requirements for fulfilling those tasks. The process of requirements specification consists of mapping real-world phenomena as described in the requirements document onto basic concepts of a specification language, i.e. describing a certain problem in an as precise, concise, understandable and correct as possible manner. The COLOR-X method divides the requirements specification stage in two parts: a natural language approach and a scenario based approach. In this section we will limit ourselves to the natural language approach, which equals most how the ORM method specifies a conceptual model. The COLOR-X natural language approach for specifying requirements consists of four steps:

1. Select the words and sentences from the requirements document that are relevant for the COLOR-X models.
2. Break up complex sentences and / or combine several redundant or overlapping sentences into understandable ones (i.e. structured sentences).
3. Annotate additional syntactic and semantic information, retrieved from the lexicon, to the words selected from the requirements document.
4. Transform the structured sentences into formal specifications.

In this section, a possible acquisition task as part of step *one* is discussed. Furthermore a synthesis task and a testing task as part of step *two* are dealt with. Suppose that actor a is a *requirements modeler* and wishes to go through the requirements specification phase and therefore applies the COLOR-X method. Assume that the following snippet is part of the requirements document of the `DEXAR` application:

```
A partial knowledge profile should be represented by a lattice also
referred to as a power index expression. Such a lattice should be
constructed by using index expressions. A power index expression
contains all index expressions, including the empty index expression
and the most meaningful index expression. An example of an index
expression is '(identification of a patient) with (Q fever
pneumonia)'. Simply put, (power)index expressions are used by DEXAR
as a representation for a knowledge profile.
```

While walking through the first step as mentioned above, the requirements modeler selects the words and sentences from the requirements document snippet. This is part of an acquisition task instance *acquire words and sentences* denoted by i_1, thus $\mathsf{Task}(i_1) = \mathtt{acquisition}$. The requirements modeler has a *need* for those words and sentences. The acquired words and sentences i.e. knowledge assets can be depicted as follows:

k_1 A partial knowledge profile is represented by a lattice.
k_2 A lattice equals a power index expression.
k_3 A power index expression contains all index expressions.
k_4 A power index expression includes the empty index expression and the most meaningful index expression.

When executing the acquisition task instance above, the requirements modeler needs to satisfy the *satisfaction* property, denoted as: $\forall_{n\in\{1,2,3,4\}}[\mathsf{Need}_t(\mathcal{S}, k_n) > 0 \wedge k \in \mathsf{In}_t(a) \Rightarrow \mathsf{Need}_{t\ltimes k_n}(\mathcal{S}, k_n) = 0]$. In order to acquire knowledge that is not irrelevant, the modeler should satisfy the *relevance* property as follows: $\forall_{n\in\{1,2,3,4\}}[k_n \in \mathsf{In}(a) \Leftrightarrow \mathsf{Need}(\mathcal{S}, k_n) > 0 \wedge k_n \notin \mathcal{S}]$.

Step one can be seen as an intensive knowledge acquirement step, i.e. the requirements document is sifted for relevant words and sentences. It is not until step two of the requirements specification process as prescribed by COLOR-X that a synthesis task can be identified. Task instance i_1 is now followed by a task instance i_2. Task instance i_2 can be referred to as *create structured sentences* and is part of step two. Table 2 represents the knowledge assets following from task i_2. Knowledge assets k_5 up to and including k_9

Table 2. The created structured sentences

	Subject	Predicate	Direct object
k_5	A lattice	represents	a knowledge profile
k_6	A lattice	equals	a power index expression
k_7	A power index expression	contains	all index expressions
k_8	A power index expression	includes	the empty index expression
k_9	A power index expression	includes	the most meaningful index expression

are mostly similar with assets k_1 up to and including k_4, but the knowledge assets of table 2 include additional *grammatical* knowledge instead. The *applicability* property now determines if the structured sentences are applicable for task i_2: $\forall_{n\in\{5,6,7,8,9\}}[\mathsf{Out}(a) = \{k_n\} \Leftrightarrow \mathsf{Applicable}(i_2, k_n) > 0 \wedge k_n \in \mathcal{S}]$. Once applied, the *correctness* property determines if the structured sentences meet the requirements: $\forall_{n\in\{5,6,7,8,9\}}[\mathsf{Applicable}(i_2, k_n) > 0 \wedge k_n \in \mathsf{Out}(a) \Leftrightarrow (k_n, \mathcal{R}) \in \mathsf{Requirement} \wedge k_n \in \mathcal{S}]$. The set R contains the requirements for correctly conceiving structured sentences in COLOR-X. Two possible requirements $r_1, r_2 \in \mathcal{R}$ can be:

r_1 **Annotate a main sentence structure, i.e. the subject, predicate and direct object.**
r_2 **Annotate special grammatical elements, i.e. the adjectives, adverbs and nominal predicates.**

Knowledge assets k_5 up to and including k_9 do not meet requirement r_2, however, because no special grammatical elements are shown in table 2. In this case the correctness property fails and the requirements modeler should first add special grammatical elements.

When altering k_5 up to and including k_9, the requirements modeler fulfills a testing task instance i_3 denoted as *correct omitted special grammatical elements.* The resulting special grammatical elements are displayed in table 3 after completing testing task instance i_3. Now the properties of task instance

Table 3. The created special grammatical elements

	Grammatical concept	Word	Category
$k_{5'}$	Adjective	Partial	Property
$k_{6'}$	Nominal predicate	A lattice is a power index expression	Specialization
$k_{7'}$	Adverb	All	Quantity
$k_{8'}$	Adjective	Empty	Property
$k_{9'}$	Adjective	Most meaningful	Property

i_3 should be analyzed to determine how they are satisfied. For asset k_5, the *faultiness* property stipulates that the asset does not meet requirement r_2: $\mathsf{In}(a) = \mathcal{K} \wedge (k_5, \{r_2\}) \notin \mathsf{Requirement} \wedge k_5 \in \mathcal{K} \Rightarrow \mathsf{Out}(a) = \{k_5\}$. To be able to meet the requirement, the modeler, currently in a state t, has a desire to create another knowledge asset $k_{5'}$ that includes special grammatical elements for the sentence included in k_5. The concatenation of k_5 and $k_{5'}$, i.e. $k_5 + k_{5'}$ should meet both requirements r_1 and r_2. The concatenated asset should be part of the modeler's profile $\mathcal{S}$ at state $t \ltimes k_5 + k_{5'}$. Therefore the *satisfaction* property for $k_5 + k_{5'}$ results in: $\mathsf{Need}_t(\mathcal{S}, k_5 + k_{5'}) > 0 \wedge k_5 + k_{5'} \in \mathsf{In}_t(a) \Rightarrow \mathsf{Need}_{t \ltimes k_5 + k_{5'}}(\mathcal{S}, k_5 + k_{5'}) = 0$. When the concatenated knowledge asset $k_5 + k_{5'}$ is applied during the task, it should be relevant enough to reach the task's goal. This is expressed by the *applicability* property: $k_5 + k_{5'} \in \mathsf{Out}(a) \Leftrightarrow \mathsf{Applicable}(i_3, k_5 + k_{5'}) > 0 \wedge k_5 + k_{5'} \in \mathcal{S}$. Finally, the *rectification* property determines if requirement r_2 has been met by creating asset $k_{5'}$ and concatenating it with k_5: $\mathsf{In}(a) = \{k_5\} \wedge (k_5, \{r_2\}) \notin \mathsf{Requirement} \Rightarrow \mathsf{Out}(a) = \{k_5 + k_{5'}\} \wedge (k_5 + k_{5'}, \{r_2\}) \in \mathsf{Requirement}$. Following the same approach as above, properties k_6 up to and including k_9 can be concatenated with the created grammatical elements. So k_6 should be concatenated with $k_{6'}$ and so on. This completely satisfies the properties of task instance i_3 eventually.

Now that the theoretical part and possible applications of it in methods for specific tasks have been discussed, it is appropriate to compare our approach with other approaches in the field. The next section therefore deals with this matter.

5 Discussion

Literature indicates that characterizing tasks on a cognitive basis is possible in several different ways. The research of Weir et al. [10] includes a characterization of *information management tasks* by studying activities of workers in the primary care setting. This has resulted in an abstraction of several information management tasks during the research, such as: assignment tasks, determination tasks, organization tasks, etc. First, Weir et al. [10] show that they have analyzed tasks in primary clinical care and from that specialized analysis an abstraction has been made constituting a general categorization of tasks. Compared to our study, this is a bottom-up approach from analyzing tasks in a certain context to the eventual abstraction of tasks. We have analyzed tasks using a top-down approach by generalizing tasks based on parallels made with an inductive-hypothetical research approach before materializing the theory in methods for specific tasks. An advantage of our approach is that the theory is not stemming from a study in a specialized context and thus does not run the risk of being useful only in a certain context. Therefore, it is assumed that our theory is applicable in numerous contexts and can be adapted to that context if desired. For instance, sections 3 and 4 are an indication that this is possible.

Especially when methods for specific tasks are concerned, it is difficult to identify significant research related to matching an actor's cognitive abilities with the cognitive abilities required to perform a certain task. However, the research of Zhang et al. [11] shows that the *human-centered distributed information system design* methodology includes *user analysis* and *task analysis* as part of information system design. The methodology has a much broader focus than only dealing with the match / mismatch between a user's cognitive abilities and the cognitive abilities necessary to fulfill a specific task. An important function of task analysis in human-centered distributed information system design is to ensure that the system implementation includes only the necessary and sufficient task features that match user capacity and are required by the task. This contrasts with our research, because we do not wish to exclude the situations in which an actor / task combination does not match very well, but instead we would like to provide support for it in the future. We assume that instead of excluding the situations in which an actor / task combination does not match it is better to provide *support* for it, simply because it occurs often enough in everyday practice. An early attempt by e.g. Harris and Brightman [3] shows a preliminary attempt to couple potential automated support with cognitive task fulfillment by academics. The proposed automated support however consists of existing tools only and suggestions for future, possibly better, tools are not made. Hence it seems that our longer term research goals, as mentioned in section 1, are worth pursuing.

6 Conclusion

This paper describes a categorization and characterization of knowledge intensive tasks, illustrated by definitions of task properties indicating cognitive requirements for task fulfillment. Proceeding from these definitions method application scenarios in conceptual modeling of information systems respectively requirements engineering show how the theory can be materialized.

References

1. J.F.M. Burg. *Linguistic Instruments in Requirements Engineering.* PhD thesis, Vrije Universiteit Amsterdam, The Netherlands, EU, 1997.
2. T. Halpin. *Information Modeling and Relational Databases, from Conceptual Analysis to Logical Design.* Morgan Kaufmann, San Mateo, CA, USA, 2001.
3. S.E. Harris and H.J. Brightman. Design implications of a task-driven approach to unstructured cognitive tasks in office work. *ACM Transactions on Information Systems*, 3(3):292–306, 1985.
4. T.Y. Liang. The basic entity model: A fundamental theoretical model of information and information processing. *Information Processing & Management*, 30(5):647–661, 1994.
5. P. Loucopoulos and V. Karakostas. *System Requirements Engineering.* McGraw-Hill Book Company Europe, Berkshire, UK, EU, 1995.
6. N. Meiran. Modeling cognitive control in task-switching. *Psychological Research*, 63(3–4):234–249, 2000.
7. S.J. Overbeek, P. van Bommel, H.A. Proper, and D.B.B. Rijsenbrij. Knowledge discovery and exchange – Towards a web-based application for discovery and exchange of revealed knowledge. In J. Filipe, J. Cordeiro, B. Encarnação, and V. Pedrosa, editors, *Proceedings of the Third International Conference on Web Information Systems and Technologies (WEBIST)*, pages 26–34. Barcelona, Spain, EU, INSTICC Press, Setúbal, Portugal, EU, 2007.
8. J. Schraagen, S. Chipman, and V. Shalin. *Cognitive Task Analyis.* Lawrence Erlbaum Associates, Mahway, NJ, USA, 2000.
9. H.G. Sol. *Simulation in Information Systems.* PhD thesis, University of Groningen, The Netherlands, EU, 1982.
10. C.R. Weir, J.J.R. Nebeker, L.H. Bret, R. Campo, F. Drews, and B. LeBar. A cognitive task analysis of information management strategies in a computerized provider order entry environment. *Journal of the American Medical Informatics Association*, 14(1):65–75, 2007.
11. J. Zhang, V.L. Patel, K.A. Johnson, J.W. Smith, and J. Malin. Designing human-centered distributed information systems. *IEEE Intelligent Systems*, 17(5):42–47, 2002.

Partial Evaluation in Meta Modeling

Manfred A. Jeusfeld
Tilburg University, Department of Information Systems and Management,
Warandelaan 2, 5037 AB Tilburg, The Netherlands
jeusfeld@uvt.nl
WWW home page: http://infolab.uvt.nl/~jeusfeld

Abstract. Meta modeling is a well-established technique to describe the structure modeling languages. Method engineering environments utilize the technique to provide a flexible environment for defining and adapting modeling environments. We show that basing meta modeling strictly on first-order logic provides not only clean semantics but also the ability to define high-level constructs such as transitivity at the meta model, or even meta meta model level and to efficiently map the constructs to lower levels by partial evaluation. We show that it applies both to universally and existentially quantified expressions. Examples are included to demonstrate the usefulness. A full implementation is available in the ConceptBase meta modeling environment.

1 Introduction

A model is a structured representation of statements about some world, be it real or imagined. A meta model is a model about models, i.e. it contains some statements about some set of models, in particular models that conform to the same modeling language.

Typically, meta models are denoted in a style similar to models. Graphical notations are dominant providing rather few features to encode the desired meaning of constructs in the meta model. In this paper, we are concerned about extending the usefulness of meta models by enriching them with first -order logical expressions. Such expressions can both be used for defining some syntax rules and for defining the logic-based semantics of the use of the constructs in models conforming to the meta models.

This paper shall first recap the use of models and meta models as inspired by the model-driven architecture. The analogy of instantiation to variable substitution

---

Please use the following format when citing this chapter:

Jeusfeld, M. A., 2007, in IFIP International Federation for Information Processing, Volume 244, Situational Method Engineering: Fundamentals and Experiences, eds. Ralyté, J., Brinkkemper, S., Henderson-Sellers B., (Boston Springer), pp. 115-129.

allows for a simple partial evaluation technique borrowed from deductive databases that translates high-level logical expressions, i.e. expressions ranging over objects at more than two meta modeling layers, to lower-level expressions down to simple expressions that relate just two meta modeling layers.

We demonstrate some generic examples to show its applicability to various meta modeling scenarios, e.g. the definition of required attributes and transitivity of attributes, which can be used to specify the semantics of the PartOf concept as well as the IsA concept. Throughout the paper, we assume Herbrand interpretations of the logical formulas. Even more, we restrict ourselves to those first order formulas that can be translated to Datalog with negation, i.e. to logical theories that have a unique minimal Herbrand interpretation. The technique has been implemented in the ConceptBase system (Jarke et al., 1995).

We claim that the incorporation of a sound meta modeling component is essential for method engineering, in particular in cases where dedicated modeling languages have to be constructed.

2 Meta Modeling Layers

The OMG meta object facility MOF [OMG 2006] organizes expressions in models with respect to their abstraction level. The lowest level M0 contains expressions that are such concrete that they do not have examples. They are representations of *examples* or *example objects*. The next level M1 contains expressions that classify or constrain the expressions at the M0 level. Expressions at the M1 level are also called *classes*. The M2 level organizes the classes of the M1 level into so-called meta classes. Meta classes are used to make statements about classes and we associate the term meta model to this level. Finally, the M3 level classifies meta classes into meta meta classes (or meta models). From a formal language point of view, the M2 level contains definitions of modeling languages, and the M3 level contains facilities to define modeling languages. The layer hierarchy can in principle continue to M4, M5 etc. but these levels are rarely used in the literature. Apparently four abstraction levels are regarded as sufficient by most authors.

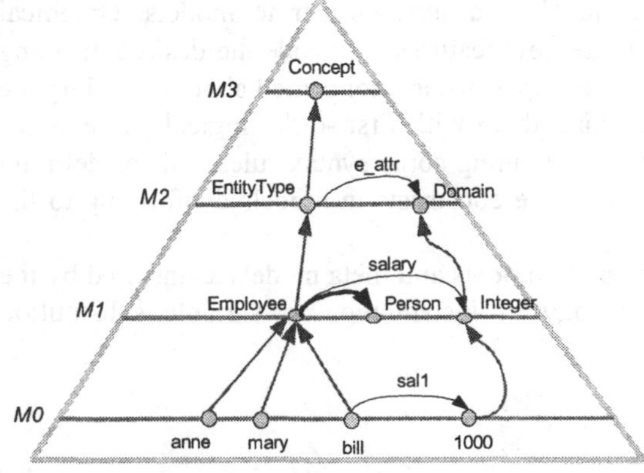

Figure 1: An interpretation of the MOF abstraction levels

Figure 1 motivates the four MOF layers. The triangular display symbolizes the expectation that the number of concepts decreases with the layer index. Intuitively, an M1 model (e.g. an entity-relationship diagram) has less elements than a M0 object model that conforms to it (e.g. the tuples of a database). This numerical relation continues with the other layers. Since each layer constrains the subsequent layer, the scope of an expression increases with the layer at which it is defined. For example, if we define the meaning of ERD cardinality constraints at the M2 layer, then it will range in principal over all databases that are conforming to some ERD model at the M1 layer.

Our goal is to allow for the efficient management of logical expressions at any MOF abstraction layer. The higher the degree of abstraction, the higher will be the degree of reuse of the expression and ultimately the more efficient will be the design of new modeling languages.

3 Models and Logic

The higher a concept is located in the MOF abstraction layers, the more abstract is also its meaning. For reasons of simplicity, we will interpret all objects at any abstraction level by itself, i.e. we assume a Herbrand interpretation where each object as shown in figure 1 is a constant being its own interpretation.

Rather than defining a predicate c(x) to denote that object x is an instance of concept c, we introduce a binary predicate In(x,c) . In figure 1, the instantiations are displayed in green color. They correspond to the following facts being a possible Herbrand interpretation of the predicate In:

```
{In(anne,Employee),
In(mary,Employee), In(1000,Integer),
In(Employee,EntityType),
In(Integer,Domain), In(EntityType,Concept),...}
```

We introduce two further predicates Isa(c,d) for declaring c as specialization of d, and AL(x,m,n,y) for declaring an attribution link (x has an attribute labelled n to y and this attribute has the category m). Applied to the example of figure 1, we would get the following Herbrand interpretation of these two predicates

```
{Isa(Employee,Person),
AL(bill,salary,sal1,1000),
AL(Employee,e_attr,salary,Integer),
AL(EntityType,attribute,e_attr,Domain)}
```

The three predicates are capable to represent concepts at *any abstraction layer* and are the basis for defining the meaning of abstract features such as inheritance, transitivity of partOf, cardinality constraints, and so forth.

To represent the meaning of concepts, we need to refer to attributes as being concepts. This is also called *reification*. If x is concept and n is the label of some attribute of x, then x!n is the constant denoting the attribute as a concept. In our running example, we have the attribute concepts `bill!sal1`, `Employee!salary`, `EntityType!ent_attr`. Like any other concept, attribute concepts can occur in the In, Isa, and AL predicates. For example `In(bill!sal1,Employee!salary)` states that the sal1 attribute of bill is an instance of the salary attribute of Employee. If o is an attribute, then the predicate P(o,x,l,y) returns the source x, the label l and the destination y of the attribute o. The following examples are true:

```
P(Employee!salary,Employee,salary,Integer)
```

```
P(bill!sal1,bill,sal1,1000)
```

Let us recall some implications of basing the semantics on Herbrand models. We demand that any model is finite we also have a finite number of constants. This is an important restriction. While finiteness for M1, M2 and M3 models is intuitive, the M0 layer might be regarded as infinite, e.g. containing all *possible* database states. For our purpose however, we strictly demand finiteness. It implies that any Herbrand interpretation of the three base predicates is also finite.

First order logic can be used to provide additional information about the concepts in a model. They are statements over the three base predicates. For example, we can express that each employee must have a salary:

[Formula 1] ∀ e In(e,Employee) ⇒ ∃ s,n In(s,Integer) ∧ AL(e,salary,n,s)

At the M2 level, we can demand that any entity type has at least one entity attribute:

[Formula 2] ∀ et In(et,EntityType) ⇒ ∃ t,n In(t,Domain) ∧ AL(et,e_attr,n,t)

The first formula contains constants from the M1 level and the variables are substitutable by constants from the M0 layer. The second formula contains constants from the M2 layer and the variable range over constants from the M1 layer. We call such formulas type 1 formulas since they relate two neighbouring abstractions layers. Apparently, both formulas have the same structure. Instead of copying the same formula code, we aim for a facility were we only code a *meta formula* once and re-use it wherever required. There more of such formulas are defined, the richer is the meta modeling environment since the meaning of modeling constructs can be recombined from the meta formulas.

Definition 1: A variable occurrence x1 in a predicate P is called a *meta variable* iff P=In(x,x1), or P=AL(x,x1,n,y). A *meta formula* is a first order formula with at least one meta variable.

There are plenty of examples for meta formulas. We use the following example for discussing the method (meta variables are c,d and m):

[Formula 3] ∀ x,a,c,m,d In(a,required) ∧ P(a,c,m,d) ∧ In(x,c) ⇒ ∃ y,n In(y,d) ∧ AL(x,m,n,y)

4 Partial Evaluation of Meta Formulas

A meta formula has no peculiar property except that it has constants and variables ranging over more than 2 abstraction layers. To understand this, we show how a meta formula can be compiled to a type 1 formula by means of partial evaluation. There are a few reasons why partial evaluation is useful for meta modeling:

1. By translating a meta formula to a type 1 formula, one can understand its meaning in terms of the context in which it is used. For example, the

formulas 1 and 2 are partially evaluated from formula 3. They are more understandable than formula 3 because they use constants from the appropriate abstraction layer.

2. The partially evaluated formulas have less variables than the corresponding meta formula. Since the computational complexity grows exponentially in the number of variables, the partially evaluated formulas are more efficient to evaluate.
3. View maintenance on the basis of meta formulas is virtually intractable since the predicate occurrences In(x,c) will match facts of any model base update. An important example of view maintenance is integrity checking.

The last reason is the most relevant one: if we want to efficiently check the integrity of a set of models in an incremental way, then we have to restrict to type 1 formulas.

Our partial evaluation technique is inspired by the 'simplification' method for deductive integrity checking. The simplification method generates from an update and a formula that matches some facts in the update a new formula. The matching binds variables to constants. In our case, the new formula is not just evaluated against the database but it becomes part of the logical theory that represents our model base. Assume that MF is a meta formula and C is the list of some meta variables in MF.

> **Step 1:** Rearrange MF into one of the two possible normalized forms (called input formula subsequently)
>
> `∀ C E(C) ⇒ F(C)`
>
> `∃ C E(C) ∧ F(C)`
>
> where E(C) is a predicate and F(C) is the rest of the formula. It is allowed to define auxiliary deductive rules for E(C) in order to match one of the two forms.

The normalized forms are ensuring that the meta variables in C are restricted to those values V for which E(V) is in the interpretation of the E-predicate. The syntactic form is now as 'range-restricted' or 'domain-independent' in deductive database literature (Nicolas, 1979; Bry, 1989). To continue the example, step 1 rearranges formula 3 to

[Formula 4] `∃ c,d E1(c,d) ⇒ (∀ x In(x,c) ⇒ ∃ y,n In(y,d) ∧ AL(x,m,n,y))`

with the auxiliary deductive rule

`∀ a,c,m,d In(a,required) ∧ P(a,c,m,d) ⇒ E1(c,d,m)`

In the next step, we compute the interpretation of the E-predicate (also called the extension). The goal is to replace the E-predicate by its extension.

> **Step 2:** Compute the Herbrand interpretation for the E-predicate, say $I_E=\{E(V_1),E(V_2),..,E(V_K)\}$ and replace the predicate E(C) in the normalized meta formula by the disjunction $((C=V_1) \vee (C=V_2) \vee ... \vee (C=V_K))$.

The Herbrand interpretation shall be finite because the base predicates are finite. If C has more than one variable, then C=V is a the pairwise equality of variables in C with values in V, i.e. ((c1=v1) ∧ (c2=v2) ∧ ...).

Example: Assume that `In(EntityType!e_attr,required)` is true. Then, `E1(EntityType,Domain,e_attr)` becomes derivable via the auxiliary deductive rule. As a consequence, the partially evaluated formula is:

[Formula 5] `∀ c,d ((c=EntityType ∧ (d=Domain) ∧ (m=e_attr) ⇒ ∀ x (In(x,c) ⇒ ∃ y,n In(y,d) ∧ AL(x,m,n,y))`

If the meta formula is universally quantified, then each entry (C=V) in the value disjunction leads to a substituted subformula F(C)[V/C], i.e. the formula F(C) where all occurences of variables of C are replaces by the corresponding values of V.

Lemma 1: If the input formula is a universally quantified meta formula, then the conjunction F(C)[V1/C] ∧ F(C)[V2/C] ∧ ... ∧ F(C)[VK/C] of all such substituted subformulas is equivalent to it.

Proof: The follows directly from the fact that ∀ x (x=v) ⇒ F(x) is equivalent to F(v) and the finiteness assumption.

Example: Let I_{E1}=`{E1(EntityType, Domain,e_attr), E1(Employee, Integer,salary)}`. By lemma 1, formula 4 is equivalent to the conjunction

[Formula 6]

```
∀ x In(x,EntityType) ⇒ ∃ y,n In(y,Domain) ∧ AL(x,e_attr,n,y))
∧
∀ x In(x,Employee) ⇒ ∃ y,n In(y,Integer) ∧ AL(x,salary,n,y))
```

Except variable naming, these two formulas are exactly formulas 1 and 2 of our initial example!

Lemma 2: If the input formula is an existentially quantified meta formula, then the disjunction F(C)[V1/C] ∨ F(C)[V2/C] ∨ ... ∨ F(C)[VK/C] of all such substituted subformulas is equivalent to it.

The proof is analogous to lemma 1. Not any meta formulas can be partially evaluated. Some meta formulas can simply not transformed into the normalized form of step 1. An example is

```
∃ c ∀ x In(x,c)
```

> **Step 3:** Generate the target formula as specified in Lemma 1 (universal quantification) and Lemma 2 (existential quantification).

Steps 1 to 3 constitute a term rewriting system where a meta formula MF is transformed to a representation with less meta variables. Note that the rewriting is also applicable to sub-formulas of a meta formula MF. As noted above, the term rewriting system is not complete, i.e. there are meta formulas that can't be rewritten.

If a meta formula is range-restricted, then there is always a rewriting to a formula without meta variables (proof pending).

5 Complexity Considerations

The above method has been implemented in the ConceptBase system. The crucial problem is the transformation in step 1, i.e. the selection of the E-predicate. In general, there is more than one candidate. So the question is, which candidate is the best one. We realized a strategy where the candidate is chosen that binds the maximum number of meta variables.

A second criterion in the selection is the size of the interpretation I_E of the meta predicate. The larger the size, the more subformulas `F(C)[V/C]` will be generated. One can easily think of scenarios where the number of generated subformulas grows to the size of the model base itself. In such a case, partial evaluation is intractable. We have to demand that the abstraction layers of figure 1 are indeed *decreasing in size*, i.e. layer 0 has many more objects than layer 1, layer 1 has many more objects than layer 2, etc. Since the concepts become more and more abstract, this is true in most meta modeling scenarios, in particular in the scenario of specifying modeling languages (layer 2). If one has a large number of concepts in layer 2 (e.g. an elaborated ontology of concepts occurring in information systems development), and only few concepts in layer 1 and 0, then it makes less sense to apply the technique. It would be analogous to run a large set of queries against a tiny database.

Another issue is the incremental maintenance of the partially generated formulas. When an update to the model base changes the extension of some E-predicate, then step 3 has to be executed again. If the interpretation I_E gets more entries $\{E(V_{K+1}),E(V_{K+2},...\}$, then one only has to re-apply incrementally step 3 to the new entries. If the interpretation shrinks, then one has to remove the corresponding subformulas. ConceptBase attaches triggers to the E-predicate to achieve this type of formula maintenance. If the majority of updates to the model base include updates to the interpretation of E-predicates, then the partial evaluation method is rather expensive. Fortunately, the 'triangular' nature of layers in figure 1 suggests that this is not the case in 'normal' applications of meta modeling.

6 Application to Meta Modeling Cases

The benefit of meta formulas is that they encode the meaning of abstract concepts such as the concept of 'required' attributes encoded in formula 3. It was possible to partially evaluate this formula to a conjunction of type 1 formulas by a single E-predicate. We call such a meta formula a type 2 formula. If the meta formula has predicate occurrences `In(x,c)`, `In(c,mc)` where c and mc are meta variables, one has to apply the partial evaluation method successively until the result is a type 1 formula. The first iteration eliminates mc as a variable, and subsequently c is eliminated. Such a meta formula is called a type 3 formula. If we have a predicates like `In(x,c)`, `In(c,mc)`, and `In(mc,mmc)` with all c, mc, mmc being meta variables, then we speak of a level 4 formula. A type 4 formulas has variables ranging over 4 different abstraction levels.

6.1 Meta level instantiation and attribution

It is useful to define some formulas that describe the relative instantiation between layers:

[Formula 7] `∀ x,c,mc In(mc,Concept) ∧ In(c,mc) ∧ In(x,c) ⇒ In2(x,mc)`

There are two meta variables in this example: c and mmc. The E-predicate is In(mc,Concept) where Concept is some constant denoting the class of all concepts in the model base. The normalized form is

[Formula 8] `∀ mc In(mc,Concept) ==> (∀ x,c In(c,mc) ∧ In(x,c) ⇒ In2(x,mc))`

Let In(EntityType,Concept) be in the interpretation of the E-predicate. Then, the partial evaluation yields

[Formula 9] `∀ x,c In(c,EntityType) ∧ In(x,c) ⇒ In2(x,EntityType))`

Formula 9 happens to be again a meta formula (type 3). The meta variable is c and the E-predicate is `In(x,c)`. Let `In(Employee,EntityType)` be in the interpretation. The partial evaluation will then yield

[Formula 10] `∀ x In(x,Employee) ⇒ In2(x,EntityType)`

The derived predicate `In2(x,mc)` has an important contribution to meta modeling. It defines the relation of a concept x to its meta class `mc`. It can be used to define the meaning of being an entity or being a value:

[Formulas 11] `∀ x In2(x,EntityType) ⇒ In(x,Entity)`
[Formulas 12] `∀ x In2(x,Domain) ⇒ In(x,Value)`

Note that the variable x ranges over concepts at the M0 abstraction layer. Thus, formulas 11 and 12 really separate entities from values. It is defined independently from the M1 level and works for any M1 model instantiated to the M2 model. One can now easily express a condition that an entity may never be a value and vice versa. We leave this exercise to the reader. The In2 predicate can be accompanied by a similar predicate AL2 on attribution.

[Formula 13] `∀ c,d,x,m,mm,n,y In(x,c) ∧ In(y,d) ∧ AL(c,mm,m,d) ∧ AL(x,m,n,y) ⇒ AL2(x,mm,m,y)`

Here AL(c,mm,m,d) can serve as E-predicate. For AL(Employee,e_attr,salary,Integer) it is partially evaluated to

[Formula 14] ∀ x,m,n,y In(x,Employee) ∧ In(y,Integer) ∧ AL(x,salary,n,y) ⇒ AL2(x,e_attr,salary,y)

With AL2, we can now define a predicate A2 as follows:

[Formula 15] ∀ x,mm,y AL2(x,mm,m,y) ⇒ A2(x,mm,y)

This predicate is using an attribute label from the meta class layer (e.g. M2) while x,y are ranging over concepts two levels below (e.g. M0). Applied to our running example, `A2(x,e_attr,y)` subsumes all attribute links between objects x and y from the M0 level. Again, the A2 predicate is independent from the middle layer M1. If we extend our running example at the M2 level by an attribute 'key' between EntityType and Domain, then the predicate A2(x,key,y) precisely defines the key values y for a given entity x. The formula

[Formula 16] ∀ x1,x2,k A2(x1,key,k) ∧ A2(x2,key,k) ⇒ (x1 = x2)

axiomatizes the key property based on the A2 predicate. Figure 2 illustrates this application. It implies that `A2(bill,key,130606)` is true.

The two predicate In2 and A2 may also be used to query the M0 level from the M2 level, i.e. to formulate queries to a database that are independent from the database schema. For example, one can find those entities that are identified by a key that occurs as normal attribute value (e_attr) in another entity.

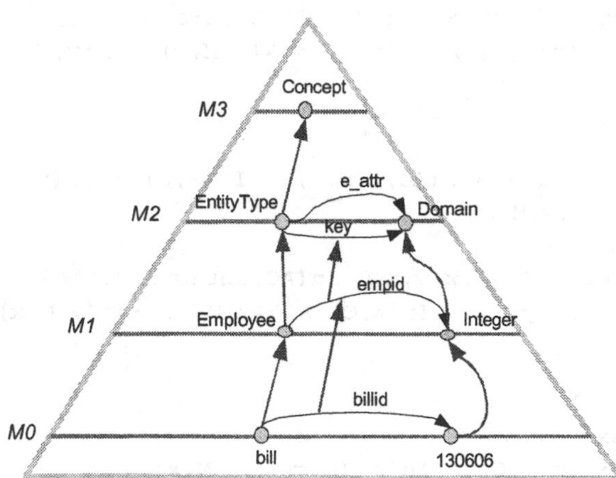

Figure 2: Formalizing the key property

Analogous to In2 and A2, one can define In3 and A3 predicate that relate concepts from the M3 layer and the M0 layer. We do not provide their definition but state that it allows to express properties of concepts from the M0 layer that are not only independent from the M1 layer (e.g. database schema) but also independent from the M2 layer, i.e. the modeling language. For example, one can define the fact that two concepts are linked to each other regardless of the type of the link.

We have applied meta formulas to provide a complete definition of the ERD modeling language including specialization (ISA), key attributes, and cardinalities. Apparently data modeling languages with their static semantics are affined to predicate logic with Herbrand interpretation. The same is not true for dynamic modeling languages like Petri nets[1]. While the semantics of ERDs can be explained in terms of the finite M0 models, dynamic modeling languages are defined on M0 layers encoding potentially infinitely many states of the execution of the dynamic model.

6.2 Relation properties

Some constructs in meta modeling are defined by re-usable patterns. For example, both the IsA relation between classes and subclasses and the PartOf relation between classes are transitive. However, while the IsA relation is reflexive, the partOf relation is anti-symmetric. Meta formulas easily cope with this partial semantic overlap of concepts. All that one has to do is to define the appropriate meta formulas and then instantiate the modeling constructs to those meta formulas that are applicable to them. Let us first define the relation properties by adapting their textbook definitions to our base predicates. To do so, we introduce the A predicate in terms of the AL predicate.

```
[Formula 17] ∀ x,m,n,y AL(x,m,n,y) ⇒ A(x,m,y)
```

There is nothing special about the A predicate. It is simply a projection on AL. Analogous to the AL predicate, we regard a variable in `A(x,m,y)` to be a meta variable.

```
[Formula 18: transitivity] ∀ AC,x,y,z,M,C In(AC,transitive) ∧
P(AC,C,M,C) ∧ In(x,C) ∧ In(y,C) ∧ In(z,C) ∧ A(x,M,y) ∧ A(y,M,z)
⇒ A(x,M,z)
```

```
[Formula 19: symmetry]
∀ AC,x,y,M,C In(AC,symmetric) ∧ P(AC,C,M,C) ∧ In(x,C) ∧ In(y,C)
∧ In(z,C) ∧ A(x,M,y) ⇒ A(y,M,x)
```

```
[Formula 19: antisymmetry] ∀ AC,x,y,M,C In(AC,antisymmetric) ∧
P(AC,C,M,C) ∧ In(x,C) ∧ In(y,C) ∧ In(z,C) ∧ A(x,M,y) ∧ A(y,M,x)
⇒(x = y)
```

```
[Formula 20: reflexivity]
∀ AC,x,M,C In(AC,reflexive) ∧
P(AC,C,M,C) ∧ In(x,C) ∧ In(y,C) ∧ In(z,C) ⇒ A(x,M,x)
```

Figure 3 shows how the meta formulas are applied to a the `IsA` and `PartOf` relations of classes. It is sufficient to declare

```
{In(Class!IsA,transitive), In(Class!IsA,reflexive),
```

[1] The ConceptBase system is capable to model the dynamic semantics of languages such as Petri nets by so-called active rules. They are however of a procedural nature and therefore beyond the scope of this paper.

```
In(Class!PartOf,transitive),
In(Class!PartOf,antisymmetric)}
```

for encoding the desired meaning of the two constructs. Hence, the more meta formulas are available, the higher are the chances of re-use for multiple cases.

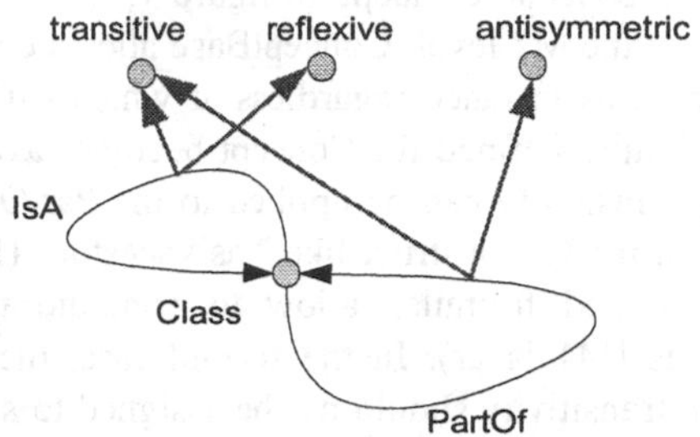

Figure 3: Configuring semantics via instantiation

7 Implementation

The method of partially evaluating meta formulas has been fully implemented in ConceptBase since 2003 for universally quantified formulas. The generated formulas are incrementally maintained when an update to an E-predicate occurs. This works both for additions and deletions. The bulk of the implementation work was not the partial evaluator but the code that selects the best E-predicate out of multiple candidates.

Except for pathological cases with large extensions of the E-predicate, there are no performance penalties when using meta formulas like the one on transitivity. We did tests with large model bases where version I defined transitivity 'by hand' and the version II used the meta formula. Both versions exhibit virtually the same evaluation times for queries over the transitive attribute. In the table below, reponse times of four queries are reported. Query Q1 is computing the dead ends of a network, i.e. those nodes that are connected only to nodes that lead to leave nodes. Query Q2 is an incomplete test on cliques and Q3 computes the transitive closure. Finally, Q4 returns the inverse of the transitive closure, i.e. nodes that are not reachable to each other. The size of the network is about 1400 nodes with about 5000 links. The table shows that there is no performance penalty to use the partially evaluated meta formulas.

Version	Q1	Q2	Q3	Q4
I	0.084	0.812	4.31	1.417
II	0.083	0.820	4.39	1.418

The universally quantified meta formulas are slightly easier to handle since they produce conjunctions of subformulas. Hence, each individual subformula can be maintained as a separate formula in the (deductive) theory. Existentially quantified meta formulas produce disjunctions of subformulas that must remain in one formula. ConceptBase currently does not support this case.

We used the MOF layers to motivate meta models and meta meta models. The implementation does not require this view. In fact by abandoning the strict association of concepts to MOF layers, one gets a more expressive meta modeling framework. Consider the concept 'Concept' in figure 1. It is located at the M3 layer and classifies concepts of the M2 level. ConceptBase allows objects like 'Concept' to have any another concept as instance regardless at which MOF layer we prefer to locate it. By this, any feature defined for Concept becomes available to any defined concept. For example, transitivity can be applied to the PartOf relation (M2 layer), but also to some domain model construct like 'hasAncestor' (M1 layer). In the first case, the partially evaluated formulas allow to compute the transitive closure between model elements (M1 layer). In the second case, they operate on the M0 layer. So, concepts like transitivity should not be assigned to strictly one abstraction layer. They constitute a relation between pairs of abstraction layers: M2 to M0, M3 to M1, M4 to M2, and so forth. Once defined, meta formulas can be used in ConceptBase by just making sure that the corresponding E-predicate is populated.

8 Related Work

While the partial evaluation technique itself is an adaption of the simplification method for deductive datab9ases (Nicolas, 1979), our contribution is to apply it to meta modeling. By our technique abstract constructs like transitivity can be defined once and forever. While the simplification method generates simplified formulas for any predicate occurrence, the partial evaluation method requires determining a single so-called E-predicate to compile a meta formula. The flat representation of the model base by predicates is inspired by Telos (Mylopoulos et al, 1990). In contrast to Telos, we have no predefined axioms to make the approach generally applicable. In particular the P predicate has a purely auxiliary function in our approach whereas it is central in the Telos axiomatization.

There are other ways to represent models and meta models by flat facts. The approach by (Bezivin, 2006) uses predicate names to encode concept names. As pointed out in section 2, such representations are preventing a management of first-order meta formulas.

Meta formulas are also treated by ontology management systems, in particular Protégé (Protégé, 2006). Protégé has predefined expressions for transitivity, symmetry etc. They are however not evaluated against some database as we do.

In linguistic semantics, so-called generalized quantifiers (Barwise and Cooper, 1981) have been investigated to descripe higher-order predicates, in particular to express properties of properties. Lambda parameters expressions abstract the predicate names from the logical formula. By substituting the parameters by actual predicate names, one yields a first order expression. For example,

```
lambda.X lambda.Y (X subset Y)(Student)(Person)
```

would be reduced to

```
Student subset Person.
```

We note that our definition of meta formulas is completely embedded into first order logic and does not require additional abstractions such as the lambda operator.

The HiLog logic programming language (Chen et al, 1993) deals with properties of properties much in the spirit of generalized quantifiers. Properties like transitive closure are expressed in a higher-order syntax of logic. HiLog has a mechanism to encode such higher-order expressions to predicate calculus using the `apply` predicate that shifts the higher order predicate symbol like 'transitive' to an argument position. The difference to our approach is that HiLog has a one-to-one encoding, i.e. the higher order formula is mapped to a single first order formula. In our approach, the meta formula (expressing the same principle of transitive closure) is mapped to many first order formulas, each specialized for one element of the extension of the E-predicate. So, we stick to first-order syntax to express higher order features and we provide for an efficient evaluation of the meta formulas via partial evaluation. On the other hand, HiLog is not limited by a finiteness assumption. HiLog is a Turing-complete programming language while our approach is defined for a deductive theory with finite perfect model semantics.

9 Application to Method Engineering

Partial evaluation of meta-level formulas has a somewhat theoretic flavor as it deals with highly abstract concepts. The most obvious application of the technique is for designing new modeling languages or formally defining existing modeling languages. The abstract concepts such as transitivity and multiplicity of relationships can be employed directly to define constructs like specialization and part-of in modeling languages. The added value of the meta-level formulas is that they only have to be defined once. Instantiating them leads to the automatic generation of a formula (either a rule or a constraint) specialized for the modeling language. In essence, the meta level formulas are the building blocks for the semantics of formally defined modeling languages.

The modeling languages are the product side of a method to be engineered. There is also a production side, namely the guidelines or processes that create and manipulate the products. The two sides are dependent on each other leading to amalgamated model such as process-data diagrams (Weerd et al., 2006) or software process models (Jarke et al, 1990). The amalgamated model constitutes a method fragment subject to be incorporated in complex methods. Such models also conform to some schema, i.e. there is a meta model in the sense of MOF that describes how the product side and the production side may be linked to each other. The link types themselves are elements of a modeling language, namely the language to describe the connection between a process and its products. This language has a meaning that should be reflected in the defininition of its constructs. Not surprisingly, the abstract concepts like transitivity are applicable to define the desired semantics. As an example, we focus on the traceability of products, i.e. of models and their elements. Traceability is has been a hot topic in the requirements engineering community. It allows following the development of the products of a development process. Each product (and each element of a product) depends on other products (and their elements). This is essentially the transitivity concept. All we would need to do would be to define a predicate `A(p1,dependsOn,p2)` in the meta model of the amalgamated process/product diagrams and to declare that dependsOn is transitive, i.e. `In(Product!dependsOn,transitive)`.

As a second example consider the versioning of product models as described in (Saeki, 2006). A product model is versioned by applying change operations on it. Let's assume that the version relation is represented by a predicate `A(p1,versionedTo,p2)` where p1 and p2 are product models. Then, one would define the versionedTo relation to be transitive and assymetric (a product model cannot be versioned to itself). The newest version of a given product model p can then be retrieved simply by querying

`A(p,versionedTo,pv)` $\wedge \neg \exists$ `px (pv,versionedTo,px)`

10 Conclusions

We presented an approach to manage first order formulas defining the meaning of modeling constructs at the meta and meta meta class levels. It turned out that it is sufficient to demand range-restrictedness in order to partially evaluate the meta formulas into conjunctions or disjunctions of non-meta formulas that are more efficient to evaluate.

The flat representation of the model base with predicate facts is powerful enough to capture the MOF abstraction layers. Since instantiation is stated explicitly, our method is more general by allowing models that *link concepts* of different abstraction layers. To apply the partial evaluation approach, one simply has to encode that one concept is an instance of another concept rather than by specifying to which MOF layer a concept belongs. It is perfectly possible to define a meta class (or even a meta meta class) that has an attribute link to a concept that one would regard as M0 concept. For example, a meta class can have an attribute 'createdBy' that links it to its creator. This phenomenon systematically occurs when one superimposes a product meta model (e.g. ERD) with a process meta model, i.e. a specification of operations that manipulate instances of the product meta model. This is the common case in method engineering as it links process models (the procedural steps of the method) with product models (the input and output of the steps).

The greatest benefit of our method arises when meta formulas are defined at the most generic layer. Then, the semantics of modeling language constructs is generated by instantiating them to the meta formulas. This level of re-use of meta formulas makes meta modeling itself a more productive activity: instead of coding formulas one simply declares a construct as an instance of the abstract concepts defined by the meta formulas. As an additional bonus, the generated formulas are materialized and can be attached to the meta model describing the modeling language.

As mentioned earlier, semantics of dynamic modeling languages are not covered by our technique because they require to reason about infinite extensions. We plan to investigate whether certain principles like state transitions can be defined as an abstract concept, i.e. independently from the specific modeling language, and then be instantiated to a specific modeling language by an analogous approach. That capability would further enrich the toolbox for engineering modeling languages from pre-fabricated building blocks. For example, languages like event-process chains should be definable from building blocks that can also be used to define petri nets.

The partial evaluation technique described in this paper is fully implemented in the ConceptBase system and has been used in various meta modeling scenarios. Some details are on the web page http://conceptbase.cc.

Acknowledgements: We cordially thank René Soiron for implementing a major part of the meta formula compiler in ConceptBase.

References

Barwise, J. and Cooper, R., 1981. Generalized quantifiers and natural language. Linguistics and Philosophy 4: 159-219.

Bezivin, J., 2006. On the Unification Power of Models. Software and System Modeling (SoSym) 4(2):171--188.

Bry, F., 1989. Logical rewritings for improving the evaluation of quantified queries. Proc. 2nd Intl. Symposium on Mathematical Fundamentals of Database Systems, Visegrád, Hungary, 1989, Springer-Verlag, LNCS 364.

Chen, W., Kifer, M., Warren, D.S., 1993. HiLog: A foundation for higher-order logic programming. Journal of Logic Programming 15(3):187-230.

OMG, 2006. Meta Object Facility. Online http://www.omg.org/mof/, June 2006.

Protégé, 2006. The Protégé ontology editor and knowledge acquisition system. Online http://protege.stanford.edu/, June 2006.

Jarke, M., R. Gallersdörfer, R., Jeusfeld, M.A., Staudt, M., Eherer, S, 1995.: ConceptBase - a deductive object base for meta data management. Journal of Intelligent Information Systems, 4, 2, 1995, pp. 167-192.

Jarke, M., Jeusfeld, M.A., Rose, T., 1990: A software process data model for knowledge engineering in information systems. In Information Systems, 15, 1, 1990, pp. 85-116.

Mylopoulos, J., Borgida, A., Jarke, M., Koubarakis, M., 1990. Telos - a language for representing knowledge about information systems. In ACM Trans. Information Systems, 8, 4, 1990, pp. 325-362.

Nicolas, J.-M., 1979. Logical formulas and integrity constraints: the range restricted property and a simplification method. Technical report T-R CERT-LBD/79-1, Toulouse, France.

Saeki, M., 2006: Configuration management in a method engineering context. Proceedings CAiSE 2006, Springer-Verlag, LNCS 4001/2006, pp. 384-398.

Weerd, I. van de, Versendaal, J., Brinkkemper, S., 2006. A product software knowledge infrastructure for situational scpability maturation: vision and case studies in product management, Technical Report UU-CS-2006-008, Utrecht University, The Netherlands.

Representation of Method Fragments

A Comparative Study

Anat Aharoni and Iris Reinhartz-Berger
Department of Management Information Systems,
University of Haifa, Haifa 31905, Israel
anatah@mis.haifa.ac.il, iris@mis.haifa.ac.il

Abstract. The discipline of situational method engineering promotes the idea of retrieving and adapting fragments, rather than complete methodologies, to specific situations. In order to succeed in creating good methodologies that best suit given situations, fragment representation and cataloguing are very important activities. This paper presents and compares three existing approaches to fragment representation. It further provides a set of evaluation criteria for comparing fragment representation approaches. These criteria include expressiveness, consistency, formalism, situational cataloguing, adaptability and flexibility to changes, comprehensibility, and connectivity. Based on this comparison, we introduce a new visual approach that combines the benefits of the three reviewed approaches and attempts to overcome their limitations. This approach relies on a specific domain engineering method, called Application-based DOmain Modeling (ADOM), which enables specification of fragments at various levels of details, specification of fragment types and their constraints, and validation of specific fragments against their relevant fragment types. All these activities are done using a well known modeling language (UML), increasing user accessibility (and consequently comprehensibility).

1 Introduction

As the complexity and variety of computer-based systems have increased, the need for well-defined guidelines that will make the development process most efficient and effective has become crucial. Although sticking to an individual methodology has potential advantages, such as reducing learning and training times and improving the expertise of developers in the chosen methodology, there is no single methodology that can be uniquely pointed as "the best". Furthermore, the possible existence of a universally applicable methodology has been doubted by many researchers, such as [0], and, hence, different types of "local" adaptations and modifications have to be made in order to adjust a methodology to the specific requirements and constraints of a project. The area of *method engineering* [00] aims at providing effective solutions for building, improving, and supporting evolution of development methodologies. *Situational method engineering* [0], which can be viewed as a sub-field of method

---

Please use the following format when citing this chapter:

Aharoni, A., Reinhartz-Berger, I., 2007, in IFIP International Federation for Information Processing, Volume 244, Situational Method Engineering: Fundamentals and Experiences, eds. Ralyté, J., Brinkkemper, S., Henderson-Sellers B., (Boston Springer), pp. 130-145.

engineering, focuses on creating methodologies especially for specific situations. Both regular and situational method engineering refer to *fragments*, the building blocks of methodologies, rather than to complete methodologies. They offer ways to represent fragments, catalogue them according to different features, retrieve the most appropriate ones to given situations, and organize them into complete methodologies. In order to succeed in creating good situational methodologies, i.e., methodologies that best fit given situations, fragment representation and cataloguing are very important activities. In particular, the fragments have to be represented in a uniform way that includes all the necessary information that may influence their retrieval and assembling. This paper focuses on these activities, presenting and comparing three existing approaches to fragment representation. Based on this comparison, which involves criteria such as expressiveness, consistency, and situational cataloguing, we introduce a new visual approach that combines the benefits of the three reviewed approaches and attempts to overcome their limitations. The contribution of this paper is two folded. First, it provides evaluation criteria for comparing and analyzing situational method engineering approaches that concentrate on fragment representation and cataloguing. To the best of our knowledge, such criteria have not been suggested yet and the comparison of situational method engineering approaches is done based on general method engineering criteria. We use the evaluation criteria for comparing the three reviewed fragment representation methods and for explaining the benefits and limitations of the new introduced approach. Second, the new introduced approach brings further advantages that are not exhibited by the three reviewed representation approaches (or by others): it improves the situational cataloguing ability; it enables constraining and specifying fragment types; and it enables validating the completeness and correctness of fragments (against their fragment types).

The structure of the rest of the paper is as follows. Section 2 motivates the need for situational method engineering. We later use this example for exemplifying the different approaches, their limitations, and advantages. Section 3 lists seven evaluation criteria for comparing fragment representation approaches, while Section 4 uses these criteria for presenting and comparing three particular fragment representation approaches. Section 5 introduces and exemplifies our approach, discussing its benefits and limitations in the light of the other three approaches and the evaluation criteria. Finally, Section 6 concludes and refers to future research plans.

2 The need for situational method engineering: a motivation example

As already noted, situational method engineering deals with creation of methodologies that best fit given situations. The situation can be given as a vector of different properties related to the project, the customer, the developing team, the developing organization, etc. Examples to researches that list such properties can be found at [0, 0]. To motivate the need for situational methodologies, consider the following simple Obsert Oglesby case [0].

Obsert Oglesby is an art dealer who requests an information system to assist him in buying and selling paintings for his gallery. After consulting with an independent consultant, Obsert decided to turn to a well-known development company in order to buy a system which will enable him calculating the minimal and maximal prices of a painting and will also serve in detecting new trends in the art market as soon as possible. The development company which was chosen is familiar with the art world and has developed similar systems. The company mainly works with eXtreme Programming (XP) [0] for small projects which need to be developed quickly in an environment of rapidly changing requirements and with RUP [0] for complex projects which are developed by large teams and require detailed documentation. Since Obsert's case does not completely fit to any of these options, the development team decided to use suitable fragments from both methodologies and to adapt them for the particular case. In order to succeed in this mission, the development team has to tackle three main questions: (1) How to divide a methodology into different fragments that can be reused in various contexts? (2) What are the properties that best characterize each fragment? (3) How (or to what extent) can different fragments be adapted and organized into a complete, consecutive methodology? In the context of fragment representation, these questions can be transformed into the following ones: (1) What are the expressiveness and consistency requirements needed for specifying all kinds of method fragments? (2) What are the situational cataloguing abilities required to be supported at the fragment representation level? (3) How (or to what extent) can the possible adaptation (that a fragment may undergo in a situational methodology) be constrained?

Returning to our Obsert's case, the required system is small, the client (Obsert Oglesby) requests his involvement during the development process, and detailed documentation, especially of the business model and system requirements, is required. Hence, the fragments which may be found as relevant to the early development stages of the requested system are "extract requirements" and "build a business model" from RUP and "on-site customer" from XP. The "extract requirements" fragment may be selected due to the generality of the requirements and their extraction by an external consultant. The “building a business model” may be chosen due to the explicit request of the client to receive a detailed documentation of his business. Finally, the “on-site customer” fragment may be selected due to the client's request to be involved throughout the entire development process. However, since the company has already previous obligations and since the client is relatively small, the "on-site customer” fragment cannot be followed literally. Instead, the company may suggest that the client representative will have the authority and ability to provide information pertaining to the system and to make timely decisions regarding the requirements and their prioritization. However, he/she will not be able to physically present in the development site. This limitation will be overcome by creating a time schedule that defines slots and places for collaboration during the development period.

In order that all these selections and modifications will finalize in a complete, consecutive methodology, the way the fragments are presented and constrained is very crucial. In the next section, we list and elaborate on evaluation criteria for examining and comparing fragment representation approaches.

3 Evaluation criteria for fragment representation approaches

The set of evaluation criteria listed here aims at supporting correct, complete, and consistent representation and cataloguing of method fragments, as well as supporting the successive activities of retrieval, adaptation, and building situational methodologies. These criteria were derived from works on qualities of representation models or languages, especially from [0] and [0].

Expressiveness. Although using the same term, fragments differ from each other. Brinkkemper et al. [0] refer to three orthogonal dimensions when modeling and classifying fragments: perspective, abstraction, and granularity. According to the *perspective* dimension, a fragment can be either product- or process-oriented: product fragments relate to the structural and static aspects of methodologies (e.g., deliverables, documents, and models), whereas process fragments capture the behavioral and procedural aspects of methodologies (e.g., stages, tasks, and activities to be carried out). The *abstraction* level of a fragment can be conceptual or technical: conceptual fragments are descriptions and specifications of methodology parts, while technical fragments are implementations of operational parts of the methodology in the form of tools. Finally, a fragment can reside in one of five possible *granularity* levels: method, stage, model, diagram, or concept. The expressiveness of a fragment representation approach can be measured as how much of this variety of fragment types can be specified using the approach. For specifying process fragments, for example, means for expressing branching, loops, and concurrency are required. For expressing fragments at different granularity levels, encapsulation and generalization mechanisms are required for combining several concepts to one (aggregated or generalized) concept. Furthermore, the relations between different fragments, mainly the interactions between process and product fragments, should be specified somehow.

Consistency. Consistency refers to the fact that the same fragment can be (re)used in different contexts, e.g., while describing a specialized or an aggregated fragment, while defining the relations between process and product fragments, while adapting the fragment to the situation at hand, etc. It is important that all these occurrences of the fragment will be consistent with each other, meaning that changes in one place will be applied to all the other places as well. However, if those changes regard to a specific situation, a separate version of the fragment should be maintained.

Formalism. There are different ways to represent things: graphically, textually, logically, mathematically, etc. Generally speaking, representation formalism is a set of syntactic and semantic conventions that allows describing and specifying things. It can be formal, semi-formal, or completely informal, affecting comprehensibility and non-ambiguity of the specifications. In the context of situational method engineering, the presented fragments have to be retrieved, adapted, and tailored latter and, hence, it is important that their representation will be formal or at least semi-formal.

Situational cataloguing. In order to make fragment retrieval easy, effective, and optionally (semi-)automated, fragment representation approaches should wisely catalogue and index the different fragments according to characteristics and features that may define and distinguish different situations. This criterion checks the ability to describe for each fragment the different organizational, human, and project-related features that best characterize it and are likely to be used for retrieval purposes [0, 0]. These lists of characteristics may be modified over time and location (the developing organization) and may vary when different types of fragments are considered.

Adaptability and flexibility to changes. Situational method engineering mainly deals with two ways for integrating fragments to new methodologies, customization and assembling. *Customization* includes operations that have to be carried out on the original method fragments in order to create new (usually slightly different) versions of that fragments that suit the given situations. *Assembling* deals with attaching and connecting methodology fragments, while transformation and gluing parts between the fragments can be added in order to create complete, consecutive methodologies. This criterion checks the ability to support these operations in the representation level.

Comprehensibility. This criterion checks how easy it is to learn and use the fragment representation approach. This is derived from the approach complexity (number of different concepts), ambiguity, and expected stakeholders (users). Although both regular and situational method engineering are perceived as the responsibility of method engineers only, involving other stakeholders, such as software engineers, developers, and even managers, in the associated method engineering processes and decisions may improve their commitment to the chosen constructed methodologies, so they will actually follow them.

Connectivity. Connectivity measures the ability of the method to tailor fragments derived from different source methodologies [0]. Since different methodologies have different assumptions and characteristics, the ability to represent fragments from various source methodologies is not a trivial task. Furthermore, assembling them to consecutive situational methodologies often requires maintaining transformation and gluing fragments. Although this type of fragments can be analyzed and described in terms of product and process fragments, it has also special requirements which need to be considered by the representation approach, such as storing the associated source and target fragments.

4 Fragment representation approaches

There are several works in the area of method engineering and situational method engineering whose focus is fragment and/or methodology representation. We chose to use three particular approaches in this paper which are consistently cited in the literature and refer to (at least) several of our evaluation criteria, discussed in Section 0. Next, we briefly present each approach, exemplify how it represents the "extract requirements" fragment from RUP, and discuss its benefits and limitations according to the seven evaluation criteria. The main outcomes of this comparison are summarized in the appendix.

4.1 An assembly-based situational method engineering approach

The assembly-based situational method engineering approach [0] aims at supporting the development of web-based Content Management Systems (CMS). The four main stages in this approach are identification of the implementation situation, selection of candidate methods, analysis and storage of relevant fragments in the method base, and assembly of the fragments into a complete methodology using route maps for tuning the fragments to the situation at hand [0]. Regarding fragment representation, the approach uses process-data diagrams, which integrate the process model described by UML activity diagrams with the product model described by UML class diagrams. The relations between these two parts are described by dotted arrows that connect activities with the artifacts they create or adjust. Figure 1 for example, describes the "extract requirements" fragment in this approach.

Several adjustments have been made to the standard UML notation in this approach. First, the approach allows specifying unordered activities. The sub-activities "set priority", "estimate risk", and "set status" in Figure 1, for example, are unordered, but they are all sequential to the sub-activity "categories to functional/nonfunctional requirements". Second, the approach uses three different types of symbols for indicating simple vs. compound concepts. A simple concept, denoted by a rectangle, is atomic and, hence, does not contain other (sub-)concepts. An open concept, denoted by a white shadowed rectangle, consists of a collection of (sub-)concepts. Finally, a closed concept, denoted by a black shadowed rectangle, is an unexpanded compound concept, which consists of (sub-)concepts in other fragments. "Value", "Requirement", and "Priority" in Figure 1 are simple concepts, "Domain Glossary" and "Requirement Document" are open concepts, and Business Model is a closed concept.

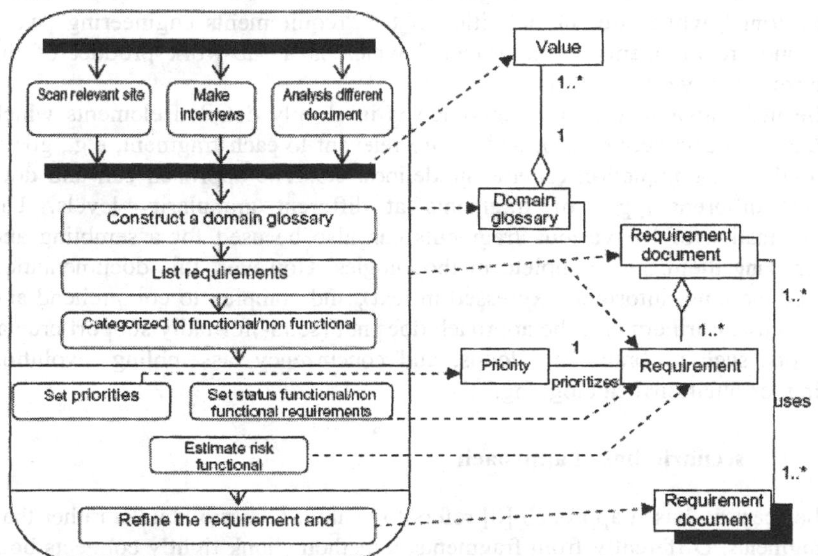

Figure 1. The "extract requirements" fragment of RUP expressed in the assembly-based situational method engineering approach [0].

The approach enables expression of both process and product fragments, as well as the mutual relationships among them. It uses a well known semi-formal, modeling language (UML) with minor changes, which might slightly affect the approach comprehensibility and accessibility. However, it only partially refers to consistency issues by introducing closed concepts, and does not enable specification of the allowed adaptations and changes that a fragment may undergo when assembling or customizing it to a given situation. It further misses the ability to specify the situational features that characterize each fragment, leaving the selection process to the user (i.e., the method engineer).

4.2 The OPEN Process Framework (OPF)

The OPEN Process Framework (OPF) [0] is a large repository for supporting flexible creation of numerous tailored methodologies. Although OPF started as a method engineering approach, we decided to choose it in our research due to its good informational website, its large, diverse, and free repository, and its lately adaptation to situational method engineering requirements.

The OPF consists of three main parts, which are: (1) a repository of reusable method components documented as hierarchical linked Web pages, (2) a meta-model describing the organizational structure of the repository, and (3) construction and usage guidelines. Being a general method engineering approach, OPF does not explicitly refer to method fragments. However, work products, which are significant elements that are described using fields such as contents, stakeholders, and conventions, can be considered as product fragments. Work units, on the other hand, which are described using fields such as completion criteria, tasks, and work products to be produced, can be considered as process fragments. To implement the "extract requirements" fragment, for example, one can consider the following Web pages from the OPF repository: “application requirements engineering” and “business requirements engineering”, which are sub-activities of the “requirements engineering” work unit, and “requirements work product” which is a sub-work product of the “requirements” work product.

The main advantage of this approach is its deeply detailed elements which include a wide variety of aspects that are relevant to each fragment, e.g., goals, preconditions, completion criteria, guidelines, etc. The approach can and does support different types of fragments at different granularity levels. The documentation of the various fragments can also be used for assembling and customizing them into complete methodologies. However, this documentation may be too long, informal (expressed in text), and complex to comprehend and learn to use. Furthermore, the approach does not (semi-)formally support crucial concepts, such as branching, loops, and concurrency, assembling, evolution tracing, or situational cataloguing.

4.3 The scenario-based approach

The scenario-based approach [0] refers to method scenario chunks rather than to fragments. Differently from fragments, a method chunk tightly connects both product and process parts, allowing specifying mutual relations between them. The scenario method base is organized in two levels, the *method knowledge* and the *method meta-knowledge*. The method knowledge level includes for each chunk its interface and body. The *chunk body* describes the product to be delivered and the guidelines to be applied in order to produce the product. The guidelines are defined as hierarchies of related contexts which are connected through three types of links: refinement, composition, and action. The *chunk interface* describes its conditions for applicability to different situations and the ‘intention’ the chunk aims to fulfill. The method meta-knowledge aims at supporting the retrieval process and deals with the context in which method knowledge can be (re)used. This is done by using *chunk descriptors* which express the situation to which the chunk is suitable in terms of the application domains and the design activities in which the chunk can be reused. The chunk interface, body, and descriptor are specified using Standard Generalized Markup Language (SGML) [0].

exemplifies the approach for the "extract requirements" chunk. For the sake of clarity and brevity, we brought here only parts of the SGML description, emphasizing the representation template.

```
(a) <DESCRIPTOR_SITUATION>
  <APPLICATION_DOMAIN> all types of application </APPLICATION_DOMAIN>
  <DESIGN_ACTIVITY> requirements </ DESIGN_ACTIVITY>
  </DESCRIPTOR_SITUATION>
  <DESCRIPTOR_INTENTION>
      <VERB> capture </VERB>
      <TARGET role=<<result>>Type=<<non-scenario-based>>>App. Requirements
      </TARGET>
      <COMPLEX_MANNER>
          <VERB> Produce </VERB>
          <TARGET role=<<result>>Type=<<scenario-based>>...>requirements doc.
          </TARGET>
          <SIMPLE_MANNER> by the requirement workflow of RUP
          </SIMPLE _MANNER>
      </ COMPLEX_MANNER >
  </DESCRIPTOR_ INTENTION >
(b)
<CHUNK name=<< produce requirements document >>
type=<<formal>>  informal description= << produce requirements document by obtain an
initial understanding of the domain than draw up an initial set of requirements and finally refine
the requirements artifacts >>  >
   <GRAPHICAL_REPRESENTATION><AHREF=<<fileName.gif>> ></A>
   </GRAPHICAL_REPRESENTATION >
<INTERFACE>
 <CHUNK_SITUATION> <CHUNK_SITUATION>      ...
</CHUNK_INTENTION>          ...        <CHUNK_INTENTION>
</INTERFACE>
 <BODY>
<PRODUCT name=<< Requirements document>>
informal description=<< informal description of the requirements document
structure>>>...
       </ PRODUCT>
<PRODUCT_GRAPHICAL REPRESENTATION>
<A HREF =<<grapich_rep.gif>>>.....
</ GUIDELINE >          ...          <GUIDELINE>
    </BODY>
</CHUNK>
```

Figure 2. The "extract requirements" chunk of RUP expressed in the scenario-based approach: a partial SGML code of (a) the chunk descriptor (b) chunk interface and body

This approach supports specification of method chunks, including their product and process parts, at different granularity levels. It uses a (semi-)formal language in the form of SGML code that might be complex to understand and manage by human users. Each chunk can be reused in a more complex aggregated chunk. Furthermore, the approach enables adapting and changing chunks to specific situations by supporting the definition of parameters within the SGML code. However, the tight coupling between product and process fragments in the approach may cause redundancy and difficulties in reusing the same process or product fragment in different contexts, raising consistency issues that must be handled. Furthermore, at the current stage, the situational cataloguing capabilities of the approach are limited to the application domain and the relevant design activities only.

5 A domain engineering-based approach for fragment representation

As discussed in the previous section, the main limitations of existing method representation approaches are in their user accessibility and comprehensibility, their situational cataloguing abilities, and their ability to constrain the structure and behavior of fragments in order to support a smooth transition to the successive situational method engineering activities (mainly assembling and customization). In order to overcome these limitations, we propose a holistic, visual, domain engineering-based approach for managing, representing, retrieving, customizing, and integrating method fragments in order to create new methodologies that best suit a situation at hand. The fragment representation part of this approach provides the ability to express different types of methodologies and their fragments, their associated characteristics and values, their pre- and post-conditions, and other fragment-related requirements, such as mandatory participants, recommended (optional) participants, triggers, etc. This is done by using a domain engineering approach called Application-based DOmain Modeling (ADOM) and the standard notation of UML 2.0 [0].

Domain engineering [0] is a software engineering discipline concerned with building reusable assets and components that fit to a family of applications, termed a domain. The purpose of domain engineering is to identify, model, construct, catalog, and disseminate a set of software artifacts that can be applied to existing and future software in a particular application domain. As such, it is an important type of software reuse, knowledge representation, and validation. ADOM [0, 0] is a particular domain engineering approach perceiving that applications and domains are similar in many aspects, thus it enables modeling domains with regular software engineering techniques. The application models use domain models mainly for creation (instantiation, reuse) and validation purposes. ADOM is based on a three layered architecture: application, domain, and language. The application layer consists of models of particular applications, including their structure and behavior. The language layer includes meta-models of modeling languages, such as UML. The intermediate domain layer consists of specifications of various domains (i.e., application families). These specifications describe the commonality as well as the variability allowed among applications in the domain. The ADOM approach further enforces constraints among the different layers; in particular, the domain layer enforces constraints on the application layer, while the language layer enforces constraints on both domain and application layers.

ADOM is a quite general architecture and can be applied to different modeling languages that support element classification. ADOM-UML, in which ADOM is used in combination with UML 2.0 [0], was chosen in this context due to the familiarity and establishment of UML in the software development area.

5.1 ADOM-UML

In ADOM-UML, UML stereotypes are used both for classifying application elements according to their relevant domain elements and for specifying the allowed variability among applications in the domain.

In the *language layer*, a new stereotype of the form <<multiplicity min=m max = n>> is defined in order to represent how many times, constrained by the lowest and upper most multiplicity boundaries, a model element of this type can appear in a specific context[1].

In the *domain layer* the main concepts of the domain and the relations among them are specified using UML. The allowed variability within the domain is also specified in this layer by attaching multiplicity stereotypes to the various domain concepts and by adding additional logical constraints (such as "or" to denote variations and "xor" to denote alternatives).

In the *application layer*, the stereotype mechanism is used in order to classify the application elements according to the pre-defined domain elements. The classified application elements are required to fulfill the constraints induced by their classifying domain elements at the domain layer. In addition, the ADOM approach allows adding to application models non-classified elements which are specific to the application at hand and, hence, do not appear in the domain model. These additions are allowed as long as they do not violate the domain constraints.

5.2 Representing and cataloguing fragments in ADOM-UML

The structure and guidelines of fragments are described within the domain layer of ADOM, while their instantiations, which specify particular situational methodologies, are defined in the application layer. In these two layers, process and product fragments are respectively described by UML activity and class diagrams, while the lowest (simple, atomic) fragments may link to Web pages, similar to those exist in the OPF repository. The dependencies among process and product fragments can be concluded from the consistency constraints required to be maintained between the relevant class and activity diagrams in UML (e.g., the classes of object nodes that appear in the activity diagrams have to be described in the class diagrams). Furthermore, the different features that characterize each fragment are represented and associated to the fragment models as UML templates, i.e., parameterized elements that can be used to generate other model elements using binding relationships. The exact lists of features that characterize the different types of fragments can be derived from works that were done in the area of situational method engineering, such as [0, 0], and from practitioners.

Figure 3 and Figure 4 respectively exemplify process and product fragments taken from RUP [0]. Figure 3 describes the "extract requirements" process

---

[1] For clarity purposes, we defined four commonly used multiplicity groups on top of this stereotype: <<optional many>>, where min=0 and max=unbounded, <<optional single>>, where min=0 and max=1, <<mandatory many>>, where min=1 and max=unbounded, and <<mandatory single>>, where min=max=1.

fragment, including its optional inputs, required participants, expected deliverables, skeletal steps and flow of control[2].

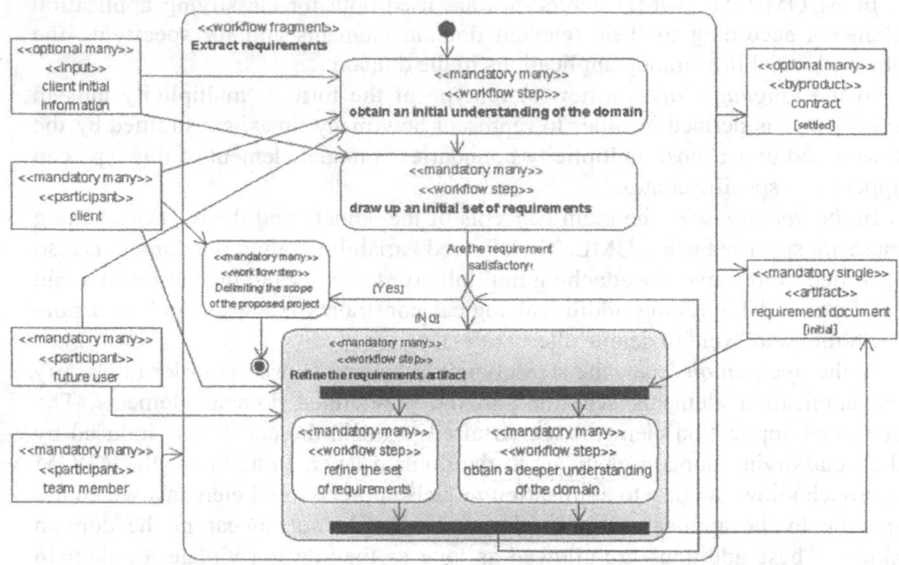

(b) **<SITUATION_CHARACTERISTICS** fragmentType=<<process>>
fragmentName=<<extract requirements>> >
<PROJECT_CHARACTERISTICS>
<APPLICATION_DOMAIN>All</APPLICATION_DOMAIN>
<PROJECT_SIZE>greater or equal 2 sub systems</ PROJECT_SIZE >
<FLEXIBILITY_TO_CHANGES>low</ FLEXIBILITY_TO_CHANGES >
. . .
</ PROJECT_CHARACTERISTICS>
<METHOD_CHARACTERISTICS>
<SOURCE_METHOD>RUP</ SOURCE_METHOD >
<DEVELOPMENT_ACTIVITY>requirements
</DEVELOPMENT_ACTIVITY>
<PRE-ACTIVITIES>signed contract</ SOURCE_METHOD >
. . .
</ METHOD_CHARACTERISTICS>
</SITUATION_CHARACTERISTICS

Figure 3. (a) A description of the "extract requirements" process fragment of RUP in the ADOM-UML-based approach. (b) Its associated characterization file.

Figure 4 describes the "requirement document", which is an artifact that may be produced by the "extract requirements" fragment or another process fragment. The fragment model constrains the general structure of a requirement document, including its possible variability, without referring to its production way. A requirement document, for example, may relate to several business models and business domain glossaries, which are also types of artifacts. Figure 4 also specifies, using UML templates, the situations in which usage of the

[2] Note that UML enables associating separated icons to the various stereotypes in order to help differentiate among them (e.g. humans vs. deliverables). However, in this paper, we preferred using the full (meaningful) stereotype labels so that readers who are not familiar with ADOM will easily understand the models.

"requirement document" product fragment is desirable: the project life cycle is at least one year, the project size is at least two sub systems, and the flexibility to change is low. As this description might become long and embedding it within the graphics may badly affect the comprehensibility of the diagram, we also support the possibility to define the situations to which the fragment is suitable in a separate XML or SGML file. Figure 3 (b) exemplifies such a characterization file for the "extract requirements" process fragment.

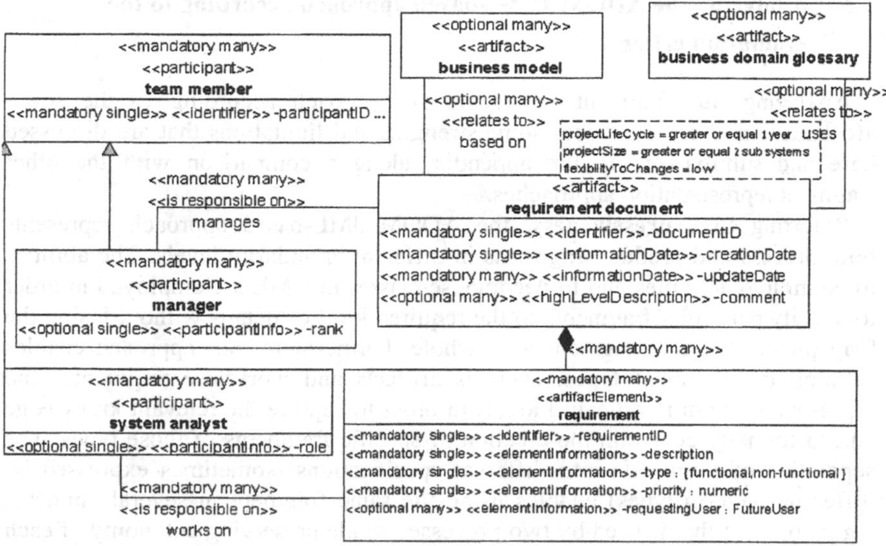

Figure 4. A description of the "requirement document" product fragment of RUP in the ADOM-UML-based approach

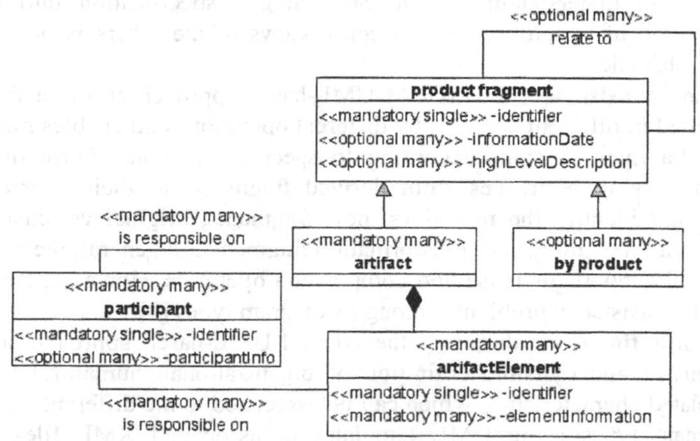

Figure 5. A description of an artifact, which is a specialization of a product fragment, in the ADOM-UML-based approach

Note that all the stereotypes that are used in these diagrams, except from the multiplicity stereotypes discussed earlier, are meaningful concepts in the situational method engineering area. Hence, they can (and may) be generalized and constrained, so that the particular method fragments will be specified in a uniform way. These specifications can be done within ADOM-UML as more general domain models. Figure 5, for example, presents a partial model of an artifact. As can be seen, this meta-model is in yet a more abstract level than the fragment models depicted in Figure 3 and Figure 4, allowing its usage for different kinds of artifacts, e.g., business models and domain glossaries. However, note that the model given in Figure 4 uses the stereotypes defined in Figure 5 and fulfills all the constraints imposed by this figure.

5.3 Analyzing the ADOM-UML-based approach according to the evaluation criteria

Analyzing our fragment representation approach according to the seven aforementioned criteria raises some strengths and limitations that are discussed here and summarized in the appendix, along a comparison with the other fragment representation approaches.

Referring to **expressiveness**, the ADOM-UML-based approach represents both process and product fragments in different granularity levels. The abilities to zoom into activities and to decompose classes in UML are employed in order to specify particular fragments to the required level of details without losing the "big picture" of the fragment as a whole. Furthermore, our approach enables refining the fragment types, such as artifacts and workflow fragments, and representing them in domain models in order to capture the relevant knowledge and to formally constrain the creation of specific fragments of those types. The separation of fragments into different specifications (sometimes expressed by different diagram types) enables using the same fragment in several contexts, e.g., a product that is used by two processes, while preserving autonomy of each part. However, as the fragments might become very complex, this approach also has to deal with visibility problems in the diagrams, both in developing the models and in understanding them. Separating a specification into several diagrams some of which are more specific views of the others is one way to tackle this obstacle.

Regarding **consistency**, the ADOM-UML-based approach allows a fragment to be (re)used in different contexts by different operations and enables managing separated fragment versions according to specific situations. Furthermore, it enables preserving references from derived fragments to their source ones, helping easily identify the reused vs. new fragments, original vs. customized fragments, and the gluing and transformation fragments. In general, the approach provides full support for reuse and composition operators. However, it inherits from UML consistency problems among its diagram types [0].

As for **situational cataloguing**, the ADOM-UML-based approach supports comprehensive and dynamic definition of organizational, human-related, and project-related characteristics, which can be associated to the different fragments and fragment types using UML templates or associated XML files. These features may be used latter for retrieving and assembling the fragments.

Referring to **formalism**, the ADOM-UML-based approach is visual and semi-formal. However, since it applies the well-known modeling language UML, its accessibility to different types of users, such as developers or managers with technical background, is increased over other more formal fragment representation approaches. As noted, the approach accessibility is important for increasing the probability of using the resultant situational methodologies and for making the process of learning and using the fragment representation method easy (earlier referred to as the **comprehensibility** criterion).

Regarding **adaptability and flexibility to changes**, the ADOM-UML-based approach enables all its fragment types to be specialized, adapted, and customized. These operations create new fragments that can be modified as requested by allowing specification of gluing and transformation fragments, customization parts, etc., but without violating the core constraints of the fragment types and of the fragments from which they were derived.

Regarding **connectivity**, the uniform representation of all fragments in the ADOM-UML-based approach enables assembling and connecting fragments that are derived from different source methodologies as long as their pre- and post-conditions fit. Even if they do not exactly fit, the approach allows defining transformation and gluing fragments that help create complete and consecutive situational methodologies.

6 Conclusions and future work

As there is no (and probably will not be) a single universally applicable methodology, the importance of situational method engineering and fragment representation approaches has been increased. In this paper, we listed seven important criteria for evaluating and comparing fragment representation approaches, used them for analyzing the benefits and limitations of three known approaches, and proposed a new approach that aims at overcoming the shortcomings and offering some additional benefits. In the new ADOM-UML-based approach, the fragments are generalized and specified in a domain layer, while the situational methodologies, which assemble and customize the relevant, retrieved fragments, are specified and modeled in the application layer. Due to space limitations, we have not exemplified here a situational methodology, but such an example can be found at [0] along with a description of the supporting CASE tool. Fragment types are also generalized in ADOM as more abstract domain models that guide and constrain the creation of particular fragments of those types. We used UML class and activity diagrams in order to be able to express both product and process fragments and to maintain their consistency. Our comparative analysis shows that the ADOM-UML-based approach supports comprehensive and dynamic definition of characteristics and situational cataloguing information; it better guides the creation of different types of fragments; it is accessible to both method engineers and other potential stakeholders; and it may enable a smooth transition to the successive situational method engineering activities (mainly assembling and customization) by constraining and guiding fragment creation.

As for the future, we plan to elaborate the evaluation criteria to other situational method engineering activities, as well as to show how our extended ADOM-based approach supports these activities in a semi-automatic manner.

References

1. Aydin MN, Harmsen F. Making a Method Work for a Project Situation in the Context of CMM. LNCS 2559, Springer, pp. 158–171, 2002.
2. Brinkkemper, S. Method Engineering: Engineering of information systems development methods and tools. Information and Software Technology, 38(4), pp. 275-280, 1996.

3. Brinkkemper, S. Saeki, M., Harmsen, F. Meta-modelling based assembly techniques for situational method engineering. Information Systems, 24(3), pp. 209-228. 1999.
4. Bryan, M. SGML - An Author's Guide to the Standard Generalized Markup Language. Addison-Wesley publishers Ltd., 1995.
5. Carnegie Mellon Software Engineering Institute. Domain Engineering: A Model-Based Approach, http://www.sei.cmu.edu/domain-engineering , 2002.
6. Extreme Programming Web Site, Extreme Programming: A gentle introduction, http://www.extremeprogramming.org, 2006.
7. IBM, Rational Unified Process, http://www-306.ibm.com/software/awdtools/rup/
8. Krogstie, J. and Arnesen, S. Assessing Enterprise Modeling Languages using a Generic Quality Framework. In J. Krogstie, K. Siau, & T. Halpin, (Eds.), Information Modeling Methods and Methodologies, Idea Group, pp. 63-79, 2005.
9. Krogstie, J., Lindland, O.I., and Sindre, G. Defining Quality Aspects for Conceptual Models. In E. D. Falkenberg, W. Hesse, & A. Olive (Eds.), Proceedings of the IFIP8.1 working conference on Information Systems Concepts (ISCO3): Towards a consolidation of views, pp. 216-231, 1995.
10. Malouin, J.L., Landry, M. The mirage of universal methods in system design. Journal of applied systems analysis, 10, pp. 47-62, 1983.
11. Mirbel, I. Rethinking ISD methods: Fitting project team members profiles. I3S technical report I3S/RR-2004-13-FR, 2004. Available from http://www.i3s.unice.fr/~mirbel/publis/im-isd-04.pdf.
12. Mirbel, I., Method chunk federation. Available at http://www.i3s.unice.fr/~mh/RR/2006/RR-06.04-I.MIRBEL.pdf, 2006.
13. OMG, "Unified Modeling Language: Superstructure", Version 2.0, 2005, http://www.omg.org/docs/formal/05-07-04.pdf
14. OPEN Process Framework (OPF) Web Site. http://www.opfro.org/.
15. Ralyté, J., Deneckere, R., Rolland, C., Towards a generic model for situational method engineering, CAiSE 2003, LNCS 2681, pp. 95-110, 2003.
16. Reinhartz-Berger, I. Conceptual Modeling of Structure and Behavior with UML – The Top Level Object-Oriented Framework (TLOOF) Approach, 24th International Conference on Conceptual Modeling (ER'2005), LNCS 3716, 1-15, 2005.
17. Reinhartz-Berger, I. and Aharoni, A. Representation of Method Fragments: A Domain Engineering Approach. Accepted to the EMMSAD'07 workshop in conjunction with CAiSE'07, 2007.
19. Reinhartz-Berger, I., Sturm, A. Behavioral Domain Analysis – The Application-based Domain Modeling Approach, UML'2004, LNCS 3273, pp. 410-424, 2004.
20. Rolland, C., Plihon, V., Ralyté, J., Specifying the reuse context of scenario method chunks, Proceedings of the CAiSE'98, LNCS 1413, Springer, pp. 191, 1998.
21. Schach, S. R. An Introduction to Object-Oriented Analysis and Design with UML and the Unified Process. McGraw-Hill/Irwin, pp. 56, 2004.
22. Sturm, A., Reinhartz-Berger, I., Applying the Application-based Domain Modeling Approach to UML Structural Views, ER'2004, LNCS 3288, pp. 766-779, 2004.
23. Wistrand, K. Karlsson, F. Method Components – Rationale Revealed. Proceedings of the CAiSE 04, LNCS 3084, Springer, pp. 189-201, 2004.
24. Weerd, I. Brinkkemper, S., Souer, J., Versendaal, J. A situational implementation method for web-based content management system-application: method engineering and validation in practice. Software process: improvement and practice 11(5): 521-538, 2006.

Appendix: The main outcomes from the comparative analysis of the four fragment representation approaches

Criterion	Weerd et al. [0]	OPF [0]	Rolland et al. [0]	ADOM-UML-based approach
Expressiveness	Product and process fragments and the relations among them; different granularity levels; unordered activities and three types of concepts	Product and process fragments; different granularity levels; does not formally support controlling constructs	Method chunks; different granularity levels; supports branching and loops	Product and process fragments; different granularity levels; supports branching, looping and concurrency; preserves references to original fragments
Consistency	Does not support reuse & assembly operations, only the overall route maps contributes to prevent from inconsistencies	Does not support evolution tracing	Each fragment can be reused while aggregating fragments	Full support for reuse and composition operations
Formalism	A visual, semi-formal UML-based language; Some unique adjustments are introduced	A structured hierarchy of Web pages integrated into a visual meta-model	A semi structured, markup language (SGML)	A visual, semi-formal UML- based language; fragment types are specified by domain models
Situational cataloguing	Limited to 7 characteristics that refer to the organization, the technique and the context	No explicit support	Limited to 2 characteristics: application domain and design activity	Supports dynamic lists of characteristics according to the fragment types
Adaptability and flexibility to changes	Supports customization of the process-data diagrams and the route maps are flexible to situational changes	Provides only construction and usage guidelines	Supports parameters	Supports specialization, adaptation, and customization of fragments
Comprehensibility	Only the unique adjustments to UML have to be studied and comprehend	The repository structure helps learn and use the fragments; provides information on stakeholders' involvement	The visual part facilitates fragment usage and learning; does not support stakeholders' involvement	The used language is familiar to the different stakeholders, including method and software engineers
Connectivity	Does not include any rules for connecting fragments; the route maps support assembling of fragments	Does not provide rules or guidelines for connecting fragments	Does not provide rules or guidelines for connecting fragments	Supports customizing and assembling of fragments, as well as specification of transformation and gluing fragments

Taxonomic Dimensions for Studying Situational Method Development

Mehmet N. Aydin[1], Frank Harmsen[2] and Jos van Hillegersberg[1]
1 University of Twente, Department of Information Systems and Change Management. P. O. Box 217, 7500 AE, Enschede, The Netherlands, {m.n.aydin, j.vanhillegersberg}@utwente.nl
2 Cap Gemini, Practice Manager Technology Advisory Services, The Netherlands, frank.harmsen@capgemini.nl

Abstract. This paper is concerned with fragmented literature on situational method development, which is one of fundamental topics related to information systems development (ISD) methods. As the topic has attracted many scholars from various and possibly complementary schools of thought, different interpretations and understandings of key notions related to method development are present. In this paper, we regard such understandings as both challenges and opportunities for studying this topic. Upon the extensive review of relevant research, this paper shows how this literature fragmentation has resulted in and what needs to be done to make sense of the various understandings for studying situational ISD methods. For the latter, we propose the use of a number of taxonomic dimensions. We argue that these dimensions can help to ease the conduct of literature review and to position disparate research endeavors concerning situational method development properly. In particular, we discuss three basic studies to demonstrate how the taxonomic dimensions can be useful in studying the subject matter.

1 Introduction

IS development (ISD) methods have been of interest to IS scholars and practitioners for a long time since they are essential to structuring method users' thinking and actions in projects and achievement of desired information systems. Among other topics, there is a specific subject, which we call method development, addressing all kinds of problems, issues, and solutions with ISD methods. This particular subject

---

Please use the following format when citing this chapter:

Aydin, M. N., Harmsen, F., van Hillegersberg, J., 2007, in IFIP International Federation for Information Processing, Volume 244, Situational Method Engineering: Fundamentals and Experiences, eds. Ralyté, J., Brinkkemper, S., Henderson-Sellers B., (Boston Springer), pp. 146-160.

has a long tradition in several schools of thought. Over the last decades, academics have been urged to investigate the effectiveness of methods as they are not used in practice as prescribed. This research is concerned with fragmented literature for studying method development (MD) and situational method development (SMD) in particular, with a focused research endeavor aiming at studying adaptation of a method to a project situation.

The problem, as perceived and addressed in this paper, is a fragmented body of knowledge (literature) on MD and SMD, which has accumulated significantly over the last two decades. By fragmented literature we mean to say that various research schools of thought do exist, but are disparate and utilization of the existing studies from these schools is lacking. We believe that this fragmentation in turn hinders the advances in the intellectual development on studying method development. Our goal in this paper is two fold. First, it is to bring up this issue and make academics aware of it. Second, it is to propose a means for making sense of literature fragmentation and to draw a generic picture where the academic endeavors are heading.

2 Review Studies Concerning Method Development

2.1 Existing Review Studies and Approaches for MD

Let us first discuss the concepts of method development (MD) and situational method development (SMD). MD is a subject matter concerning the way through which method stakeholders (such as method experts, project managers and other method users) develop a method in a specific context. Technically, this 'way' can be considered as a mental activity by which method stakeholders analyze [1], adapt and assemble [2] [3] appropriate means to support ways of thinking and actions for ISD projects. SMD is a sub-subject of method development and refers to this adaptation process of method development. It is this process or ability through which (human and non-human) agents determine a system development approach for a specific project situation through responsive changes in, and dynamic interplays between, contexts, intentions, and method fragments [4]. SMD especially employs the input of the analysis and provides the output for the assembly, rather than focuses on method analysis or assembly of method fragments *per se*. The key issue of situational method development is not exclusive focus on the analysis or the assembly, it is how method fragments, context, and method stakeholders are *adapted* to each other in a project situation. Thus, what lies at heart of SME is method adaptation [4].

Kumar and Welke [5], and Van Slooten [6] have provided classifications of the approaches to method development. They argue that the "method engineering approach" in Kumar and Welke's terminology and the "situated method engineering" in Van Slooten's terminology are promising approaches for method development. Additionally, Harmsen's [7] and Tolvanen's [8] classifications are specifically for SMD. Harmsen et al. [9] positions various approaches in what they call a "situational method spectrum". As the most flexible or most radical approach to achieve effective method, he proposes an approach, which is central to his thesis and called "situational method engineering". Tolvanen's [8] classification uses criteria applied to achieve the methodical requirements of ISD.

Two review studies are worth to mention as they show how MD literature has evolved. One is about the progress of information systems development (ISD) research [10] and the other is concerned with method engineering (ME) research [11]. The progress of ISD research over the past 15 years is referred in terms of the early methodical era (until 1988), the methodical era (until 1995), and the era of method assessment. It is argued that at the end of the methodical era, researchers studying ISD methods questioned and 'listened to' what the field really needed, how practitioners felt about methods, and how they dealt with ISD from a method use perspective. Thus, as they claim, the relevance of exposed methods to practice has been undervalued and not studied thoroughly until 1995. The other review draws a picture of what method engineering research has focused up until 1996 [11]. They claim that most of the studies focus on *the technical context* (which is about how to efficiently process and store data or sign related concerning method development) and *the language* context (which concerns different topics such as metamodelling formalisms [12], integration of methods, evaluation of methods, and representational paradigms of ME languages (i.e., supporting a multiparadigmatic representational metamodelling environment- e.g., metaEdit+ and metaCASE [13]). They urge the researchers in the method engineering field to study *the organisational context* (which concerns human activities, interactions, etc) [14] and actual use methods, tools in fields.

The review studies summarized above provide limited "sense making" (that is, each discusses the subject matter from its own perspective) about the classification of relevant research. The articulations are partial in that they are limited to their schools of thought. They also lack focus on understanding what accounts for situational method development. There is a need for a classification of studies broader on incorporating ideas on method development in various domains. To do this, we visit not only ME and ISD literature, but IS implementation literature that provides insights into the course of implementing (situational) method in an empirical setting.

2.3 Classification of (Situational) Method Development Related Studies

At a high level, we distinguish three research domains (the ISD research, Method Engineering, and Implementation research domain (see table 1)) that contribute to an understanding of (situated) method development. The ISD and ME research domains provide insights into the way (situated) method development takes places (that is, a model or process describing how to arrive at a situated method). The ISD and Implementation research domains study the content of such a way (including characteristics and/or elements used in this process).

Having stated the contributions of the three research domains, we examine each domain by using certain elements of the codification schema. The research domains differ in terms of motives, the phenomenon of interest, the label or metaphor used, and associated researchers.

ISD Research. The main motives in ISD research are to improve IS and ISD, and to reveal and resolve issues concerning them. The ISD research includes two kinds of research focusing on IS, ISD, and ISD method: the variance and process research. The variance research (e.g., [10 15]) aims to build and/or test a model by which cause-effect relationships among dependent, independent, and mediating factors essential to the subject matter are studied. In contrast, the process strategy [16, 17, 18, 19] is used to study the phenomenon as a process, a number of events, actions, or episodes that occur in an actual setting where the phenomenon is realized and observed.

The ISD research domain employs ideas and theories from sociology, economics, psychology, and system sciences. One of the earliest uses of this model for determining Management Information Systems design approaches is in [21]. Having stated an overview of this research domain, we posit that their contribution to the theoretical basis of our research may be summarized as follows. The ISD research literature provides: (1) insights into what problems of methods should be targeted in (situated) method development, (2) insights into the functioning, use of method and in work practice, (3) alternative ways of characterizing a target work system, (4) alternative ways of characterizing a method, and (5) alternative ways of selecting the elements of a method.

Method Engineering Research. Under this research domain, we distinguish the following sub- domains: Software Engineering, Requirements Engineering, and SME. Even though the object of interest of these sub-research domains varies with respect to the scope of method under investigation, they often provide procedures for the selection, assembly of components of a method. We briefly discuss the three sub-research streams, but it should be noted that SME is different in that the research efforts are directed to customization of a method to better suit a project situation. Often in this research stream, constituents of method are specified with a certain degree of formality to achieve unambiguous descriptions of the constituents (see e.g., [7], [22]).

Recently, in the *Software Engineering (SE)* research sub-domain, number of methods has been promoted as the solution to the long-standing problem of the so-called conventional software development methods characterized as complex, rigid to change for different project types, technology oriented, and inappropriate for post modern forms of organisations whose distinctive character was adaptable to continual change [23]. The reaction of software engineers and associated researchers [24] has been presented as a manifesto for agile software development. The 'new' methods have been described as 'agile' methods in that they adopt lightweight development processes based on iterative and incremental development, active user involvement, prioritized requirements, etc. [25]. Software engineering literature pays more attention to the stage of application construction and selection of elements of development process by applying techniques in a pragmatic manner. For instance, CMMI (Capability Maturity Model Integration) is used as a model to standardize and measure maturity of the practices for software development. Among a number of key process areas, software product engineering (SPE) indicates the need of tailoring a method. For this purpose, a matrix is often used to match project characteristics to the standardized elements of a software development process [26, 27].

Table 1. Classification of Method Development Related Studies

Research streams	Motives	Phenomenon of interest	Metaphors or Key Terms used	Proposed ideas, theories, or alike for method development	Examples of Studies
The ISD Research					
Variance Research	To identify the antecedents of method and ISD and their implications on better IS use in an organisational setting	- Analysis and evaluation of an ISD approach or method - Description of ISD with an emphasis on a socio-organisational dimension of the development process - Selection of MTTs by using contingencies of a project situation	approach determination, contingency-based approach, techniques, tools selection	- Models for the selection of methods, tools, and techniques (MTTs) - Factors influencing the determination of ISD approach - Success/failure factors in ISD - Evolution of ISD in practice and academy	[10, 15]
Process Research	Examining a rich picture of the basis and development of IS	Elements of method Intellectual structures of method Aspect and levels of method Characterization of ISD Experienced-based method dev.	emergent ISD, emancipation, fitness of approach to a project context, amethodical, against methodism, design ideals for a method	- Approaches or models for determining the ISD approach - Frameworks or taxonomies for characterizing ISD and/or methods	[16, 17, 18, 35]
The Method Engineering					
Situational ME	Supporting situational method development	Design, construction, assembly of components of, maintenance of a method	Route map, scenario, tailoring, approach determination	- Models for the selection, modification of MTTs - Formulize the constituents of a method	[2, 7, 9, 22, 33, 36, 49]
Requirements Engineering (RE)	Supporting RE activities by selecting and/or creating MTTs	Analysis of and support for the process of the selecting MTTs developed for RE	Selection of MTT, tool-box based selection design rationale for RE	Contingency-based selection of MTTs used for RE	[29, 30, 50]
Software Engineering (SE)	Supporting SE at later stages (construction, maintenance, etc.) by MTTs	Analysis and development of software engineering method	Tailoring, balancing agility and planned approach, spiral model	- Risk-based model for SE method, tailoring or customizing method - A list of software project risks	[20, 26, 27, 28]
The Implementation Research					
	Understanding problems regarding the use of IS and examining IS implementation in organisational setting	IS use, socio-organisational implications of IS, implementation approach, Implementation of Enterprise Systems (ERP, CRM,) and IOS (E-commerce applications)	Plan approach, Phase models, Mapping of methods, tools, techniques for ERP, BPR	- A Process theory of ES success - Situation-Activity Framework for BPR - A Taxonomy of ERP implementation	[37, 38, 39, 40, 52]

Another example cited is an experience-based approach to method development by which method use-experiences concerning development processes and associated elements such as activities, roles, and deliverables are collected, stored, maintained, and distributed. To facilitate the choice of the appropriate method elements by developers, a case-based reasoning technique is often used through which characteristics of the situation realized are linked to the applied process model and its constituents [28].

The *Requirements Engineering (RE)* research sub-domain has produced many methodical means for major requirements engineering activities such as requirements elicitation, analysis, triage, specification, and verification. Two orientations are seen with regard to method development: the way to support the requirements engineering process along with the design process and the way to select, engineer tools as part of a method. For the requirements engineering process, researchers aim to capture the design rationale and provide the systems developer and project manager with potential benefits in understanding and monitoring the RE process [29]. Several models and support environments (e.g., REMAP: Representation and Maintenance of Process knowledge) are proposed for capturing and supporting design decisions [30]. Rossi et al. [31] adopt REMAP for method rationale in method engineering. For selecting and engineering tools as part of the method, [21] points out the need for developing strategies for information requirements.

The *Situational Method Engineering (SME)* research sub-domain plays a central role in this work; it provides accounts, approaches, and models for studying method adaptation. The proposed research approaches are of primary importance to this work and called alternately situated method engineering [32], situational method engineering [14], context-specific method engineering [22], and incremental method engineering [13], method configuration [23]; roadmap-driven approaches [33, 34]. In the literature there are a few known accounts that these efforts have been fully utilized [35] and this challenges the applicability of the proposed procedures, models, instruments, and support means concerning method development. This limitation is mentioned in both the ISD (e.g., [35]) and ME literature (e.g., [36]).

Implementation Research. This particular literature (see, exemplary studies [38, 39]) refers to those studies that examine method development in particular domains for certain application types. We use the term implementation because studies in this research domain consider applications as ready-made solutions and often focus on later stages of ISD (e.g., modifications and installation). The level of analysis is limited to a general description of phases, stages, key activities, and tools used in implementation.

We identify a number of sub-research areas that provide relevant studies usually related to enterprise systems implementations, IT-enabled business process (re)engineering, and inter-organisational systems implementation. With regard to method development, the implementation research focuses on risk and success factors of implementation projects and relates them to 'implementation approach' or 'implementation strategy' which is a high level description of the way in which implementation is carried out. Considering an implementation project as technology adoption appears to be the dominant view in studying implementation projects. Taxonomies of implementation approaches are provided based on these theories, (see, for instance, [37]). In fact, these phase models or taxonomies (see, e.g., [38, 39]) provide implementation strategies (e.g., big-bang, evolutionary) concerning the development process and essential activities for ISD where the focus is on organisational change-related activities. There are few studies in this domain that specifically examine method development in the context of enterprise systems implementation (especially in relation to enterprise resources planning applications).

This classification of relevant studies and their review indicate that:

- ISD literature (e.g., [10, 15, 16]) provides a partial examination of situational method development as both process and content wise. Most of the proposed models of SME adopt a contingency-based approach which appears to fall short in detailing situated method development.
- ME literature (e.g., [2, 7, 9, 22, 33]) provides an elaborate examination of situational method development as process wise. A few models proposed for situational method development are actually adopted or extended by most of the studies in the ME research domain.
- Implementation literature (e.g., [37, 38, 39]) provides a partial examination of situational method development as content-wise. Most of the proposed models of method development adopt a contingency-based approach.

3 Manifestation of Taxonomic Dimensions for Studying Situational Method Development

In this section we propose what we call taxonomic dimensions, which allow to position situational method development related studies (Table 2). The proposed dimensions are induced from those studies which are concerned about comparison of accounts, models for SME [7, 8, 14, 23]. We use taxonomic dimensions to critically examine three studies ([2], [7], and [41]), which are considered as prevailing models. The three studies are chosen because: they are found to be the most relevant studies for our purpose (illustrating the usefulness of the proposed dimensions) and they provide underpinnings of SME in terms of basics models.

The first dimension (level of abstraction) has already been mentioned in method engineering. Harmsen [7] introduces three levels of the method engineering hierarchy each of which contains different method knowledge. These levels are: classes of method concepts are described at the *method engineering* (ME) level, instances of the concepts at the ME level are examined at the *ISD method* (ISDM) level, and the third level is the *information system development* (ISD) level at which the actual method fragments of an IS project are located. Notice that the IS situation in which actual business activities are performed is not included in the hierarchy. Most of the IS method engineering studies stay at the ME and ISDM levels, while studies in ISD research and implementation research stay mostly at the ISD level, only few stay at the ISDM level.

The second dimension concerns types of method knowledge [8] in relation with typology of method aspects or components as described in [51]. The shell model on method knowledge has six types of method knowledge: *conceptual structure* including the fundamental concepts of a method and their interrelations; *notation* with which modelling techniques can be represented; *process* which indicates how models are created, adopted, and used; *participation and roles*; *development objectives and decisions* concerning design choices; and finally *assumption and values* embedded in a method. For this work, method knowledge concerning development objectives and decisions is central to the examination of situational method development. Related to this dimension, one might consider the level of details or granularity level (fine or coarse grained, see [7]) and degree of formulization via modelling techniques for each type of knowledge.

Table 2. Taxonomic Dimensions for Studying Situational ISD Method

Taxonomic Dimensions	Operationalisation
Level of Abstraction	Method Engineering Hierarchy [7]: Method Engineering Level, IS Development Method Level, IS Development Level
Knowledge Types	The Shell Model [8]: Conceptual Structure, Notation, Process, Participation and Roles, Development Objectives and Decisions, Assumptions and Values
Adaptation Situation	Project Specific, Project Independent [4]
Aspects of a Situational Method	The Philosophy, The Framework, The Techniques [43]
Adaptation Stage	Pre- or Early Stage, Later Stage, Final or Post-Stage
Decision Support Aspect	Descriptive, Prescriptive, Normative [42]

In addition to these two dimensions, we suggest four additional taxonomic dimensions specifically for situational method development: types of the situation in which adaptation takes place, aspects of a method, adaptation stage, and decision-making and support orientation on situational method development. The last dimension is particularly essential for situational method development as it relates to possible viewpoints of decision-making and support on situational method development.

The third dimension, *adaptation situation*, has two generic variants: project-independent and project-specific method adaptation. Project-independent refers to the situation in which some predefined situations are taken for granted and for which some contextual attributes are used as a priori knowledge (e.g., types of applications, types of problem situation, target domain characteristics, or other typical project characteristics such as size of project, degree of time pressure) [43]. The latter refers to the consideration of method adaptation in an actual ISD project where the knowledge used for method adaptation is situational in the course of the project rather than based on a priori knowledge. Mirbel and Ralyté [34] propose a typology of (generic model for) various processes and strategies for this kind of adaptation. While this work concerns both types of situations, in the following section we especially focus on those studies examining project-specific method adaptation.

Consider the fourth and fifth dimensions, *the aspects of a method* along with granularity level and *the development level of an IS*. For the first, we distinguish three essential aspects at a high level: the philosophy, the framework and essential techniques, and we adopt Wijers' way of thinking, modelling, working, supporting, and controlling [44]. The philosophy aspect is akin to the way of thinking, the essential techniques aspect is more or less similar to the way of controlling and supporting, and the other ways of Wijers [44] are subsumed in the framework aspect.

The fifth dimension indicates the positioning of situational method development on the ISD timeline. Several notions or terms are used to logically split the timeline or workflow of ISD. For instance, Harmsen [7] used the term 'stages of ISD' referring to decreasing level of abstraction (e.g., business modelling, functional design, technical design, and implementation) or increasing level of detail (e.g., global analysis, detailed analysis, global design, detail design). Van Slooten [2] uses 'the levels' as he adopts Zachman's framework [46] (e.g., scope, object system and analysis and design level (OSAD), information system analysis and design (ISAD) level and so on). The implementation literature (e.g., [39]) uses several stages or phases. Given the multiplicity of the terms, we prefer to use the timeline notion in terms of beginning, earlier, during, and later time in ISD.

The final dimension is decision-making and support orientation on situational method development. We address three basic views on decision-making and decision support: normative, descriptive, and prescriptive. These are cited as key orientations pertaining to the decision-making and support model (e.g., [42]). We closely examine these three orientations later and outline them now to see how method adaptation can be analysed from a decision-making and support point of view. The normative view is mainly concerned with the question "How should people ideally make decisions?"; the descriptive view focuses on "How and why people make decisions" whereas the prescriptive view addresses "How can we help people make better (not necessarily ideal) decisions while still taking human cognitive limitations into account".

3.1 Examining Prevailing Models for Situational Method Development

In this section we examine each of the three models based on the proposed taxonomic dimensions (see table 2, which summarizes the examination). While articulating these dimensions we show how to characterize and in turn compare them.

"Situated Method Engineering" and Configuration Procedure for a Scenario

Van Slooten introduces "Situated Method Engineering", a particular model of situation-specific approach to method development. Four notions (project context, configuration process, project performance, and method engineering information systems consisting of formalized rules and a method base that includes method and route map fragments) are suggested to describe the process of SME. The configuration procedure, acknowledged as the heart of method engineering, that includes other notions such as (method) fragments, route maps, intermediate variables (aspects, levels, constraint, and development strategy) scenarios, and their relations.

Positioning Along With Taxonomic Dimensions. With a concise and in-depth presentation of SME, we are ready to explicate the taxonomic dimensions. Notice that Van Slooten [2] has not used or mentioned the proposed taxonomic dimensions in his work. Given the fact that he was one of few researchers investigating the idea of situation-specific approach to method adaptation in the 1990s, his works can be seen as explorations of this idea in an organisational setting and the introduction of a new model, new notions, and new concepts without always providing their clear cut definitions as his findings have been conceptualized and perpetuated during the course of an investigation that goes back to 1987 [47]. Nevertheless, we are now able to apply the taxonomic dimensions to better understand his endeavors.

Table 3. Applying the taxonomic dimensions to the three models proposed for SME

Taxonomic dimensions	The Configuration Procedure for a Scenario [2]	The S3 (Situation Scenario and Success) Model [7]	A Social Process for Method Fragment Adaptation [41]
Level of Abstraction	The ISD Method and ISD levels	The ME, ISD Method levels	The ISD Method and ISD levels
Knowledge Types	Mainly development objectives and decisions	All types, except assumptions and values	Mainly conceptual structure, notation
Adaptation Situation	Project independent and to a certain extent project specific	Project independent and to a certain extent project specific	Project specific
Aspects of a Situational Method	The framework and techniques	The framework and techniques	The framework
Adaptation Stage	Mainly early stage	Mainly early stage	Not specifically mentioned
Decision Support Aspect	Mainly prescriptive	Mainly prescriptive	Descriptive

With regard to the level of abstraction, the SME proposed appears to stay at the ISDM level for which he provides a 'configuration procedure' model and at the ISD level for which he has described how (route map or method) fragments have been used in an actual project context. With regard to the type of method knowledge, we contend that the proposed SME emphasizes the method knowledge type pertaining to the development objectives and decisions concerning design choices of a situational method. With regard to the adaptation situation, it suggests the use of a configuration process in the course of the project situation, but appears that project execution is a black box for method adaptation: only the output of the black box is used to feed 'method base' and 'project characterization'. The SME proposed employs on the one hand a priori knowledge (known or foreseen contingencies, project characteristics) about the project that implies project-independent method adaptation, while on the other hand it acknowledges the unprecedented project situation and includes a feedback mechanism but is not fully operationalized to accommodate method adaptation in the progress of ISD. With regard to the aspect of a method, the SME proposed supports all aspects except the way of thinking, along with a variety of fragments. With regard to the adaptation stage, it is clearly proposed for the beginning or earlier time. With regard to the final dimension, we contend that the decision-making model behind the configuration procedure is prescriptive, but the decision-making model behind the framework is descriptive as mentioned in [2]. The

SME proposed does not exclusively focus on what/how or by whom decision support is or can be provided for situational method development.

Situational Method Engineering and the S3 -Situation, Scenario and Success-Model

Harmsen and his colleagues [7, 9] have worked on the idea of the situation-specific approach to method adaptation by adopting a slightly different orientation on the subject. Most of their work seems to provide clear-cut definitions of the models, notions, and concepts suggested for what they call "Situational Method Engineering" (SME), referring to the research discipline focus on development of situational methods. In Harmsen [7] basic concepts of SME are described. Among other things, his works include an ontology for product fragments and a process classification system to anchor fragments with their semantics, Method Engineering Language (MEL) to enable method fragment representation, the SME process indicating the necessary steps needed to achieve situational method, and the S^3 model relating the three key notions- *S*ituation, *S*cenario, and *S*uccess, which is proposed for the selection and assembly of method fragments

Positioning Along With Taxonomic Dimensions. SME is one of the first attempts to provide a full-fledged description of the basic concepts needed for the design and construction of a situational method. Harmsen and his colleagues' endeavours have often been cited as a significant attempt for formalization of the basic concepts required for a situational method or as a limited view on the way a method adaptation can be realized (see, for instance, [22], [33], [36]). With regard to the level of abstraction, SME stays at the ME level where it provides descriptions of basic concepts and their relationships for a situational method. With regard to knowledge type, SME does not limit itself to any particular type of method knowledge, but appears to employ a special conceptual structure and notation pertaining method knowledge probably due to the need for a degree of formalization of concepts and their relationships often expected by the IS ME community. The level of detail preferred is fine grained in terms of semantics of method fragments in SME. With regard to the adaptation situation, situated and situational method engineering have some similarities. Nevertheless, this approach puts more attention on project-specific adaptation as it acknowledges changes in project situation in the later stages of ISD. Given the characteristics mentioned, the adaptation stage is clearly proposed for the beginning or earlier time of ISD. Finally, SME includes procedures for method adaptation with a reservation that human and/or inanimate agents have some freedom to adhere to these procedures with regard to decision-making and support. In general, however, SME opts for a prescriptive view and even uses some normative techniques like cluster analysis on method adaptation. We believe that decision-making support for situational method development is not the central focus of these suggested CAME tools.

A Social Process for Method Fragment Adaptation

Baskerville and Stage put more emphasis on the emergent aspect of ISD and argue that much of the literature on method development is normative, conceptual and that empirical work is lacking [41]. One of the central notions in their work is 'work practice'. This refers to the way in which a concrete development process is actually conducted in practice. They show that this notion may be best understood together with two additional concepts: situation and constraint. Though they do not provide clear definitions of these terms, they discuss how the concepts are related. They assert that "The conditions and work practice influence the situations that occur, the situations may change conditions and work practices, and work practices may filter the influence of conditions on the situations that occur (p. 15)". Their work focuses on the way work practice is supported and the selection of a method fragment. Such a selection process is seen as a sociological process in their work. They acknowledge that method engineering endeavours are directed towards such a selection process and have some limitations on the way method adaptation is treated.

Positioning Along With Taxonomic Dimensions. Baskerville and Stage's [41] comment on the limitations of 'method engineering' on method adaptation appears in R. Baskerville's earlier work. For instance, Baskerville [48] already mentions the need to look into work practice, which corresponds to the level of ISD in method engineering hierarchy, to identify ISD conflicts and fit these conflicts to structural artefacts at the third level of abstraction which corresponds to the ISD method engineering hierarchy. So, with regard to level of abstraction, their work concerns method adaptation at the ISD method and ISD levels. With regard to the types of method knowledge, their framework does not emphasize certain types, but examples in their work are related to conceptual structure and notational types of method knowledge. The degree of formality used in their illustrative case is coarse grained and expressed in terms of narratives. The proposed process model aims for a project-specific method adaptation and does not focus on particular aspects of method. Even though there is no clear emphasis on the timeline dimension of method adaptation in their work, from the illustrative case study it appears more attention is given to the earlier time of ISD. Concerning the decision-making and support dimension, the object of interest in terms of method stakeholders is extended to a broader audience including designers, users, programmers, method engineers, and other people involved in the project and/or the target IS domain. Their work does not mention any decision-making support in method adaptation and the decision rational behind their model reflects a descriptive view on method adaptation.

4 Concluding Remarks

This research is aimed to bring up the issue of fragmented literature on method development in general and situational method development in particular. We show three basic research domains studying method development, as each domain its own motives, research concerns, research approaches and methods. We argue that the academics in these domains do rarely refer to cross domains. Their endeavors are diverging rather than overlapping. As we regard these domains as complementary rather than competing, they need to be utilized. For instance, one can study how these domains understand and adopt certain notions (situation, context, agency, method fragment) for their theoretical underpinnings. We suspect that such notions have been incorporated with different interpretations in their domains.

To make sense of the fragment literature, we propose taxonomic dimensions for studying situational method development. One might argue completeness of the taxonomic dimensions, but in this work we consider them as a means to characterize and compare models of SME. That is, one can evaluate these dimensions in terms of their relevance to the subject examined and so the dimensions can be extended. To demonstrate how to use these dimensions we have examined three basic studies and showed that they are providing three alternative approaches to studying the subject matter. For instance, by employing the decision support dimension we point out that the models of [2, 7] are aimed to support SME practice in a prescriptive manner. On the other hand, the model of [41] is directed towards identifying and understanding of the SME practice in a project situation (that is, a descriptive view on the decision support dimension). In a similar way, the other proposed dimensions can help one to better understand the existing accounts, models and alike related to method development. In particular we contend that fragmented literature can be seen as an opportunity for utilizing complementary views on and enhancing the understanding of method development. It is this understanding that can help academics to know where their research stands and where research endeavors are heading towards.

References

1. N. Jayaratna, *Understanding and Evaluating Methodologies* (McGraw-Hill, Berkshire, 1994).
2. C. van Slooten, Situated *Methods for Systems Development*, Doctoral Dissertation, University of Twente (1995).
3. S. Brinkkemper, M. Saeki and F. Harmsen, Assembly Techniques for Method Engineering. CAiSE 1998, 381-400 (1998).
4. M. N. Aydin, F. Harmsen, C. van. Slooten R. A. Stegwee, On the Adaptation of An Agile Information Systems Development Method, *Journal of Database Management*, Special issue on Agile Analysis, Design, and Implementation, **16**(4): 24-40 (2005).
5. Kumar and R. J. Welke, Methodology Engineering: A Proposal for Situation-Specific Methodology Construction. in: Challenges and Strategies for Research in Systems Development Method, edited by W. W. Cotterman, J. A. Senn (John Wiley & Sons, 1992).
6. C. van Slooten and B. Schoonhoven, Contingent Information Systems Development, *Journal of Systems and Software*, **33**(2) 153-161 (1996).
7. F. Harmsen, *Situational Method Engineering* (Moret Ernst & Young Management Consultants, Utrecht, 1997).
8. J. –P. Tolvanen, Incremental Method Engineering with Modeling Tools - Theoretical Principles and Empirical Evidence. Computer Science, Economics and Statistics. ER-Paino Ky, University of Jyväskylä: 301 (1998).
9. F. Harmsen, S. Brinkkemper, and H. Oei, Situational Method Engineering for Information Systems Projects. in: Methods and Associated Tools for Information Systems Life Cycle, edited by T. W. Olle and A. V. Stuart (North-Holland, Amsterdam, 1994) pp.169-194.
10. D. Avison and G. Fitzgerald, Reflections on Information Systems Development 1988-2002, in: Information Systems Development - Advances in Methodologies, Components, and Management, edited by M. Kirikova et al. (Kluwer Academic Publishers, 2002) pp.1-11.
11. J. –P. Tolvanen, M. Rossi, and H. Liu, Method Engineering: Current research directions and implications for future research, in: Principles of Method Construction and Tool Support, edited by S. Brinkkemper, K. Lyytinen and R. J. Welke (Chapman & Hall: 1996).

12. J. van Hillegersberg and K. Kumar, Using metamodeling to integrate object-oriented analysis, design and programming concepts, *Information Systems,* **24** (2), 113-129 (1999)
13. S. Kelly, A Matrix Editor for a metaCASE Environment, *Information and Software Technology*, **36**(6), 361-171 (1994).
14. K. Lyytinen, A Taxonomic Perspective of Information Systems Development: Theoretical Constructs, in: Critical issues in information systems research, edited by R. J. Boland, R. A. Hirschheim (John Wiley & Sons Ltd., 1987) pp. 3-41.
15. J. Iivari, R. Hirschheim, and H. K. Klein, A Dynamic Framework for Classifying Information Systems Development Methodologies and Approaches, *Journal of Management Information Systems*, **17**(3), 179-218 (2001).
16. A. G. van Offenbeek and P. L. Koopman, Scenarios for system development: matching context and strategy, *Behavior & Information Technology*, **15**(4), 250-265 (1996).
17. L. D. Introna and E. A. Whitley Against method: Exploring the limits of method, *Information Technology & People*, March **10**(1), 31-45 (1997).
18. D. R. Truex, R. Baskerville, and J. Travis, Amethodical system development: the deferred meaning of systems development method, *Accounting, Management & Technology*, **10**,: 53-79 (2000).
19. G. F. Lanzara and L. Mathiassen, Mapping Situations. *Information and Management*, **8**(1): 71-107 (1985).
20. L. Mathiassen, and J. Stage, The Principle of Limited Reduction in Software Design, *Information, Technology and People*, *6*(2) (1992).
21. G. B. Davis, Strategies for Information Requirements Determination, *IBM Systems Journal*, **20**(1), 4-30 (1982).
22. C. Rolland, and N. Prakash, A proposal for context-specific method engineering, in: Principles of Method Construction and Tool Support, edited by S. Brinkkemper, K. Lyytinen and R. J. Welke (Chapman & Hall: 1996) pp.191-208.
23. F. Karlsson and P.J. Ågerfalk, Method Configuration: Adapting to situational characteristics while creating reusable assets, *Information and Software Technology*, **46**(9): 619-633 (2004).
24. Beck, K. et al., Manifesto for Agile Software Development [Online Web Site]. The Agile Alliance. Available WWW: http://agilemanifesto.org/ (2001)
25. P. Abrahamsson, J. Warsta, M. T. Siponen, J. Ronkainen, New Directions on Agile Methods: A Comparative Analysis. ICSE 2003, May 3-10, Portland, Oregon, USA., 244-254 (2003).
26. C. Larman, V. R. Basili, Iterative and Incremental Developments: A Brief History, *IEEE Computer*, **36**(6), 47-56 (2003).
27. T. Kaltio and A. Kinnula, Deploying the Defined SW Process, *Journal of Software Process: Improvement and Practice*, **5**(1), 65-83 (2000).
28. S. Henninger and K. Baumgarten, A Case-Based Approach to Tailoring Software Processes. International Conference on Case-Based Reasoning, Vancouver, Canada, 249-262 (2001).
29. L. Nguyen and P. A. Swatman, Managing the Requirements Engineering Process. *Requirements Engineering Journal*, **8**, 55-68 (2003).
30. C. Potts and G. Bruns, Recording the reasons for design decisions. the Proceedings of 10th Int. Conf. Software Eng., IEEE Comp. Soc. Press (1998).
31. M. Rossi et al., Method Rationale in Method Engineering. Proceedings of the HICSS-33, Maui, HI, IEEE Computer Society (2000)
32. C. van Slooten, B. Hodes, Characterizing IS development projects, in: Principles of Method Construction and Tool Support, edited by S. Brinkkemper, K. Lyytinen and R. J. Welke (Chapman & Hall: 1996) pp. 29-44.
33. J. Ralyté, R. Deneckèr, C. Rolland, Towards a Generic Model for Situational Method Engineering. CAiSE 2003, Springer-Verlag Berlin Heidelberg (2003).
34. I. Mirbel and J. Ralyté, Situational Method Engineering: Combining assembly-based and roadmap driven approaches, *Requirements Engineering* **11**(1):58-78 (2006).

35. R. Hirschheim, H. K. Klein, and K. Lyytinen, Exploring the Intellectual Structures of Information Systems Development: A Social Action Theoretic Analysis. *Accounting, Management & Technology* **6**(1/2), 1-64 (1996).
36. B. Henderson-Sellers, Method Engineering for OO Systems Development. *Communications of the ACM*, **46**(10), 73-78 (2003).
37. A. Parr, G. Shanks, and P. Darke, Identification of Necessary Factors for Successful Implementation of ERP Systems. New Information Technologies In Organisational Processes - Field Studies And Theoretical Reflections On The Future Of Work, Kluwer Academic Publishers, 99-119 (1999).
38. H. C. Lucas, J. Walton, and M. J. Ginzberg, M. J., Implementing Packaged Software., *MIS Quarterly*, **12**(4) 537-549 (1988).
39. M. L. Markus et al. Learning from Adopters' Experiences with ERP–Successes and Problems, *Journal of Information Technology*, **15**(4) (December) 245-265 (2000)
40. W. J. Kettinger, J. T. C. Teng, and S, Guha, Business Process Change: A Study of Methodologies, Techniques, and Tools, *MIS Quarterly*, **21**(3): 55-80 (1997).
41. R. Baskerville and J. Stage, Accommodating emergent work practices: Ethnographic choice of method fragments. In realigning research and practice: The social and organisational perspectives, Boston, Kluwer Academic Publishers, 11-27 (2001).
42. D. E. Bell, H. Raiffa, and A. Tversky, Descriptive, normative, and prescriptive interactions in decision making, in: Decision making: Descriptive, normative, and prescriptive interactions, edited by Bell, Raiffa, and Tversky (Cambridge University Press , New York, 1988).
43. M. N. Aydin, F. Harmsen, Making a Method Work for a Project Situation, in: the Context of CMM, edited by Oivo and Komi-Sirvio, LNCS: 2559, Springer Verlag Berlin, 158-171 (2002).
44. G. M. Wijers, Modelling Support in Information Systems Development, *Delft University of Technology*, Delft (1991).
45. M. Leppänen, Conceptual Evaluation of Methods for Engineering Situational ISD Methods, in*: Software Process: Improvement and Practice*, **11** (5), 539-555 (2006)
46. J. A. Zachman, A Framework for Information Systems Architecture. *IBM Systems Journal*, **26**(3) (1987).
47. C. van Slooten, Systeemontwikkelingsmethoden (In English: Systems Development Methods) *Informatie*, **4** (1987).
48. R. Baskerville, Structural artifacts in method engineering: the security imperative in: Principles of Method Construction and Tool Support, edited by S. Brinkkemper, K. Lyytinen and R. J. Welke (Chapman & Hall: 1996) pp. 8-28.
49. I. van de Weerd, S. Brinkkemper, J. Souer, and J. Versendaal,. A Situational method for web-based content management system-applications: Method engineering and validation in practice. Software Process Improvement and Practice, 11:521-538 (2006).
50. T. Tsumaki and T. Tamai. Framework for matching requirements elicitation techniques to project characteristics, *Software Process Improvement and Practice*, **11**, 505-519 (2006).
51. K. Wistrand and F. Karlsson, Method Components – Rationale Revealed. In: A. Persson and J. Stirna (Eds.). CAiSE 2004, LNCS: 189-201 (2004).
52. A. Parr, G. Shanks, and P. Darke, Identification of Necessary Factors for Successful Implementation of ERP Systems. New Information Technologies, in: Organisational Processes - Field Studies and Theoretical Reflections on the Future of Work (Kluwer Academic Publishers, 1999), pp. 99-119.

Component-based Situational Methods

A framework for understanding SME

Yves-Roger Nehan and Rébecca Deneckere
CRI, University Paris 1 - Panthéon Sorbonne
90, rue de Tolbiac, 75013 Paris, France,
Habas.Nehan@malix.univ-paris1.fr,rebecca.deneckere@univ-paris1.fr
WWW home page: http://crinfo.univ-paris1.fr/

Abstract. The work presented in this paper is related to the area of Situational Method Engineering (SME) which focuses on project-specific method construction. We propose a faceted framework to understand and classify issues in system development SME. The framework identifies four different but complementary viewpoints. Each view allows us to capture a particular aspect of situational methods. Inter-relationships between these views show how they influence each other. In order to study, understand and classify a particular view of SME in its diversity, we associate a set of facets with each view. As a facet allows an in-depth description of one specific aspect of SME, the views show the variety and diversity of these aspects.

1. Introduction

Method Engineering aims to bring effective solutions to the construction, improvement and modification of the methods used to develop information and software systems. Several authors tried to design methods that would be as effective and as adapted as possible to the development needs of information systems [0,0]. This goal was not always reached, especially because the methods were not always well adapted to projects specificities. The situational methods were designed to correct this weakness. The situational approach finds its justification in the practical field analysis which shows that a method is never followed literally [0, 0]. The discipline of Situational Method Engineering (SME) promotes the idea of retrieving, adapting and tailoring components, rather than complete methodologies, to specific situations [0]. In order to succeed in creating good methodologies that best suit given situations, components (building blocks of methodologies) representation and cataloguing are very important activities. In particular, the components have to be represented in a uniform way that includes all the necessary information that may influence their retrieval and assembling. This paper is an attempt to explore some of the issues underlying component-based approaches to Situational Method Engineering (SME) and to propose

---

Please use the following format when citing this chapter:

Nehan, Y.-R., Deneckère, R., 2007, in IFIP International Federation for Information Processing, Volume 244, Situational Method Engineering: Fundamentals and Experiences, eds. Ralyté, J., Brinkkemper, S., Henderson-Sellers B., (Boston Springer), pp. 161-175.

a framework for their classification. This framework is 4-dimensional as it advocates that a SME approach can be defined by four views, each capturing a particular aspect of SME. Each view has multiple facets and the associated metric. The idea of a four views framework and its facets has been used in several domains such as: requirements engineering for understanding and classifying scenario based approaches [0], system engineering [0], etc.

When used in the SME domain, a facet provides a means of classification. For instance, the formalism facet of the system view (see section below) helps in classifying SMEs according to the underlying paradigm used: informal, semi-formal and formal. Each facet has values which are defined in a domain. A domain may be a predefined type, an enumerated type, or a structured type.

We use the four views framework as a baseline and attach an aspect of SME to each of the views and a set of facets to each view. As a result, it is possible to identify and investigate four major viewpoints of SME: what is the objective of SME, , how are represented the method components, how can the methods be developed and used and finally what does SME achieve.

This paper is organised as follows: Section 2 describes our four views framework. Section 3, 4, 5, 6 explain each view and list a set of their facets for comparing and evaluating the component representation approach. Section 7 presents and illustrates eight of the most recent situational methods, then further analyses each SME approach according to these four different views of our framework. A conclusion is done in Section 8.

2. The Four-views Framework

The four views framework, originally proposed in [7], has proved its efficiency in enhancing the understanding of various engineering disciplines such as information systems engineering [0], requirements engineering [0], IS development process engineering [0] and method engineering [0].

In the original SE framework [0], the views where described as follows.

- The subject view contains knowledge of the domain about which the proposed IS has to provide information. It contains real-world objects which become the subject matter for system modeling.
- The system view includes specifications of what the system does, at different levels of detail. It holds the modeled entities, events, processes, etc. of the subject world as well as the mapping onto design specifications and implementations.
- The usage view describes the organizational environment of the information system, i.e. the activity of agents and how the system is used to achieve work, including the stakeholders who are system owners and users.
- The development view focuses on the entities and activities which arise as part of the engineering process itself.

Our point of view is that this framework concept can be used to help in understanding the field of SME disciplines which consists of applying engineering approaches, techniques, and tools to the construction and representation of components. The purpose of this work is then to present a state of the art in Situational Method Engineering. The four views composing the 4-dimensional framework proposed in this work try to answer the following questions about component-based situational methods:

- what is a component-based situational method ?
- how is represented a situational method component ?
- how can situational methods be developed and used ?
- what is the rationale of component-based situational method engineering ?

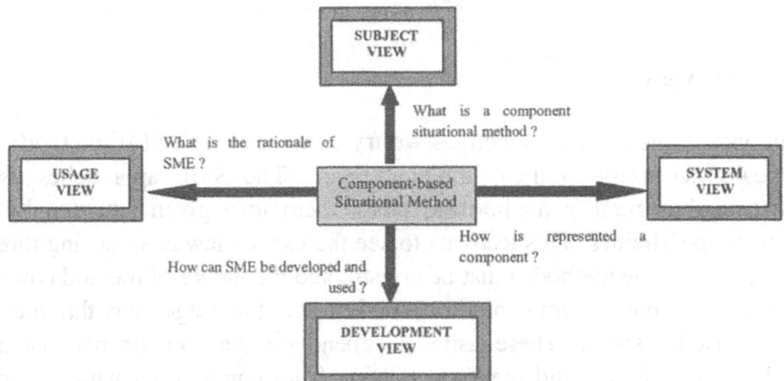

Fig. 1: The four views of SME

For our purpose, we define the SME 4-dimensional framework as follows.

- The subject view as the dimension which deals with the situational method definition, its nature.
- The representation of method component is described in the system view.
- In the usage view, we will investigate the reasons, the rationale for SME and relate users needs to the situational methods that can best meet them.
- The development view deals with the process of constructing component-based situational methods. This process is a meta-process in that it supports the construction of components which will in turn support the development of methods. The way this process might be supported by a tool environment is also relevant in this view.

This allows us to discuss in a focused manner the different concerns of SME: the definitions of components, their representations, the way of developing these representations, and the rationale for using these representations. This is done in the subject, system, development, and usage views respectively. Each view is described by a set of facets that allow a more detailed study of the situational methods. However, this set is not exhaustive and can be completed by other studies.

3. The Subject view

This view of SME deals with the notion of method nature.

In [0], I. Mirbel defines different objectives that are targeted by the approaches. Following this typology, we define a facet representing the nature of the SME methods.

- A first family of approaches aims at *documenting methods* through well-defined components [0, 0]. This kind of method does not state precisely how to retrieve and reuse a component but offers a good effort of specification with regards to the elements a method is made of.

- The second category focuses on the *retrieving* of components to reuse them and *evaluating* their similarity [0].
- The third category focuses on method fragmentation with the definition of *guidelines for reusing* the different components in daily developer tasks by project team members [0,0].

The nature of SMEs can thus be classified as follows:

Nature: SET (ENUM {Documenting, Retrieving and evaluating, Reuse guiding})

4. The Usage view

The usage view concerns the objectives we try to achieve with SME methods as well as the means necessary to their implementation. The SME approaches use high flexibility and thus modify methods to adapt them to a given situation by taking account of its specificities. This leads us to see the usage view as imposing three strict requirements : how the methods must be constructed the nature of method components and how these components must be developed. It is in the usage view that the method objectives must be stated. These aspects depend on the components management policy. This policy is to build methods starting from components whose names and contents vary according to the design. The use of components allows capturing knowledge which changes with time. The use of a library allows capitalizing the experiments of prior projects. A particular policy may be formalised with the two following facets: *Construction technique* and *knowledge representation.*

4.1 Construction technique facet

This facet represents the various ways of building a method which are instantiation, assembly, extension and reduction.

- *The instantiation approaches* use an identification of the common and generic method characteristics and represent them by a system of concepts called meta-model. These approaches allow the creation of a whole set of methods sharing the same properties [0, 0, 0].
- *The assembly approaches* concentrate on the grouping of method components belonging to complementary methods [0,0]. They assemble separate selected method components with regard to the studied specific project to form a unique method. To be successful, it is necessary to have a modular process model.
- *The extension approaches* allow the transformation of a basic method into a new method adapted to the project's needs [0, 0] with addition of new functionalities in a base method.
- *The reduction approaches* allow removal of basic method operators in order to transform it to match the engineer's needs [0, 0].

A method can be classified according to its defined type of construction:

Construction technique: SET (ENUM {instantiation, assembly, extension, reduction})

4.2 Knowledge representation facet

The question of the component retrieval is an important issue of the SME field. Three possibilities have emerged in the literature : (1) the project is globally characterized with use of contingency factors, (2) the components are described with use of descriptors and (3) patterns are used to instantiate the right componant following the project needs. We can then define three SME categories following the knowledge representation.

- *An SME fragment based method* consists in encouraging a global analysis of the projects while basing itself on contingency criteria. The projects and the situations are characterized by means of factors associated with the methods. [0] uses a contingency model based on 17 contingency factors which take value between Low and High as 'Importance of the Project', 'Knowledge and Experience', 'Stability' and so on. According to the authors, the characterization of the project allows them to select the method components appropriate to the project. Construction is supported by component assembly rules and constraints having to be satisfied by the created method.
- *An SME chunk based method* aim at associating these reusable components to their description in order to facilitate component research and extraction according to the user's needs. [0] uses the concept of descriptor [0] like a means to describe method components. The descriptors are organized in a contextual way: each one of them defines the situation in which the component can be employed and describe its usage intention.
- *An SME pattern based method.* A pattern describes a recurring problem with his associated solution [0]. It provides a solution which becomes reusable for any situation concerned with this problem. By developing patterns, the users condense part of their knowledge on the field of the problem and allow its availability for the other users.

The knowledge representation can thus be classified as follows:

Knowledge representation : ENUM {fragment, chunk, pattern}

5. The System view

This specific view is focused on the component representation by defining what is represented, at what level of abstraction, how is it represented and what properties should have the representation. These aspects are captured by the following three facets : Dimension, Abstraction and Formalism.

5.1 Dimension facet

A component is not always viewed with the same dimension. The situational methods use various techniques to represent knowledge: fragments, chunks and patterns. Although terminology between research groups differs, typically a chunk [0, 0] will encapsulate both a process and a product part whereas a fragment [0] can be either a product or a process fragment:

- *product* fragment relate to the structural and static aspects of methodologies (e.g.; deliverables, documents, models, diagrams, and concepts), whereas
- *process* fragment capture the behavioral and procedural aspects of methodologies (stage, tasks, activities, and techniques to be carried out) [0].

Dimension can thus be classified as follows:
Dimension: SET (ENUM {product-oriented, process-oriented})

5.2 Abstraction facet

In [0], this notion in SME is related to the abstraction level of a component that can be :

- *conceptual*, as in [0] where components are expressed with descriptions and specifications of methodology parts, or
- *technical* as in [0, 0] where there is an implementation of operational parts with tools.

Abstraction can thus be classified as follows:
Abstraction: ENUM: {conceptual, technical}

5.3 Formalism facet

Generally speaking, representation formalism is a set of syntactic and semantic natural language, semi-formal such as diagram [0] or completely formal [0, 0].

A formal formalism is required to support the verification of the expected properties of the process model and validation of the process model using, for instance, simulation or enactment techniques. The use of informal notations has made it difficult for process models to be followed systematically. Formal or semi-formal formalism make these efforts considerably more effective as a formal formalism is necessary for providing automatic enactment support.

In the context of SME, the presented components have to be retrieved, assembled, tailored, and customized later and, hence, it is important that the representation approach will be formal or at least semi-formal.

The formalism facet helps classifying SME by one of the three values of the following enumeration:
Formalism: ENUM {formal, semi-formal, informal}

6. The Development view

The development view deals with two specific issues: the process of constructing component method, and the enactment of process as the SME methods are carried out with an aim of assisting the application engineers. The environment to offer assistance to the process in its execution course thus forms part of the problems whose solutions are provided by the development view. Three facets allow covering these aspects: *Flexibility, knowledge construction, knowledge organisation.*

6.1 Flexibility facet

Traditional methods (also named *rigid* methods) follow a static approach, which consist in prescribing entirely and statically the method, whereas SME methods use a contingency approach which consist in defining contingency factors defined on an application development. This is strongly related to the library of method components which must be enriched by the specific projects experiments.

[0] proposed a spectrum to organize the engineering methods approaches according to their degree of flexibility towards a new situation. The methods are organized on a scale of flexibility varying of "low" to "high". At the "low flexibility" level are the rigid methods while, at the "high flexibility" level, we find the SME methods. They are represented with the two last types of this spectrum:

- either the method engineer performs operations that have to be carried out on the original methodologies in order to create a new one, process that we will call *Customization*, as in [0] or
- he refers to methodology components, including their retrieval and assembly, process called *Modularity,* as in [0, 0]. In this last case, each component is usually treated as a closed unit that cannot be modified, while transformation and gluing parts between the components can be added in order to create "consecutive" methodologies.

This typology may be captured by a facet called *Flexibility* witch classifies the methods in two distinct categories.

Flexibility: ENUM {customization, modularity}

6.2 Knowledge construction techniques facet

The traditional knowledge construction is the expression of the application engineer experience. As long as this experience is not formalized and that a basic available knowledge does not constitute an available part for the various applications, one can say that this knowledge is the result of a *ad-hoc* construction technique [0]. This has two major consequences: ignorance in the way in how was carried out the construction and dependence on the field of expertise. If this knowledge must be independent of the expertise field and rapid to built, it is then necessary for construction techniques based on the experiment to use more *formalized* techniques [0].

The techniques of knowledge construction can thus be classified as follows:

Knowledge Construction: ENUM {formalised, ad hoc}

6.3 Knowledge organization techniques facet

The knowledge used during SME construction can be stored in library or *repository* to be reused later. Those provide the basic functions for the management of a components repository. As these libraries can contain a large number of components, they generally offer research techniques, as indexation techniques or the use of keywords.

Other approaches, in addition to the component extraction formalism, have an *organisational process* which helps to manage the knowledge coherence. The organization processes thus allow managing this problem in a more formal way [0, 0].

The knowledge organization technique can be classified as follows:

Knowledge organisation: SET (ENUM {repository, organization process})

Figure 2 summarizes the views and facets of the framework presented:

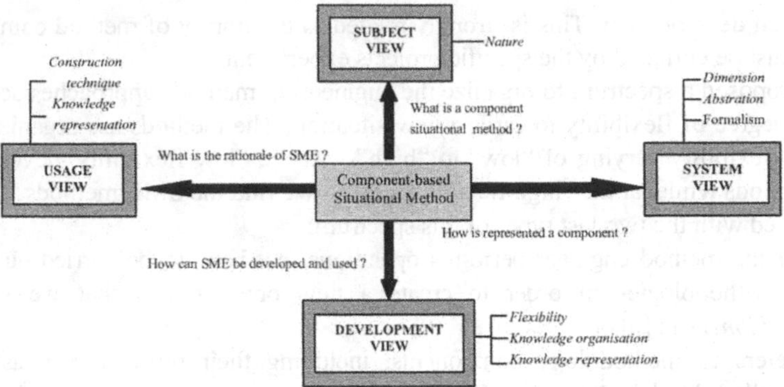

Fig. 2: Views and Facets of SME framework

This framework is used in the following section to evaluate a panel of SME approaches.

7. Review of SME approaches according to the framework

We propose a review of eight component-based SME approaches. We choose our method panel in the set of the most recent approaches and with the intention to offer a more complete study of the different views and their facets.
The aim is, firstly, to get a 'big picture' of the SME research area and to help understanding the achievements gained from currently developed SME based approaches in the literature. It is, secondly, to check the framework against eight SME approaches.

7.1 SME approaches

7.1.1 Method configuration approach

[0] proposed a meta-method called Method for Method Configuration, which is based on the concept of Configuration Packages and Configuration Templates. These concepts are used to configure methods following the specificities of a project while creating reusable assets. Method configuration uses a specific base method as a basis for creating specific configurations. The reusability advantage is obvious since pre-made configurations can be used over and over again. Hence, there is no need to perform a complete method assembly or method configuration for each new project. Experiences can be gathered and reused more efficiently since they can be attributed to coherent set of prescribed actions common in the organization, rather than to context-free actions.

7.1.2 Process Configuration approach

[0] proposes an approach called process configuration that tells how to create a project-specific methodology from an existing one, taking into account the project circumstances.

The idea that lies behind is: for each individual project a specific process configuration (project-specific methodology) is create. This is done by selecting component from methodology that has been specifically designed for the organization and thus reflects the actual ways of working in the organization (base methodology). The configuration is done by processing the rules (in the engine) that are part of the base methodology. The rules define, for each methodology component, in what circumstances (project situations) its use is compulsory, advisable or discouraged.

7.1.3 Method extension approach

This approach [0] guides the method engineer by providing extension patterns that help identifying typical extension situations and provide advises to perform the required extension. In the extension-based, there is two ways to extend a method: directly through the pattern-matching strategy or by using some generic knowledge related to the domain for which the extension is to be done through the path select a meta-pattern, extend a method with the pattern-based strategy. The former help to match extension pattern stored in a library to the extension requirements whereas the latter select first, a meta-pattern corresponding to the extension domain and then, guides the method extension by applying the patterns suggested by the meta-pattern. Both way-of-working use a library of extension patterns but do it in different ways.

7.1.4 Method chunks approach

This approach [0] for assembly-based SME aims at constructing a method 'on the fly' in order to match as well as possible the situation of the project at hand. It consists in the selection of method components (called method chunks) from existing methods that satisfy some situational requirements and their assembly. This approach is requirements-driven, meaning that the method engineer must start by eliciting requirements for the method. Next, the method chunks matching these requirements can be retrieved from the method base. And finally, the selected chunks are assembled in order to compose a new method or to enhance an existing one. As a consequence, the three key intentions in the assembly-based method engineering process are: specify method requirements, select method chunks and assemble method chunks.

7.1.5 Application-based Domain Modeling (ADOM) approach

ADOM [0] is a domain engineering approach and uses the standard notation of UML 2.0 [0]. This approach is a visual methodology for managing representing, retrieving, customizing and tailoring situational method components. ADOM allows to express different types of methodologies and their components, their associated characteristics and values, their pre and post-condition and other component-related requirements, such as mandatory participants, recommended participants, triggers, etc. The structure and guidelines of components are described within the domain layer of ADOM, while their instantiations, which specify particular situational methodologies, are defined in the application layer.

7.1.6 Evolution-Driven (or Paradigm-Based) approach

This approach [0] uses meta-modelling as an underlying method engineering technique. The hypothesis of this approach is that the new method is obtained either by abstracting from an existing model or by instantiating a meta-model. Meta-modelling is known as a technique to capture knowledge about methods. It is a basis for understanding, comparing, evaluating an engineering method. A new methodology is then created by first constructing a product model and then a process model. There is different strategies available to construct both product and process model.

7.1.7 OPEN Process Framework (OPF) approach

The OPEN Process Framework [0] uses a meta-model to generate method components that are stored in a repository. OPEN offers a set of construction guidelines that are considered to be part of existing methodologies used to construct new methods. The OPF meta-model is composed of five main meta-classes [0] [0]: Stage, Producers, Work Units, Work Products and Languages; a method component is produced as soon as a meta-class is instantiated. An OPEN guideline helps method engineers both to instantiate the meta-model element to create method components and to select the best method components (from the repository) in order to create the situational method.

7.1.8 FIPA (Foundation for Intelligent Physical Agent) approach

FIPA [0] entered the IEEE computer Society Standards Committee with the mission of promoting agent-based technologies and the interoperability of agents with other technologies. FIPA defines the method fragment with a process meta-model [0, 0]. In this model, a process is composed of a set of activities performed by some active entities whose task is to produce a well-defined state of an Artefact as input/output. A process is defined as strongly oriented to the production of products. As a result, a method component [0] is defined as a reuse part of a design process composed of two elements: the structure of the product and the necessary procedures to construct this product [0].

7.2 Review of component-based SME approaches according to the framework

In this section, we propose a review of eight component-based SME approaches. Table 1 evaluates these eight approaches with respect to the four view defined facets and the four following sub-sections give more details about it, each one corresponding to a specific view of the framework.

Subject View

The subject view contains only one facet concerning the SME objectives. We can notice that almost all the approaches aims at documenting methods through well-defined fragments. Their strength resides in the effort of specification with regards to the elements a method is made of (tasks, activities, resources, etc.). In the method chunks approach, the focus is on the operators provided to allow a new combination of existing process fragments and on mechanisms to evaluate the similarity among them. Finally, five over the eight studied approaches focuses on method fragmentation for project team members, to provide them with guidelines which are to be reused while performing their daily task. We see here that only the Method chunks approach is addressing the particular aspect of the component retrieving with a formalized evaluation strategy. However, we think that the retrieval and selection of a component is a very important issue of the SME field and that a particular attention had to be drawn on it.

Usage View

The objective for the methods engineers, in situational approaches, is to make methods completely flexible and situation adaptable. This is possible with the components that enrich method library or repository and are reused for method construction. Thus, method chunks use directives and signatures. Its method construction technique is done by *instantiation* and chunks *assembly*. The following methods use the same technique: Evolution-Driven, ADOM-UML and OPEN. Method configuration and processes configuration build their method through the technique of *reduction* and *extension* and they propose a combination of the cancellation and extension operators. All of this show that the construction techniques are often combined, which increase the flexibility of the SME approaches.

The components representation of these methods varies. Thus the method extension uses extension *patterns* and the FIPA method defines its components like a set of activities. As knowledge representation model, method configuration uses packages and templates as *method components* and process configuration uses *process components* which are then to enrich by a set of rules which define how the component has to be used. More than half the approaches studied use a chunk knowledge representation, which allows to describe more effectively the component.

System View

Six of the studied methods (chunks, extension, OPF, Evolution-Driven, FIPA, ADOM) integrate two aspects of the method fragment, the *product* and the *process*, so they represents a portion of process together with its related product(s). Process configuration tends to bring the construction *process* closer to its users by providing facilities for managing the rules. Method configuration is based rather on the *product*.

Regarding the abstraction, we notice that some methods (Process Configuration, OPF, Evolution driven, ADOM) define their fragments as *technical* fragment i.e. in the form of tools. ADOM-UML has to develop a supporting CASE tool for managing the activities. On the same way, Evolution-Driven develop the LyeeALL CASE tool in order to generate programs, as a set of well-formatted software requirements are given. OPF use the tool OPENPC (OPEN Process Construction) that use the OPEN repository of methodological components (firstly conceived for the development of directed objects but used widely for other applications).

Three methods (configuration, chunks and evolution-Driven), have a *formal* representation approach. These approaches deals with the definition, the representation, the cataloguing of components according to different features, the retrieval of the most appropriate ones, and the customization and tailoring of them to complete methodologies that best fit a given situation. In these approaches, component representation and cataloguing are very important activities. The others approaches are *semi-formal*.

Views	Subject	Usage		System			Development		
Facet	Nature	Construction technique	Knowledge representation	Dimension	Abstraction	Formalism	Flexibility	Knowledge Construction	Knowledge organization
Process Configuration	Documenting + Reuse Guiding	Extension + Reduction	Chunk	Process	Technical	Semi-formal	Customization	Ad hoc	Repository
Method configuration	Reuse Guiding	Extension + Reduction	Fragment	Product	Conceptual	Formal	Customization	Formalised	Repository + Organization process.
Method Extension	Documenting + Reuse Guiding	Instantiation + Extension	Pattern	Product + Process	Conceptual	Semi-formal	Customization	Formalised	Repository + Organization process
OPEN Process Framework	Documenting, + Reuse Guiding	Instantiation + Assembly	Chunk	Product + Process	Technical	Formal	Modularity	Formalised	Repository
Method chunks	Documenting + Reuse Guiding + Retrieving and evaluating	Instantiation + Assembly	Chunk	Product + Process	Conceptual	Formal	Modularity	Formalised	Repository
FIPA	Documenting + Reuse Guiding	Assembly	Chunk	Product + Process	Conceptual	Semi-formal	Modularity	Ad hoc	Repository
Evolution-Driven	Documenting + Reuse Guiding	Instantiation + Assembly	Chunk	Product + Process	Technical	Formal	Modularity	Formalised	Repository + Organization process
Method ADOM	Documenting	Instantiation + Assembly	Fragment	Product + Process	Technical	Semi-formal	Customization	Formalised	Repository

Table 1 Review of SME methods

Development View

Regarding flexibility, four approaches (method extension, method configuration, process configuration) enable all their components to be specialized, adapted and *customized*. These operations create new components that can be modified as requested by allowing specification of gluing and transformation components, customization parts. They start with a particular basic method as initial point of departure, then configure them with different reusable components. In that case, there is no assembly but rather a configuration from different parameters or reusable components. In Method configuration, the configuration of a methodology is supported by configuration packages and configuration templates which present reusable assets that can be used in particular software development situation. In process configuration, each process component or components is supplemented by a set of rules that define when to use the component. Method extension uses the patterns as reusable components to configure the method. On the other hand, the other methods (ADOM-UML, OPEN, method chunk, Evolution-Driven, FIPA) use *modularity* construction strategy's which focus on consistent and congruent method modules. Project-specific methodology is created from fragments that might come from different methodologies. These approaches design their final approaches starting from a set of different and reusable modules to assemble them. This illustrates that authors do not favour one approach to the other, they either use customization or modularity.

All methods use a *library* to organize the components. Some of them also use an *organization process* to manage the coherence. Thus, method extension and Evolution-Driven use the process organization based on the "Map" process of [0] to organize their components. Method configuration proposes an organization based on three *repositories* of components (characteristic, configuration packages and templates). This is showing that the use of a library is required when using an SME approach, as all the components have to be stored somewhere. However, the use of an organization process is not always offered. This may be an issue that authors should work on.

8. Conclusion

Our study has shown that component-based SME approaches are very complex, multi-dimensional entities. They cannot be treated adequately with simple predicate based classification techniques. Rather, the need is for a 4-dimensional framework for a component-based approach to be well described.

Every view is itself multi-faceted. Some facets have been proposed by other researchers earlier, others have been introduced by us here. We believe that we have incorporated in our proposals a comprehensive set of facets which cover all the dimensions of our framework.

Through the notion of a view and a facet, we are able to successfully capture the global view and the more detailed view of a component-based SME approach. In this way, the individual characteristics of these approaches are captured within the larger view of SME nature, component management policy, component use and knowledge representation and construction.

Applying the framework on eight recent approaches shows that they all share some of the properties that characterise component-based SME methods. However, they differ in a lot of the selected parameters and their application to this framework allow a precise inventory of their differences.

One of our objectives for our further researches is to review more of the existing SME approaches in order to apply our 4-dimensional framework on a panel as complete as possible. This will allow us to test the validity of our framework and maybe to identify more facets to compare more effectively the methods. Moreover, discussion with other SME approaches authors will help to check the validity, or the invalidity, of our facets.

The main perspective of this work is to identify the real key facets of SME in order to identify reusable components *from* these construction approaches. As a result, components would be of two types, either a capture of method knowledge or a capture of method construction knowledge. This will offer the possibility to the method engineer to reuse them in order to create a new approach to construct SME methods, perfectly adapted to his way of working.

References

1. D. Firesmith and B. Henderson-sellers, The OPEN Process Framework. An Introduction, Addison-Wesley (2001).
2. C. Rolland and C.Cauvet, Object-Oriented Conceptual Modelling, CISMOD'92, International Conf. on Management of Data, Bangalore (July, 1992).
3. J. Ralyte, Method chunks engineering, PhD thesis, University of Paris 1-Sorbonne (2001).
4. I. Mirbel and V. de Rivieres, Adapting Analysis and Design to Software Context : The jecko Approach, In 8th International Conference on Object Orirented Information Systems (2002).
5. C. Rolland and J. Ralyté, An Assembly Process for Method Engineering, Proc. of the 13th CAISE, Springer, pp.267-283 (2001).
6. C. Rolland, C. Ben Achour, C. Cauvet, J. Ralyté, A. Sutcliffe, N.A.M. Maiden, M. Jarke, P. Haumer, K. Pohl, Dubois and P. Heymans, A proposal for a scenario classification framework. Requirements Engineering Journal 3:1 (1998).
7. M. Jarke and K. Pohl, Information systems quality and quality information systems, In Proc. Of the IFIP 8.2 working conference on the impact of computer-supported techniques on information systems development, Mineapolis, NM (june 1992).
8. M. Jarke and K. Pohl, Requirements Engineering: An Integrated View of Representation, Process and Domain, Proc. 4th European Software Conf., Springer Verlag (1993).
9. C. Rolland, A comprehensive view of process engineering, proceeding of CAISE'98, Pisa, Italy, (1998).
10. C. Rolland, A primer for method engineering, proceeding of INFORSID' 97, Toulouse, France (1997)
11. J. Mirbel, Rethinking ISD methods, Fitting project team members profiles. I3S technical Report I3S/RR-2004-13-FR, (2004).
12. B. Henderson-Sellers, Process meta-modelling and process construction: examples using the OPF. Ann. Software Engineering 14(1-4) (2002) 341-362
13. H. Storrle, Describing process paterns with UML, in ESWT, (2001).
14. M. Gnatz, F. Marshall, G. Popp and W. Schwerin, Modular process paterns supporting an evolutionary software development process. Lectures notes in Computer sciences, 2188, (2001)
15. C. Rolland, J. Ralyte and M. Ayed, Construction the Lyee method with a method engineering approach, Knowledge-Based System, 17 (2004) 2396248
16. J. Ralyte, Towards Situational Methods for Information Systems Development: Engineering Reusable Method Chunks. Proc. of ISD'04, Vilnius, Lithuania, September 9-11, 2004. pp. 271-282. ISBN 9986-05-762-0

17. I. Reinhartz-Berger and A. Sturn, Applying the Application-based Domain Modeling Approach to UML Structure Views, ER'2004, Springer, pp. 766-779
18. R. Deneckere, Approche d'extension de méthodes fondée sur l'utilisation de composants génériques, PhD thesis, University of Paris 1-Sorbonne (2001).
19. J. Ralyté, R. Deneckere and C. Rolland, Towards a Generic Model for Situational Method Engineering, *International Conference on Advanced information Systems Engineering (CAISE)*, Springer Verlag, Velden, Austria, (2003).
20. F. Karlsson and Pär J., Ågerfalk, Method Configuration: Adapting to Situational Characteristics while Creating Reusable Assets, In Information and Software Technoloy, Volume 46, Issue 9.
21. B. Marko, An approach for creating project-specific software development methodologies, TPSE Cairo (2005).
22. K. Van Slooten and B. Hodes, Characterising IS develop. project, IFIP WG 8th Conf. on Method Engineering, Chapman and Hall, pp. 29-44, (1996).
23. V. De Antonellis., B. Pernici and P. Samarati, F-ORM METHOD : A methodology for reusing specifications, in Object Oriented Approach in Information Systems, F. Van Assche, B. Moulin and C. Rolland (eds), North Holland, (1991)
24. S. Brinkkemper, M, Saeki and F. Harmsen, Meta-Modelling based assembly techniques for situational method engineering, Information Systems 24 (1999) 209-228
25. B. Henderson-Sellers, SPI – A role for Method Engineering, Proceedings of the 32nd EUROMICRO, SEAA'06, (2006).
26. A. F. Harmsen, S. Brinkkemper and H. Oei, , SME for IS projects, In T.W. Olle & A.A. Verrijn Stuart (Eds.), Methods and associated tools for the IS life cycle — Proceedings of the IFIP WG8.1 Working Conference (CRIS'94) (pp. 169-194). Amsterdam: North-Holland (1994).
27. OMG, « unified Modeling Language : Superstructure », Version 2.0 (2005); http://www.omg.org/docs/formal/05-07-04.pdf
28. M. Cossentino, S. Gaglio, B. Henderson-sellers, V. Seidita, A metamodelling approach for method fragment comparison, Proceedings of the 11th International Workshop on Exploring Modeling Methods in Systems Analysis and Design (EMMSAD), Luxembourg (june 2006).
29. B. Henderson-Sellers, M. Serour, T. McBride, C. Gonzalez-Perez and L. Dagher, Process construction and customization, Journal of Universal Computer Sciences, 10(3), online journal accessible at http://www.jucs.org (2004)
30. B. Henderson-Sellers, C. Gonzalez-Perez and McBride, A meta-model for assessable software development methodologies. Software Quality Journal, 13(2) (2005)
31. M. Cossentino and V. Seidita, Composition of a new process to meet agile needs using method engineering. Software Engineering for Large Multi-Agent Systems Vol. III. LNCS Series, Vol. 3390. Springer-Verlag GmbH (2005)
32. http://www.fipa.org/
33. G. Terracina, A. Garro and D. Ursino, A multi-agent system for supporting the predition of protein structures. ICAE, 11(3) IOS Press, Amsterdam, The Netherlands (2004), 256-280
34. Method fragment definition, FIPA Document (Nov 2003) ; http://www.fipa.org/activities/methodology.html
35. C. Rolland, N. Prakash and A. Benjamen, A multi-model view of process modeling, Requirements Engineering Journal, pp. 169-187 (1999).

Connecting method engineering knowledge: a community based approach

Isabelle Mirbel

I3S Laboratory
UMR 6070 UNSA-CNRS
Les Algorithmes - Route des Lucioles, BP 121
F-06903 Sophia Antipolis Cedex, France
Isabelle.Mirbel@unice.fr

Abstract. Current practices in the field of information system development reveal a crucial need for spreading and sharing methodological knowledge in addition to existing proposals about formalizing, building and tailoring methods. Currently, the methodological knowledge is mostly shared and spreaded inside an organization by organizing training sessions, attending to conferences and reading manuals. Moreover, it is not very interactive and do not provide efficient support for evolution. The methodological knowledge under consideration ranges from very formal descriptions to informal experience report, empirical knowhow and best practices. But in reality, feedbacks about methods in practice are most of the time neither captured nor integrated to the corporate knowledge. And finally, method bases which have been developed to store predefined method fragments to support method tailoring inside organizations have not been very successful in the industrial context. For all these reasons we propose an approach to share and spread methodological knowledge based on the concept of community of practice. Our proposal aims at supporting exchange of knowledge outside of the boundaries of the organization and deepens members knowledge and expertise about methodological knowledge by interacting on an ongoing basis. In this paper, we focus on the lightweight top ontology we propose to specify the core concepts required to qualify any piece of knowledge about method.

1 Introduction

Current practices in the field of Information System Development (ISD) show that methods are almost never suited literally and that there is a wide difference between the formalized sequences of steps prescribed by the method and their real application in practice. Indeed, there is a tension between the 'method-in-concept' (the method as formalized in manual) and the 'method-in-action' (as interpreted by practitioners) [4]. And even among the different practical applications of a specific method, differences exist : methods are often uniquely tailored to the project and organizational characteristics [3]. Moreover, practitioners have a negative perception of methods which are seen as too rigid and

Please use the following format when citing this chapter:

Mirbel, I., 2007, in IFIP International Federation for Information Processing, Volume 244, Situational Method Engineering: Fundamentals and Experiences, eds. Ralyté, J., Brinkkemper, S., Henderson-Sellers B., (Boston Springer), pp. 176-192.

too prescriptive [24]. Even if a method is decomposed into fragments, practitioners must apprehend the method as a whole and understand all its concepts in order to use it. It can have negative impact and discourage practitioners from using methods. Methods are often criticized for the emphasized focus on the method artifacts as such, making them look cumbersome. Methods should not be in the forefront during ISD, it should be viewed as heuristic procedures [11]. Most of the provided approaches have been devoted to method engineering (ME) while method use (MU) needs also dedicated approaches [27,7]. Methods need to be maintained based on reflection from practice, transforming tacit knowledge into explicit knowledge. The importance of tacit knowledge partly explains the low acceptance and use of methods [21]. MU is a learning process in which an individual or an organization creates new knowledge about methods and how to apply them [21].

All these tendencies reveal a crucial need for spreading and sharing methodological knowledge (MU) in addition to existing proposals about formalizing, building and tailoring methods (ME).

Currently, the methodological knowledge is mostly shared and spreaded inside an organization by organizing training sessions, attending to conferences and reading manuals. These basic transmission means require that the practitioners are present (to attend to the training or the conference). It is not very interactive and do not provide efficient support for evolution. Therefore, we propose an approach which allows to collect heterogeneous contributions and to make them evolve collaboratively in a more interactive way.

The methodological knowledge under consideration ranges from very formal descriptions to informal experience report, empirical know-how and best practices. But in reality, feedbacks about methods in practice are most of the time neither captured nor integrated to the corporate knowledge. By providing means to exploit different kinds of methodological knowledge in a homogeneous way, we aim at reducing the gap between 'method-in-concept' and 'method-in-action'. As emphasized in [3], although a method focus is important for obtaining coherence in the organization, it is the practice of people that brings the method to life. Integrating the different kinds of methodological knowledge in a common framework will encourage practitioners to be active in documenting, using and keeping the method alive and the related knowledge up to date. It will also contribute to make methods look less cumbersome and less prescriptive. Among our aims, one is to provide means to integrate emerging feedback from practitioner situations to various materials describing methods.

Exisiting works dealing with feedback from practitioner situations (method rationale) capture, represent and analysis this kind of knowledge in order to support method evolution [27]. Therefore they propose to formalize the method knowldge with the help of a meta model and they provide means to relate the method rationale knowledge to the method meta model in order to explicit it [21]. Such a proposal is willing to support evolution inside the frame of a specific method. Our aim is slightly different as we want to facilitate methodological knowledge sharing accross different methods. We want our approach for instance to allow to bring together knowldge about two different object-oriented notations which would be represented by two different meta models but which may have points to share because of their common paradigm. Moreover we focus on MU and therefore we are focusing on MU rationale [27]. We propose an approach based on an ontology which allows to share concepts among methods, models, notations, meta-models or whatever is related to method knowledge. In addition, we exploit the capabilities of a semantic search engine to bring knowledge together. Indeed, this need to share and exchange methodological knowledge goes beyond the scope of a particular method, project or organization. Therefore, our aim is to provide support for collecting contributions from the whole ISD community (researchers, method engineers, developers, ...) : actors from this community may face similar problems independently of their environment (project, team, organizational unit, ...). In addition, method bases which have been developed to store predefined method fragments to support method tailoring inside organizations have not been very successful in the industrial context [23]. Therefore, we do not want to provide a centralized approach based on a repository of resources about methods. On the contrary, we propose a distributed approach based on a shared representation of methodological knowledge and means to annotate resources with regards to this shared representation.

In this context, our aim is twofold: we want to improve the support dedicated to practitioners in order to help them in their daily activities and we also want to improve the corporation support about methodological knowledge by providing means to integrate various kinds of methodological knowledge and to keep the corporate knowledge up to date.

We contribute in supporting the collect of MU experiences, the recording of comments and observations. These experiences may then be for instance analyzed in the way it is proposed in [27] in order to support evolution in ME, but not only. Our focus is mainly on MU. Therefore we aim at capitalizing knowledge to explain and transmit way of working without only focusing on ME evolution aspects. Our proposal aims at giving unexperimented practitioners a way to learn about best practices related to method. We contribute to experience-based learning and to explicitly collect MU rationale across different use contexts and populations.

The paper is organized as follows. Section 2 presents the concept of community of practice our work is based on. The context of our work is presented in Section 3. The concepts of our top ontology, which is the backbone of our approach, are discussed in Section 4. Section 5 presents a motivating example to demonstrate the feasibility of the proposed approach. Section 6 is a conclusion and a summary of the important points dealt with in this paper and introduces perspectives on the future work.

2 Communities of Practice

The concept of a community of practice (abbreviated as CoP in the following) refers to the process of social learning that occurs when people who have a common interest in some subject or problem collaborate over an extended period to share ideas, find solutions, and build innovations [1].

Recently, CoP have become associated with knowledge management as people have begun to see them as ways of developing social capital, nurturing new knowledge, stimulating innovation, or sharing existing tacit knowledge within an organization [9].

These communities aim at capitalizing individual knowledge, increasing the number of exchanges among people and allowing the identification of domain experts. They help in storing and preserving know-hows through a collective distributed and dynamic process. They create connections among people beyond the geographical and organizational structures.

A community is characterized by its domain (ISD methodological knowledge in our case), its practice (methodological pratice through ISD experiences), its members (all the actors participating in the ISD process), its external environment (the organization the actors belong to, the other CoPs and networks the actors are involved in, ...), its resources (documents and tools about methodological aspects of the ISD process) and its history and life. CoPs differ from business or functional units, from teams and networks because people belong to CoPs at the same time as they belong to other organizational structures. An effective organization comprises a constellation of interconnected CoPs, as these are privileged nodes for the exchange and interpretation of information [12]. The concept of CoP seems promising for methodological knowledge management because it is an effective support of transmission of knowledge from expert to novice, especially in terms of practices. It also makes the participating actors more active and implicated, not undergoing the method in our case. It allows exchange of knowledge outside of the boundaries of the organization and deepens members knowledge and expertise in the CoP domain by interacting on an ongoing basis.

Web-based technologies have allowed the emergency of virtual CoPs. Virtual CoPs (VCoPs) are informal networks, existing outside of any one particular organisation, that support professional practionners to develop a shared meaning and engage in knowledge building among their members by providing opportunities for relationship building and interaction through the use of internet based information and communication technology's as well as other methods [28].

A distributed network of practice (DNoPs) consists of a larger, geographically dispersed group of participants engaged in a shared practice or common topic of interest. CoPs and DNoPs share the characteristics of being emergent and self-organizing, and the participants create communication linkages inside and between organizations that represent a kind of "invisible" net existing beside the formal organizational hierarchies [8].

Virtual CoPs, as well as DNoPs, are concepts which allow to share tacit knowledge [28], albeit to a lesser degree than CoPs : they are for instance particularly suitable for transmitting internet specific soft skills; they provide quick and easy comment systems in blogs and interactive environment provided in online forums for instance and they help feedback mechanisms by reducing first the cost of communication and second the cost of storing and retrieving them efficiently.

But efforts have still to be made to fully exploit the potential of web-based technologies. Dedicated solutions have to be provided to answer the needs related to the domain of knowledge under consideration. Tools have been proposed to support CoP [10] (VCoPs and DNoPs). Some of them are generic enough to be suitable whatever the domain of knowledge is, for instance tools ensuring individual participation or tools ensuring community cultivation [10]. Other tools may be customized to match the requirements of the methodological knowledge.

Formality of the ME design is increased rationally in approaches where it is modeled as an argumentation process organized into specific discourse structure [27]. CoP dedicated tools are promising to answer this need. They may provide good support to adequately capture the context in which decisions are made and support method rationale during ME as well as MU.

Whatever the situation, creation, accumulation and diffusion of knowledge cannot be achieved without a good description of this knowledge which is the purpose of this paper.

3 Context of the work

Our aim is to provide means for practitioners to share and exchange knowledge about method engineering. Similar attempts have been made in the field of requirement engineering [23] and in the field of business interoperability [20] to spread and share successful solutions to requirement engineering or interoperability problems.

In [20], a repository of method chunks is suggested as a knowledge management application for projects within the interoperability domain. In this approach the knowledge about interoperability, based on experience and best practices is formalized in the form of reusable method chunks stored in a method chunk repository. A meta-model for interoperability problem classification is provided to support method chunk qualification and ease the indexing and retrieval of the pieces of knowledge stored in the repository.

In [23], the pieces of knowledge are formalized in the form of patterns which are stored in a common repository. Patterns are mainly described through a problem description, a context, references and keywords. Different versions of patterns are managed in association with feedbacks information in terms of comments and evaluations. An original and polymorphic way to link patterns among them is also provided.

On the contrary of the proposals discussed above, we don't want to encapsulate the heterogeneous resources we are dealing with into chunks or patterns to get uniform pieces of knowledge. We rely on annotation mechanisms to qualify them and allow their exploitation.

In addition, we don't propose to keep the knowledge inside a unique repository. We want the resources to be kept at the practitioners side, making them responsible of it.

As in the discussed approaches, we provide a way to classify the pieces of knowledge we are dealing with. We choose to represent this classification as an ontology, as it will be explain in the remaining of this paper, in order to take advantage of the web semantic techniques and tools and fully rely on annotation mechanisms and semantic search engine capabilities.

Our aim is to provide a sound basis to build dedicated knowledge management services (or tools) to support the cultivation of CoPs (or DNoPs) dedicated to methodological knowledge.

In our approach, data is collected from various sources participating in the CoP and stored in a resource description collection belonging to the CoP (semantic storage in Figure 1). It is collected from the practitioners that want to spread their methodological knowledge. As we don't want to centralize the resources but only their descriptions and in order to let all the practitioners be aware about the referenced knowledge, we assume only descriptions of resources are stored in the repository shared by the community.

As our aim is to help practitioners to share and spread methodological knowledge, the descriptions need to be expressed using a commonly agreed set of concepts. It is the purpose of the ME ontology to preserve in the CoP a shared set of terms and concepts about ME. In this lightweight ontology, the shared vocabulary is expressed in terms of concepts, relationships and constraints. When importing new resource descriptions, practitioners browse the ontology and find suitable concepts or enrich the ontology with new concepts or label in order to annotate the resources they are dealing with.

A semantic search engine can easily exploit the ontology to search the resource description collection. Indeed, such an engine supports applications allowing practitioners to exploit the resource description collection and find pointers on methodological knowledge meaningful for them, thus keeping the community aware and alive about each one contribution. The ontology and the search engine constitute the semantic enrichment part of our framework on top of which dedicated knowledge management services may be developed, as summarized in Figure 1. The knowledge management services form the set of tools dedicated to the CoP cultivation. Examples of such knowledge management services are ontology creation and annotation, cooperative knowledge creation to support collaborative problem solving, knowledge retrieval, knowledge dissemination, knowledge visualization, knowledge evaluation, evolution and maintenance.

The architecture we presented has several advantages with regards to our concern:

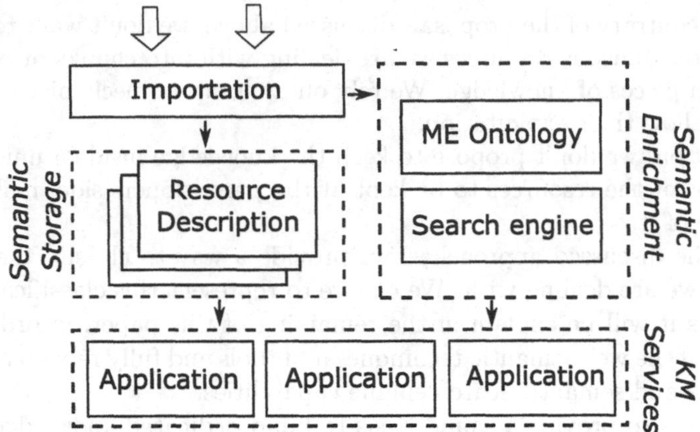

Fig. 1. System Architecture

- It is open and allows easily new practitioners to contribute to the community by exporting the description of their resources in a standard language.
- It is not fully centralized since it does not hold the resources. Resources are kept at the practitioner side, making them responsible of it.
- It allows to reference and qualify in a same way different kinds of knowledge ranging from very formal descriptions to informal experience report, empirical know-how and best practices.

4 A method engineering top ontology

The aim of our work is to provide support to practitioners to help them qualifying the knowledge they own in order to share it with other practitioners. Our approach is based on a lightweight ontology that is shared by all practitioners. We provide a top ontology holding the core concepts we thought required to qualify any piece of knowledge about method. This top ontology will be enrich by the practitioners: they will add new labels for the core concepts and also refine them in order to be able to precisely qualify the knowledge they are dealing with. In this section we discuss the core concepts that constitute the top ontology. In the next section we will show on an example how the top ontology may be refined while importing resource descriptions and how it allows to join heterogeneous resources together.

Our purpose is nor to provide a general ontology about ME or ISD, as it has already been carefully studied in [26,25] for instance, nor to provide a survey of existing approaches about ME or ISD, as good surveys have already been proposed [5,29]. Our aim is to provide the core concepts required in order to support the cultivation of a CoP about ME, that is to say, in a first time, the spreading and sharing about various and heterogeneous pieces of knowledge about methods.

According to the literature about CoP [12], different actors participate in a community which aim is to support the creation, accumulation and diffusion of knowledge *resources* about a domain. The resources or outcomes developed by the CoP (artifacts, stories, routines, documents) constitute the *practice* of the CoP. In the ME domain, we are dealing with *method* of course and *models* which are used to formalize the content of method deliverables as well as to formalize the different steps recommended to built the deliverables. A method may be viewed as a set of loosely coupled method components expressed at different levels of granularity. A *method component* is an autonomous and coherent part of a method supporting the realization of some specific ISD activities. Such a modular view of methods favors the exchange of knowledge about it among different practitioners. The significance of situationality of a method and even more of method components has been clearly enlightened in the literature [30,19]. Therefore, the concept of *context* has to be associated to each practice in order to increase its reusability. These main concepts constitute the backbone of our top ontology. They are summarized in Figure 2 and will be discussed more in detail in the following.

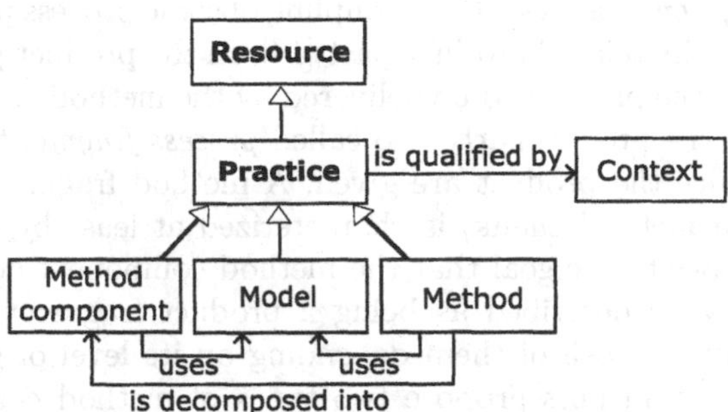

Fig. 2. Top of the ontology

The main information that will help practitioners to understand a *method* usefulness is its *purpose*. One can for instance want to share a feedback about an approach to build a situational method, an experience report about an Xtreme Programming framework or simply advertise a web site about an ISD process. In addition to the purpose of the method, indication about the *manner* the problem is tackled in the method may be interesting to understand the suitability of the piece of knowledge under consideration (while describing it or while searching for methodological knowledge). Method for building methods, for instance, are classified into ad-hoc, by evolution, by extension or by assembly approaches [5]. Requirements engineering methods are usually classified into goal-based, scenario-based or goal-and-scenario based approaches [6]. Similar purposes and manners can be supported by different approaches and different pieces of knowledge. By providing these concepts in the top ontology, as it is shown in Figure 3, it will be possible to join resources together based on these concepts.

A method is considered as a couple of two interrelated models : *product model* and *process model*. The product model of a method defines a set of concepts, relationships between these concepts and constraints for a corresponding schema construction. The process model describes how to construct the corresponding product model. Different notations and languages exist to specify products and processes. Different *paradigms* have been proposed to model products and processes. The relational, functional, intentional and object-oriented paradigms are examples of well-known *product model paradigms*. Activity-oriented, product-oriented, decision-oriented, context-oriented and strategy-oriented paradigms are examples of *process model paradigms*. Different object-oriented notations have been for instance proposed to model products. Different pieces of knowledge, each of them expressed with a different object-oriented model, may be referenced in our CoP. And even if slightly different from the notation point of view, the resources may contain information that could be shared by the different practitioners because of the common paradigm. Figure 3 illustrates the concepts related to the model specification.

A *method fragment* ensures a tight coupling of some process part of a method process model and its related product part [14]. In the product part, also called *product fragment*, the product to be delivered by the method component is captured whereas in the process part, also called *process fragment*, the guidelines allowing to produce the product are given. A method fragment, also called a method bloc or a method chunk, is characterized at least by a name and an intention which specify the goal that the method component achieves. A piece of knowledge may be described as being a product fragment only or a process fragment only or both of them depending on its level of granularity and focus. Indeed, some authors propose two types of method components while others consider only process aspects. Integrated approaches also exist [14]. The resources described with the help of these concepts (method fragment, product fragment and process fragment) consist in guidelines about how to use the meta models (to build models) in addition to references to appropriate parts of product and/or process meta-models. Another way to reuse methodological knowledge is based on generic elements [18]. The *method pattern* concept aims at describing resources which capture generic lows governing the construction and adaptation of methods. Decision-making patterns capturing the best practices in enterprise modeling and domain-specific *process patterns* and *product patterns* [14] are examples of patterns. Fragments as well as patterns may be respectively decomposed into more refined fragments and patterns. Figure 3 summarizes the different concepts suitable for characterizing method components. The relationships between method components and models is summarized in Figure 4.

As our aim is to help practitioners to spread and share methodological knowledge, it is important to provide means for them to express in which context the resource may be useful. Therefore we introduce the concept of *context*.

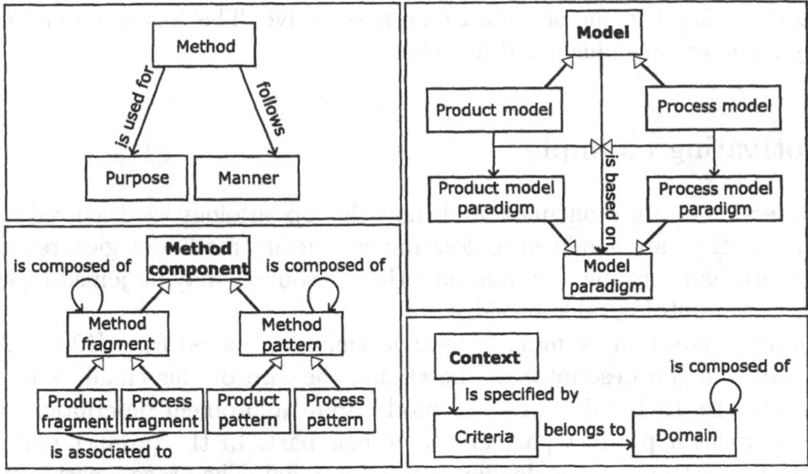

Fig. 3. Content of the ontology

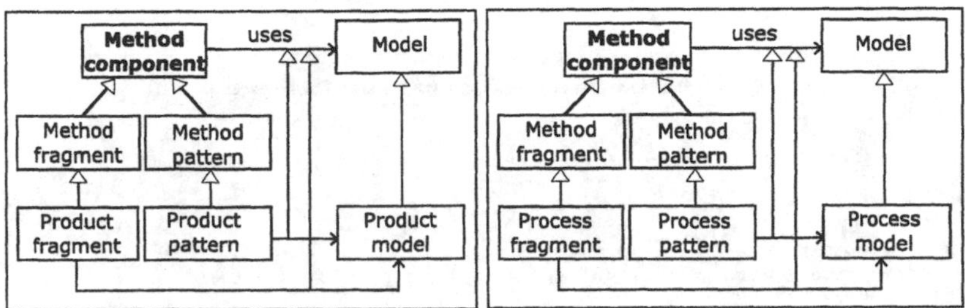

Fig. 4. Relationships among models, fragments and patterns

It is useful for defining potential reuse situations when describing a resource and importing its description into the resource description collection. It is also profitable when searching for resources : it allows to specify the situation in which the resources could be reused. It contributes to better specify what the practitioner is searching for, in addition to the kind of knowledge (model, method, method component, ...) and features about the element under consideration (intention of a method component, paradigm of a model, ...). The context also allows to specify characteristics which are not dependent on the kind of concept under examination and therefore allows to join together heterogeneous knowledge. By heterogeneity we mean resources about different concepts (model, method component, purposes, etc) as well as resources with different levels of formalization ranging from formal descriptions to informal experience report. A context is defined by a set of *criteria* belonging to different *domain* of interest [13]. The organizational perspective (and especially contingency factors [22]) and the human dimension are examples of domain. The practitioner involvement in the ISD project or the time pressure on the project are examples of criterias related to the organizational perspective. The concepts required to specify a context are illustrated in Figure 3.

5 Motivating example

In this section we show on an example how the top ontology we discussed in the previous section can be refined to describe two specific methodological resources in a generic and reusable way and how these resources may be joined together thanks to the ontological knowledge.

Figure 5 shows an example of method chunk extracted from [19,14]. As it is indicated in the descriptor of the chunk, the aim of this chunk is to provide guidelines to build a use-case model from a problem description. This chunk contains a product part and a process part. In the product part, the use-case model the chunk is dealing with is specified. The process part is specified through tactical guidelines. This formalism is part of the NATURE process model and allows to express complex guidelines through a set of steps.

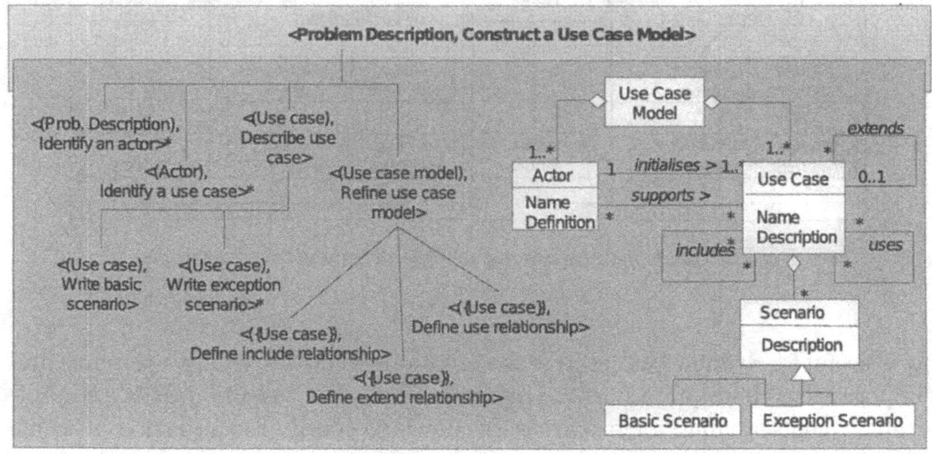

Fig. 5. A method chunk

The description of this resource in a graphical way is given in Figure 6. The name and intention of the chunk have been represented, as well as the *use-case* and *NATURE* model referred to in the chunk body. A context has been specified to help in understanding the reuse context of the method chunk. It has been described with regards to the *design activities* it is suitable for : *requirement elicitation* and *analysis*. It has also been qualified with regards to the kind of *application domain* it is suitable for: when designing an *information system* or *human computer interfaces*. Of course, in parallel with the specification of this description, the top ontology has to be enriched to take into account the new concepts the chunk contains : *use-case model, NATURE model, Information system, Human computer interfaces, Analysis, Requirement elicitation, design activity* and *Application domain.*

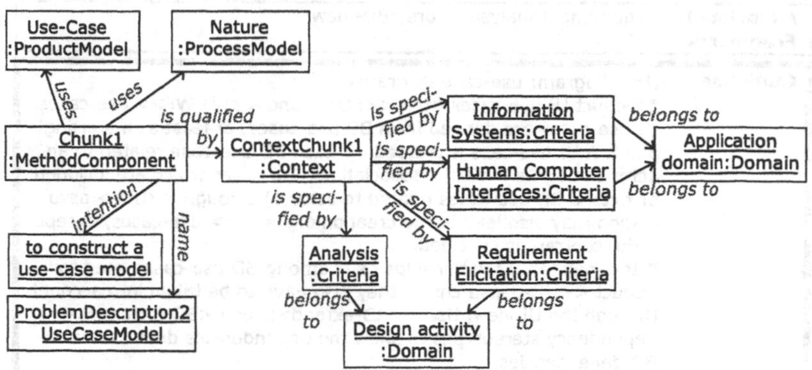

Fig. 6. The chunk description

Figure 7 shows another example of resource about methodological knowledge. It is a method fragment which has been extracted from the JECKO framework [2]. This framework, which is the result of a collaboration between Amadeus SAS and the I3S research laboratory [16], is a context-driven approach to analysis and design to address the problem of adapting methodology to specific development environment. Dedicated method fragments as well as dedicated UML profiles have been proposed to deal with different criteria qualifying the application under development [15,17]. The method fragment shown in Figure 7 is dedicated to applications with a graphical user interface (*situation: when dealing with GUI*) and provides guidelines to help in defining the user interface specification by starting from the business domain specification, as it is explained in the *intention* of the method fragment. The method fragment provides textual guidelines about this specification activity during the *requirement analysis phase* (in this framework fragments are grouped by phases and steps that are recalled in the name of the fragment). It assumes the *use-case model* is used to support this activity.

A graphical view of the description of this resource is given in Figure 8. The name and intention of the fragment have been represented, as well as the *use-case* model referred to in the fragment guidelines. A context has been specified to help in understanding the reuse context of the method fragment. It has been described with regards to the *design activity* it is suitable for : *requirement analysis*. It has also been qualified with regards to the kind of *application domain* it is suitable for : when dealing with a *graphical user interface.*

Again, in parallel with the specification of the method fragment description, the top ontology is enriched to take into account the new concepts the chunk refers to : *Requirement analysis*. The part of the top ontology enriched to take

Name	RequirementAnalysis::Core::UI-View
Situation	When dealing with GUI
Intention	Define User Interface (UI) specifications from Business Domain (BD) ones
Associated Fragments	RequirementAnalysis::Core::BD-View
Guideline	UML diagram: use-case diagrams * Deduct UI use-cases from <<BD>> and <<BD-WF>> use-cases. UI use-cases are derived from BD use-cases, at least as a starting point. A UI use-case is created for each BD use-case related to an actor through a <<UI>> association. Use-cases which are included or extend BD use-cases related to actor(s) through <<UI>> asso ciation may also lead to the creation of <<UI>> use-cases, except if the contrary is specified. * If dependency relationships exist among BD use-cases used to deduct <<UI>> use-cases, they also have to be taken into account through the UI view. Use <<BD-extend>> or <<BD-include>> dependency stereotypes to show the dependencies deducted from BD dependencies. * If a BD use-case has been stereotyped <<BD-WF>>, then the deducted UI use-case is stereotyped <<UI-WF>>. * Group the models related to the UI View in <<UI>> package(s). * When UI use-cases have been deducted from BD use-cases, show it explicitly via <<For>> dependencies.

Fig. 7. A method fragment

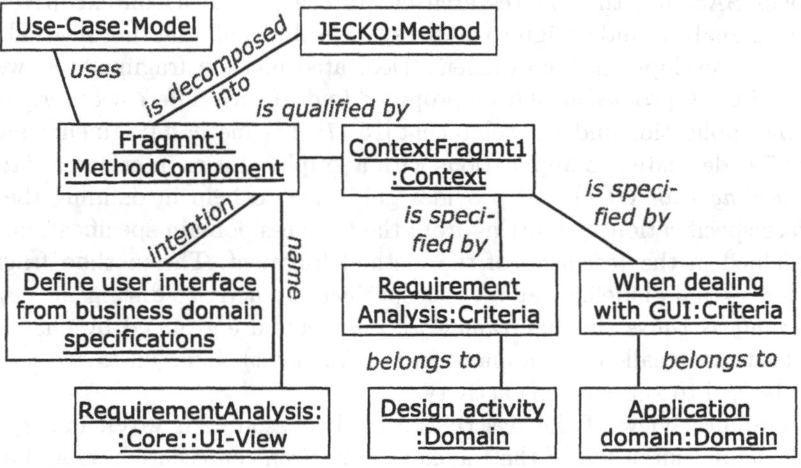

Fig. 8. The fragment description

into account the concepts required to qualify the chunk and the fragment under concern is shown in Figure 9.

With the help of a semantic search engine the collection of resource descriptions can be searched and similarities between the two method components

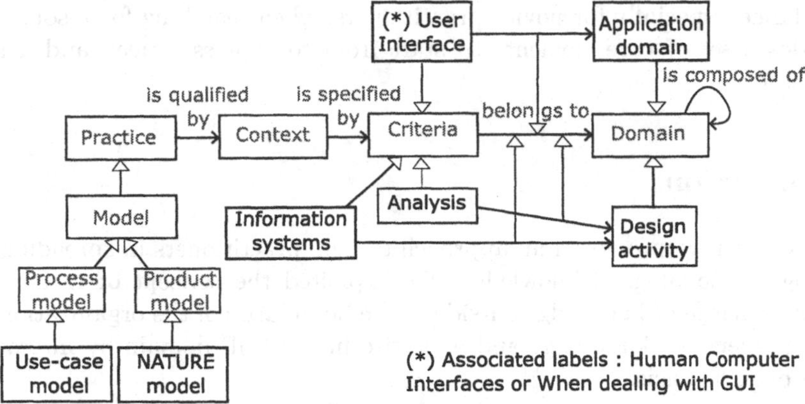

Fig. 9. The extended ontology

under consideration could be found. The chunk and the fragment would be considered as close because of their common product model of course, but also because they share part of their context (the user interface concept) and because they cover design activities which are join together by generalization relationships (analysis in the chunk context and requirement analysis in the fragment context).

The proposed top ontology makes a difference to current practice because pieces of knowledge not expressed with the same formalism (NATURE process model in one case textual description in the other), not belonging to the same method may still be joined together and presented to practitioners as two possible answers to a single query.

Compared to a localized Google search engine, our approach allows experts to provide, through the refinement of the top ontology, a set of meaningful concepts to describe the ME domain. It could be especially useful for novice practitioners when looking for resources about methods. Moreover, as we deal with heterogeneous kinds of resources ranging from very formal descriptions to informal experience report, empirical know-how and best practices, it could be difficult to index all of them in a homogeneous and meaningful way. Keywords extracted from the text body would not lead to good retrieval results. By following an ontology-based approach to capture domain concepts we aim at improving resource indexing and retrieval.

Thanks to our lightweight top ontology, which is very basic and concise, each practitioner participating in the community can contribute to the methodological knowledge description by refining the top ontology when exporting descriptions of resources. Each CoP will then obtain an ontology which reflects the knowledge cultivated in this CoP. It will make possible to reference heterogeneous pieces of knowledge in a common framework and let practitioners exchange pieces of knowledge whatever the formalism, the granularity, the level of detail of what they want to spread and share are. The ontology also constitutes a guidance, especially for novice practitioners, when searching for resources. It provides a set of core elements to start from to express a need and a reuse situation.

6 Conclusion

In this paper we presented an approach to help practitioners in spreading and sharing methodological knowledge. We exploited the concept of CoP, which allows exchange of knowledge outside of the boundaries of the organization and deepens members knowledge and expertise in the CoP domain by interacting on an ongoing basis.

Our concern is more precisely on providing an interactive and evolutive support to integrate heterogeneous contributions about ME to encourage practitioners to be active in documenting, using and keeping the method alive.

In this context, our contribution deals with a lightweight top ontology to specify the core concepts required to qualify any piece of knowledge about method. This top ontology is refined by practitioners when they import resource descriptions which constitute the CoP practice. It allows practitioners to join together resources with different levels of formalization and notations. An access to a large amount of practices, not inevitably partitioned by models, notations or approaches is gained. Moreover, the ontology provides a guidance for defining practitioner need and specifying practitioners situation when searching the resource description collection.

Future works will proceed in both theoretical and practical directions. The theory will focus on providing core concepts to describe actors and ISD activities and techniques in order to extend the scope of our top ontology and better handle all the key element of a CoP [12] devoted to ME. Associated dedicated tools will also be studied. The practical work will consist in testing this approach through several case studies.

References

1. http://fr.wikipedia.org.
2. http://www.i3s.unice.fr/ mirbel/jecko/jecko.html.
3. A. de Moor and H. Delugach (2006) Software Process Validation: Comparing Process and Practice Models. 18th Conference on Advanced Information Systems Engineering - CAISE 2006 Workshop on Exploring Modeling Methods in Systems Analysis and Design - EMMSAD.
4. B. Lings and B. Lundell (2004). Method-in-Action and Method-in-Tool: Some Implications for CASE. 6th International Conference on Enterprise Information Systems - ICEIS 2004, Porto, Portugal.
5. C. Rolland (2005). L'ingénierie des méthodes : une visite guidée. e-TI - la revue électronique des technologies d'information, http://www.revue-eti.netdocument.php?id=726, (1).

6. C. Rolland and C. Salinesi (2001). Ingénierie des systemes d'information. Hermes.
7. A. Järvi and H. Hakonen and T. Mäkilä (2007). Developer driven approach to situational method engineering. IFIP WG8.1 working conference on situational method engineering: fundamentals and experiences (ME07), Geneva, Switzerland.
8. E. Hustad (2007). A conceptual framework for knowledge integration in distributed networks of practice. 40th Hawaii International Conference on System Sciences.
9. E. Wenger (1998). Communities of practice: learning, meaning, and identity. Cambridge University Press, Cambridge, U.K. and New York, N.Y.
10. E. Wenger, N. White, J. Smith, K. Rowe (2005). Technology for communities. CEFRIO.
11. E. Hustad (2007). A conceptual framework for knowledge integration in distributed networks of practice. 40th Hawaii International Conference on System Sciences.
12. E. Wenger (1998). Communities of practice: learning, meaning, and identity. Cambridge University Press, Cambridge, U.K. and New York, N.Y.
13. E. Wenger, N. White, J. Smith, K. Rowe (2005). Technology for communities. CEFRIO.
14. F. Karlsson and K. Wistrand (2006). Combining method engineering with activity theory : theoretical grounding of the method component concept. European Journal of Information Systems, (15), 2006, pp. 82-90.
15. G. Vidou, R. Dieng-Kuntz, A. El Ghali, C. Evangelou, A. Giboin, A. Tifous and S. Jacquemart (2006). Towards an Ontology for Knowledge Management in Communities of Practice.. 6th International Conference on Practical Aspects of Knowledge Management - PAKM 2006, Vienna, Austria, 2006, pp. 303-314.
16. I. Mirbel (2004). A polymorphic context frame to support scalability and evolvability of information system development processes. 6th International Conference on Enterprise Information Systems - ICEIS 2004, Porto, Portugal, April, 2004, pp. 131–138.
17. I. Mirbel and J. Ralyté (2006). Situational method engineering : combining assembly-based and roadmap-driven approaches. Requirement Engineering Journal, 11(1), 2006, pp. 58–78.
18. I. Mirbel and V. De Rivieres (2003). Conciliating User Interface and Business Domain Analysis and Design. 9th International Conference on Object-Oriented Information Systems - OOIS 2003, Geneva, Switzerland, September, 2003, pp. 383-399.
19. I. Mirbel and V. de Rivieres (2002). Adapting Analysis and Design to Software Context: The JECKO Approach.. 8th International Conference on Object-Oriented Information Systems - OOIS 2002, , Montpellier, France, Sept., 2002, pp. 223-228.
20. I. Mirbel and V. de Rivières (2003). UML and the unified process. IRMA Press, 2003.
21. J. Ralyteé and R. Deneckere and C. Rolland (2003). Towards a Generic Model for Situational Method Engineering.. 15th International Conference on Advanced Information Systems Engineering (CAISE 2003), 2003, pp. 95-110.
22. J. Ralyté (2001). Ingénierie des méthodes à base de composants. Université Paris I - Sorbonne, January, 2001.
23. J. Ralyté and P. Backlund and H. Kühn and M. A. Jeusfeld (2006). Method Chunks for Interoperability. 25th International Conference on Conceptual Modeling, ER 2006, 2006, pp. 339-353.

24. J.P. Tolvanen (1998). Incremental Method Engineering with Modeling. Tools: Theoretical Principles and Empirical Evidence. University of Jyvskyl, Finland, 1998.
25. K. van Slooten, B. Hobbes (1998). Characterizing IS development projects. IFIP WG8.1 Working Conference on Method Engineering: Principle s of method construction and tool support, Great Britain, 1996, pp. 29-44.
26. L.H. Jean-Baptiste, C. Salinesi and G. Fanmuy (2005). Sharing Methodological Knowledge with REGAL: "Requirements Engineering Guide for All". 13th IEEE International Conference on Requirements Engineering, Paris, France, 2005, pp. 461-462.
27. M. Bajec, D. Vavpotic and M. Kirsper (2004). The scenario and tool-support for constructing flexible, people-focused system developement methodologies. 13th International Conference on Information Systems Development - ISD 2004, Vilnius, Lituania, September.
28. M. Leppanen (2005). Conceptual Analysis of Current ME Artifacts in Terms of Coverage: A Contextual Approach. 1st International Workshop on Situational Engineering Processes Methods, Techniques and Tools to Support Situation-Specific Requirements Engineering Processes (SREP), in conjunction with 13th IEEE International Requirements Engineering Conference, pp. 75-90.
29. M. Leppanen (2006). Towards an Ontology for Information Systems Development. 18th Conference on Advanced Information Systems Engineering - CAISE 2006 Workshop on Exploring Modeling Methods in Systems Analysis and Design - EMMSAD.
30. M. Rossi and B. Ramesh and K. Lyytinen and J.P. Tolvanen (2004). Managing evolutionary method engineering by method rationale. Journal of the Association for Information Systems, 5(9), pp. 356-391.
31. M.P. Zarb (2006). Modelling participation in Virtual Communities of Practice. London, UK.
32. S. Brinkkemper (1996). Method Engineering: Engineering of Information Systems Development Methods and Tools. Information and Software Technology, 38(4), 1996, pp. 275-280.
33. S. Brinkkemper and M. Saeki and F. Harmsen (1998). Assembly techniques for method engineering. 10th International Conference on Advanced Information Systems Engineering, Pisa, Italy, 1998.

Situational Method Quality

Liming Zhu and Mark Staples
1 NICTA, Australian Technology Park, Eveleigh, NSW 1430, Australia
2 School of Computer Science and Engineering
University of New South Wales, NSW, Australia
[Liming.Zhu, Mark.Staples]@nicta.com.au
WWW home page: http://www.cse.unsw.edu.au/~limingz/

Abstract. Some overall method characteristics, such as agility and scalability, have become increasingly important. These characteristics are different from existing method requirements which focus on the functional purposes of individual method chunks and overall methods. Characteristics like agility and scalability are often not embodied in the function of a single method chunk but are instead reflected in constraints over one or more method chunks, connections between method chunks and cross-cutting aspects of the overall method. We propose the concept of method tactics, which are techniques for achieving certain method quality attributes. We identify a list of method tactics focusing on agility and scalability by considering factors that affect these quality attributes. We validate the feasibility of using method tactics by applying them to traditional software development method chunks and deriving practices for agile development. We examine the effectiveness of the tactics by comparing our derived practices with existing practices for agile development. The comparison results show that most of the derived practices are found in existing agile methods. We also identify new practices that may have potential for use in agile methods. The results demonstrate initial support for our proposal for the use of method tactics, and for the extraction or invention of further cross-cutting primitive method tactics for more flexible situational method engineering.

1 Introduction

Method quality is often considered to be functional conformance to method requirements or industry best practices. However, in system development, quality is defined not only in terms of correctness (conformance to functional requirements) but also satisfaction of non-functional requirements. Non-functional requirements are equally important for method engineering. Some examples of non-functional characteristics for methods include:

Please use the following format when citing this chapter:

Zhu, L., Staples, M., 2007, in IFIP International Federation for Information Processing, Volume 244, Situational Method Engineering: Fundamentals and Experiences, eds. Ralyté, J., Brinkkemper, S., Henderson-Sellers B., (Boston Springer), pp. 193-206.

- Agility: the ability of a method to accommodate expected change rapidly and efficiently
- Scalability: the ability of a method to retain its effectiveness with larger (or smaller) team size and product size
- Interoperability: the ability a method to interact with other methods and environments
- Usability: the ease of use of the method by human agents to achieve the goals supported by the method

The current approach to improve quality characteristics of a method is to tailor an existing method or select and integrate existing method chunks [20] that posses some degree of the desired quality characteristic. For example, in the software development domain, existing agile practices can be added to a method, or a particular agile method can be tailored.

However, this approach has some limitations. A method engineer should be able to directly and systematically improve specific quality attributes of a method, rather then rely solely on selecting and integrating method chunks from among existing practices. This can not be achieved if method engineers do not understand the underlying reasons why an existing method chunk supports those quality attributes. This limits the flexibility and precision of a method engineer's ability to improve the quality characteristics of a method.

In this paper, we propose a new concept called "method tactic". A method tactic is a technique for method engineering, intended to achieve specific method qualities. Method tactics can apply to an existing method chunk, a collection of method chunks, or an entire method. Although some method tactics can themselves be realized as method chunks, usually method tactics manifest as constraints over a method chunk, or more frequently as cross-cutting constraints over multiple method chunks. We observe that the cross-cutting nature of these tactics also makes it difficult to treat them as a single method chunk in a method repository. Thus this approach complements existing approaches for method engineering that rely mostly on selecting method chunks from a method repository.

We have collected an initial collection of tactics for agility and scalability. We have not intended to collect a complete set of such tactics or to rigorously categorize them. Our goal has been to identify some practical techniques that a method engineer can use to improve the non-functional quality of a method. We have conducted an initial validation of our method tactics by applying them to software development methods. Using the method tactics we have been able to derive practices that exhibit the desired method qualities and that match industry best practices and methods that promote the same qualities. We have also been able to identify new practices that have not yet been included in software development processes. These new practices can be further empirically validated and considered as candidates to be included in future software development methods. Our work has a number of contributions:

- Method tactics characterize why methods achieve specific method quality characteristics.
- Applying method tactics directly allows more flexible method design, and can potentially identify new reusable method chunks as best practices.

- A method tactic may affect multiple method quality characteristics in different directions. Our approach makes such trade-offs explicitly understood for resolution by method engineers. For example, the trade-offs between agility and scalability in software development methods is an area of growing interest [5, 12].

This paper is organized as follows. We first discuss related work in section 2. In section 3, we introduce the concept of method tactics and illustrate them by providing a list of tactics that affect agility and scalability. In section 4, we apply these tactics to general activities (method chunks) in software development processes in order to achieve specific method characteristics. We demonstrate that the derived practices closely resemble existing software development practices that promote those characteristics. We discuss the limitations of our work in section 5, and present conclusions and future work in section 6.

2 Related Work

Methods possess both functional and non-functional characteristics. Situational method requirements often specify non-functional requirements of methods, such as being able to handle large team size, large project size, high product requirement volatility, fast responsiveness to change, and flexibility.

Many approaches to method engineering focus on assembly techniques [6, 8, 13, 21, 24]. Such approaches propose strategies such as association and integration to bridge or merge method chunks [20], and use configuration packages [11] during assembly and adapting. Such approaches do not include atomic means to achieve cross-cutting concerns such as method qualities. Our work addresses this issue by identifying and using method tactics, which complement method chunks and bridging/merging-based assembly techniques.

Method engineering theories have been successfully applied to software development domains to create situation and project specific methods [1-3, 9, 17]. Assembly approaches have been used to investigate support for product qualities, such as system interoperability [19]. Certain method quality attributes, such as agility has been investigated [10, 22] and compared among methods. However, the agility of these methods has only been analyzed at the phase and practice level. The atomic and primitive reasons why these practices are "agile" has not been explicitly captured and analyzed. Our work is the first attempt to extract these underlying reasons and to use them in the context of method engineering.

The concept of tactics for design is not new. Atomic architectural and design tactics have been used to achieve non-functional cross-cutting product quality at the architectural level [4]. These tactics have been useful because most non-functional product requirements can not be achieved by selecting and assembling functional components. The analogy between products and methods (processes) is well-recognized [18]: a method should be designed to satisfy method requirements [20] just as products are designed to satisfy product requirements. By further following this analogy, we observe that applying the concept of tactics to method engineering can provide atomic means of achieving cross-cutting method quality.

3 Method Tactics

As defined previously, a method tactic is a technique for method engineering, intended to achieve specific method qualities. Ideally, it should be possible to systematically analyze a specific quality of a method by using a method quality reasoning model. Such a model would represent how a method tactic could manipulate parameters leading to the quality, and would help to explain the effectiveness of such tactics. However, no formal method for reasoning about method quality exists. Nonetheless, some informal factors can be identified.

In this paper, we use the method qualities of agility and scalability as illustrative examples. We have chosen from the software development methodology literature a number of well-recognized factors that affect these two qualities:

- Efficiency of information flow (speed, responsiveness and leanness)
- Type of feedback
- Frequency of activity/feedback/auditing
- Incremental completion of tasks
- Reversible actions
- Task interdependency

By inventing techniques to try to affect these factors, we have identified a preliminary list of method tactics. This list is not intended to be a complete list. As expected, most tactics affect multiple method qualities in different directions. That is, by achieving one quality method engineers may have to sacrifice another quality. The analysis of method tactics that we present using these informal factors should be taken as general analyses – we note where counter-examples may exist in some circumstances. In presenting our list of method tactics, we have grouped them for ease of analysis.

Method Tactic: Use verbal communication and "light" informal documentation
Method Tactic: Use formal documentation

Verbal communication can increase the agility of a method through increased speed of information flow, responsiveness and leanness. Relying primarily on verbal communication does not necessarily remove documentation completely. Many industry practices that promote verbal communication tactics are also conveyed as practices about using less documentation. "Light" informal documentation can include forms such as email or instant messaging logs, and wiki pages. Verbal communication can suffer from poor scalability to larger team size and longer project durations. Purely verbal communication on complex topics among a large number of people is not highly effective, and informal documentation is prone to obsolescence through poor maintenance. Longer project durations present an increased risk of higher personnel turnover, leading to a decrease in the effectiveness of organizational memory and knowledge. Verbal communication and informal documentation can also negatively affect method reliability. Verbal communication and informal documentation is often used in smaller projects and for methods that require extremely high agility in terms of responsiveness and leanness. Formal documented communication manifests the opposite quality attributes. Extensive and rigorous documentation usually decreases method agility but can increase reliability and scalability. (However, counter-examples to this can exist if documentation is poorly maintained.)

Method Tactic: Downstream-driven input (feed-back)
Method Tactic: Upstream-driven input (feed-forward)

The inputs into an activity can be based on downstream activities/artifacts or upstream activities/artifacts. For example, in the software development method context, design activities could rely solely on the upstream requirements to verify design output against the requirements. However, design activities could also rely on inputs from downstream activities such as coding (Code Smell) or testing (Design for Test).

Downstream-driven inputs effectively establish a feedback loop. Downstream feedback can provide rich information that is quite different to that from upstream activities. Exiting an activity with low quality outputs may lead to higher downstream or overall cost due to unnecessary rework not caused by changing environment and requirements. In such situations, the longer and less frequent the feedback loop, the greater the overall cost. Thus, downstream-driven input is often used with a very short loop and with frequent feedback.

This tactic may not scale well for large systems when rework cost is not linear due to the effects of complexity. The cost of rework may outweigh the richer feedback obtained through "trialing" downstream activities. On the other hand, the value of downstream feedback may decrease when a domain is very mature or a team is very experienced. This is why large projects in mature domains often still follow waterfall methods to some degree, with less frequent iterations.

Method Tactic: Introduce continuous feedback/auditing
Method Tactic: Introduce staged feedback/auditing

Continuous feedback is effectively a very small feedback loop between interconnected method chunks. For example, in software development methods, it is possible to maintain such feedback loops between designing and coding or between coding and testing. Continuous feedback improves agility tremendously. In terms of scalability, it works well if the activities within a loop are performed by one individual. However, if it involves multiple people, the communication overhead, synchronization issues and potential resource contention will harm the scalability of the method. For example, continuous integration in software development involves a coding/building continuous feedback loop. This can suffer from scalability due to the reasons mentioned above.

Method Tactic: Allow a single method chunk to be carried out incrementally

Method chunks may be carried out incrementally to fit with tactics for iteration or feedback. However, there are other reasons for incremental execution. For example, requirements change volatility can lead to a risk that early work might be rendered obsolete. Incremental execution allows certain decisions to be deferred until required. Just-in-time elaboration and maximizing work-not-to-be-done are practices that employ this tactic. Some product properties have an emergent nature (especially in large scale systems [16]) and are difficult to plan. Incremental execution can be useful in these situations.

This tactic improves method agility but may suffer from scalability over the long run on certain activities. Long-term incremental refinement of large products may reach a breaking point that can only be solved by a comprehensive overhaul [5].

Method Tactic: Use configuration management

In order to allow reversible changes, configuration management should be used to track all changes. This tactic increases method agility by enabling managed changes. Configuration management may introduce additional cost and overhead. However, for any project involving multiple working in parallel on the same artifacts, the benefits of configuration management normally outweigh its costs.

Tactics such as configuration management clearly have it's a cross-cutting aspect. Introducing a single method chunk called "configuration management" won't work. Although initial method chunks may be required to plan and establish a configuration management environment, configuration controls influence many existing method chunks, for example to support "check-out" and "check-in" activities before and after their execution.

Method Tactic: Reduce task dependencies between multiple resources.

Task dependency between multiple resources introduces communication and synchronization overhead. Method chunks should be designed to support maximum parallelism not only among method chunks but also among instances of a single method chunk. Although the nature of the task often has a major impact on its ability to be partitioned and executed in parallel, process analysis techniques can improve this. As we have demonstrated, method tactics can be applied in different ways:

- One can add constraints to a single method chunk. For example, to make an activity shorter or allow it to be carried out incrementally.
- One can add constraints to a block of method chunks. For example, to introduce continuous feedback loop or fixed iteration times in an area of method chunks.
- One can add method elements to many method chunks to realize cross-cutting tactics. For example, to apply configuration management activities to each of the method chunks in a method that are affected by configuration control policies.

Figure 1 shows relationships between method tactics and method chunks in method engineering. Tactics can also be applied to instances of method or method chunks. None of these method transformations can be easily modeled using traditional method chunks and integration/association-based assembly techniques.

4 Applying Method Tactics to Software Development Methods

In order to validate the feasibility and effectiveness of using method tactics, we now apply method tactics to general software development method chunks. We have only selected tactics listed in section 3 that improve method agility. Some of these also harm scalability. The generic method chunks include eliciting and defining requirements (R), design (D), coding (C), testing (T), and product and project management (P). This is shown in Table 1. Each cell represents the practice derived from applying the corresponding method tactic to the generic activity. Multiple related method chunks can be involved during the process due to the cross-cutting nature of the tactics and non-functional method requirements. We then determine if the derived practices match existing agile practices in industry, and consider if they suffer from poor scalability. We looked at eight agile methods:

1. Feature Driven Development (FDD)
2. Extreme Programming (XP)
3. Dynamic Systems Development Method (DSDM)
4. Scrum (Scrum)
5. Agile Software Development (ASD)
6. Crystal (Crystal)
7. Lean Software (Lean)
8. Agile RUP (ARUP)

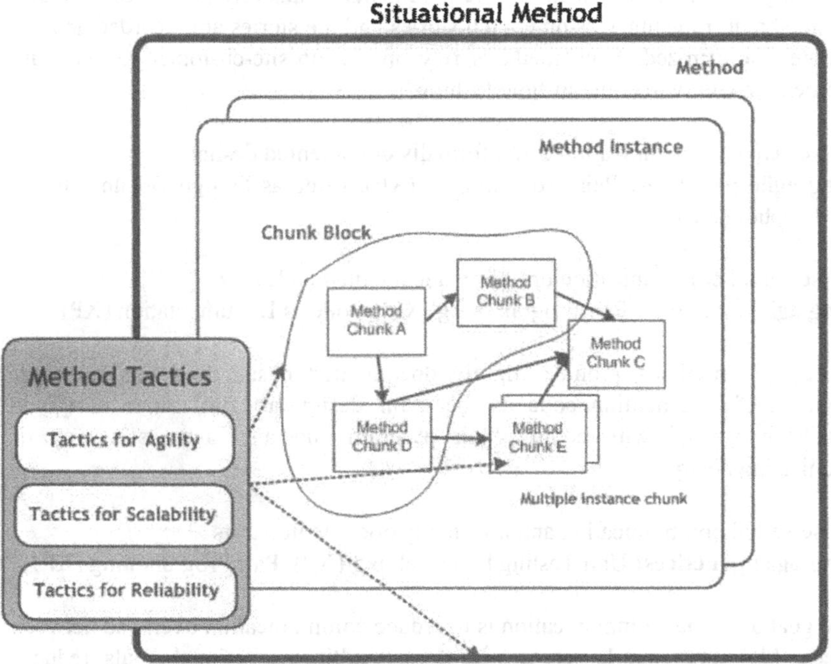

Figure 1 Method Tactics

Due to a high degree of overlap, we only include the first four in the following report. All eight methods were considered when we try to identify potential missing practices.

Table 1. Applying method tactics to generic software development method chunks

	R	D	C	T	P
1 Verbal communication	1xR	1xD	1xC	1xT	1xP
2 Downstream driven feedback	2xR	2xD	2xC	2xT	2xP
3 Frequent feedback/checking	3xR	3xD	3xC	3xT	3xP
4 Incremental completion	4xR	4xD	4xC	4xT	4xP
5 configuration management					
6 Reduce task dependency					

1xR: Use verbal communication and informally documented requirements
Existing Agile Practices: On-Site Customer (XP), User Stories (XP), Active User Involvement (DSDM), Collaboration and Cooperation among stakeholders (DSDM), Domain Object Modeling (FDD)

Applying verbal communication to requirements means relying less on formally documented requirements. Customers tell stories and the stories are recorded and not immediately scrutinized. Such methods rely on the on-site-customer to elaborate requirements verbally in a just-in-time fashion.

1xD: Use verbal communication and informally documented design
Existing agile practices: Pair Programming (XP), Code as Design Documentation (XP), Metaphor (XP)

1xC: Use verbal communication or lightly documented code
Existing agile practices: Pair Programming (XP), Code as Documentation (XP)

Most agile methods promote lightly documented design and use standard-complying self-documenting code as the main design artefact. Since design is essentially integrated with coding, pair programming also acts as a way of communicating designs.

1xT: Use verbal communication and informally documented tests
Existing agile practices: Unit Testing by Developer (XP), Pair Programming (XP)

The goal of verbal communication is to reduce communication overhead between resources. Making a single resource perform multiple functional goals reduces communication overhead to zero since only one person is involved. Making developers do unit testing is an example of applying this tactic.

1xP: Use verbal communication and informally documented products
Existing agile practices: Co-location (XP), On-site Customer (XP), Code as Documentation (XP)

When this tactic is applied cross-cuttingly to the overall project, co-location is the result. However, providing co-location and on-site customers is difficult for large projects, and in global development and outsourcing contexts.

2xR: Design/Coding/Testing/Product driven requirements validation with user
Existing agile practices: Just-in-time requirements elaboration (XP – design/coding driven), Testable Requirements (XP –testing driven), Short Release (XP –product driven), Productionizing (XP – product driven), Frequent Product Delivery (DSDM – product driven)

The downstream activities for requirements are design, coding, testing and product. We consider them separately as indicated in the brackets. Products are considered have the richest feedback because: 1) productionizing leads to more intermediate steps to be carried out which may reveal more issues; and 2) products can be used to seek feedback from users directly. The second point is especially important for requirements activities. However, the cost of constantly producing working and tested products can be costly for large projects. The trade-off between cost and agility should be considered here.

2xD: Coding/Testing/Product driven design validation
Existing agile practices: Spiking (XP – coding driven), Code Smell (XP – coding driven), Design for Test (XP – testing driven),
Potential missing practices: Release driven design review, non-functional requirements validation through design review

2xC: Testing/Product driven coding
Existing agile practices: Test Driven Development (XP – testing driven), Continuous/Nightly Build (XP – product driven)

2xT: Product driven testing
Existing agile practices: Acceptance Testing (XP)

Coding and designing are often intertwined activities in agile processes. Although testing is extensively used for driving all upstream activities (requirements, design and coding), there is no emphasis on using the product feedback to improve design and coding directly. Products are often used as a way to elicit feature-based feedback rather than systematic non-functional requirements, e.g. performance, reliability, scalability validation through design review. We identify this as a potential missing agile practice.

3xR: Continues requirement validation
Existing agile practices: On-Site Customer (XP), Active User Involvement (DSDM), Collaboration and Cooperation among stakeholders (DSDM), Domain Object Modeling (FDD)

3xD: Continuous design validation
Existing agile practices: Refactoring/Code Smell (XP)

3xC: Continuous code validation
Existing agile practices: Test Driven Development (XP), Pair Programming (XP), Regression Testing (XP), Continuous Integration (XP)

The continuous method tactic can be applied in two ways:

1. By creating immediate feedback loop between adjacent method chunks. Refactoring and test driven development are two examples.
2. By adding extra resources on the same task to provide immediate feedback. Pair programming and on-site customers are two examples.

Continuous feedback will improve software development agility. The cost and scalability of this very short feedback loop is affected by whether multiple people are involved. For example, one benefit of continuous integration is that messages about build failures can be sent to the specific individual(s) who caused the failure. The entire development team need not be involved. However, continuous integration may not scale well due to resource contention on build servers and synchronization issues during a long build. Adding extra resources is also costly and can only be justified in certain circumstances. For example, the increased cost of pair programming is often justified by mentoring and training benefits.

3xT: Continuous test code validation
Existing agile practices: Pair Programming (XP)
Potential missing practices: Continuous test quality check, test refactoring, test smell.

It has been argued that test driven development will produce code as good as the test design. Since test code is not as rigorously examined as other part of the development, low quality code could be produced due to low quality test code. Currently, test design largely depends on experience. Employing more rigorous test design techniques or auto-test-generation can mitigate the risks involved.

3xP: Continues product validation
Existing agile practices: Short Release (XP), Productionizing (XP), Sprint/Sprint Review (Scrum), Frequent Product Delivery (DSDM)

Continuous product validation has appeared in almost all agile methods. However, it is not exactly continuous, but instead usually a very short release iteration. Different methods put different constraints or use different criteria for the length of iterations.

4xR: Incremental requirement definition
Existing agile practices: Just-in-time requirement elaboration (XP), Accept Requirement Changes (all agile methods)

4xD: Incremental design
Existing agile practices: YAGNI/Simple Design (XP), Refactoring (XP)

4xC: Incremental coding

Existing agile practices: Short Release (XP), Developing by Feature (FDD), Iterative and Incremental development (DSDM), Product Backlog (Scrum)

4xT: Incremental testing
Existing agile practices: N/A
Potential missing practices: Simple Testing.

Incremental execution of method chunks has been an important practice in all agile methods due to a number of reasons:

- Constantly changing environment and requirements
- Emergent properties instead of planned properties of a system [16]
- Inevitable programming rework [7]

The focus of incremental work has been on all activities except testing. This might be due to the fact that testing is essential in quality assurance. However, it has been observed that one difficulty in test driven development is the amount of time taken to setup testing infrastructure, including high quality skeletons, stubs and mock objects. Due to the high volatility of requirements change and design refactoring (which affects interfaces), testing code can become obsolete quickly. There is a need to balance the sophistication of the testing code and its ability to perform high quality testing. The XP YAGNI principle (You Aren't Gonna Need It) can be applied cautiously to progressively improve the coverage and quality of testing code.

4xP: Incremental product development
Existing agile practices: Short Release (XP), Developing by Feature (FDD), Iterative and Incremental development (DSDM), Product Backlog (Scrum)

Tactics such as configuration management and task dependency are overall cross-cutting tactics. Thus, we try to apply them to the overall method.

5: Configuration management
Existing agile practices: Reversible Changes (DSDM), Configuration Management (FDD).

6: Task Dependencies:
Existing agile practices: Collective ownership (XP)
Potential missing practices: Architecture driven process planning

Task dependency in software development is very much related to the architecture of a product [27]. Architecture is usually not systematically used to optimize method parallelism and concurrent development. However, there has been some preliminary research [15] into the issue.

As discussed in section 3, some tactics promoting agility suffer from scalability issues. The software development agile practices we derived here inherit these scalability issues. Some issues can be mitigated [12]. Others have to be accepted on balance [5].

Overall there is a high degree of fit between our derived practices and existing industry practices. Variants or different elaborations exist in industry for most of our derived practices, but they achieve agility through the same means. This supports our claim that method tactics can be and should be discovered and used in situational method design. By applying these method tactics systematically to relevant method chunks, we can potentially identify new practices. The quality trade-offs documented for each tactic can be used to analyze practice trade-offs within new situations. Certain situations may exacerbate quality problems while others may make them less relevant. We have demonstrated that agility and scalability trade-offs in software development methods can be better understood through method tactic analysis.

5 Discussion

The discovery and accumulation of method tactics should be based on both theoretically sound grounds and also empirical observation and validation. Because there is little existing theory on non-functional method quality, we have conducted our initial work by observing important factors in practices within existing software development methods. Similar general observations have also been made in other specific development domains such as product line development [23] and COTS-based development [14]. However, the observations are usually too high-level to be useful in validating fine-grained practice-level method chunks. There are a number of limitations of our work due to this.

- Our list of tactics may appear to be arbitrary in terms of their orthogonality and level of abstraction. Some of the tactics are overlapping and some others have close relationships. Some tactics may be able to be divided into more atomic ones. This limitation could be addressed by the development and validation of reasoning models and parameters for each method quality attribute. Then, method tactics could be organized around their influence on these parameters. We are currently working on establishing such reasoning models.
- Our list may omit some important kinds of tactics, especially those used in other method domains. We are looking into other method engineering domains and may expand our use of method tactics to these broader domains.

6 Conclusion

Just like a product, a method has to be designed to satisfy situational requirements. These situational requirements include both functional requirements and non-functional requirements. Achieving scalability, agility, reliability and usability of a method is equally important as achieving functional requirements. We observe such non functional requirements can often be achieved only through using cross-cutting techniques rather than changing or adding single method chunks. We propose the concept of method tactics to capture these cross-cutting techniques. Our preliminary work identified a number of such tactics for achieving agility and scalability. Most of the tactics affect both -ilities in different directions. This raises interesting trade-off analysis opportunities in situational method design. We validated these general tactics by applying them to general software development methods. The result demonstrates that agile practices can be designed intentionally and these derived agile practices match existing agile methodologies. This opens a new door to designing new method chunks in more flexible and creative ways. We plan to visualize these tactics and affected development processes in process definition languages such as Little-JIL[25] or goal-oriented languages such as i*[26]. We also plan to include a more systematic evaluation framework to evaluate newly proposed techniques which claim certain cross-cutting ilities.

Acknowledgements

NICTA is funded by the Australian Government's Department of Communications, Information Technology, and the Arts and the Australian Research Council through Backing Australia's Ability and the ICT Research Centre of Excellence programs.

References

1. M. N. Aydin and F. Harmsen, "Making a Method Work for a Project Situation in the Context of CMM," in *Product-Focused Software Process Improvement (PROFES)*, 2002 pp. 158-171.
2. M. Bajec, R. Rupnik, and M. Krisper, "A Framework for Reengineering Software Development Methods " in *International Conference on Software Engineering Advances (ICSEA'06)*, 2006 p. 28.
3. M. Bajec, D. Vavpotič, and M. Krisper, "Practice-driven approach for creating project-specific software development methods," *Information and Software Technology,* vol. 49(4), pp. 345-365, 2007.
4. L. Bass, P. Clements, and R. Kazman, *Software Architecture in Practice*, 2 ed.: Addison-Wesley, 2003.
5. B. W. Boehm and R. Turner, *Balancing agility and discipline : a guide for the perplexed.* Boston: Addison-Wesley, 2003.
6. S. Brinkkemper, M. Saeki, and F. Harmsen, "Assembly Techniques for Method Engineering," in *10th International Conference Advanced Information Systems Engineering (CAiSE'98)*, 1998.
7. A. Cass and L. Osterweil, "Programming Rework in Software Processes," Department of Computer Science, University of Massachusetts UM-CS-2002-025, 2002.
8. E. Domínguez and M. A. Zapata, "Noesis: Towards a situational method engineering technique," *Information Systems,* vol. 32(2), pp. 181-222, 2007.
9. B. Henderson-Sellers and C. Gonzalez-Perez, "A comparison of four process metamodels and the creation of a new generic standard," *Information and Software Technology,* vol. 47, pp. 49-65, 2005.
10. B. Henderson-Sellers and A. Qumer, "An Evaluation of the Degree of Agility in Six Agile Methods and its Applicability for Method Engineering," *Information and Software Technology,* vol. In Press, 2007.
11. F. Karlsson and P. Agerfalk, "Method configuration: adapting to situational characteristics while creating reusable assets " *Information and Software Technology,* vol. 46(9), pp. 619-633, 2004.

12. D. Leffingwell, *Scaling software agility : best practices for large enterprises*. Upper Saddle River, NJ: Addison-Wesley, 2007.
13. I. Mirbel and J. Ralyte, "Situational Method Engineering: Combining Assembly-based and Roadmap-driven Approaches," *Requirements Engineering*, vol. 11(1), pp. 58-78, 2006.
14. F. Navarrete, P. Botella, and X. Franch, "Reconciling Agility and Discipline in COTS Selection Processes " in *the Sixth International IEEE Conference on Commercial-off-the-Shelf (COTS)-Based Software Systems (ICCBSS'07)*, 2007.
15. M. Nonaka, L. Zhu, M. A. Barbar, and M. Staples, "Project Delay Variability Simulation in Software Product Line Development,," in *International Conference on Software Process (ICSP'07) co-located with ICSE'07*, 2007.
16. L. Northrop, R. Kazman, M. Klein, D. Schmidt, K. Wallnau, and K. Sullivan, "Ultra-Large Scale Systems: The Software Challenge of the Future," 2006.
17. B. Nuseibeh, A. Finkelstein, and J. Kramer, "Method engineering for multi-perspective software development," *Information and Software Technology*, vol. 38(4), pp. 267-274, 1998.
18. L. Osterweil, "Software Processes Are Software Too," in *International Conference on Software Engineering (ICSE)*, 1987.
19. J. Ralyte, P. Backlund, H. Kuhn, and M. Jeusfeld, "Method Chunks for Interoperability," in *International Conference on Conceptual Modeling (ER)*, 2006.
20. J. Ralyte, R. Deneckere, and C. Rolland, "Towards a Generic Model for Situational Method Engineering," in *International Conference Advanced Information Systems Engineering (CAiSE'03)*, 2003.
21. M. Rossi, J.-P. Tolvanen, B. Ramesh, K. Lyytinen, and J. Kaipala, "Method Rationale in Method Engineering," in *33rd Hawaii International Conference on System Sciences (HICSS)*, 2000.
22. M. K. Serour and B. Henderson-Sellers, "Introducing Agility: A Case Study of Situational Method Engineering Using the OPEN Process Framework," in *28th Annual International Computer Software and Applications Conference (COMPSAC '04)*, 2004.
23. K. Tian and K. Cooper, "Agile and Software Product Line Methods: Are They So Different?," in *the First International Workshop on Agile Product Line Engineering (APLE'06)*, 2006.
24. I. v. d. Weerd, S. Brinkkemper, J. Souer, and J. Versendaal, "A Situational Implementation Method for Web-based Content Management System-applications: Method Engineering and Validation in Practice," *Software Process Improvement and Practice*, vol. 11, pp. 521-538, 2006.
25. A. Wise, "Little-JIL 1.5 Language Report," Department of Computer Science, University of Massachusetts, Amherst, MA 2006.
26. E. Yu, "Towards Modeling and Reasoning Support for Early-Phase Requirements Engineering," in *the Third International Symposium on Requirements Engineering (RE'97)*, 1997.
27. L. Zhu, R. Jeffery, M. Huo, and T. T. Tran, "Effects of Architecture and Technical Development Process on Micro-Process," in *International Conference on Software Process (ICSP'07) co-located with ICSE'07*, 2007.

Complete Methods for Building Complete Applications

Naveen Prakash
1 Knowledge Park Phase II, Greater NOIDA 201306, India
praknav@hotmail.com

Abstract. nformation systems development methods (ISDMs) produce a product, the application, by following a development process model. We argue that in failing to produce the application process model that supports the application product, ISDMs only address part of the IS development problem. Additionally, we show that there is, in fact, a range of abstractions of the application product and process and ISDMs do not build these abstractions.. To address these issues, we define the completeness principle that integrates the 100% and conceptualization principles of conceptual modelling. This principle states that an information system should be a faithful representation of the product and process models at the required level of conceptualization. A method that complies with this principle is called a complete method. We develop a complete method and discuss issues raised in developing such methods.

1 Introduction

The development of products embedded in business is an issue taken up by the Information Systems community. We have put in considerable effort in product development and in modelling IS development processes for producing products. The approach to product development is to build a schema, given an application and a data model. Thus, for example, for the Oberoi Hotels Reservation System an Oberoi schema in ER form is built. Several process models have been built to define the process to be followed in constructing such schemata. Two points are to be noticed:

In developing an application product, our concern is the immediate application and not the larger domain of which the application is a part. Thus we develop the

Please use the following format when citing this chapter:

Prakash, N., 2007, in IFIP International Federation for Information Processing, Volume 244, Situational Method Engineering: Fundamentals and Experiences, eds. Ralyté, J., Brinkkemper, S., Henderson-Sellers B., (Boston Springer), pp. 207-221.

Oberoi Hotel schema but not a generic hotel reservation schema. Extending this, we find that there is in fact a range of abstractions above the Oberoi Hotel schema: the hotel reservation schema, the more abstract 'reservation' schema, the even more abstract resource allocation schema and so on. Yet the IS development process aims to develop an application product and not the range of schema abstractions as *products*.

Interest in process models is centred on *our* problem of product development. We investigate process models that help *us* in solving *our* problem of developing schemata. However, there is an application views point that we totally ignore. To illustrate, consider a hotel reservation schema and assume that it meets its requirements. When installed in an organization, this schema is instantiated for the different hotel booking requests. Let the hotel be a transit hotel that gives bookings for one day only. Then, upon getting a reservation request, we can instantiate the schema components in two different orders. We refer to a schema instantiation order as an Application Process Model (APM). The two APMs in our example are shown in Table I.

Table I: Two Application Process Models

APM1	APM2
Requestor (name, address)	Booking(date, price)
Booking(date, price)	Availability(number of rooms, type of room)
Availability(number of rooms, type of room)	Requestor (name, address)

The application process models of Table I show two strategies for room reservation. APM1 considers booking issues like availability, prices etc. only after all requestor information is obtained whereas APM2 considers booking issues first and thereafter, once the booking is notionally done, considers requestor information to complete it. Evidently, these constitute two different ways of doing business. The APM selected should be the one that best fits into the business process in which the reservation system is embedded.

The foregoing shows an APM plays an important role in the success of an IS product. Yet the IS community ignores these. Consequently, methods that produce an APM have not been engineered

We believe that complete application development cannot be restricted to development of application products only but must also have the capability to support the range of schema abstractions and associated APMs. We propose *the completeness principle* that states **t***hat an information system should be a faithful representation of the product and process models at the required level of conceptualization.* A diagrammatic representation of this principle is shown in Fig. 1. As shown, at abstraction level i, $0 \leq i \leq n$, both the APM and product models are to be represented.

The completeness principle subsumes *both the 100% and conceptualization principles* (Gri82, Hoe94) of conceptual modelling. According to the *100% principle*, everything that is relevant should be represented, and the representation should contain only that which is relevant. Traditionally, this principle has been applied to product aspects only and the completeness principle here proposes to extend it to the process aspects of applications as well: when developing the product model of an application, one should develop the APM as well. This is shown in the boxes of Fig. 1 and implies that an application is the integration of the product and application process models.

The *conceptualization principle* says that the representation should be independent of any implementation issues. In conceptual modelling, this has been interpreted to mean independence of the conceptual schema from the underlying implementation platform. The *completeness principle* proposed here extends this to cover every pair of abstraction levels of the representation. This is shown on the left side of Fig. 1. Consider abstractions at level n and level (n-1). The completeness principle treats level (n-1) as the 'implementation platform' of the abstraction at level n. When n=1 then we get the conceptual modelling view of the conceptualization principle: the schema at the first level is the conceptual schema whereas the 0th level is its implementation platform.

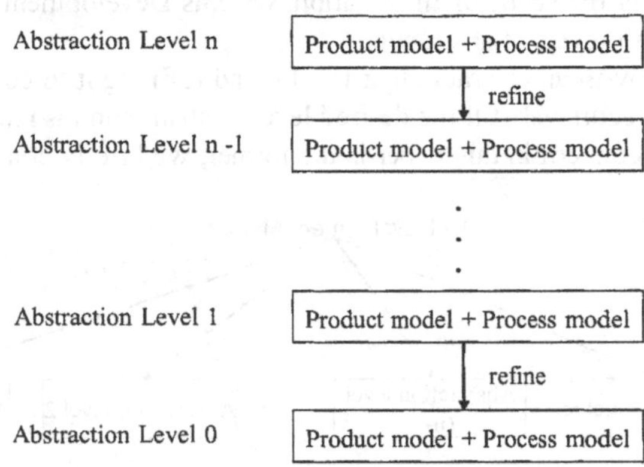

Fig. 1: The completeness principle

Taken as a whole, the completeness principle says that applications can be visualized at different levels of abstraction and at each level modelling is complete if and only if both the application product and application process models have been developed. The application at level (n-1) is a refinement of its abstraction at level n.

In this paper, we consider the impact of the completeness principle on Information Systems Development Methods (ISDM). We shall refer to an ISDM that complies with the completeness principle as a complete method. That is, *a complete method is one that provides capability to develop both the product and associated application process model at the stated level of conceptualization.* We show that method engineering approaches that integrate the product and process aspects of methods have the capacity to build complete methods. In doing this, we use the generic method model (Pra06). This model treats a method as a triple <M, Dep, E> where M is a set of method blocks, Dep is a set of dependencies between these methods, and E is an enactment mechanism. M and Dep can be organized in a dependency graph. This graph is the set of all routes that can be followed in the method; it is the set of all process models that can be built by performing a walk through the dependency graph.

The layout of this paper is as follows. In the next section we consider the impact of the completeness principle on IS development. In section III contains a brief overview of the generic model that highlights those features that we shall use here. In section IV we illustrate the completeness principle by taking the example of issuing permits. We build product and process models at two abstraction levels. In section V, we outline a tool that takes process information as input and produces the process model for a product. In section VI, we consider related work and show how the completeness principle brings new issues to the forefront.

2 Implication of the Completeness Principle

The completeness principle implies that information systems can be developed in two ways

1. By extending the scope of Information Systems Development Methods to cover systems at all levels of abstraction.
2. By starting with an abstraction at level n and refining it to construct abstraction level (n-1) recursively till the desired level of abstraction is reached.

Though the concern in this paper is the former, we briefly consider each of these in turn.

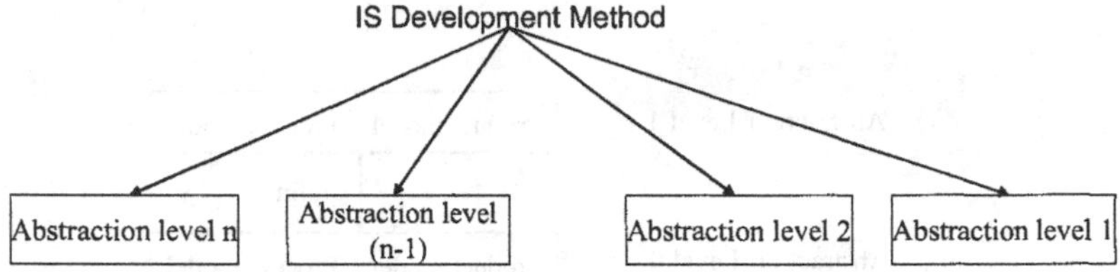

Fig. 2: Scope of an IS Development Method

Fig. 2 shows the scope of an ISDM. Whereas today, an ISDM builds only abstraction level 1, the completeness principle says that it should have the capability to build any level. An example of this is shown in Fig. 3.

Meta domain model	Resource allocation
Application Domain model	Reservation domain
Application	Oberoi, Taj reservation

Fig. 3: Example of Levels of Abstraction

On the left hand side of this Figure, we see three abstraction levels. The lowest is the Application layer, the next higher is the Application Domain layer and the highest is the Meta domain layer. On the right hand side is an example of each of these. As shown, the lowest layer is inhabited by the Oberoi Hotels application; its domain is the Reservation domain at the next higher level and finally, its meta domain is that of Resource Allocation. The completeness principle says that an ISDM should be able to develop all the models on the right hand side of Fig. 3.

The second implication of the completeness principle is illustrated in Fig. 4. As shown, the Meta layer is converted to the domain layer through a domain development process and the latter is in turn converted to the application by an application development process.

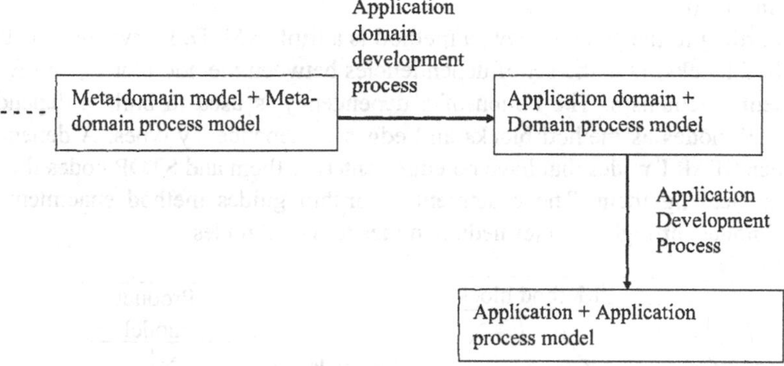

Fig. 4: Progressing through Meta Levels

This is exemplified in Fig. 5. As shown, the resource allocation meta domain is converted to the reservation domain by the reservation domain development process which, in turn, is converted to the application proper by the hotel reservation development process.

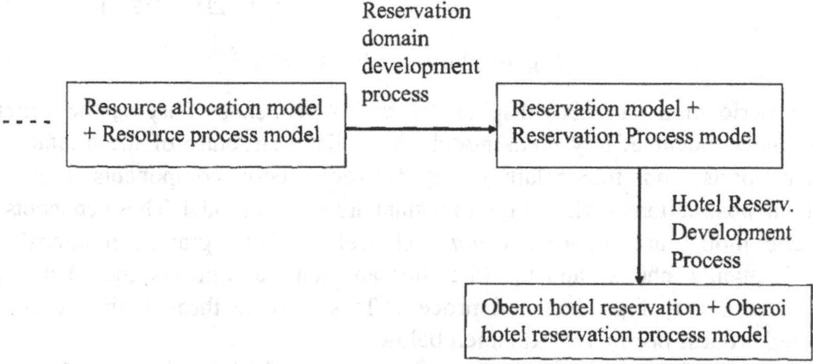

Fig. 5: Building an Application through Progression

As mentioned earlier, the focus of this paper is on elaborating the scope of an ISDM and the second approach indicated here shall be the subject of another paper.

3 The Generic Method Model

The generic method model was developed (Pra06) as means to capture the essential nature of methods, devoid of any commitment to meta concepts as in meta-models. The generic method model integrates product and process aspects together. We shall provide only a broad view of the generic model so as to show its capability to meet the completeness criterion. For full details of the generic model please refer to (Pra06). However, it must be noted that we have extended the generic model to explicitly represent the relationship of process primitives with the process model as shown in Fig. 6.

According to the generic view, a method is a triple <M, D, E> where M is the set of method blocks, D is the set of dependencies between method blocks, and E is the enactment mechanism. The notion of a dependency is used to build a dependency graph with nodes as method blocks and edges as dependency types. A dependency graph has START nodes that have no edges entering them and STOP nodes that have no edges leaving them. The enactment algorithm guides method enactment from START nodes through the intermediate nodes to STOP nodes.

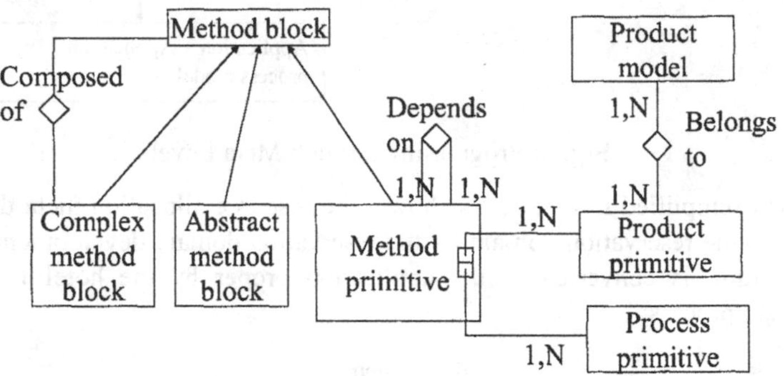

Fig. 6: The Generic Model

The generic model (Pra06) displays *class independence*. That is, the generic model is independent of any meta-model: the holistic structure of the artefact, its component parts and inter-relationships between these components must be expressed in abstractions high enough to instantiate a meta-model. These concepts of the generic model are *themselves not* technical artifacts, graphs, relationships, objects, fragments, chunks and the like. Instead, generic concepts should directly capture the notions of product and process. This is done through the notion of product and process primitives explained below.

As shown in Fig. 6, there are three kinds of method blocks, complex ones composed out of other simpler ones, abstract ones that are generalizations/specializations of method blocks and method primitives that are atomic method blocks. A method primitive is a pair <product primitive, process primitive>. Extending this to all method blocks, a method block can be considered as having two parts, an argument part and an action part where the action part is capable of manipulating the argument in the desired way. These two parts correspond to product primitive and process primitive respectively of Fig. 6. For example, <entity, attribute, attach> is a method block. It specifies that an attribute can be attached to an entity. In order for a method block to be enacted, it is necessary that instances of arguments are available. In our example, instances of attribute attributes and entity to be attached to one another must be available in the product under construction. In order to handle method blocks like <entity, create> a special product instance called 'don't care' is postulated that exists in all products. Such method blocks assume the availability of 'don't care'.

Product primitives have their origin in the product model and depending on the abstraction level and the nature of the product to be developed. Process primitives originate from the process model, and capture the kinds of operations one wants to do in the application. For a corporate system these may be Recruit and Promote for operating on Employee and Allot Budget for Department.

Table 1: Types of Dependencies

Type	Urgency	Necessity	Abbreviation
1	Immediate	Must	IM
2	Immediate	Can	IC
3	Deferred	Must	DM
4	Deferred	Can	DC

Now consider the notion of a dependency. Two attributes, urgency and necessity, are associated with each dependency type. Urgency refers to the time at which the dependent method block, O_2, is to be enacted. If O_2 is to be enacted immediately after O_1 is enacted then this attribute takes on the value *Immediate.* If O_2 can be enacted any time, immediately or at any moment, after O_1 has been enacted, then urgency takes on the value *Deferred.* Necessity refers to whether or not the dependent method block O_2 is necessarily to be enacted after O_1 has been enacted. If it is necessary to enact O_2, then this attribute takes the value *Must* otherwise it has the value *Can.* This gives rise to four dependency types displayed in Table 1.

Using the notion of a dependency, a method can be organized as a dependency graph. We illustrate this by considering a method with the set of method primitives O = $\{O_1, O_2, \ldots., O_{14}\}$. Let there be two dependency types IM and IC respectively. Let the following dependencies be defined:

IM dependencies		**IC dependencies**	
$O_1 \rightarrow O_2$	$O_1 \rightarrow O_3$	$O_1 \rightarrow O_6$	$O_1 \rightarrow O_9$
$O_1 \rightarrow O_4$	$O_1 \rightarrow O_5$	$O_6 \rightarrow O_{13}$	$O_6 \rightarrow O_{14}$
$O_6 \rightarrow O_7$	$O_6 \rightarrow O_8$		
$O_9 \rightarrow O_{10}$	$O_9 \rightarrow O_{11}$		
$O_9 \rightarrow O_{12}$			

The organization of the method as a dependency graph for our method is shown in Fig 7. So as not to clutter up the Figure, only the IC dependencies are labelled. The non-labelled ones are assumed to be IM dependencies.

To summarize, from the perspective of the completeness principle, the generic model brings two key notions, meta-model independence and dependency graph. The former contributes to product and process construction at any abstraction level. Thus, it is a matter of choosing the abstraction level of the product, determining the interesting product model concepts and carrying out the instantiation of the generic model. Similarly, process concepts comprising the process model at the same level of abstraction as the product are to be determined and instantiation performed. Thus, meta-model independence is the basis for development of product and process models at any abstraction level.

The dependency graph contributes to the construction of the process model associated with the product model. A path from START to STOP node represents a process model. In this sense, the dependency graph is the set of all process models that are permissible under the method.

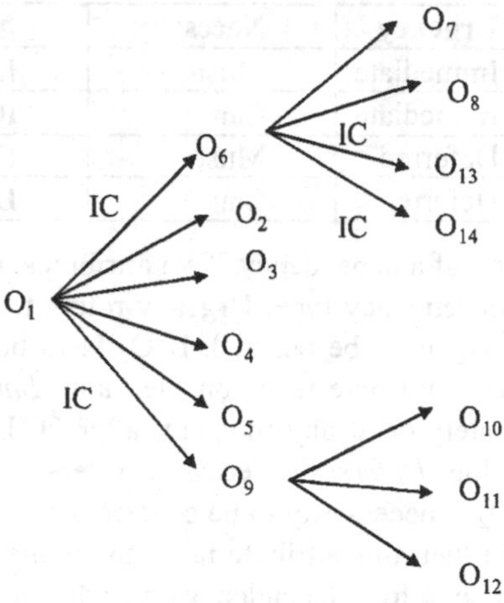

Fig. 7: A Dependency Graph

4 Illustrating Completeness Principle

In this section we present an example to show that the generic model follows the completeness principle: it can support the construction of a product and the associated process model at any level of abstraction. We do this by presenting a small example at different levels of abstraction as in Fig. 8. At the second abstraction level of Fig. 1, let us consider the domain of governance systems for issuing permits of different kinds, driving licenses, passports, election identity cards, running a restaurant, etc. Since all these issue permissions, we shall refer to their domain as the permit domain. We shall develop a product model and associated process model for this domain. Thereafter, at abstraction level 1, we shall consider the passport application as a refinement of the permit domain.

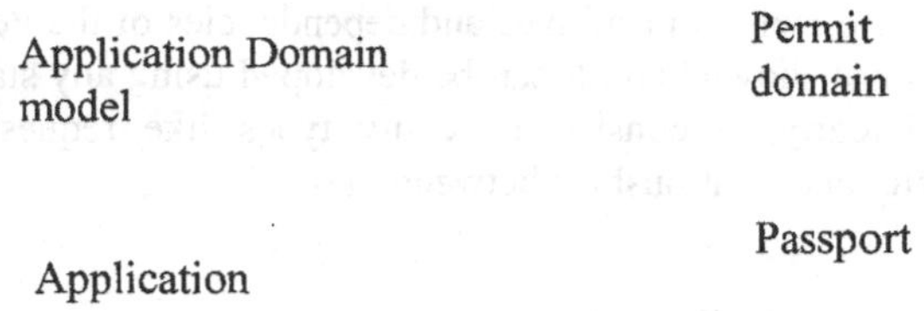

Application Domain model

Permit domain

Application

Passport

Fig. 8: The Permit Domain and its Refinement

4.1 The Permit Domain

In the domain of permits, a request is received for obtaining the permit. Usually, a permit is issued to an individual who may be a person, a company, a society etc. The request is processed to see that it can be further treated, that all information required is supplied, and statutory requirements are met. To check fraud or to enforce standards, verifications/inspections are carried out. There may be transaction costs associated with the issue of permits that are recovered from the requestor in the form of fees. Finally, if the requestor is found fit to receive the permit then it is issued. Permits may be lost or damaged. So, a facility for issuing duplicate permits is required. Similarly, certain permits may have to be issued on an emergency basis.

The following set of product primitives are of interest:

P = {Request, Permit, Emergency Permit, Duplicate Permit}

The Process primitives are

A= {Receive, Verify, Refuse, Issue, Terminate}

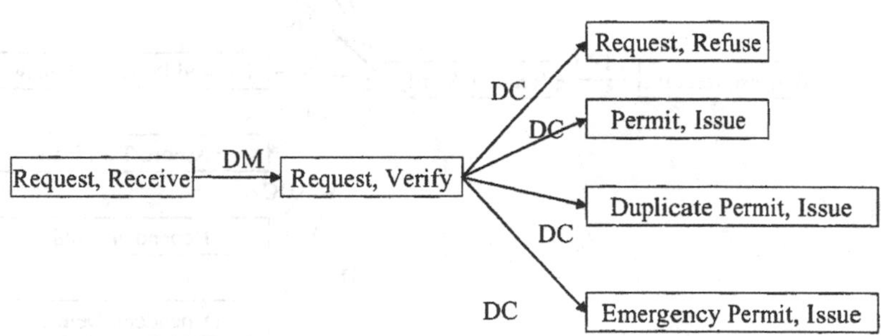

Fig. 9: The Permit Process Model

The set of method primitives is obtained by associating meaningful process types with their product types. The set of meaningful method primitives for our example is as follows:

O = {<Request, Receive>, <Request, Verify>, <Permit, Refuse>, <Permit, Issue>, <Duplicate Permit, Issue>, <Emergency Permit, Renew>, <Permit, Terminate>}

Fig. 9 shows the method primitives and dependencies of the Permit domain. The product model is not shown here. It can be developed using any standard data model like the ER. Clearly, it consists of entity types like request, permit and its specializations etc. and relationships between these.

4.2 The Passport Application

In this section we consider building a method for issuing Passports. The Passport Office has forms in which an application for passport services can be made. These services may be the issue of a fresh passport, renewal of an expired passport, issue of a duplicate passport, termination of a valid passport. The passport office verifies the details of the requestor and checks that there is no police record that might disallow the issue of the passport. Thereafter, the passport is issued. It is possible to add dependents of the passport holder on his/her passport or to delete them from the passport. The set of product primitives, P, is as follows:

P = {Request, Passport, Expired passport, Duplicate Passport, Dependent}

The set of process primitives, A, is

A= {Receive, Verify, Refuse, Issue, Renew, Terminate, Add, Delete}

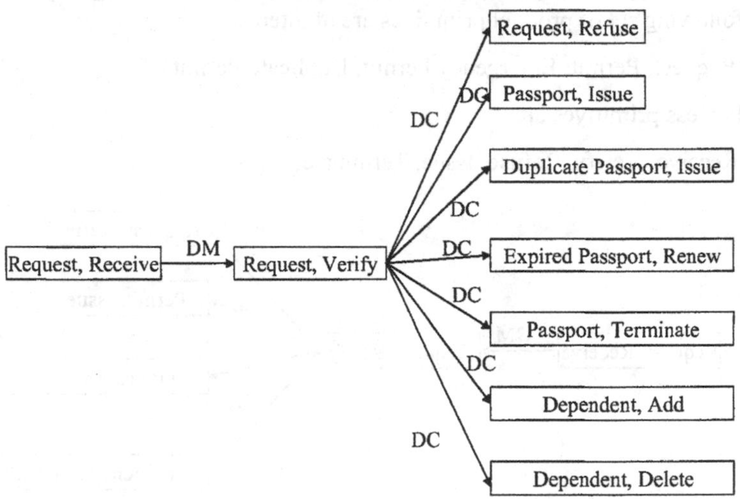

Fig. 10: The Passport Process Model

The set of method primitives is as follows:

O = {<Request, Receive>, <Request, Verify>, <Request, Refuse>, <Passport, Issue>, <Duplicate Passport, Issue>, <Expired Passport, Renew>, <Passport, Terminate>, <Dependent, Add>, <Dependent, delete>}

Fig. 10 shows the dependencies as well as the set of method primitives organized as a process model. Again, as for the permit domain, the product model is not shown here.

5 A Complete CASE Tool

Information Systems Development methods present user interfaces in their CASE tools. Regarding the process model adopted by these tools, at least three attitudes exist:

1. Assume a process model. Indeed, many methods and their CASE tools assume the Linear, Cartesian one.
2. Prescribe the set of process models that can be adopted. The application engineer selects the needed one from this assembly.
3. Make no commitment to a process model. The method provides the basic structure for the application engineer to follow any process model.

Notice that all these continue to work in the case of complete methods as well.

We illustrate a CASE tool interface that obtains dependency information during application engineering. This interface (see Fig. 11) has been designed for the generic method model introduced earlier.

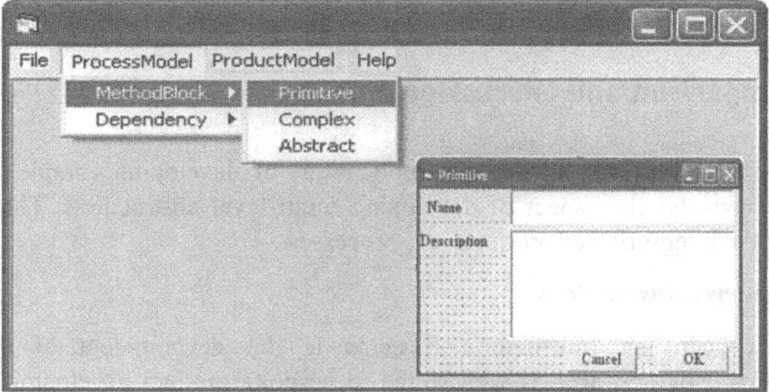

Fig. 11: Defining Method Blocks

This interface is similar to that of MetaEdit (Met93) and uses a menu bar that consists of combo boxes. As shown in the Figure, there are two menu items called Product Model and Process Model respectively. The combo box of the former contains concepts used for developing the product. Since it well understood, we do not consider this aspect here and elaborate the Process Model combo box that helps us develop the process model.

In order to produce the process model, information about method blocks and dependency information must be captured. This is achieved by the Process Model option. Clicking on the Process Model option causes the model components, Method Block and Dependency to be displayed (Fig. 11). Clicking further on method blocks enables selection of the kind of method block desired, method primitive, abstract or complex method block. Selection of these enables a pop-up box that asks for the name, description etc. of the method block. In case of abstract and complex method blocks, information about the components and specialized method blocks respectively is also asked for.

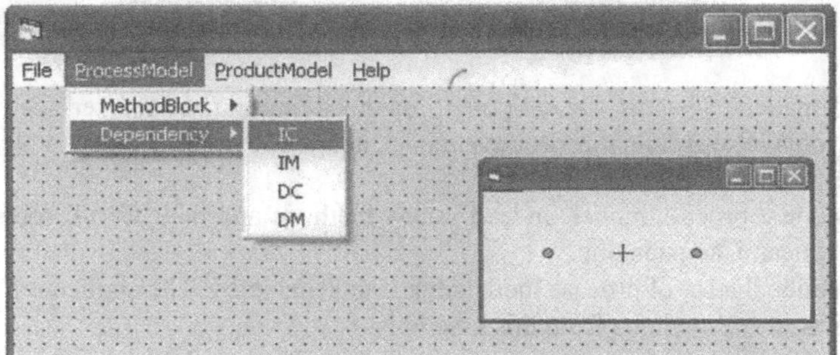

Fig. 12: Defining Dependencies between Method Blocks

Clicking on the Dependency choice (Fig. 12) invokes two capabilities. First, a cursor is enabled that is used to select two method blocks, the first of which is the source of the dependency and the second is its sink. Thus, the direction of the dependency is displayed. Second, the application engineer is asked to make a selection of the dependency type, DM, DC etc. from the displayed combo box.

6 Comparison and Discussion

In this section we consider the implications of developing complete methods. First we consider the aspect of developing multi-level abstractions. Thereafter we consider the integration of products and processes.

Multi-level Abstractions

The concern in Information Systems is the development of the instant application. This approach is well suited to bespoke product development: domain knowledge, technical capability, and organizational functional/non-functional requirements are all brought together to build the new product. If there is any reuse then this involves picking up components of legacy products. The point is that development is concerned exclusively with products and not with abstractions of these.

The completeness principle proposes multi-level abstractions of products. By analogy with meta models of methods that abstract out common features of methods, it can be seen that application concepts can also be meta modeled, thus giving rise to an application abstraction. Extending this argument to pairs of levels, the completeness principle proposes multi-levels of application abstractions. From the perspective of the conceptualization principle, this can be understood as its application to levels above the traditional conceptual one.

ERP systems (ASA99) model the wider context of applications. Thus, if an organization wants to use an ERP system for materials management, then a general framework exists that must be customized to the specific needs of the organization. Additional functionality can be introduced by using adaptation features like ABAP of SAP. Further, ERP systems are defined at relatively low, operational levels of abstraction. However, the problem of the Information Systems community is different from that solved by ERP systems. This community gives primacy to conceptualization and abstractions and leaves the task of converting these into operational systems to downstream stages in the life cycle. Complete methods and the completeness principle addresses the conceptualization/abstraction concerns of the Information Systems community.

Enterprise modeling (Fox97, Fox 98, Lou95) is again different from developing abstractions of applications because of its emphasis on modeling the larger information context of the enterprise within which the system To-Be is embedded. It is not interesting per se to look at the information system to be developed which is only a fall out of enterprise modeling. In contrast, complete methods limit themselves to multi-level abstractions of information systems. As to whether or not enterprises can be usefully abstracted for each level of application abstraction is an open issue.

We can draw an analogy between product families and product lines on the one hand and method abstractions on the other. Consider a path from the root of the abstraction hierarchy to a leaf. A method on this path is a variant of another irrespective of whether it is above or below it in the hierarchy. In this sense, we obtain a method line that is analogous to product lines.

Balancing Products with Processes

The area of method engineering lays great emphasis on meta models (Har94, Gro97, Pra98). Depending on the nature of the meta model, we can instantiate methods that can build exclusively the application product, or the Information System Development process, or both of these. Irrespective of this, for the application engineer, the end result of the application of a method is the Information Systems product that can eventually be installed and operated upon. Even the 100% principle that lays emphasis on an exact representation of the real world does so in terms of the IS product: application concepts, inter-relationships between these, and constraints. Complete methods give equal emphasis to the IS product and the application process. It argues for an equal treatment to be given to process concepts, inter-relationships between these and constraints, heuristics etc.

The process model is represented in its full richness and variations as a dependency graph. This enables us to look at each individual method feature and its relationship with other features. There is a successor-predecessor relationship between method features. However, this relationship is controlled by the urgency and necessity properties. These properties specify the time delay in the relationship and also identify whether a feature must necessarily be enacted or is only a possibility, a choice.

The dependency graph looks similar to the notion of a map [Rol99]. However, the map is at a completely different level of abstraction. Its nodes are intentions and edges are strategies for fulfilling these intentions. This is in contrast to a dependency graph where nodes represent the capability of operating on given product elements and edges are dependencies of different types. Again, in a map, there is a successor-predecessor relationship between intentions and this relationship is controlled by different map topologies: bundles, multi-paths, etc. In contrast, a dependency graph uses the properties of dependencies to exercise control of what can/must be enacted next. It can be seen that there is no notion in a map corresponding to that of the property, urgency, of our dependencies.

Impact on Method Engineering

The completeness principle introduces two new problems in method engineering, corresponding to the two aspects of multiple level of abstractions and application process models respectively. Consider the former. When a new method is to be engineered, its position in the abstraction hierarchy is to be determined. If it is a refinement of another method, then an appropriate relationship between the two is established. If it is an abstraction of another method, then it is to be placed at a higher level of refinement than this one. Finally, if none of these two conditions is satisfied then the new method is the root of a new abstraction hierarchy.

The organization of and retrieval from the method repository now becomes more complex than in traditional method engineering. Whereas earlier we were concerned with issues of keeping method descriptors or project characteristics in the repository, we now have to additionally move to a different kind of information. Descriptor/characteristic data only becomes relevant after the method is located in the abstraction hierarchy first. One way of handling this is to partition the repository into two parts, a meta method data part that contains abstraction hierarchy information and another, the method data part that contains descriptor/characteristic information. However, this is an open issue connected with the implementation of the completeness principle.

Now consider the issue of application process models. Any new method that we build must be engineered to accept information about the APM to be followed. We see two possible strategies. The first is the one we have adopted in this paper: generate the set of all possible application process models from which the desired one can be chosen. The second strategy is to produce the unique application process model that shall be used. Experience with the Map shows that the first strategy is perhaps better. One reason for this is the possibility of capturing variations in the set of models. However, we believe that this issue needs to be investigated further.

7 Conclusion

Traditional methods are limited in two ways (a) they fail to produce the application process model, and (b) they do not consider product abstractions. Complete methods attempt to address both these. The completeness principle provides:

Tight integration of the product and process aspects: Research in methods has pointed out the need to integrate product and process aspects of methods together. The completeness principle combines the existing 100% and conceptualization principles to put this integration on a firm conceptual basis.

Better product fit: Products are to be embedded in organizational processes. The completeness principle requires methods to build the application process model associated with the product under development. This shall provide a basis to verify that the process model built is in conformity with the business process of the organization. The closer these two are to one another the more likely it shall be that the product shall smoothly fit in the organization.

Support for process re-engineering: The ability to build the APM makes it possible to determine the extent of its fitness with organizational processes. Any differences between these can form the basis for informed debate on APM selection/process re-engineering.

References

(ASA99) ASAP World Consultancy and J. Blain et al, *Using SAP R/3,* Prentice Hall of India, 1999

(Fox97) Fox M.S. & Gruninger M., On Ontologies and Enterprise Modelling, Intl. Conf. On Enterprise Integration Modelling, Italy, 1997

(Fox98) Fox M.S. & Gruninger M., Enterprise Modelling, AI Magazine, 19, 3, 109 – 121, 1998

(Gri82) Griethuysen JJ van (ed.) Concepts and Terminology for the Conceptual Scheme and the Information Base, Publication Nr. ISO/TC97/SC5/WG3-N695, ANSI, New York

(Gro97) Grosz G., et al, Modelling and Engineering the Requirements Engineering Process: An Overview of the NATURE Approach, Requirements Engineering Journal, 2, 3, 115-131

(Har94) Harmsen F., et al, Situational Method Engineering for Information System Project Approaches, in Methods and Associated Tools for the Information Systems Life Cycle, Verrijn-Stuart and Olle (eds.), Elsevier, 169-194

(Hoe94) ter Hoefstede, Propoer AHM., van der Weide, Formal Description of a Conceptual Language for the Description and Manipulation of Information Models, Information Systems, 18(7) 489-523

(Lou95) Loucopoulos P., & Kavakli E., Enterprise Modeling and the Teleological Approach to Requirements Engineering, IJCIS, 45 – 79, 1995

(Met93) MetaEdit version 1.2, MetaCase Consulting, Jyvaskyla, FInland

(Pra99) Prakash N., (1999) On Method Statics and Dynamics, Information Systems Journal, 24, 8, 613-637.

(Pra06) Prakash Naveen, On Generic Method Models, Requirements Engineering Journal, 11, 4, 221-237, 2006

(Rol99) Rolland C., Prakash N., and Benjamen A., A Multi-model View of Process Modelling, Requirements Engineering Journal, 4, 4, 169-187, 1999

(Ral03) Ralyté J; Deneckère R., Rolland C., Towards a Generic Model for Situational Method Engineering, Proc. CAiSE 2003, Eder J. & Missikoff M. (eds.) LNCS 2681, Springer, 95-110.

Process Patterns for Agile Methodologies

Samira Tasharofi[1] and Raman Ramsin[2]
1 University of Tehran, Department of Electrical and Computer Engineering
North Karegar, Tehran, Iran, stasharofi@ut.ac.ir
2 Sharif University of Technology, Department of Computer Engineering
Azadi Avenue, Tehran, Iran, ramsin@sharif.edu

Abstract. The need for constructing software development methods that have been tailored to fit specific situations and requirements has given rise to the generation of general method fragments, or *process patterns*. Process patterns can be seen in some third-generation integrated methodologies (such as OPEN) and in Method Engineering approaches where they are used as *process components*. They have also been presented as components in generic software development lifecycles where they represent classes of common practices in a specific domain or paradigm; object-oriented process patterns are well-known examples. Agile methodologies, however, are yet to be thoroughly explored in this regard. We provide a set of high-level process patterns for agile development which have been derived from a study of seven agile methodologies based on a proposed generic Agile Software Process (ASP). These process patterns can promote method engineering by providing classes of common process components which can be used for developing, tailoring, and analyzing agile methodologies.

1 Introduction

A *pattern* is a "general solution to a common problem or issue, one from which a specific solution may be derived" [1, 2]. *Process Patterns* are results of applying abstraction to recurring software development processes and process components; they are an effective mechanism for highlighting and establishing methods and approaches that have proven to be successful in practice [2].

Process patterns were first introduced by Coplien in 1994 [1], and were defined as "the patterns of activity within an organization (and hence within its project)". Coplien's patterns were relatively fine-grained techniques for exercising better organizational and management practices. Therefore, they did not constitute a comprehensive and coherent whole for defining a software development process.

Process patterns were later focused upon in the object-oriented paradigm. In his two books on object-oriented process patterns, Ambler defined an object-oriented process pattern as "a collection of general techniques, actions, and/or tasks

Please use the following format when citing this chapter:

Tasharofi, S., Ramsin, R., 2007, in IFIP International Federation for Information Processing, Volume 244, Situational Method Engineering: Fundamentals and Experiences, eds. Ralyté, J., Brinkkemper, S., Henderson-Sellers B., (Boston Springer), pp. 222-237.

(activities) for developing object-oriented software" [2, 3]. The proposed object-oriented patterns were categorized as belonging to three different types, commonly ordered by ascending level of abstraction and granularity as *tasks*, *stages*, and *phases*. A *task* process pattern depicts the detailed steps to execute a specific fine-grained task of a process. A *stage* process pattern defines the steps that need to be executed in order to perform a stage of the process and is usually made up of several task process patterns. Finally, a *phase* process pattern represents the interaction of two or more stage process patterns in order to execute the phase to which they belong. The process patterns introduced by Ambler constitute a proposed generic Object-Oriented Software Process (OOSP), which helps make sense of the relative position of the patterns in a general lifecycle, and their interrelationships. The approach relates to the one later put forward, in a more detailed and formal fashion, by Prakash [4]. Although these patterns have been intended to abstract common practices over a vast range of object-oriented methodologies, and are consequently rather general, their object-oriented-software-development nature makes them more tangible to software practitioners than Coplien's patterns.

Process patterns create means for developing methodologies through composition of appropriate pattern instances [5], a practice also commonly seen in *assembly-based* Situational Method Engineering [6, 7, 8]. One of the core elements in situational method engineering is a repository of reusable building blocks (also called method fragments or method chunks) from which method elements can be instantiated [9, 10]. Process patterns can provide a rich repository for the purpose of process assembly and/or tailoring. One of the main concerns with this repository is the provision of a good classification of building blocks so that it leads the method engineer to better selections. Classification of process patterns according to different domains of application (methodology types) can aid the method engineer in addressing this problem.

Process patterns have already been used to great effect in methodologies such as OPEN [11, 12] and are rapidly gaining popularity as process building blocks in method composition/configuration approaches such as the Rational Method Composer (RMC) [13]. Agile development, however, has enjoyed little attention in this regard: efforts have mostly been confined to Software Process Improvement (SPI) [14] and dual-methodology integration/customization [15]. A generic view on agile methodologies can only be seen in Ambler's proposed Agile System Development Life Cycle (ASDLC) [16], which is not only rather cursory in its treatment of the constituent process patterns, but also lacks ample coverage, as the abstraction and generalization it provides is mainly based on just two methodologies: XP [17, 18] and AUP [19].

In this work, we identify process patterns commonly encountered in agile methodologies. Because of common defining characteristics and basic underlying principles – as presented in [20] and set out in the Agile Manifesto [21] – Agile methodologies share many common constituents, which if extracted in terms of process patterns, can be used in constructing and/or tailoring other agile methodologies. In order to achieve this goal, we start from a generic model for agile software processes, which has resulted from inspecting seven prominent, widely-used agile methodologies. We then extract the recurring process patterns in a top-down fashion according to the three abstraction levels suggested by Ambler [2]. The approach is similar to that applied in [2], yet the main contribution of our work is that the process patterns thus defined are agile-specific.

The organization of this paper is as follows: In Section 2, the proposed generic Agile Software Process (ASP) will be described. Section 3 introduces the process patterns derived from the ASP. Section 4 shows how different agile methodologies can be realized using the proposed patterns. Section 5 discusses the benefits obtained from the proposed agile process patterns, and finally, Section 6 contains the conclusions and suggestions for future work.

2 Agile Software Process (ASP)

The Agile Software Process (ASP), depicted in Fig. 1, is the proposed generic process model of agile methodologies. This model is obtained as a result of investigating seven agile methodologies: DSDM [22], Scrum [23], XP [17, 18], ASD [24], dX [25], Crystal Clear [26], and FDD [27].

ASP is composed of three serial phases which are in turn composed of internal iterative stages. According to these phases, an agile process begins with initiating the project; in the activities that follow, the software will be developed and deployed into the user environment through multiple iterations. In most agile methodologies, maintenance does not appear as a separate phase, but is rather performed through further iterations of the main development phases. Therefore, in ASP, maintenance is supported by a transition from the *Release* phase to the *Initiation* or the *Development Iterations* Phase. The other intention behind the transition from *Release* phase to *Development Iterations* phase is to accommodate frequent releases of software, which is followed as a principle in most agile methodologies.

The arrow at the bottom of the diagram indicates umbrella activities (expressed as task process patterns) which are critical to the success of a project and are applied to all stages of development. The phase and stage process patterns in ASP, as well as the tasks specified in the arrow, can in turn be detailed by delving into their constituent task process patterns.

ASP can be compared with Ambler's Object Oriented Software Process (OOSP) [2]. They are similar in several aspects: Some common stages can be found in their constituent phases, e.g., *Justify* and *Define Infrastructure*, and they are especially quite similar in the umbrella activities that they propose. But that is where the similarity ends. Since OOSP is proposed for all object-oriented methodologies regardless of their types, it is more general and consequently more abstract. This means that the patterns extracted from OOSP belong, more or less, to all object-oriented methodologies, whereas in ASP we have limited the extracted patterns to those found in agile methodologies. Therefore, ASP and OOSP are different in their structure and pattern content. The differences arise from the principles that define agility: For example, continuous verification and validation requires the existence of a review stage in the Development Iterations phase, the need for early and frequent releases of software necessitates the possibility of deploying working software increments into the user environment before deploying the complete system, and the change-based nature of agile methodologies has resulted in the absence of maintenance as a separate phase (as mentioned earlier). In the following sections, the agile process patterns obtained from ASP are described in more detail. These patterns are classified, according to [2], as phase-, stage-, and task process patterns, and have been extracted from the generic ASP in a top-down fashion.

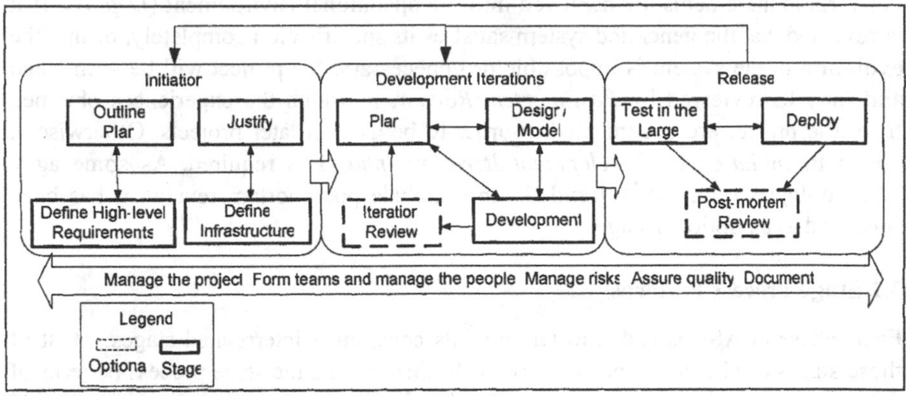

Fig. 1. The proposed Agile Software Process (ASP)

3 Agile Process Patterns

In this section, the agile process patterns extracted from the ASP will be described. For sake of simplicity and brevity, we use a more abstract notation than that used for describing object-oriented process patterns in [2]. For the same reason, we have avoided delving into the details of task process patterns and umbrella activities.

3.1 Phase Process Patterns

ASP consists of three phase process patterns: *Initiation, Development Iterations*, and *Release*. These are described below.

Initiation Phase

The goal in this phase is to initiate the project through preliminary analysis of the system. This phase consists of four iterative stages for providing an *outline plan, justifying* the project, and defining *high level requirements* and the *infrastructure* of the project.

Development Iterations Phase

In this phase, the working software is generated in multiple iterations. Each iteration is made up of planning, design, coding, testing and (optionally) review activities. These activities are covered by *Plan, Model/Design, Development*, and *Iteration Review* stage process patterns. As noted earlier, the transition from this phase to the *Release* phase and vice versa provides the possibility of deploying the newly generated software into the user environment after one or multiple iterations; the choice of the multiplicity depends on many factors, including the project type, and lies with the developer/manager.

Release Phase
Deployment activities of software engineering are performed in this phase. System-level testing (*Test in the large*) is done to verify and validate the system, and deliverable increments are deployed into the operational environment (*Deploy*). If it is revealed that the generated system satisfies its specification completely, or that the evolution of the system is impossible or unnecessary, the project will be terminated and may be reviewed by *Post-mortem Review*, in which the experiences obtained from the project are documented in order to be used in later projects. Otherwise, a return to *Initiation* or *Development Iterations phases* is required. As some agile methodologies (e.g., DSDM and Scrum) exclude post-mortem review, it has been specified as an optional stage.

3.2 Stage Process Patterns

Each phase in ASP is stated in terms of its constituent interrelated stages. Most of these stages can be performed iteratively. In this section, the stage process patterns of ASP are described in terms of their interrelated constituents – consisting of tasks and other nested stages – and the work products produced in and/or transferred among phases and stages.

Justify
In this stage (Fig. 2), the intention is to justify the project via a feasibility study and gain initial support and funding for the project.

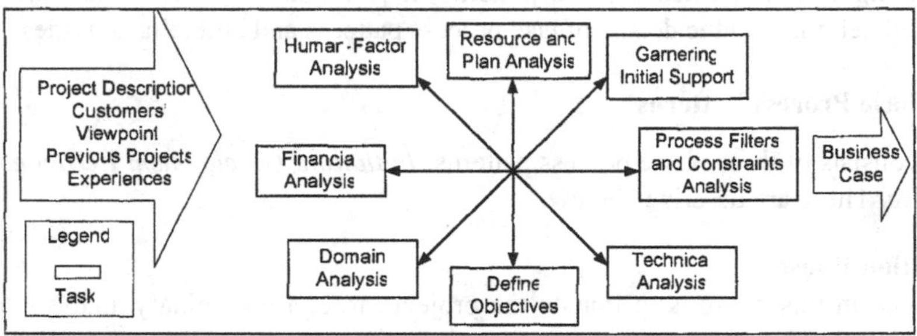

Fig. 2. Components of the *Justify* stage process pattern

As can be seen from Fig. 2, the input work products to this stage are *Project Description*, *Customers' Viewpoint* about the project, and the documented *Previous Projects Experiences*. The result of this stage is the project *Business Case* which represents the business value of the project. In this stage, feasibility study is performed through risk analysis which involves *Resource and Plan Analysis*, *Human-Factor Analysis*, *Financial Analysis*, and *Technical Analysis*. These tasks are coupled with the application of project constraints and process suitability filters in *Process Filters and Constraints Analysis, Defining Objectives*, and a domain walkthrough in the *Domain Analysis* tasks. At the end of this stage, customer approval and initial support for the start of the project will be obtained in the *Garnering Initial Support* task.

Define High-level Requirements

The requirements form the basis for other steps of the project. At the start of the project, initial high-level requirements are defined which will later be detailed and refined (Fig. 3). The required work products for this stage are *Project Description*, *Customers' Viewpoints* about the project, the *Business Case* defined in the Justify stage, and other related *Projects Experiences*; these documented experiences are often provided by the post-mortem reviews at the end of projects.

The requirements are identified and defined in *Problem Domain and Solution Domain Analysis*, and require active customer collaboration (*Get Customer Approval*). Examination of the problem and solution domains can be performed more precisely with the aid of modeling which is specified as the *Design/Model* stage in Fig. 3. A description of this stage will be given in the next section. Because of the model-phobic nature of many agile methodologies, this stage has been specified as optional. The products of this stage are a document of discriminated requirements (*Requirements Document*) and the generated models (*Models*).

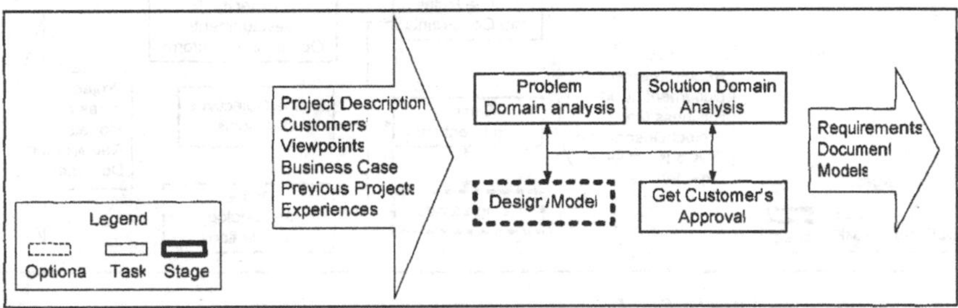

Fig. 3. Components of the *Define High-level Requirements* stage process pattern

Design/Model

Design and modeling may be used for defining and/or refining the requirements, the architecture, the design of the system, and the plans. Prototyping can also be considered as a task belonging to this stage. The iterative tasks of this stage, as depicted in Fig. 4, are defining the goal of design/modeling, designing and defining the alternatives, (optionally) using tools and prototyping to propose different alternatives, and reaching an agreement on the produced designs/models. The generated designs, models, and prototypes are packaged in the *Models* document.

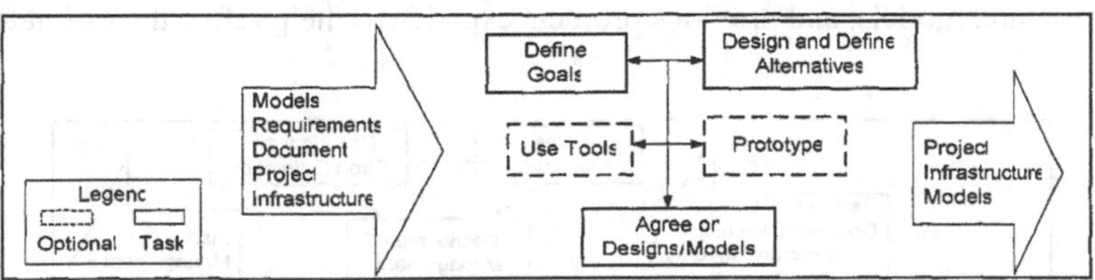

Fig. 4. Components of the *Design/Model* stage process pattern

Define Infrastructure

In this stage, project constraints, standards, and the system architecture are defined. As shown in Fig. 5, it uses the *Requirements Document*, *Business Case*, *Project Description* and *Previous Projects Experiences* to provide the *Project Infrastructure*.

This stage is performed through iterative tasks for defining rules and constraints, designing the architecture, specifying the development and operational platforms, defining goals and objectives, and (optionally) defining methodology conventions. The task *Define Methodology Conventions* is not found in all agile methodologies, yet it is considered an essential activity in some agile methodologies, such as Crystal. It has therefore been specified as optional. To define the system architecture, modeling, designing or prototyping may be needed. Therefore, the possibility of moving from *Define Architecture* to the *Design/Model* stage and vice versa has been accommodated. As a consequence of applying this stage, the requirements document may be changed or refined.

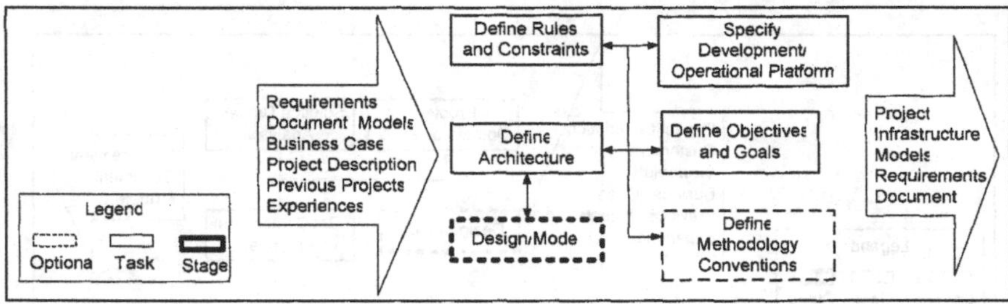

Fig. 5. Components of the *Define Infrastructure* stage process pattern

Outline Plan

In this stage the preliminary plan and schedule of the project are defined. As results of this stage, the initial project management document (*Management Document*) and the project plan and schedule (*Plan*) are produced. As deduced from Fig. 6, the required tasks include estimating the time, resources, and the effort needed for project completion, and preparing the management document according to these estimates. The management document contains all the information needed for project management (e.g., project schedule, plan, people communication paths, etc.). It may be needed to perform these tasks in multiple iterations. The requirements, project infrastructure, models, and previous projects experiences help refine the estimates.

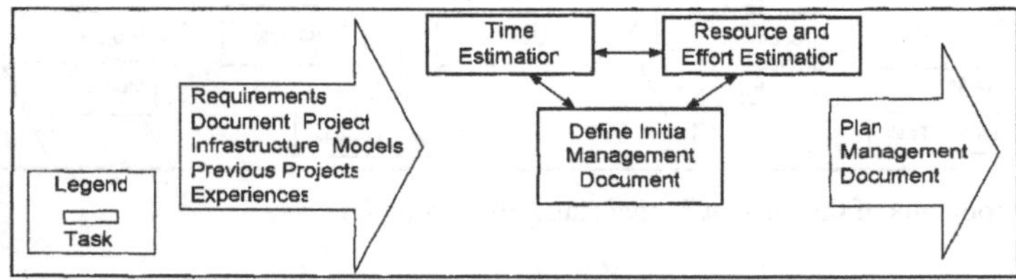

Fig. 6. Components of the *Outline Plan* stage process pattern

Requirements Analysis

The detailed analysis of requirements is carried out in this stage (Fig. 7). Existing requirements are refined and some new ones may also be added. Additionally, the requirements are prioritized according to different criteria depending on the project at hand, e.g., interdependencies, business value, or risks associated with the requirements. Designing and modeling can be used to gain a better understanding of the requirements. The requirements document is refined and completed in this stage.

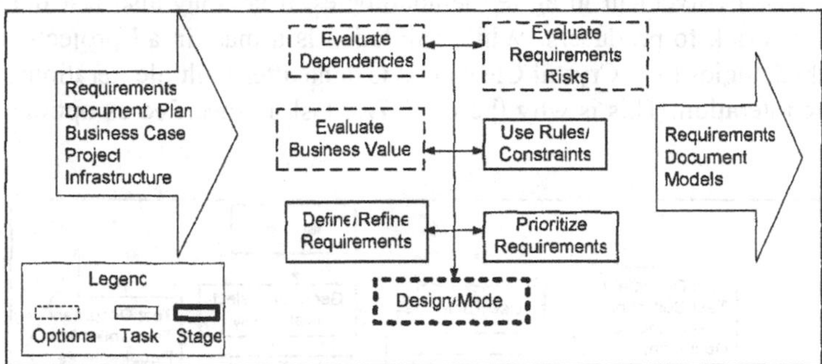

Fig. 7. Components of the *Requirements Analysis* stage process pattern

Plan

Because of frequent reviews in the development iterations of agile methodologies, the plan is likely to be refined or otherwise modified during the iterations. Therefore, at the start of each iteration in the *Development Iterations* phase, the project plan and schedule are reviewed and revised. This stage is shown in Fig. 8. The *Requirements Analysis* stage refines or otherwise changes the requirements document. Time boxes and artifacts of the next iteration(s) are then specified. The documented lessons learnt from previous iterations (*Iteration Review Document*), if existing, form an important artifact, based on which planning and scheduling decisions are made in this stage. The stage also involves the definition of tasks and their assignment to project team members. Some agile methodologies, e.g. DSDM, exclude defining and assigning tasks in each iteration; the two tasks are therefore specified as optional.

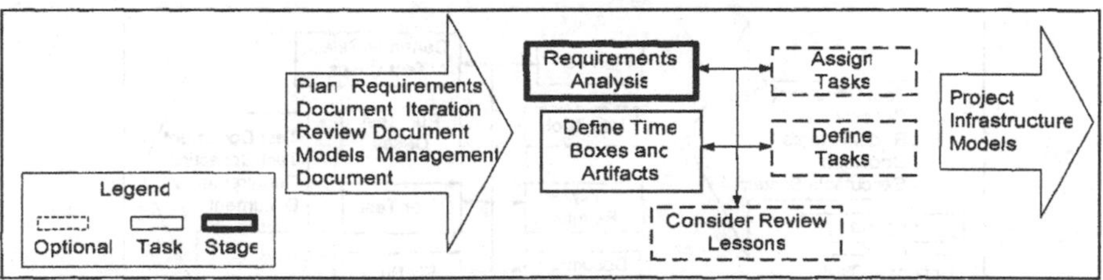

Fig. 8. Components of the *Plan* stage process pattern

Test in the Small

During the stages in which the system is evolved, the generated increments must be tested. These tests are not system-level, and specifically consist of unit testing, black-box testing, regression testing, and integration testing. Testing may be performed with the aid of tools, as seen in XP. The constituent tasks and artifacts of this stage are demonstrated in Fig. 9. The requirements document is the basic artifact for this stage. If any test collections and documented results exist, they too will be used for regression testing or in repeating the failed tests. At the start of this stage, the goal of testing and the targets must be defined through planning the test. Test cases are then generated or may be selected from test collections according to the test plan. The results of running test cases are documented in the *Test Document* artifact. Because of active user involvement in agile methodologies, users may also test the product and give feedback to producers. While validation is a must in all projects, in some agile methodologies (e.g. Crystal Clear) this is done after multiple iterations, and not during each iteration. This is why the *User Test* task is specified as optional in this stage.

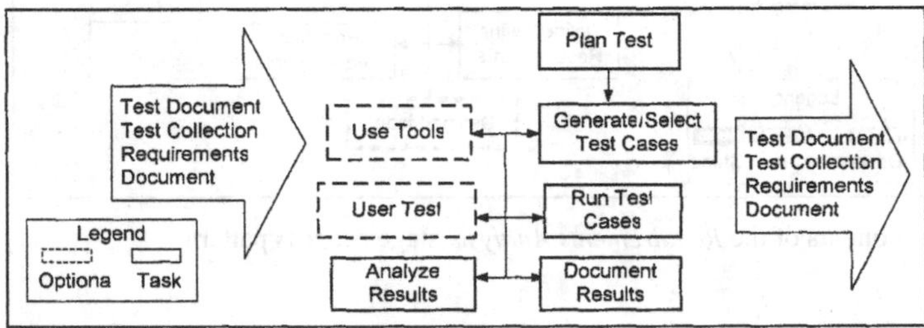

Fig. 9. Components of the *Test in the Small* stage process pattern

Test in the Large

This stage (Fig. 10) is where system-level testing is performed. The defects found in testing may be resolved by the *Fix Bugs* task in this stage, or deferred to the *Development Iterations* phase. The constituent tasks in this stage are similar to the *Test in the Small* stage with some differences: 1) the *User Test* task is not optional, 2) the defects found may be resolved in this stage, 3) Planning and generating test cases is based on system-level tests strategies, and 4) because of the need for bug fixing, the constituent tasks may be performed iteratively.

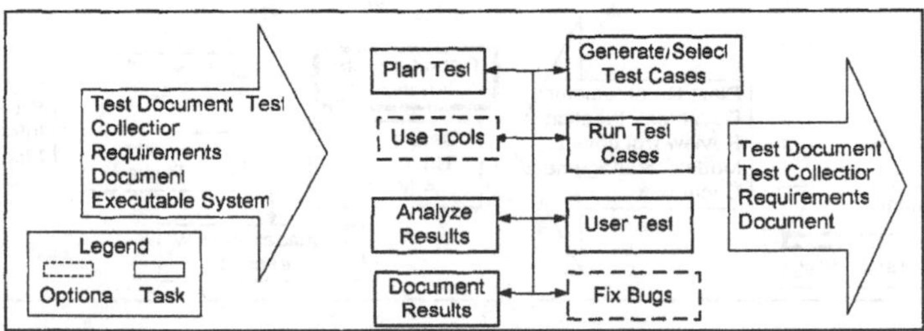

Fig. 10. Components of the *Test in the Large* stage process pattern

Review

Reviews play an important role in agile methodologies. Different types of reviews extracted from agile methodologies are: *Product Review*, *Process/Plan Review*, and *Project Review* (*Post-mortem Review*).

Product Review

The product is reviewed via analyzing the test results, validating the product through delivery to customers, comparing the results with defined goals, and documenting the conclusions in the *Product Review Document* (Fig. 11). As a consequence, the requirements and project infrastructure may be changed.

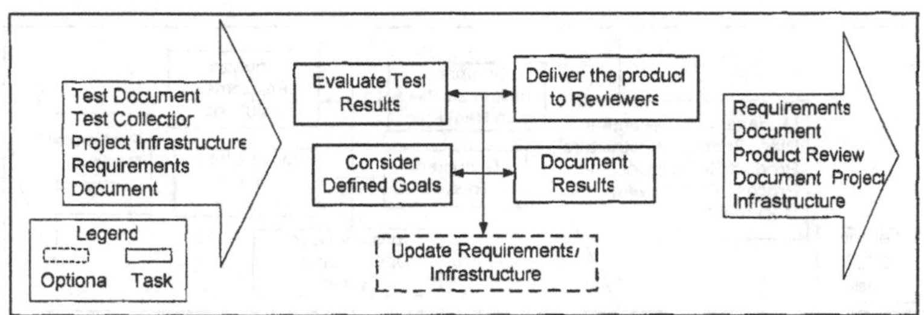

Fig. 11. Components of the *Product Review* stage process pattern

Process/Plan Review

Process/Plan Review, as shown in Fig. 12, aims at adapting the applied process/plan with the current state of the project. The plan of the project, management document, project infrastructure, and product review document help assess the process/plan. Therefore, the project plan and schedule must be compared with the current state of the project and the project velocity, the encountered problems must be analyzed, and the tuning points of the process/plan must be specified. The results are recorded in the *Process/Plan Review Document*.

Post-mortem Review (Project Review)

At the end of the project, the project will be investigated and the lessons learned are documented in the *Post-mortem Review Document*. This stage, as illustrated in Fig. 13, uses the product- and process/plan review documents, management document, project plan and infrastructure to make a tour of the system, compare the initial estimates with the current state of the project, using users' opinion on the system, and analyze the problems and solutions. This stage provides a good protection against the *Reinvent the Wheel* process antipattern [28].

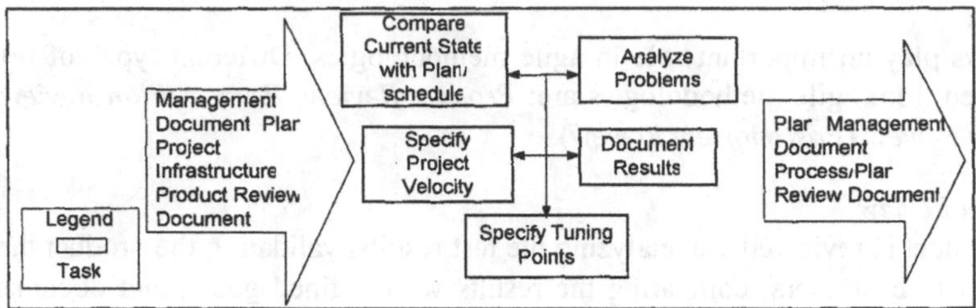

Fig. 12. Components of the *Process/Plan Review* stage process pattern

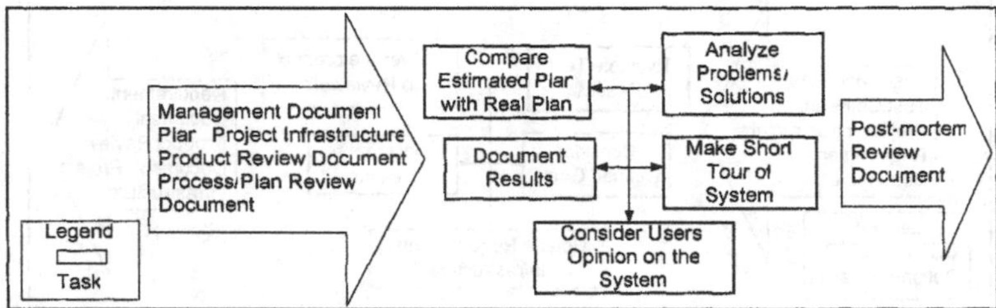

Fig. 13. Components of the *Post-mortem Review* stage process pattern

Implement

Implementing the requirements and resolving the defects are performed in this stage (Fig. 14).

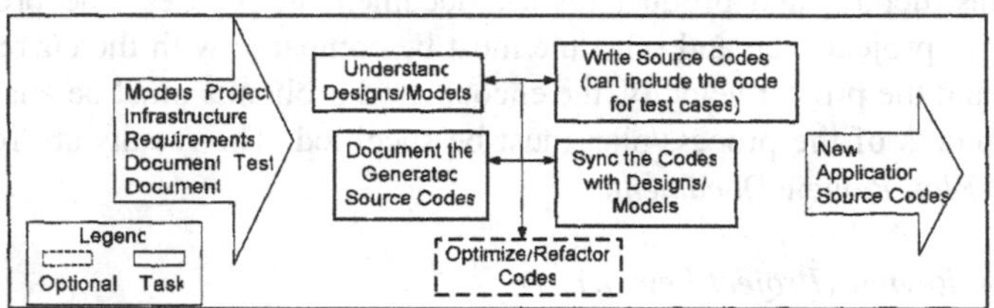

Fig. 14. Components of the *Implement* stage process pattern

The test document is used for fixing the bugs diagnosed during test activities. The generated code (which may include the test code, as commonly seen in Test-Driven Development) must conform to the requirements/defects and models/designs. Code inspection with the aim of refactoring and code optimization is a practice used in most agile methodologies after generating the source code (e.g., XP and ASD). The outcome of this stage is a new version of the product.

Integrate

Integration of newly generated increment(s) with the current system is handled in this stage (Fig. 15). Inputs to this stage are the new increment, the current integrated system, and the project infrastructure which contains the standards and constrains governing integration. The environment must first be prepared for the new increment; the new application is then integrated with the current system (this may be done iteratively) and the new system is prepared for testing (e.g., integration test, regression test, etc.). The strategy governing the time and frequency of integration is dependent on the nature of the process, the plan, and the project itself.

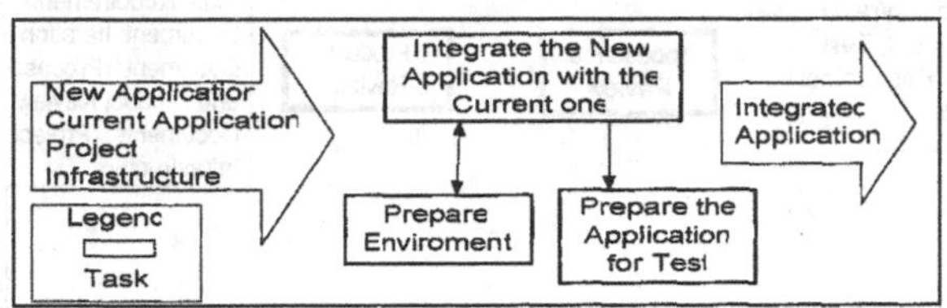

Fig. 15. Components of the *Integrate* stage process pattern

Deploy

This stage, as seen in Fig. 16, is made up of all the tasks related to the deployment of the system into the user environment. It consists of setting up the user environment, deploying the system, preparing user documents, and training the users. Tasks must be performed with attention to the constraints delineated in the project infrastructure.

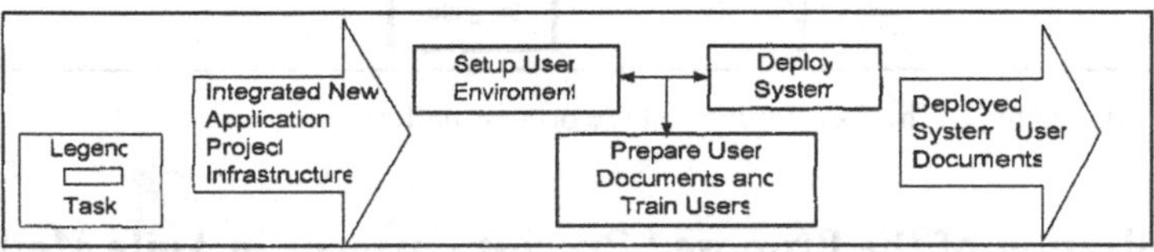

Fig. 16. Components of the *Deploy* stage process pattern

Iteration Review

This type of review is carried out after performing the iteration(s) in the *Development Iterations* phase. The aim is to adapt the plan and the process with the project and the development team in order to enhance product quality. Therefore, as shown in Fig. 17, it consists of *Process/Plan Review* and *Product Review* stages performed in an iterative manner.

Development

This stage (Fig. 18) is preformed via iterative application of the *Implement, Test in the Small*, and *Integrate* stages. The input and output work products are the union of the inputs and outputs of the constituent stages. The goal is to produce, integrate and test different parts of the system.

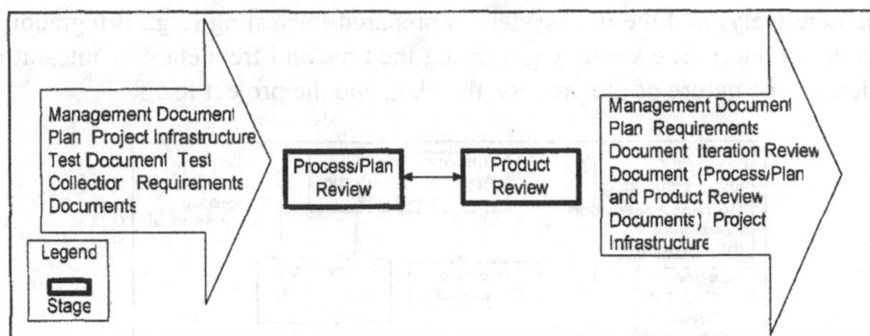

Fig. 17. Components of the *Iteration Review* stage process pattern

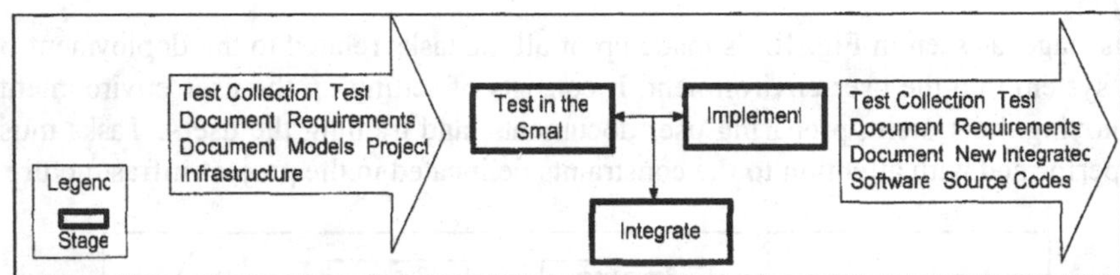

Fig. 18. Components of the *Development* stage process pattern

4 Realization of the Proposed Process Patterns in Agile Methods

Table 1 shows how different phases of the agile methodologies studied in our work can be realized by our suggested process patterns. We abstract away from umbrella activities, e.g., people and project management, which span all phases of the project and correspond to task process patterns. Therefore, they do not appear in this table. The realization table has been used to verify that the extracted process patterns indeed cover the methodologies used as the bases.

5 Applications of the Proposed Agile Process Patterns

The Agile process patterns proposed herein can facilitate situational method engineering (SME) when aimed at constructing agile methodologies to match given organizational settings or specific development projects [8, 29]. The process patterns can be used in the *assembly-based* approach of SME [29, 9] as classes of agile method chunks which can be used for composing agile methodologies. Furthermore, ASP and agile process patterns can be used in enacting the *paradigm-based approach* of SME [29] for instantiation and adaptation of process and product models.

The process patterns can also provide the basis for a rich component library for instantiating process components according to a predefined framework, typically depicted as a method engineering meta-model; much in the fashion of OPEN/OPF [11, 12].

Table 1. Realization of the proposed agile process patterns in agile methodologies

Methodology	Phases	Corresponding Stage Process Patterns
DSDM	Feasibility Study	Justify, Outline Plan
	Business Study	Define High-level Requirements, Plan, Define Infrastructure
	Functional Model	Plan, Requirements Analysis, Design/Model
	Design and Build	Plan, Development, Design/Model
	Implementation	Test in the large, Deploy, Product Review
	Post-Project	Further iteration of previous five main phases
Scrum	Pre-game: planning	Define High-level Requirements, Requirements Analysis, Outline Plan
	Pre-game: Architecture/ High-level Design	Define Infrastructure
	Development	Plan, Process/Plan Review, Design/Model ,Implement, Test in the Small, Iteration Review
	Post-game	Integrate, Test in the large, Deploy
XP	Exploration	Define High-level Requirements, Define Infrastructure
	Planning	Outline Plan, Plan
	Iterations to First Release	Plan, Design/Model, Development, Process/Plan Review
	Productionizing	Deploy, Test in the Large
	Maintenance	Repetition of three previous phases
	Death	Post-mortem Review
ASD	Project Initiation	Justify, Define High-level Requirements, Define Infrastructure
	Iterative Development Phases	Plan, Development, Iteration Review
	Final Q/A and Release	Test in the large, Deploy, Post-mortem Review
dX	Inception	Define High-level Requirements, Define Infrastructure, Outline Plan
	Elaboration	Plan, Design/Model, Development, Iteration Review
	Construction	Plan, Design/Model, Development
	Transition	Deploy, Test in the large
Crystal Clear	Chartering	Justify, Outline Plan, Define High-level Requirements, Define Infrastructure, Plan
	Delivery Cycle	Plan, Design/Model, Development, Iteration Review
	Wrap-up	Test in the large, Deploy, Post-mortem Review
FDD	Develop an Overall Model	Design/Model
	Build a Features List	Requirements Analysis
	Plan by Feature	Plan
	Design by Feature	Design/Model
	Build by Feature	Implement, Test in the Small

Finally, because of their abstract nature, the proposed process patterns lend themselves better to adaptation and tailoring, thereby enhancing configurability and dynamic flexibility; a feature which can be indispensable in agile methodologies, where the process itself needs to be adaptable based on the circumstances surrounding different project situations.

6 Conclusion

We have proposed a set of agile-specific process patterns that can be used for method engineering purposes. Pattern extraction was based on detailed inspection of seven prominent agile methodologies, and a generic Agile Software Process (ASP) was identified and used as the starting point for the extraction process. We have also demonstrated how each studied agile methodology can be realized using the proposed process patterns. Our suggested process patterns thus provide classes of reusable agile process building blocks that can be instantiated and used for composing and tailoring agile processes.

This work can be further extended to investigate the full details of the task process patterns, and especially address the umbrella activities covered in the generic ASP. Future work can then be directed towards developing a Computer Aided Method Engineering (CAME) environment [7, 30] that facilitates assembly-based engineering of agile methodologies using the agile process patterns introduced herein as reusable method fragments stored in a method base. ASP's role will be that of a generic method model providing a general template for agile methodologies, thus adding the support for paradigm-based SME. Another strand can focus on defining extension points for agile process patterns, further layering the patterns architecture into *core* process patterns and available *extensions*, thereby enhancing complexity management and promoting the production of lighter methodologies.

Acknowledgment. We wish to thank the Research Vice-Presidency of Sharif University of Technology for sponsoring this research.

References

1. J. O. Coplien, A Generative Development Process Pattern Language, in: Pattern Languages of Program Design (ACM Press/Addison-Wesley, 1995), pp. 187-196.
2. S. W. Ambler, Process Patterns: Building Large-Scale Systems Using Object Technology (Cambridge University Press, 1998).
3. S. W. Ambler, More Process Patterns: Delivering Large-Scale Systems Using Object Technology (Cambridge University Press, 1999).
4. N. Prakash, On generic method models, Requirements Engineering 11(4), 221-237 (September 2006).
5. K. Bergner, A. Rausch, M. Sihling, and A. Vilbig, A Componentware Development Methodology based on Process Patterns, in: Proceedings of PLoP-98 (1998).
6. K. Kumar and R. J. Welke, Method engineering: a proposal for situation-specific methodology construction, in: Systems Analysis and Design: A Research Agenda, (Wiley, 1992), pp. 257-268.
7. A. F. Harmsen, Situational Method Engineering (Moret Ernst & Young, 1997).
8. I. Mirbel and J. Ralyté, Situational method engineering: combining assembly-based and roadmap-driven approaches. Requirements Engineering 11(1), 58–78 (March 2006).
9. S. Brinkkemper, M. Saeki and F. Harmsen, Assembly techniques for method engineering. in: Proceedings of CAiSE'98 (1998), pp. 381–400.
10. S. Brinkkemper, Method engineering: Engineering of information systems development methods and tools. Information and Software Technology 38(4), 275–280 (Apr.1996).
11. D. Firesmith and B. Henderson-Sellers, The OPEN Process Framework: An Introduction (Addison-Wesley, 2001).
12. B. Henderson-Sellers, Method Engineering for OO Systems Development, Communications of the ACM 46(10), 73-78 (October 2003).

13. P. Kroll, Introducing IBM Rational Method Composer, published on the web at: http://www-128.ibm.com/developerworks/rational/library/nov05/kroll (2005).
14. B. Henderson-Sellers and M. K. Serour, Creating a dual-agility method: The value of Method Engineering, Journal of Database Management 16(4), 1-23 (Oct./Dec. 2005).
15. B. Fitzgerald, G. Hartnett and K. Conboy, Customizing agile methods to software practices at Intel Shannon, European Journal of Information Systems, 15(2), 200-213 (April 2006).
16. S. W. Ambler, The agile system development lifecycle, published on the web at: http://www.ambysoft.com/essays/agileLifecycle.html (2006).
17. D. Wells, Extreme programming: A gentle introduction, published on the web at: http://www.extremeprogramming.org (2006).
18. K. Beck and C. Andres, Extreme Programming Explained: Embrace Change, 2nd Ed (Addison-Wesley, 2004).
19. S. W. Ambler, The agile unified process, published on the web at: http://www.ambysoft.com/unifiedprocess/agileUP.html (2005).
20. D. Turk, R. France and B. Rumpe, Limitations of agile software processes, in: Proceedings of XP (2002), Alghero, Italy.
21. K. Beck, et al, Manifesto for agile software development, published on the Web at: http://agilemanifesto.org (2001).
22. DSDM Consortium, J. Stapleton, DSDM: Business Focused Development, 2nd Ed. (Addison-Wesley, 2003).
23. K. Schwaber and M. Beedle, Agile Software Development with Scrum (Prentice-Hall, 2001).
24. J. Highsmith, Adaptive Software Development: A Collaborative Approach to Managing Complex Systems (Dorset House, 2000).
25. G. Booch, R.C. Martin and J. Newkirk, Object Oriented Analysis and Design with Applications, 2nd ed. (1998), (Unpublished).
26. A. Cockburn, Crystal Clear: A Human-Powered Methodology for Small Teams (Addison-Wesley, 2004).
27. S. R. Palmer and J. M. Felsing, A Practical Guide to Feature-Driven Development (Prentice-Hall, 2002).
28. W. J. Brown, R. C. Malveau, H. McCormick, T. Mowbray, Antipatterns: Refactoring Software, Architectures, and Projects in Crisis (Wiley, 1998).
29. J. Ralyté, R. Deneckére and C. Rolland, Towards a generic model for situational method engineering, in: Proceedings of CAiSE2003 (2003), pp. 95-110.
30. S. Kelly, K. Lyytinen, M. Rossi, MetaEdit+: A Fully Configurable Multi-User and Multi-Tool CASE and CAME Environment, in: Proceedings of CAiSE'96 (1996), pp. 1-21.

Domain-specific Adaptations of Product Line Variability Modeling

Deepak Dhungana, Paul Grünbacher and Rick Rabiser
Christian Doppler Laboratory for Automated Software Engineering
Johannes Kepler Universität, Linz, Austria
dhungana@ase.jku.at

Abstract. Despite its increasing popularity the widespread adoption of product line engineering is still hampered by a lack of flexible and extensible approaches that can be tailored to deal with diverse organizational specifics such as architectural styles, languages, or modeling notations. Many existing product line approaches focus on process aspects and provide general-purpose modeling approaches. In this paper we present a flexible and extensible variability modeling approach that can be adapted to domain-specific needs. The approach is supported by the meta-tool DecisionKing. The tool treats variability as a prime modeling concept and supports the domain-specific definition of dependencies between model elements. We demonstrate the feasibility of our approach with two case studies in the areas of industrial automation and service-oriented systems.

1 Introduction

Conventional single-system software engineering is often insufficient to meet the tight budget and schedule constraints faced by software industry. Companies therefore aim at understanding the relationships between similar products to exploit commonalities regarding marketing, technical, or end-user aspects. Software product line engineering (PLE) is based on creating and managing artifacts and processes such that they can be reused for building different yet related products. It has been shown that PLE can increase productivity, reliability, and quality of software development thereby also reducing cost and time-to-market [3, 4, 14, 17, 22]. This is achieved by modeling techniques for capturing the variability of reusable core assets such as requirements, architecture, code, processes, documents, or models.

Please use the following format when citing this chapter:

Dhungana, D., Grünbacher, P., Rabiser, R., 2007, in IFIP International Federation for Information Processing, Volume 244, Situational Method Engineering: Fundamentals and Experiences, eds. Ralyté, J., Brinkkemper, S., Henderson-Sellers B., (Boston Springer), pp. 238-251.

While there is a strong consensus on the benefits of PLE, it remains challenging for organizations to identify methods and techniques applicable for their particular context, to adapt these methods and techniques to address the specific needs of their domain, and to integrate them with their current practices, tools, and standards [16]. A reason for these problems lies in the inflexibility of existing product line modeling approaches and tools which often do not support the diverse needs of different organizations. A key goal of our research is thus to make our methods and tools as flexible as possible.

Variability modeling is central in PLE to capture commonalities and variability of a product line's core assets. Variability has to be understood and modeled at different levels (e.g., requirements, architecture, or implementation level) and for diverse domain-specific artifacts [7]. The traceability between variation points, i.e., decision points describing possible choices about assets' functions or qualities, and the management of variability mechanisms implementing these points are important aspects. The need for a flexible variability modeling approach becomes evident when considering the heterogeneous languages, modeling notations, or architectural styles used by different organizations. There are two important problems faced by both research and industry [7]: (1) there is a lack of integrated variability modeling approaches that work well with arbitrary and heterogeneous types of assets in the product line; (2) there is a lack of flexible and extensible tools that can be tailored to support a particular organization's needs.

In our ongoing research collaboration with Siemens VAI we are developing an approach addressing these issues. DOPLER (**D**ecision-**O**riented **P**roduct **L**ine **E**ngineering for effective **R**euse) is an approach that works with heterogeneous domain-specific artifacts while being independent of specific architectural styles, languages, or modeling notations. The approach is supported by the meta-tool DecisionKing [7] supporting the identification, design, implementation, and maintenance of a product line's assets. Unlike existing general purpose meta-tools [11, 21, 26] DecisionKing provides support for variability as a first class modeling concept. Furthermore, it adopts a rule engine to master the complexity of dependencies in the models. Organizations can also incorporate company-specific capabilities by exploiting the tool's plug-in architecture.

This paper is organized as follows: We describe our variability modeling approach and show how it allows domain-specific adaptations. We present the meta-tool DecisionKing [7] and discuss method engineering concepts used in our approach. Two case studies illustrate the benefits and feasibility of our approach in two significantly different domains: (i) Together with Siemens VAI, the world's leader in building plants for the iron, steel, and aluminum industries, we are using DOPLER to model the variability of their automation software for continuous casting in steel plants; (ii) In an ongoing research project [5, 10] we are modeling service variability by complementing the *i** modeling language [25] with variability modeling. We conclude the paper with a discussion of related work and an outlook on future work.

2 Product Line Variability Modeling

Leveraging reuse in PLE relies on documenting tacit knowledge about variability and making it explicit and manageable in models [4]. Variability models cover the product line's problem space (stakeholder needs and desired features) and its solution space (architecture and components of the technical solution). Variability models define a product line's assets with organization- and domain-specific properties and dependencies. They capture different variants of features and solution components and their valid combinations, i.e., the possible variants together with constraints and dependencies. Variability models also document fundamental system-wide decisions for the configuration and derivation of a product [8] and the rationale for these decisions.

DOPLER can deal with diverse product line assets and allows arbitrary dependency links between the assets. It relates the assets with decisions for product derivation and customization. The approach is based on a generic variability meta-model (Fig. 2) which has to be extended and adapted to organizational needs. The meta-model does not encompass every modeling element that may be relevant in certain organizations. It defines just the basic concepts to be modeled on a higher level of abstraction. Unlike a general-purpose meta-model, our approach treats variability as a prime concept by modeling decisions. Fig. 1 depicts the DOPLER modeling process encompassing domain modeling (the adaptation of the meta-model), asset modeling (the definition of the PL's assets based on the meta-model), and decision modeling (the definition of variability):

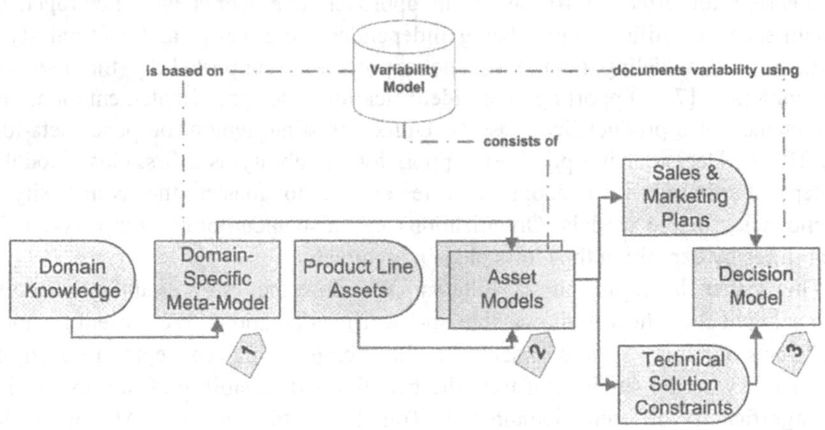

Fig. 1 DOPLER variability modeling approach [7].

(1) Domain Modeling. Managing different kinds of assets in a PL relies on the precise definition of their specific characteristics in a domain-specific meta-model. Building such a model requires knowledge about the domain and the organization's settings and specifics. The meta-model defines the types of assets to be included in the product line (e.g., Components, Services, Documents, Properties, etc.) and the possible relationships between the different asset types.

(2) Asset Modeling. An asset model is created on the basis of a domain-specific meta-model and describes the concrete reusable elements in a product line and dependencies among them. Asset models can often be created semi-automatically if product line development does not start from scratch and core assets already exist. For example, call dependencies defined in existing system configuration files can be utilized to automatically derive *requires* dependencies among software components that reflect the underlying technical restrictions (cf. Section 5.1). Modeling these dependencies is essential for later product derivation.

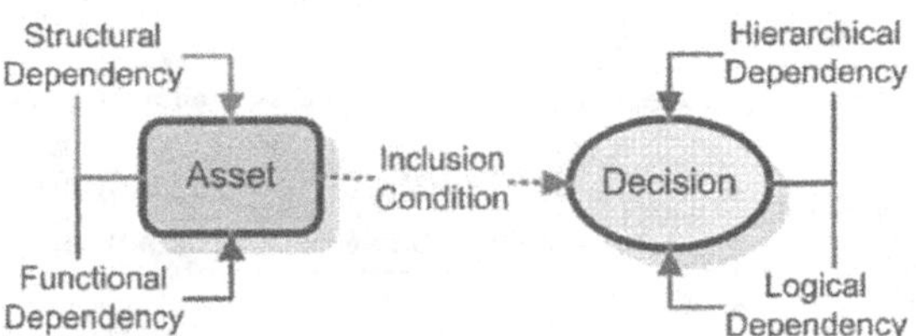

Fig. 2 Core meta-model for variability [8].

(3) Decision Modeling: Variability stemming from technical or marketing considerations is expressed using decisions to be taken when deriving products from the product line [19]. Decision models link external variability (visible to customers, sales people, or marketing staff) with internal variability (visible to engineers). A decision model is a graph where the nodes represent decisions and the edges represent relationships between them. Decisions are variables which can have special dependencies to other variables. These dependencies are expressed using a rule language. Decisions are presented to decision-takers in the form of questions. Validity conditions restrict the range of possible values. In order to link assets and decisions, assets specify an *inclusion condition* which has to be satisfied for a particular asset to be included in the final product. This expression can be composed of arbitrary decisions. Decisions and inclusion conditions also establish trace links between user demands and assets [8]. Decision models reduce modeling complexity as they represent variability at a higher level of abstraction. For instance, variability mechanism in the asset base can be changed without having to change the variation points of the system. Experience also shows that fewer decisions are necessary to reach the desired variability than adding variability specifications to all assets [8]. The core meta-model (Fig. 2) currently supports *hierarchical dependencies* specifying how the decisions are organized and *logical dependencies* specifying the known consequences of taking decisions:

Hierarchical dependencies are Boolean expressions that specify when a particular decision is visible to the user. For example, the user needs to decide if an archiving feature is required before taking more specific decisions on the type of database used for archiving. Considering the example in Fig. 3, this kind of relationship is modeled between the decision DeburrerPredecessor and Deburrer. The decision DeburrerPredecessor is visible to the user only if the value of decision Deburrer is true.

Logical dependencies specify actions that need to be executed after a decision has been taken. Typically, these are business rules that need to be checked (before and) after a decision is taken. In the example presented in Fig. 3, we can see such a relationship between DeburrerPredecessor and MarkingPredecessor. If the user enters INPUT as the value for DeburrerPredecessor the value of the variable MarkingPredecessor is also set to INPUT. After a decision is taken, its effects are propagated automatically to all the other affected decisions in the model. This is important to guarantee the consistency of selected options and taken decisions during product derivation.

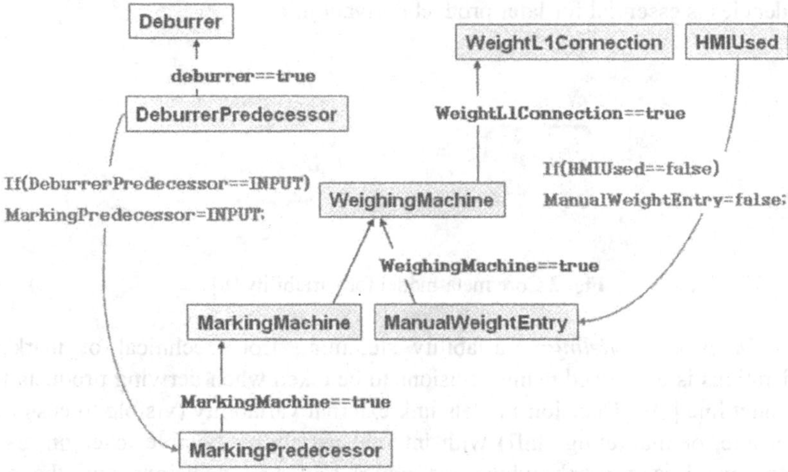

Fig. 3 Example of a Decision Model based on an existing variability model of the Siemens VAI subsystem Runout. Decision variables (nodes) are modeled with their hierarchical and logical dependencies (edges) thereby forming a graph.

3 Adopting Method Engineering Concepts

Method Engineering offers important concepts for achieving a higher level of flexibility: (i) Meta-models have proven to be useful to identify and describe the concepts of a generic method, (ii) Generic methods can be adapted to the actual situation of a project using concepts of Situational Method Engineering (SME) [15], and (iii) Meta-tools provide a automated support for such adaptations. Our approach is based on these concepts: we provide a generic meta-model, which has to be adapted to domain-specific needs. We also offer tool support through adaptations of our meta-tool DecisionKing.

Meta-model adaptation and evolution. Every domain has its own concepts, dependencies, and rules. These characteristics are defined by a meta-model specifying the attributes, dependencies, syntax, and semantics of these concepts. A meta-model defines the "language" in which domain models can be expressed and from which tools for writing domain models can be generated. While the meta-model is specified by method experts, the models are developed by domain experts using the generated domain-modeling tools. For example, in our approach the core meta-model (Fig. 2) is refined using new asset types together with attributes and relationships among them to support domain-specific concepts. The behavior of model elements is defined by semantic classes, i.e., model element interpreters and dependency resolvers for relationships between the assets.

Meta-models can change just like other models. Variability modeling tools and techniques must be adaptable to provide an effective model-driven development cycle. We allow domain evolution via updates to the meta-model [20] thereby also adapting the variability modeling tool. This allows us to react to changing requirements of the problem domain. For instance, the introduction of new asset types as well as the modification of existing assets requires techniques for schema evolution of already existing models, automatic adaptation of tools, and methods for checking the semantic consistency of the evolved models. The evolution of the meta-model is of particular interest when introducing a new product line. In order to master the complexity, one can begin with a relatively simple meta-model which is extended as the product line evolves.

Meta-tools and tool extensions. Meta-tools are needed to benefit from the flexibility offered by meta-modeling and meta-model evolution. Such meta-tools allow the generation of specific tools for a target environment. Recent developments in the area of software tools such as the Eclipse platform allow the development of extensible meta-tools that can be augmented with domain-specific capabilities. For instance, the plug-in approach supports a compact core that can be extended with plug-in components tailored to the users' needs to improve focus and reduce clutter by providing a customized user environment [24]. In DOPLER we used a plug-in approach to incorporate a domain-specific rule language, an off-the-shelf rule engine, a model visualization system, and domain-specific tools for semi-automatically creating initial decision models from existing assets.

4 DecisionKing: A Meta-Tool for Variability Modeling

DecisionKing can be configured to support domain-specific variability modeling with domain meta-models specifying relevant characteristics of the application domain. DecisionKing distinguishes itself from more general-purpose meta-tools like MetaEdit+ [21] or Pounamu [11, 26] by treating variability as a primary modeling concept. Also, the dependencies among model elements are not just plain trace links as they are interpreted using a rule engine. The plug-in-based architecture of the tool makes it flexible and extensible to domain-specific adaptations (cf. Fig. 4). The result of adapting DecisionKing for a particular organization is a domain-specific variability model editor for domain-specific assets. Implementing tool-extensions allows a tight integration of this editor with current practices, standards, and existing tools of the organization. Fig. 4 shows an overview of the DecisionKing's capabilities for domain-specific adaptations:

Meta-model editor. An editor allows the creation of domain-specific meta-models by specifying domain-specific asset types (e.g., components, services, data, code, settings, documents, component descriptions), their attributes (e.g., description, URL, cost), and dependencies (e.g., component *requires* component). Domain-specific behavior can be added to model elements and relationships by providing model element interpreters and dependency resolvers as domain-specific plug-ins.

The meta-model adaptation framework (cf. Fig. 4) adjusts the variability modeling editor according to the domain-specific meta-model.

Domain-specific tool extensions and plug-ins. The DecisionKing customization framework supports two types of extensions:

(i) We provide extension points for adapting the functionality of the tool. Default implementations of these capabilities can easily be replaced with domain-specific plug-ins without having to touching the tool's implementation. We have created default plug-ins of a rule language, a constraint editor, a rule engine, and a model visualizer. For example, one can provide a model viewer with domain-specific graphical layouts and symbols. Another example is the rule specification language needed to model dependencies among decisions. The language used for this purpose and choice of technology depends highly on the domain and current practices of the organization. We have experimented with different domain-specific languages for rule specification, using JBOSS[1] Rules as the rule engine. We have also tried JESS[2], where we modeled our decisions as facts of an expert shell.

(ii) A generic extension point is provided in the form of a model API which allows arbitrary tools to manipulate, use, or create models. This API has for instance been useful to develop model importers, which analyze the existing asset base to semi-automatically create asset models. The integration of existing domain-specific tools is another important aspect.

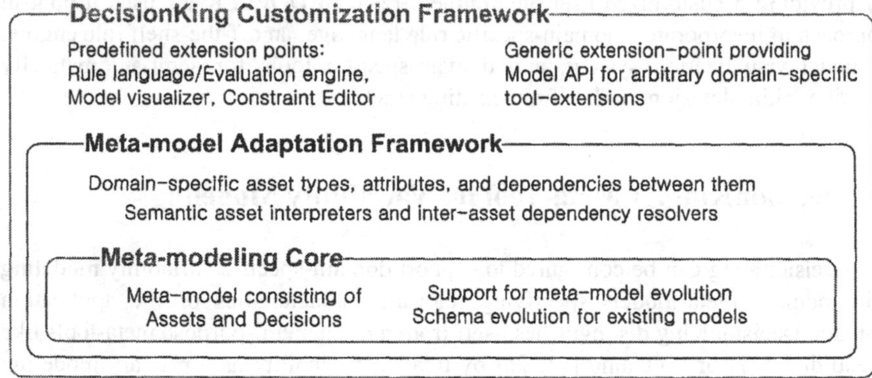

Fig. 4 Overview of DecisionKing's adaptation mechanisms.

5 Case Studies

To demonstrate the feasibility of our approach, we present two case studies from two different contexts. The goal of the case studies was to validate the generic meta-model and to gain experience with method engineering concepts (cf. Section 3) in practical settings. The case studies were also instrumental to demonstrate the usefulness and usability of our tools in different contexts. We describe the meta-

[1] http://www.jboss.com/products/rules
[2] http://herzberg.ca.sandia.gov/jess/

model adaptations and domain-specific extensions of our tools developed for the case study contexts, as well as key experiences gained.

5.1 Case study 1: Industrial automation

Siemens VAI[3] is the world's leading engineering and plant-building company for the iron, steel, and aluminum industries. In an ongoing research project, we are modeling the variability of their software product line for process automation, optimization, supervision, and material tracking of continuous casting in steel plants.

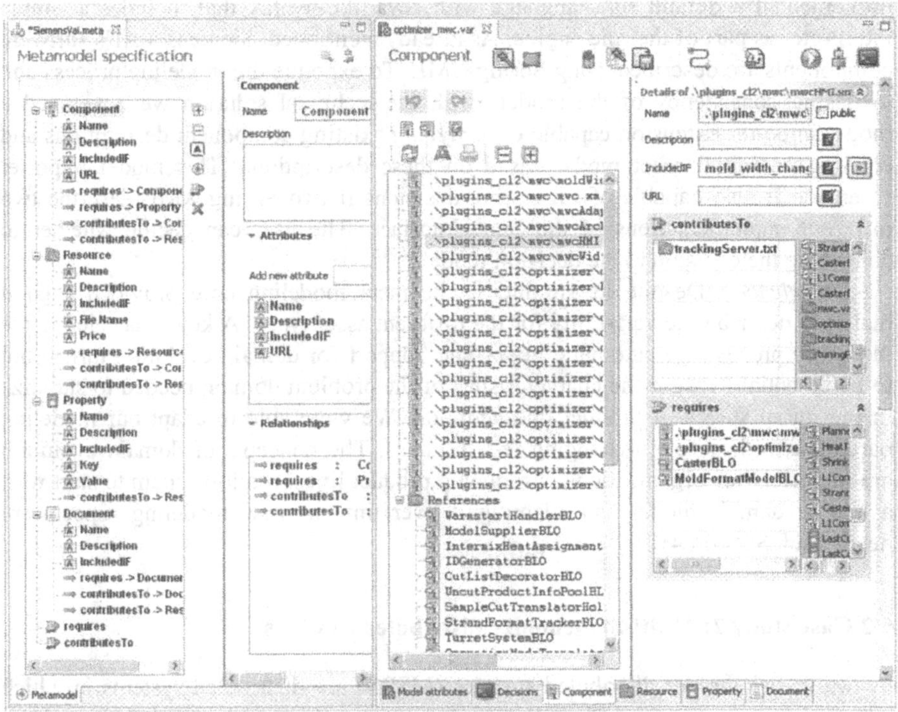

Fig. 5 DecisionKing's Meta-Model Editor (left) and Variability Model Editor (right). The variability model on the right is based on the meta-model on the left.

Meta-model adaptation. In various workshops conducted with the engineers and sales experts of Siemens VAI, we identified the types of core assets to be reused in the product line: *Components* (specified using Spring[4] XML files), *Properties* (configuration parameters for components), *Resources* (legacy hard- or software elements, configuration files, etc), and *Documents* (e.g., descriptions of components, notes, fragments of end user documentation, etc). We also identified the functional dependency *requires* between assets. E.g., a software component may rely on another component to function properly (similar modeling capabilities are available

[3] http://www.industry.siemens.com/metals/en/

[4] http://www.springframework.org/

in architecture description languages such as xADL [6]). A domain-specific resolver for the relationship *requires* adds all components required by a certain component as soon as the parent is added to the final system (i.e., by taking a decision during product derivation). Information about the deployment structure of the system is modeled using the relationship *contributesTo (e.g.,* a component contributes to the sub-system it belongs to).

Domain-specific extensions and plug-ins. We developed a tree-based graphical viewer for Siemens VAI variability models based on GEF viewers[5] which is seamlessly integrated in the modeling environment of DecisionKing. In order to represent the relationships between the decisions needed to derive a product, we have implemented a default rule language with Java-like syntax that includes a simple interpreter as part of the rule engine. As already mentioned, Siemens VAI's software components are described using Spring XML. To expedite the modeling process and to ensure consistency of the models with the technical solution we developed a model importer extension capable of analyzing existing component descriptions and creating an initial asset model based on these descriptions. This model importer extension is also capable of suggesting decisions if two Spring XML describe two different implementations of the same interface. The user can decide whether to contribute the decision to the decision model.

Experiences. Despite its simplicity, the meta modeling core provided a good match to describe the variability for the different asset types. A key to accelerate the modeling process are automatic importers. Support for domain evolution turned out to be essential because the characteristics of the problem domain needed to stabilize in the initial stages of product line adoption. We were able to adapt our modeling paradigm to these often-changing requirements. The concepts of domain evolution are important for organizations introducing product lines. It allows them to start with a simple domain-model and adapting it over time as new modeling aspects are needed (cf. Section 4).

5.2 Case study 2: Multi-Stakeholder distributed Systems

Multi-stakeholder distributed systems (MSDS) are distributed systems in which subsets of the nodes are designed, owned, or operated by distinct stakeholders [12]. MSDS are quickly gaining importance in today's networked world as, e.g., shown in the field of service-oriented computing. We have been using the *i** language [25] to model a service-oriented multi-stakeholder distributed system in the travel domain to validate the usefulness of *i** for that purpose. A major goal of the project was to enhance *i** with capabilities for variability modeling in the context of our MSDS framework [5].

Meta-model adaptation. We identified four asset types in our framework relevant to variability modeling: goals, service types, services, and service instances. The element *Goal* in DecisionKing's meta-model maps to the element "actor goal" in *i**. Different *Service types* contribute to fulfilling these goals. Available services realizing a service type are modeled as a *Service*. Finally, available runtime implementations of services can be modeled as *Service instances*. We also identified

[5] http://www.eclipse.org/gef/

two kinds of relationships between the assets: A *requires* relationship is used whenever the selection of a service leads to the selection of another service. This can be the result of logical dependencies between goals, conceptual relationships between service types, relationships between services, or functional dependencies between service instances. The *contributesTo* relationship is used to capture structural dependencies between assets of different levels. Service instances for example contribute to services. Services contribute to service types which themselves contribute to goals. It is however also possible that a goal is split up into sub-goals. Such compositional relationships between goals can also be modeled using the *contributesTo* relationship.

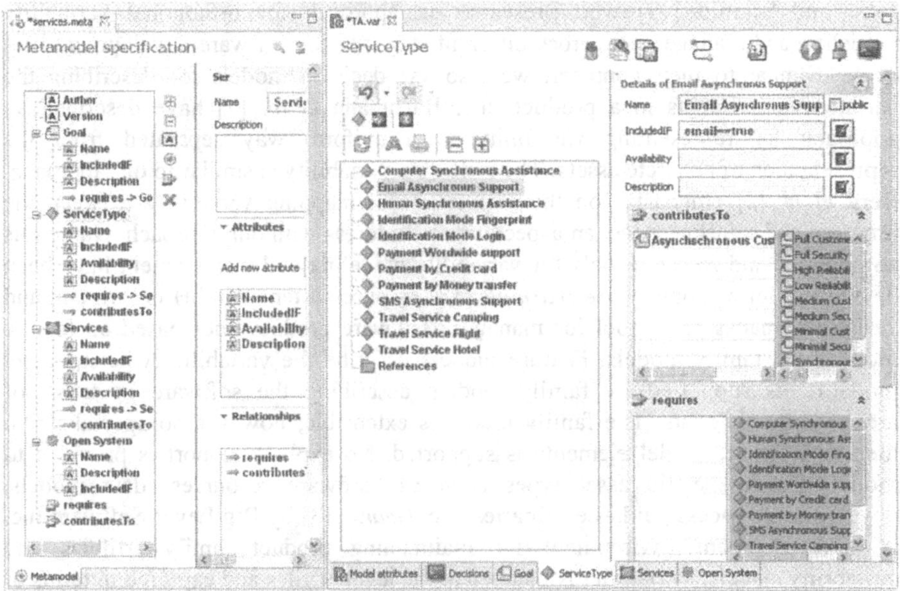

Fig. 6 DecisionKing's Meta-Model Editor (left) and Variability Model Editor (right). The variability model on the right is based on the meta-model for service-oriented systems on the left.

Domain-specific extensions and plug-ins. The dependencies among decisions were expressed using a domain-specific language; the rules were transformed to JBOSS rules using a rule-converter. We use the JBOSS rule engine to evaluate the dependencies among decisions and the inclusion conditions between assets and decisions (cf. Section 2). We have not yet implemented a specific visualization for service-oriented variability models. The model can however be visualized using the default model viewer. We will develop a connector to tools for the *i** modeling approach, e.g., the REDEPEND tool [9] that is capable of storing *i** models in XML.

Experiences. The use of DecisionKing in the project confirmed the need for a general-purpose model API that allows arbitrary external tools to update and query the variability model. This capability will allow us to use DecisionKing as one component in our framework for service monitoring and adaptation. We are planning to utilize variability models to support the controlled runtime adaptation of service-oriented systems, e.g., by replacing a malfunctioning service with a similar service specified in the variability model.

6 Related Work

We focus the discussion of related work on variability modeling approaches and tools, meta-tools, and plug-in frameworks.

Variability modeling approaches and tools. Many variability modeling approaches have been proposed. Our work was strongly influenced by the work of John and Schmid [19] who presented an approach for orthogonal variability modeling and management across different stages of the software development life-cycle. Similar to their approach we also use decision models for describing the variation of products in a product line. Bachmann *et al.* [1] have described an approach for representing variability in a uniform way separated from the representation of concrete assets. Their view on variability is similar to our approach. Berg *et al.* [2] emphasize on the importance of mapping variability between the problem and solution space, an aspect we also address with our approach. Numerous commercial and research tools for variability modeling and management have been developed, for example: *Pure::variants* [18] by pure-systems GmbH is a variant and variability management tool for managing software product lines based on feature models and family models. Feature models describe the variability whereas asset modeling is supported by family models describing the software in terms of architectural elements. The family model is extensible; however no specialization hierarchy for the model elements is supported. No explicit support is provided to model domain-specific asset types such as hardware resources, data models, development process guidance, libraries, etc. *Gears* [13] by Big Lever Software Inc. is a development environment for maintaining product family artifacts and variability models. Variability is handled at the level of files and captured in terms of features, product family artifacts, and defined products that can be derived from the variability model. The tool supports the identification of common and variable source code files. Our approach differs form this because we treat all assets as model elements and don't deal with them at file level.

Meta-Tools. Meta-tools can be seen as generators for domain-specific tools. Examples for Meta-tools are MetaEdit+ [21] and Pounamu [11, 26]. MetaEdit+ [21] is a tool for designing a modeling language, its concepts, rules, notations, and generators. The language definition is stored as a meta-model in the MetaEdit+ repository. MetaEdit+ follows the given modeling language definition and automatically provides full modeling tool functionality like diagramming editors, browsers, generators, or multi-user support. Pounamu [26] is a meta-tool for the specification and generation of multiple-view visual tools. The tool permits rapid specification of visual notational elements, the tool information model, visual editors, the relationships between notational and model elements, and behavior. Tools are generated on the fly and can be used for modeling immediately. Changes to the meta-tool specification are immediately reflected in tool instances. Typically meta-tools provide support for their target domain environments but are restricted in their flexibility and integration capabilities with other tools [23]. They do not treat variability as a prime modeling concept, which hampers their use for product line modeling.

Plug-in frameworks. Plug-in concepts are widely used in modern development platforms. DecisionKing is an Eclipse[6] Rich Client Application based on the Eclipse plug-in platform [24]. It uses the platform's plug-in mechanisms to define extension points allowing the integration of different domain-specific plug-ins.

7 Conclusions and Further Work

In this paper we described the DOPLER approach which adopts method engineering concepts supporting the creation of domain-specific variability modeling tools. We presented DecisionKing, a meta-tool that can easily be tailored to a particular organization's needs by refining its core meta-model and exploiting its plug-in architecture. DOPLER provides tools for the creation and management of the models. The approach does not assume any particular approach to software product line engineering beyond the basic tenets implied by the definition of a software product line. We showed the adaptability of the approach using two case studies in different domains. It is noteworthy mentioning that an automated approach is only as good as the model underlying the approach. Meta-model evolution capabilities allow us to start with a small language first that can be extended in the project after the team has gained some experience and confidence.

We are currently working on the following issues and will report about them in the future:

Use of variability models to support runtime adaptation of systems. We are currently adapting DecisionKing to the domain of ERP systems. We are developing plug-ins allowing to adapt an ERP system at runtime based on variability models.

Validation of the model evolution capability. Our model evolution framework is a great help in coping with changing architectures and implementations of a product line under development. We are currently refining and evolving the variability models for Siemens VAI to further validate our capabilities for model evolution and meta-model evolution.

Improvement of generic visualization support. We intend to make the current model visualization more generic. The graphical representation of a model has to be changed for different domains because of domain-specific symbols and layouts. This enables the use of symbols and layouts which stakeholders of the domain already know and understand. In particular, we are interested in using graphical ways to specify variability to overcome shortcomings of a purely text-based approach.

[6] http://eclipse.org

Acknowledgements

This work has been conducted in cooperation with Siemens VAI and has been supported by the Christian Doppler Forschungsgesellschaft, Austria. We would like to express our sincere gratitude to Klaus Lehner, Christian Federspiel, and Wolfgang Oberaigner from Siemens VAI for their support and the valuable insights.

References

1. F. Bachmann, M. Goedicke, J. Leite, R. Nord, K. Pohl, B. Ramesh, and A. Vilbig, "A Meta-model for Representing Variability in Product Family Development," in *Lecture Notes in Computer Science: Software Product-Family Engineering*. Siena, Italy: Springer Berlin / Heidelberg, 2003, pp. 66-80.
2. K. Berg, J. Bishop, and D. Muthig, "Tracing Software Product Line Variability – From Problem to Solution Space," presented at 2005 annual research conference of the South African institute of computer scientists and information technologists on IT research in developing countries, White River, South Africa, 2005.
3. G. Böckle, P. Clements, J. D. McGregor, D. Muthig, and K. Schmid, "Calculating ROI for Software Product Lines," *IEEE Software*, vol. 21, pp. 23-31, 2004.
4. P. Clements and L. Northrop, *Software Product Lines: Practices and Patterns*: SEI Series in Software Engineering, Addison-Wesley, 2001.
5. R. Clotet, F. Xavier, P. Grünbacher, L. López, J. Marco, M. Quintus, and N. Seyff, "Requirements Modelling for Multi-Stakeholder Distributed Systems: Challenges and Techniques. ," presented at RCIS'07: 1st IEEE Int. Conf. on Research Challenges in Information Science, Quarzazate, 2007.
6. E. M. Dashofy and A. van der Hoek, "Representing Product Family Architectures in an Extensible Architecture Description Language," presented at 4th International Workshop on Software Product-Family Engineering, Bilbao, Spain, 2001.
7. D. Dhungana, P. Gruenbacher, and R. Rabiser, "DecisionKing: A Flexible and Extensible Tool for Integrated Variability Modeling," in *First International Workshop on Variability Modelling of Software-intensive Systems - Proceedings*, K. Pohl, P. Heymans, K.-C. Kang, and A. Metzger, Eds. Limerick, Ireland: Lero - Technical Report 2007-01, 2007, pp. 119-128.
8. D. Dhungana, R. Rabiser, and P. Grünbacher, "Decision-Oriented Modeling of Product Line Architectures," presented at Sixth Working IEEE/IFIP Conference on Software Architecture, Mumbai, India, 2007.
9. G. Grau, X. Franch, N. A. M. Maiden, and " REDEPEND-REACT: an architecture analysis tool," presented at 13th IEEE International Conference on Requirements Engineering, 2005. Proceedings.
10. P. Grünbacher, D. Dhungana, N. Seyff, M. Quintus, R. Clotet, F. Xavier, L. López, and J. Marco, "Goal and Variability Modeling for Service-oriented System: Integrating i* with Decision Models," presented at Software and Services Variability Management Workshop: Concepts, Models, and Tools, Helsinki, 2007.
11. J. Grundy, J. Hosking, N. Zhu, and N. Liu, "Generating Domain-Specific Visual Language Editors from High-level Tool Specifications " presented at 21st IEEE International Conference on Automated Software Engineering (ASE'06), Tokyo, Japan, 2006.

12. R. J. Hall, "Open modeling in multi-stakeholder distributed systems: requirements engineering for the 21st Century," presented at First Workshop on the State of the Art in Automated Software Engineering, Irvine, California, 2002.
13. C. W. Krueger, "Software Mass Customization," BigLever Software, Inc 2005.
14. C. W. Krueger, "New Methods in Software Product Line Development," presented at 10th International Software Product Line Conference, Baltimore, USA, 2006.
15. K. Kumar and R. J. Welke, "Method Engineering: a proposal for situation-specific methodology construction " in *Systems Analysis and Design : A Research Agenda*: John Wiley & Sons, Inc., 1992 pp. pp257-268.
16. D. Muthig, I. John, M. Anastasopoulos, T. Forster, J. Dörr, and K. Schmid, "GoPhone - A Software Product Line in the Mobile Phone Domain," *IESE-Report No. 025.04/E*, 2004.
17. L. Northrop, "SEI's Software Product Line Tenets," *IEEE Software*, vol. 19, pp. 32-40, 2002.
18. pure-systemsGmbH, "Technical White Paper, Variant Management with pure::variants,," 2004.
19. K. Schmid and I. John, "A Customizable Approach to Full-Life Cycle Variability Management," *Journal of the Science of Computer Programming, Special Issue on Variability Management*, vol. 53, pp. 259-284, 2004.
20. D. C. Schmidt, A. Nechypurenko, and E. Wuchner, "MDD for Software Product-lines: Fact or Fiction?," presented at 8th international Conference on Model driven Engineering Languages and Systems (MODELS '05), Jamaica, 2005.
21. J.-P. Tolvanen and M. Rossi, "MetaEdit+: defining and using domain-specific modeling languages and code generators," presented at Conference on Object Oriented Programming Systems Languages and Applications, Anaheim, CA, USA, 2003.
22. F. van der Linden, "Software Product Families in Europe: The Esaps & Cafe Projects," *IEEE Software*, vol. 19, pp. 41-49, 2002.
23. A. I. Wasserman, "Tool integration in software engineering environments," presented at Proceedings of the international workshop on environments on Software engineering environments Chinon, France, 1990
24. R. Wolfinger, D. Dhungana, H. Prähofer, and H. Mössenböck, " A Component Plug-in Architecture for the .NET Platform," presented at Proceedings of 7th Joint Modular Languages Conference, (JMLC'06), Oxford, UK, 2006.
25. E. S.-K. Yu., "Modeling Strategic Relationships for Process Reengineering," vol. PhD Thesis. Toronto: University of Toronto 1996.
26. N. Zhu, J. Grundy, and J. Hosking, " Pounamu: A Meta-Tool for Multi-View Visual Language Environment Construction," presented at 2004 IEEE Symposium on Visual Languages and Human Centric Computing, 2004.

A Look at Misuse Cases for Safety Concerns

Guttorm Sindre
Dept of Computer and Info Science, Norwegian University of Science and Technology, NO-7491 Trondheim, Norway, guttors@idi.ntnu.no
WWW home page: http://www.idi.ntnu.no/~guttors

Abstract. Given the huge industrial take-up of UML, it has become less feasible to invent entirely new methods and modeling languages to address systems development challenges not covered by that language. Instead, the most fruitful way to go often seems to be to adapt UML to address such special challenges. In the security and safety domain, various such adaptations have been proposed. In this paper we look at misuse cases, originally proposed for security, with the purpose of investigating whether they are also useful for safety, and to what extent they can complement existing diagrammatic modeling techniques in the safety domain. Misuse cases is thus compared to several traditional techniques for safety analysis, such as fault trees, cause-consequence diagrams, HazOp, and FME(C)A, identifying strengths and weaknesses of either.

1 Introduction

As observed in [1] an increasing number of safety-critical systems are being fielded as IT penetrates more and more into the core operations of industry and society. Many problems with such systems stem from requirements defects. Although safety concerns may have been taken into account in the development of a system, unforeseen combinations of external events, system faults, and human failure may sometimes lead to disastrous effects [2]. There are many methods for safety analysis, some quite rigorous and other informal. Both have their advantages and disadvantages. The rigorous methods allow for formal analysis, perhaps automated. Informal methods may be better for creativity, e.g., imagining possible hazards, and for involving a diverse set of stakeholders in the discussion of safety concerns. Indeed, [3] points out both a better integration of formal and informal methods and a better integration of safety techniques with mainstream software engineering as important directions for improving the engineering of safety-critical software systems.

Please use the following format when citing this chapter:

Sindre, G., 2007, in IFIP International Federation for Information Processing, Volume 244, Situational Method Engineering: Fundamentals and Experiences, eds. Ralyté, J., Brinkkemper, S., Henderson-Sellers B., (Boston Springer), pp. 252-266.

One proposal for a technique towards the informal end of the spectrum, but which can easily be integrated with mainstream software engineering practices, is that of misuse cases [4]. These were originally proposed for looking at security threats, but in some case studies by Alexander [5, 6] the problems investigated were just as much concerned with safety hazards – the distinction being that security considers threats from malicious attackers, while safety considers hazards resulting from accidental human or system failure. The same notation can be used for safety-oriented as for security-oriented misuse cases, i.e., the misuse case uses an oval icon of the same shape as a use case icon, only inverted, and the actor performing the misuse case is similarly inverted compared to a normal use case actor. If addressing security and safety concerns in the same diagram, one might also distinguish between the two – as it might be of some importance whether something happens as a result of a malicious attack or because of an accident. One possible way of doing this is shown in Figure

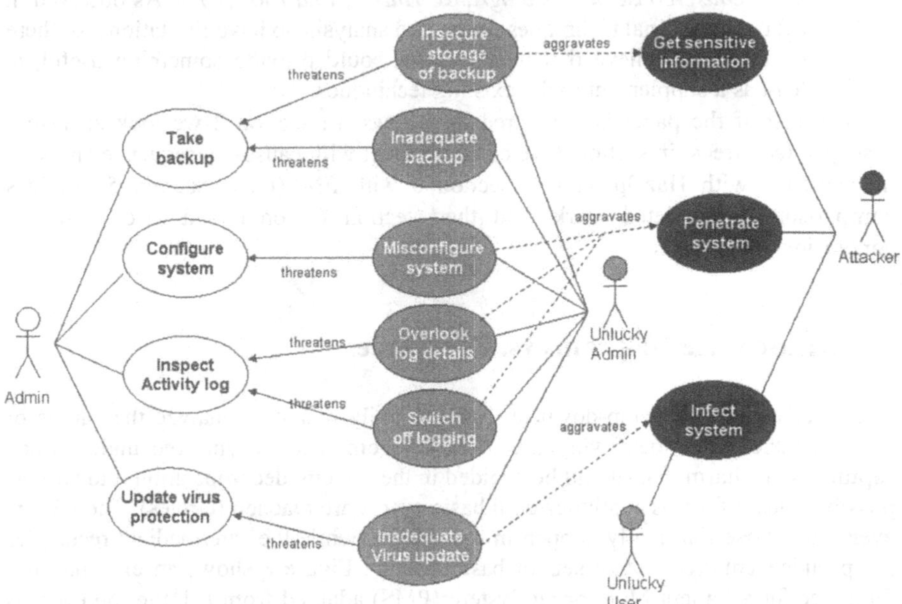

1, using black nodes for security threats and grey nodes for safety hazards.

Fig. 1. Misuse case diagram with both safety and security threats

The diagram of Fig 1 does not show all the use cases of the system in question, only some of those relating to a system administrator, who in this case is responsible for backup, configuration, virus protection, and the inspection of activity logs. Middle and right it then shows safety-related misuse cases (grey) and security-related misuse cases (black). The difference between these would be that the grey ones result from human or system failure, while the black ones result from a malicious attack. Alternatively, all these might have been shown as black, not distinguishing the notation of various types of misuse cases. However, the explicit distinction between safety and security makes the picture clearer, in particular demonstrating how human error on the system administrators side ("Unlucky Admin")[1], such as misconfiguring the system, may in turn increase the possibility for malicious attacks such as "Penetrate system". This is often the case: Many organizations have adequate firewalls, virus protection software etc., but vulnerabilities exist because the software is not used properly, necessary updates not done frequently enough, or similar.

It can be noted that diagrams quickly grow complex when trying to look at realistic examples and including both safety and security problems. In the rest of the paper we will therefore restrict ourselves to looking only at misuse cases for safety. Our research questions are as follows:

- *RQ1: Can misuse cases, both diagrammatic and textual, be applied in the safety domain?* (i.e., can they faithfully capture hazards and mitigations)
- *RQ2: Do misuse cases add value to other textual and diagrammatic representations traditionally used for safety hazard analysis, such as fault trees, cause-consequence diagrams, HazOp, and FME(C)A?* As observed in [2] the traditional techniques for hazard analysis do have limitations, so there is reason to believe that misuse cases could provide something useful, at least as a supplement to the existing techniques.

The rest of the paper is structured as follows: In section 2 we look at misuse cases vs. fault trees, in section 3 we compare them with cause-consequence analysis, in section 4 with HazOp, and in section 5 with FME(C)A. Section 5 provides comparison with related work, and then section 6 contains a discussion and conclusion to the paper.

2 Misuse Case Diagrams vs. Fault Trees

Fault tree analysis is a top-down method primarily meant to analyze the causes of hazards rather than identifying the hazards. From a top event (rectangle) which captures some harm that should be avoided in the system, decomposition into various possible causes for this continues until basic events are reached (circles). These basic events are those that really happen in the system, while the intermediate rectangles are pseudoevents (collective sets of basic events). Figure 2 shows an example of a fault tree for a Patient Monitoring System (PMS) adapted from [2], the top event is that wrong / inadequate treatment is given to the patient. This is then decomposed until basic events are reached. The gates with concave bottoms are OR-gates, i.e., the top event can occur if either of the two pseudo-events on level 2 happen, while gates with flat bottoms are AND-gates, i.e., for vital signs not to be reported, it is necessary that both the basic events below occur: the sensor failing and the nurse failing. We use a textbook fault tree rather than a self-developed one, to pose a less biased challenge for misuse cases. With a home-made example, there would be a greater risk that we either consciously or unconsciously made up one that could be represented elegantly with misuse cases.

[1] Of course, the Admin might not only be "unlucky" but possibly also incompetent, overworked or something else. The chosen phrasing, however, appears more sympathetic, and it must be remembered that in concrete projects the system admin in question will be one important stakeholder in the analysis.

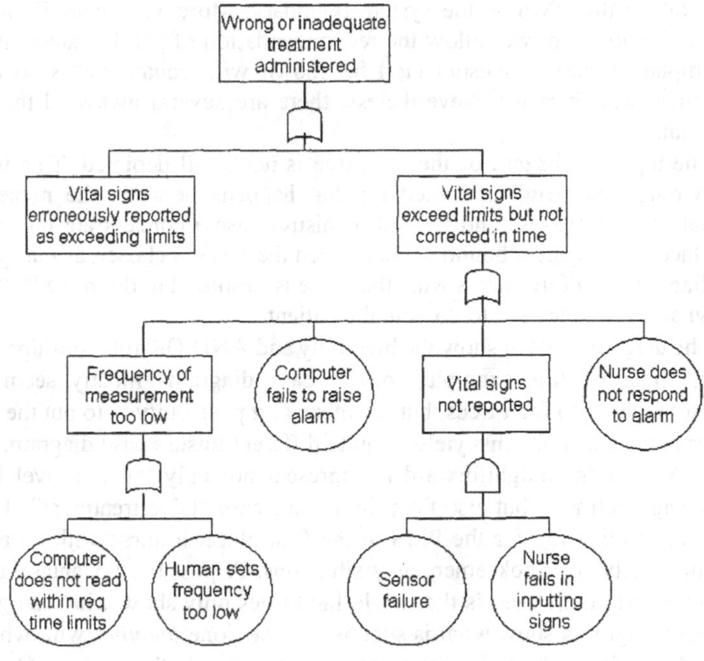

Fig. 2. Partial fault tree for Patient Monitoring System (PMS), adapted from [2]

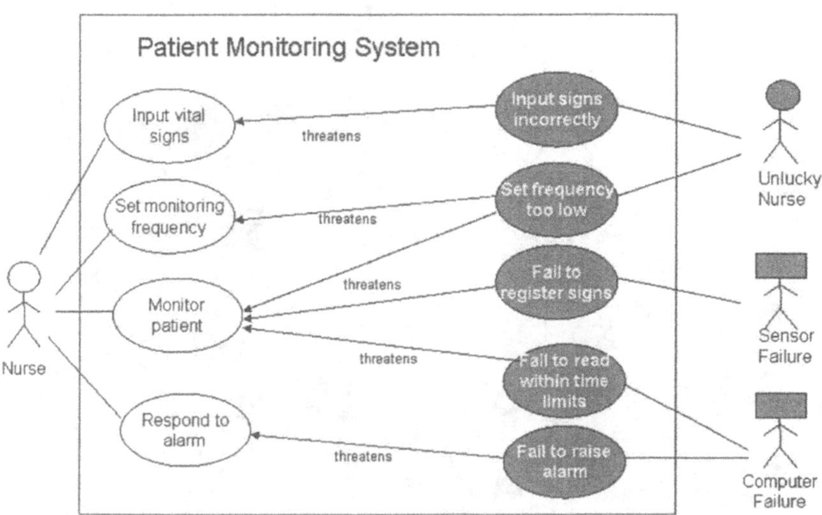

Fig. 3. First attempt at a MUC diagram for the PMS

A first attempt to represent the same problem domain with misuse cases is shown in figure 3, taking the PMS as the system boundary. Moreover, apart from standard UML diagram notation, we follow the recommendation of [7] that automated actors (e.g., computer systems, sensors etc.) be shown with square heads so as not to confuse them with humans. Nevertheless, there are several awkward things about this diagram:

- The top level hazard of the fault tree is not at all depicted. This is because "wrong treatment" is something that happens between the nurse and the patient. Use cases (and thus also misuse cases) concentrate on what takes place at the system boundary, and when the PMS is chosen as the system, the diagram therefore shows what the nurse is supposed to do in the PMS, but not what she is supposed to do with the patient.
- The diagram fails to show the hierarchy and AND/OR-relationships.

In the light of this example, misuse case diagrams mostly seem to have weaknesses relative to fault trees, but an interesting possibility is to put the patient at the center of the analysis. This yields a quite different misuse case diagram, shown in Figure 4. Now it is straightforward to represent not only the top level hazard of giving wrong treatment, but also the primary use case "Give treatment". This better discloses the motivation for the PMS in the first place: a nurse with no automated help would easily overlook emergency situations. A possible advantage of misuse case diagrams vs. fault trees is that while fault trees only show what can go wrong, misuse case diagrams show what is supposed to be done *together* with what can go wrong and can also indicate how use cases might mitigate the hazards. On the other hand, the diagram of figure 4 fails to show the interaction between the Nurse and the PMS. Combining the two views yields Figure 5. This would soon become too complex if taking more hazards into account, so it is most practical to develop diagrams looking at one system boundary at a time.

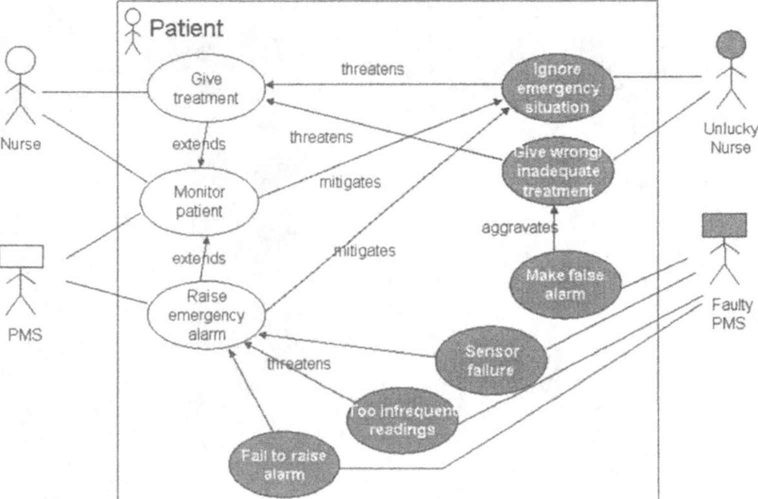

Fig. 4. New misuse case diagram, now with the Patient as system boundary

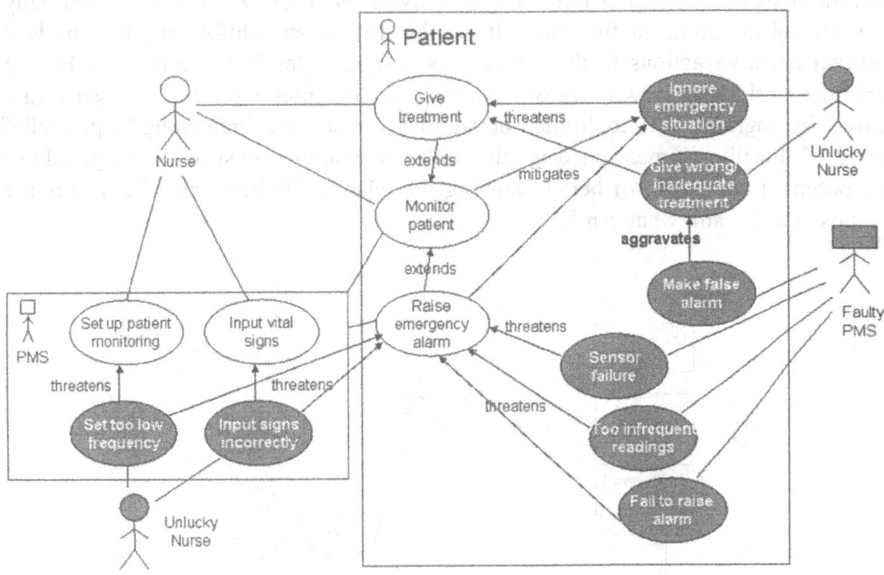

Fig. 5. Combining the two perspectives of Figure 3 and 4

3 Misuse Case Diagrams vs. Cause-Consequence Diagrams

Figure 6 shows an example cause-consequence diagram for a boiler system, again taken from [7]. Such diagrams are focused on a critical event – in this case "Pressure too high" – and look both at causes of the event (backward search) and results of the event (forward search). In the example, the cause is "Uncontrolled action", while the final harm if everything fails is "Explosion". Hence, the reading direction is from top to bottom, implying both a timeline and causal development. In addition to the square events, the diagram shows conditional boxes (with Yes/No continuations), basic conditions (circles), and OR-connectors. There are also AND-connectors, as well as several other symbols available which are not used in this small example.

Figure 7 shows a misuse case diagram representation of the same system. In this case, it is quite straightforward to represent the same phenomena in the misuse case diagram with one single system boundary. Each representation has advantages and disadvantages. The CCD explicitly shows the timeline and causal relationship between various events, and also has explicit Yes/No choices. In the misuse case diagram causal relationships are implicit in "threatens" and "mitigates" relationships, but no so easy to spot quickly since there is no standard reading direction for such causal chains. In addition to the OR (shown), AND, and XOR nodes, there are several other kinds of nodes available in CCD's that would be difficult or impossible to capture in a misuse case diagram, such as time delays.

On the other hand, the CCD only shows events or conditions that directly affect the critical event. Misuse case diagrams can also easily include mitigations with an indirect effect – as exemplified by "Raise alarm" in Figure 8 – which will make it less likely that the Operator fails to open Valve 2. With CCD's one would normally use several diagrams in this case. It would also be straightforward to introduce indirect negative actions in the misuse case diagram, for instance that the Failing Operator accidentally switches off computer auto-response for high pressure (not shown in diagram), this could then be another misuse case threatening "Open relief valve 1". Finally, as mentioned for the fault tree example, misuse cases again have the potential advantage of better showing the relationship between what actors are supposed to do, and what can fail.

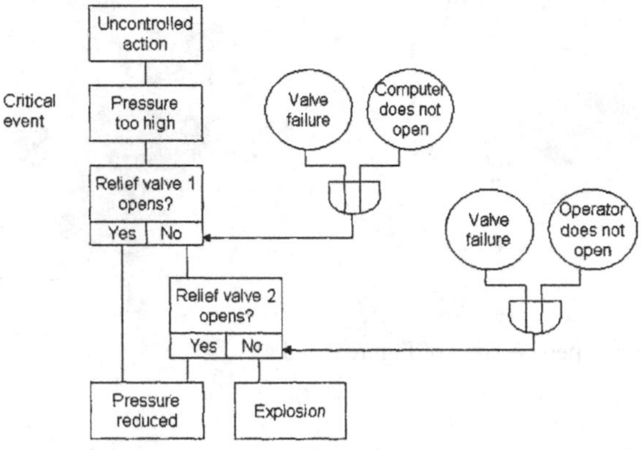

Fig. 6. Cause-consequence diagram (CCD) for a boiler system

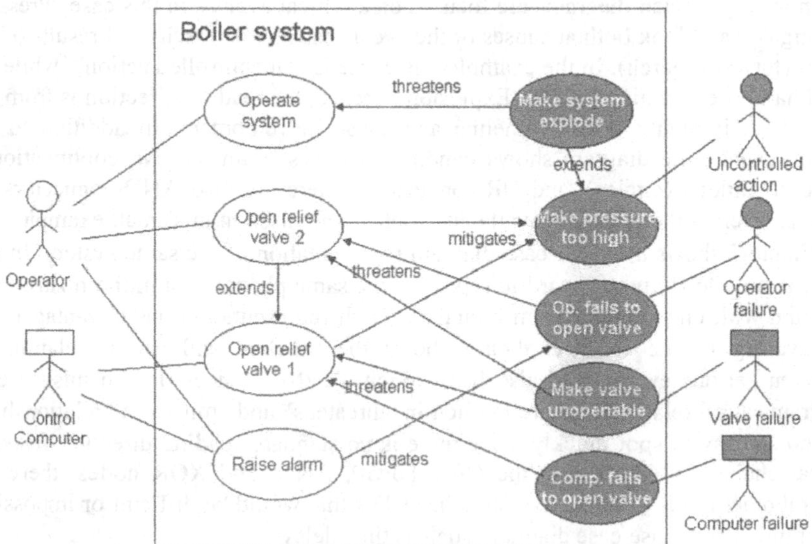

Fig. 7. Misuse case diagram for the boiler system

An overall observation here is that misuse case diagrams and cause-consequence diagrams have quite different purposes, the former meant for a high level overview of a system, while the latter is for a detailed exploration of specific chains of causation. Also, cause-consequence diagrams appear as a design level technique rather than requirements level, in that it must already be known which components the system consists of. For a requirements level misuse case diagram it would for instance be more appropriate to have a generic use case "Relieve pressure" than the two use cases assuming the existence of specific valves. Hence, rather than suggesting that one technique is better than the other here, a more natural question for further investigation would be whether they could be combined.

4 Textual Misuse Cases vs. HazOp

HazOp (Hazards and Operability Analysis) does not use diagrams but a textual representation, and would therefore be more relevant to compare with textual misuse cases. HazOp looks at the design of a system, e.g., a plant, and considers this system node by node, tentatively trying a number of guidewords for each node:

- NO: intended result not achieved
- MORE: more of a relevant physical property than there should be, e.g., pressure, voltage, temperature, flow, ...
- LESS: opposite of MORE
- AS WELL AS: something comes in addition to what was intended
- PART OF: only part of the intended result is achieved
- REVERSE, e.g., backflow instead of forward flow, closing valves instead of opening them
- OTHER THAN: the intended result is not achieved – as with NO – moreover, something completely different happens

A full HazOp requires that it is known exactly which nodes the system consists of, i.e., the design must be quite finished. This means that it is often too costly to change the design to avoid a hazard, so instead the outcome is to add protective measures. Many therefore prefer to do a preliminary HazOp considering early design sketches when it is still possible to change to a safer design. Still, even this preliminary HazOp is normally a design phase technique – although one could imagine looking at use cases as "nodes" for investigation rather than design components. The report produced by a HazOp will contain a number of table formed entries, an example of such an entry is shown in Table 1.

Table 1. Example HazOp entry, adapted from [7]

Guide word	Deviation	Possible causes	Possible consequences
NO	No flow	1. pump failure 2. suction filter blocked 3. isolation valve closed	1. overheating in heat exchanger 2. loss of feed to reactor

A direct attempt to translate the above into textual misuse cases is shown in Table 2. Clearly, the HazOp entry is more compact and easier to understand in this case, and not surprisingly, since misuse cases are not intended for describing systems at the design level, and especially not continuous physical systems like this one. Misuse cases share with use cases a primary suitability for systems where action is performed in discrete chunks. It can also be noticed that there is hardly any scenario path here.

Table 2. Textual misuse case reflecting the HazOp entry

Misuse Case Name: Pump failure causes flow loss
Basic path: bp–1. A pump fails. bp–2. Flow is lost.
Alternatives: a–1. Instead of pump failure, flow loss is caused by **a blocked suction filter.** a–2. Instead of pump failure, flow loss is caused by **a closed isolation valve.**
Hazards: **h1.** heat exchanger is overheated. **h2.** feed to the reactor is lost.

On the other hand, textual misuse cases can again do something else better than the traditional safety techniques, namely relate threats directly to the actions to be performed in the system. For instance, this could be done through the lightweight textual misuse case notation suggested in [4]. Table 3 shows an example where the normal use case is described in the two leftmost columns, following the format of an essential use case, as proposed by [7]. Then, an additional column is added on the right, describing the potential hazards. An advantage of this, compared to the HazOp entry format of Table 1, is that it becomes clear which specific step in an activity the hazard relates to. Also, the practice of looking for threats for each use case step can in itself contribute to creativity in brainstorming threats – as can be seen, 11 different hazards are identified only for this quite small use case. If one had been asked to imagine hazards just based on the use case name "provideEmergencyTreatment", not relating the hazards to the various steps, there is high chance that some of these hazards might have been overlooked.

Table 3: Example of lightweight misuse case notation including hazards per step

provideEmergencyTreatment		
Nurse intention	*PMS Response*	*Hazards*
Stay on guard		Nurse falls asleep
	Alarm nurse of emergency condition	PMS fails to raise alarm Alarm not noticed
Acknowledge alarm		Nurse fails to take action Nurse busy with other alarm
	Show patient and location	Wrong patient shown Wrong location shown
Administer treatment		Wrong treatment given Treatment to wrong patient
	Condition normalizes	Patient status incorrectly displayed
Log treatment		Erroneous logging, misinforming next shift

Clearly, HazOp and misuse cases thus complement each other, at least for systems where it is natural to apply use cases in the first place. A further possibility to consider would be if they could be combined more systematically, for instance whether HazOp guidewords could be applied for each use case step. When thinking about physical variables such as temperature, voltage and flow, it is quite clear what MORE, LESS, REVERSE etc. would mean, but this could be fuzzier when talking about actions involving information and human interaction, such as use case steps. For instance, looking at the sentence "The nurse administers the necessary treatment to the patient", we could have:

- NO: nurse fails to administer treatment
- MORE: administers too much of the treatment, e.g., giving an overdose of medication, or using too high voltage at defibrillation
- LESS: administers too little of the treatment.
- AS WELL AS: does something else in addition to the needed treatment, e.g., administration of another drug, too
- PART OF: gives only one of several treatments that were needed in conjunction. Another guideword that is sometimes used for time dependent systems, and which would clearly be of relevance in this example, is TOO LATE.
- REVERSE: not always applicable, e.g., cannot do the reverse of defibrillation, but might be relevant in some cases, e.g., decreasing rather than increasing the intensity of a drip
- OTHER THAN: meant to cover "something completely different", i.e., this should be wider than just the combination NO + AS WELL AS. Looking at the starting sentence, several OTHER THAN's could be imagined, e.g.,

OTHER SUBJECT: somebody else than the authorized nurse treats the patient, OTHER VERB: nurse does something else to the patient than giving treatment, OTHER DIRECT OBJECT: nurse gives something else to the patient than the treatment, OTHER INDIRECT OBJECT: nurse gives the treatment to another patient than the one intended.

As can be seen, not all of the hazards above are equally relevant in the given case, and for the latter bullet some seem partly overlapping. Yet, such a combination of use cases and guidewords may inspire the analysts to consider hazards that would otherwise have been overlooked, and these could then be captured in use cases like the one shown in Table 3.

5 Textual misuse cases vs. FME(C)A

Failure Modes and Effects Analysis (FMEA) uses forward search where the initiating events are failures of individual components (i.e., failure modes), then deriving from this what harm this could possibly lead to on a higher level (i.e., effects). Failure Modes, Effects, and Criticality Analysis (FMECA) is an extension of the same technique, where the criticality of each effect is analyzed in more detail. Table 4 shows a sample FMECA for a missile system, again adapted from [2].

Table 4: Sample FMECA for a missile system, from [2]

Failure Modes and Effects Criticality Analysis Subsystem: ______ Prepared by: ________ Date: ___________						
Item	**Failure Modes**	**Cause of Failure**	**Possible Effects**	**P**	**Level**	**Mitigation**
Motor case	Rupture	a. poor work b.defective materials c.transport damage d.handling damage e.overpressurization	Destruction of missile	0.0006	Critical	Closely control manufacturing ...

This is difficult to translate to a misuse case, since "The missile's motor case ruptures" is a single event, not a use case style step by step action. Similar to HazOp the focus is also on design (and not on the requirements level) – one needs to be able to list all the components in the system and then perform FME(C)A on each of them. Still, the previous section suggested that a combination of misuse cases and HazOp might be useful, so the same might be the case for FME(C)A and misuse cases. Indeed, there already exists a proposal combining FMEA and use cases [8], but then looking at the use case as a whole when generating ideas for possible threats, and considering the use case as a "node" for investigation rather than looking at design components as nodes. A possible extension of this idea could be to look at threats per step and document the results in a textual misuse case similar to that of Table 3, or similar to Table 2 if more details are needed. For each use case step one could then ask:

- What are the possible causes for failure of this step?
- What are the possible consequences of failure of this step?

This analysis could for instance prompt the inclusion of more alternative or exceptional paths in the use case, to address safety concerns and ensure that the use case as a whole might succeed even if one planned step fails. However, for space reasons the further exploration of this opportunity is beyond the scope of this paper.

6 Related Work

There are several techniques that seek to combine use cases or scenarios with safety analysis. [9] and [10] propose to apply use cases as input for performing safety analysis by means of safety engineering techniques such as Functional Hazard Assessment (FHA) [11] and HAZOP [12]. [13] proposes to formalize use cases to deal with the specification of fault-tolerant systems. In the CORAS project misuse cases were combined with other UML notations such as sequence diagrams, also specifically adapted for safety analysis [14].

Other adaptations of UML have also been proposed to address safety concerns, but then more on the design level. [15] extends UML specifically for safety, primarily achieved by profiles of packages, class and component diagrams. Safe-UML for modeling in the railway domain is proposed in [16]. Similar adaptations have been made for UML with respect to security in UMLsec [17] and SecureUML [18]. This work is different from the abovementioned in trying to compare the advantages and disadvantages of misuse cases relative to traditional safety analysis techniques.

7 Discussion and conclusions

In this paper we have mainly looked further at the possibility of applying misuse cases (both diagrams and text) for identifying safety hazards, which can be seen as a prerequisite for eliciting safety requirements. Several examples of safety-related misuse case diagrams and textual descriptions have been shown, comparing misuse cases with traditional safety techniques such as fault trees, cause-consequence diagrams, HAZOP, and FME(C)A. The examples show that these techniques, specially geared towards safety analysis, have many advantages versus misuse cases, and that it would certainly not be a good idea to throw away previous safety-analysis techniques and use misuse cases instead. In particular, it appears that misuse cases will be of little use in describing physical systems of continuous nature, where the accidents are sudden events rather than mistakes made in step-by-step processes. In short: if use cases are not suitable for the activity that goes on, neither will misuse cases be suitable for describing hazards of those activities.

Yet, on the other hand it has been indicated that misuse cases do also have something to offer for problems involving step-by-step activities. Better than the traditional safety techniques, misuse cases show the relationships between the normal activities on the one side and faults and hazards on the other side. Also, it provides a simple intuitive notation which is well geared towards brainstorming, and if use cases or use case diagrams are anyway used in the project in question, the additional effort needed to apply misuse cases is small. Hence, it provides a good possibility for including safety concerns in the requirements phase of mainstream projects, in a similar way to what has previously been discussed for security. So, to answer the research questions:

RQ1: Can misuse cases, both diagrammatic and textual, be applied in the safety domain? Yes, but not necessarily for all problems. If the problem is dominated by continuous processes and physical concerns – and it is anyway not natural to apply use cases – then misuse cases are not likely to be suitable. On the other hand, for systems where activity is performed in a typical step-by-step manner appropriate for use cases, misuse cases can be suitable for early discussion of safety problems.

RQ2: Do misuse cases add value to other textual and diagrammatic representations traditionally used for safety hazard analysis...? Yes, but it is not all advantages – there are both pros and cons to misuse cases compared to other description formats. Hence, misuse cases cannot replace other techniques, but it could be useful in combination with other techniques. Typically, one could first use misuse cases for an early brainstorming of hazards, then follow up with other techniques such as fault trees, cause-consequence analysis, HAZOP, and FME(C)A. This also makes sense since these other techniques are primarily meant to be applied in the design stage, whereas misuse cases are intended for the requirements analysis stage.

Further investigation is of course needed to suggest in detail how misuse cases should be combined with other techniques. A particular weakness of the current paper is that all the examples looked at are small and simple. But at least, the examples were not invented by the author but taken from a textbook [2] which offered only one example for each of the techniques looked at. This means that the possibility for the author consciously or unconsciously to invent or pick examples that would be particularly fitting for misuse cases was removed, so at least the examples provide an unbiased challenge for misuse cases with examples that are representative of the safety field. But the most interesting topic for further work would of course be to investigate the application of misuse cases in real projects with significant safety concerns.

It can also be argued that safety issues might cause particular needs for situational method engineering [19-21], due to the following:

- Much variation in expertise: In some projects there are team members with much previous experience in safety analysis with traditional / heavyweight methods. In other projects this is lacking. And even in projects with high expertise, it may be necessary to use lightweight informal approaches at some stages to involve diverse groups of stakeholders with no competence in safety analysis.
- Variation in the degree of importance of the safety concerns. In some projects these are essential to every aspect of the software, while in others safety issues only apply to certain modules.
- Variation in the stage where safety analysis would take place. In some projects it might be natural to do some safety analysis very early (e.g.,

requirements elicitation stage), whereas in other projects participants might need to see some possible designs to be able to reason about safety issues.

One interesting topic for further work would therefore be to establish systematized criteria on the selection of safety modeling techniques such as those compared in this paper, based on task and stakeholder characteristics.

References

1. D.G. Firesmith, Engineering Safety Requirements, Safety Constraints, and Safety-Critical Requirements, *Journal of Object Technology*, 3 (3), 27-42 (2004).
2. N.G. Leveson, Safeware: System Safety and Computers (Addison-Wesley, Boston, 1995).
3. R.R. Lutz, Software Engineering for Safety: A Roadmap, in: The Future of Software Engineering, edited by A. Finkelstein (ACM Press, New York, 2000), pp. 213-226.
4. G. Sindre and A.L. Opdahl, Eliciting Security Requirements with Misuse Cases, *Requirements Engineering*, 10 (1), 34-44 (2005).
5. I.F. Alexander, Initial Industrial Experience of Misuse Cases in Trade-Off Analysis, in: 10th Anniversary IEEE Joint International Requirements Engineering Conference (RE'02), Essen, Germany, 9-13 Sep, edited by K. Pohl (IEEE, 2002).
6. I.F. Alexander, Misuse Cases, Use Cases with Hostile Intent, *IEEE Software*, 20 58-66 (2003).
7. L.L. Constantine and L.A.D. Lockwood, Software for Use: A Practical Guide to the Models and Methods of Usage-Centered Design (ACM Press, New York, 1999).
8. J. Zhou and T. Stålhane, A Framework for Early Robustness Assessment, in: 8th IASTED Conference on Software Engineering and Application, MIT, Cambridge, MA, 8-10 Nov, edited by M.H. Hamza (Acta Press, 2004).
9. K. Allenby and T. Kelly, Deriving Safety Requirements Using Scenarios, in: Fifth IEEE International Symposium on Requirements Engineering (RE'01), Toronto, Canada, edited by B. Nuseibeh, and S. Easterbrook (IEEE, 2001), pp. 228-235.
10. H.-K. Kim and Y.-K. Chung, Automatic Translation from Requirements Model into Use Cases Modeling on UML, in: Computational Science and Its Applications (ICCSA'05), Singapore, 9-12 May, Lecture Notes in Computer Science Vol. 3482, edited by O. Gervasi, M.L. Gavrilova, V. Kumar, A. Laganà, H.P. Lee, Y. Mun, D. Taniar, and C.J.K. Tan (Springer-Verlag, 2005), pp. 769-777.
11. SAE, Guidelines and Methods for Conducting the Safety Assessment Process on Civil Airborne Systems and Equipment, Society of Automotive Engineers, Technical report, ARP4761, 1996 (unpublished).
12. F. Redmill, M. Chudleigh, and J. Catmur, System Safety: HAZOP and Software HAZOP (Wiley, Chichester, UK, 1999).
13. A. Ebnenasir, B.H.C. Cheng, and S. Konrad, Use Case-Based Modeling and Analysis of Failsafe Fault-Tolerance, in: 14th IEEE International Requirements Engineering Conference (RE'06), St.Louis, USA, 11-15 Sep, edited by M. Glinz (IEEE, 2006), pp. 343-344.
14. B.A. Gran, R. Fredriksen, and A.P.-J. Thunem, An Approach for Model-Based Risk Assessment, in: Computer Safety, Reliability, and Security, 23rd International Conference, SAFECOMP 2004, Potsdam, Germany, 21-24 Sep, Lecture Notes in Computer Science Vol. 3219, edited by M. Heisel, P. Liggesmeyer, and S. Wittmann (Springer, 2004), pp. 311-324.

15.J. Jürjens, Developing Safety-Critical Systems with UML, in: The Sixth International Conference on The Unified Modeling Language (UML'03), San Francisco, USA, 20-24 Oct, Lecture Notes on Computer Science Vol. 2863, edited by P. Stevens, J. Whittle, and G. Booch (Springer-Verlag, 2003), pp. 144-159.
16.K. Berkenkötter, U. Hannemann, and J. Peleska, HYBRIS - Efficient Specification and Analysis of Hybrid Systems - Part III: RCSD - A UML 2.0 Profile for the Railway Control System Domain (Draft Version), Univ. Bremen, Germany, 2006 (unpublished).
17.J. Jürjens, UMLsec: Extending UML for Secure Systems Development, in: The Unified Modeling Language, 5th International Conference (UML 2002), Dresden, Germany, Sep 30 - Oct 4, Lecture Notes in Computer Science Vol. 2460, edited by J. M. Jezequel, H. Haussmann, and S. Cook (Springer, 2002), pp. 412-425.
18.T. Lodderstedt, D. Basin, and J. Doser, SecureUML: A UML-Based Modeling Language for Model-Driven Security, in: The Unified Modeling Language, 5th International Conference (UML 2002), Dresden, Germany, Sep 30 - Oct 4, Lecture Notes in Computer Science Vol. 2460, edited by J.M. Jezequel, H. Haussmann, and S. Cook (Springer, 2002), pp. 426-441.
19.C. Rolland and N. Prakash, A proposal for context-specific method engineering, in: IFIP TC8, WG8.1/8.2 working conference on Method engineering: principles of method construction and tool support, Atlanta, edited by S. Brinkkemper, K. Lyytinen, and R.J. Welke (Chapman & Hall, 1996), pp. 191–208.
20.S. Brinkkemper, M. Saeki, and F. Harmsen, Assembly techniques for method engineering, in: 10th international conference on advanced information systems engineering (CAiSE'98), Pisa, Italy, Lecture Notes in Computer Science Vol. 1413, edited by B. Pernici, and C. Thanos (Springer, 1998).
21.I. Mirbel and J. Ralyté, Situational method engineering: combining assembly-based and roadmap-driven approaches, *Requirements Engineering*, 11 (1), 58-78 (2006).

Engineering Medical Processes to Improve Their Safety

An Experience Report

Leon J. Osterweil[1], George S. Avrunin[1], Bin Chen[1], Lori A. Clarke[1], Rachel Cobleigh[1], Elizabeth A. Henneman[2] and Philip L. Henneman[3]

1 Laboratory for Advanced Software Engineering Research (LASER)
University of Massachusetts at Amherst, Amherst, MA 01003
{ljo, avrunin, chenbin, clarke, rcobleig} @ cs.umass.edu

2 School of Nursing, University of Massachusetts at Amherst, Amherst, MA 01003, henneman@nursing.umass.edu

3 Baystate Medical Center, Springfield, MA and Tufts University School of Medicine, Boston, MA, philip.henneman@bhs.org

Abstract. This paper describes experiences in using precise definitions of medical processes as the basis for analyses aimed at finding and correcting defects leading to improvements in patient safety. The work entails the use of the Little-JIL process definition language for creating the precise definitions, the Propel system for creating precise specifications of process requirements, and the FLAVERS systems for analyzing process definitions. The paper describes the details of using these technologies, employing a blood transfusion process as an example. Although this work is still ongoing, early experiences suggest that our approach is viable and promising. The work has also helped us to learn about the desiderata for process definition and analysis technologies that are intended to be used to engineer methods.

1 Introduction: The Problem and Our Proposed Approach

Medical errors cause approximately 98,000 patients to die each year [1] in the United States. US Institute of Medicine (IOM) reports have suggested that the delivery of healthcare must fundamentally change to address medical error (eg. see [1, 2]). In particular, these studies suggest that many serious medical errors result from *system* rather than individual failures, leading the IOM to advocate the development of healthcare systems that directly address patient safety. In particular, the IOM report states, "what is most disturbing is the absence of real progress… in information technology to improve clinical *processes* [italics ours]" ([1 pg. 3]).

Please use the following format when citing this chapter:

Osterweil, L. J., Avrunin, G. S., Chen, B., Clarke, L. A., Cobleigh, R., Henneman, E. A., Henneman, P. L., 2007, in IFIP International Federation for Information Processing, Volume 244, Situational Method Engineering: Fundamentals and Experiences, eds. Ralyté, J., Brinkkemper, S., Henderson-Sellers B., (Boston Springer), pp. 267-282.

Encouraged by these findings, the authors of this paper began a project to investigate how software engineering research in process definition and analysis might be applied and extended to help reduce errors and improve safety in medical processes.

Our preliminary research (eg. [3]) showed that in many cases current medical processes are often described only at a high-level of generality and are usually not defined completely and precisely. These processes typically describe standard practices, but usually do not address how healthcare providers should react when unusual, yet expectable, situations arise. Because of this, healthcare providers can often find themselves in situations that are not directly addressed by the processes they learned, and thus are often unsure of whether or not their actions conform to recommended care guidelines. In addition, aspects of current care process descriptions are frequently vague, ambiguous, or inconsistent, allowing different providers to arrive at different understandings about their specifics. Such descriptions may lead workers to believe they are following recommended care guidelines when, in fact, their care has deviated, increasing the possibility of error.

In the work we describe here, software engineering researchers and medical experts developed precise, rigorous definitions of medical processes that capture not only the standard cases, but also the exceptional situations that can arise. The process definitions also captured the inherent concurrency and multi-tasking frequently undertaken by busy healthcare providers, as well as details of the complex use of resources in performing medical processes. The processes defined covered different aspects of medical care, such as blood transfusion, chemotherapy, and emergency department patient flow. In all of these domains, the literature indicates that errors can be frequent and can result in serious negative consequences [1, 4, 5].

This preliminary investigation indicated somewhat different goals for the engineering of methods in these different areas of medical practice, and thus suggested somewhat different approaches. The Emergency Department (ED) sought to reduce patient waiting time, as delay is a safety hazard (and a source of pain and inconvenience). Moreover, the highly concurrent nature of Emergency Department activities is believed to increase the chance of incorrect process execution, which also leads to safety hazards. Other concerns included identifying bottlenecks and improving resource utilization. This suggested the desirability of analyzing precise, rigorous process definitions to study their concurrency and resource utilization.

In blood transfusion and chemotherapy there was concern for the identification and removal of process defects that create hazards to patient health and safety. These concerns suggested the value of at least two complementary engineering approaches, namely fault tree analysis and finite-state verification, each applied to a precise definition of safety-critical processes. Analysis of fault trees promises to indicate possible effects of incorrect performance of process steps [6, 13], while finite state verification (eg., [8, 9]) promises to identify sequences of tasks that, even if performed perfectly, could still lead to safety hazards [1610].

Our project aims to evaluate the effectiveness of defining medical processes using a rigorously defined language, carrying out rigorous analysis of the processes to detect defects, and then improving the processes by defect removal. Here we address in detail only one research activity, namely our work in improving processes related to blood transfusion in a clinical setting and only touch briefly upon some of our other activities. In the next section we present the Little-JIL process definition language and provide some examples of how it was used to define a blood transfusion process. Section 3 describes and evaluates our experiences, and Section 4 summarizes some related work. Section 5 summarizes some of our other work on medical processes, and suggests future directions for this research.

2 An Example: A Clinical Blood Transfusion Process

The administration of blood and blood products is a common, high-risk, resource-intensive medical intervention. Despite strict regulation by the US Food and Drug Administration as well as healthcare accreditation agencies, the error rate in transfusion medicine is significant and believed to be underreported [11]. To investigate whether the precise definition and analysis of this process could help identify defects that lead to such errors, we used the Little-JIL process definition language [12, 13] to define a transfusion process in detail. We then used the Propel property definition system [14] to specify desired properties, and then used the FLAVERS finite-state verification system [9] to determine whether the properties could ever be violated by any path through the defined process.

2.1 Principal Features of Little-JIL

Little-JIL [12, 13] is a language originally developed for defining the processes by which software is developed and maintained. Wise [13] provides full technical details of the language. Here we outline its salient features. A Little-JIL process is defined by means of specification of three components, an artifact collection, a resource repository, and a coordination specification. Each addresses a different area of concern. The artifact collection contains the various items, initial, intermediate, and final, that are the focus of the activities carried out by the process. The resource repository specifies the agents and other capabilities available to support performing the activities. The coordination specification ties these together by specifying which agents, aided by which supplementary capabilities, will perform which activities upon which artifacts at which time(s). Because of its central role in specifying this, the coordination diagram is generally the central focus of a Little-JIL process definition.

A Little-JIL coordination specification has a visual representation, but is, nevertheless, precisely defined using finite-state automata. This renders processes defined in Little-JIL amenable to definitive analyses that are analogous to those used to evaluate application software. Among the key features of Little-JIL that distinguish it from most process languages are its 1) use of abstraction to support scalability and clarity, 2) use of scoping to make the use of step parameterization clear, 3) facilities for specifying parallel processing, 4) extensive capabilities for defining how to handle exceptional conditions, and 5) clarity and precision in specifying iteration.

A Little-JIL coordination specification is defined using hierarchically decomposed steps (Figure 1), where a step represents a task to be done by an assigned agent. Each step has a name and a set of badges to represent control flow among its sub-steps, its interface (a specification of its input/output artifacts and the resources it requires), the exceptions it handles, etc. A step with no sub-steps is called a leaf step and represents an activity to be performed by an agent, without any guidance from the process.

Resources and Agents—Each Little-JIL step contains as part of its interface a specification of the types of resources that are required in order to support the execution of the step. Some examples of resources are physicians, blood units, beds, and accesses to medical records of various sorts. The assignment of an actual resource instance is carried out by a separate Resource Manager, which maintains a repository of available resources and their capabilities, and identifies a specific resource instance to be assigned in response to the step's request. Each step always requires one specially designated resource instance, called its agent, which is the resource that is assigned responsibility for the performance of the step. Little-JIL agents may be either humans or automated devices. In some cases either might be appropriate, and the choice is then made by the Resource Manager, rather than being dictated by the process definition.

Substep Decomposition—Little-JIL steps may be decomposed into substeps of two different kinds, ordinary substeps and exception handlers. The ordinary substeps define the details of how the step is to be executed. The substeps are connected to their parent by edges, which may be annotated by specifications of the artifacts that flow between parent and substep and also by cardinality specifications. Cardinality specifications define the number of times the substep is to be instantiated and may be a fixed number, a Kleene *, a Kleene +, or a Boolean expression (indicating whether the substep is to be instantiated). Exception handlers define how exceptions thrown by the step's descendants are handled. The edge from exception handler to parent is annotated with the type of the exception being handled, parameters being passed, and an indication of how execution continues after the exception has been handled.

Step sequencing –A non-leaf step has a sequencing badge (an icon embedded on the left of the step bar; e.g., the right arrow in Figure 1), which defines the order of substep execution. For example, a sequential step (right arrow) indicates that its substeps execute from left to right. A parallel step (equal sign) indicates that its substeps execute in any (possibly interleaved) order. A choice step (circle slashed with a horizontal line) indicates that step execution is by choosing any of the alternative substeps. A try step (right arrow with an X on its tail) mandates a sequence in which substeps are to be tried as alternatives.

Artifacts and artifact flows – An artifact is an entity (e.g., a physical entity or data item) that is used or produced by a step. Parameter declarations are specified in the interface to a step (circle atop the step bar) as lists of the artifacts used by the step (IN parameters) and the artifacts produced by the step (OUT parameters). Artifact flow through steps can be defined to take place in one of two different ways, 1) hierarchically, as the flow of artifacts between parent and child steps, and 2) by means of data channels. The flow of artifacts along a parent-child edge is indicated by attaching to the edge identification of the artifacts and their direction of flow.

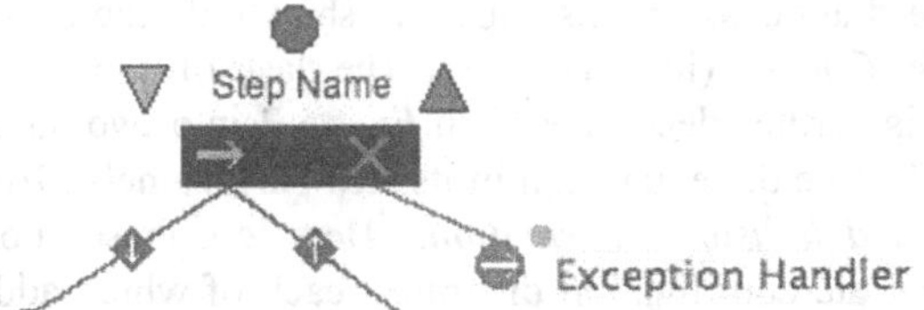

Figure 1 – A Little-JIL step icon.

Data Channels—Data Channels are named entities that directly connect specifically identified source step(s) with specifically identified destination step(s). A data channel acts much like a buffer, with some steps using the data channel as an output and others using it as an input. This construct helps define how streaming data, for example, is handled by a process. It can also be used to synchronize concurrently executing steps, since steps may choose to block when sending or receiving.

Requisites – A Little-JIL step optionally can be preceded or succeeded by a step that is executed before or after execution of the main body of the step. A prerequisite is represented by a down arrowhead to the left of the step bar, and a post-requisite is represented by an up arrowhead to the right of the step bar. Requisites facilitate checking for a condition either before executing a step or to assure that execution has been acceptable. The failure of a requisite triggers the occurrence of an exception.

Exception Handling – A step in Little-JIL can signal the occurrence of exceptional conditions when some aspect of the step's execution fails (e.g., the violation of one of the step's requisites). This triggers the execution of a matching exception handler associated with an ancestor step that throws the exception (and represented as a step attached by an edge to an X on the right of the step bar in Figure 1). Little-JIL also incorporates a facility for specifying in which, of a variety of ways, execution should proceed after completion of the exception handler. This is an important feature that is difficult to represent in many other languages.

Scoping – The parent step and its descendants represent a scope in Little-JIL, enabling specification that certain entities and datasets can be considered local to that scope. Little-JIL also supports recursive specifications of steps within its own scope, which clarifies the iterative application of a process step to its defined arguments.

2.2 An Example Using Little-JIL to Define a Blood Transfusion Process

Figure 2 is a blood transfusion process coordination diagram. The actual process has 112 Little-JIL steps, and is too large to present here. Thus, we present a version that fits the needs of terse exposition, but is still representative of the actual process.

Figure 2 shows that the full transfusion process, *Single-Unit Transfusion Process*, consists of four substeps to be executed in sequence (note the right arrow in the step bar), namely *Bedside Checks, Prepare for Infusion, Transfuse Blood,* and *Post Transfusion Work.* The first three are all decomposed into subprocesses that are defined by separate diagrams. In this paper we show only the decomposition of the first step, *Bedside Checks* (in Figure 3). The last of the four substeps, *Post Transfusion Work* is further decomposed in Figure 2 into two substeps that can be executed in parallel (note the equal sign in its step bar), namely *Discard Transfusion Materials* and *Record Infusion Information.* Here too, these substeps are further decomposed in separate coordination diagrams, each of which adds further details. Substeps are the primary method of supporting the incorporation of details into Little-JIL process definitions, since decomposition can proceed to any level of abstraction.

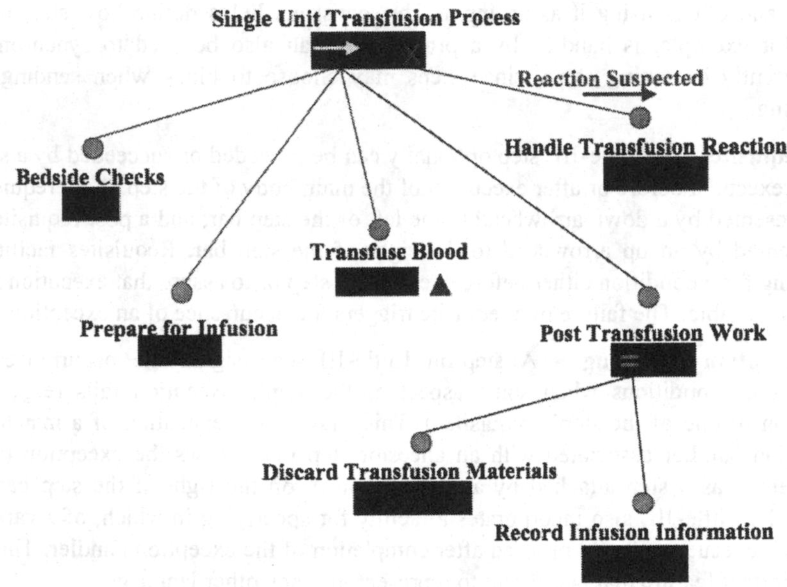

Figure 2: A coordination diagram of a Little-JIL blood transfusion process.

Note also that the *Transfuse Blood* step has a postrequisite (indicated by the fact that the arrowhead on the right of its step bar is colored in). We do not show the decomposition of this step, but the postrequisite defines the activities to be performed after this step's execution to determine whether there has been an adverse reaction to the blood transfusion. If so, this postrequisite will throw a *Reaction Suspected* exception, causing control to be transferred to the *Handle Transfusion Reaction* exception handler, which is another substep of the parent, *Single-Unit Transfusion Process*. *Handle Transfusion Reaction* is also elaborated by a structure of substeps, again not shown here for lack of space. But, as might be expected, this handler is of significant size and thus represented by a non-trivial structure. Note that the exception handler edge is annotated with the type of exception that is handled and with a right arrow icon indicating that execution continues as though the step that threw the exception finished execution. Thus, the next step executed is *Post Transfusion Work.*

We note that the diagrams in Figures 2 and 3 do not contain all the information comprising a complete coordination specification. The Visual-JIL editor is used to create Little-JIL coordination diagrams, and it can elide much information in the interests of reducing visual clutter. In particular the step's agent and resource requirements are not shown in these diagrams, but are represented iconically by the circle above the step. Likewise, the artifacts that are arguments to the various steps must be specified on the edges of a Little-JIL diagram and as part of the information attached to the circle above each step. This information too is elided here for clarity.

While the process depicted in Figure 2 presents a straightforward top-level view of the transfusion process, this view is somewhat illusory. There is considerable additional complexity that must be defined in detail in order to capture salient issues in blood transfusion, thereby rendering them amenable to definitive analysis. To illustrate this, we decompose the first substep, *Bedside Checks*. This step, depicted in Figure 3, represents the checking that is to be done prior to a transfusion, and is thus of central importance in establishing a good basis for safety analysis.

Note that the hierarchical elaboration of *Bedside Checks* makes it clear that this step consists of two separate checks, one to assure the transfusion is being given to the right patient and one to assure the blood to be transfused is correct. The equal sign in the *Bedside Checks* step bar indicates that these two checks can be performed in any order, and indeed can be interleaved with each other. The details of the two checks are interesting and important, and also indicate the value of some of the semantic power of a language such as Little-JIL. Note, for example, that the first substep, *Check Patient ID*, consists of the execution of *Get Patient ID*, followed by the execution of *Check ID to Patient Match*. Each of these requires considerable further elaboration (not shown for lack of space), as they can be seriously complicated by various combinations of situations such as an unconscious patient, a patient who is bleeding profusely, and a patient who has no ID band. The full elaboration of these substeps deals with combinations of these situations, using language features such as exception handling. Of central concern to this step, however, is the possibility that the *Check ID to Patient Match* step might fail. This may happen for many different reasons, but here we indicate that it might happen as a consequence of the evaluation of this step's postrequisite, in which case this contingency is handled by throwing the *ID and Patient Don't Match* exception. The handling of this exception is done by recursively calling the *Check Patient ID* step. Here we note that, because Little-JIL steps are abstractions, and thus function very much like procedure calls, this recursive call of *Check Patient ID* occurs in the scope and context of the exception handler, thus making available to the step information that may be carried along as arguments to the recursive call. Thus, Little-JIL supports sending information about the reasons that the check has failed. This is a faithful representation of what would happen in the real-world situation, where this information would be used to guide the next execution of the *Get Patient ID* step (eg. gathering new information on the patient),and the next invocation of the *Check Patient ID* step. This shows the value of providing strong support for abstraction.

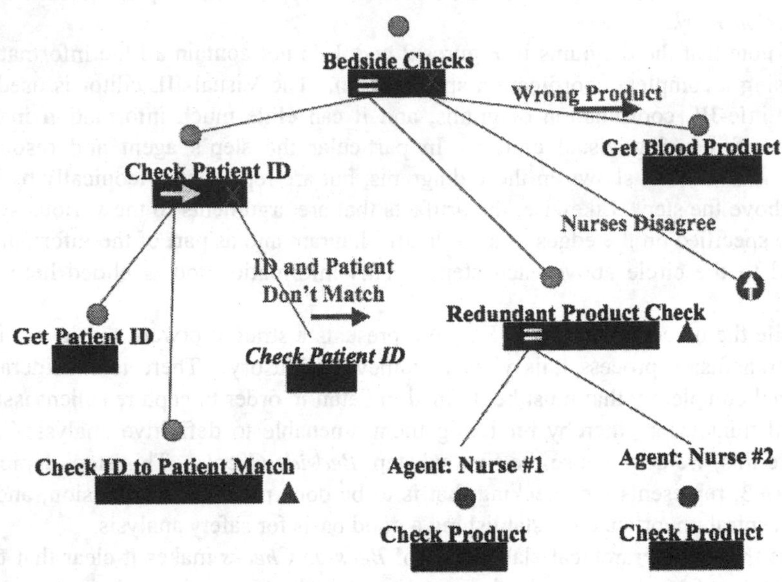

Figure 3: The hierarchical elaboration of the *Bedside Checks* step

The other checking step, *Redundant Product Check*, provides examples of the value of other Little-JIL language features. Here we note that this step consists of the parallel execution of two different instances of the *Check Product* step, not elaborated here for lack of space. But we have specified that the resources required as agents for the two steps are two different nurses (*Nurse #1* and *Nurse #2*),who are obliged to perform the identical check to be sure that the blood product is correct.

Redundant Product Check has a postrequisite, a comparison (not shown here) of the reports from the two nurses to make sure that both agree that the blood product is correct. We show two possible exceptions that can be thrown. If the two nurses disagree, a Nurses Disagree exception is thrown, and is handled by rethrowing (upward arrow) the exception to an ancestor step for resolution. If there is agreement that the blood product is incorrect, a *Wrong Product* exception is thrown, and is handled by the *Get Blood Product* step, which is a reinstantiation of the step defining how a blood product is requested from the blood bank. That step appeared previously in this process definition, but is not shown for lack of space. Again, note that the fact that *Get Blood Product* is called in the context of the handling of this exception means that the report from the nurses providing details about what was wrong with the blood product can now be transmitted to the blood bank.

2.3 Using Propel and FLAVERS Analysis to Look for Process Defects

We now provide a very brief and simplified example of how we applied finite-state verification to the blood transfusion process definition. Our approach to finite-state verification is described in detail in [9]. In that paper we describe how FLAVERS performs exhaustive checks of all possible paths through a system in order to determine whether or not the execution of any path would cause a violation of a desired property. For our purposes, a property is a specification of the requirements for some aspect of the behavior of a system. As a requirement, the property is a specification against which a system is to be verified. For example, a property may specify that a certain event may not occur until another event has occurred. In our work we compare a process against such properties. In cases where the property is violated we modify the process (note, we ignore for the moment the possibility that the property may be incorrectly specified) and verify the modified process to the property again, continuing until the verification succeeds, thereby improving the process. For our analysis, properties are represented as finite-state automata and describe certain sequences of events that must (or must not) occur in every execution of the process. Figure 4 shows an example of one such property for our blood transfusion process. This automaton specifies that after executing the *Get Patient ID* step, executing the *Check ID to Patient Match* step moves the process into a state where *Transfuse Blood* is acceptable as the next step. The automaton also specifies, however, that *Transfuse Blood* is not acceptable if *Get Patient ID* or *Check ID to Patient Match* has not yet been executed. This would cause the automaton to be moved to the error state. Note also that if *Check ID to Patient Match* is followed by *Get Patient ID*, the automaton is moved back into the initial state, from which *Transfuse Blood* again causes a transition to the *ERROR State*. This event sequence occurs if *Check ID to Patient Match* is followed by the throwing of an exception, because the match has failed. The exception is handled by reinvoking the *Check Patient ID* step. Because its first substep is *Get Patient ID*, this repeated execution of *Get Patient ID* indicates that the *Check ID to Patient Match* step has failed and that *Transfuse Blood* is not acceptable now. Automata such as that indicated in Figure 4 were generated with the aid of our Propel system [14], which facilitates the generation of such automata by using a question tree to elicit specifics of the properties. Propel also features a natural language facility to describe the semantics of the automaton in natural English. Note, that for this example there are several other important properties that need to be verified, including one that states that *Check ID to Patient Match* must always be immediately preceded (e.g., no intermediate *Transfuse Blood* events) by *Get Patient ID.*

Once a process and an automaton are defined, using Little-JIL and Propel respectively, we use the FLAVERS finite-state verification system to determine whether any execution of the process could drive the automaton to the error state. While the verification may appear straightforward for this example, we note that even this small example poses serious challenges. The parallel step allows all possible interleavings of substep executions, and the recursive invocation adds further complexity. Finally, the sheer size of the final process (112 steps) makes the verification problem very large. A verifier such as FLAVERS, which employs a number of optimization techniques, is usually able to handle the verification of properties of modest-sized processes such as this one.

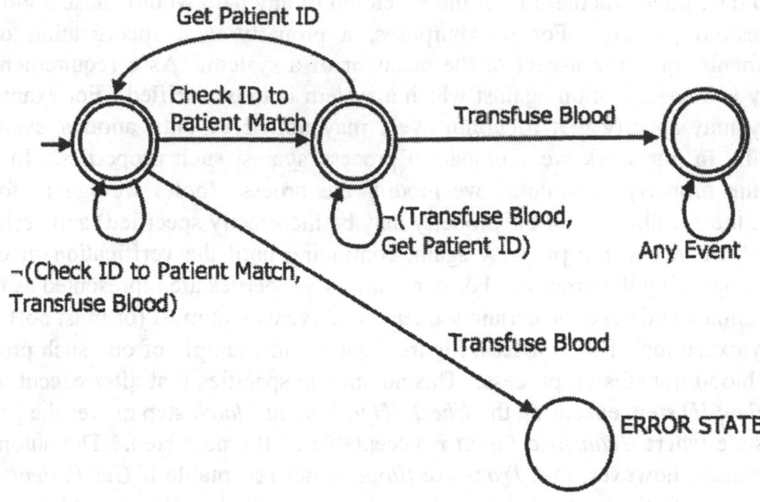

Figure 4: This finite-state automaton requires *Transfuse Blood* to happen only if *Check ID to Patient Match* has executed, but NOT been followed by *Get Patient ID*.

3 Experiences and Evaluation

Our experience in defining and analyzing the blood transfusion process suggests the value in this approach, as it has resulted in detection and correction of process defects. Some of our experiences were as expected, but many were unexpected.

3.1 Process Elicitation

Many process deficiencies were realized just in the interviewing that was necessary to elicit the complete, detailed process. We quickly found that the original process guidelines often did not use terms consistently. For example, we found that a word such as "check" sometimes was used in the same way as the word "verify", but sometimes it had different connotations. Careful elicitation of what was meant, by using Little-JIL to clarify the exact meanings, often led to the desired understandings. This led the medical professionals to examine their terms, to define them more carefully, and to use them more consistently. In doing so, the resulting process definitions left less room for confusion, misunderstanding, and ambiguity.

It was not uncommon for the process guidelines to leave responses to exceptions unspecified. For example, in some cases a process required a "check" for a condition, with the understanding that some alternative processing was necessary if the "check" fails. In many cases, however, the existing process description assumed that check would always succeed and provided little or no guidance about what to do in case of a failure. Here again specifying details of the process quickly raised such issues and led the medical professionals to synthesize responses, thereby improving the process.

We note that the Little-JIL language itself was very helpful in this regard. We found that bundling resource specification, exception management, pre- and post-requisites, and artifact flow together in the definition of a step caused interviewers to ask about each of these issues each time the need for a new step was recognized. In asking such questions as "where is this exception handled?" and "what kind of agent is responsible for execution of this step?" important issues were raised, and significant process improvements were made. We have concluded that a language offering rich semantics can be important in suggesting the absence of important details from a process definition and in suggesting the need for elaboration.

The semantic features of Little-JIL were useful in this work. In particular we found that the facilities for handling exceptions were valuable and generally effective in representing exceptional behavior. The facilities for specifying agent types for each step were also useful and important. As we proceeded with the detailed elaboration of the blood transfusion process, the value of abstraction, scoping, and hierarchy became increasingly apparent. While this example gives only a hint of scaling issues, as our process became larger, the problems posed by increasing size became more apparent. Hierarchy is a well-established device for dealing with scaling issues, and its use in Little-JIL underscored that point. But hierarchy in Little-JIL also incorporates the use of abstraction. Thus, for example, specifying the same step in more than one place causes the elaboration of that step, but Little-JIL's use of scoping causes each elaboration to be done in the context of its enclosing scope(s). The previous example indicated how useful this can be.

Thus our experience suggested that a process definition language should offer facilities for abstraction, scoping, hierarchy, exception management, resource specification, and artifact specification—at the very least. This experience also suggested the value of other features not present in Little-JIL, for example transaction semantics and real-time specification.

Finally it seems important to note that the Little-JIL pictorial notation proved to be quite accessible to the medical professionals. Although we expected to find medical professionals unwilling to learn the semantics and iconography of Little-JIL we discovered that within an hour most were relatively comfortable with the language and were becoming increasingly adept at using its features skillfully.

3.2 Property Elicitation

Our work also indicated the importance of eliciting the properties that are required of the process being elicited. We were especially interested in properties that are stated at a high enough level to apply not just to the specific process we had elicited, but to other processes intended to achieve the same goals. In particular, we would like to use finite-state verification not just to detect possible problems with the existing process but also to evaluate proposed modifications to that process. Our experience demonstrated that property elicitation is valuable additionally as another vehicle for drawing out important process details. We found that it was not uncommon for medical domain experts to specify the details of what they do without having a clear idea of what higher-level goals they are trying to achieve when they perform certain activities in certain ways. By using property specification as a way to place a focus on the goals, motivations, and desiderata for a process, we were often able to cause process performers to think about their processes in a new light, sometimes leading to realizations of possible improvements. In other cases we found that the careful specification of process desiderata, phrased in terms of required or forbidden sequences of steps, led quickly to a realization that some of the steps were missing from the process definition, were misnamed in the process definition, or were used incorrectly in the process definition. Thus, property elicitation also led to improvements in the process. It complemented the focus on "what do you do?" with "why do you do that?" or "what are you really trying to do here?".

We found that Propel was an important aid to the elicitation of precise property specifications. Experience with other projects had demonstrated that it is quite common to specify a property formally in terms of a finite-state automaton or some form of temporal logic, only then to find that important property details were not captured correctly. For example, the property, "A consent form must be signed prior to blood transfusion", leaves unanswered such questions as, "does one consent form suffice for multiple transfusions?" and "can the consent be revoked prior to transfusion?". Propel uses a question tree to automatically pose such questions, thus improving the likelihood that the specified property will correctly reflect the full intent of the person specifying the property. Propel's use on this project supported this conclusion.

3.3 Verification of the Process

Our work on this project is just beginning to employ the FLAVERS finite-state verifier to analyze the blood transfusion process for adherence to some properties. To date we have been able to verify adherence to a small number of properties, most of which have been relatively trivial. There have been numerous verification failures, but most have been due to errors in the process definition itself or the property definition. Although to date we have not yet uncovered serious defects in the process itself, we expect that process defects will start to appear once we begin to verify larger portions of the process and verify them against more stringent properties.

In analyzing larger portions of the process, however, it has become increasingly clear that it is important to employ the services of a reasoning system that can handle this scale. We note that processes, such as blood transfusion, that entail substantial amounts of concurrency and exception handling have accordingly very large execution state spaces, thus making scaling an important issue. Indeed the underlying graph structures that we generated from our process definitions and used as the basis for our finite-state verification often had tens of thousands of nodes and edges. The relative terseness of Little-JIL often serves to mask the size of this state space, but it is this state space that must be explored in order to verify properties.

Our experiences so far suggest that the performance of FLAVERS does seem to scale acceptably well.

4 Related Work

There has been some prior work in using process definition and analysis to improve medical processes. For example, the Protocure II project [15] has goals that are quite similar to ours, but uses a rather different, AI-based, linguistic paradigm for defining processes. Noumeir has also pursued similar goals, but using a notation like UML to define processes [16]. Others (eg. [17]), view medical processes as workflows and use a workflow-like language to define processes and drive their execution. But, we note that these projects seem to place less emphasis on analysis.

There have been other approaches to improving medical safety, as well, but much of the emphasis of this work has been targeted towards quality control measures [5,18], error reporting systems [19], and process automation in laboratory settings [20], such as those where blood products are prepared for administration. In other work, Bayesian belief networks have been used as the basis for discrete event simulations of medical scenarios and to guide treatment planning (eg. [21]).

We note that many languages and diagrammatic notations have been evaluated as vehicles for defining processes. It was suggested that processes be defined using a procedural language [22]. In MARVEL/Oz [23] processes were defined using rules. SLANG [24] used modified Petri Nets to define processes. More recently, the workflow [25] and electronic commerce [26] communities have pursued similar research. This work has shown that some notations aid process understanding, while others provide the semantic rigor needed to support verifying processes to varying degrees of certainty. None, however, seems able to support process definitions that are clear and precise enough. Main failings of these approaches include inadequate specification of exception handling, weak facilities for controlling concurrency, lack of resource management, and inadequate specification of artifact flows.

We also note that there has been a great deal of work on the analysis of software artifacts. Most of this work has been focused on analysis of code or models of systems. Finite-state verification, or model checking, techniques (eg. [8, 9, 27]), work by constructing a finite model that represents all possible executions of the system and then analyzing that model algorithmically to detect executions that violate a particular property specified by the analyst. As noted above one of the major concerns of these techniques is controlling the size of the state-space model, while maintaining precision in the analysis result. Our team has been involved in the analysis and evaluation of various finite-state verification approaches [9], and the development of verifiers such as FLAVERS [9] and INCA [28]. Our work seems to be among the first that has applied FSV approaches to process definitions [10].

5. Extensions of the Work

We have used the blood transfusion process definition to automatically generate a fault tree representation of the process and have used the fault tree to identify single points of failure. This shows the use of process definitions to improve the robustness of a process by identifying and removing single points of failure. Work with chemotherapy processes has confirmed most of the findings stated above. Work with patient flow in the Emergency Department, however, has led to realization of the centrality and complexity of issues pertaining to resources.

We have applied our process improvement approach to processes to a broad range of domains such as labor-management negotiation, elections, and scientific data processing. The work in each domain has shown the need for additional language facilities and a broader research focus, but has confirmed the general applicability of our approach, thus, pointing to the need for interesting complementary work.

In conclusion, we observe that this work has shown considerable promise and has suggested extensions in several directions. We propose to pursue further research in this domain. We expect that this research will lead to notable improvements in the quality of medical processes, and we also expect it to lead to better understandings of how process definition and analysis technology can become key components in the more effective engineering of methods in this critically important domain.

Acknowledgements

This research was supported by the US National Science Foundation under Award Nos. CCR-0204321 and CCR-0205575 and by the U. S. Department of Defense/Army Research Office under Award No. DAAD19-03-1-0133. The U.S. Government is authorized to reproduce and distribute reprints for Governmental purposes notwithstanding any copyright annotation thereon. The views and conclusions contained herein are those of the authors and should not be interpreted as necessarily representing the official policies or endorsements, either expressed or implied, of the U.S. National Science Foundation, U. S. Department of Defense/Army Research Office, or the U.S. Government.

The authors gratefully acknowledge the work of Sandy Wise, who had major responsibility for the development of Little-JIL, as well as Barbara Lerner and Aaron Cass, who also made major contributions. Many students participated in the case studies described here, and major contributions were made by Irene Ros, Ethan Katz-Bassett, Huong Phan, M.S. Raunak, and Dave Miller.

References

1. L.T. Kohn, J.M. Corrigan, M.S. Donaldson (Eds). *To Err is Human: Building a Safer Health System.* Washington, DC: National Academy Press, 1999.

2. P.P. Reid, W.D. Compton, J.H. Grossman, G. Fanjiang (Eds). *Building a Better Delivery System: A new Engineering/Healthcare Partnership.* Nat. Academies Press, Washington. DC, 2005.
3. E.H. Henneman, R.L. Cobleigh, K. Frederick, E. Katz-Bassett, G.A. Avrunin, L.A. Clarke, L.J. Osterweil, C. Andrzejewski, K. Merrigan, P.L. Henneman, Increasing patient Safety and Efficiency in Transfusion Therapy using Formal Process Definitions, *Transfusion Medicine Reviews*, **21**, 1, pp. 49-57, January 2007
4. J.L. Callum, H.S. Kaplan, L.L. Merkley, et.al. Near-miss Event Reporting for Transfusion Medicine: Improving Transfusion Safety, *Transfusion*, **41**,1204-1211, 2001.
5. D. Voak, J.F. Chapman, P. Phillips, Quality of transfusion practice beyond the blood transfusion laboratory is essential to prevent ABO-incompatible death. *Transfusion Medicine* **10**: 95-96, 2000.
6. J. Burgmeier, Failure Mode and Effect Analysis: An Application in Reducing Risk in Blood Transfusion. *Quality Improvement* **28**, 331-339, 2002.
7. B. Chen, G.S. Avrunin, L.A. Clarke, L.J. Osterweil, Automatic Fault Tree Derivation from Little-JIL Process Definitions, SPW/PROSIM 2006, Shanghai, China, May 20-22, 2006, Springer-Verlag LNCS. **3966**, pp. 150-158.
8. A. Cimatti, E. Clarke, E. Giunchiglia, F. Giunchiglia, M. Pistore, M. Roveri, R. Sebastiani, A. Tacchella, NuSMV vers. 2: An Open-Source Tool for Symbolic Model Checking, *Computer Aided Verification Conf.*, Springer-Verlag, 2002, 359-365.
9. M.B. Dwyer, L.A. Clarke, J.M. Cobleigh, G. Naumovich, Flow Analysis for Verifying Properties of Concurrent Software Systems. *ACM Trans. on Software Engineering and Methodology*, **13**(4) 359-430, 2004.
10. J.M. Cobleigh, L.A. Clarke, L.J. Osterweil, Verifying Properties of Process Definitions, *ACM SIGSOFT Intl. Symp. on Software Testing & Analysis*, Portland, OR, ACM Press, 2000:96-101
11. J.V. Linden, K. Wagner, A.E. Voytovich, et.al., Transfusion Errors in New York State: An Analysis of 10 Years' Experience, *Transfusion*, **40** (10), 1207-1213, 2000.
12. A.G. Cass, B.S. Lerner, E.K. McCall, et al. Little-JIL/Juliette: A Process Definition Language and Interpreter, *Intl Conf. on Software Engineering*. Limerick, Ireland, 754-758, 2000.
13. A. Wise, Little-JIL 1.5 Language Report, Lab. for Advanced SW Eng. Research (LASER). Dept. of Comp. Sci., UMass, Amherst, Tech. Report, 2006.
14. R.L. Smith, G.S. Avrunin, L.A. Clarke, L.J. Osterweil, PROPEL: An Approach To Supporting Property Elucidation, 24th Intl. Conf. on Software Engineering, Orlando, FL, 11-21, 2002.
15. A. ten Teije, M. Marcos, M. Balser, J. van Croonenborg, C. Duelli, F. van Harmelen, P. Lucas, S. Miksch, W. Reif, K. Rosenbrand, A. Seyfang, Improving Medical Protocols by Formal Methods. *Artificial Intell. in Medicine*, **36** (3), 193-209, 2006.
16. R. Noumeir, Radiology interpretation process modeling. *Journal of Biomedical Informatics* **39**(2) 103-114, 2006.
17. M. Ruffolo, R. Curio, L. Gallucci, Process Management in Health Care: A System for Preventing Risks and Medical Errors, *Business Process Mgmt.* 334-343 2005.
18. M.L. Foss, S.B. Moore, Evolution of Quality Management: Integration of Quality Assurance Functions Into Operations, or "Quality is Everyone's Responsibility". *Transfusion* **43** 1330-1336, 2003.
19. J.B. Battles, H.S. Kaplan, T.W. van der Schaaf, C.E. Shea, The Attributes of Medical Event Reporting Systems for Transfusion Medicine. *Arch Pathology Laboratory Medicine* **122**, 231-238, 1998.
20. S.A. Galel, C.A. Richards, Practical Approaches to Improve Laboratory Performance and Transfusion Safety, *Am. J. Clinical Pathology* **107** (Suppl 1):S43-S49, 1997.

21. L.C. van der Gaag, S. Renooji, C.L.M. Witteman, B.M.P. Aleman, B.G. Taal, Probabilities for a Probabilistic Network: A Case-Study in Oesophageal Cancer, *Artificial Intelligence in Medicine*, **25**(2), 123-148.
22. S.M. Sutton Jr., D.M. Heimbigner, L.J. Osterweil, APPL/A: A Language for Software-Process Programming, *ACM Trans. on Software Engineering and Methodology*, **4** (3), 221-286, 1995.
23. I.Z. Ben-Shaul, G. Kaiser, A Paradigm for Decentralized Process Modeling and its Realization in the Oz Environment, *16th Intl. Conference on Software Engineering*, 179-188, 1994.
24. S. Bandinelli, A. Fuggetta, C. Ghezzi, Process Model Evolution in the SPADE Environment. *IEEE Transactions on Software Engineering* **19**(12) 1993.
25. S. Paul, E. Park, J. Chaar, RainMan: A Workflow System for the Internet, *Usenix Symposium on Internet Technologies and Systems*, 1997.
26. B. Grosof, Y. Labrou, H.Y. Chan, A Declarative Approach to Business Rules in Contracts: Courteous Logic Programs in XML, *ACM Conf. on Electronic Commerce (EC 99)*, Denver, CO, 68-77, 1999.
27. G. J. Holzmann, *The SPIN Model Checker*, Addison-Wesley, 2004.
28. J.C. Corbett, G.S. Avrunin, Using Integer Programming to Verify General Safety and Liveness Properties, *Formal Methods in System Design*, **6**, 97-123, 1995.

Software Process Improvement Based on the Method Engineering Principles

Marko Bajec, Damjan Vavpotič, Štefan Furlan and Marjan Krisper
University of Ljubljana, Faculty of Computer & Information Science
Trzaska 25, 1000 Ljubljana, Slovenia
{marko.bajec, damjan.vavpotic, stefan.furlan, marjan.krisper}@fri.uni-lj.si

Abstract. While it used to be a common belief that the use of rigorous methods in software development is beneficial if not compulsory to assure success of software development projects, the investigations in practice reveal developers often avoid to follow prescribed methods and that there is a wide gap between the organisations' official methods and the work actually performed by their developers in IT projects. According to the literature, there are many reasons contributing to this rather undesirable situation. The two of them are *rigidity* of methods and their *social inappropriateness*. In the *MasterProc* project we have addressed these issues by developing a framework and tool-support for the reengineering of software development methods. Using the framework an organisation can reengineer its existing ways of working into a method that is *organisation-specific* and *auto-adjustable* to specifics of its projects. The evaluation that was performed in five partner companies is motivating, as it shows the framework can be very useful in improving software development practice. This paper describes the framework philosophy and its main components.

1 Introduction

It was decades ago when the software development became acknowledged as a complex process that needed disciplined methodological approaches. Since then a number of software development methods have emerged. Interestingly, in the last ten years, software development methods are not seen anymore as a panacea for software development and the wave of enthusiasm about their practical value has started to decrease. It has been empirically proved that in real practice the use of methods is actually low (see e.g. [1 – 5]). In the research community, several reasons have been identified as explanatory for this situation (see e.g. [4 – 5]). The two of them that seem to be the most important are: *inflexibility*, which is a characteristic of

---

Please use the following format when citing this chapter:

Bajec, M., Vavpotič, D., Furlan, Š., Krisper, M., 2007, in IFIP International Federation for Information Processing, Volume 244, Situational Method Engineering: Fundamentals and Experiences, eds. Ralyté, J., Brinkkemper, S., Henderson-Sellers B., (Boston Springer), pp. 283-297.

methods that permits virtually no adjustments to specific circumstances (a.k.a. *rigidity*), and *social inappropriateness*, i.e. unsuitability of the prescribed method to the company's actual performance or to the characteristics of the company's development team.

In this paper we present a framework for reengineering software development methods that we have developed under the *MasterProc* project[1]. Building on the established principles of the software process improvement initiatives and specifically of the method engineering, the framework facilitates companies that wish to improve their software development processes with guidelines and tools for acquiring their ways of working, for their continuous improvement, and for their adaptation to circumstances of a particular project or team.

The paper is organised as follows. In Section 2 we describe the research approach adopted in our work. Next is the related works section that briefly describes related research areas and explains how our work fits into this research. The core of the paper is in Sections 4 where the philosophy and main components of the suggested framework are described. The paper ends with concluding remarks and ideas for further work on the subject.

2 Research Method

The MasterProc project was organized as a *collaborative practice research* [6] using a combination of *action research, experiments* and *study practices*. *Interviews* and *surveys* were used to carry out the assessment of the existing state of the art of software development methods in each of the participating software companies. The main focus of the assessment was to determine how socio-technically suitable are the methods for typical projects carried out by each of the software companies. Furthermore, the goal was to identify the level of flexibility of the existing processes. The information that we received from the interviews and surveys was complemented by action research. For each of the participating software companies a working team was set up comprising two researchers and two practitioners. The main responsibility of the team was to take part in real projects to get firsthand information. The practitioners acted as project managers and methodologists, while the researchers were more or less observers.

In the organization of the MasterProc project the principles of a general *learning cycle* have been adopted, i.e. interpret current situation, find ways to improve practice, plan and implement improvements, and learn from the actions taken. The CPR supports such learning cycle by the three goals it identifies: to understand the current state of software development, to build new knowledge that can support practice, and finally to plan changes and implement them as necessary. After implementing the improvements, the interpretation of the lessons learned have to take place, hopefully leading into the next learning cycle.

[1] The MasterProc is a research project which is carried out under the umbrella of the Centre of excellence. The project was co-founded by the Slovenian Ministry of Higher Education, Science and Technology, European Commission and the participating Software Companies.)

3 Related work

The main principles on which we build our research can be found in two autonomous but related research areas: *Software process improvement* (SPI) and *Situational method engineering* (SME). While the main purpose of the SPI is to facilitate the identification and application of changes to the software development process in order to improve the product, the SME primarily deals with developing or tailoring software methods in order to facilitate specific projects and circumstances. The introduction of a specific SME approach into a software company to improve the flexibility of its existing methods can be thus seen as a specific step towards SPI. In this section we shortly describe both research fields and their relation to our work.

3.1 Software Process Improvement

Today, many organisations are trying to adopt models of *total quality management* (TQM) principles. In the software development arena these efforts typically manifest through software process improvement (SPI) initiatives of software companies that strive to improve the quality, safety, and reliability of the software they develop and in this way try to increase productivity and customer satisfaction with their products.

One of the commonly known models in the SPI is the *capability maturity model* (CMM), which represents a central framework for software quality and process improvement (see e.g. [7-8]). The CMM introduces five levels of maturity into which an organisation can fall according to the quality of their software processes. The five levels are: *initial*, *repeatable*, *defined*, *managed* and *optimised*. While in the initial level (level 1) the process is typically ad-hoc and chaotic, the repeatable level (level 2) introduces basic project management processes to track cost, schedule and functionality. The necessary process discipline is in place to repeat earlier successes on projects with similar applications. In level 3 (defined), the software process for both management and engineering activities is documented, standardized and integrated into a standard software process for the organization. All projects use an approved, tailored version of the organization's standard software process for developing and maintaining software. In level 4 (managed), detailed measures of the software process and product quality are collected. Both the software process and products are quantitatively understood and controlled. Finally, in level 5 (optimized), continuous process improvement is enabled by quantitative feedback from the process and from piloting innovative ideas and technologies[2].

In our framework we use CMM as a model against which we evaluate how mature are specific software processes and identify desired maturity levels, i.e. the maturity levels the evaluated organisations want to achieve. Building on the empirical studies that have shown there is a correlation between CMM levels and software quality [9-10], we assume the increased maturity will lead also to the improved software quality. The use of the framework for method reengineering inherently leads to at least level 3 (defined) while it includes also activities, such as constant measurement of success and continuous evaluation and feedback from the

[2] The description of CMM maturity levels is based on [7].

process that can lead to higher levels of CMM maturity, i.e. level 4 (managed) and level 5 (optimised).

3.2 Situational Method Engineering

As described above, if we want to achieve the maturity level 3 or more, all projects must be performed according to an approved, tailored version of the organization's standard software process for developing and maintaining software. This is where SME fits in. In the SME literature, a number of approaches can be found that propose how to create project-specific methods. One that is probably the most popular is based on the so-called *reuse strategy*. In this approach a new method is constructed from the fragments of existing methods. The notion of method fragment was introduced by Harmsen et al [11] who defined it as a reusable part of a method. Fragments can be further categorized into product and process fragments depending on the perspective they cover. Much effort has been put into decomposing existing methods into fragments [12]. Also, different repositories have been proposed for their storage (e.g. [11-13]). The method construction using the reuse strategy is, however, far from easy, as the fragments have to be first retrieved from the repository, changed if necessary and than assembled together into one consistent and congruent method.

Another approach to SME, known from the literature as the *extension-based approach*, uses the *extension strategy*. In this approach, method engineers are provided with extension patterns that help them to identify typical extension situations and provide guidance to perform extensions. In [13], Ralyté describes two possible ways to perform extensions: (a) directly through matching extension patterns stored in a library to satisfy the extension requirements, and (b) indirectly through first selecting a meta-pattern corresponding to the extension domain and then guiding the extension applying the patterns suggested by the meta-pattern. Karlsson and Ågerfalk have, however, criticized this approach for not considering situations that are actually very frequent in practice, i.e. when a method is both extended in some fragments and reduced in others [14]. As a solution they proposed a new method for SME that uses a combination of the cancellation and extension operators. They named it *method for method configuration* (MMC). The MMC differs from the aforementioned approaches also in the fact that it does not deal with modular construction of a method but rather with method tailoring taking a particular method as the starting point. From the literature, it is clear that this approach has been somewhat overlooked by the method engineering research in the past.

Finally, the approach to SME that seems to be a result of the most recent efforts in the method engineering research is the *paradigm-based approach* [13] a.k.a. *evolution-based approach* [15]. This approach is founded on the idea that the new method can be obtained either by abstracting from an existing model or by instantiating a metamodel. A new method is then created by first constructing a product model and then process model while for the construction of both product and process model different strategies are available.

For the purpose of our framework we created our own approach to SME which uses a combination of the meta-modelling and extension/reduction based approaches.

The approach shares several commonalities with other approach to SME, but most notably with MMC. Both, our approach and MMC suggest configuring an existing method rather then assembling fragments from different methods to construct a new one. Detailed description as well as comparison between our approach and other SME approaches can be found in [16].

4 A framework for method reengineering

The idea that lies behind the framework for reengineering software development methods is relatively simple. It is based on the assumption that in each software development company, patterns of work could be found that tell how the company is developing software. While a large percentage of software companies own some kind of formalized methods (typically commercial methods), empirical investigations show that what they really do on IT projects differs a lot from what is written in the methods they own (e.g. [4, 17]). Our assumption in the suggested framework is that in a typical software company the ways of working are sufficiently repeatable to be captured into a formalized method (*base method*) reflecting how the company actually performs its IT projects. If base methods are captured and represented in the way we suggest in this paper then project-specific methods can be created on-the-fly almost without any need for method engineers to intervene. This is done by processing the rules that define, for each method component, in what circumstances its use is *compulsory*, *advisable* or *discouraged*. The configuration process is however interactive. The questions that are subjective in their nature and influenced by particular developers involved in the project can be addressed when they arise and users may intervene as they wish.

The framework consists of four distinct but related phases: (I) *Method Construction*, (II) *Method Configuration*, (III) *Method Use* and (IV) *Method Evaluation and Improvement*. In the remaining part of this section each of the phases will be described in more detail.

4.1 Method Construction

Method construction is probably the most important phase of the method reengineering framework and a prerequisite for the other phases. Its aim is to construct a base method that will provide formal description of how the organization that is being analyzed is performing its project. Furthermore, the construction of a base method is crucial as it presents a foundation for creating project-specific methods on-the-fly. Due to the limits of space we will provide here only a brief description of the main activities of the method construction process. For details please refer to [17] and [16].

The construction of a base method is a process that has to be done for each organization individually. It starts with the analysis of existing practice in the company and leads into identification of the parts that are technically and socially sound and those that are in these respects problematical. For the analysis of the socio-technical suitability of the existing practice an evaluation model has been designed that facilitates the evaluation [18]. Possible improvements to the existing practice are then suggested and discussed with the company's development team. Once the vision for the new method is developed and accepted, a *metamodel* is designed that helps to formalize the method. The metamodel can be developed either from scratch or from existing metamodels that have been recently constructed to both underpin and to help formalize methods. Those represent a good source for selecting generic concepts for method formalization. Finally, the metamodel is instantiated and fragments of the base method are captured. Besides the fragments of the existing practice that have been previously approved as technically and social appropriate, many new fragments may emerge. These are based on the suggestions for improvements that have been identified within the analysis of the existing practice. The fragments are first classified according to the underlying metamodel and then described using templates. The templates, which belong to the metamodel, outline how elements of a certain metamodel type should be described.

For the purpose of representing a base method we designed a generic data structure that can be used to underpin any metamodel. The idea of a generic data structure is to allow method engineers to design metamodels according to their perception of how their methods should be formally represented.

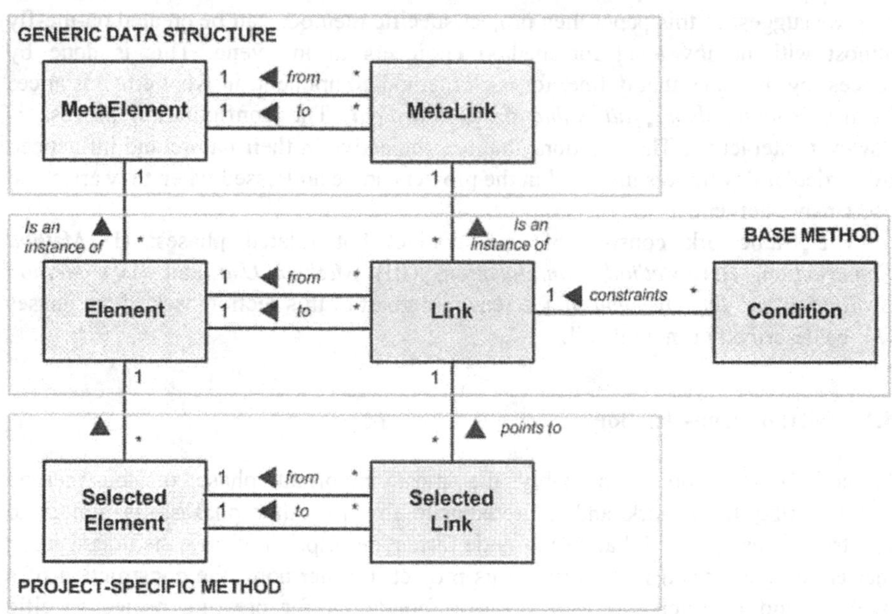

Fig. 1. A generic data structure

Fig. 1 illustrates the main components of the aforementioned *generic data structure*, *base method* and *project-specific method*. The classes representing metamodel are: a *metaelement* (it can be of two types: *content element*, such as activity, tool, discipline, role, etc. or *process flow element*, such as decision node, join and synchronization) and *metalink* (links between metaelements). By using such a generic data structure, a base method is represented as a structure of instances of the metaelements and metalinks, and a project-specific method is represented as a selection of the elements and links of the base method.

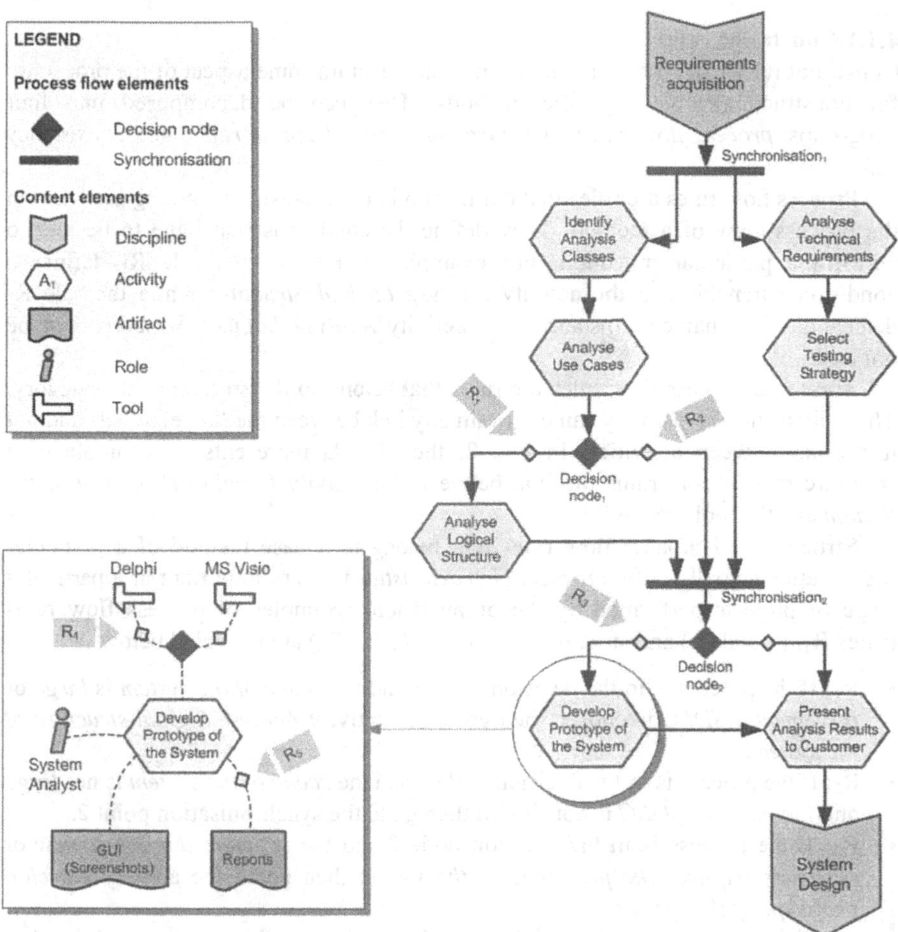

Fig. 2. Representation of a base method

As mentioned before, a base method encompasses various situations that may occur when projects are performed. In other words, it comprises a number of elements and their alternatives which describe several possible ways to perform a particular project (similar to *project paths* as defined by Hares [12]). The paths and method structure, however, are not static. They are defined by the rules that tell which elements to consider in specific circumstances and consequently which path to take. As depicted in Fig. 1, rules apply directly to the links that bind elements of the method (see the element *Condition*).

Besides the rules that put constraints on the links between elements of the method there are also other types of rules that play important role in the suggested framework. In general, they can be categorised into *constraint rules* and *facts*. Since in configuring the base method for the needs of a particular project or situation these rules play essential role we will explain their taxonomy in more detail.

4.1.1 Constraint rules

Constraint rules can be seen as assertions that constrain some aspect of the procedure for constructing project-specific methods. They can be decomposed into four subgroups: *process flow rules*, *structure rules*, *completeness rules*, and *consistency rules*.

Process flow rules are rules that define conditional transitions among activities in the process view of a method. They define the conditions that have to be met to perform a particular transition. For example, in Fig. 2., the rule R_1 defines a conditional transition to the activity *Analyse Logical Structure* while the rule R_2 determines in what circumstances the activity *Analyse Logical Structure* can be omitted.

Similar to process flow rules are rules that belong to the structure rule category. Their distinction is that they can constrain any link between method elements and not just links between activities. In Fig. 2, the rule R_4 represents an example of a structure rule. It constrains the link between the activity *Develop Prototype of the System* and the tool *MS Visio*.

Structure and process flow rules that belong to a base method of a particular organisation actually define *project characteristics* that are important at a particular stage of projects performed by the organisation. Examples of process flow rules (rules R_1, R_2 and R_3) and structure rules (rule R_4 and R_5) are provided below[3].

- R_1: If the process is in the decision node *1* and the *scope of the system* is *large* or *incremental SDLC* is chosen then go to the activity *Analyse logical structure of the system.*
- R_2: If the process is in the decision node *1* and the *scope of the system* is not *large* and *incremental SDLC* is not chosen then go to the synchronisation point *2*.
- R_3: If the process is in the decision node *2* and the *problem domain* is *new* or *customer requires the prototype of the system* then go to the activity *Develop prototype of the system.*
- R_4: If the process is in the activity *Develop prototype* of the system and the *time frame for producing the prototype* is *more than 1 month* then develop the prototype of the system using *Delphi tool.*
- R_5: If the process is in the activity *Develop prototype of the system* and *important reports are to be developed* then create output artifact *Reports* as a part of the prototype.

Project characteristics, such as *project length*, *project risk*, *project complexity*, *the scope of the system*, *the number of parties involved*, etc. and their respective domains are defined within the organisation's base method. However the values that

[3] The rules are here written in natural language to ensure their understanding.

these characteristics receive are project-specific and are thus defined during the configuration process.

Besides process flow rules and structure rules that both put constraints on associations between elements of a base method the constraint rule category comprises also *completeness* and *consistency rules*. The purpose of these two subcategories is to assure that each project-specific method, created from the elements of a base method, is complete and consistent.

Completeness rules apply – in contrast to the process flow rules and structure rules – to a metamodel and not to a base method (see Fig. 1). Their responsibility is to define the conditions that must be met when creating a project-specific method. Completeness rules actually help to check whether a project-specific method that has been created includes all required components. For example, an organisation may decide the following rules have to be followed when creating methods for projects:

- R_6: each *activity* except the last one must have at least one *successor activity*.
- R_7: each *activity* must be linked with exactly one *role*.
- R_8: each *technique* must be linked with at least one *tool*, etc.

Consistency rules are the last category in the group of constraints. They are similar to completeness rules. Their goal is to assure that the selection of fragments comprising a project-specific method is consistent. While completeness rules only apply to elements that are linked together, consistency rules deal with interdependency between any two elements. In other words, for each element e they determine a set of other elements *E* that need to be included into a project-specific method if *e* is included. In the example below the rule R_9 asserts that *the deliverable Business model is dependent on the activity Business modelling*.

- R_9: The deliverable *Business Model* depends on the activity *Business modelling*.

This means that if the deliverable Business model is selected for the inclusion into a project-specific method, the activity Business modelling has to be selected too. While such a dependency may seem trivial it is important as it helps to avoid conflicting situations.

4.1.2 Facts

Another important group of rules that are considered during the configuration process are facts. Facts are assertions that define characteristics of the project for which we create a project-specific method. Depending on how they define project characteristics they can be classified into *base facts* or *derived facts*. Base facts define project variables directly while derived facts are derived from base facts using inferences or calculations. In the examples below, the rule R_{10} is a base fact while the rule R_{11} is a derived fact.

- R_{10}: The *project domain* is *well known.*
- R_{11}: If the *project field* is *telecommunications or healthcare* then the *project domain* is *well known.*

In the method configuration process facts are very important as they are checked when structure and process flow rules are processed. For example, a structure rule might state that “when performing requirements validation there is no need to produce a prototype if the problem domain is well known". To be able to perform this rule we must first check the facts about the project domain to find out whether the domain is well known or not.

As indicated in the examples of the constraint rule category (see e.g. rules R_3 or R_5) facts can describe virtually any condition that is important for the project. Furthermore, they are created dynamically during the method configuration process. For example, when an element *e* is selected to be included into a project-specific method this becomes a fact (*e is selected*) which could become important latter on in the method configuration process.

4.2 Method configuration and use

Once a base method has been successfully established and discussed with its users it is ready for use. However before it is actually applied to a specific project or situation it has to be configured so that it includes only the components that are relevant to the situation in question. At this point the representation of a base method that was described before reveals its value. With an appropriate tool the adjustment can be done automatically. In this section we describe the algorithms that facilitate the auto-adjustment process.

The algorithm that supports the method configuration process is relatively simple. It starts with an element in the base method (typically this would be a starting activity) and ends when there is no link that would connect the current element further with any other element. If such links are found they are examined for constraints they might have. When a particular link has no constraints or when constraints exist but are satisfied than the element at the end of that link is processed in the same way using recursion.

```
PROCEDURE CreateProjectMethod(pm,e);
//pm - project method, e - starting element of the base method
BEGIN
  Find links for the element e
  For each Link l
     IF conditions are satisfied for the link l
     THEN
       Mark the output element of the Link l as selected for the pm
       Mark the link l as selected for the pm
       CreateProjectMethod(output element of the Link l,pm)//recursion
       END IF
  NEXT
END;
```

When a project-specific method is created using the algorithm above, the elements that have been selected has to be checked for consistency and completeness. The verification algorithms below show how this can be done.

```
PROCEDURE CheckCompletness (pm);
```

```
// pm - project method
BEGIN
  //completeness verification
  Select all links from the pm
  For each Link l
       //Check the completeness constraint for the link l
       Count the links that connect the input element of the Link l with the
output    elements of the same type as is the output element of the
Link l
    IF the number of links is outside the min, max limits
    THEN mark the Link l as problematical.
  NEXT;
END;

PROCEDURE CheckConsistency (pm, e);
// pm - project method, e - starting element or
// link of the project-specific method
BEGIN
  //consistency verification
  Select the set of elements and links D that e is dependent on
  For each element or link d from D
       IF d is not selected THEN Mark d as problematical
       CheckConsistency(pm, d) //recursion
  NEXT;
END;
```

For detailed description on the process configuration approach, its comparison with other SME approaches, as well as on the experiences with its application in practice, please see [16].

4.3 Method evaluation and improvement

In the suggested framework it is essential that the underlying base method and corresponding rules continuously evolve as a reflection of knowledge and experiences acquired through project performance. This means that when using the framework new fragments may emerge as a result of situations that are specific and thus not yet supported by a current base method. In such cases, additional fragments are captured and circumstances for their use are determined. In practice, it actually takes some time for a base method to become *all-inclusive* in terms of providing guidelines for all kinds of situations that may happen in projects a particular company is performing. This phase, in which the base method rapidly evolves, is called the *learning phase*. It takes place in the first few projects after the framework has been introduced into a company. Eventually however, the base method would become more stable and changes on a large scale less frequent.

For the aforementioned reasons the framework provides specific activities for the continuous method evaluation and improvement. To retain social and technical suitability base methods are regularly evaluated and improved. The evaluation is performed on a level of a single method element, which enables precise identification of less suitable method elements, determination of reasons for their unsuitability and creation of improvements consequentially.

The evaluation activities are based on the *method evaluation model*. Although various method evaluation models have been proposed in the past, they tend to consider either only technical [19 – 21] or only social [22 – 24] dimension of a method. However, such partial evaluation does not provide a complete understanding of method's suitability. Therefore, an *evaluation model* was created that facilitates simultaneous evaluation of method suitability on a *social* and *technical dimension*. The social dimension focuses on method's suitability for social and cultural characteristics of a development team and facilitates determination of the level of method's adoption. The technical dimension considers suitability of a method for technical characteristics of a project and an organization, and helps to determine the level of method's efficiency.

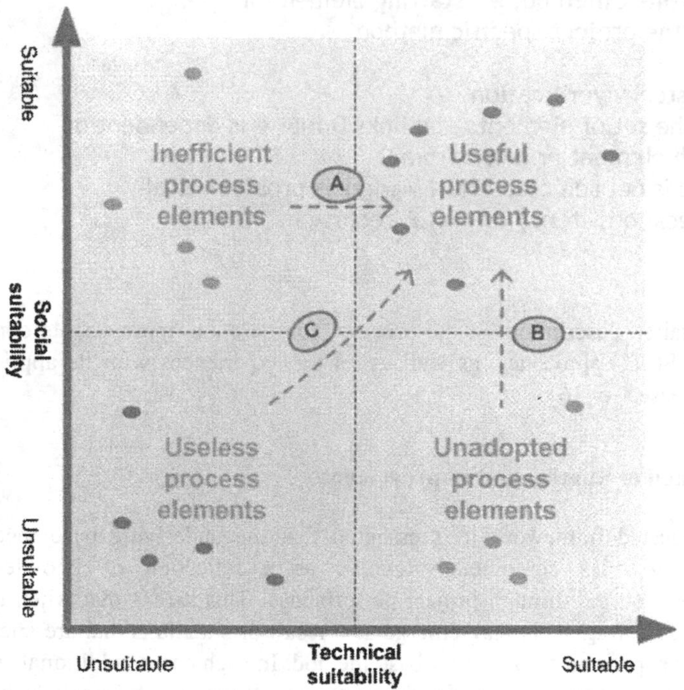

Fig. 3. Application of the evaluation model

Fig. 3 depicts application of the evaluation model in practice. After an evaluation is completed, all method elements are positioned in a scatter plot diagram that is divided into four quadrants distinguishing between four different types of method elements (regarding their value):

- A *useless method element* is both technically and socially unsuitable. Different reasons for such unsuitability can be identified. For instance, unsuitability can be caused by constant technology change that eventually renders a method element technically unsuitable. Consequently, developers stop using the element, which finally results in its complete unsuitability. Alternatively, an element might have been technically unsuitable from the beginning and therefore never used.
- An *inefficient method element* is socially suitable, but does not suit technical needs of a project or an organisation. For instance, these can be method elements that have been technically suitable in preceding projects and are well adopted among users, but are technically inappropriate for the current project.
- In contrast to an inefficient element, an *unadopted method element* is technically suitable, but its potential users do not use it because it is socially unsuitable. Many reasons why potential users do not adopt a technically efficient method element can be identified. The element might be overwhelmingly complex, it might be difficult to present advantages of its use to the potential users, it might be incompatible with existing user experience and knowledge, etc.
- A *useful method element* is socially and technically suitable. Such method element is adopted among its users and suits technical needs of the project and the organisation.

A method element that is perceived as not suitable can be improved by using different *improvements scenarios.* These depend on the quadrant where the element is positioned. In case of an *inefficient method element* (see Fig. 3, arrow A.), its technical suitability should be improved and social suitability retained. Since users already adopted the element, it should be modified only to the extent that it becomes technically efficient again. In case of an *unadopted but technically suitable method element* (see Fig. 3, arrow B.), the causes for element's rejection among its potential users should be explored. For instance, potential users of the element might lack knowledge and experience to use it. Consequentially the improvement should focus on training of element's potential users rather than on altering the element. In case of a *useless element* (see Fig. 3, arrow C.) that is both socially and technically unsuitable the most reasonable action would be to replace or discard it completely. Most likely a technically and/or socially more suitable element can be found or the element is not needed at all.

After application of improvement scenarios most method elements are expected to move to useful method elements quadrant, though some of the elements might still need further improvements or even replacement.

Two distinctive qualities of the proposed model can be identified. Firstly, it simultaneously considers social and technical suitability of a method; and secondly, it facilitates evaluation on a scale of a single method element. These allow a software development organization to observe value of its method in detail, to identify technically and/or socially inappropriate parts, and to create customized improvement scenarios based on the evaluation of each method element. For the detailed information on the method evaluation model please see [18] and [25].

5 Conclusions and further work

In this paper we presented a framework for reengineering software development methods. Using the framework organisations can reengineer their existing ways of working and establish formalised methods that are *organisation-specific* and *auto-adjustable* to specifics of their projects.

In respect to the method engineering field the contribution of the framework should be seen in the integration of the method engineering principles within the software process improvement scenario. This way we assure the improved methods are not rigid but adjustable to specific circumstances. Furthermore, the framework encapsulates activities for continuous method evaluation and improvement based on the organisation's technical and social characteristics. Specifically the latter have been very often neglected by the traditional approaches to method engineering.

There are several directions in which we tend to continue the existing research work. Firstly, we wish to extend the framework to cover not only the creation and configuration of software development processes but rather arbitrary IT processes or even business processes. The research on this subject has started and is reported in a separate paper submitted to this conference. Next, we wish to improve the framework by incorporating a repository of best practices in software development which will facilitate (following assembly-based method engineering principles) semi-automatic creation of base methods. Finally, our goal is to employ the framework, specifically the method configuration phase, in the research project aimed at software development in rapidly created virtual teams.

6 References

1. C. J. Hardy, J. B. Thompson, and H. M. Edwards, The use, limitations and customization of structured systems development methods in the UK, Information and Software Technology, 37(9), 467-477 (1995).
2. M. Huisman and J. Iivari, The individual deployment of systems development methods, Lecture Notes in Computer Science, (Springer 2348, 134-150, 2002).
3. M. Huisman and J. Iivari, The organizational deployment of systems development methods, Information Systems Development: Advances in Methods, Components, and Management, (Kluwer 87-99, 2003).
4. B. Fitzgerald, An empirical investigation into the adoption of systems development methods, Information & Management, 34(6) 317-328 (1998).
5. P. Middleton, Managing information system development in bureaucracies, Information and Software Technology. 41(8), 473-482 (1999).
6. L. Mathiassen, Collaborative practice research. Information Technology and People, 15, 321-345 (2002).
7. M.C. Paulk, B. Curtis, M. B. Chrisis, C. V. Weber, Capability Maturity Model for Software, version 1.1, CMU/SEI-93-TR-24, February, Software Engineering Institute (1993).
8. R. S. Pressman, Software Engineering: A Practitioner's Approach. McGraw-Hill, New York (2004).
9. D. E. Harter, M. S. Krishnan, S. A. Slaughter, Effects of process maturity on quality, cycle time, and effort in software projects. Management Science April 46 (4), 451 (2000).

10.M. J. Parzinger, R. Nath, R., A study of the relationships between total quality management implementation factors and software quality. *Total Quality Management* 11 (3), 353–371 (2000).
11. F. Harmsen, S. Brinkkemper, and H. Oei, Situational Method Engineering for IS Project Approaches, in: Methods and Associated Tools for the IS Life Cycle, edited by A. Verrijn-Stuart and T. W. Olle (Elsevier, 1994), pp. 169 – 194.
12. S. Brinkkemper, K. Lyytinen, and R. J. Welke, Method engineering: principles of method construction and tool support. Conf. on Principles of Method Construction and Tool Support, selected papers. Edited by S. Brinkkemper, K. Lyytinen, and R. J. Welke, (Kluwer Academic Publishers, Boston, MA, 1996).
13. J. Ralyté, R. Deneckère, and C. Rolland, Edited by J. Eder et al, Towards a generic model for situational method engineering (CAiSE 2003), Klagenfurt, Austria, June 16-18, 2003, (Springer, Haidelberg, 2003), pp 95-110.
14. F. Karlsson, and P. J. Ågerfalk, Method configuration: adapting to situational characteristics while creating reusable assets, *Information and Software Technology*, 46(9), 619-633 (2004).
15. M. B. Ayed, J. Ralyte, C. Rolland, Constructing the Lyee method with a method engineering approach, *Knowledge-Based Systems* 17(7-8), 239-248 (2004).
16. M. Bajec, D. Vavpotič, M. Krisper, Practice-driven approach for creating project-specific software development methods, *Information and Software Technology*, 49(4), 345-365 (2007).
17. M. Bajec, D. Vavpotič, and M. Krisper, The scenario and tool-support for constructing flexible, people-focused systems development methodologies, in: Proc. ISD'04, Vilnius, Lituania, (2004).
18. D. Vavpotič, M. Bajec, M. Krisper, Measuring and improving software development method value by considering technical and social suitability of its constituent elements, in: Advances in theory, practice and education: proc. of the 13th Inter. Conf. on IS Development, edited by O. Vasilecas, J. Zupančič, (Technika, Vilnius, 2004), pp. 228-238.
19. CMU/SEI-2002-TR-029, Capability Maturity Model ® Integration (CMMISM), Version 1.1. SEI., (2002)
20. ISO/IEC-15504, Information technology – software process assessment, (1998)
21. ISO/IEC-FCD-9126-1, Software product quality – Part 1: Quality model, (1998)
22. E. M. Rogers, Diffusion of innovations, (Free Press, New York, 2003).
23. I. Ajzen, The Theory of Planned Behavior, *Organizational Behavior and Human Decision Processes*, 50, 179-211 (1991).
V. Venkatesh, and F. D. Davis, A theoretical extension of the Technology Acceptance Model: Four longitudinal field studies, *Management Science* 46(2), 186-204 (2000).
24. D. Vavpotič, M. Bajec, M. Krisper, Scenarios for improvement of software development methodologies, in: Advances in information systems development. Vol. 1, Bridging the gap between academia and industry, edited by A.G. Nilsson, R. Gustas, W. Wojtkowski, W.G. Wojtkowski, S. Wrycza and J. Zupancic, (Springer, New York, 2006), pp. 278-288.

Defining a Scope for COTS Selection Methods

Fredy Navarrete, Pere Botella and Xavier Franch
Universitat Politècnica de Catalunya
{fjnavarrete, botella, franch}@lsi.upc.edu
http://www.lsi.upc.edu/~gessi

Abstract. The specification of a methodology defines a set of procedures and techniques that are associated to a specific domain. As part of this specification, it is advisable to establish a scope that allows identifying the set of roles and activities that should be covered to develop a life-cycle for a specific domain. If such a scope is not clearly defined in a methodology, some problems may arise, e.g., the set of roles in charge of carrying out the processes may lack of coordination, cooperation, and communication during the development of the life-cycle for the domain. In the Commercial Off-The-Shelf (*COTS*) components selection domain, there are currently different methodologies which define procedures and techniques to select or to license a COTS component from the marketplace. The application of these COTS selection methods results in processes that are different from usual development ones, yielding to new activities and responsibilities that should be defined in a scope which covers the interactions of specialized roles. However it may be observed that these methods do not put emphasis neither on the identification of these roles, nor on their subsequent interactions, nor on their combination to form a selection team. Furthermore, activities differ from one method to another. The contribution of this work is to define a scope for COTS selection processes, identifying and defining the undertaken activities, the roles that take place, their interactions and their responsibilities, and to organize a life-cycle around them. We use a goal-oriented approach, the *i** notation, and a framework to model the engineering process, the OPEN Process Framework (*OPF*), with the purpose of issuing a well-defined work team that can adapt itself to the internal processes of a particular organization.

1 Introduction

Commercial Off-The-Shelf (COTS) components are software components that may be purchased or licensed from the marketplace [13]. COTS-based systems require some specific software activities, and among them COTS components selection play a crucial role [14]. In some previous work [1, 2], we studied some of the most widespread COTS selection methods (CARE [3], SCARLET [4], OTSO [5], EPIC

Please use the following format when citing this chapter:

Navarrete, F., Botella, P., Franch, X., 2007, in IFIP International Federation for Information Processing, Volume 244, Situational Method Engineering: Fundamentals and Experiences, eds. Ralyté, J., Brinkkemper, S., Henderson-Sellers B., (Boston Springer), pp. 298-312.

[6], STACE [7], PECA [8]) with the purpose of analyzing if the agile principles and values briefed in the agile manifesto [9] influence them. We observed in this analysis that neither the human factor, nor the conformation of a selection team, were clearly defined within the processes suggested by those methods. But in fact, even a more relevant observation not specifically bound to this agile perspective, was concluding that COTS selection projects need specific roles and new activities to support a successful selection [10] but that in fact we may say that current methods either do not address this issue because they emphasise the analysis of the artifacts generated during the process, or they just outline some general recommendations but do not provide a comprehensive framework.

To tackle this point, we may recall that a methodology specifies a set of procedures, techniques, rules, and postulates employed by a discipline [11] which influences the development of a specific domain. In [12], Cockburn proposes to use structural terms (*Process, Milestones, Quality, Activities, Teams, Products, Techniques, Roles, Standards, Tools, Skills, Personality* and *Team Values*) to embrace a methodology to be applied to any team endeavour. Some of these structural elements are defined by a specific *Scope*. Cockburn defines the scope of a methodology as: *...consists of the range of roles and activities that it attempts to cover* [12]. Then, he characterizes the scope of a methodology along three axes:

- o *Role coverage:* describes the set of roles that fall into the coverage of a methodology.
- o *Activity coverage:* defines which activities of a specific project fall into the coverage of the roles in a methodology.
- o *Life-cycle coverage:* mainly, specifies the coverage of a methodology over a life-cycle in a specific project.

Therefore, our attempt to clarify which are the roles, activities and life-cycle specifities in the domain of COTS components selection, may be rephrased as identifying and defining a scope for COTS selections methods, and this is the goal of our paper. Building such a scope requires taking into account the concrete roles and the main activities that must be assigned to cover a life-cycle of COTS selection processes. To define formally a scope for COTS selection methods, we have started by modelling COTS selection processes in a high level, to identify their main activities. We have used a process-focussed OO methodology, the OPEN Process Framework (*OPF*) [15], to formalize these activities. Next, we have identified the roles proposed by current COTS selection methods, describing some activities that they do not cover. Next, we have used a widespread goal-oriented notation, the *i** framework [16], to put together the roles conforming a selection team, and to state the interactions among these roles, and also among the selection team and its environment, obtaining a scope from a highly strategic perspective. Finally, we have considered the life-cycle perspective in order to complete the scope.

2 The Activity Dimension in the COTS Selection Scope

In some recent work [2] we have identified the most relevant processes that appear during COTS selection methods, we have decomposed these processes into tasks, and finally we grouped these tasks into five categories. We summarize the result in this section.

2.1 Market Exploration

The COTS marketplace is composed of different kinds of technology segments from which COTS components are acquired or licensed. Currently, we may find a significant quantity of COTS information from the marketplace. Nevertheless, the market dynamics and continuous updates of COTS components, makes this information obsolete quickly. For this reason, we need selecting the necessary information produced in the market exploration process taking into account the provider information, the COTS component features themselves, and other aspects that we can reuse. In Table 1, we summarize the main activities undertaken in the market exploration process.

Table 1. MARKET EXPLORATION ACTIVITIES

Activities	Description
Candidate Component Identification	It identifies the candidate components from the market, classifying them into suitable categories and domains that fit to main requirements of the problem at hand.
Candidate Component Solution Identification	It identifies ensembles of related COTS components from the marketplace that conform to the required type of system.
Candidate Vendor Analysis	This task analyzes the main aspects of vendors from the marketplace.
Component Vendor Monitoring	Monitoring COTS vendors helps to establish relationships with mutual benefit in which users and vendors work together with each other.

2.2 Requirements Engineering

Requirements engineering applied to COTS projects heavily depends on the dynamics and evolution of the components available from the marketplace. The processes and technical tools that we use to steer the elicitation and specification of requirements must try to adapt user needs to the real state of marketplace. In table 2, we describe the main tasks involved in COTS requirements engineering.

2.3 System Architecture Analysis

Before integrating a component from the marketplace into a specific information system, we must consider the constraints, restrictions and composition of the system architecture. For this reason, we need a system description to know the main features over which we integrate the new components. In Table 3, we describe the five main activities that take part of the system architecture process.

Table 2. REQUIREMENT ENGINEERING ACTIVITIES

Activities	Description
Requirements Elicitation	This task comprises the set of activities necessary to carry out the requirements formulation. Therefore, activities such as to identify properly the user requirements, to hold a continuous requirements analysis, and to negotiate the requirements with user representatives, are essential activities in COTS projects to maintain the system architecture integrity, to understand the user needs, and to seek suitable components from the marketplace.
Business Analysis	It specifies the set of tasks necessary to compare the user requirements against organizational goals. For this reason, the market analysis is performed, identifying the suitable providers, analyzing the specific market technology segment where the organization technology is developed. Furthermore, user goals are analyzed throughout the COTS project to preserve the user vision.
Requirements Management	It includes the set of activities needed to manage properly user requirements; for example, activities to negotiate, to store and to control requirements are proposed.
Vision	This requirements engineering task produces and documents the vision of user representatives about a required component.

Table 3. SYSTEM ARCHITECTURE ACTIVITIES

Activities	Description
Architecture Reuse	It is focused on seeking reusable elements and artefacts within the system architecture. In order to carry out this task, we need an architecture description timely updated.
Architecture Prototyping	Considering this task can help us to support and validate the decisions that can impact over the system architecture
Architecture Production	This task identifies the set of features that compose the system architecture, determining their advantages, restrictions, and constraints against the user requirements.
Architecture Documentation	The purpose of this task is gathering the architecture information that we must store to obtain the component that we can reuse, and the added functionality of the system components
Architecture Integrity Assurance	This task preserves the architecture integrity to be not violated when we select or we integrate a new component in the system architecture

2.4 Candidate Component Evaluation

As suggested in previous categories, we can find different components in the marketplace that adjust to user requirements. The evaluation process must take into account techniques and tools that help to discriminate between the different options. The team that steers component evaluation must have either knowledge or experience in the component domain under evaluation. Therefore, the team members must be able to handle technical tools; besides, they must have a good understanding of the users' needs to evaluate components according to them. In Table 4, we describe the main tasks performed in candidate component evaluation.

Table 4. CANDIDATE COMPONENT EVALUATION ACTIVITIES

Activities	Description
Candidate Component Evaluation	Its responsibility is evaluating the COTS candidate component features with respect to user requirements.
Candidate Solution Component Evaluation	Ensembles of COTS candidate components which may be part of the possible final solution are evaluated.
Business Impact Analysis	This task analyzes the impact of component candidates over objectives of the business.
Candidate Vendor Analysis	This represents the main aspects of possible vendors, which influence component evaluation criterion.

2.5 Component Selection

We need considering different criteria to choose a suitable component, because neither the most expensive component nor the cheapest one are necessarily the most advisable components to integrate into the information system. There are a lot of aspects that play a crucial role when selecting a candidate component, such as the contract, the component aggregated functionality, the verification of the functionality offered by the COTS vendor and the integration ability, among other factors. In Table 5, we describe briefly the main tasks that are part of selection processes.

Table 5. COMPONENT SELECTION ACTIVITIES

Activities	Description
Component Vendor Monitoring	It represents the set of tasks to control and monitor the vendor representative in the selection processes and component integration.
Component Monitoring	It undertakes the tasks to control the component performance during the evaluation processes and selection. Besides, it proposes the control of future versions and releases of selected components.
Business Process Modification	Its responsibility is measuring the impact of selected components over the business goals.
Component Selection	It comprises the set of tasks for discarding or selecting the candidate components that are part of the possible final solution
Update Definition of System Architecture	This definition is relevant to maintain updated the changes of the system architecture when the COTS components are selected for integration.

3 The Role Dimension in the COTS Selection Scope

After addressing the activity dimension of the scope, we cope with roles. The situation is fairly different. Nowadays, the most used COTS selection methods have their own set of practices and suggested processes and activities. But as we have pointed out in previous work [1], these methods do not fully succeed in considering individual motivations, as well as in defining the human factor, within their suggested processes. In fact, building a work team is considered a secondary aspect in conventional methodologies [19]. Although a set of roles is included in some methods, they are more focused on the artifacts produced by the roles than on the formalization of the specific scope and the composition of the team in which all the roles will develop their activities. In table 6 we summarize the most relevant statements about COTS selection roles found in these approaches [3, 6, 8, 20], complementing them with some roles specified in the RUP-for-COTS proposal:, for lack of space we have highlighted some roles that take part in the selection processes and that not overlap with other roles [21].

Table 6. DEFINITION OF ROLES IN SEVERAL COTS SELECTION METHODS

COTS Method	Roles Suggested
CARE [3]	"Requirements engineer: complete and correct description of users needs with a technical background"
	"Software architect: defining the outline for the software architecture and defining the baseline software architecture"
	"Engineer component: maintaining the component repository"
	"Component vendor: complete and correct information about the component products"
IEEE 1062 Software Acquisition Standard [20]	"Acquirer: a person or organization that acquires or procures a system or software product (which may be part of a system) from a supplier"
	"Developer: a person or organization that performs development activities (including requirements analysis, design, testing through acceptance) during the life cycle process"
	"Supplier: a person or organization that enters into a contract with the acquirer for the supply of a software product (which may be part of a system) under the terms of the contract"
EPIC [6, 21]	"Acquirer: identify relevant COTS packages and vendors"
	"System architect: oversees the entire system and all factors that might affect its development"
	"Designer: specify the COTS package configuration requirements"
	"Data designer: ...mapping between the data sources and the target databases..."
PECA [8]	"Evaluator: should have technical experience"
	"Charter: defines the scope and constrains of the evaluation"
	"Evaluation stakeholders: are those individuals or groups with vested interest in the results of a COTS evaluation..."

The roles of this set are mainly concerned on their work products, rather than defining the interactions that take an important part at the moment of selecting a COTS component. For example: in activities as "candidate component identification", "business process modification", "update definition of system architecture", and "architecture production" (among others), the specific contribution of all team members to develop these activities is not defined.

In the rest of the section, we propose a set of roles primarily based on Table 6 but complemented with some missing roles covering the activities not included in current COTS selection methods. As a result, we have identified nine specific roles for COTS selection, which are identified in Table 7 with the following capital letters:

A *System Architect:* Defines the structure of the information system, identifying constraints and technological specifications that compose it.

B *Market Watcher:* Explores the marketplace segments involved in the undertaken selection process to find the candidate COTS components which are to be evaluated and assessed with respect to user specifications.

C *COTS Component Evaluator:* Evaluates candidate COTS components which are assessed with respect to user requirements using the appropriate techniques. Experience in the component domain under evaluation is required.

D *Requirements Engineer:* Guides the elicitation, negotiation and validation of user requirements. To do so, he or she needs a minimum technical background and socialization ability.

E *COTS Vendor Interface:* Communicates with a particular COTS component provider company, trying to involve it inside the project, looking for mutual benefits of both parts.

F *Stakeholder Representative:* Someone who has an interest on the system-to-be and, as a consequence, has an interest on the success of the selection process.

G *COTS Data Expert:* Evaluates and stores the information that is produced during the process, part of which may be used in future selection projects taking place in the same or similar domains.

H *COTS Lawyer:* Protects the company interests at the moment of acquiring or licensing a component, collaborating in the writing and review of contracts.

I *COTS Provider:* for providing detailed information and demos of components during detailed analysis.

In Table 7 we show the correspondence of those proposed roles with the ones identified in Table 6 (each column stands for a role using the capital letters introduced above). Besides this set of roles specific for COTS selection, other transversal ones can be incorporated in the selection team. Among them, we consider at least the Project Manager [22] and the COTS Quality Engineer. The existence of these roles will be made explicit in the next section.

Once the roles that compose a COTS selection team have been identified, we address the different interactions that may occur among them. With this purpose, we use the *i** framework [16] basically because of two reasons: 1) it includes roles as part of its model elements; 2) it is possible to declare both high-level and low-level interactions, using the same model element (dependencies). For this reason, we use Strategic Dependency (*SD*) models to identify the *Strategic Dependencies* that arise inside a selection team. We use the R*i*SD methodology to construct this SD model [23], because R*i*SD suggests a construction guide and specific syntax for each constructor of an SD model.

Table 7. MAPPING THE PROPOSED ROLES WITH EXISTING ONES

COTS Method	Roles Suggested	A	B	C	D	E	F	G	H	I
CARE [3]	Requirement engineer				X					
	Software architect	X								
	Engineer component							X		
	Component vendor					X			X	X
IEEE 1062 [20]	Acquirer						X			
	Developer	X		X	X					
	Supplier					X			X	
EPIC [6]	Acquirer		X							
	System architect	X								
	Designer				X					
	Data designer							X		
PECA [8]	Evaluator			X						
	Charter			X						
	Evaluation stakeholders						X			

In our scope, *i** models consists of a set of nodes that represent roles and a set of *dependencies* that represent the relationships among them, expressing that an actor (*depender*) depends on some other (*dependee*) in order to achieve some objective (*dependum*). The *dependum* is an intentional element that can be a: *resource* (a physical or informational entity), *task* (particular way of doing something), *goal* (condition or state of affairs in the world that the actor would like to achieve) or *softgoal* (a condition in the world which the actor would like to achieve, but the criteria for the condition being achieved is not sharply defined a priori, and is subject to interpretation) [16, 23] (see Figure 1 for a legend).

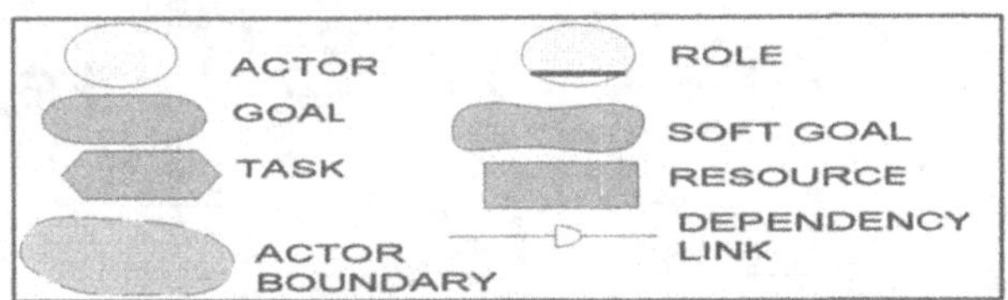

Fig. 1. Graphical representation of *i** constructs.

In Figure 2 we can observe the SD model that identifies the interactions among the members of a selection team. In the model we may distinguish the selection team (whose boundary is drawn in green) that contains the different roles defined in previous sections. Furthermore, some external actors appear, which represent the environment in which the selection team operates: the *Organization* interested in the selection, the *Information System* under construction, the COTS *Marketplace* and the *Vendor Representative* company. Dependencies among these actors and the roles inside the selection team are also included in the model.

We explain next, the most important interactions that appear in the model (we use the capital letters to identify the abbreviations of each role):

- *Stakeholder Representative* (**UR**): depends on *Requirements Engineer* to validate his/her requirements, because the *Requirements Engineer* must negotiate and steer the user needs.
- *System Architect* (**SA**): depends on *Market Watcher* to compare the candidate components with the system architecture, for this reason the *Market Watcher* has to explore the marketplace to find components that will be evaluated.
- *Requirements Engineer* (**RE**): depends on *Stakeholder Representative* to negotiate user requirements, because the *Stakeholder Representative* has to adapt his/her requirements to the market.
- *COTS Component Evaluator* (**CE**): depends on *Market Watcher* to evaluate candidate components, because the *Market Watcher* must explore the marketplace to find components to be evaluated.
- *Market Watcher* (**MW**): depends on *Requirements Engineer* to locate the candidate components, since the *Requirements Engineer* must define user requirements with the purpose of driving the component search in the market.
- *Vendor Representative* (**VR**): depends on *COTS Vendor Interface* to answer to the organization needs, since the *COTS Vendor Interface* is the communication bridge between the organization and the provider.

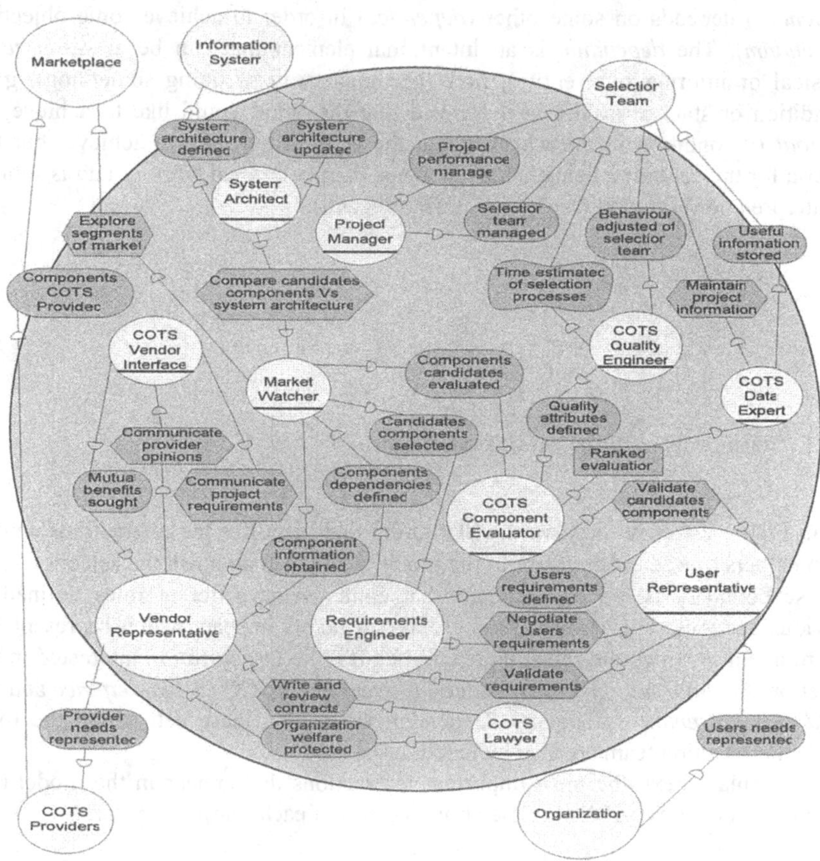

Fig. 2. Interaction of roles in a strategic *i** model.

- *COTS Vendor Interface* (**VI**): depends on *Vendor Representative* to communicate him/her the project requirements, because the *Vendor Representative* can provide information to select a suitable component.
- *COTS Lawyer* (**LW**): depends on *Vendor Representative* to write and review the acquisition contracts since the *Vendor Representative* is the owner of components that the organization wants to acquire or license.
- *COTS Quality Engineer* (**QE**): depends on the whole selection team to estimate the time for each process, because the selection team has the knowledge for doing this task.
- *COTS Data Expert* (**DE**): depends on the whole selection team to store useful information, since the selection team must take advantage of this information.
- *Project Manager* (**MN**): depends on the whole selection team, because only with its help, the project manager can achieve his objectives.

4 Defining a scope formally

In this section we aim at formalising the scope for COTS methods, defining the roles and the activities to cover the main selection processes. To do so, we use OPEN, a framework consolidated in the field of process modelling. OPEN was created by a group of methodologists, researchers, tool vendors and practitioners [17], which includes concepts bound to business modelling, business decision making, maintenance, and application development. Our main purpose is to take the OPEN processes repository defined in [18] (OPF, the Open Process Framework) making stress in the activities that should be undertaken to carry out COTS selection processes, which belong to the five categories mentioned in section 2. On the other hand, in OPF, the roles compose teams and these teams are part of organizations; for lack of space, we focus on the roles hierarchy without specifying what kind of organizations or what kind of teams the roles compose.

In Figure 3, we present our COTS selection role hierarchy. We identify which roles are taken from the OPF (shaded boxes) and which are specific COTS selection roles (thick-lined boxes). These roles are classified according to two kinds of OPF roles, *Internal Role ("it is a producer internal")* and *External Role ("it is a producer external, outside of the work product to be developed but it is relevant to the development process")*. As a class of *External Role*, OPF proposes the *Representative* abstract class, which corresponds to a person that represents a specific type of organization or group of people that have common interests. Some of the roles identified in the previous section are defined as concrete classes that inherit directly from *Representative*:

- o ***Vendor Representative*** (OPF), is a representative of the COTS provider company, with the purpose of providing detailed information and demos of components, among others benefices;

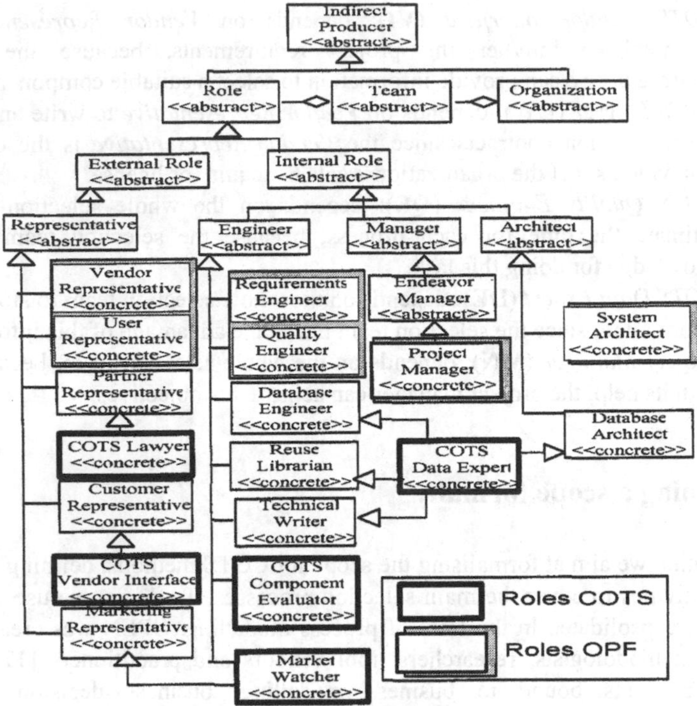

Fig. 3. Formalization of COTS selection roles using the OPF.

- ***User Representative*** (OPF), representing the needs of the stakeholders in the selection team;
- ***COTS Lawyer*** (COTS), this class inherits from *Partner Representative* (OPF) the knowledge about the contracts that are carried out with the *Vendor Representative* (OPF);
- ***COTS Vendor Interface*** (COTS), this class makes part of organization that requests a component, thus it inherits from *Customer Representative* (OPF);
- ***Market Watcher*** (COTS), this class inherits from two OPF classes: as a representative, it inherits from *Marketing Representative* (OPF), because it uses the knowledge about the marketplace where the organization technology is developed; as an *Engineer* (OPF), it needs technical skills to perform marketplace exploration, e.g. classifying technological segments therein.

On the other hand, among the *Internal Roles*, we find in OPF three abstracts classes of interest for our work. The first of them is *Engineer*, and as descendants we define:

- ***Requirements Engineer*** (OPF);
- ***COTS Quality Engineer*** (COTS), helps in the definition of quality attributes of COTS components. This class inherits from *Quality Engineer* (OPF) the skills to provide improvement and time estimates of each selection activity;
- ***COTS Data Expert*** (COTS), this role inherits from *Database Engineer* (OPF), *Technical Writer* (OPF) and *Database Architect* (OPF) because is the role for a person who creates, maintains and plans the data structure that will support the

information that somebody can reuse inside the project or in future projects (for the project it is very important storing the information that someone can use without documenting each process excessively);

- *COTS Component Evaluator* (COTS) and *Market Watcher* (COTS) are very-specific COTS roles that we define them as direct heir of *Engineer*.

The next abstract class that inherits from *Internal Role* is *Manager* (OPF), which makes reference to the administration activities carried out by a person. We find a class that inherits from *Manager*:

- ***Project Manager*** (OPF), which corresponds to the person in charge of representing the selection team at the organization. A person playing this role drives the work team through the selection process. This class inherits from other abstract class *Endeavor Manager* (OPF), because this class has the necessity of carrying out the project goals.

The final abstract class that inherits of *Internal Role* is *Architect*, which makes reference to the person that produces a specific architecture. We can find a concrete class in this hierarchy:

- ***System Architect*** (OPF), because this class has to describe the structure of information system.

With the model depicted in Figure 4, we are able to identify the abstract activities that roles must undertake during specific projects, where concrete activities have a set of task to make a work (*Work Unit*) during COTS process, and where we can classify them to be reused in future projects.

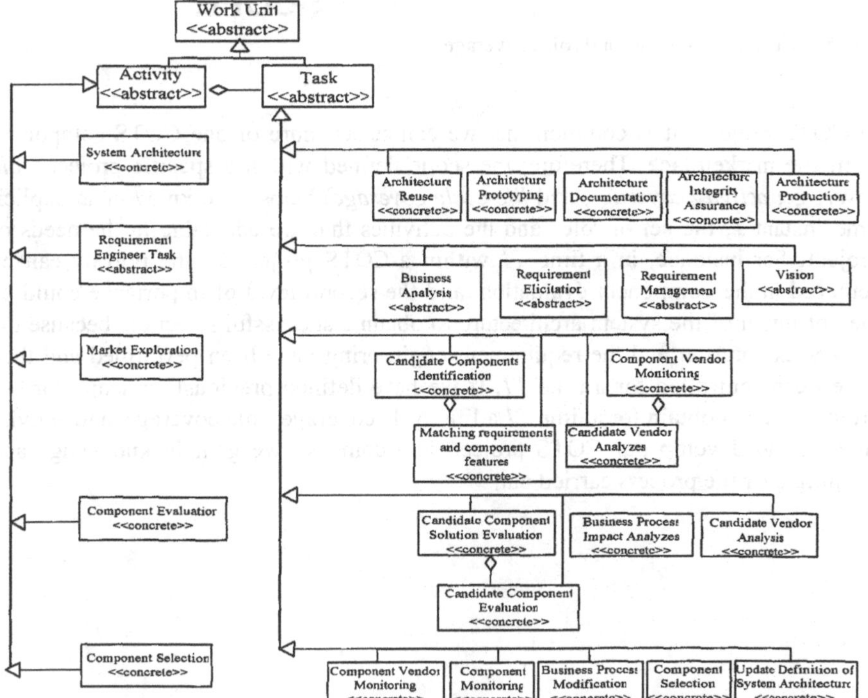

Fig. 4. Formalization of activities using the OPF.

6 Life-cycle coverage

COTS selection processes are continuous processes, and usually they arrive at their end when the development of the information system under study does not evolve across the time. For that reason, the interaction of the roles during the life-cycle of an information system is constant. Therefore, we want in this section to represent the continuous movement of COTS process as a kind of orbital system, with activities gravitating around the project at the center, where capital letters ***SA*** represent software architecture, ***RE*** requirement engineering, ***ME*** market exploration, ***CE*** component evaluation, and ***CS*** component selection (see Figure 5).

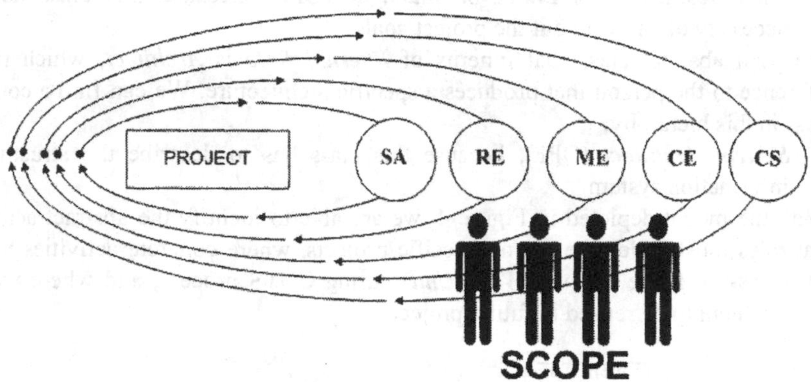

Fig. 5. Life-cycle coverage and roles coverage.

In COTS projects it is common that we can select more of one COTS component from the marketplace. Therefore, the scope defined within a specific project (*role coverage, activity coverage,* and *life-cycle coverage*) helps us to know in an explicit time instant *T*, the set of roles and the activities that are adaptable to the needs of project. For instance, in a time *T1* within a COTS project X, the priority can be centered in the component evaluation, and the second level of importance could be the definition of the system architecture to obtain a successful selection, because the market exploration and the requirement engineering have been performed and they have been controlled for a time *T1*. If we have defined previously a scope for our project, we can obtain for a time *T1* a life-cycle coverage, role coverage, and activity coverage to develop our COTS project, and doing so we gain in knowledge and learning over the process carried out.

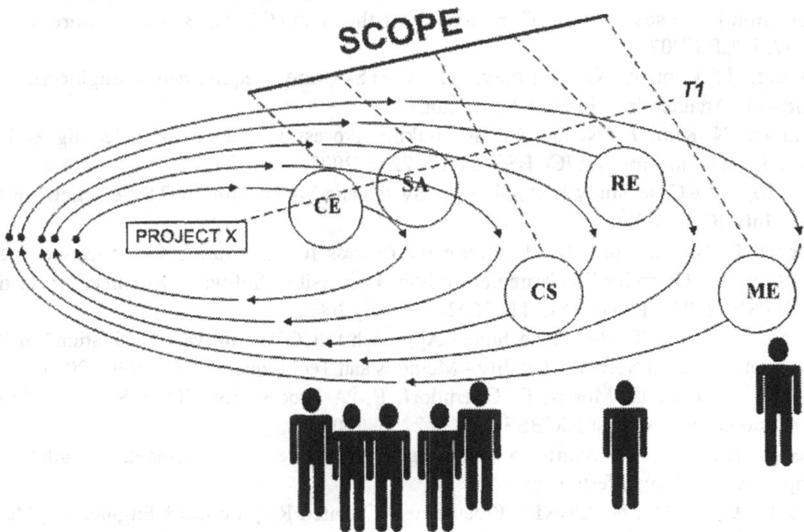

Fig. 6. Identifying a scope for a specific time *T1*

7 Conclusions

There are several COTS selection methods available, but they do not define formally the interactions among the roles and the activities needed to cover the life-cycle in the COTS projects. For this reason, we have proposed the definition of a scope to improve the process engineering perspective of those methods. Defining and identifying the roles and the activities that may be needed in COTS selection projects provides an improvement in the maturity of COTS processes and helps to identify the endeavors that are needed during the COTS project development. The use of formal or at least rigorous frameworks such as OPF and *i** has been of great help to identify the roles and the activities involved in selection processes, and as a result, we have defined the roles and the activities identified in the previous section by contextualizing them in the OPF.

Our research agenda primary includes the definition of a COTS selection method built upon our presented proposal, based in a model able to consider what scope is necessary for a whole COTS-based development life-cycle.

References

1. Navarrete, F., Botella, P., Franch, X. "How Agile COTS Selection Methods are (and can be)?" in Proc. Euromicro 2005. Porto, Portugal.

2. Navarrete, F., Botella, P., Franch, X. "Reconciling Agility and Discipline in COTS Selection Processes" in Proc. Commercial-off-the-Shelf (COTS)-Based Software Systems, 2007. ICCBSS '07.
3. Chung, L. Cooper, K. Courtney, S. "COTS-Aware Requirements Engineering and Software Architecting" in Proc. SERP 2004.
4. Maiden, N. Kim, H. Ncube, C. "Rethinking Process Guidance for Selecting Software Components" in Proc. 1st ICCBSS, LNCS 2255, 2002.
5. Kontio, J. "A Case Study in Applying a Systematic Method for COTS Selection" in Proc 18th Intl' ICSE, 1996.
6. Albert, C. Brownsword, L. "Evolutionary Process for Integrating COTS-Based System (EPIC): An Overview". Carnegie Mellon University, Software Engineering Institute CMU/SEI-2002-TR-099 ESC-TR-2002-009, July 2002.
7. Kunda, D. "STACE: Social Technical Approach to COTS Software Evaluation" in Proc. Component-Based Software Quality - Methods and Techniques, LNCS 2693, 2003.
8. Dorda, C. Dean, C. Morris, E. Oberndorf, P. "A Process for COTS Software Product Evaluation." in Proc. 1st ICCBSS, LNCS 2255, 2002.
9. Beck, K., et al. Manifesto for Agile Software Development. Available at: http://www.agilemanifesto.org
10. Ncube, C. Maiden, N. "PORE: Procurement Oriented Requirements Engineering Method for a Component-Based System Engineering Development Paradigm." in Procs. 2nd International Workshop on Component-Based Software Engineering (CBSE), 1999
11. Merriam-Webster, On-Line Dictionary http://www.m-w.com/dictionary/methodology. Last Update April 2007.
12. Cockburn, A. "Agile Software Development". Addison Wesley 2000-2001.
13. Meyers, B., Oberndorf, P., Managing Software Acquisition: Open Systems and COTS Products, Addison-Wesley, 2001.
14. Finkelstein, A., Spanoudakis, G., Ryan, M., "Software Package Requirements and Procurement", in Procs. 8th IEEE IWSSD, 1998.
15. Firesmith, D. Henderson-Sellers, B. Graham, I. "OPEN Modeling Language (OML) Reference Manual". Cambridge Univ. Press, New York, 1998.
16. Yu, E. "Towards Modelling and Reasoning Support for Early-Phase Requirements Engineering" in Proc 3rd IEEE Int. Symp. on Requirements Engineering, RE'97. Washington, USA.
17. Henderson-Sellers, B. "The OPEN framework for enhancing productivity" Software, IEEE 17(2), March-April 2000 Page(s): 53 – 58
18. Firesmith, D. Henderson-Sellers B. Graham, I. OPEN Process Framework (OPF). Available: http://www.opfro.org/. Last update April 2007.
19. McBreen, P. "Questioning Extreme Programming". Addison Wesley, 2003.
20. IEEE recommended practice for software acquisition, IEEE Standard 1062, 1998.
21. Pannone, R. Peraire. C. "The IBM Rational Unified Process for COTS-based projects: An introduction". Available at: http://www-128.ibm.com/developerworks/rational/library/aug05/peraire-pannone/
22. Albert, C. Brownsword, L. "Evolutionary Process for Integrating COTS-Based System (EPIC): An Overview". Carnegie Mellon University, Software Engineering Institute CMU/SEI-2002-TR-099 ESC-TR-2002-009, July 2002.
23. Grau, G., Franch, X., Mayol, E., Ayala, C.P., Cares, C., Haya, M., Navarrete, F., Botella, P., Quer, C.. "RiSD: A Methodology for Building i* Strategic Dependency Models". In Proc 17th International Conference on Software Engineering and Knowledge Engineering (SEKE), 2005.

Developing a Reference Method for Game Production by Method Comparison

Inge van de Weerd, Stefan de Weerd and Sjaak Brinkkemper
Department of Information and Computing Sciences, Utrecht University,
PO Box 80.089, 3508TB Utrecht, The Netherlands
{i.vandeweerd, sweerd, s.brinkkemper}@cs.uu.nl
WWW home page: http://www.cs.uu.nl/

Abstract. In this research, we use a formal method comparison approach to construct a reference method for game production. First, we analyze four game production methods by using a meta-modelling technique: three documented methods and one method obtained via a case study at a game production company. By developing a super method, containing all activities and concepts of four analyzed methods, we compare the four methods. Based on the super method, a reference method is constructed to give a complete overview of all possible steps and deliverables in a game production process: the reference method for game production.

1 Method Comparison

Several motives exist for evaluating and comparing methods. In literature many reasons are listed; see for example [1] and [2]. We can order these motives according the point of view form the actor that is involved. From the method user's point of view, method comparison can aid in selecting the best method for a particular situation. A tangle of methods exists in the IS development world. To know which method is best in a certain situation, one has to now the strengths and weaknesses of candidate methods. Furthermore, method users might want to use a tool to support their method. Method comparison makes it easier to select the right tool.

From the developer or researcher's point of view, comparing methods leads to a better understanding of methods and their rationale. Also, existing methods can be improved and new situational methods can be assembled. Ultimately, it allows the researcher to develop a reference method, which can be used to identify the similarities and differences between the various methods in a systematic way.

Several empirical and non-empirical approaches exist for method evaluation [1]. Empirical approaches for method evaluation are often time-costly. A laboratory setting, for example, is almost unfeasible. Case studies take a lot of time to get

Please use the following format when citing this chapter:

van de Weerd, I., de Weerd, S., Brinkkemper, S., 2007, in IFIP International Federation for Information Processing, Volume 244, Situational Method Engineering: Fundamentals and Experiences, eds. Ralyté, J., Brinkkemper, S., Henderson-Sellers B., (Boston Springer), pp. 313-327.

enough case studies for a reliable result. Another drawback from some empirical approaches is that the evaluation of the method can be highly influenced by the performers and their experience, and the domain or project in which the method is used. Non-empirical methods are in general less time-costly.

In this paper we use a qualitative and formal approach to develop a reference method for game production; namely a comparison approach based on conceptual differentiation of meta-models, as described in [3]. In this comparison, we compare three documented methods for game production. A fourth method is obtained via a case study at a game developer company. We develop a super method, based on the four analyzed methods, which we use for the method comparison. Finally, we construct a reference method that can be used to a) give an overview of the steps and deliverables in a game production process, b) develop a uniform terminology field within the game production domain, c) serve as input for a public knowledge infrastructure on development methods, and d) give recommendation to the game production company that was researched in the case study.

The remainder of this paper presents our approach to the development of the reference method. Related work in the method engineering and method comparison domain is described in Section 2. Then, in Section 3, we describe our approach. We present the resulting reference method for game production in Section 4, and discuss the results in Section 5. Finally, in Section 6, we present our conclusions and future research.

2 Related Work

Siau and Rossi [1] give an extensive overview of empirical and non-empirical method evaluation techniques. They distinguish the following empirical techniques: surveys, laboratory experiments, field experiments, case studies and action research. The non-empirical methods are: feature comparison, meta-modeling, metrics approach, paradigmatic analyses, contingency identification, ontological evaluation and approaches based on cognitive psychology. They state that none of these techniques is inherently superior to others, but that the choice to use a certain technique should be based on the research questions, the environment, the strengths of the researchers, and the opportunities available. Also Fettke and Loos [2] compare the different approaches on evaluation. They propose a framework for the multi-perspective evaluation of frameworks, in which the same perspectives as Siau and Rossi are used. However, the framework is extended with an economic-based evaluation, a master reference model-based evaluation, and a plain text-based evaluation.

In [3], a formal approach to the comparison of six object-oriented analysis and design methodologies is presented. From all six methods a meta-process model and a meta-data model is created in order to obtain a uniform and formal representation of the methods. The meta-models are then used to compare the analysis and design steps, the concepts, and the techniques provided in each method. The result is a set of tables that reveal the similarities and differences between the methods.

Several method comparison frameworks have been developed; see for example the ACRE framework for selecting the right requirements acquisition method [4], the Method Characteristics Framework for evaluating information engineering methods [5], and the Cataloging Framework for software development methods [6]. All these frameworks use a number of features or properties which are used to characterize the methods.

3 Method Comparison: A More Formal Approach

In this section we describe the approach that we followed to come to a systematic method comparison. The approach we use was first applied in [3] for the comparison of Object-Oriented methods as described in Section 2.

3.1 Approach

Based on the formal approach for method comparison, proposed by Hong, van den Goor and Brinkkemper [3], we use the following steps to come to a complete method comparison:

1. *Method selection*
   In this research we compare four methods. Three of these methods are documented in game production literature, namely Game Development and Production [7], Introduction to Game Development [8], and The Game Production Handbook [9]. The reason for this choice lies in the fact that all three books are written from a management perspective, rather than a technical development perspective. All three methods have received good reviews and they complement each other in the topics that are covered. The fourth method is proprietary method used at a game production company.
2. *Method modeling*
   For the analysis of methods, we use process-deliverable diagrams (PDDs), a meta-modeling technique that is based on UML activity diagrams and UML class diagrams. This meta-modeling technique is clear, compact and consistent with UML standards. The resulting PDDs models the processes on the left-hand side and deliverables on the right-hand side, see for examples figure 1 and 2. Details on this modeling technique can be found in [10] and [11]. The process and deliverables are explained by accompanying activity and concept tables, in which all activities and deliverables are described.
3. *Development of super method*
   The four methods, modeled in PDDs, are decomposed in activities and concepts. From both activities and concepts a comparison table is created that lists all activities and concepts of all four methods, using a similar approach as is described in [3].
4. *Comparison of methods*
   The method comparison is performed by filling in the fields in the comparison tables with comparison symbols: an '=' symbol to indicate that the concept or activities are the same; the '<' and '>' symbols to indicate whether an activity in

the super method comprises more or less than the activity in the concerning method; and the '><' symbol to indicate that the activity in the supermodel partly overlaps the activity of the process model. In case a field in the comparison table is left blank it means that the activity or concept is not present in the concerning method.

The comparison is as formal as can be at the moment at a large scale. Even more formal would be that all concepts tabulated in step 2 are formally described using an ontological language like [12]. The activities of step 2 can be sequentially formalized as manipulations (create, modify, delete) of concepts. Then, the comparison of concepts and activities can be executed at the *most* formal level. However, it is debatable whether this most formal comparison would really provide valid results, as the field of game production is young and dynamic, which makes the formal comparison outdated the moment it is presented.

3.2 Meta-models of documented methods

In this section, an overview is given on the game development methods derived from the theories in the three books. Altogether, the analysis of game development methods resulted in 13 PDDs.

Chandler [9] describes in 'The Game Production Handbook' four main processes in the game production cycle. These are Pre- Production, Production, Testing and Post-Production. The pre-production phase encompasses the definition of the game concept, the definition of the game requirements and the definition of the game plan. After pre-production there is production, in which builds of the game are created and localized. In the successive testing phase quality assurance tests are performed and the final game code is released, after which in the post-production phase post mortems are conducted and closing kits created. In Figure 1, the PDD of the Game concept definition is depicted to give an example of a PDD.

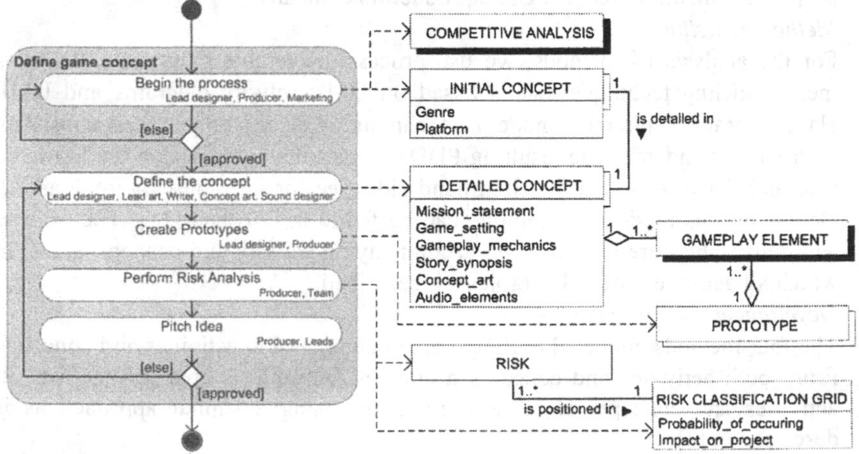

Fig. 1. Process-deliverable diagram of the Concept Phase in "The Game Production Handbook" [9]

The main activity *Define game concept* consists of five sub activities that all result in one or more deliverables and/or a decision point. In Tables 1 and 2, we describe the activities and the deliverables respectively.

Table 1. Activity table for Define game concept

Activity	Sub-Activity	Description
Define Game Concept	Begin the Process	At the start of the process, the Lead designer, Producer and Marketing manager develop an INITIAL CONCEPt for the new game. In the INITIAL CONCEPT the genre and platform on which the game is supposed to run are described. They also perform a COMPETITIVE ANALYSIS.
	Define the Concept	When the INITIAL CONCEPT is approved, the Lead designer, Lead art, Writer, Concept art, and Sound designer define the concept in a DETAILED CONCEPT.
	Create Prototype	The Lead designer and Producer create a PROTOTYPE, based on the DETAILED CONCEPT.
	Perform Risk Analysis	The Producer develops together with the rest of the Team a RISK CLASSIFICATION GRID, in which all RISKS are plotted.
	Pitch Idea	The Producer and Lead pitch the idea to the management. When it is approved, they can carry on with defining the game requirements.

Table 2. Concept table for Define game concept

Concept	Definition
INITIAL CONCEPT	A not detailed concept of the game that needs to present a compelling goal for the game to achieve.
DETAILED CONCEPT	A definition of the concept of a game that specifies the game mechanics, setting, characters, storyline, and major features.
COMPETETIVE ANALYSIS	An identification of the strengths and weaknesses of your game's competition, market opportunities for your game, and any threats that might impact the game's success in the market.
GAMEPLAY ELEMENT	Elements that are defined in the detailed concept, like mission statement, game setting, gameplay mechanics, story synopsis, concept art, and audio elements.
PROTOTYPE	An original type, form, or instance serving as a basis or standard of the full game for later stages.
RISK CLASSIFICATION GRID	The result of performing risk analysis, where risks have been identified, analyzed and classified on probability of occurring and impact on the project.
RISK	The possibility of suffering harm or loss.

The second method, described in 'Game Development and Production' (Eric Bethke [7]) recognizes four main steps in game development project life cycles; Business Context, Game Design, Game Implementation and Post Release Support.

Finally, in 'Introduction to Game Development', edited by Steve Rabin [8], the game development process is divided in five phases; the Concept Phase, Preproduction Phase, Production Phase, Postproduction Phase and After-Market Phase.

In Table 3 we give an overview of the amount of activities, sub activities and concepts per method. The method derived from Game Development and Production

[7] is referred to as GD&P; Introduction to Game Development [8] is abbreviated to ITGD; and The Game Production Handbook [9] is referred to as TGPH.

Table 3. Method statistics

	GD&P	ITGD	TGPH
Activities	6	10	9
Sub activities	23	37	36
Concepts	36	42	49

3.3 Processes of the Zylom case study

We carried out a case study at a developer and publisher of casual games: Zylom, which is part of RealNetworks Inc. Zylom develops retro arcade games, new games inspired by retro games, card and board games, puzzle games, and the like. These games are often referred to as "casual games" because it is possible for the casual consumer to pick them up and learn to play quickly [13]. The Zylom Media Group was established in 2001 in the city of Eindhoven, the Netherlands, and still has its headquarters there nowadays. The company currently employs over 60 people.

3.3.1 Case Study Design

The case study was carried out in a period of three weeks. Resulting from the case study, activities and deliverables are identified, which are used to compare to literature on game development. The research is done by means of an exploratory-explanatory case study. The case study concentrates on the game development process, from the initial idea for a game until the final release of it. The primary goal of this case study is to obtain an overview of the game development processes at Zylom at present. The procedure in the case study is as follows:

a. Perform explorative interviews
b. Analyze documentation
c. Perform feedback interviews to affirm and explain results

The explorative interviews were conducted with seven employees: a game designer, three game developers, an employee of the localization department, an employee responsible for Q&A and support and a member of the Management. Each employee answered the following questions

- What are the chronological steps taken in your specific part of the game development process?
- What are typical activities that are performed in your department?
- What are the dependencies between these activities?
- What deliverables are created and/or used by your department?

Complementary documentation was provided by access to the internet and via email.

After modeling the activities and deliverables in PDDs, a second interview session was carried out to check the results. Eight employees were interviewed, of which 4 were the same employees as in the first interview round.

3.3.2 Results

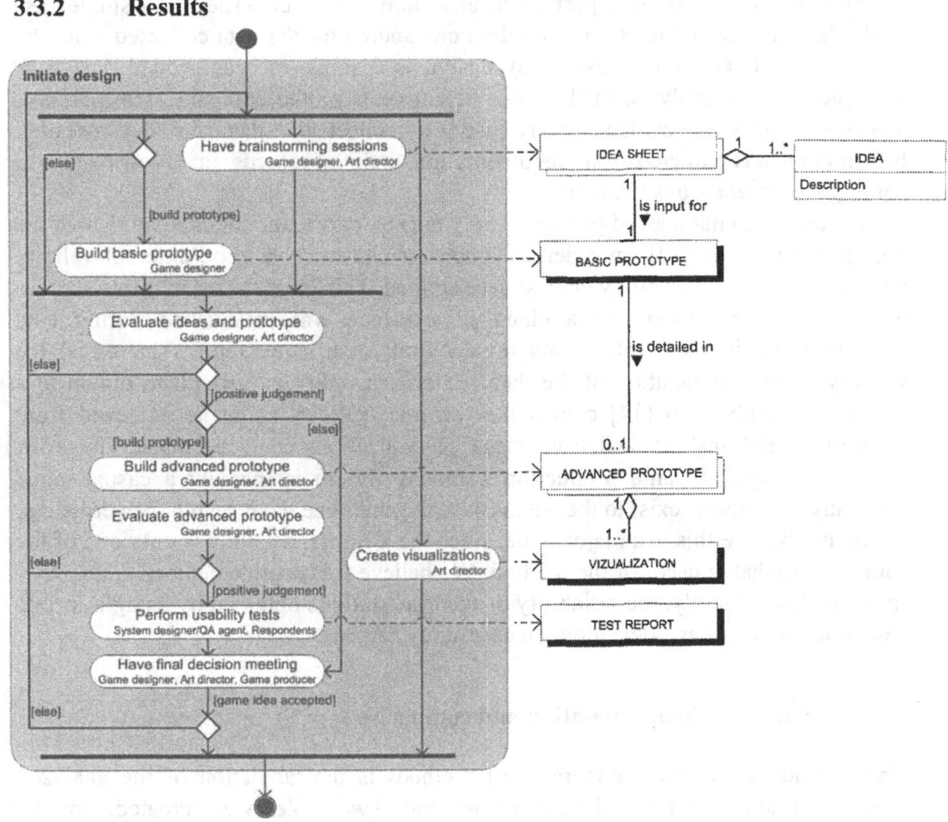

Fig. 2. Process-deliverable diagram 'Initiate design'

The game production process as it is carried out at Zylom is divided into four phases, namely Design, Development, Quality assurance and Localization. The method process consists of 11 activities, 59 activities, and 60 concepts.

In Figure 2, the PDD that illustrates the activity of the Design activity, namely 'Initiate design'. We identify one main activity, 'Initiate design' and eight sub activities. Each sub activity results in a deliverable (e.g. BASIC PROTOTYPE), or proceeds to decision point (e.g. 'Evaluate ideas and prototype'). In each sub activity, roles are added, which describe the actor(s) that carries out the activity. Roles in the 'Initiate design' activity are: Game designer, Art director, System designer, QA agent, Respondent, and Game producer.

3.3.3 Validity Issues

To make sure that the gathered information about Zylom and the game development theories is valid, the research design applies to the case study tactics defined by Yin [14]. These case study tactics encompass various facets that underwrite the validity of four research design tests; construct validity, internal validity, external validity and reliability. By making sure that the collected data from the research met the case study tactics, the validity of the scientific research is vouched for.

The case study that was performed at Zylom can be classified as a single-case study design, since there is no more than one source for the data collected from the case study. Moreover the case study design is a single-case embedded design as multiple units of analysis, in this case departments of the company, are included. Various sources of evidence were used to collect the data for the research. Information was gathered from documentation, archival records, interviews and – to some lesser extent – observations.

Because the character of this case study is exploratory, the internal validity of the design is irrelevant [14]. In order to vouch for construct validity, external validity and reliability, the case study tactics were applied. This implies that multiple sources of evidence were used and a chain of evidence was established during data collection. Having key informants review draft case study reports increased the validity of the composition of the data. External validity is difficult to obtain in a single-case study. Yin [14] claims that external validity could be achieved from theoretical relationships, and from these generalizations could be made. However, due to the type of game production company Zylom is, namely a casual game company, limitations exist to the extent we can generalize the research. Nevertheless, we do not believe this is a major issue, since the Zylom case study is only one of the four sources that is used for the method. We believe it is complementary to the other three methods. Finally, the reliability of the case study is obtained by using a formal case study protocol and developing a case study database.

3.4 Super method: tabulation and comparison

The second step in the comparison of methods is the tabulation of the analyzed methods, leading to a so-called super method. Two tables were created. For the activity table the procedure is as follows: In case a field in the comparison table is left blank it means that the activity on that particular row is not present in the process model of the corresponding column. When a field is not blank, these are the notations that describe the comparative relationship between two methods:

- An '=' symbol indicates that a similar activity to the one in the super method is available in the concerning method.
- The '<' and '>' symbols indicate whether the activity in the super method comprises more than the activity in the concerning method or less than the activity in the concerning method, respectively.
- The '><' symbol is used when a part of the activity in the supermodel overlaps a part of the activity of the process model, but other parts don't overlap.

For the comparison of concepts a similar approach is used; a super set of concepts is derived from the meta-deliverable models and forms the basis for the comparison of concepts. The notation is somewhat different than for the activities. A blank field is representing that a concept from the super method is not available in the concerning method. Other notations used in the concept comparison table are:

- The '=' symbol is still used to indicate that a concept in the super method is also included in the concerning method.

A string in a field indicates the same; however the naming for the concept is different than in the super method.

In Tables 4 and 5, we show excerpts of the resulting activity comparison and concept comparison table respectively. We use the same abbreviations as in Section 3.2 to refer to the different methods.

Table 4. Activity comparison table (excerpt)

2. Preproduction Phase	**GD&P**	**ITGD**	**TGPH**	**Zylom**
2.1 Create game design				
2.1.1 Brainstorm	=			
2.1.2 Delegate design	=			
2.1.3 Write game design document	=	>		=
2.1.4 Evaluate game design document				=
2.1.5 Write technical design document	=	><		<
2.1.6 Create visualizations				=
2.1.7 Present game design				=
2.1.8 Evaluate technology			=	
2.1.9 Define tools and pipeline			=	
2.1.10 Create documentation			=	

Table 5. Concept comparison table (excerpt)

2. Preproduction Phase	**GD&P**	**ITGD**	**TGPH**	**Zylom**
2.1 Create game design				
2.1.1 GAME DESIGN DOCUMENT	=	=	DESIGN DOC.	=
2.1.2 CORE GAMEPLAY	=			
2.1.3 CONTEXTUAL GAMEPLAY	=			
2.1.4 STORY	=			
2.1.5 TECHNICAL DESIGN DOCUMENT	=	=	TECHNICAL DOC.	=
2.1.6 REQUIREMENT	ASSET	FEATURE	FEATURE	ASSET
2.1.7 VISIBLE REQUIREMENT	=			
2.1.8 NONVISIBLE REQUIREMENT	=			
2.1.9 FEATURE LIST			=	ASSET LIST
2.1.10 DOCUMENTATION			=	
2.1.112 PROTOTYPE				=

The super method consists of four phases, in which we can identify 13 activities and 96 sub activities. These sub activities have the following distribution over the four comparison methods: GD&P: 26; ITGD: 37; TGPH: 37; and Zylom: 40. The activities result in a total of 117 concepts, which are distributed as follows: GD&P: 32; ITGD: 40; TPGH: 49; and Zylom 46. Please note that these statistics do not match the statistics described in Section 3.2. This is due to two reasons: a) only relevant activities and concepts are included in the comparison table, and b) some activities in the comparison methods are listed more than once, due to the fact that this activity covers more activities in the reference method.

One important observation from the comparison of activities of the different methods is that some methods cover areas or phases in the game production process that are neglected by other methods. It can be concluded that GD&P is clearly written from a management perspective; most processes in the method focus either on the preparation, measuring or monitoring of tasks. The more basic tasks that directly relate to game development are mainly omitted. The focus in the theory is also clearly on deliverables that need to be completed in game production projects.

The ITGD method is the only one to address in detail the hiring of staff members as part of the game production process and performing marketing and sales related activities. Activities are not only management specific; also the actual game development process is covered in quite some detail. However, the localization of finished games is described very briefly and is therefore too basic to be really useful. Still, ITGD covers many important parts of the game production process and is therefore quite complete.

In TGPH some extra activities in the pre-production phase are suggested; the evaluation of technology, creation of documentation and definition of tools and pipelines to be used during the project are available in this method. Management related activities in this method are quite basic and high-level. The TGPH method excels when it comes to the localization process and the finalization of the game production project. The localization steps and the definition and creation of closing kits are thoroughly discussed. Finally, the part of the project in which code is released is also well explained in TGPH compared to other methods.

The Zylom method contains very detailed descriptions of the localization and quality assurance testing activities. Besides that, prototyping during several phases in a game production processes and usability testing using these prototypes are fragments that are only available in Zylom and valuable for the reference method.

3.5 Determination of reference method

The final step is the creation of the reference method. This reference method is an executable method that includes the best method fragments from the super method, based on the comparison of the four methods. In the next section we present the method.

4 Reference method

4.1 A Reference Method for Game Production

The resulting reference method for game production consists of thirteen main activities, expressed in four PDDs, which correspond to the four production phases. In Figure 4, we provide a high-level overview of the game production process, comprising four phases: Concept phase, Pre-production phase, Production phase and Post-production phase. The reference method consists of 13 main activities and 69 sub activities, which result in 93 deliverables. In the concept phase first the business parameters are identified, which comprises, among others, the budget, recourses and competitive analysis. A detailed game concept is defined and presented by means of prototypes. Then, in the pre-production phase, the game design document is developed, which described the story, gameplay and requirements. Also, a project plan and staffing plan is created. This late moment for project planning and staffing has to do with the nature of the game production process. Rather than the straightforward development process from requirements to implementation that is used in the information systems domain, first the game concept needs to be approved. Developing this game concept is a creative activity, comparable with the production of movies. Someone has to approve or invest in the idea that is developed in this phase, before you can think about a project and staffing plan.

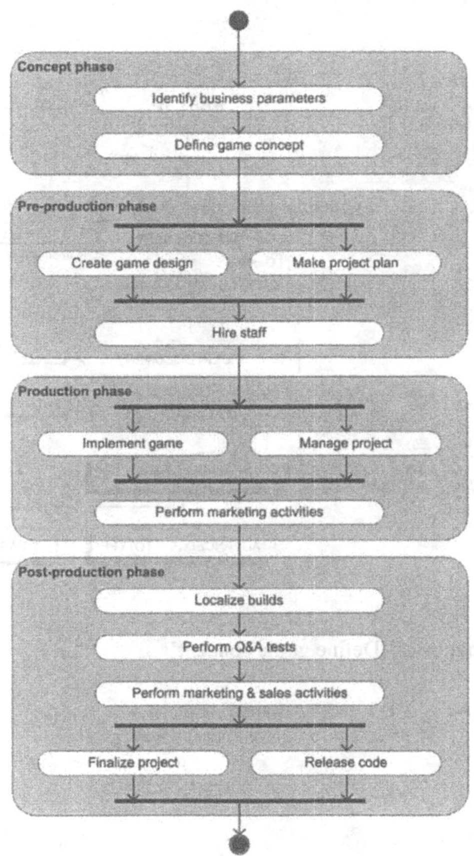

Fig. 3. Reference Method for Game Production: Process Overview

Next, in the production phase, the game is implemented in a working game; the final version. During the implementation scope changes are managed. At the end of this phase, a demo is developed for marketing purposes. Finally, the fourth phase comprises the typical post-production activities. The game needs to be localized so it can be released in different countries, QA tests are done and promotion material for the marketing department is created. Finally, the project concludes with developing a closing kit and releasing and shipping the game.

4.2 Define game concept

To elaborate the reference method a bit further, we illustrate one of the main activities, namely 'Define game concept' (Figure 4). When we compare this PDD with the PDD of Zylom's first development activity, described in Section 3.3.2, we see that the first has more activities and deliverables. The process is more structured and there are less decision points. Furthermore, usability tests are included very early in the process. An important issue is the formal definition of a game concept, which is missing in the Zylom method.

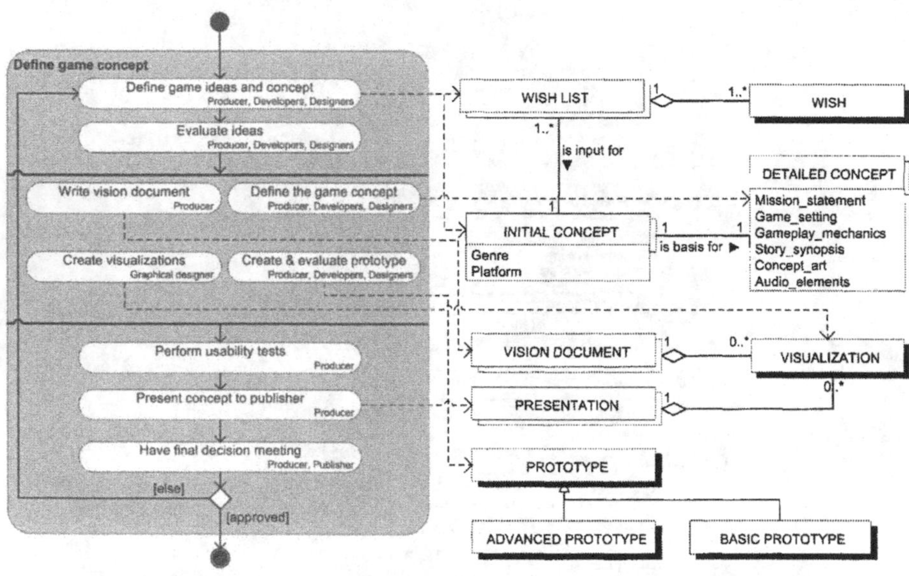

Fig. 4. Process-deliverable diagram of 'Define game concept'

5 Discussion

5.1 Reference Method

Theories on game production are not unambiguous; there exist quite some differences in elements of the game production domain between the various sources. For example, the importance of localization of a game was stressed in some theories, while the localization process was completely omitted in others. Also, the importance of defining your business parameters before commencing with the design phase was not indicated in all methods. However, globally there are many similarities between the methods when it comes to the main game production process. All fragments from the methods have been included in the reference method, leaving the duplicates out. In case there were more than one fragments representing one and the same activity, the clearest and most comprehensible fragments have been selected and included in the reference method. This has resulted in a complete reference method of the game production process that should quickly provide people with insight in what game development projects exactly encompass. Note that we do not want to prescribe this method as the best game production method, but rather as a complete reference of all activities and deliverables, showing how the method could be organized.

5.2 Public Knowledge Infrastructure

The result of this research, the reference method and the method comparison can be of great value for game companies. Various employees of Zylom that were interviewed indicated that task descriptions and templates would be useful to include in the project planning. Providing employees with proper, unambiguous descriptions of the tasks that they need to perform in a specific period of time can improve the process. In our vision this is realizable by developing a public knowledge infrastructure for game production methods, consisting of process descriptions, templates and best practices. Currently, we are working on such an infrastructure in the domain of product software [11].

5.3 Uniforming Terminology

During the analysis of the four game production methods, we encountered a wide range of terms that often are used for the same concepts. Especially in the comparison of the deliverables this was a problem, since it was difficult to detect whether two concept with different names, meant the same thing and vice versa. A de facto standardization of the terms would make the comparison of methods considerable easier.

5.4 Method Comparison

The comparison technique that is used in this research has some great advantages. The visibility and intelligibility that was already signaled in the comparison study of object-oriented analysis and design methodologies [3] also shows in this research. Moreover, the use of the activity and concept tables, improved the comparison method. However, the actual comparison of activities and concepts proved to be quite complex. When comparing activities, it was hard to identify whether two activities were totally similar, or if one activity encompassed more or less than another. For concepts it was often not easy to see whether or not two concepts with different names actually represent one and the same thing, due to the different terminologies that were used. Finally, after completing the comparison process, the resulting tables provide a good overview of the differences between the various activities and concepts.

5.5 Recommendations Zylom

A major observation from the processes at Zylom is that there are many decisions in a game development project whether or not to continue with the project. Especially in the designing phase of development projects these so called go – no go decisions occur often which might result in starting over the whole design process from scratch. In some cases it might prove useful not to reject a game idea as a whole, but refine or redefine a game idea by adjusting a prototype or brainstorm about other features or concepts.

In the current situation at Zylom the project plan is defined after the design phase. This means that design activities are not as properly planned as the rest of the game development activities. A suggestion is to create the project plan before the designing of a game takes place, in order to improve the managing and progress tracking of projects. It was indicated by various interviewees that game development projects are commonly significantly over time and thus that predefined targets in terms of numbers of games that need to be completed are not met.

5.6 Game Production versus Standard Information Systems Development

When it comes to the differences between managing the game production process and software development for other types of software, there are some differences that are identified. First of all, the concept phase in game production projects is quite different and more complex, because a game's atmosphere has to be defined and an initial concept version of a game is far less representative for the final game than in other software engineering projects. Especially the determination of the future 'look-and-feel' of a game and its atmosphere implies that the concept is likely to be changed more often during the concept phase than in other types of software products. The inventive and creative character of games also results in a design phase that is different from other software production projects. Because the atmosphere of a game needs to be defined, lots of art work and gameplay prototypes are created already during the design phase. Because creativity in game production plays an important role, and (elements of) games can be seen as kind of art, defining a basic concept with some wishes for requirements is not enough. Game production projects contain many decision moments during the design phase whether or not to cancel a project and start up with a complete new idea, while ideas for other types of software products are more easily defined in a product design and then developed.

6 Conclusions and Future Research

In this paper we presented an approach to the development of a reference framework for game production. We used a more formal approach to method comparison by using activities and concept tables. We analyzed three documented game production methods and carried out a case study at a game production company to analyze a fourth method. By developing meta-models with accompanying activity and concept tables, we were able to carry out a method comparison and develop a reference method.

We can conclude that all methods are written from different perspectives, which causes a difference in the activities and concepts they contain. The reference method integrates these perspectives and can be used as a complete reference of how a method could be organized.

The use of activity and concept tables improves the method comparison approach as described in [3]. In future research, the method can be improved by making it more formal by using ontologies. This will also solve the problem of the ambiguous terminology that is used in the domain. Finally, we aim to develop a knowledge infrastructure for game production methods, containing process descriptions, templates and best practices.

References

1. K. Siau and M. Rossi, Evaluation of Information Modeling Methods - A Review, *Proceedings of the 31st Annual Hawaii International Conference on System Sciences* **5**, (1998), p. 314.
2. P. Fettke and P. Loos, Multiperspective Evaluation of Reference Models - Towards a Framework, *LNCS* **2814**, 80-91 (2003).
3. S. Hong, G. van den Goor, and S. Brinkkemper, A Formal Approach to the Comparison of Object-oriented Analysis and Design Methodologies, *Proceeding of the 26th Hawaii International Conference on System Sciences* **4**, (1993), pp. 689-698.
4. N.A.M. Maiden and G. Rugg, ACRE: Selecting Methods for Requirements Acquisition, *Software Engineering Journal* **11**(3), 183–192 (1996).
5. R.D. Hackathorn and J. Karimi, A Framework for Comparing Information Engineering Methods. *MIS Quarterly* **12**(2), 203-220 (1988).
6. G.M. Karam, R.S. Casselman, A Cataloging Framework for Software Development Methods, *Computer* **26**(2), 34-45 (1993).
7. E. Bethke, Game Development and Production (Wordware Publishing, Inc., Plano, Texas, 2003).
8. S. Rabin, Introduction to Game Development (Charles River Media, Boston, 2005).
9. H. Chandler, The Game Production Handbook (Charles River Media, Boston, 2006).
10. I. van de Weerd, S. Brinkkemper, J. Souer, and J. Versendaal, A Situational Implementation Method for Web-based Content Management System-applications, *Software Process: Improvement and Practice* **11**(5), 521-538 (2006).
11. I. van de Weerd, J. Versendaal, and S. Brinkkemper, A Product Software Knowledge Infrastructure for Situational Capability Maturation: Vision and Case Studies in Product Management, *Proceedings of the 12th Working Conference on Requirements Engineering: Foundation for Software Quality (REFSQ'06)*, Luxembourg (2006)
12. I. Horrocks, P. F. Patel-Schneider, and F. van Harmelen, From SHIQ and RDF to OWL: The Making of a Web Ontology Language, *Journal of Web Semantics* **1**(1), 7–26 (2003).
13. G.E. Mills et al., 2005 Casual Games White Paper (IGDA Casual Games SIG, 2005).
14. R.K. Yin, Case Study Research: Design and Methods (Sage Publications, Thousand Oaks, CA, 2003).

Towards Evidence Based Splitting of Organizations

Martin Op 't Land
Delft University of Technology, Netherlands
Capgemini, P.O. Box 2575, 3500 GN Utrecht, Netherlands

Abstract. The reported research program aims at finding and testing principles for adequately splitting organizations. Using actors from Enterprise Ontology as organization building blocks on one hand and criteria from organization science on the other hand, an expert-meeting was presented the organization-splitting choices for a part of the Dutch Agency of Public Works and Water Management. The experts could construct their own free-format (gut-feeling) organization choice and they could choose from predefined alternatives, based on the *High Internal Cohesion / Low External Coupling* criterion and calculated using the min-cut algorithm from graph-theory. The gut-feeling alternative appeared to be close to the (non-trivial) calculated organization alternative, with *separation of functions* as main reason for difference. Also, business service dependencies appeared to determine organization-splitting far more dominantly than information dependencies.

1 Introduction

Organizations increasingly [1] split off parts and start cooperating with those parts, for instance in Shared Service Centers or by in- or outsourcing activities. Splitting organizations is believed to make organizations more agile [2] in offering complex products, in participating in complex product-offerings of another party or in timely dropping current products. Such agility has become a business requirement in many lines of business [3], from Defense via car industry to banking industry [4]. Splitting organizations in units with clear customer-supplier-responsibilities, clear competencies and geo-flexibility in operations and ICT also improves its current operations, stimulates entrepreneurship and gives those units a customer-oriented focus, with the potential to broaden the customer base [5]. Through a reduction of

---

Please use the following format when citing this chapter:

Op't Land, M., 2007, in IFIP International Federation for Information Processing, Volume 244, Situational Method Engineering: Fundamentals and Experiences, eds. Ralyté, J., Brinkkemper, S., Henderson-Sellers B., (Boston Springer), pp. 328-342.

redundancy in processes and ICT, this results in saving costs, simplifying operations and making those operations more manageable [6].

The question *where to split an organization* is not an easy one: what criteria and what organizational building blocks should be used? Already in a simple example we can see a complex trade-off in motives of customer intimacy, efficiency, product uniqueness, broadening the product portfolio, cost control and equalizing capacity. And even if the (functional) priorities chosen in those motives are clear, it is not immediately clear how this mix of priorities leads to choices in splitting the enterprise [7]. Dietz [8] proposes to use actors of an Enterprise Ontology according to the Design & Engineering Methodology for Organizations (DEMO) [9] as organization building blocks. Mulder [10] actually tested the use of actors in organization design, letting the criteria appear bottom-up while discussing the positioning of actors. Op 't Land [11] adds to this method the test on previously defined situational criteria.

In this paper we extend the method to include testing previously defined *general* criteria. The extended method is applied in a real-life case study in splitting an organization by an expert-meeting in a Group Decision Support (GDS) room. The participating experts were presented a choice in assigning organizational building blocks, using actors from a DEMO Construction Model. We summarized general criteria from organization science and system theory and tested its use in the actual expert choices. Especially we tested an operationalization of the *High Internal Cohesion / Low External Coupling* (HICLEC) criterion, as introduced into IS development by Stevens et al [12] and into organizational studies by Karl Weick [13]. We measured the strength of business service dependencies compared with information dependencies. This operationalization took the shape of prepared graph alternatives, using the min-cut algorithm. We found that business service dependencies determined the organization splitting far more than information dependencies. We found also that (non-trivial) calculated organization alternatives appeared to be close to the gut-feeling alternative with *separation of functions* as the main reason for difference.

The remainder of this paper is structured as follows. Section 2 explains the research design applied, from the level of the research program until the level of an individual case. For each individual case in the program we discern an intervention- and a measurement-phase; in this case-study we describe the intervention-phase. Section 3 introduces the actual intervention in the case Rijkswaterstaat- Deltares[1]: what was its context, how did the models and criteria specific for its situation look like and how was the expert-meeting constructed? Section 4 discusses the results of the intervention: how was the expert-meeting conducted, which of the prepared alternatives were chosen and what were the underlying hypotheses. Finally, section 5 provides the conclusions as well as directions for further research.

[1] Rijkswaterstaat is the Dutch Agency for Public Works and Water Management; this Directorate-General is the implementing organisation of the Ministry of Transport, Public Works and Water Management. Deltares is a Dutch-based international institute for applied research and specialist consultancy in the field of water and the subsurface. For further details, see section 3.

2 Research Design

This case-study is part of the CIAO-research program [14] “Applying Architecture and Ontology to the Splitting and Allying of Enterprises” [7]. We look for answers to the question “which organization-construction rules lead to adequate splitting of enterprises?”. In this section we will first introduce the research design of the research program as a whole, which has the shape of action research. In this action research cycle we then position this individual case study. Next we formulate for this case study the desired exploration and the hypothesis we wanted to test. Finally we explain the structure of the expert meeting used.

2.1 Position of case study in research program

The research program “Applying Architecture and Ontology to the Splitting and Allying of Enterprises” aims at finding validated principles and organization construction rules, whose application leads to adequate splitting of enterprises. We define an *enterprise* as a goal-oriented cooperative of people and means. Splitting and allying enterprises are two sides of the same medal: the moment the work for an enterprise is split over parties, those parties have to ally in order to stay that “goal-oriented cooperative of people and means”.

Let’s now further introduce the basic concepts of the program (see Figure 1). For a *specific enterprise E* we want to arrive at an *adequate splitting proposal (E)*. *Adequate* is defined as being compliant with professional principles, enterprise specific principles, situational process requirements and situational result

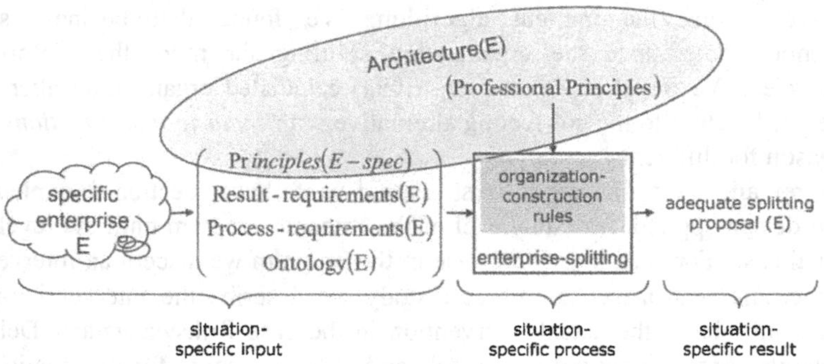

Figure 1. Concepts of Enterprise Splitting

requirements. A *professional principle* is broadly applicable and not situation specific, e.g. "minimize need for tuning"; it will typically originate from general systems theory and organization sciences. Enterprise specific principles (*Principles(E-spec)*) are the operationalization of enterprise E’s strategic choices and policies, e.g. “re-use before buy before build” or “all employees should be able to work everywhere in our country in the same way”. Situational process requirements (*Process-requirements(E)*) are specific for a specific process or project of splitting, e.g. project costs, timeliness, effectiveness and quality. Situational result requirements (*Result-requirements(E)*) are the goals to be reached by splitting the enterprise, including the constraints to be complied with. As mentioned in section 1, the goals for splitting of enterprises can be quite diverse and include saving costs (location, people, tax), improving quality (right people with right qualifications in e.g. language, training and experience) and improving agility and flexibility. Constraints will typically originate from the ecosystem of the organization, like from (legal or branch-) supervisors, customers, suppliers and other network partners. Following xAF [15], *architecture* is understood (1) conceptually as a *normative restriction* of *design freedom* and (2) operationally as a consistent and coherent set of design *principles* that embody general requirements, where these general requirements hold for a class of systems. Therefore the architecture of enterprise E (*Architecture(E)*) consists of the professional principles and the enterprise-specific principles. By the ontology of the enterprise E (*Ontology(E)*) we understand a model of E's construction that is completely independent of the way in which it is realized and implemented. After Dietz [8], we will use a DEMO Construction Model for such an ontology. *Organization-construction rules* guide the decisions where to split, e.g. "don't cut the enterprise on a spot with heavy information-exchange, because this will increase the error-rate". In the organization-construction rules the trade-offs are made between all requirements and principles, using the ontology as language of the essence of the enterprise and delivering finally that adequate splitting proposal.

To find the organization-construction rules, which is in the black-box of the enterprise-splitting process, we have to repeatedly execute that splitting process, controlling the in- and output. This fits in the notion of *action research*, defined by Avison et al [16] as a repeating cycle of intervention, measuring, evaluation and improvement. In action research, the researcher selects or develops new concepts and tools, in our research program organization-construction rules for splitting enterprises, to use it (or let it be used) in new situations. Each case study in the program, including this one, has its own sub problem, method, result and conclusions and therefore also each case has its own research design. As Lee [17] shows, studying single cases can satisfy the standards of the natural science model of scientific research.

Where does this case-study fit in the action research cycle? Dietz [8] proposed to use actors of an Enterprise Ontology according to the Design & Engineering Methodology for Organizations (DEMO) [9] as organization building blocks. Mulder [10] actually tested the use of actors in organization redesign, letting the criteria appear bottom-up while discussing the positioning of actors. Op 't Land [11] earlier added to this method the test on previously defined situational criteria. In this case-study we extend the method by a test of previously defined *general* principles and organization-construction rules. And we apply this method in an intervention, the actual splitting of an organization by an expert-meeting in a Group Decision Support (GDS) room. This case-study should have results on two levels, a case-result and a research result. The intended case-result is an adequate splitting proposal, including an underpinning why that proposal is advisable. This splitting proposal will in turn be the basis for drafting SLA's and for migration planning. The intended research-result is (1) explorative: which professional principles and organization-construction-rules have been applied and why (2) validating the well-known general construction principle "high internal cohesion, loose external coupling" (HICLEC) as hypothesis.

2.2 Using DEMO modelling in the organizational building blocks

We will now briefly introduce the required concepts of the DEMO Construction Model (CM), using Figure 2. A DEMO Construction Model expresses the coherence (chain/network) of business services, delivered by actors to other actors within a defined scope. E.g. actor A01 executes transaction T01, which delivers a business service to actor A00. Actor A00 is called the *initiator* and actor A01 the *executor* of transaction T01. The execution of transaction T01 results in a new fact in reality. Another actor A07, for its responsibility in executing transaction T07, needs information about those facts from transaction T01; this *information link* between actor A07 and (the fact bank of) transaction T01 is indicated by a dashed line. In the fact bank of T01 we find both the production facts and the coordination facts (like status "requested", "promised", "stated", "accepted") of transaction T01.

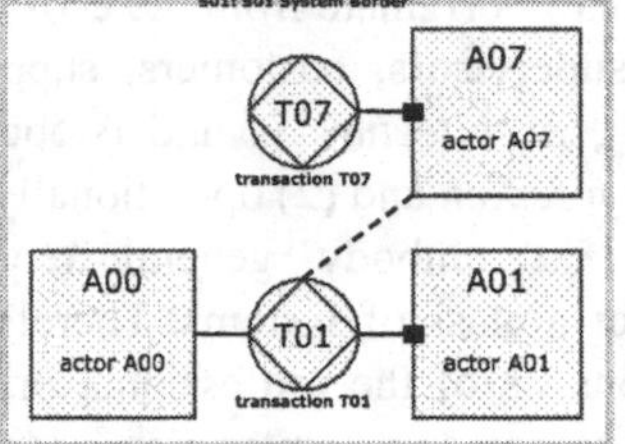

Legend DEMO CM

symbol	name
	system border
S	aggregated actor
A	elementary actor
T	transaction type
	initiator link
	executor link
	information link

Figure 2. Typical DEMO Construction Model

In terms of a DEMO CM, making an organization-split is the assigning of actors to separate organizational units. Parnas states [18] that in modularization the modules should be structured in such a way that changes in reality influence the modules in an isolated way, so that modules are islands of stability. In a DEMO CM actors fulfill Parnas' "information hiding" principle, because they have a relatively simple outside interface – a new fact brought about in reality – and potentially hidden complexity on the production process needed to produce that fact.

2.3 The general criteria for splitting and their application

Based on the scripts of several case studies [10, 11, 19] and supplemented by organization science and systems theory literature (a/o [20], [21]), Op 't Land [22] summarized organization construction rules and professional principles (see Tables 1 and 2).

Table 1. Professional principles

nr	Professional principle
G01	better quality of operations
G02	more flexibility in service levels
G03	accelerated operations
G04	accelerated time-to-market
G05	lower operational costs
G06	increased turnover
G07	client centricity
G08	customer ownership
G09	multi-channel offering ability

Table 2. Organization-construction rules

nr	Organization-construction rule: keep actors together, when …
C01	... their mutual *interface* cannot well be standardized, due to *complexity*
C02	... their mutual *interface* cannot well be standardized, due to *frequent change*
C03	… they *cannot have a supporting role* for other actors
C04	… they use the *same language / culture*
C05	… they operate under the *same regulatory, legal and tax-regime*
C06	… those actors more or less *work on the same case / deal with the same event*
C07	… the *risk to fail* (in banking sector: *operational risk*) of a split is unacceptable high
C08	… they need *comparable competencies*
C09	… a *transaction-relationship* exists between those actors
C10	... an *information-relationship* exists between those actors

The general criteria mentioned (G01-G09 and C01-C10) should be tested in the organization-splitting case study, except for the criteria C09 and C10. Indeed, rules C09 and C10 can directly be derived from the DEMO CM and therefore didn't need not be tested by the expert-meeting. And as we will see, these two criteria play a special role in the operationalization of the HICLEC-criterion.

Galbraith [21] brings his four organization-design strategies (1. Slack Resources; 2. Self-Contained Tasks; 3. Vertical Information Systems; 4. Lateral Relationships) ultimately back to a trade-off between two variables: either build in / accept slack in cooperation relationships or strengthen the information-relationship. This inspired our curiosity: how important would those cooperation-relationships (freely translated by us to transaction-relationships) be compared with information relationships in deciding about the organizational split? We suppose Galbraith considered information to be an important organization-design variable, because implementing information relationships at that time (1974) was very costly. That could be different today, since the costs of implementing information relations are considerably lower, caused by emerging standards and widely available cheap and reliable ICT-infrastructure.

We therefore like to test the following hypothesis: *transaction relations are more important than information relations, when deciding about organizational splits*. We did that by calculating several organization-alternatives in which the transaction- and information-relationships got different weights. During the expert-meeting, the experts were asked to choose which calculated organization-alternative they preferred, thus implicitly choosing for a certain weight-ratio between transaction- and information-relationships. This procedure is an application of the so-called *conjoint analysis*, also called multi-attribute compositional models or stated preference analysis [23].

The hypothesis is made operational in the following way.

1. We assigned a weight to each transaction and information relationship in the DEMO CM. A simple example is "all Transaction relationships (T) get the weight 9, all Information relationships (I) get the weight 1"; for short, we code this as TI=91.
2. We interpret those weights as follows (see Figure 2). A high weight of a *transaction relationship* between actor roles A00 and A01 is an indication that those actor roles A00 and A01 should stay together in one organization /

department. A high weight of an *information relationship* between actor role A07 and the fact bank of transaction T01, we interpret as an indication that the actor roles A07 and (the executing actor role of T01 =) A01 should stay together in one organization / department. The underlying assumptions are that (1) information in an information link mostly deals with the production information of the transaction, not its coordination information (2) production information of transaction T01 is caused by its executor A01, not by its initiator A00 (3) coordination information is caused as much by initiator A00 as by executor A01.

3. A certain organizational-splitting solution S, which splits the organization in two parts - say Org1 and Org2 -, is fully characterized by the collection of actor roles which reside in Org1 and (therefore automatically the remainder of actor roles) in Org2. We consider a relationship between actors to be broken if those actors reside in different organizations. Now we can define the penalty function P of solution S, P(S), as the sum of weights of broken relationships in Org1 and Org2 in solution S. As an example, see Figure 3: in solution S_1, the relationships A28-A31 and A27-A31 have been broken, therefore $P(S_1) = 2+8 = 10$; in solution S_2 only the relationship A31-A33 has been been broken, therefore $P(S_2) = 4$.

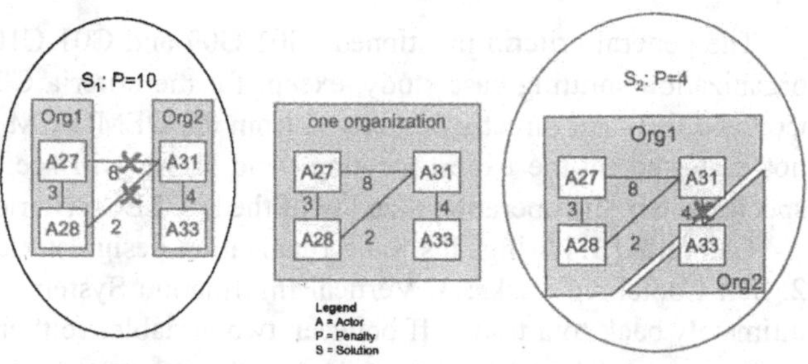

Figure 3. Penalties in Organization Splitting

4. Now we use the HICLEC-criterion: we consider the split better iff the penalty of the splitting-solution is lower. The optimal organization therefore would be the one with the minimum penalty, given that a split has to occur anyhow (the one-organization alternative doesn't count). This restating of the problem is known in graph-theory as the *min-cut problem* and a *min-cut algorithm* exists to solve that [24]. For each weight-distribution (like TI=91, TI=55), the optimal solution (so with the minimal penalty) could be calculated, also using Gomory-Hu trees [25].
5. Finally it must be possible to state in advance that certain actors should stay with Org1 or Org2 and to enforce that as a boundary constraint for further optimizations.

2.4 Structure of the expert-meeting

In the expert-meeting the following steps should be executed.

1. After an explanation of the Construction Model for the area of splitting, as the first step the experts should formulate the gut-feeling alternative. No calculated or other alternative is presented at beforehand, to prevent influencing the experts.
2. Then the gut-feeling alternative should be tested by both situation-specific and general criteria.

3. After explanation of the calculated organization-alternatives, the experts should express their preference and test the alternatives against the same criteria as the gut-feeling alternative.
4. Finally the experts were asked to answer questions on the way of working.

3 The intervention: case Rijkswaterstaat – Deltares

Rijkswaterstaat (RWS), the Directorate-General for Public Works and Water Management is the executive branch of the Ministry of Transport, Public Works and Water Management (V&W). Under the command of a departmental Minister and State Secretary, it constructs, manages, develops and maintains the Netherlands' main infrastructure networks. RWS aims to prevent flooding, ensure adequate good quality water, ensure safe & unimpeded movement on roads and waterways and generate reliable information in a user friendly format. RWS has an annual expenditure of approximately € 4 billion, number of staff approximately 10,500, 17 departments and 160 offices in the Netherlands.

From mid-2007, the Netherlands will gain an institute for applied research and specialist consultancy named Deltares (Dlt) [26]. Its goal is to improve the habitability of vulnerable delta areas, contributing to the sustainable management, use and design of low-lying, densely-populated deltas. Deltares wants to be in the international top flight in the field of water and the subsurface. It will use an integrated approach to develop innovative solutions. Deltares brings together Dutch knowledge, experience and specialists in the area of water and the subsurface. The Deltares workforce will be 700 to 800 FTEs in the initial stages. Turnover is projected at € 80 million a year.

Deltares will bring together WL | Delft Hydraulics, GeoDelft, parts of TNO Built Environment and Geosciences and parts of specialist services of RWS. At the time of this case-study, it had to be decided and validated which responsibilities of RWS exactly had to be split off from RWS and added to Deltares.

To guide us in the choice for an area for our case study (which area, which size, when, who to involve) we had to balance the following considerations:

- what is the "right size" of the area for the case study; the good choice here would make it sufficiently interesting and relevant for the RWS-/Dlt-policy makers and at the same time feasible in time;
- political visibility: to what extent and in which phase did we want what attention from what stakeholders to this case study; e.g. the right moment could enable a fruitful discussion between management and Works Council about a major BPO or IT-outsourcing proposal;
- availability of material; during the case study we would have to use existing DEMO CM-models of Rijkswaterstaat, tested by subject matter experts, and also existing situational principles, process requirements and result requirements.

Waterquantity has been chosen as area of our case-study. This RWS-area is responsible for the hydrological and morphological state of the Dutch national waters. This covers a wide range of activities, varying from a/o modelling hydrology and morphology, measuring and reporting water heights, controlling dikes, operating sluices/locks, via the Storm Surge Warning Service to integral consulting on all this.

For the area Waterquantity, a DEMO Construction Model validated by subject matter experts was available. The model emerged from an application consolidation project, in which it was used to structure the current application portfolio, seeking for rationalization-opportunities. The model contained 43 (elementary) actors, 59 transactions and 69 information links.

As boundary constraints for graph-construction RWS-experts in advance chose:

- RWS-BED: all operations of construction works (like sluices, locks and storm surge barriers) should remain with RWS;
- DLT-MOD: all modelling of hydrology and morphology of national waters should go to Deltares.

We chose quite distributed values as parameters for the graph-construction, namely TI=91, TI=55 and TI=19. This delivered three calculated splitting-alternatives, named by us α (small RWS), β (intermediate) and γ (small Deltares). Alternative α (small RWS) only consisted of RWS-BED and alternative γ (small Deltares) only consisted of DLT-MOD. Alternative β brings all modelling, all consulting services and the SLA-management for hydrology and morphology to Deltares. Both the alternatives α and γ are trivial, because they simply reflect the boundary constraint. The alternatives α and γ appear as min-cut alternatives for all values of TI (19, 55 and 91). Alternative β only appears for TI=91, as second choice (penalty P = 11); the first choices for TI=91 were α and γ (both P=4). The participants of the expert-meeting were asked to express and underpin their preference for organization-alternative α, β or γ, of course without knowing the value of the TI-parameters underlying those alternatives.

RWS introduced 9 strategic principles and 16 business principles, Deltares introduced 5 principles. Two examples of situation-specific criteria are:

- DR01 = better focus of RWS on networkmanagement (its core-business);
- DR05 = Deltares should be an authoritative knowledge-institution in Europe.

For the expert-meeting we invited ± 20 persons, representing 4 groups:

1. subject matter experts, like RWS-management and business staff;
2. subject matter and ontology experts from Enterprise Architecture RWS (EAR);
3. ontology-experts and
4. organization scientists.

This variation in expertise should enable us to perform several analyses like:

- to what extent is it possible to propose meaningful organization-alternatives, only possessing ontology-knowledge;
- how much do the evaluations of subject-matter experts differ, depending if they have ontology knowledge or not;
- to what extent do organization scicentists share the opinion of the group – they don't share the ontology-view or the subject matter knowledge, but they have experience with organization design, so with the underlying professional principles and organization-construction rules.

To enable these analyses we used a Group Decision Support Room, in which all argumentation, comments and scores could be systematically collected and subdivided by group. Also it should enable us to direct the facilitation of discussions.

The duration of the expert-meeting had to be limited to 4 hours, in which a complete scoring of all actors and organization-alternatives on all (42) criteria was not considered feasible. Therefore in the meeting-planning steps were added to select the top 7 from the 42 criteria and to select 8 more or less representative actors.

4 Results of the intervention

On January 29, 2007 08:30-12:30, the expert-meeting on splitting RWS-parts concerning Waterquantity to Deltares has been held, supported by the GDS-system MeetingWorks, which collected all contributions of participants electronically.

The longlist of (42) criteria had been sent before the meeting to the experts to comment on that; comments were received neither before nor during the workshop and no new criteria appeared. In the step to select the shortlist (top-7) criteria from the professional principles and organization-construction rules only C07 (*keep actors together when ... the risk to fail (in banking sector: operational risk) of a split is unacceptable high*) got selected; all other shortlist-criteria were situation-specific.

In the testing of the gut-feeling organization-alternative 8 out of actors were selected: 2 for which all agreed to keep the actors at RWS, 2 for which all agreed to move the actors to Deltares and 4 from a middle group on which opinions differed.

Due to time constraints the step "test calculated organization-splits on shortlist-criteria" could not be executed.

In drafting the gut-feeling organization-alternative everyone agreed on the boundary constraints RWS-BED and Dlt-MOD. Most participants agreed that Advice-roles belong to Deltares and that Data-gathering should remain at RWS. On information supply the opinions differed; a small minority positioned suppliers of information and drafters of information strategy in Deltares. Controlfunctions (morphological and hydrological) were mainly placed in RWS, though a small minority put its quality control in Deltares: "don't test your own meat" (*separation of functions*). Also a new actor role was discovered "establisher required Delta-knowledge".

In the comments given several characteristics of RWS and Dlt emerged, which we consider the basis for additions to enterprise-specific principles. For RWS as catchwords were mentioned control, directing, coordination demand-side, executore of policy and steering, control data. For Deltares as catchwords were mentioned specialized consultancy, execution, knowledge-supplier, trusted advisor, models and model data, specialized statistical analyses, strategic knowledge function, should know state of affair watersystems.

Let's now turn to the choices for the calculated organization-alternative. The calculated organization-alternative β was preferred and got report-mark 6.2 with a variance 36% (see Table 3). Because this alternative only appeared with TI=91, our hypothesis *transaction-relations are more important than information-relations, when deciding about organization-splits* could not be falsified.

Table 3. "Give an over-all report mark (scale 1 to 10) to the organization-alternative"

Organization-alternative		Average rating	Variance
α "small RWS"	(TI=19, 55 or 91)	2.2	32%
β "intermediate"	(TI=91)	6.2	36%
γ "small Deltares"	(TI=19, 55 or 91)	5.4	55%

How close was the gut-feeling alternative to the calculated organization-alternative β? Four actors were differently positioned, which could be explained mainly by separation of functions. We then recalculated graphs to see if different TI-weights could generate the gut-feeling alternative. The answer is no, for only one out of four actors this made a difference; the other three actors could not "switch organization" for any TI-weight.

From the prepared professional principles and organizational construction rules, we noticed the use of two of them. The term "need to know" as in "Deltares needs to know the state of the water systems" we saw as C10 "keep actors together when ... an information-relationship exists between those actors". And sometimes specific expertise was mentioned, which pointed to C08 "keep actors together when … they need comparable competences".

Some criteria arose which might have a more general value, e.g. "best fit with purposes of organization", "separation of functions", "keep responsibility with the one who is doing the job" and "establishing information needs always by the demand-side". On "establishing information strategy always by the demand-side" discussion arose; some argued that information strategy deals with *how* information will be supplied, and subject matter expertise of the supplier should play an important role in that, e.g. in the choice of means for monitoring and data collection.

The participants appreciated the way of working in this expert-meeting. The offering of the calculated (α-, β-, γ-) alternatives helped to get more clarity on the motives of the preferred organization-split. Also the contribution of non subject matter experts was valued e.g. their comparison of the RWS-Dlt-relationship with the relationship between an airline and the National Airspace Laboratory (NLR).

The results of the scoring of the gut-feeling alternative were consistent with the scoring of the selected actors on the shortlist-criteria. We further noticed that subject matter experts scored outspokenly and homogeneously (low variance). Also we noticed that the method experts more often abstained from voting, explaining that more subject matter insight was required.

A method-expert suggested to better order the list of criteria, e.g. to add the categories function-/ product-requirements, performance-indicators (like lead time or MTBF) and some organization-construction rules (like technical coherence and failure sensibility).

In preparing the next time workshop the following improvements could be made:

- make the criteria SMART in a small group before the expert-meeting;
- test the DEMO Construction Model in a smaller group, especially on the places where discussions on organization-splits can be expected; for this "borderline" actors, put effort in more precisely defining the (direct object of the) transaction-result; e.g. is *A027 Supplier statistics* the supplier of standard statistics or of specialized statistics? is *A024 SLA Manager information supply* serving the demand-side or the supply-side or both?

During the next time workshop the following improvements could be made:

- start with an explanation on the strategic directions of RWS and Deltares;
- then explain consequences for making an organizational split, e.g. "cooperation and allying over the split remain necessary", "introduce SLA's on the split";
- let the splitting of the organization be done top-down, so first at the level of aggregated actors; where the scores on aggregated actors are not unambiguous, drill down to the level of elementary actors; use the time thus saved for more interaction and discussion;
- the question "should this actor go to Deltares or stay with RWS?" is too binary; indeed an actor role can next to *sequentially* and *concurrently* also be fulfilled *collectively* [8: 125], so introduce the option of collective fulfilment of roles;
- during the workshop let the participants first score the actors with business roles, then the actors with informational roles; then participants will be better aware of their assumptions and score more consistently.

5 Conclusions and further research

5.1 Conclusions on the level of this case

The half-day expert-meeting was considered productive and effective by the participants. Vagueness in criteria and strategic starting points of Rijkwaterstaat and Deltares were revealed and discussed. The use of actors from the DEMO Construction Model as organizational building blocks – which was new for about 50% of the experts – was generally clearly understood and appreciated. The discussion got an objective basis, responsibilities and dependencies became clear and also new actors were discovered. The pre-calculated organization-alternatives (graphs) made the discussions on the organization-split more directed. E.g. the roles of RWS and Deltares and the underlying situational principles became articulated more clearly than reached by the gut-feeling exercise.

The (non-trivial) calculated organization-alternative β came close to the gut-feeling alternative. The min-cut algorithm delivered 3 organization-alternatives, of which 2 were the trivial ones, namely the smallest ones fulfilling the minimum boundary constraints of actor-roles remaining in an organization. The deviation of the β-alternative to the gut-feeling alternative could be explained almost fully by the criterion *separation of functions*.

What can we say about our hypothesis "transaction-relations are more important than information-relations when deciding about organization-splits" (section 2)? The (non-trivial) calculated organization-alternative β appeared only when giving transaction-relationships a far higher weight than information-relationships (TI=91 and TI=90). As soon as information links were assigned a higher weight (TI≥92), then only the trivial organization-alternatives appeared. This case-study therefore was not able to falsify our hypothesis.

No calculation of organization-alternatives with whatever uniform weights for transaction- and information-relationships could exactly produce the gut-feeling alternative. Therefore a completely calculable advise on organization-splitting, based on the strength of transaction- and information-relationships, which also is recognized by experts as good, has been proven to be impossible.

On the value and the power of discernment of the general criteria (general principles and construction rules), no conclusion can be drawn from this case-study. Because of time-constraints, the expert-group had to select the criteria which they felt to be most important. From the general criteria only one out of 18 was selected and its score did not noticeably differ from the scores on the other (situation-specific) criteria in positioning an actor on either side of the gut-feeling organization-split.

5.2 Conclusion on the level of the action research

Situational Method Engineering [27] is characterized by (1) definition of *reusable method chunks* by reengineering existing methods and models as well as by capturing new ideas, experience and best practices; (2) engineering of new *situation-specific methods* by assembling method chunks stored in the repository. From existing method chunks [10] [11] we reused (a) the use of actors from a DEMO Construction Model as organization building blocks (b) the use of a Group Decision Support Mechanism. We added to this in section 2 (c) the use of general principles and construction rules, (d) the operationalizion of the HICLEC-criterion on transaction and information links and (e) the use of the min-cut algorithm from graph theory. Sitation-specific in the method applied is a/o the goal of organization-splitting, which caused us not to ask for optimal multi-clusters, but to request a binary choice ("stays with organization X" versus "goes to organization Y").

We have discovered that theoretically underpinned organization-alternatives can be calculated, which look plausible in the real-life situation. That calculated alternative need not be the best; many criteria can play a role, which are not part of the starting point, the DEMO Construction Model. The calculated alternatives, represented in graphs, at least then give the insight which penalties are paid in terms of broken or hampered transaction- or information-relationships. These penalties can then be explicitly weighed against the other criteria. Summarizing: if someone wants to deviate from the calculated alternative, he now will be aware of the penalties of that deviation, which enables him to make conscious trade-offs.

5.3 Future research directions

To validate the hypothesis "transaction-relations are more important than information-relations when deciding about organization-splits", replication of this research is necessary with variation in organization types and sectors.

To test the value and the power of discernment of the general criteria (general principles and construction rules), these criteria have to be used again in future case-studies in a way which guarantuees scores on all criteria. At the same time the research design for those case-studies have to stay open for discovering new general criteria.

Another interesting question is what would happen when we apply other criteria and other algorithms to the graphs instead of the min-cut algorithm. E.g. in social networks the criterion of "betweenness" appeared to be successful in predicting the structure of communities [28]; could this also be applied to the question of organization-splitting? And now we have also restricted ourselves to a binary choice ("should this actor stay with organization X or move to organization Y"), resulting in two clusters. We might broaden the question to an open choice ("what actors have close transaction- / information-relationships"), resulting in multi-clusters, which then could be translated to departments or separate legal entities.

Acknowledgements

We want to acknowledge Richard Jorissen, acting managing director Rijkswaterstaat / National Institute for Coastal and Marine Management (RWS/RIKZ), and Hero Prins, corporate change-manager Deltares, for their sponsorship of the expert-meeting. Karin Middeljans and Kees Buursink generously made available all relevant materials of the Enterprise Architecture Rijkswaterstaat (EAR) team. And Wim Vree, Hans Mulder, Bart Kusse and Martijn Faay supported us greatly in preparing the expert-meeting and analyzing its results.

References

1 Hackett, *BPO-outlook for finance and accounting 2006-2008* (The Hackett Group, 2006)
2 A. Umar, IT infrastructure to enable next generation enterprises. *Information Systems Frontiers* 7(3), 217-256 (2005).
3 Thomas L Friedman, *The World is Flat: A Brief History of the Twenty-first Century* (Farrar, Straus and Giroux, 2005).
4 Martin Op 't Land, Bert Arnold, Ariane Engels, FPS: another way of looking at components and architecture in the financial world. *Congress paper for the Dutch National Architecture Congress 2000 (LAC2000).* www.serc.nl/lac/LAC-2001/lac-2000/3-realisatie/fps.doc
5 Carolien van Straten, *Disaggregating the firm by means of Business Process Outsourcing.* Master thesis Erasmus University Rotterdam, 2002. www.strategie-vsb.nl/pdf/8.pdf
6 Lance Travis and Jim Shepherd, *Shared Services, Cost Savings, Compliance Relief and Prelude to Outsourcing* (AMR-research, 2005).
7 Martin Op 't Land (2006) Applying Architecture and Ontology to the Splitting and Allying of Enterprises; Problem Definition and Research Approach. *Proceedings of the OTM Workshops Montpellier France 2006, (R. Meersman, Z. Tari, P. Herrero et al., Eds.), LNCS, Springer Berlin Heidelberg.* http://dx.doi.org/10.1007/11915072_46
8 J.L.G. Dietz, *Enterprise Ontology – theory and methodology* (Springer, 2006).
9 DEMO (=Design & Engineering Methodology for Organizations)-website, www.demo.nl
10 J.B.F. Mulder, *Rapid Enterprise Design* (Dissertation Delft University of Technology, 2006).
11 Martin Op 't Land, Bert Arnold, Jan Dietz, Effects of An Architectural Approach to the Implementation of Shared Service Centers. *Financecom05 Regensburg, Germany (2005).* http://www.iw.uni-karlsruhe.de/financecom05/contributions/opt-land-paper.pdf
12 W.P. Stevens, G.J. Myers and L.L. Constantine, Structured design. *IBM Systems Journal* **13**(2) pp. 115-139 (1975).

13 K.E. Weick, Management of Organizational Change Among Loosely Coupled Elements. In: Goodman PS Associates (Eds) Change in Organizations, Jossey-Bass, San Francisco, CA, pp 375-408. (1982)
14 CIAO! program (2004) Research program on Cooperation & Interoperability - Architecture & Ontology. www.ciao.tudelft.nl.
15 xAF (2003) Extensible Architecture Framework version 1.1 (formal edition); report of the NAF-working group xAF. See http://www.naf.nl/content/bestanden/xaf-1.1_fe.pdf
16 D. Avison, F. Lau, M. Myers, P.A. Nielsen PA, Action research. *Communications of the ACM* **42**:94-97 (1999).
17 Allen S Lee, A Scientific Methodology for MIS Case Studies. *MIS Quarterly* **13**(1) pp. 33-50 (1989).
18 D.L. Parnas, On the Criteria To Be Used in Decomposing Systems into Modules. *Communications of the ACM* **15**(12) (1972).
19 Erwin van der Graaf Architectuurprincipes voor de afbakening van outsourcebare kavels (2006). http://www.architecture-institute.nl/master-lab/pdf/ErwinVanDerGraaf.pdf.
20 Pierre van Amelsvoort, *De moderne sociotechnische benadering – een overzicht van de socio-technische theorie* (ST-Groep, Vlijmen, 1999).
21 Jay R Galbraith, *Het ontwerpen van complexe organisaties* (Samson Uitgeverij Alphen aan den Rijn – Brussel, 1976).
22 Martin Op 't Land, Organization science and systems theory on the splitting of enterprises (unpublished, 2006).
23 Wikipedia on Conjoint Analysis, http://en.wikipedia.org/wiki/Conjoint_analysis
24 L.R. Ford Jr. and D.R. Fulkerson, Maximal Flow Through a Network, *Canadian Journal of Mathematics* **8**:399-404 (1956).
25 R.E. Gomory and T.C. Hu, Multi-Terminal Network Flows. *J. SIAM* **9** pp. 551-570 (1961)
26 Deltares-website, http://www.deltares.eu.
27 Situational Method Engineering website, http://matis.unige.ch/research/SME
28 Michelle Girvan and M.E.J. Newman, Community structure in social and biological networks. *Proc Natl Acad Sci U S A* **99**(12), pp. 7821—7826 (2002) http://www.santafe.edu/research/publications/workingpapers/01-12-077.pdf

A Formal Framework for Modeling and Analysis of Organizations

Viara Popova and Alexei Sharpanskykh
Vrije Universiteit Amsterdam, Department of Artificial Intelligence,
De Boelelaan 1081a, 1081 HV Amsterdam, The Netherlands
{popova, sharp}@cs.vu.nl

Abstract. This paper introduces a formal framework for modeling and analysis of organizations. It allows representing a great variety of organizational concepts and relations that are structured into a number of dedicated perspectives (or views), similar to the ones defined in GERAM [3]. In contrast to many existing enterprise architectures the proposed framework has formal foundations based on the order-sorted predicate logic. This formal basis enables different types of analysis of organizational specifications both of particular views and across different views. Furthermore, the framework provides support for real time management of organizational processes. The framework has been applied in a number of case studies, one of which is discussed in this paper.

1 Introduction

Nowadays, many organizations employ automated management systems, based on a great variety of enterprise architectures [3] (e.g., CIMOSA, ARIS, Zachman, PERA, GRAI/GIM, TOVE). Based on the analysis of a large number of the existing architectures, the IFIP/IFAC Task Force has developed the Generalized Enterprise Reference Architecture and Methodology (GERAM) [3], which forms a basis for comparison of the existing architectures and serves as a template for the development of new architectures. GERAM identifies the essential characteristics for methods, models and tools required to build and to maintain the integrated enterprise at different phases of its life-cycle. Moreover, to reduce the complexity of enterprise modeling GERAM identifies a number of particular views on enterprises (e.g., function, information, resource, organization) and defines a standard vocabulary of concepts that may be used in the context of these views. The existing architectures conform to the recommendations of GERAM to a variable degree [3]. Although many architectures include a rich ontological basis for creating models of different views, most of them provide only a limited support for automated analysis of these models, addressed in the category *Enterprise Engineering Tools* of GERAM,

Please use the following format when citing this chapter:

Popova, V., Sharpanskykh, A., 2007, in IFIP International Federation for Information Processing, Volume 244, Situational Method Engineering: Fundamentals and Experiences, eds. Ralyté, J., Brinkkemper, S., Henderson-Sellers B., (Boston Springer), pp. 343-358.

primarily due to the lack of formal foundations in these frameworks. Formal analysis is particularly useful for checking the correctness of enterprise models, for inspecting and improving efficiency and effectiveness of the enterprise operation by identifying inconsistencies and performance bottlenecks, as well as for controlling the actual execution of organizational scenarios and evaluating organizational performance. Moreover, analysis methods (e.g. simulation) may be used to investigate and predict organizational behavior and performance under different conditions.

Within several frameworks analysis methods limited to particular views have been developed (e.g., process-oriented modeling techniques for the function view [1, 2, 3, 10], ABC-based techniques for the performance view [26]). However, since different modeling views are related to each other, this should also be reflected in the analysis methods. Analysis performed across different views allows investigating a combined influence of factors from different views on the organizational behavior, thus, the designer is provided with more rigorous and manifold analysis possibilities than by using analysis techniques dedicated to a particular view only. The need for such analysis techniques is identified in [12]. A uniform formal basis (syntax and semantics) underlying different views facilitates the development of cross-view analysis methods. In [12] an integrated framework for process and performance modeling is described that incorporates accounting/business parameters into a formal process modeling approach based on Petri-nets. However, key aspects as authority and power relations, organizational and individual goals, individual behavior are not considered. Another formal framework for business process modeling is described in [14] focusing on the formal goal-oriented modeling using the situation calculus. Modeling and analysis of processes and other organizational concepts are not properly addressed in this framework. A formal framework for verifying models specified in Unified Enterprise Modeling Language (UEML) is proposed in [9]. It identifies a general idea to use conceptual graphs for verifying enterprise models; however, neither technical nor experimental results are provided to support this idea.

Since individuals often exert a significant influence on the organizational dynamics, also aspects related to human behavior should be explicitly considered in enterprise architectures. In particular, by modeling motivational and intentional aspects of humans, an organization can flexibly (re)organize the work of its employees to improve the productivity. The extensive theoretical basis on modeling humans in organizational context developed in social science (e.g., theory of needs [17], expectancy theory [27]) is largely ignored in the existing architectures.

To address the issues and shortcomings identified above, this paper proposes a formal framework for organizational modeling and analysis that:

(1) has a high expressivity to represent static and dynamic aspects of different views on organizations, similar to the ones defined in GERAM;
(2) allows the representation and analysis of organization models at different levels of abstraction in order to handle complexity and increase scalability;
(3) enables formal verification and validation of models of different views;
(4) enables simulation for experimenting and testing hypothesis on the organizational behaviour under different circumstances;
(5) proposes manifold computational analysis methods across multiple views;
(6) incorporates agent-based models of individuals based on social theories;
(7) supports and controls the execution of organizational scenarios and the evaluation of organizational performance.

The framework addresses design, implementation and operation life-cycle phases of GERAM to a greater extent than identification, concept and requirements phases.

The framework proposes a wide spectrum of means for modeling and analysis of structures and dynamics of organizations of different types. In particular, the framework allows modeling mechanistic organizations that represent systems of hierarchically linked job positions with clear responsibilities that operate in a relatively stable (possibly complex) environment. At the same time the framework proposes modeling and analysis means for organic organizations characterized by highly dynamic, constantly changing, organic structure with non-linear behavior. Although the structure and behavioral rules for organic organizations can be hardly identified and formalized, nevertheless by performing agent-based simulations with changing characteristics of proactive agents useful insights into functioning of such organizations can be gained. Furthermore, the framework supports reuse of parts of models constructed within particular organizational views.

The focus of this paper is on the general framework design and analysis methods involving concepts and relation of more than one view, thus, integrating the four views in a coherent and consistent modeling framework. The separate views with their analysis techniques are presented in details elsewhere [6, 18, 19, 20, 21, 23, 24].

The paper is organized as follows. Section 2 describes the formal foundations of the proposed framework. The case study used for the illustration of the framework is introduced in Section 3. Section 4 gives a brief overview of the four modeling views. The issues of design of organization models using the framework are discussed in Section 5. The methods for the organizational analysis using the framework are described in Section 6. Finally, Section 7 concludes the paper.

2 Formal Foundations of the Proposed Framework

In line with GERAM, the proposed framework introduces four interrelated views: performance-oriented, process-oriented, organization-oriented, and agent-oriented. The first-order sorted predicate logic [16] serves as a formal basis for defining dedicated modeling languages for each view. These languages provide high expressivity for conceptualizing a variety of concepts and relations and allow expressing both quantitative and qualitative aspects of different views.

To express temporal relations in specifications of the views, the dedicated languages of the views are embedded into the Temporal Trace Language (TTL) [4, 6, 25], which is a variant of the order-sorted predicate logic. In TTL the organizational dynamics are represented by a trace, i.e. a temporally ordered sequence of states. Each state is characterized by a unique time point and a set of state properties that hold (i.e., are true). State properties are specified using the dedicated language(s) of the view(s). Temporal (or dynamic) properties are defined in TTL as transition relations between state properties. For the description of the formal syntax and semantics, and examples of use of TTL we refer to [25].

Both specifications in the dedicated languages of the views and in TTL are suitable for performing computations. In particular, in [25] it is shown that any TTL formula can be automatically translated into executable format that can be implemented in most commonly used programming languages.

Within every view a set of structural and behavioral *constraints* imposed on the specifications of the view can be identified. Formally, this set is represented by a *logical theory* that consists of formulae constructed in the standard predicate logic way [16] from the terms of the dedicated language of the view (and of TTL if temporal relations are required). Since the views are related to each other by sets of common concepts, also these concepts can be used in the constraints expressions. A specification of the view is *correct* if the corresponding theory is satisfied by this specification, i.e., all sentences in theory are true in the logical structure(s) corresponding to the specification. The constraints are divided in two groups: (1) *generic constraints* need to be satisfied by any specification of the view; (2) *domain-specific constraints* are dictated by the application domain and may be changed by the designer. Two types of generic constraints are considered: (1) *structural integrity and consistency constraints* based on the rules of the specification composition; (2) *constraints imposed by the physical world.* Domain-specific constraints can be imposed by the organization, external parties or the physical world of the specific application domain. The algorithms for the verification of the correctness of specifications of every view w.r.t. different types of constraints have been developed and implemented, and will be discussed in Section 6.

3 Introduction to the Case Study

The proposed approach was applied for modeling and analysis of an organization from the security domain within the project CIM (Cybernetic Incident Management, see http://www.almende.com/cim/). The main purpose of the organization is to deliver security services to different types of customers. The organization has well-defined multi-level structure that comprises several areas divided into locations with predefined job descriptions for employees (approx. 230.000 persons).

The examples in this paper are related to the planning of assignment of security officers to locations. The planning process consists of forward (long-term) planning and short-term planning. Forward planning is the process of creation, analysis and optimization of forward plans for the allocation of security officers based on custommer contracts. It is performed by forward planners from the forward planning group. During the short-term planning, plans for the allocation of security officers in a certain area for a short term (a week) are created and updated based on a forward plan and up-to-date information about the security officers. Based on short term plans, daily plans are created. Short-term planning is performed by area planning teams.

4 Modeling Views

In this section, the views of the proposed framework will be presented. Three of them, process-oriented, performance-oriented and organization-oriented, have prescriptive character and define the desired behavior of the organization. The fourth view, agent-oriented, describes and integrates agents into the framework.

4.1 Process-oriented View

The process-oriented view of the framework contains information about the organizational functions, how they are related, ordered and synchronized and the resources they use and produce. The main concepts are: task, process, resource type and resource which, together with the relations between them, are specified in the formal language L_{PR}. A *task* represents a function performed in the organization and is characterized by *name*, *maximal* and *minimal duration*. Tasks can range from very general to very specific. General tasks can be decomposed into more specific ones using AND- and OR-relations thus forming hierarchies.

A *workflow* is defined by a set of (partially) temporally ordered *processes*. Each process is defined using a task as a template and inherits all characteristics of the task. Decisions are also treated as processes associated with decision variables taking as values the possible decision outcomes. The (partial) order of execution of processes in the workflow is defined by sequencing, branching, cycle and synchronization relations specified by the designer. Part of the workflow describing the short-term planning process in the organization from the case study is given in Fig. 1 seen at two different levels of abstraction.

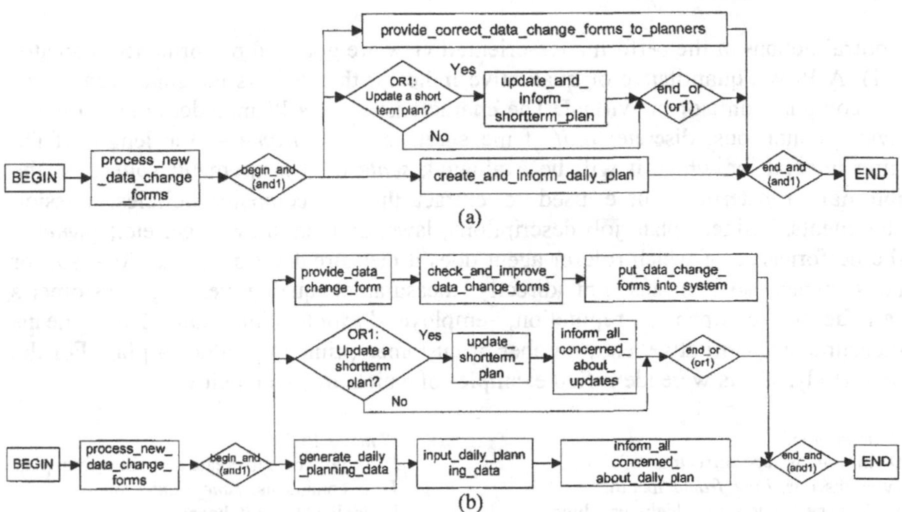

Fig.1 Part of the workflow describing the short-term planning process for the case study

Tasks use/consume/produce resources of different types. Resource types describe tools, supplies, components, data or other material or digital artifacts and are characterized by *name*, *category* (discrete, continuous), *measurement_unit*, *expiration_duration* (the length of the time interval when a resource type can be used). Resources are instances of resource types and inherit their characteristics, having, in addition, *name* and *amount*. Some resources can be shared, or used simultaneously, by a set of processes (e.g., storage facilities, transportation vehicles). Alternative sets of processes sharing a resource can be defined.

Using the language, generic and domain-specific constraints can be defined. Generic constraints include structural constraints on the correctness of the workflow, task and resource hierarchies and constraints from the physical world. An example of a structural generic constraint is: "For every and-decomposition of a task, the minimal duration of the task is at least the maximal of all minimal durations of its subtasks". An example of a physical world generic constraint is: "For every process that uses certain amount of a resource as input, without consuming it, either at least that amount of resource of this type is available or can be shared with another process at every time point during process execution". Domain-specific constraints can be added by the designer using templates.

L_{PR} has some similarities with and distinctions from other process modeling languages [1, 2, 10]. In particular, it realizes the most commonly used workflow patterns identified in [2] extended with time parameters (e.g., sequence and parallel execution, synchronization, loops). In comparison with other approaches [1, 3], L_{PR} provides a more extensive means for resource modeling (e.g. shared resources). More details on the process-oriented modeling using L_{PR} can be found in [21].

4.2 Performance-oriented View

Central notions in the performance-oriented view are goal and performance indicator (PI). A PI is a quantitative or qualitative indicator that reflects the state/progress of the company, unit or individual. The characteristics of a PI include, among others: *type* – continuous, discrete; *unit* of measurement; *time_frame* – the length of the time interval for which it will be evaluated; *scale* of measurement; *source* – the internal or external source used to extract the PI: company policies, mission statements, business plan, job descriptions, laws, domain knowledge, etc.; *owner* – the performance of which role or agent does it measure/describe; *hardness* – soft or hard, where soft means not directly measurable, qualitative, e.g. customer's satisfaction, company's reputation, employees' motivation, and hard means measurable, quantitative, e.g., number of customers, time to produce a plan. For the case study, 33 PIs were identified examples of which are given below:

PI name: PI5;
Definition: average correctness of plans
Type: discrete; *Time_frame:* month;
Scale: very_low-low-med-high-very_high;
Source: mission statement, job descriptions;
Owner: forward/daily planning departments
Hardness: soft; ...

PI name: PI27;
Definition: time to create new short-term plan
Type: continuous; *Time_frame:* month
Scale: REAL; *Unit:* hour;
Source: job descriptions
Owner: daily planning departments
Hardness: hard; ...

PIs can be related through various relationships. The following are considered in the framework: (strongly) positive/negative causal influence of one PI on another, positive/negative correlation between two PIs, aggregation – two PIs express the same measure at different aggregation levels. Such relationships can be identified using e.g. company documents, domain knowledge, inference from known relations, statistical or data mining techniques, knowledge from other structures of the framework. Using these relations, a graph structure of PIs can be built.

Based on PIs, PI expressions can be defined as mathematical statements over PIs that can be evaluated to a numerical, qualitative or Boolean value. They are used to define goal patterns. The *type* of a goal pattern indicates the way its property is checked: *achieved (ceased)* – true (false) for a specific time point; *maintained (avoided)* – true (false) for a given time interval; *optimized* – if the value of the PI expression has increased, decreased or approached a target value for a given interval.

Goals are objectives that describe a desired state or development and are defined by adding to goal patterns information such as desirability and priority. The characteristics of a goal include, among others: *priority*; *evaluation type* – achievement goal (based on achieved/ceased pattern – evaluated for a time point) or development goal (based on maintained/avoided/optimized pattern – evaluated for a time interval); *horizon* – for which time point/interval should the goal be satisfied; *hardness* – hard (satisfaction can be established) or soft (satisfaction cannot be clearly established, instead degrees of *satisficing* are defined); *negotiability*. Examples of goals identified for the case study are given below:

Goal name: G3.2
Definition: It is required to maintain high efficiency of allocation of security officers
Priority: high; *Horizon:* long-term
Evaluation type: development goal
Perspective: management, customer
Hardness: soft; *Negotiability:* negotiable, ...

Goal name: G3.1.1.1
Definition: It is required to achieve that the time to update a short-term plan given operational data is at most 48 hours
Priority: high; *Horizon:* short-term
Evaluation type: achievement goal
Perspective: management
Hardness: hard, *Negotiability:* negotiable, ...

A goal can be refined into sub-goals forming a hierarchy. Information about the satisfaction of lower-level goals can be propagated to determine the satisfaction of high-level goals. A goal can be refined into one or more alternative goal lists of AND-type or balanced-type (more fine-tuned ways of decomposition - inspired by the weighted average function) [19]. For each type, propagation rules are defined. Fig. 2 shows a part of the goals hierarchy built for the case study.

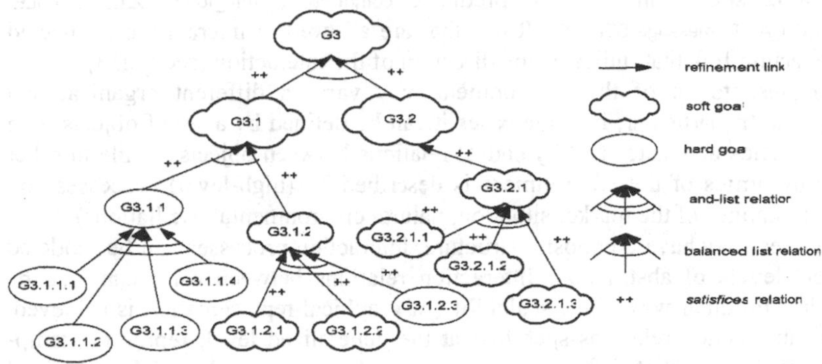

Fig. 2 A part of the goal hierarchy for the case study

Using the concepts and relations of the performance-oriented view, constraints can be formulated. An example of a generic structural constraint is: "If two PIs are related by an aggregation relation then they should have the same type and measurement unit."

Modeling goals is supported to a various degree by a number of existing frameworks in enterprise modeling; however the concept of a PI has been largely ignored. Our approach [19, 20] differs in explicitly representing PIs and the link between a goal and the PI that will measure its satisfaction. Besides the relationships between PIs can be represented and used for reasoning at the design phase.

4.3 Organization-oriented View

In the organization-oriented view organizations are modeled as composite roles that can be refined iteratively into a number of (interacting) composite or simple roles, representing as many aggregation levels as needed. The refined role structures correspond to different types of organization constructs (e.g., groups, units, departments). Yet many of the existing modeling frameworks are able to represent only two or three levels of abstraction: the level of a role, the level of a group composed of roles, and the overall organization level, as in [13]. The organization-oriented view provides means to structure and organize roles by defining interaction and power relations on them. First, interaction relations are discussed.

One of the aims of an organizational structure is to facilitate the interaction between the roles that are involved into the execution of the same or related task(s). Therefore, patterns of role interactions are usually reflected in an organization structure. Each role has an input and an output interface, which facilitate in the interaction (in particular, communication) with other roles and the environment. Role interfaces are described in terms of interaction (input and output) ontologies: a signature specified in order-sorted logic. Generally speaking, an input ontology determines what types of information are allowed to be transferred to the input of a role (or of the environment), and an output ontology predefines what kinds of information can be generated at the output of a role (or of the environment). In particular, to specify a special type of interaction – a speech act s_act (e.g., inform, request, ask) with the content message the ontologies of both role-source r1 and role-destination r2 should include the predicate communicate_from_to(r1:ROLE, r2:ROLE, s_act:SPEECH_ACT, message:STRING). Roles that are allowed to interact are connected by an interaction link that indicates the direction of the interaction (see Fig. 3).

The representation of the environment may vary in different organizational specifications. In particular, in some cases it can be defined by a set of objects with certain properties and states and by causal relations between objects. While in other cases the dynamics of the environment is described by (high-level) processes and trends (e.g. changes of the market situation, natural environmental oscillations).

Since roles may have composite structure, interaction processes can be modeled at different levels of abstraction. Interaction relations between roles can also be depicted in a modular way; thus, scalability of graphical representation is achieved. Moreover, interaction relations specified at the generalized level, represent templates that can be instantiated for a particular case. An instantiated model is obtained from a template by unfolding generic relations between roles and by creating new role instances. For example, the documents of the organization from the case study define standard patterns of interaction between the forward planner and the daily planner roles that can be modeled at the generalized (template) level. However, for a more detailed analysis of the organizational dynamics, a more specific representation defining interaction relations between particular role instances of the forward planner and the daily planner roles (e.g., from different planning teams) is needed (see Fig. 3). For a more detailed description of the modeling of interaction relations at different levels of abstraction and generalization we refer to [6].

Besides interaction relations, also power relations on roles constitute a part of the formal organizational structure. Formal organizational power (authority) establishes and regulates normative superior-subordinate relationships between roles. Authority relations are defined w.r.t. tasks. In the context of the running example the relation is_subordinate_of_for(Daily_PlannerA, Team_Leader1, daily_planning) means that role Daily_PlannerA is a subordinate of role Team_Leader1 w.r.t. the task daily_planning.

Roles have rights and responsibilities related to different aspects of tasks (e.g., execution, monitoring, consulting, and making technological and/or managerial decisions). For example, is_responsible_for(Daily_PlannerB, execution, inform_about_daily_plan) expresses execution responsibility of role Daily_PlannerB for task inform_about_daily_plan.

A number of generic constraints have been identified in this view. For example, "to assign responsibility for some aspect of a task, a role should have the responsibility to make managerial decisions and be the superior of a role, to which the responsibility is assigned".

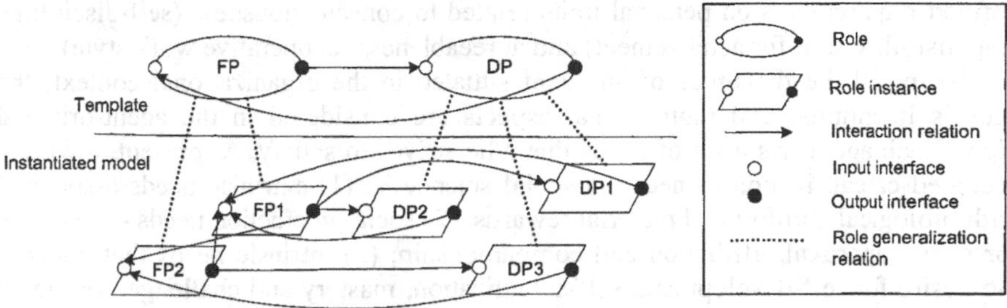

Fig. 3 The graphical representation of interaction relations between the roles Forward Planner (FP) and Daily Planner (DP) (the template) and their instances (the instantiated model)

Roles with managerial rights may under certain conditions authorize and/or make other roles responsible for certain aspects of task execution. In many modern organizations rewards and sanctions form a part of authority relation, thus, they are explicitly defined by appropriate language constructs. Specific conditions (e.g., temporal, situational) under which authority relations may be created/maintained/dissolved are defined by executable rules expressed by TTL formulae. For more details on specifying authority relations in organizations of different types see [23].

4.4 Agent-oriented View

To create realistic organization models, in addition to formal (explicitly identified, documented) aspects, also informal aspects of human behavior in the organizational context should be considered. The computational organization theory [7] has a long tradition of modeling human organizations using the agent paradigm, also used in the proposed framework. Models of agents defined in the agent-oriented view are based on psychological and social theories receiving the most empirical support [17, 27].

An agent is defined as an autonomous entity able to interact (e.g., by observations and actions) with other agents and the environment. Agents are characterized by a set of capabilities (i.e., knowledge and skills) and personal traits. Knowledge of an agent comprises facts and procedures, of which the agent has confident understanding. Skills describe developed abilities of agents to use effectively and readily their knowledge for the performance of tasks. In the literature four types of skills relevant in the organizational context are distinguished: technical, interpersonal, problem-solving/decision-making and managerial skills. Every skill of an agent is associated with a performance indicator. Furthermore, for each skill a numerical value of the skill development that changes over time is defined.

Personal traits are divided into five broad categories discovered in psychology [22]: openness to experience, conscientiousness, extroversion, agreeableness, and neuroticism. Using sets of capabilities and traits, several characteristic types of agents (e.g. "self-confident professional", "intrinsically motivated novice", "submissive employee") are defined that are relevant in different organizational settings.

An agent can be allocated to an organizational role if s/he possesses the necessary capabilities and traits defined as requirements for the role. In the case study, the role Daily_Planner requires the agent to have knowledge and technical skills related to daily planning, as well as some interpersonal skills. The company also defined requirements on personal traits related to conscientiousness (self-discipline, responsibility, aim for achievement) and agreeableness (cooperative work style).

To model the dynamics of an agent situated in the organizational context, the agent's intentional and motivational aspects are considered in the agent-oriented view. Each agent has a set of needs that s/he strives to satisfy. At present, a widely accepted categorization of needs in social science is: (1) extrinsic needs associated with biological comfort and material rewards; (2) social interaction needs - the desire for social approval, affiliation and companionship; (3) intrinsic needs that concern the desire for self-development, self-actualization, mastery and challenge. The level of satisfaction and importance of different types of individual needs change with time causing change in priorities of individual goals related to these needs. The highest motivation is demonstrated by an agent w.r.t. actions (e.g., the execution of organizational tasks) that (significantly) contribute to the satisfaction of his/her primary goals. An organization that recognizes primary goals of its agents often can arrange their work and provide incentives so that the agents are constantly stimulated to adopt the behavior that also ensures the satisfaction of organizational goals.

For reasoning about the agent motivation and work behavior, Vroom's version of the expectancy theory [27] is used which establishes causal dependencies between a number of individual, organizational and environmental parameters and the agent's motivation to perform certain action (e.g., process). The expectancy theory is one of the few organization theories that can be made operational and used for simulation.

5 Design Issues

The general approaches to organization design differ w.r.t. the presence and involvement of the concerned agents. The design can be performed without having in mind specific agents - the necessary agent profiles are composed at the later design stages based on the considered/designed tasks. Organizational design can also be performed w.r.t. a (partially) known set of agents who will take roles in the organization. Thus agents' skills and traits can be taken into account. Sometimes the agents are not only known but they have some degree of power to steer the design process.

The design process often starts with the identification of one or more high-level goals which play the role of the driving force behind the design process. These goals (initially still informally defined) should answer the question: why should the organization exist and what purpose will it serve? Such goals can be identified by the designer or emerge through communication and/or negotiation between the involved agents. In the second case the resulting organizational goals reflect to some extent the individual goals of the participating agents. In this way some possible future conflicts between individual and organizational goals are prevented early. If conflicts do appear, they can be dealt with through negotiation and redesign at the later stages.

The higher-level goals are often more abstract and, through refinement, more specific, easier to evaluate, goals are formulated. Also, often the higher-level goals are long-term, strategic goals while their sub-goals are shorter-term tactical or operational goals. The leaves of the hierarchies should be goals formulated so that the corresponding PIs can clearly be associated to the processes in the workflow. In this way the satisfaction of every goal in the hierarchies can be evaluated.

Also at the earlier stage of the design process one or more general tasks are identified giving an answer to the question: what should the organization do? For identifying these tasks sometimes only the defined goals are considered. However when the involved agents are (partially) known, the definition of tasks can be based on the available skills and experience as well. These tasks are later refined to task hierarchies. For the tasks, the used / produced resource types are identified which can also form hierarchies. Based on the tasks, processes are defined and organized into workflows that can represent different levels of abstraction. The level of elaboration of these structures can depend on the type of the organization. In mechanistic organizations [22] the procedures are prescribed to a great degree of detail which should result in more elaborate structures refined to simple tasks and processes. In organic organizations (e.g., adhocracies) the procedures are described at a higher level of abstraction leaving more freedom to the agents to choose how to perform them which should result in less deep task hierarchies and less elaborate workflows.

The design process can follow different paths through the views and concepts but several general guidelines can be formulated. When an informally defined goal is being formalized and made more precise this should be reflected on the PI structure - often this means that a new PI is defined or an existing one is revised. A change in the goal hierarchy should also be reflected on the task hierarchy by identifying new or existing tasks that can realize the new or revised goals. A change in the task hierarchy often brings changes to the current workflow design. Adding or revising processes in the workflow might give rise to new PIs that need to be monitored. When a PI is proposed it should be decided on its level of importance in order to find out if a new goal should be formulated based on it. The definition of roles is based on the currently defined tasks and processes. Fig.4 shows the main dependencies between concepts and structures in the framework which guide the design process.

Power and authority relations between the defined roles are usually assigned at the later stages of the design process. However different general schemes can be predefined and committed to by the designer at the earlier stages as well leaving the details for later. Such schemes reflect different types of organizations identified in organization theory such as: hierarchical, flat or team-based organizations which differ in the way the power is distributed, granted or accepted by the roles (agents).

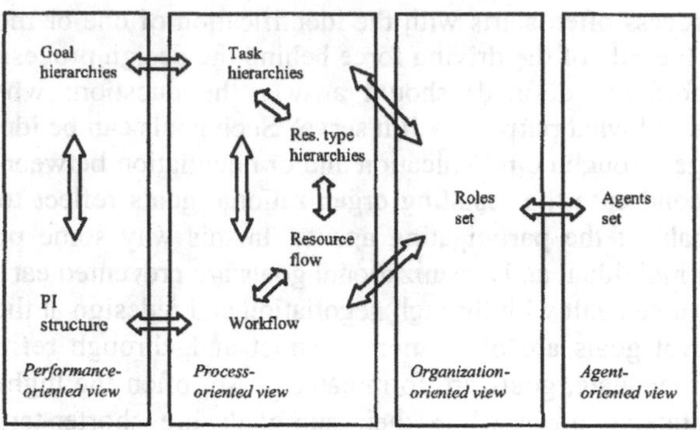

Fig. 4 Dependencies between the structures of the four views

The choice of scheme should be driven by an analysis of the environment in which the organization should operate. For example a relatively stable environment tolerates a well-defined hierarchical structure which can help the organization to operate more efficiently. A changing environment can be addressed by designing a lighter, more flexible and dynamic structure that can easily adapt to the changes. Obviously the environment in which the organization will be situated plays an important role not only in defining power and authority relations. It needs to be taken into account at every step of the design process and in every view of the framework.

Sometimes instead of designing an organization from scratch, a specification of an existing one needs to be created. Here a wide range of internal or external documents are used, e.g., company policies, job descriptions, mission statement, business plans, procedure descriptions, laws. However even the richest documentation leaves some information unspecified thus it is essential to involve domain experts and managers. In organizational redesign, the issue of maintaining the consistency and correspondence between the structures of different views becomes more complex and the tools for automatic analysis become indispensable.

The framework allows reuse in a number of ways. Libraries of commonly appearing parts of structures (goals and tasks hierarchies, PI-structures, workflow graphs, etc.) can be stored and reused for organizations in the same domain. The research in identifying and classifying important PIs for different domains [e.g. 8, 15] can easily be applied here. Reuse can also be supported by predefined templates for various aspects of different types of organizations (mechanistic, organic, etc.). For example templates for domain-specific constraints can be provided for each view to be customized by the designer. The used tool allows defining parameterized templates (macros) for TTL formulae that can be instantiated in different ways which can also be used as support for designers not skilled in logics. For more details see [21].

6 Analysis Methods

The formal foundations of the proposed framework enable three types of automated analysis. The first type focuses on the verification of specifications of every view (i.e., establishing the correctness w.r.t. a set of constraints). The second type addresses the validation of (combined) correct specifications of different views by simulation. Finally, the third type focuses on the analysis of actual executions of organizational scenarios based on (combined) specifications from different views. The three types of analysis are discussed in this order in the rest of this Section.

The verification of the consistency of a PI structure is performed by checking constraints based on the inference rules described in [20]. The inference rules allow generating all correct causality relations between PIs that should hold in the PI structure. Since goal and PI structures are closely related, it is important to guarantee consistency and correspondence of these structures to each other. For this a dedicated consistency check can be performed, based on the constraints described in [19]. For organizations that do not allow conflicts between goals, a number of dedicated techniques for the identification and the resolution of conflicts are proposed in [19].

In the process-oriented view constraints are defined for the three types of structures: workflow, task and resource hierarchies [21] that should be satisfied by specifications. The verification of the correctness of a specification is performed during or at the end of the design process, depending on the type of constraint. Some domain-specific constraints might not (yet) be satisfied for incomplete specifications. The designer can choose when they should be checked. The syntactical check of a specification and the verification of generic constraints are performed at each design step.

Note that workflow specifications can be represented and analyzed at different levels of abstraction. In general, the verification of higher-level specifications is computationally cheaper than that of more detailed lower-level specifications. Furthermore, a correct high level workflow specification can be refined to a lower level by using the correct hierarchy of tasks, on which the processes of the workflow are based. In such a case the correctness verification of the obtained workflow is guaranteed without additional verification. The verification of interaction relations in composite (multi-level, hierarchical) organizational structures is addressed in [6].

The algorithms developed for the verification of constraints of different types in the proposed framework are more efficient than general-purpose methods for verifying specifications (e.g., model checking [11]).

As shown in [18], correct organizational specifications can be used to guide and to control the actual execution of processes in organizations. The execution data recorded by an enterprise information system and structured in the form of a trace can be checked for conformity to a formal organization (i.e., specifications and constraints defined in particular views). To this end, the relations and constraints specified for particular views are translated into properties expressed in the execution language used for the formalization of the trace [18]. They are checked in real time on the trace. Depending on the type of event that (should) occur(s) in the trace at a certain time point, only a subset of relevant properties is checked at this time point. Moreover, the designer may specify additional properties to be checked in real time.

A trace can also be analyzed after the execution of an organizational scenario is completed. For this type of analysis, next to the properties obtained from the formal organization, the designer may specify in TTL and check other properties. The traces are used to evaluate the PIs associated with the executed processes. These PIs are related to the leaves of the goals hierarchy, thus the satisfaction of these goals can be evaluated. The satisfaction values are propagated upwards to establish the satisfaction of higher-level goals determining the overall organizational performance [18].

Based on correct (combined) specifications of the views, simulation can be performed, in which different types of agents, defined using the concepts from the agent-oriented view, are allocated to the organizational roles. By considering different simulation scenarios of organizational behavior, the validation of organizational specifications can be performed (i.e., checking if the model behaves as expected, corresponds to reality) using the dedicated tool [4, 5].

In the context of the case study the behavior of different types of planners under different organizational and environmental conditions was investigated [24]. The simulation results in Fig.5 are related to a planner agent with initially lacking skills but good learning abilities to improve through processes execution. In the simulation comparable amounts of simple and complex tasks and equal arrival rates of tasks are.used. Fig.5a shows the change of the satisfaction level of the intrinsic needs of the agent, performing tasks under the control of a team leader. The simulation results show that the more experience the agent gains, the less s/he appreciates the leader's involvement. Fig.5b shows a growth of the agent satisfaction when the leader exercises direct control only if the agent lacks experience. The simulation results conform to the empirical evidence [27], which supports the specification's validity.

The simulation tool also provides the possibility to generate the simulation results in the form of a trace. Traces can be used for the validation of specifications by checking dynamic properties in the environment TTL Checker [4]. Such properties should be specified in TTL and may be expressed using the concepts and the relations defined in different views. A detailed explanation can be found in [4, 6].

Simulation based on a correct and valid specification can also be used for predictions on the organization's behavior in different environmental conditions and with different agents as well as for investigating theories from the social sciences.

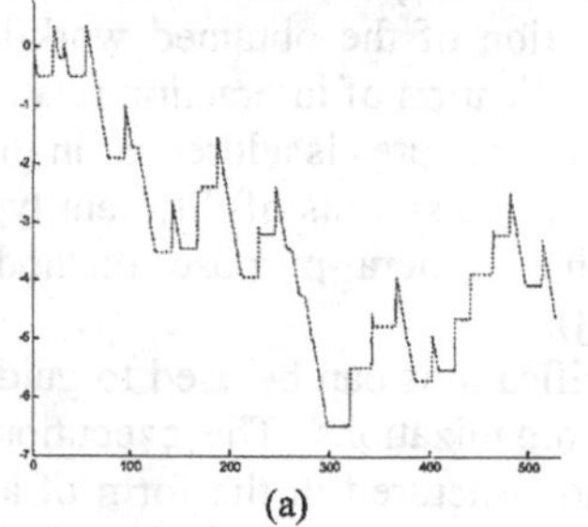

(a)

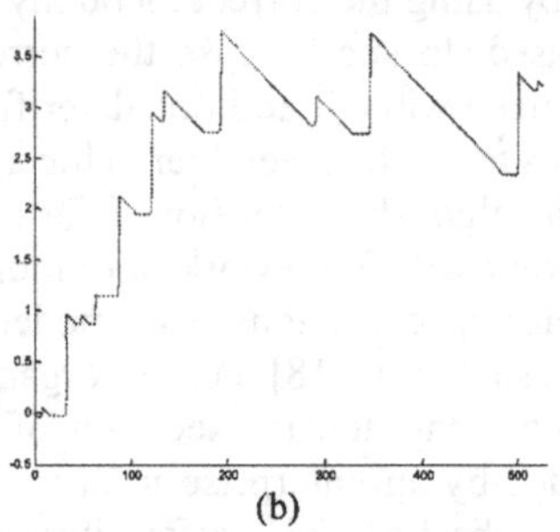

(b)

Fig. 5 Change of the satisfaction level of the agent's intrinsic needs (the vertical axis) over time (the horizontal axis) in the case of constant supervision (a) and temporary supervision (b)

7 Conclusions

This paper describes a formal framework for modeling and analysis of organizations. The framework has a rich ontological basis that comprises concepts and relations partitioned into a number of dedicated views similar to the ones defined in GERAM. The introduced modeling framework allows representing different types of organizations ranging from mechanistic to organic. In contrast to many existing architectures, the proposed framework allows performing different types of automated analysis of organizational models (e.g. by verification, validation and simulation) both of particular views and across different views. Moreover, the framework incorporates agent-based models of individuals based on social theories. Organizational models of different views can be represented and analysed at different abstraction levels, which allows handling high complexity and increases scalability of modeling. Finally, the framework allows model reuse that accelerates and facilitates the modeling process.

The views of the proposed framework are formalized based on intuitive, close to the natural, predicate languages, with concepts and relations that can be represented graphically. Currently, the graphical interface is provided for the performance-oriented view, whereas other views are specified textually using the dedicated tools. In the future, modeling related to other views will be also supported graphically.

The application of the proposed framework has been illustrated by an example of an organization from the security domain. The framework was also applied in the context of a case study in logistics (*http://www.almende.com/deal/*). Currently, the framework is used for modeling and analysis of an air traffic control organization.

References

1. W. van der Aalst and K.M van Hee, *Workflow Management: Models, Methods, and Systems* (MIT press, Cambridge, MA, 2002).
2. W. van der Aalst, A. ter Hofstede, B. Kiepuszewski, and A.P. Barros, Workflow patterns, *Distributed and Parallel Databases* 14(3), 5–51 (2003).
3. P. Bernus, et al. (eds.): *Handbook on Architectures of Information Systems*, Springer-Verlag, Heidelberg (1998) 209-241.
4. T. Bosse, C.M. Jonker, L. van der Meij, A. Sharpanskykh, and J. Treur, Specification and Verification of Dynamics in Cognitive Agent Models. In: *Proceedings of the 6th Int. Conf. on Intelligent Agent Technology, IAT'06* (IEEE Computer Society, 2006), pp. 247-254.
5. T. Bosse, C.M. Jonker, L. van der Meij, and J. Treur, LEADSTO: a Language and Environment for Analysis of Dynamics by SimulaTiOn. In: *Proc. MATES'05*. LNAI 3550, edited by T. Eymann et al. (Springer Verlag, 2005) pp. 165-178.
6. E. Broek, C. Jonker, A. Sharpanskykh, J. Treur, and P. Yolum, Formal Modeling and Analysis of Organizations. In *Coordination, Organization, Institutions and Norms in Agent Systems I*, LNAI 3913, (Springer, 2006).
7. K.M. Carley: A comparison of artificial and human organizations. *Journal of Economic Behavior & Organization*, 31(2) 175-191 (1996).
8. F.T.S. Chan, Performance measurement in a supply chain, *International Journal of Advanced Manufacturing Technology* 21(7), 534-548 (2003).
9. V. Chapurlat, B. Kamsu-Foguem, and F. Prunet, A formal verification framework and associated tools for enterprise modeling: Application to UEML, *Computers in industry*, 57, 153-166 (2006).
10. Y.-H. Chen-Burger, A. Tate, and D. Robertson, Enterprise Modelling: A Declarative Approach for FBPML, *European Conference of Artificial Intelligence, Knowledge Management and Organisational Memories Workshop*, 2002.
11. E.M. Clarke, O. Grumberg, and D.A. Peled, *Model Checking* (MIT Press, 2000).
12. N. Dalal, M. Kamath, W. Kolarik, and E. Sivaraman, Toward an integrated framework for modeling enterprise processes, *Communications of the ACM*, 47(3), 83-87 (2004).
13. J. Ferber and O. Gutknecht, A meta-model for the analysis and design of organizations in multi-agent systems. In: *Proceedings of Third International Conference on Multi-Agent Systems (ICMAS'98)* (IEEE Computer Society 1998), pp.128-135.
14. M. Koubarakis and D. Plexousakis. A formal framework for business process modeling and design. *Information Systems*, 27(5), 299–319 (2002).

15. E. Krauth, H. Moonen, V. Popova, and M. Schut, Performance Measurement and Control in Logistics Service Providing, *Proceedings of ICEIS 2005*, pp. 239-247 (2005).
16. M. Manzano, *Extensions of First Order Logic* (Cambridge University Press, 1996).
17. A. H. Maslow, *Motivation and Personality*, 2nd. ed. (New York, Harper & Row, 1970).
18. V. Popova and A. Sharpanskykh, Formal analysis of executions of organizational scenarios based on process-oriented models. To appear in: *Proc. of 21st European Conference on Modeling and Simulation (ECMS'07)*, 2007.
19. V. Popova and A. Sharpanskykh, Formal Modelling of Goals in Agent Organizations. In *Proc. of the AOMS Workshop* (joint with IJCAI 2007), 74-86.
20. V. Popova and A. Sharpanskykh, Modelling Organizational Performance Indicators. In: *Proc. of IMSM'07 conference*, edited by Barros, F. et al., 165–170, (2007).
21. V. Popova and A. Sharpanskykh, Process-Oriented Organization Modeling and Analysis Based on Constraints. Technical Report 062911AI, VUA, http://hdl.handle.net/1871/10545
22. W.R. Scott, *Institutions and organizations* (SAGE Publications, Thousand Oaks 2001).
23. A. Sharpanskykh, Authority and its Implementation in Enterprise Information Systems, Technical Report 070202AI, VUA.
24. A. Sharpanskykh, Modeling of Agent Behavior in the Organizational Context, Technical Report 070323AI, VUA.
25. A. Sharpanskykh and J. Treur, Verifying Interlevel Relations within Multi-Agent Systems. In: *Proc. of the 17th European Conf. on AI, ECAI'06* (IOS Press, 2006), pp. 290-294.
26. K.D. Tham, *Representation and Reasoning About Costs Using Enterprise Models and ABC*, PhD Dissertation, University of Toronto, 1999.
27. V.H. Vroom, *Work and motivation* (Wiley, New York, 1964).

Modularization Constructs in Method Engineering: Towards Common Ground?

Pär J. Ågerfalk[1], Sjaak Brinkkemper[2], Cesar Gonzalez-Perez[3], Brian Henderson-Sellers[4], Fredrik Karlsson[5], Steven Kelly[6] and Jolita Ralyté[7]

1 Lero – The Irish Software Engineering Research Centre, University of Limerick, Ireland, and Uppsala University, Sweden, par.agerfalk@lero.ie

2 Institute for Information and Computing Sciences, Utrecht University, Netherlands, S.Brinkkemper@cs.uu.nl

3 European Software Institute, cesargon@verdewek.com

4 University of Technology, Sydney, Australia, brian@it.uts.edu.au

5 Methodology Exploration Lab, Dept. of Informatics (ESI), Örebro University, Sweden, fredrik.karlsson@esi.oru.se

6 MetaCase, Finland, stevek@metacase.com

7 CUI, University of Geneva, Switzerland, jolita.ralyte@cui.unige.ch

Abstract. Although the Method Engineering (ME) research community has reached considerable maturity, it has not yet been able to agree on the granularity and definition of the configurable parts of methods. This state of affairs is causing unnecessary confusion, especially with an ever increasing number of people contributing to ME research. There are several competing notions around, most significantly 'method fragments' and 'method chunks', but also 'method components' and 'process components' are used in some quarters and have also been widely published. Sometimes these terms are used interchangeably, but there appears to be important semantic and pragmatic differences. If the differences are unimportant, we should be able to come to an agreement on what construct to promote. Alternatively, the different constructs may serve different purposes and there is a need for them to coexist. If this is the case, it should be possible to pinpoint exactly how they are related and which are useful in what contexts. This panel is a step towards finding common ground in this area, which arguably is at the very core of ME.

1 Introduction

Since its inception in the early to mid 1990s, the Method Engineering (ME) research community has reached considerable maturity. Nonetheless, there is still

---

Please use the following format when citing this chapter:

Ågerfalk, P. J., Brinkkemper, S., Gonzalez-Perez, C., Henderson-Sellers, B., Karlsson, F., Kelly, S., Ralyté, J., 2007, in IFIP International Federation for Information Processing, Volume 244, Situational Method Engineering: Fundamentals and Experiences, eds. Ralyté, J., Brinkkemper, S., Henderson-Sellers B., (Boston Springer), pp. 359-368.

some ambiguity with regards to fundamental concepts and terminology. Since situational ME is fundamentally concerned with the assembly and configuration of information systems engineering methods, understanding the basic building blocks of methods is arguably core to the discipline. In order to devise appropriate ME processes and tools, we need to understand what building blocks those processes and tools are to handle. To date, a number of different such 'modularization constructs' have been suggested. Among the most cited are 'method fragments', 'method chunks', 'method components' and 'process components'. Along with these constructs come certain interpretations of related concepts such as method, technique, notation, process, deliverable, work product, tool etc. Sometimes the constructs are used interchangeably, but there appears to be important semantic and pragmatic differences. If the differences are unimportant, we should be able to come to an agreement on what construct to promote. Alternatively, the different constructs may serve different purposes and there is a need for them to coexist. If this is the case, it should be possible to pinpoint exactly how they are related and which are useful in what contexts. This panel is a significant step towards finding common ground in this area.

The remainder of this panel introduction consists of a brief description of the four modularization constructs mentioned above, followed by a brief introduction of the panellists. The aim of this document is to provide some background and context for the panel. The actual discussion and its outcome will be reported elsewhere.

2 Method Fragments

One of the earliest and arguably most important modularization construct in ME is that of the *method fragment*. It was first proposed and elaborated by Brinkkemper and colleagues [1–4] and has since been widely adopted in ME research. Essentially, method fragments are standardized building blocks based on a coherent part of a method [1]: '... a description of an IS engineering method, or any coherent part thereof'. A complete method, such as 'OMT', is a method fragment and so is any single concept used within that method, such as 'object'. A method fragment thus resides on a certain so-called *layer of granularity*, of which five are possible: method, stage, model, diagram, or concept [4]. Consequently, 'object' resides on the concept layer while 'OMT' resides on the method layer. Furthermore, a method fragment is either a *process fragment* or a *product fragment*. Process fragments represent the activities, stages etc that are to be carried out and product fragments represent deliverables, diagrams etc that are to be produced, or that are required, during development. Method fragments are stored in a method base from which they can be retrieved using a query language, such as the Method Engineering Language (MEL) [5]. This way, a situational method can be constructed by combining a number of method fragments into a situational method. To be meaningful and useful, such a combination must follow certain assembly rules that adhere to the construction principles in the process perspective on the one hand and in the product perspective on the other hand. This has been explored by Brinkkemper *et al.* [4].

Currently the team of Brinkkemper at Utrecht University is focussing on the methodological support for product software companies, i.e. companies that develop and market software products for a particular market. About 10% of the total ICT spending is spend on software products and examples of such companies are Microsoft, SAP, Oracle, and Business Objects [6]. As these companies keep the ownership of the software code and all auxiliary materials belonging to the software product, these companies create and maintain a proprietary software development method. From the start-up phase where they begin with bug tracing to a more consolidated company with all kinds of quality engineering processes in place. The gradual growth of the product software company calls for a more incremental growth from simple method fragments to more complex fragments at a later stage [7, 8]. The evolution from simple to complex processes properly supported with development tools while keeping the historical documentation and the methodological context in place are a significant scientific challenge for the coming years.

3 Method Chunks

The *method chunk* concept was proposed by Rolland and colleagues [9–13] as a way to capture more of the situational aspects in ME and to appropriately support the retrieval process. The concept was introduced together with a contextual ME approach using scenarios [10] and suggests an organization of the method base in two levels, one method knowledge level and one method meta-knowledge level [9]. The former level is represented by the method chunk body and the latter captures the situational and intentional aspect of method chunks in the method chunk descriptor. In [9] the method knowledge level is operationalized in a three level abstraction model and method chunks are classified into component, pattern or framework. A method component is a complete method description. A pattern is, for example, a set of generic guidelines for writing test scripts. Finally, a framework is a meta-method that guides the construction of a way-of-working within a specific method.

In the latest work [11–13] the concept of method chunk is defined as autonomous, cohesive and coherent part of a method providing guidelines and related concepts to support the realisation of some specific system engineering activity (e.g. business modelling, requirements specification, design etc). In fact, the method knowledge is captured in the method chunk *body* and *interface*. The interface defines pre and post conditions of chunk application formalised by a couple <*situation, intention*>. The situation specifies the required input product part(s) while the intention defines the goal that the chunk helps to achieve. For example, the interface of the method chunk supporting identification of Business Actors and Use Cases within the RUP could be modelled as <(Business knowledge, problem description, interview results), Identify and describe business actor(s) and use case(s)>.

The body of the method chunk includes two kinds of knowledge: product and process. The product knowledge defines the work products (input and output) used by the method chunk (e.g. the definitions of the concept "actor" and "use case and their relationships). This knowledge is generally expressed in terms of meta-models.

The process knowledge captured in a method chunk provides guidelines how to obtain target product(s) from input product(s) (e.g. the guidelines how to identify system actors and their business use cases). The guideline can be represented as an informal description or expressed by using different process modelling formalisms such as NATURE context trees [14] or MAP graphs [15] depending on how rich and complex it is. The fact that a guideline can be complex (i.e. composed of a set of sub-guidelines) means that the corresponding method chunk can be an aggregate of a collection of smaller chunks.

The *descriptor* (i.e. method meta-knowledge) of the method chunk extends the contextual knowledge defined in the *interface* with a set of criteria that help to better locate the engineering situation in which the method chunk is useful. A detailed classification of these criteria related to the information systems development, named Reuse Frame, is proposed in [13].

A method chunk is selected for a specific situation based on the characterization of that situation and how relevant it is to achieve the intention of the method chunk. Hence, the intention of a method chunk, the goal that can be achieved through application of the way of working prescribed by the method chunk, is central.

Method chunks are retrieved from the method base through the use of meta-knowledge. Based on the structure of the method base, where method chunks have been clustered and described using interfaces and descriptors, it is possible to query the method base using a query language. For example, it is possible to select a chunk from the RUP if it has a representation in the method base. Hence, a method chunk query language has similarities with MEL when using method fragments.

Some initial comparisons of method fragments and method chunks are to be found in [13] and [16].

4 Method Components

First introduced by Goldkuhl and colleagues [17, 18], the *method component* concept has recently been further developed by Karlsson and others [19–22]. The basic idea is to view methods as constituted by exchangeable and reusable components. Fundamentally, each component consists of descriptions for ways of working (a process), notations, and concepts [17]. A process describes rules and recommendations for and informs the method (component) user what actions to perform and in what order. Notation means semantic, syntactic and symbolic rules for documentation. Concepts are categories included in the process and the notation. Concepts and notation together constitute what is sometimes referred to as a modelling language, such as the UML. A method component can also be used separately and independently from other components. Each method component addresses a certain aspect of the problem at hand.

Building further on this original method component concept, Karlsson [21] defines it as 'a self-contained part of a method expressing the transformation of one or several artifacts into a defined target artifact and the rationale for such a transformation.' The method component construct thus draws significantly on the idea of method rationale – the systematic treatment of the arguments and reasons behind a particular method [20, 23, 24, 25]. While the intention of a method chunk is typically expressed in terms of the action that immediately satisfies the intention, method rationale aims to direct method engineers' attention to the underlying assumptions of those actions and promote a critical attitude towards the different parts of a method.

A method component consists of two parts: its content and the rationale expressing why the content is designed as it is and what it can bring about. The content of a method component is an aggregate of method elements [21]: A method element is a part of a method that manifests a method component's target state or facilitates the transformation from one defined state to another. The concept of method element can be specialized into five categories. Firstly, there are three interrelated parts of prescribed action, concept and notation. These categories are complemented with artefact and actor role as two further sub-types of method element. Artefacts act as deliverables from the transformation process as well as input to this process. Methods are here viewed as heuristic procedures (heurithms) and consequently specified inputs are considered to be recommended inputs. However, a method component needs to have at least one input. Otherwise the method component will not have any meaningful support in the method. One exception to this is method components that initiate new activities that are later integrated with the result from other method components. The selection of actor roles are determined by the prescribed actions that need to be part of the transformation process. Actor roles are played either as drivers of the prescribed actions in the method component or as participants.

The rationale part of the method component concept consists of two parts: goals and values. Method elements exist for reasons, which are made explicit by means of associating method elements to the goals. These goals are anchored in values of the method creator [18, 25]. Taken together, goals and values are often considered important constituents of a methods underlying perspective [18] or 'philosophy' [26]. In method engineering, method rationale is more important than the deliverable as such. Through the method rationale it is possible to address the goals that are essential in order to fulfil the overall goal of a specific project. Prescribed actions and artefacts are only means to achieve something and method rationale can thus help developers not to lose sight of that ultimate result, and also help them find alternative ways forward.

It is important to point out that in our current understanding, method components always reside on the 'artefact layer of granularity' and represent a non-hierarchal concept. This is to reflect the notion that method components are the smallest coherent parts of a method that are practically useful. This design choice is based on two empirical observations [21]: The first, and most important, is that systems developers' tend to focus on the artefacts (a.k.a. deliverables) when discussing situational methods, and these are viewed as non-hierarchal patterns. Second, it has proven difficult to balance precision and cost with hierarchal concepts in situational method engineering.

5 OPF Method/Process Components

The OPEN Process Framework [27, 28] also utilizes the concept of a method fragment but stresses that each fragment needs to be generated from an element in a prescribed underpinning metamodel. This metamodel has recently been upgraded with the recent availability of the International Standard ISO/IEC 24744 'Software Engineering Metamodel for Development Methodologies' [29]. While many of the OPF fragments focus on 'process' there are also significant numbers for products and producers (people and tools involved in software development). These are the three acknowledged top-level meta-elements for methodologies leading to: process-focussed fragments (e.g. a kind of task or technique), product-focussed fragments (a kind of diagram, document or other work product) and producer-focussed fragments (e.g. a role played by a member of the software development team, a testing tool) – the last of which (producers) is not represented in other SME approaches. In the OPF, these method fragments are defined separately and then linked together using instances of metamodel classes such as *ActionKind*, representing a single usage event that a given process fragment exerts upon a given product fragment. This class contains an attribute, *Type*, that specifies what kind of action the process part is exerting on the product part. For example, imagine a methodology that contains a requirements validation task. This task takes a draft requirements document as input and modifies it accordingly through the validation process, creating, as well, a requirements defect list. Modelling this task plus the two involved products (one of which is both an input *and* an output) can be easily modelled by using two actions: one action would map the requirements validation task to the requirements document, specifying a type 'modify', and a second action would map the same requirements validation task to the requirements defect list, specifying the type as 'create'. The relationships between process- and product-oriented fragments are thus clearly specified. (It must be noted that the actions are lightweight entities in the methodology that act as mappings between heavyweight process- and product-oriented fragments. Actions are not containers, as are chunks.).

6 The MetaEdit Experience

Research in the MetaPHOR project, object-oriented ideas in the implementation of MetaEdit+, and experience with customers, led MetaCase largely to avoid the question of the size or definition of 'chunks' or 'fragments'. Rather they are able to reuse anything, from a single Property type (e.g. the 'Actor Name' field of the Actor type in UML Use Case diagrams) through Object types (e.g. Actor) to Graph types (e.g. Use Case Diagram) and interlinked sets of Graph types (e.g. UML). Accompanying these central and clearly identifiable elements go various rules that map to the 'harder' end of the process scale, generators that form the operational semantics, along with 'softer' parts of processes and things like problem domain semantics. Mainly, though, the focus has been on support for creating entirely new modelling languages, and how reuse and linking of types in the metamodel allows reuse and linking on the model level.

7 About the Panellists

Prof. Pär J. Ågerfalk (panel moderator) is a Senior Researcher at Lero – The Irish Software Engineering Research Centre and holds the Chair in Computer Science in Intersection with Social Sciences at Uppsala University. He received his PhD in Information Systems Development from Linköping University and has held fulltime positions at Örebro University, University of Limerick, and Jönköping International Business School. His current research centres on open source software development, globally distributed and flexible development methods and how IS development can be informed by language/action theory. His work has appeared in a number of leading IS journals and conferences and he is currently an associate editor of the *European Journal of Information Systems* and a senior associate editor for a special issue of *Information Systems Research* on Flexible and Distributed IS Development.

Prof. Sjaak Brinkkemper is professor of Organisation and Information at the Institute of Information and Computing Sciences of the Utrecht University, the Netherlands. Before he was a consultant at the Vanenburg Group and a Chief Architect at Baan. Before Baan he held academic positions at the University of Twente and the University of Nijmegen, both in the Netherlands. He holds a MSc and a PhD in of the University of Nijmegen. He has published five books and more than hundred papers on his research interests: software product development, information systems methodology, meta-modelling, and method engineering.

Dr. Cesar Gonzalez-Perez has been a research project leader at the European Software Institute until last June, where he led research efforts in the areas of method engineering, metamodelling and conceptual modelling. Previously, he worked over 3 years at the Faculty of IT of the University of Technology, Sydney, from where he co-edited the standardisation projects that resulted in the standard metamodels AS4651 and ISO/IEC 24744. Cesar is also the founder and former technical director of Neco, a company based in Spain specialising in software development support services, which include the deployment and use of OPEN/Metis at small and mid-sized organisations. Cesar has also worked for the University of Santiago de Compostela in Spain as a researcher in computing and archaeology, and got his PhD in this topic in 2000.

Dr. Fredrik Karlsson received his PhD in Information Systems Development from Linköping University and is currently a Senior Lecturer at Örebro University. His research focuses on tailoring of systems development methods, systems development methods as reusable assets, and CAME tools. He has developed the CAME tool MC Sandbox that supports method configuration. At Örebro University he heads the Methodology Exploration Lab and is an active member of the Swedish research network VITS. His work has appeared in, for example, *European Journal of Information Systems* and *Information and Software Technology*.

Dr. Steven Kelly is the CTO of MetaCase and co-founder of the DSM Forum. He has over a dozen years of experience of building metaCASE environments and acting as a consultant on their use in Domain-Specific Modelling. He is architect and lead developer of MetaEdit+, MetaCase's domain-specific modelling tool. Ever present on the program committee of the OOPSLA workshops on Domain-Specific Modelling, he co-organized the first workshop in 2001. He is author of over 20 articles in both academic and industry publications, and is a member of IFIP WG 8.1 and the editorial board for the Journal of Database Management. Steven has an M.A. (Hons.) in Mathematics and Computer Science from the University of Cambridge, and a Ph.D. from the University of Jyväskylä.

Dr. Jolita Ralyté is currently a senior researcher and lecturer at the University of Geneva, Department of Information Systems. She obtained a PhD in Computer Science from the University of Paris 1 – Sorbonne in 2001. The research areas of Dr. Ralyté include situational method engineering, requirement engineering, information systems evolution and interoperability and distributed information systems development. She is in charge of the International Method Engineering Task Group within the IFIP WG 8.1 and the task group TG6 dealing with methods and method engineering techniques supporting various systems interoperability issues within the European NoE INTEROP. Her work has been published in various international conferences and journals. Dr Ralyté has been involved in the organisation of a number of international conferences and workshops (ME'07, OOIS'03, EMSISE'03, Interop-ESA'05, SREP'05, SREP'07 and Doctoral Symposium at I-ESA'06) and co-edited a special issue of *SPIP* with revised best papers from SREP'05.

References

1. Harmsen, F., Brinkkemper, S., and Oei, H. (1994). Situational Method Engineering for Information System Project Approaches. In: A.A. Verrijn Stuart and T.W. Olle (Eds.), Methods and Associated Tools for the Information Systems Life Cycle. *Proceedings of the IFIP WG 8.1 Working Conference*, Maastricht, Netherlands, September 1994, IFIP Transactions A-55, North-Holland, 1994, ISBN 0-444-82074-4, pp. 169-194. Also in: *Memoranda Informatica* 94-03, ISSN 0924-3755, 34 pages, January 1994.
2. Brinkkemper, S. (1996). Method engineering: Engineering of information systems development methods and tools. *Information and Software Technology, 38*(4), 275–280.
3. Harmsen, A.F. (1997). *Situational method engineering.* Doctoral dissertation, Moret Ernst & Young Management Consultants, Utrecht, The Netherlands.
4. Brinkkemper S., Saeki, M., and Harmsen, F. (1999). Meta-Modelling Based Assembly Techniques for Situational Method Engineering, *Information Systems,* 24(3), pp. 209–228.
5. Brinkkemper S., Saeki M., and Harmsen, F. (2001). A Method Engineering Language for the Description of Systems Development Methods (Extended Abstract). In: K.R. Dittrich, A Geppert, and M.C. Norrie (eds.), *Proceedings of the 13th International Conference CAiSE'01*, pp. 173-179, Interlaken, Switzerland, 2001, Lecture Notes in Computer Science, Springer Verlag. ISBN 3-540-42215-3.
6. Xu, L. and Brinkkemper, S. (2007). Concepts for Product Software. To appear in *European Journal of Information Systems.*
7. Weerd, I. van de, Brinkkemper, S., Souer, J., and Versendaal, J. (2006). A Situational Implementation Method for Web-based Content Management System-applications: Method Engineering and Validation in Practice. *Software Process: Improvement and Practice* 11(5), 521-538.
8. Weerd, I. van de, Brinkkemper, S., Versendaal J. (2007). Concepts for Incremental Method Evolution: Empirical Exploration and Validation in Requirements Management. In *Proceedings of the 19th International Conference on Advanced Information Systems Engineering*, LNCS 4495, 469–484.

9. Rolland, C. and Prakash, N. (1996). A proposal for context-specific method engineering. In S. Brinkkemper, K. Lyytinen & R. Welke (Eds.), *Method Engineering: Principles of method construction and tool support* (Vol. 191–208): Chapman & Hall.
10. Rolland, C., Plihon, V. and Ralyté, J. (1998). Specifying the Reuse Context of Scenario Method Chunks. *Proceedings of the 10th International Conference on Advanced Information System Engineering (CAISE'98),* Pisa, Italy, June 1998. B. Pernici, C. Thanos (Eds), LNCS 1413, Springer-Verlag, pp. 191-218.
11. Ralyté, J. and Rolland, C. (2001). An Approach for Method Reengineering. Proceedings of the 20th International Conference on Conceptual Modeling (ER2001), LNCS 2224, Springer-Verlag, pp.471-484.
12. Ralyté, J., Deneckère, R., and Rolland, C. (2003). Towards a Generic Model for Situational Method Engineering, In *Proceedings of 15th International Conference on Advanced Information Systems Engineering (CAiSE 2003), Klagenfurt, Austria, June 16–18, 2003,* (Eds, Eder J, *et al.*) Heidelberg, Germany: Springer-Verlag, pp. 95–110.
13. Mirbel, I. and Ralyté, J. (2006). Situational method engineering: combining assembly-based and roadmap-driven approaches, *Requirements Engineering*, 11(1), pp. 58–78.
14. Jarke, M., Rolland, C., Sutcliffe, A., and Domges, R. (1999). *The NATURE requirements Engineering*. Shaker Verlag, Aachen.
15. Rolland, C., Prakash, N., and Benjamen, A. (1999). A multi-model view of process modelling. *Requirements Engineering, 4*(4), 169–187.
16. Henderson-Sellers, B., Gonzalez-Perez, C., and Ralyté, J. (2007). Situational method engineering: chunks or fragments? *CAiSE Forum, Trondheim, 11-15 June 2007,* 89-92
17. Röstlinger, A., and Goldkuhl, G. (1996). *Generisk flexibilitet: På väg mot en komponentbaserad metodsyn*, In Swedish: "Generic flexibility: Towards a component-based view of methods", Technical Report LiTH-IDA-R-96-15, Dept. of Computer and Information Science, Linköping University. Originally presented at VITS Höstseminarium 1994.
18. Goldkuhl, G., Lind, M., and Seigerroth, U. (1998). Method integration: The need for a learning perspective. *IEE Proceedings Software*, 145, 113–118.
19. Ågerfalk, P.J. (2003). *Information Systems Actability: Understanding Information Technology as a Tool for Business Action and Communication*. Doctoral dissertation. Dept. of Computer and Information Science, Linköping University, 2003.
20. Wistrand, K. and Karlsson, F. (2004). Method Components: Rationale Revealed. In Persson, A. and Stirna, J. (eds.) *Proceedings of the 16th International Conference on Advanced Information Systems Engineering (CAiSE 2004)*, Riga, Latvia, June 7-11, 2004. Heidelberg, Springer-Verlag.
21. Karlsson, F. (2005) *Method Configuration: Method and Computerized Tool Support*. Doctoral dissertation. Dept. of Computer and Information Science, Linköping University.
22. Karlsson, F. and Wistrand, K. (2006). Combining method engineering with activity theory: theoretical grounding of the method component concept. *European Journal of Information Systems*, 15, 82-90.
23. Ågerfalk, P.J. and Wistrand, K. (2003). Systems Development Method Rationale: A Conceptual Framework for Analysis. In Camp, O., Filipe, J., Hammoudi, S. & Piattini, M. (Eds.) *Proceedings of the 5th International Conference on Enterprise Information Systems (ICEIS 2003)*. Angers, France.
24. Rossi, M., Ramesh, B., Lyytinen, K., and Tolvanen, J.-P. (2004). Managing evolutionary method engineering by method rationale. *Journal of the Association for Information Systems, 5*(9), 356–391.
25. Ågerfalk, P.J. and Fitzgerald, B. (2006). Exploring the Concept of Method Rationale: A Conceptual Tool for Method Tailoring. In Siau, K. (Ed.) *Advanced Topics in Database Research Vol 5*. Hershey, PA, Idea Group.

26. Fitzgerald, B., Russo, N. L., and Stolterman, E. (2002). *Information systems development - methods in action*. London: McGraw-Hill.
27. Henderson-Sellers, B. and Graham, I.M. (1996). OPEN: toward method convergence? *IEEE Computer*, 29(4), 86-89
28. Firesmith, D.G. and Henderson-Sellers, B. (2002). *The OPEN Process Framework. An Introduction*, Addison-Wesley, 330pp
29. ISO/IEC (2007). *Software Engineering. Metamodel for Development Methodologies. ISO/IEC 24744*: International Standards Organization / International Electrotechnical Commission, Geneva.